Redevelopment in California

Publisher's Note

Before you rely on the information in this book, be sure you are aware that some changes in the statutes or case law may have gone into effect since the date of publication. The book, moreover, provides general information about the law. Readers should consult their own attorneys before relying on the representations found herein.

Redevelopment in California

Joseph E. Coomes, Jr. et al.

2009 (Fourth) Edition

SOLANO PRESS BOOKS

Redevelopment in California
2009 (Fourth) Edition

Copyright © 2009
McDonough, Holland & Allen
All rights reserved.

Printed in the United States of America.
No part of this publication may be
reproduced, stored in a retrieval system,
or transmitted, in any form or by any
means, electronic, mechanical, photocopied,
recorded, or otherwise, without the prior
written approval of McDonough, Holland
& Allen and the publisher.

May 2009

Solano Press Books
Post Office Box 773
Point Arena, California 95468
Phone (707) 884-4508
Fax (707) 884-4109

Cover design by Kevin J. Boyd
    and Solano Press Books
Cover illustration courtesy
    McDonough, Holland & Allen
Book design by
    Solano Press Books
Index by Julie Shell
Printed by Publishers Book
    Services, Salt Lake City

ISBN 0-923956-82-0

NOTICE

This book is designed to assist you in understanding
redevelopment law and practice. It is necessarily
general in nature and does not discuss all exceptions
and variations to general rules. Also, it may not
reflect the latest changes in the law. It is not intended
as legal advice and should not be relied on to address
legal problems. You should always consult an attorney
for advice regarding your specific factual situation.

Chapters at a Glance

1. **Introduction** ... *page 1* (1-19)
2. **Redevelopment Agencies** ... *page 21* (21-33)
3. **Adoption of Redevelopment Plan** ... *page 35* (35-47)
4. **Conflicts of Interest** ... *page 87*
5. **Property Acquisition** ... *page 105*
6. **Environmental Issues** ... *page 137*
7. **Relocation** ... *page 155*
8. **Property Disposition** ... *page 171* (177-194) (201-205)
9. **Public Improvements** ... *page 217*
10. **Financing** ... *page 231*
11. **Housing** ... *page 267* (267-277)
12. **Closed Military Bases** ... *page 299* (299-310)
13. **Validation Litigation** ... *page 311*
14. **Conclusion** ... *page 323*

(331-333)

Contents

Preface xiii
About the Authors xvii

1 Introduction 1

History 2
   Federal. 2
   State 5
      1945–1993: Pre-AB 1290 •
      1994–2006: AB 1290 • 2006–
      Present: SB 1206 and AB 1389
Why and How Redevelopment
Has Been Used 15

2 Redevelopment Agencies 21

Establishment. 21
Organization: Alternatives and
Advantages and Disadvantages. . . 21
   Legislative Body as Agency. 22
   Appointment of Separate Agency. . 23
   *Establishment of Community
   Development Commission* 23
   Compensation 23
Agency Establishment
and the Referendum
and Initiative Process 24
Agency Activation 24
General Powers and Jurisdiction . 25
Conflicts of Interest and
Disclosure of Economic Interests . 26
   Political Reform Act of 1974 . . . 26
   *Community Redevelopment
   Law: Prohibition and Disclosure* . . 27
   Incompatibility of Office. 28
Open Meeting Requirements—
The Brown Act 28
Staff and Consultants 29
Budget. 30
Reporting 30
Pass-Through Payments. 31
Major Violations 33
Dissolution of the Agency. 33

3 Adoption of Redevelopment Plan 35

What Is a
Redevelopment Plan? 35
Redevelopment Team 36
Prerequisites to
Redevelopment Plan Adoption. . . 36
Designation of Survey Area. 38
Project Area Prerequisites
and Formulation of
Preliminary Plans. 38
   Project Area Prerequisites 38
      Blight • Predominantly
      Urbanized • Agricultural
      Lands • Housing Relocation/
      Replacement/Use of
      20 Percent of Tax Increment •
      Other Considerations
Adoption of
Redevelopment Plan. 48
   *Preparation of Preliminary
   Plan; County Fiscal
   Officer's Report* 48
Project Area Committee. 50
Preparation of the
Preliminary Report. 53
Redevelopment Plan Preparation,
Owner Participation Rules,
Environmental Impact
Report, and Report to
the Legislative Body. 55
   Redevelopment Plan. 55
   *Time Limit on
   Incurring Indebtedness* 57
   *Time Limit on Effectiveness
   of the Redevelopment Plan* 59
   *Time Limit on Repayment
   of Indebtedness*. 61
   *Time Limit Extensions
   for ERAF Contributions*. 62
   *Special Procedures Applicable
   to SB 211 Amendments* 62
      Prior Determinations •
      Extended Consultations
   *Time Limit on Exercise
   of Eminent Domain* 65
   Effect of Merger on Time Limits . . 65
   *Effect of Amendments
   on Time Limits* 65
   Owner Participation Rules 65
   Environmental Impact Report . . . 66
   Report to Legislative Body 72
Public Hearings and Approval . . . 73
   Review by Other Bodies. 73
   Notice; Public Hearing 73
   Notifications after Plan Adoption. . 76
Referenda 77
Legal Actions 77

Contents

Redevelopment Plan
Amendments 78
   Mergers. 80
Joint Exercise or
Delegation of Authority
to Redevelop 81
Implementation Plans 83
Community Redevelopment
Disaster Project Law 85

4 Conflicts of Interest 87

Political Reform Act 87
   General. 87
   Disclosure. 88
   Disqualification 89
      Making or Participating in a
      Decision • Types of Economic
      Interests • Direct or Indirect
      Involvement in Decision •
      Reasonable Foreseeability •
      Materiality • Distinguishable
      from the Public Generally •
      Project Area Committees •
      Small Jurisdictions • Residential
      Properties • Examples
   Recusal. 98
   Legally Required Participation—
   The Rule of Necessity 98
FPPC Opinions, Advice 100
   Violations. 100
   Effect of Violations
   on Decisions 101
Community
Redevelopment Law 101
Other Conflict-of-
Interest Provisions 102

5 Property Acquisition 105

Introduction. 105
General Authority and
Statutory Requirements 105
Contaminated Property 107
Voluntary Sales 108
Eminent Domain 110
   Power to Take 110
      Generally • Exercise of
      Eminent Domain Authority
      by Redevelopment Agencies
   Political and Policy Concerns . . . 115
   Precondemnation Procedures . . . 115
      Statutory Requirements •
      Acquisition Team
   Eminent Domain Procedures . . . 119
      Resolution of Necessity;
      Hearing; Notice • The
      Complaint • Deposit of
      Probable Compensation;
      Order for Possession •
      Challenging the Right to Take •
      Compensation to Owner •
      Apportioning Compensation
      Between Property Owner
      and Tenant • Trial •
      Judgment and Appeal
Inverse Condemnation. 132
Interim Property
Management. 135

6 Environmental Issues 137

Introduction: Interplay
Between Redevelopment
and Environmental Law 137

Contaminated Property in
the Redevelopment Context . . . 138
   Polanco Redevelopment
   Act of 1990. 138
      Investigation • Remediation
Other Key Environmental
Statutes. 144
   Federal Superfund. 144
   State Superfund 145
AB 389—the California Land
Reuse and Revitalization Act . . . 146
State Programs to Assist
with Remediation of
Contaminated Properties 147
   Voluntary Cleanup Program . . . 147
   Expedited Remedial Action
   Program (ERAP or SB 923) . . . 147
   CalSites Validation Program . . . 147
   Institutional Controls 148
Other Statutes Applicable
to Environmental Issues
Affecting Redevelopment 148
   Mello-Roos Community
   Facilities Act 148
   Hazardous Waste
   Disposal on Public Land. 149
   Proposition 65 149
   Cleanup-Related Taxes and Fees. . 150
Other Environmental Laws
to Consider at Specific Sites . . . 150
   Reporting Requirements 150
   Local CERCLA-Like
   Ordinances. 151
   Toxic Substances Control Act . . . 151
   Asbestos and Lead 152
   Military Base
   Cleanup and Reuse 152

Contents

Paying for Cleanup of
Contaminated Property 152
*Redevelopment Project
Proponent as the Deep Pocket* . . . 152
*Responsible Parties'
Insurance Policies* 153
Governmental Funding Sources . . 153
Underground Storage Tank
Cleanup Fund • Cleanup Loans
and Environmental Assistance
to Neighborhoods Program
Conclusion. 154

7 Relocation 155
History and the Law 155
Requirements
Prior to Displacement 156
*Agency Relocation
Rules and Regulations*. 157
*Prior Determinations/
Assurances* 157
Relocation Plans 158
Relocation Assistance
Advisory Program. 159
Comparable Replacement
Dwelling Units 160
*Required Notices to
Persons Being Displaced*. 161
*Relocation Payments
to Displaced Persons* 162
Payments for Businesses 163
*Payments for
Homeowner-Occupants*. 164
*Payments for
Residential Tenants* 165
*Authority to Exceed
Minimum Payments* 166

*Time Limit for
Submitting Claims*. 166
Other Major Components of
the Relocation Law and Process . 167
Grievance Procedures 167
Eviction Policies 167
Last Resort Housing 168
Good Record Keeping 168
*Relocation Payments
Not Considered Income*. 168
Property "Offered for Sale"
by Owner-Occupant 168
Utility Relocation 169

8 Property
Disposition 171
General Rules 171
Developer Selection 173
Highest Bid/Auction 174
*Negotiation with Single
Developer without
Formal Selection Process*. 174
Request for Qualifications 175
Requests for Proposal 175
Combined RFQ/RFP. 175
Master Developers 177
Exclusive Negotiation
Agreements 178
Owner Participation 180
General Rules. 180
The "Norm's Slauson" Problem. . 184
Negotiations. 187
Objectives. 187
Preparation for Negotiation. . . . 188
*Structuring the
Negotiation Process*. 190

*Methods of Assisting
Development When Necessary*. . . 191
Prevailing Wage
Considerations 193
Documenting the Transaction . . 198
*Disposition and
Development Agreements* 198
*Owner Participation
Agreements* 199
Ground Leases 199
*Agency Participation
in Cash Flow* 201
Developer Advances 202
*Subsequent
Discretionary Approvals*. 203
Renegotiating the Deal. 204
*Dealing with Unforeseen
Contingencies*. 205
Effect of Initiatives,
Referenda, and Local
Legislative Enactments. 207
Approval Process 211
*Hearings, Reports and Special
Findings, and Determinations* . . 211
CEQA. 214

9 Public
Improvements 217
Basic Powers. 217
Background. 217
*Inadequate Public Improvements
No Longer Blight Criteria;
Must Be Linked to
Elimination of Blight* 218
*Off-Site Public
Improvements*. 218

Contents

*Land and Public
Buildings and Facilities;
Section 33445 Findings* 219
*Other Requirements
and Limitations* 222
    Redevelopment Plan
    Requirements • Implementation
    Plan Requirements • Normal
    Maintenance and Operations
    Not Authorized • Public
    Hearing Required; Use of
    Tax Increments for Public
    Buildings Other Than Parking
    Facilities • Primary Benefit
    to Project Area Required
    for Use of Tax Increments •
    Prohibition on Payment
    for Certain Services
Other Specific
Projects Authorized 223
    Air Rights Sites 224
    *Buildings for Residential,
    Commercial, Industrial,
    and Other Use* 224
Specific Applications 224
    *Typical Infrastructure
    Improvements* 224
    *Parking Facilities; Public
    Buildings Other Than
    City Halls, County
    Administration Buildings* 225
    *City Halls, County
    Administration Buildings* 226
    *Assistance to Certain
    Automobile Dealerships
    and Retail Projects Prohibited* . . . 226
    *Assistance for Relocation
    of Automobile Dealerships and
    Big Box Retailers Prohibited* . . . 227

Public Works Contracting
Requirements 227
Developer Construction
of "Integrally-Related"
Public Improvements 228

10 Financing 231

Agency Revenues 231
    Tax-Increment Financing 231
        Background •
        Limitations upon Receipt
    *Payments to
    Taxing Entities* 236
        Indebtedness • Direct
        Bonded Debt–Tax Allocation
        Bonds • Repayment Debt–
        Contracts • Reimbursement
        Debt–Obligations Incurred
        by an Agency under
        Section 33445 • Expenses
        Incurred by the Agency for
        Operation, Administration,
        and Overhead • Contingent
        or Contractual Obligations
    *Statements
    of Indebtedness* 244
        Receipt by Agency •
        Limitations upon Use •
        Payments to Educational
        Revenue Augmentation
        Fund • Miscellaneous
        Expenditure Authority
    *Sales and Use
    Tax Financing* 250
    *Transient Occupancy
    Tax Financing* 253
    *Land Sale Proceeds
    and Lease Revenues* 253

Revenues from
Governmental Agencies 254
    Community Funds 254
    State 254
    Federal 255
        Community Development
        Block Grants • Section 108(a)
        Loan Guarantee Program •
        Urban Mass Transit
        Program • Economic
        Stimulus Bill(s) • Other
        Sources of Federal Funds
Borrowing by the Agency 256
    Tax Exemption 257
    Tax Allocation Bonds 258
    Lease Revenue Bonds 259
    *Certificates of Participation
    (Lease Participation)* 260
    Assessment District Bonds 260
    Mello-Roos Bonds 261
    *Residential Mortgage
    Revenue Bonds* 261
Borrowing
from Developers 262
    Developer Advances 262
    Land Sale Proceeds 262
    *In Lieu Guarantee
    of Tax Increment* 263
    *Public Purpose or
    Governmental Bonds* 263
        Private Business Use
        Test and Private Security
        or Payment Test • Private
        Loan Financing Test
    Private Activity Bonds 264
        Use of Proceeds and Costs
        of Issuance • Volume Cap

Contents

*Tax Allocation Bonds—
Tax-Exempt or Taxable* 265
   Public Purpose or
   Governmental Tax
   Allocation Bonds •
   Qualified Redevelopment
   Bonds • Taxable Tax
   Allocation Bonds

11 Housing 267

Introduction 267
The "20 Percent
Set-Aside" Requirement 270
   *Project Areas
   Established After 1976* 272
   Exceptions 273
   "Excess Surplus" 274
   *Use of Housing
   Fund Monies* 275
   *Targeted Expenditures
   of Housing Fund Monies* 277
   *Implementation of
   "Targeting" Requirements* 278
   *Limitations of
   Housing Fund Monies* 279
   *Use of Housing Funds
   Outside the Community* 279
   Affordability 280
   Maintaining Affordability 281
   *Plans Adopted
   Prior to 1977* 283
   Merger of Project Areas 284
Redevelopment Inclusionary
Housing Requirements 284
   *Inclusionary Implementation
   Methods* 286
   Two-for-One Alternative 287

*Aggregation Between
Project Areas* 287
*Purchase of Affordability
Covenants* 287
*Sale of Owner-
Occupied Units* 288
Production Housing
Requirements 288
Replacement Housing
Requirements 288
   *Housing Unit
   Replacement* 288
   *Replacement
   Housing Plan* 289
   *Federal: CDBG
   Special Requirements* 290
Completion of
Housing Obligations 290
Special Provisions
for Time Limit
Extension Amendment 292
   *Expenditures from
   Housing Fund* 292
   *Deposits into
   Housing Fund* 292
   *Plans Adopted
   Prior to 1976* 293
Additional
Housing Authority 294
Article XXXIV 294
Reporting
and Monitoring
Requirements 297
   Reporting 297
   Findings Sent to HCD 298
   *Monitoring and
   Affordability Database* 298

12 Closed Military Bases 299

Adoption of
Redevelopment Plans 299
Integration with
BRAC Disposal Process 302
   *Establishment of
   Local Reuse Authority* 303
   *Preparation and Adoption
   of a Reuse Plan* 303
Federal EIS; EIS/EIR 304
Disposition Procedures 304
Trends in Enhancing Value . . . 305
Environmental Cleanup
Prior to Transfer 306
   *Early Transfer Pending
   Remediation; Covenant Deferral* . 308

13 Validation Litigation 311

Introduction 311
Redevelopment Plan Adoption/
Amendment Litigation 311
   Statute of Limitation 311
   Validation Procedures 312
   Standard of Review 318
   *Limitations on
   Plaintiffs: Exhaustion
   of Administrative Remedies
   and Standing to Sue* 319
Validating Acts 321
   *Limitations on Plaintiffs:
   Appeal of Validation Actions* . . . 322
Restrictions on
Filing Legal Actions 322

14 Conclusion 323

Contents

Short Articles

Key Elements
of a Successful
Relocation Program 160

Determining
Fair Reuse Value 173

Property
Disposition Process 174

Obstacles to Effective
Owner Participation 183

Financing Considerations
for Developers and Agencies . . . 187

Effective Negotiations 188

The Role of Redevelopment
Agencies in Foreclosures 203

Indebtedness 241

Federal Funding
Available 255

Financing Team
Definitions 256

Real Estate Recession
and Tax Allocation Bonds 257

Layering of
Financial Resources 260

Appendices 327

Appendix A
*Community Redevelopment
Law of the State of California* . . . 329

Appendix B
*Illustrative Time Schedule
and Procedural Guide
for the Adoption of a
Redevelopment Plan* 481

Appendix C
*Definitions of a "Displaced
Person" under Federal
DOT and HUD Guidelines* 491

Appendix D
*Key Provisions of the
California Health and
Safety Code Regarding
Affordable Housing Cost* 495

Bibliography 501

List of Acronyms 502

**Table of
Authorities 503**

Index 513

**Photography
Credits**

We would like to thank our clients for the photographs of their successful redevelopment projects and Kevin Boyd in the IT Department at McDonough Holland & Allen, PC for his help with the photography and technical support of the publishing team.

Preface

Since the third edition of Redevelopment in California was published in 2004, the practice and law of redevelopment in California have changed significantly. Annual supplements to the third edition, through 2007, noted these changes, and they are incorporated, together with changes from 2008, into this revised and expanded 2009 fourth edition.

For someone unfamiliar with the redevelopment process, understanding its evolution, complexity, and diversity can be difficult. Not only is the Community Redevelopment Law highly technical, but redevelopment is implemented by city and county officials and their consultants. Much of redevelopment practice, therefore, is administratively developed by local officials and cannot be found in the statutes, case law, or standard legal treatises. We have tried to incorporate the knowledge we gained over the last several decades and from our scores of clients and colleagues to fill this niche.

We hope that this book will be a useful and practical reference for city, county, and redevelopment agency staff; consultants and attorneys who work in the field; local public officials who are confronted with redevelopment decisions; and members of the public who seek a better understanding of redevelopment within their communities. While we have tried to be as comprehensive as possible, there inevitably will be issues that we could not address, either due to space limitations or because a discussion of law without specific facts would not be helpful. This book is not intended to be a substitute for seeking advice from legal counsel, but we hope it will assist in both framing the issues and formulating the answers about redevelopment.

The year 2008 was notable for the recession and global economic crisis that severely affected credit markets, housing prices, the building industry, consumer spending, and retailing, and caused massive fiscal intervention by the federal government on an unprecedented scale with the promise of more to come in order to stimulate the economy. Budgets of the state and local governments were hit hard as public revenues fell from sources such as property taxes, sales taxes, income taxes, building permits, and development impact fees. This has resulted in staff reductions, service cuts, and deferral of major infrastructure and development projects. The City of Vallejo filed for bankruptcy. As this edition goes to press, the State of California faces a two-year budget shortfall of $40 billion that the Governor and Legislature are struggling to resolve. State transportation and building projects were suspended as the state projected running out of money with very limited ability to borrow unless the state budget crisis is resolved, and even then, at higher interest rates. The municipal bond markets with few exceptions remained closed to redevelopment agencies and other public entities.

In December 2008 the California Redevelopment Association and others filed a major constitutional challenge to the Legislature's transfer of $350 million for fiscal year 2008–09 of redevelopment tax-increment funds to the Education Revenue Augmentation Fund (ERAF), litigation that is not expected to be resolved until 2010.

While this book is not the place to examine these matters in detail, the practice of redevelopment will likely be changed as the economy recovers and the capital markets are restructured and restored. Among the changes for redevelopment agencies and their developers could be the following:

- A slower rate of growth in most markets, a contraction in the retail sector, and an increased emphasis on in-fill development in established urban markets
- Greater due diligence and underwriting criteria for proposed tax allocation bond issues by underwriters and bond purchasers; higher costs for bond insurance, if available
- Lender requirements for more substantial developer equity, higher pre-sales and pre-leasing commitments, and sustainable cash flows in projects to be financed
- Greater difficulty in obtaining land-secured financings without significant credit enhancements
- Reliance on more conservative economic projections for projects by redevelopment agencies and their financial advisors; greater assurances of public benefits from agency investments for gap financing of development projects; and
- Increased emphasis at all levels of government on public-private projects for infrastructure and public facilities, with risk shifting to the private sector of capital costs and ongoing operations and maintenance costs in connection with revenue-producing facilities financed through development fees, user fees, and so-called "availability payments" by the public sector

This book was primarily written by several shareholders in the Redevelopment Section of McDonough Holland & Allen PC. However, we have benefited from and very much appreciate the special contributions made by several others in the firm. G. Richard Brown, a partner in McDonough's Sacramento office, and Ben Stock, a partner in MHA's Oakland office, reviewed and revised the discussion on eminent domain. Erin Quinlan Riley, an associate attorney in McDonough's Sacramento office whose real estate practice focuses on environmental and hazardous waste issues, updated chapter 6 (Environmental Issues). In addition, Catherine dela Cruz, a former paralegal with McDonough and now a consultant who specializes in relocation matters, revised chapter 7 (Relocation).

We would like to thank Kevin Boyd in McDonough's Marketing department for his technical support and unfailing good nature in helping with the production of this book. Special thanks are due to the California Redevelopment Association for making available several photographs of successful redevelopment projects. We also must acknowledge the invaluable assistance provided by Marnie Prock, a paralegal in the Public Law Practice Group, whose organizational skills are legendary throughout the firm. Marnie's dedication to this project was inspiring and much appreciated. Finally, we especially thank our clients, without whom our practice, and this book, would not be possible.

> Joseph E. Coomes, Jr.
> T. Brent Hawkins,
> Gerald J. Ramiza
> Ethan Walsh
> Iris P. Yang

Note. This all-new fourth edition includes a revised Illustrative Time Schedule and Procedural Guide for the Adoption of a Redevelopment Plan, as well as the entire text of the Community Redevelopment Law as of January 1, 2009. The Community Redevelopment Law, Brown Act, and Public Records Act are all available on the McDonough, Holland & Allen website (www.mhalaw.commha/practicespublicLaw_pubs.htm).

About the Authors

Joseph E. Coomes, Jr. helped establish the redevelopment practice at McDonough Holland & Allen PC some 40 years ago. Joe's practice is concentrated in the area of redevelopment, land use, and planning law, including military base closure and reuse. Joe, in particular, also represents both public agencies and major developers in complex land use matters and in the negotiation of development agreements. He has successfully negotiated some of the largest, most difficult urban mixed-use redevelopment projects in California, including San Francisco's Yerba Buena Gardens, and downtown San Jose's Silicon Valley Financial Center, as well as closed military base reuse projects at Hamilton Field in Novato, Mare Island in Vallejo, the Dunes Project at Fort Ord in the City of Marina, and the East Garrison Project at Ford Ord in the County of Monterey. In 2008, he received a Lifetime Achievement Award from the California Redevelopment Association.

Iris P. Yang practices redevelopment, public, and land use law (both transactional and litigation). On the transactional side, Iris has helped numerous public agencies adopt and amend redevelopment plans, and has negotiated development agreements for affordable housing projects, shopping centers, mixed-use projects, and performing arts centers. In addition, she has represented clients on a variety of litigation matters, including land use and CEQA issues, First Amendment challenges, validation actions, and conflicts of interest. She serves as City Attorney of El Paso de Robles and special counsel to public agencies and private clients on a variety of issues including conflicts of interest, lobbying, economic disclosure, and campaign finance, and has represented both public and private clients before the state Fair Political Practices Commission. She has authored the California chapter of Lobbying, PACs and Campaign Finance—Fifty State Handbook each year since 1994.

T. Brent Hawkins practices redevelopment, land use, housing, and environmental law (both transactional and litigation). Brent represents clients in California and in other western states, including Nevada and Idaho. His practice emphasizes adoption and amendment of redevelopment plans, negotiation of development transactions, development agreements, asset management, and preparation and lobbying of redevelopment legislation. Brent's litigation experience includes practice before state and federal courts relative to eminent domain law and planning and zoning law, as well as the California Environmental Quality Act, the California Relocation Assistance Act, and the Community Redevelopment Law. Brent lectures frequently for organizations such as the California Redevelopment Association, the League of California Cities, and the University of California. He is chairman of the Legal Committee of the California Redevelopment Association.

Gerald J. Ramiza is a member of McDonough Holland & Allen's Oakland office, where his practice emphasizes transactional redevelopment matters, public agency law, and real estate law. Jerry's experience includes drafting and negotiation of leases, purchase and sale, owner participation, and disposition and development agreements. He represents developers on redevelopment agency-assisted projects and advises property owners and developers on leasing, acquisition, and land use entitlement processes. He is the lead attorney for the Emeryville, Pleasant Hill, Concord, San Bruno, Vallejo, and Foster City Redevelopment Agencies and the Alameda Community Improvement Commission, and provides special counsel services to the cities of Pacifica, Truckee, Clearlake, and Los Altos in connection with real estate and land use matters and the cities of Berkeley, Pleasant Hill, San Bruno, and Emeryville on affordable housing matters.

Ethan Walsh practices in the areas of affordable housing, redevelopment, and land use law. Ethan's practice includes assisting redevelopment agencies and developers in the structuring of transactions for commercial, residential, and mixed-use projects; negotiating and drafting disposition and development agreements and owner participation agreements for commercial, residential, and mixed-use projects; advising redevelopment agencies on adoption and amendment of redevelopment plans; and providing day-to-day advice on redevelopment law issues. Additionally, Ethan has substantial experience in advising public agencies and private developers on the potential impacts of prevailing wage laws as they relate to public-private transactions.

1
Introduction

The California Community Redevelopment Act was enacted in 1945 to address problems common throughout not only California but the country.

Redevelopment legislation was born out of the deteriorating conditions existing in many American cities after World War II. Enacted in 1945, the California Community Redevelopment Act noted that California's problems mirrored those elsewhere in the country:

Redevelopment legislation was born out of the deteriorating conditions existing in many American cities after World War II.

> The decay of large areas in American cities, notably in the central sections, is one of the major problems of today. Blight and slums have spread over an estimated one-fourth of the urban America.
>
> The deterioration of property originally assessed at an estimated 40 billions of dollars has destroyed a large part of the tax base of our cities. In Los Angeles, for example, there has been a decrease of approximately three-quarters of a billion dollars in the assessed valuation of property during the past decade.
>
> Los Angeles Town Hall Report, p. 1, March 1944

In the post World War II era, public officials at the federal, state, and local levels were greatly concerned about the condition of the existing housing stock, the lack of affordable housing for returning soldiers, and urban blight. Although these conditions were not new, the nation was now ready to address them.

The Community Redevelopment Act gave cities and counties in California the authority to establish redevelopment agencies, gave these agencies the authority to attack problems of urban decay, and enabled the agencies to apply for grants and loans from the federal government.

The Community Redevelopment Act gave cities and counties in California the authority to establish redevelopment agencies, and gave these agencies the authority to attack problems of urban decay.

To remedy these domestic problems, redevelopment agencies were given certain fundamental tools that are still essential to the their operation more than 70 years later:

- The authority to acquire real property including, if necessary, the power to use eminent domain

- The authority to develop property (but not to construct private buildings)
- The authority to sell real property without bidding
- The authority and obligation to relocate persons who have interests in property acquired by the agency
- The authority to finance their operations by borrowing from federal or state governments and selling bonds
- The authority to impose land use and development controls pursuant to a comprehensive plan of redevelopment

Over the decades, redevelopment has been a powerful tool in addressing local blight, stimulating economic development, and creating affordable housing. As described in further detail throughout the book, redevelopment's success, as well as certain perceived abuses of its authority, coupled with the economic challenges faced by local government and the state, mean that redevelopment agencies now face increasing constraints both on the scope of their activities and its finances.

History

Federal

The earliest federal programs were developed during the Depression to address the problems of an inadequately housed population. The National Industrial Recovery Act of 1933 included a federal public housing component. FHA, FSLIC, and FNMA were all part of the New Deal programs established in the 1930s. The National Housing Act of 1934 created the Federal Housing Administration for the primary purpose of insuring loans for the improvement of homes. The Housing Act of 1937, which was directed to the "elimination of unsafe and unsanitary housing conditions...the eradication of slums...and the provision of decent, safe, and sanitary dwellings for families of low income," established a system of loans and grants-in-aid to local public housing authorities.

In 1941, New York became the first state to enact a statute authorizing the use of eminent domain by public entities to acquire slum property and convey that property to private, limited-dividend redevelopment corporations for the purpose of building new housing. The New York law required a plan for the area, and provided for property tax exemptions, issuance of tax-exempt bonds, regulation of rents and profits, and authority to receive federal assistance.

Other states, such as California, followed. By 1947, almost half the states had redevelopment enabling statutes. However, largely because of inadequate funds, these state programs were ineffective.

This failure on the part of the states to make significant progress helped convince Congress that only through an effective program of federal aid could real progress be made in the clearance of slums. Congress

---

Over the decades, redevelopment has been a powerful tool in addressing local blight, stimulating economic development, and creating affordable housing.

FHA = Farmers Home Administration

FSLIC = Federal Savings and Loan Insurance Corporation

FNMA = Federal National Mortgage Association

In 1941, New York became the first state to enact a statute authorizing the use of eminent domain by public entities to acquire slum property for the purpose of building new housing.

passed the Housing Act of 1949, which established the federal urban renewal program and created the structure that formed the basis for federal urban renewal programs from 1949 until 1974.

The slum clearance provisions of the Housing Act of 1949, which later became known as urban renewal, were the product of a coalition composed of two separate and conflicting groups: advocates for housing for low-income persons and real estate interests that supported a federal program for downtown commercial rejuvenation.[1] The tension at the start of the federal urban renewal programs between housing advocates and interests supporting downtown redevelopment also existed in the enactment and implementation of California redevelopment law, and continues today.

The Housing Act of 1949, like subsequent federal programs, involved efforts in three areas: planning, financial aid, and regulation of private land use. However, the basic problem for state and local governments was lack of money to implement the authority they possessed. The Housing Act of 1949 was important because it provided the first major source of federal money for redevelopment, and in California, as with the rest of the country, this money dominated redevelopment activities in the 1950s and 1960s. While federal urban renewal has always meant federal financial assistance relying on state authority, these "federal projects" in fact depended upon federal financial assistance. Thus, while all redevelopment projects were technically "state" projects because the state was the source of the authority to do the project, the federal source of money, with its accompanying restrictions, was what actually shaped and governed the programs during that period.

Between 1949 and 1957, the federal government made grants totaling $1.25 billion and loaned another $1 billion for projects nationwide. Most of these projects involved substantial or total clearance of built-up areas, usually residential, and then the construction of new buildings. Until 1954, the project areas had to be "blighted" and "predominantly residential." Congress then authorized the use of 10 percent of the grant funds for nonresidential purposes. This gradually increased to 35 percent by 1965. By 1957, out of 266 approved project areas, 239 were residential, 14 contained nonresidential blight, and 13 were vacant. Most project areas ranged from 10 acres to 100 acres, but were as small as one acre and as large as 474 acres. All but 20 projects provided for the total clearance of the project area.[2]

While the programs and restrictions were modified between 1949 and 1968, the basic framework remained. The federal government

---

1. Bernard J. Frieden and Lynn B. Sagalyn, Downtown, Inc., MIT Press (1989), p. 22.
2. Quinn Johnstone, "The Federal Urban Renewal Program" (1958), 25 University of Chicago Law Review, 301, 318–320.

advanced monies to a redevelopment agency for surveys and planning of an urban renewal project. If, after the planning was complete, the project was approved by both the federal and local governments, the two governments then entered into a loan and grant contract for implementation of the project. These funds were used to acquire property within the project area, relocate residents, demolish structures, prepare sites for development, and construct public improvements. The agency then sold the property for development through a competitive bidding process and used the proceeds to repay the federal government.

The land had to be sold at "its fair value for uses in accordance with the redevelopment plans." After the land sale proceeds were deducted from the total costs of the project, the federal government would contribute two-thirds or three-fourths (depending upon community characteristics) of the remaining costs of the project, and the local government was expected to contribute the remaining one-third or one-fourth. This local matching requirement could often be met by counting the total cost of public works constructed by the local government to serve the project area, two-thirds of which was paid by the federal government.[3]

Certain basic restrictions were included in the federal law to limit the authority of local governments and to make certain that the funds would be used "to help remove the impact of slums on human lives rather than simply assist in the redevelopment of...cities."[4] The project areas had to be blighted, not vacant, and initially they had to be "primarily residential." In addition, the federal grant and loan funds could not be used for construction, and the local government had to provide the required matching contribution.

The program was designed to offer substantial incentives to private developers to build within the project areas. By the time a developer obtained a site for development, public improvements had been installed to serve the site, and the land had been assembled and sold to the developer for a price that was substantially less than the costs of assembly, relocation, and demolition.

However, this approach had many problems—including the impact the projects had on the residents of the areas to be redeveloped. The periods of time for both planning and site assembly were too long. The planning period could extend from one to six years, and the site assembly could increase this time by an additional two to five years. As a result, an area could be planned and prepared for development over a ten-year period without involving those who would develop it. Selecting and negotiating with developers prior to the sale of land would have violated requirements that land be sold under competitive procedures. Finally, the

The land had to be sold at its fair value for uses in accordance with the redevelopment plans.

The program was designed to offer substantial incentives to private developers to build within the project areas.

3. Frieden, p. 26.
4. Frieden, p. 23.

agency's flexibility in determining the price of the land was limited by the requirement that the land had to be sold for its fair value for uses in accordance with the redevelopment plan. The interest of the federal government was to maximize land receipts in order to reduce the federal grant to the project.

In addition, during this period other federal programs—such as the interstate highway program and various programs and policies of the Federal Housing Authority—were encouraging suburban growth, which exacerbated problems in many downtown areas.

State

1945–1993: Pre-AB 1290. When California enacted the Community Redevelopment Act in 1945, the state was responding to the same post-World War II concerns that had resulted in the federal urban renewal program and in the adoption of state programs throughout the country. Since the Community Redevelopment Act contained authority to adopt projects but no money to implement them, the first California redevelopment projects occurred in cities that used funds available under the Federal Housing Act of 1949, with the cities expected to contribute one-fourth to one-third of the project costs after land sale proceeds had been received. From 1949 to the late 1960s, these projects were characterized by the same elements previously described: survey and planning, land acquisition, demolition and relocation, and substantial clearance, all of which often occurred prior to and without any knowledge of private demand.

In 1951, the Community Redevelopment Act was codified and renamed the Community Redevelopment Law (Health and Safety Code § 33000 *et seq.*).[5] Most importantly, the authority for tax-increment financing was added, although it was dependent upon the approval of a state constitutional amendment. This approval was granted in 1952 when the voters approved Article XIII, Section 19 (now Article XVI, Section 16) of the California Constitution.[6] The stimulus for this new financing technique came when voters in several cities failed to approve the local share of matching funds necessary to receive federal grants and loans. Tax-increment financing—which allows redevelopment agencies to receive and spend property tax revenues from the

Top *Capitol Mall, Sacramento, 1994*
Bottom *Capitol Mall, Sacramento, c. 1963*

---

5. All statutory references are to the Health and Safety Code, unless otherwise indicated.
6. *See* Jacobs and Levine, "Redevelopment: Making Misused and Disused Land Available and Useable" (1957), 8 Hastings Law Journal 241, for an informative description and analysis of the beginnings of redevelopment in California.

increase in assessed value that has occurred after adopting a redevelopment project—was originally intended to provide the one-third matching funds required under the federal programs. It was an original financing method, which has since been adopted by a number of states. Because it eventually allowed redevelopment agencies to finance projects without depending on federal funds, tax-increment financing remains the single most important addition to the law since its inception.

Although authorized in 1952, it wasn't until the 1960s that tax-increment financing was relied on as a principal source of finance. Only 27 redevelopment projects had been started by 1966, but in the late 1960s project areas to be financed with tax-increment funds were formed, and by 1975 approximately 100 agencies were relying on tax-increment financing as their principal method of finance.[7]

By 1976, redevelopment project areas had been established in every major urban area of the state, with 229 project areas adopted in 111 cities and two counties and plan adoption procedures started for 31 additional projects in 27 cities and one county.[8] In 1994, there were a total of 385 redevelopment agencies in California—in 359 cities, 24 counties, and two joint city-county agencies.

Prior to 1993, with the increasing number of redevelopment plan adoptions and amendments, concerns over the expansive authority of the law led to changes in five general areas:

- *Housing.* Twenty percent of tax-increment funds were required to be spent to increase and improve housing for low- and moderate-income persons unless certain exceptions were met.
- *The effect of tax-increment financing on other taxing entities.* Agencies were required to notify all public entities that levied property taxes in a proposed project area, and, more importantly, the affected taxing entities were authorized to establish fiscal review committees to meet and negotiate with the redevelopment agency regarding the fiscal impact of the proposed plan upon the taxing entities.
- *Limits on tax increment.* Redevelopment plans were required to contain limits on the total amount of tax increment that could be received, the total amount of outstanding bonded debt that could be repaid with tax increment, and a time period within which debt could be incurred.
- *Reporting requirements.* Redevelopment agencies were required to file reports with the state providing a variety of information on each project area, and to file an annual statement of indebtedness with the county as a condition of receiving tax increment.

7. Ralph Andersen and Associates, Redevelopment and Tax Increment Financing, Sacramento (1976), p. 3.
8. *Id.*, p. 26.

- *Legislative body review.* Important agency decisions—including the sale of tax-increment bonds, land disposition, and annual budgets and work programs—were required to be reviewed by the legislative body.

In 1978, with the number of redevelopment projects continuing to expand and tax increment firmly established as the principal financing tool, Proposition 13 was passed by the voters. This "tax revolt" initiative measure reduced property tax revenues to all local governments and redevelopment agencies by approximately 60 percent. While many predicted that—with the substantial decrease in property tax revenue available to redevelopment agencies—those project areas dependent on tax increments would substantially decrease, the opposite occurred. With the elimination of general obligation bonds by Proposition 13, coupled with the substantial decrease in property tax revenues available to cities and counties and reductions in state and federal funds, tax-increment financing became a major tool for capital projects, particularly public improvements. Previously used primarily by larger cities, redevelopment spread first to medium-sized and then to small cities.

In 1975, 156 redevelopment agencies had established 195 project areas and had received $50 million in tax increment during the fiscal year. By 1984, six years after the passage of Proposition 13, 293 redevelopment agencies had established 470 project areas, received $378 million in tax increment during the fiscal year, and established $3.5 billion in long-term debt. By 1988, the number of agencies had risen to 343 and the number of project areas to 585. Annual tax increment had grown to approximately $800 million. In 1988, of the 112 cities with populations over 50,000, 92 percent had active redevelopment agencies, and 111 cities with populations under 25,000 had active redevelopment agencies.

The size of project areas also increased. Projects established pursuant to federal programs had usually been small and specific. In project areas established prior to 1979, the average size was 481 acres. The average size of project areas established between 1978 and 1984 was 811 acres.[9] This increase in the number and size of project areas, many of which included a high proportion of previously undeveloped land, led to legislation enacted in 1983, requiring that 80 percent of the privately owned land in a new project area be already developed for urban uses. § 33320.1.

In addition, because taxing entities, especially counties, were increasingly concerned with the effect of tax increments upon their tax revenues, in 1983 the legislature made several changes regarding the relationship between redevelopment agencies and taxing entities,

With the elimination of general obligation bonds by Proposition 13, coupled with the substantial decrease in property tax revenues and reductions in state and federal funds, tax-increment financing became a major tool for capital projects.

---

9. California Debt Advisory Commission, Use of Redevelopment and Tax Increment Financing (1984), p. 37.

including requiring the agency to supply more complete information regarding the nature of a proposed redevelopment plan to taxing entities at the beginning stages of the plan adoption and plan amendment process; requiring an agency to follow the plan adoption process when making major amendments to redevelopment plans; allowing taxing entities to receive tax revenues that are a result of the inflationary increase in assessed value authorized by Proposition 13; and defining the term "financial burden or detriment" as it is used to determine the adverse effects of tax-increment financing upon taxing entities.

From 1984 to 1993, the major changes in the law concerned the obligation of redevelopment agencies to assist in the provision of affordable housing for low- and moderate-income persons. The general requirement that 20 percent of tax-increment funds be used to improve and increase the supply of housing for low- and moderate-income persons was made applicable to project areas established prior to 1976, and the various exceptions to this requirement were narrowed.

The requirement that redevelopment agencies replace demolished housing inhabited by persons of low- or moderate-income on a one-for-one basis was also applied to older project areas. Redevelopment agencies were directed to encumber and spend funds in the Low- and Moderate-Income Housing Fund within specific periods of time. Public improvements constructed with these housing funds had to directly benefit housing for persons of low and moderate income. Finally, covenants assuring that housing assisted with monies from the Low- and Moderate-Income Housing Funds remain affordable were required.

These changes, which were initiated by housing advocates, reflected the same tension that existed during the passage of the Housing Act of 1949. This tension between the use of the redevelopment process for housing and its use for commercial development has remained. While many of the policy considerations are also the same, it is difficult, as a practical matter, to generate large amounts of tax-increment funds to be used for housing unless commercial or industrial growth has been encouraged. A successful commercial project area can produce enough tax increment not only to pay for the subsidy required to make the project economically feasible but also to contribute funds that can be used for housing purposes. Because housing projects by themselves do not usually produce large amounts of tax increments, a successful project, as a general rule, should include both elements.

1994–2006: AB 1290. In 1993, the legislature enacted the most sweeping changes to the Community Redevelopment Law since the late 1970s. The Community Redevelopment Law Reform Act of 1993, authored by Assemblyman Phil Isenberg in AB 1290 and sponsored by the California Redevelopment Association (CRA), was enacted as Chapter 942 of the Statutes of 1993 and took effect on January 1, 1994.

From 1984 to 1993, the major changes in the law concerned the obligation of redevelopment agencies to assist in the provision of affordable housing.

CRA = California Redevelopment Association

Because housing projects by themselves do not usually produce large amounts of tax increments, a successful project, as a general rule, should include commercial development.

In one sense, AB 1290 was another unintended consequence of Proposition 13. The addition of Article XIIIA to the California Constitution in 1978 (called Proposition 13), decreased local government's ability to fund needed infrastructure and increased the pressure on cities to use redevelopment authority to assist in the provision of capital facilities. This decline in the growth of property tax revenues led communities to compete for development that produced sales tax revenues for the communities' general funds. Proposition 13 and its implementing legislation completely changed the way taxing entities reacted to the establishment of project areas and, therefore, the way fiscal review committees came to be used.

As first counties and then school districts took advantage of the fiscal review committee process to compensate for their own funding problems, caused in part by Proposition 13, the funding of redevelopment became more dependent on the state's method of funding schools. It became common practice to pass through to counties and other taxing entities a large portion of their share of the property tax dollar as a way to avoid or settle lawsuits. This left redevelopment primarily reliant upon the school district's portion of the tax dollar, since the state reimbursed school districts for any losses. Eventually, schools learned to strike their own capital facility deals and continued to receive state reimbursement, causing redevelopment finance to become even more dependent upon the state.

Proposition 13 resulted in other changes that led to specific provisions in AB 1290. Soon after the passage of Proposition 13, redevelopment agencies were given the authority to receive sales taxes generated from within a project area. The original purpose was to provide agencies with a supplemental source of revenue against which indebtedness could be secured. Instead, as the dependency of cities' general funds upon sales taxes increased, this authority was used to provide rebates to large sales tax generators such as auto malls and big-box retail developments. As another example, the so-called "two percent" inflation allocation to taxing entities, which was adopted to assist the state by requiring payments to school districts, became instead a guaranteed minimum with which to fund school facilities as redevelopment agencies and school districts entered into agreements that transferred the payments from operating to capital funds.

The CRA Board of Directors understood the link between state and redevelopment finances. For example, it was CRA-sponsored legislation in 1984 that mandated that school districts receive the two percent inflation allocation. A number of key officials in state government also understood this link. The Legislative Analyst's office concluded that the state general fund lost $400 million as a result of redevelopment; and, while that amount was questionable, new projects clearly became increasingly dependent on the schools' (and therefore the state's) share of

Proposition 13 decreased local government's ability to fund needed infrastructure and increased the pressure on cities to use redevelopment authority to assist in the provision of capital facilities.

Soon after the passage of Proposition 13, redevelopment agencies were given the authority to receive sales taxes generated from within a project area.

property taxes. Department of Finance officials were also privately concerned, and they and others questioned projects that produced sales tax revenues for city general funds but no financial benefit to the state. At the same time, both legislative staff and legislators raised concerns about plans, such as the one adopted in Coronado, that depended on the state general fund to reimburse schools that were in turn also the beneficiaries of redevelopment funds. Both the *Los Angeles Times* and the *Sacramento Bee* ran a series of articles criticizing redevelopment.

Elected officials and staff at the state level—understanding that redevelopment funds helped provide infrastructure, including school capital facilities and support for development that the state badly needed—declined to intervene in any major fashion. However, with California's deepening budget crisis, this tolerance lessened in the early 1990s.

Two separate acts illustrated this change. First, the state attorney general intervened in a case challenging a project area proposed by the City of Hemet to assist schools. Second, during the 1992 budget debate, the Legislative Analyst's office proposed to break the link between the state general fund and redevelopment by shifting property tax allocations in a way that severely penalized a community adopting a project area. It was the threat by state officials to adopt this proposal that prompted CRA to supply the language—eventually used in amended form—to shift funds from redevelopment agencies to the state in the 1992 budget bills.

This shift of $205 million from redevelopment to the state convinced a number of redevelopment officials as well as the CRA board of directors that, for redevelopment to survive, changes would have to be made.

This shift of $205 million from redevelopment to the state convinced a number of redevelopment officials as well as the CRA board of directors that, for redevelopment to survive, changes would have to be made. However clumsy, the fact that the state shifted the funds knowing the legal problems involved revealed redevelopment's vulnerability. It also reminded redevelopment officials that, although the criticism was often exaggerated or unfounded, redevelopment was a state-authorized program that could be changed, and that, even if the budget shift was ultimately determined to be unconstitutional, the legislature had a number of ways to resolve its concerns.

For these reasons, the CRA board determined to sponsor AB 1290 in 1993. While CRA hoped to eliminate or reduce the 1993 budget shift, its main goal was to assure that the core of redevelopment authority survived and that local government would continue to be authorized to implement that authority. In fact, the 1993 budget shift was only $65 million out of a total of $2.6 billion, significantly less than in 1992.

Assembly Bill 1290, enacted as Chapter 942 (1993), took effect January 1, 1994. AB 1290's changes affected both existing project areas and new project areas. In general, the changes:

- Modified the definition of blight
- Terminated the fiscal review process and instituted statutory payments to affected taxing entities

- Imposed new time limits on the life of project areas and the incurring of debt
- Repealed the authority of agencies to receive sales tax revenues
- Imposed new finding requirements for the disposition of land and the financing of public improvements
- Included a "death penalty" for agencies failing to use their housing funds

AB 1290's most important effect was on the plan adoption process, which reflected changed perceptions regarding redevelopment. It significantly revised the definition of blight, including the elimination of the need for infrastructure as a justification for a project area, thus making the adoption of project areas more difficult. Perhaps more importantly, it eliminated the fiscal review committee process and the authority to enter into "pass-through agreements" by redevelopment agencies and other taxing authorities.

These changes, together with the shift of property taxes from cities, counties, and districts to the schools—the so-called Education Revenue Augmentation Fund (ERAF) shift—lessened the impact of a plan adoption upon the general fund budget of a county. Also, because schools could use a portion of the required payments for capital facilities, the AB 1290 changes actually benefited most school districts. One result of these changes were fewer and less contentious plan adoptions. The number of project areas decreased, dropping from 86 adopted in the period 1996–2000 to 57 in the period 2001–2005.[10]

The use by redevelopment agencies of their powers to assist development that generated substantial sales tax for a city's general fund was also a source of controversy. AB 1290 eliminated the ability of redevelopment agencies to use sales tax, and expressly prohibited assistance for auto dealerships and big box stores on vacant land. Legislation passed in 2000 requires redevelopment agencies assisting in the relocation of auto dealerships and big box stores to share the sales tax with jurisdictions from which the development relocates. The fiscalization of land use was not new, but with the diminished importance of property tax, assistance by redevelopment agencies for the purpose of attracting sales tax generators raised questions about the appropriate use of redevelopment authority.

In 2001, seven years after the enactment of the reforms in AB 1290, CRA again sponsored legislation to address issues raised by AB 1290. With one of the key time deadlines established by AB 1290, the time limit to establish debt, looming for many agencies in 2004, CRA realized that, as a practical matter, this time limit would do little to stop redevelopment

AB 1290's most important effect was on the plan adoption process, which reflected changed perceptions regarding redevelopment.

ERAF = Education Revenue Augmentation Fund

AB 1290 eliminated the ability of redevelopment agencies to use sales tax, and expressly prohibited assistance for auto dealerships and big box stores on vacant land.

---

10. State Controller, Community Redevelopment Agencies Annual Report, Fiscal Year 2006–07.

activities and could in fact encourage actions designed only to avoid missing it. In response, CRA sponsored SB 211 (Chapter 741), which gave agencies the ability to expeditiously terminate this time limit. SB 211 also gave agencies the ability to extend the limit, as well as the limit to receive tax increment, by an additional ten years if a project area was adopted prior to 1994 and contained blight that could not be eliminated by the time limit on the effectiveness of the plan. The fairly narrow opening given by the legislature to extend plans was an indication that the legislature remained serious about terminating project areas.

In 2001, CRA also joined with housing advocates to sponsor AB 637 (Chapter 738). This legislation continued the trend started in 1976 to increase the housing obligations of redevelopment agencies and to assure that these obligations would be actually implemented. CRA wanted to extend the agencies' flexibility in implementing housing requirements that would otherwise sunset, and also needed support from the housing advocates for legislation that would allow agencies to eliminate the time limit to incur debt. The housing advocates understood that redevelopment housing obligations and activities constituted the single most important affordable housing program in the state. As a result, both parties worked together throughout 2001 on both SB 211 and AB 637. CRA recognized that the provision of affordable housing in a state with enormous unfilled housing needs would engender support for redevelopment across the political spectrum. Since redevelopment agencies produce thousands of housing units each year, housing advocates recognized the importance of working with CRA to assure that agencies would have the tools as well as the requirements to produce housing affordable to low- and moderate-income persons.

The state's budget crisis continued to present critical challenges for redevelopment agencies and local government during the next several years. In 2002–2003, the legislature reimposed upon redevelopment agencies a shift of funds to ERAF in the amount of $75 million. For 2003–2004, the shift to ERAF amounted to $135 million.

Redevelopment agencies again were required to shift funds to ERAF in fiscal 2004–2005 and 2005–2006, in the amount of $125 million for each of those years. Challenges to redevelopment also arose on another front.

The United States Supreme Court decision in *Kelo v. City of New London* (2005) 545 U.S. 469, precipitated a wave of proposed federal and state initiatives and legislation. The issue was whether the taking of private property for purposes of economic development satisfied the "public use" requirement of the Fifth Amendment. The State of Connecticut had declared the city of New London a "distressed municipality" and targeted it for economic revitalization.

AB 637 continued the trend started in 1976 to increase the housing obligations of redevelopment agencies.

CRA recognized that the provision of affordable housing in a state with enormous unfilled housing needs would engender support for redevelopment across the political spectrum.

In *Kelo*, a private nonprofit entity, the New London Development Corporation (NLDC), established by the city, submitted plans for the downtown's rejuvenation, which included the use of some privately-owned land. In approving the plans, the city council also authorized NLDC to acquire property by purchase or by exercising eminent domain in the city's name. While most of the property was purchased through negotiation, NLDC had to bring an action in eminent domain to acquire the few remaining single-family homes. The petitioners then brought an action claiming that the taking of their properties would violate the "public use" restriction in the Fifth Amendment.

NLDC = New London Development Corporation

In a 5–4 decision, the Supreme Court held that the taking of private property for the purpose of economic development satisfied the "public use" requirement. The majority opinion stated that "public use" was not solely determined by whether the land would be used by the public; the issue was whether the land would be used for a "public purpose." It noted that the courts had traditionally been quite deferential to legislative bodies in their determinations of what constitutes a public purpose. In *Kelo*, the city had determined that the area was sufficiently distressed to justify a program of economic rejuvenation, and that, "given the comprehensive character of the plan, the thorough deliberation that preceded its adoption and the limited scope of our review, it is appropriate for us…to resolve the challenges of the individual owners, not on a piece-meal basis, but rather in light of the entire plan." The Court found that promoting economic development had been a long-accepted function of government and that it could not find a way to distinguish economic development from other recognized public purposes.

In a 5–4 decision, the Supreme Court held that the taking of private property for the purpose of economic development satisfied the "public use" requirement.

Most legal scholars agreed that *Kelo* had little, if any, significance in California, where the well-established public purpose being served by redevelopment is to eliminate blight, rather than promote economic development. However, this did not prevent redevelopment opponents from attempting to use the unpopularity of the *Kelo* decision to win sweeping changes to eminent domain law.

The most radical proposal was Proposition 90, an initiative on the November 2006 ballot. It would have prohibited the use of eminent domain for any conveyance for private development. Even more significantly, it would have required the government to compensate property owners for decreased property values resulting from land use and other types of regulations such as downzoning, height restrictions, and environmental mitigation. Proposition 90 was defeated, but its proponents presented another similar initiative, Proposition 98, for the June 2008 ballot. In anticipation of such a measure, a broad coalition including CRA, the League of California Cities, and the California State Association of Counties co-sponsored a competing, less radical, measure, Proposition 99, which prohibited state and local governments from using eminent domain to acquire an owner-occupied residence if the owner has occupied the residence for at least one year, subject to some exceptions. Proposition 98 was defeated soundly and Proposition 99 passed.

2006–Present: SB 1206 and AB 1389. In 2006, the legislature continued to tighten the statutory definition of blight. SB 1206 stated that its purpose was "to focus public officials' attention and their extraordinary redevelopment powers on properties with physical and economic conditions that are so significantly degraded that they seriously harm the prospects for physical and economic development without the use of redevelopment." Agencies now have a greater burden of documenting the conditions of blight in a project area.

In addition, SB 1206 reflected the greater interest of the state in monitoring redevelopment activities. It requires agencies to send copies of reports and notices of public hearings to the state Department of Finance and the Department of Housing and Community Development, either of which may send comments. It also lengthens the time to challenge a redevelopment plan adoption or amendment to 90 days, whether by referendum petition or validation action, and states that the Department of Finance and the state Attorney General are "interested parties" in validation actions.

According to the State Controller, in 2006–2007 California had 397 active city, county, and joint city-county redevelopment agencies, with 745 project areas. Tax-increment revenues, the bulk of agency revenues, totaled $4.6 billion statewide; the amount of outstanding tax allocation bonds was $17 billion.[11] However, these figures, while appearing rosy, did not reflect the severe national and state economic downturn of 2008.

Faced with a then-estimated $12 billion deficit, the California legislature adopted urgency legislation requiring redevelopment agencies to make ERAF payments totaling $350 million in fiscal year 2008–2009,[12] with the state Legislative Analyst's office recommending a permanent annual shift of $400 million in redevelopment funds.[13] After the budget was adopted, the estimated budget deficit continued to balloon. Concerned that the state might try to impose ongoing shifts of redevelopment funds to help address state budgetary problems, on December 4, 2008, CRA and others filed a legal challenge to the constitutionality of the 2008–2009 transfer of redevelopment funds to ERAF.

In addition, because the state believed that redevelopment agencies had not been making their full share of pass through payments to local educational agencies (thus requiring the state to "backfill" payments to those agencies), the legislature adopted AB 1389. That bill imposed an

---

11. State Controller, Community Redevelopment Agencies Annual Report, Fiscal Year 2001–02.
12. AB 1389 (Budget Trailer bill); section 33685.
13. November 24, 2008, League of California Cities.

immediate requirement that each redevelopment agency file a report with the county auditor detailing its pass through payments to all taxing entities for the prior five years, with annual updates through 2014. If either the county auditor or State Controller does not concur with an agency's report, or if the agency has an outstanding pass through payment obligation to a local education entity, the agency is essentially prohibited from conducting any new activities until it has made all required pass through payments.

Why and How Redevelopment Has Been Used

The use and success of the redevelopment process in California to date, and of tax-increment financing in particular, has occurred for four principal reasons:

- The redevelopment process has worked because both the law and redevelopment plans provide broad authority to locally elected officials. Consequently, the process has been flexible enough to be used by communities of very different sizes and with very different needs. This has resulted in broad support of the program by city officials in communities throughout the state.

- Tax-increment financing depends upon the success of the private sector, and, therefore, encourages the establishment of plans and agreements that are based upon both the public goals of the agency and the goals and needs of the private sector.

- Federal programs and assistance have been greatly reduced, and since the adoptions of Propositions 13, 62, and 218, the ability of state and local governments to pay for needed public infrastructure has greatly diminished. In other words, there have been few alternatives.

- As land on the fringes of urban development becomes more expensive—and as both the public and private sector have understood the true costs of supporting sprawl, including the enormous cost of building infrastructure—both public officials and developers have become more interested in finding ways to make the redevelopment of existing urban areas possible.

Perhaps the most important of these reasons is the ability of local officials to design and implement a program that achieves goals established by locally-elected officials, without having to obtain approval from Sacramento or Washington. This is particularly important in small and medium-sized cities, which often have less leverage in dealing with the private sector and, therefore, must be able to respond quickly to proposed projects.

Cities of all sizes, but particularly small cities, have used tax-increment financing for needed infrastructure in downtown areas without which

The use and success of the redevelopment process in California has occurred for four principal reasons.

One important reasons for the success of redevelopment is the ability of local officials to design and implement a program that achieves goals established by locally-elected officials, without having to obtain approval from Sacramento or Washington.

private investment could not be expected. Small cities, using their own staff and outside consultants as needed, have:

- Determined that the principal goal of the agency was job creation and, therefore, adopted a redevelopment plan that included, in addition to the central business district, land containing a mix of older housing and declining or abandoned industrial uses. Tax increments were used to improve access to and circulation within the area. When a small manufacturing business showed interest in locating in the project area, the agency proposed a specific agreement designed to meet the needs of the manufacturer, including land acquisition by the agency, below-market land lease to the business with the favorable terms tied to job creation, assistance with off-site improvements, and assistance and support in obtaining construction financing. Tax increments were also used to assist in the relocation of residents within the area as well as to assure that affordable housing would be available for all persons displaced.

- Determined that the principal goal of the agency was the improvement and expansion of an existing shopping center and, therefore, adopted a redevelopment plan for the primary purpose of providing a portion of the funds necessary to redesign and reconstruct a nearby freeway interchange and improve access, without which the expansion of the retail center could not occur. Authority to acquire property by eminent domain was included to assure that land needed for the expansion could be obtained. Surplus revenues received by the agency from the expansion were to be used to improve and rehabilitate housing for low- and moderate-income persons located within the project area.

- Determined that a principal goal of the agency should be to assist the central business district. The agency was able to develop a facade improvement program in cooperation with downtown business owners, purchase land for and install walkways allowing access from the rear of the block where parking was located to the sidewalk on the main shopping street, and purchase (and then sell to a developer for rehabilitation) a historic landmark hotel in the center of the retail area, which was then changed from a transient hotel to apartments for senior citizens.

- Determined that the redevelopment of several parcels totaling more than 20 acres, some of which were severely contaminated with hazardous materials, would require intervention by the agency. The agency acquired the land using eminent domain where necessary, and used its authority under the Polanco Act[14] to both require prior

---

14. The Polanco Act was added to the Community Redevelopment Law, section 33459 *et seq.* in 1990.

owners to clean up the soils and to spend funds to clean the land itself, and then sued successfully for reimbursement by those owners. The agency then sold the property for the development of a large mixed-use project composed of a regional retail center, residential above the retail, a multiplex cinema and hotel, and structured parking.

- Started a single-family rehabilitation program that continued for many years, transforming a severely blighted part of the city block by block until the entire residential portion of the project area had been rehabilitated with the assistance of the agency and the cooperation of the residents.

In medium-sized cities, redevelopment agencies have:

- Combined the need for a community auditorium and meeting facilities with the desire to encourage regional conventions. The city, therefore, adopted a redevelopment plan authorizing the agency to acquire land, remove hazardous wastes, lease land for a hotel development, and construct parking and traffic circulation improvements needed to serve the hotel and auditorium.

- Encouraged more nighttime uses in the downtown and provided parking for daytime shoppers. The agency entered into an agreement under which land was acquired and leased to a developer who constructed a multiplex cinema under a public parking structure. Although operated and maintained by the city, the structure was financed in part by an assessment district, because it provided parking for nearby stores during the day; in part by the developer, because it provided night parking for the cinema; and in part by the agency, from tax increments the project generated.

- Assisted a school district in the abandonment of an old junior high school located in the downtown area and the construction of a new school within a residential area. The city adopted a redevelopment plan with the principal purpose of acquiring the school from the district. The district could then use the funds to obtain a new site, select a developer, and approve plans for the development of the site, sell or lease the site to the developer, and assist the development with needed off-site improvements. Development of the site could be used to stimulate development within the project area, which in turn could be facilitated with agency-assisted parking structures.

An outdated shopping center in Corona's downtown was completely renovated. The agency's assistance totaled $1.75 million, the developer invested $20.5 million.

- Prevented the loss of housing needed for low-income persons and improved the quality of the existing housing stock. The agency entered into an agreement with a nonprofit corporation that agreed to purchase an existing multi-family complex, rehabilitate the units, and manage the complex, which could then be rented to persons of low income. The acquisition, rehabilitation, and operation of the project was financed with a combination of tax-increment funds, mortgage revenue bonds, city assistance, and federal Section 8 rent subsidy payments.
- Stimulated the development of both office and retail projects in the central business district by using the agency's authority to assemble sites, sell or lease the sites at less than fair market value, and provide public parking.

Large cities have used the authority granted in the Community Redevelopment Law to plan and implement projects similar to those described above and have, in addition:

- Assembled large downtown sites for new regional shopping centers, with the agency's assistance consisting of land acquisition and reduced land costs to the developer, relocation of occupants and businesses, and the provision of public parking facilities. The Horton Plaza Project in San Diego is one of the many examples of this type of redevelopment. The stimulus of these projects has created jobs, encouraged new commercial development, and created a new market for central city housing.
- Undertaken large mixed-use projects with master developers to leverage the public income and private returns from such developers to provide public amenities such as museums, open space, and recreational and cultural facilities of benefit to the community. Examples of this type of redevelopment are the California Center Project in Los Angeles and the Yerba Buena Gardens Project in San Francisco.
- Enabled major first-class hotel complexes to locate in downtown areas, often in conjunction with new convention center facilities, with the agency making land available on favorable terms, financially assisting the public facilities of the project, and absorbing the costs of public areas in the hotel. Examples of this type of redevelopment are the Long Beach Hyatt Regency convention center hotel and the downtown San Jose Fairmont hotel.
- Leveraged the substantial tax increment available from successful downtown retail and office projects to undertake programs throughout the city to produce low-income housing. Examples of this type of redevelopment are the extensive housing programs of the Los Angeles Redevelopment Agency.

- Created a special joint powers redevelopment agency to deal in a focused and comprehensive manner with a large core area vital to the city. An example of this is the Capitol Area Development Authority created by a joint powers agreement between the State of California and the City of Sacramento to administer a plan for residential and state office uses in a 40-block area around the State Capitol.

Since 1988, in response to the latest round of military base closings, communities either singly or with adjacent communities have established redevelopment project areas that included the closed military base. These bases typically contain buildings that do not meet present building standards, have enormous hazardous waste problems, and lack adequate infrastructure to serve private development needs. While the problems are somewhat different from issues found in declining downtowns or neighborhoods, the expertise of agencies in transferring property, encouraging private sector investment, and financing infrastructure is relevant.

The above examples are illustrative. They do not begin to encompass the wide variety of redevelopment projects undertaken by small, medium-sized, and large cities and counties in California. However, given the increasing restrictions placed on redevelopment agencies, combined with the existing downturn in all segments of the economy, the challenges facing redevelopment practitioners in the coming years, perhaps more than ever before, are indeed daunting.

Since 1988, in response to the latest round of military base closings, communities either singly or with adjacent communities have established redevelopment project areas that included the closed military base.

2

Redevelopment Agencies

The authority to establish a redevelopment agency is granted by the Community Redevelopment Law of the State of California.

Establishment

The authority to establish a redevelopment agency—and the authority for a redevelopment agency to function as an agency, adopt a redevelopment plan, and implement the plan—is granted by the Community Redevelopment Law of the State of California. Health and Safety Code § 33000 *et seq.* Redevelopment agencies are, therefore, creations of the state. *Andrews v. City of San Bernardino* (1959) 175 Cal. App. 2d 459, 462. Every city and county within the state is authorized to establish a redevelopment agency by adopting an ordinance (subject to referendum) declaring that there is a need for a redevelopment agency to function in that jurisdiction. §§ 33101, 34115.

After a city or county adopts an ordinance establishing a redevelopment agency, a certified copy of the ordinance is to be filed in the office of the county clerk. § 33102.

Every city and county within the state is authorized to establish a redevelopment agency by adopting an ordinance declaring that there is a need in that jurisdiction.

Organization: Alternatives and Advantages and Disadvantages

The legislative body has three options: It may establish itself as the governing body of the redevelopment agency (§ 33200), establish a separate governing body of the redevelopment agency (§ 33110), or establish a community development commission, which allows the legislative body or a separate appointed body to function jointly as a redevelopment agency and a housing authority.

When redevelopment agencies were established in the 1950s and 1960s to implement federal financing programs, it was common for a city council to appoint a separate governing board of the redevelopment agency. In addition, many of the first redevelopment agencies were established in larger cities, where the numerous and complex duties of the city council made establishing a separate governing board an efficient and politically acceptable solution. This was particularly true where most of the funds spent were from federal, not local, tax revenue.

Since then, however, the vast majority of legislative bodies establishing redevelopment agencies have appointed themselves as the governing body. In addition, in several cities in which separate governing bodies were previously appointed, the city council has decided to appoint itself as the governing body. This trend results from several factors.

It is often neither efficient nor politically acceptable for legislative bodies to appoint separate governing boards in small or medium-sized cities.

It is often neither efficient nor politically acceptable for legislative bodies to appoint separate governing boards in small or medium-sized cities. Separate governing bodies can mean more meetings, more staff (or greater burdens on existing staff), and a lengthier approval process, since important decisions often have to be made by both the agency and the legislative body. In addition, legislative bodies are held politically accountable for redevelopment decisions, often among the more important decisions they make, and the control of agency activities is important. They know that this accountability cannot be avoided by appointing a separate governing body because major decisions regarding plan adoption and tax-increment expenditures require legislative approval of the governing board's actions. *See*, for example, §§ 33367 and 33433.

Nevertheless, in certain instances, the appointment of a separate redevelopment agency board may be desirable.

Nevertheless, in certain instances, the appointment of a separate redevelopment agency board may be desirable. It has worked well in several communities, for example, by isolating redevelopment decisions from some of the political give-and-take of a legislative body. A separate board should have more time to devote to redevelopment decisions than a legislative body that has many issues competing for attention. In addition, when a separate board with strong community support makes a recommendation, the decision of the legislative body can often be made more easily. All of this may result in simplified and accelerated development.

Legislative Body as the Agency

At the time the ordinance declaring the need for the agency is enacted, the legislative body may declare itself to be the agency. § 33200. If an agency with a governing board separate from the legislative body is in existence, the legislative body by ordinance may declare itself to be the agency and thereafter govern the agency. If a separate governing board has been in existence at least three years, then prior to declaring itself to be the agency, the legislative body must hold a public hearing on the proposed ordinance and prepare a report supporting this decision. § 33200.

If a member of the legislative body resigns as a member of the agency, the legislative body must appoint a replacement to serve the remainder of the term. § 33200(a).

Appointment of Separate Agency

The legislative body may appoint a separate governing board at the time the ordinance declaring the need for the agency is enacted by having the mayor or chairman of the board of supervisors appoint, with the approval of the legislative body, either five or seven members to the agency. § 33110. Of the approximately 349 redevelopment agencies that existed in 1989, 13 communities reported the establishment of separate governing boards.

Establishment of Community Development Commission

As a third alternative, California law authorizes the establishment of a community development commission for the purpose of giving the community the option of governing its redevelopment agency and housing authority with a single operating board. § 34110. The legislative body may grant to the commission the power to act as only a redevelopment agency or the power to act as both a redevelopment agency and a housing authority. § 34115.5. Similar to the establishment of a redevelopment agency under the Community Redevelopment Law, the legislative body can either appoint itself as the commission (§ 34120(a)) or appoint a separate board. § 34130(a). In either case, if the community development commission has been granted the power to act as the housing authority, the governing board of the commission must be expanded to include two commissioners who are tenants of the housing authority. This alternative is used by only a few communities within the state.

Compensation

If it is specifically approved by the legislative body establishing the agency, agency members are authorized to receive compensation for serving on the agency governing body. § 33114. However, in cities or counties with a population of less than 200,000, if the legislative body acts as the agency, the compensation received by each member cannot exceed $30 for each meeting of the agency attended by the member for a maximum of four meetings during a calendar month. § 33114.5. In addition, members may receive their actual and necessary expenses, including travel expenses, incurred in the discharge of the agency member's duties. §§ 33114, 33114.5.

Some city councils that also serve as agency members have voted themselves the additional compensation authorized by these sections because of the increased amount of work and responsibility directly resulting from their redevelopment duties. However, other council members, viewing these responsibilities as part of their council duties, have declined to approve additional compensation.

Del Paso Nuevo Before and After
The City and Sacramento Housing and Redevelopment Agency received an award of $10.5 million in federal grants and loans for the development of a new homeownership community. Since 1998, more than two-thirds of the 33 properties needed for the infrastructure and first phase home development have been purchased and assembled.

Agency Establishment and the Referendum and Initiative Process

The ordinance establishing the need for an agency is subject to referendum. § 33101. Because a legislative body, acting in accordance with the Community Redevelopment Law, is carrying out state policy, the courts have recognized the area to be one of statewide concern. *See* chapter 3 for a discussion of the relationship between agency projects and the referendum process. Therefore, this right to obtain a referendum on the activation of the agency is based upon this specific statute and, in its absence, no such right would exist. Moreover, a redevelopment agency cannot be established by initiative.

Agency Activation

After the ordinance establishing the redevelopment agency has become effective, and prior to taking the steps to adopt a redevelopment plan, a redevelopment agency should adopt certain organizational and procedural documents:

- Approve the chairman and vice-chairman by resolution. § 33113. When a separate agency is established, the first chairman is designated by the presiding officer of the legislative body, and thereafter the chairman is elected. If the legislative body is the agency, any agency member may be approved as chairman or vice chairman; however, as a practical matter, many agencies prefer to appoint the mayor or board chairman as chairman of the agency and the vice mayor or vice chairman of the board as vice chairman of the agency to assist in running meetings smoothly. Legislative bodies and agencies often move quickly from the agenda of one entity to the agenda of the other and occasionally conduct joint public hearings.

- Adopt bylaws to appoint officers, including the executive director, secretary, and other personnel, and establish basic procedures for meetings and organization. § 33125.

- Adopt personnel rules. § 33126. Often, agencies adopt the personnel rules of the community, particularly if no separate staff is involved.

- Adopt guidelines for considering environmental issues. Since the agency is a separate legal entity from the community and will often be considering environmental documents, sometimes as the lead agency, it is important to establish procedures or guidelines for the preparation and review of environmental documents under the California

Environmental Quality Act. Pub. Resources Code § 21000 *et seq.* Some agencies adopt their communities' guidelines because staff and officials are familiar with the procedures. Others prefer guidelines specifically tailored to the agency's needs, particularly with regard to plan adoption.

- Adopt a general agreement between the agency and the community, often called a cooperation agreement. This authorizes the community to give the newly formed agency financial and personnel assistance, use of facilities, and other aid, and may be used to establish agency indebtedness required to obtain tax increments. These agreements often obligate the agency to reimburse the community for all or a portion of the assistance.
- Designate a newspaper of general circulation for the publication of official notices. Gov. Code § 6040 *et seq.*
- Adopt a conflict of interest code under the state's Political Reform Act of 1974. Gov. Code § 87300 *et seq.*
- Inform the agency and legislative body in writing of the financial interest disclosures required by section 33130
- If additional compensation is to be received by agency members, the legislative body should approve the amount of the compensation by resolution. §§ 33114, 33114.5
- Approve a resolution that authorizes filing a statement of organization with the Secretary of State and county clerk. Gov. Code § 53051

General Powers and Jurisdiction

After the ordinance establishing the agency has become effective and after the agency has approved the organizational documents enabling it to function as a legal entity, it may exercise its general authority within the jurisdiction of the agency. The jurisdiction of the agency is the jurisdiction of the community. However, most of the activities commonly associated with redevelopment projects occur in conjunction with and after adoption of a redevelopment plan that establishes a project area boundary. The specific authority for these powers—such as eminent domain, tax-increment financing, and property disposition—are discussed in separate chapters throughout this book; this section summarizes general powers not contingent upon the adoption of a redevelopment plan.

A redevelopment agency is a separate legal entity from the community within which it exists although its jurisdiction is the same. § 33120. One case, *Nolan v. Redevelopment Agency* (1981) 117 Cal. App. 3d 494, tended to blur this legal distinction between a city and its redevelopment agency. A more recent and better reasoned case, *Pacific States Enterprise, Inc. v. City of Coachella* (1993) 13 Cal. App. 4th 1414, makes it clear that the two are entirely separate and distinct legal entities.

Most of the activities commonly associated with redevelopment projects occur in conjunction with and after adoption of a redevelopment plan that establishes a project area boundary.

A redevelopment agency is a public body, corporate and politic, that exercises governmental functions and has the powers prescribed in the Community Redevelopment Law.

A redevelopment agency is a public body, corporate and politic, that exercises governmental functions and has the powers prescribed in the Community Redevelopment Law. §§ 33100, 33112. It is, therefore, a creature of statute, and direct or implied authority for its actions must be found within the Community Redevelopment Law. A redevelopment agency is "an agency of the state for the local performance of governmental or proprietary function within limited boundaries." *Kehoe v. City of Berkeley* (1977) 67 Cal. App. 3d 666, 673.

An agency may sue and be sued and make contracts (§ 33125); appoint and employ permanent and temporary officers and employees (§ 33126); purchase or rent office space, equipment, and supplies and pay expenses (§ 33127); accept financial or other assistance from public or private sources, including the application for federal grants (§§ 33131, 33132, 33133); and carry insurance (§ 33134).

Finally, an agency may prepare and carry out plans for the improvement, rehabilitation, and redevelopment of blighted areas. § 33131. Once the plan adoption process has begun, an agency may exercise certain additional powers, such as acquiring property (§ 33391); and, once the redevelopment plan has been adopted, an agency may exercise the full authority granted by the Community Redevelopment Law within, and in certain cases outside of, the project area.

Conflicts of Interest and Disclosure of Economic Interests

Political Reform Act of 1974

Redevelopment agencies and agency members, officials, and employees are governed by the provisions of the Political Reform Act of 1974.

Redevelopment agencies (as entities) and agency members, officials, and employees (as individuals) are governed by the provisions of the Political Reform Act of 1974. Gov. Code § 81000 *et seq.*; *see* Gov. Code §§ 82003 and 82048. Redevelopment agencies must therefore adopt conflict of interest codes, and agency officers and employees must comply with both disqualification and disclosure requirements found in the Political Reform Act. The legislative body serves as the code-reviewing body for the agency.

The conflict of interest code for the agency must designate the positions within the agency that involve the making or participation in making of decisions that may foreseeably have a material effect on any financial interest of the person holding that position. These would include the members of the redevelopment agency board. If the legislative body also serves as the agency board, the members of the city council or board of supervisors, whichever is applicable, can state on their annual Statements of Economic Interests that they are filing in both capacities. In addition, the will need to determine which employees and consultants are "designated employees" within the meaning of the Political Reform Act, and what economic interests (investments, business positions, interests in

real property, and income) should be disclosed on their annual Statements of Economic Interests. Gov. Code § 87302.

The list of designated employees should include members of the project area committee (*see* chapters 3 and 4). If officers and employees are designated employees of the community, and their interests will be affected similarly by their decisions as designated employees of both entities, the agency should adopt an identical code. Alternatively, the agency could adopt by reference the code already covering the designated employee, so that one person is not subject to two codes with different provisions, a situation that could be problematic when wearing two hats.

An initial statement filed under a conflict of interest code must be filed by each designated employee within 30 days after the effective date of the code. The designated employee also must file an annual statement at the time specified in the code and an additional statement within 30 days after leaving office. Gov. Code § 87302(b).

While conflict of interest codes must be adopted after the agency is established, and initial statements must be filed immediately after code adoption, the disqualification provisions of the adopted code and the Political Reform Act will not disqualify agency members or officials from making or participating in decisions regarding agency establishment and organization. This is because, as a practical matter, the agency cannot exercise its important powers until after the redevelopment plan adoption process has been initiated. Prior to the community, the agency, or its staff taking the initial step in the plan adoption process—the adoption of a survey area—the economic interests of community and agency members and designated employees should be carefully reviewed to determine if anyone should be disqualified from participating in the process. This process and the applicable rules are discussed in greater detail in chapter 4.

Community Redevelopment Law: Prohibition and Disclosure

The Community Redevelopment Law contains important requirements regarding conflicts of interest that are different from and in addition to the provisions of the Political Reform Act of 1974. Section 33130 (discussed in detail in chapter 4) states in part that "No agency or community officer or employee who in the course of his or her duties is required to participate in the formulation of, or to approve plans or policies for, the redevelopment of a project area shall acquire any interest in any property included within a project area within the community." Because the prohibition is so definite, it is important that members of the agency, legislative body, and planning agency understand this provision when the agency is established. The officers and employees it affects should be identified as soon as possible.

Section 33130 also contains a disclosure requirement: Any officer or employee covered by the prohibition and who owns or has any direct or indirect financial interest in property included within a project area is required to make a written disclosure of that interest to the agency and the legislative body, which shall include that disclosure in the minutes of the respective bodies. Failure to disclose such an interest constitutes misconduct in office. § 33130(a).

Incompatibility of Office

The common law theory of incompatibility of offices is also applicable to officers and employees of a redevelopment agency. This theory prohibits officeholders from holding two offices when the duties of one office would conflict with or impede the unbiased exercise of discretion in the other. *People ex rel. Chapman v. Rapsey* (1940) 16 Cal. 2d 636.

A related provision in the Community Redevelopment Law states that a member of an agency separate from the legislative body may not be an elective officer or an employee of the community. However, notwithstanding any other law, he or she may be a member, commissioner, or employee of any other community agency or authority. § 33111.

Open Meeting Requirements— The Brown Act

California has a comprehensive statute—the Ralph M. Brown Act— that governs the conduct of all local legislative bodies, including a redevelopment agency, guaranteeing that public decisions be made in public. The Brown Act strictly limits the circumstances under which the redevelopment agency may take any official action outside public view. Gov. Code § 54950 *et seq*. Accordingly, the adoption of a redevelopment plan, and any amendments to the plan, must be done at a properly noticed regular meeting of the redevelopment agency.

If the agency is considering the "purchase, sale, exchange, or lease" of real property, the Brown Act allows the agency board to meet in closed session with its negotiator (who may be a member of the board) to provide instructions "regarding the price and terms of payment for the purchase, sale, exchange, or lease." However, the property and the names of the negotiator(s) must be disclosed publicly before the closed session takes place. Gov. Code § 54956.8.

The Brown Act requires that prior to meeting in closed session to discuss the purchase, sale, or lease of real property, the

An abandoned gas station and rail yards in Emeryville provided a site for ground floor retail space and 220 units at the Bridgecourt Apartments.

The adoption of a redevelopment plan, and any amendments to it, must be done at a properly noticed regular meeting of the redevelopment agency.

redevelopment agency shall disclose certain information in an open session. Government Code section 54954.5 requires, among other things, that the names of each of the negotiators attending the closed session be specified.

In *Stockton Newspapers, Inc. v. Members of the Redevelopment Agency of the City of Stockton* (1985) 171 Cal. App. 3d 95, the court held that an alleged series of one-to-one nonpublic telephone conversations between the redevelopment agency's attorney and a majority of the legislative body for the commonly agreed purpose of collectively deciding to approve a transfer of property violated the Brown Act and constituted a cause of action.

If the agency plans to acquire property through eminent domain it may meet with its legal counsel in closed session to discuss the litigation. Gov. Code §§ 54956.8, 54956.9. In addition, an agency may meet with its legal counsel to discuss pending litigation. Pending litigation can comprise either a formal adjudicatory proceeding or potential litigation against the agency or where the agency is deciding whether to initiate litigation. Gov. Code § 54956.9.

If the agency plans to acquire property through eminent domain it may meet with its legal counsel in closed session to discuss the litigation.

The agency board may also meet in closed session to discuss the hiring or termination of one of its employees or charges made against one of its employees (unless the employee requests the matter be heard publicly). Gov. Code § 54957.

Finally, the Brown Act contains provisions requiring the posting of an agenda 72 hours prior to a meeting. With certain limited exceptions, the agency may only take action on items that appear on the posted agenda. Gov. Code § 54954.2.

Staff and Consultants

An agency is authorized to appoint and employ both permanent and temporary officers, employees, consultants, and counsel and to determine their qualifications, duties, and compensation. § 33126. The legislative body may exercise control through approval of the budget. As described earlier, an agency is required to adopt both personnel rules and regulations and conflict of interest codes. *See* chapter 4 for further discussion on Conflicts of Interest.

An agency is authorized to appoint and employ both permanent and temporary officers, employees, consultants, and counsel and to determine their qualifications, duties, and compensation.

An agency is also authorized to have access to the services and facilities of the various departments and offices of the community. § 33128. As a practical matter, while some large agencies have their own staff supplemented by consultants, the majority of agencies rely upon city or county staff, who often charge time spent on agency projects to the agency. Agencies typically use legal and financial consultants, and most use planning or redevelopment consultants, particularly during the plan adoption process. Bond counsel and underwriters will also be necessary when the agency sells long-term debt.

Agencies should be careful when selecting redevelopment consultants and legal counsel.

Agencies should be careful when selecting redevelopment consultants and legal counsel. Perhaps because the plan adoption process is highly technical and, therefore, city and county staff are often unfamiliar with its requirements, and because such large amounts of money are involved, it is easy for consultants to offer what appears to be an irresistible program with many advantages and no apparent disadvantages or risks. However, there are risks and disadvantages in establishing overly ambitious redevelopment projects that may strain both the letter and intent of the law, and communities should engage consultants who are willing to work within these limits to achieve the goals of the community. This is especially critical now given the requirements for detailed and specific documentation of blight for any new plan adoption or amendment.

Budget

Each agency is required to adopt an annual budget containing activities to be financed by the Low and Moderate Income Housing Fund, proposed expenditures and indebtedness, anticipated revenues, a work program, and a comparison between the previous year's achievements and goals. The budget may be amended. Expenditures and indebtedness of the agency are to be in conformity with the budget. If the legislative body is not the agency, the legislative body must approve the annual budget and amendments to it. § 33606.

Reporting

The legislature has required agencies to file annual reports with the legislative body and the state emphasizing both the financial condition and transactions of the agency and information regarding housing for low- and moderate-income persons. The reports on housing are described in greater detail in chapter 11.

Section 33080.1 requires that each agency prepare a report to its legislative body within six months of the end of the agency's fiscal year.

Section 33080.1 (as well as Government Code § 53891) requires that each agency prepare a report to its legislative body within six months of the end of the agency's fiscal year. *See* chapter 3. A copy of this report is to be filed with the State Controller within the same time period. The report must contain:

- An independent financial audit, including an opinion regarding the agency's compliance with laws, regulations, and administrative requirements
- The fiscal statement for the previous year, which contains very specific information required by section 33080.5
- A description of the agency's activities affecting housing that contains the detailed information required by sections 33080.4 and 33080.7
- A description of the agency's progress, including specific actions and expenditures, in alleviating blight in the previous fiscal year

- A list of, and status report on, all loans made by the agency of $50,000 or more that, in the previous fiscal year, were in default or not in compliance with the loan terms
- A description of the total number and nature of the properties that the agency owns and those properties the agency acquired in the previous fiscal year
- A list of the fiscal years that the agency expects the time limits to expire for (1) commencement of eminent domain proceedings; (2) establishment of debt; (3) effectiveness of the redevelopment plan; and (4) repayment of indebtedness
- Any other information the agency wishes to include

Section 33080 requires agencies to provide a copy of the report required to be filed with the Controller under section 33080.1 to any person, including a taxing agency, who requests a copy and pays for it. If the report does not include detailed information regarding administrative costs or costs for professional or other expenditures, the agency is required to provide this information upon request.

Section 33080 also requires each agency to file a copy of the independent financial audit required by section 33080.1(a) with the State Department of Housing and Community Development (HCD). Section 33080.1(a) requires that this financial audit be prepared by a certified public accountant or public accountant, licensed by the State of California, in accordance with Government Auditing Standards adopted by the Comptroller General of the United States. The audit must, at a minimum, meet the audit guidelines prepared by the State Controller's office. HCD must publish its annual report in May and send executive summaries of this report to each agency unless the agency requests a full copy. § 33080.6.

HCD = Department of Housing and Community Development

Pass-Through Payments

On or before October 1, 2009, and annually thereafter through 2014, agencies with redevelopment plans that either were (1) adopted on or after January 1, 1994, or (2) amended to add area on or after January 1, 1994 must file a report with the county auditor detailing the tax increments received and pass-through payments made to every taxing entity. Section 33684 requires the county auditor to review each agency's reports and determine whether it concurs with the information included in the reports. If it does not concur, the auditor must give the agency at least 15 days to respond to concerns raised by the auditor, and to revise and resubmit the report. If the auditor and the agency do not agree regarding the pass-through requirements, an agency may submit a report, along with a statement of dispute identifying the issues needing resolution. § 33684(e).

After submitting a statement of dispute, the county auditor and the agency can attempt to resolve the issue on their own. The agency may then amend the report to reflect the resolution, and the county auditor may issue a finding of concurrence. However, the State Controller has the authority to revoke a finding of concurrence. § 33684(e)(5).

The county auditor is charged with preparing and submitting an annual report to the State Controller regarding each project area subject to section 33684, including information such as those agencies for which the auditor has and has not issued a finding of concurrence, and which agencies owe outstanding pass-through obligations to a local education agency. § 33684(f). The Controller then compiles the data from all of the county auditors and submits a report to the Legislative Analyst's Office and Department of Finance, with a copy to the Board of Governors of the California Community Colleges.

After February 1, 2009, all agencies listed on the Controller's report as either (1) having not received a finding of concurrence from the county auditor on all projects, or (2) having an outstanding pass-through payment obligation to one or more local educational agencies, may not do any of the following:

- Adopt new project areas or expand an existing one
- Issue new bonds
- Encumber any funds except to pay:
  - Existing bonds
  - Loans or moneys advanced to the agency
  - Contractual obligations that, if unpaid, could subject the agency to damages or other liability
  - Obligations to pay for certain public improvements or facilities
  - Affordable housing obligations
  - Obligations to make payments in lieu of property taxes on agency-owned property pursuant to section 33401
  - Monthly operational and administrative expenses not to exceed 75 percent of the average monthly amount spent in the previous fiscal year

§ 33684(i)(1)

In addition, agencies will be charged interest on any outstanding pass-through payment made to a local educational agency more than 60 days after the close of the fiscal year in which the payment was owed. § 33684(i)(2).

Under certain limited circumstances, the State Controller, with the concurrence of the state Director of Finance, may waive the restrictions listed above, for up to 12 months. The Controller must find that (1) the auditor has made a finding of concurrence on all of the agency's reports;

(2) the agency has filed a statement of dispute that the Controller believes will be resolved in the agency's favor; (3) the agency has made all required outstanding pass-through payments except the one in dispute; and (4) the agency would suffer a financial hardship if it had to make the payment estimated by the auditor. § 33684(i)(3).

Major Violations

Section 33080.8 requires the Controller to compile a list of agencies that, based on the financial audit reports, appear to have major violations of the Community Redevelopment Law. The section defines "major violations," and establishes a procedure for consultation between the Controller's office and the appropriate redevelopment agency, referral of these matters to the Attorney General, a court hearing, and the issuance of court orders designed to remedy the major violation.

Dissolution of the Agency

If an agency has not conducted any redevelopment activities, including entering into a contract, within two years after being established, the legislative body may dissolve the agency by declaring in an ordinance that no need for the agency exists. § 33140.

In addition, the legislative body may order the deactivation of an agency by declaring, in an ordinance, that no need for the agency exists, provided, however, that the agency has no outstanding financial or legal obligations, such as bonded or other indebtedness, unpaid loans or advances, or legally binding contracts with persons other than the community. If any of these obligations exist, the agency may still be deactivated if the community assumes all of these financial and legal obligations. The ordinance is subject to referendum. § 33141. An ordinance adopted pursuant to either section should be filed with the Secretary of State. § 33142. The legislative body may not adopt an ordinance dissolving an agency until the agency has fully complied with its housing obligations. §§ 33140, 33141, and 33333.8.

If an agency has not conducted any redevelopment activities within two years after being established, the legislative body may dissolve the agency.

3
Adoption of Redevelopment Plan

As the fundamental document governing the activities of a redevelopment agency, a redevelopment plan basically acts as the agency's charter.

What Is a Redevelopment Plan?

As the fundamental document governing a redevelopment agency's activities, a redevelopment plan functions as the agency's charter. Adopted by the local legislative body (a city council or county board of supervisors), the plan establishes long-term planning goals as well as implementation policies and procedures for the redevelopment of a designated project area. It also serves as a financing plan by authorizing the agency's use of particular financing tools to implement projects and policies. A redevelopment plan may also establish certain limitations on the authority of a redevelopment agency to conduct activities within a project area. It follows from this description that a redevelopment plan is typically a very general document, providing the agency with maximum flexibility. As the court stated in *County of Santa Cruz v. City of Watsonville* (1985) 177 Cal. App. 3d 831, 841:

A redevelopment plan is typically a very general document, providing the agency with maximum flexibility.

> By exercising certain of its powers to implement redevelopment, a redevelopment agency may induce private investment in an area. The success of any redevelopment project is dependent upon whether private lenders, developers, owners, and tenants can be persuaded to participate in the process. Thus, a redevelopment agency is unique among public entities since in order to achieve its objective of eliminating blight it must rely upon cooperation with the private sector. Redevelopment is also a process which occurs over a period of years. These realities dictate that a redevelopment plan be written in terms that enhance a redevelopment agency's ability to respond to market conditions, development opportunities and the desires and abilities of owners and tenants. Such a plan then cannot always outline in detail each project that a redevelopment agency will undertake during the life of

the plan. (§§ 33132, 33133, 33339, 33339.5, 33380, 33381, 33601; *In re Redevelopment Plan for Bunker Hill* (1964) 61 Cal. 2d 21 [37 Cal. Rptr. 74, 389; P.2d 539].)

The Community Redevelopment Law requires certain formal procedures to ensure that there are opportunities for taxing agencies and citizens to provide input and comments. In addition, the redevelopment agency must prepare certain detailed reports and documents regarding the proposed redevelopment plan. Consequently, the procedure for the adoption of a plan is normally a lengthy and complicated process requiring approximately one year to complete. An illustrative time schedule describing the procedural steps involved in the plan adoption process is included as Appendix B.

A redevelopment plan can be adopted either by a county, with respect to its unincorporated area, or by a city for an area within its territorial limits. § 33214. The legislative body of one jurisdiction may also authorize the redevelopment of an area within its jurisdiction by a neighboring jurisdiction, if the area is contiguous. § 33213. Cities and counties may also jointly undertake redevelopment activities for a project area consisting of both incorporated and unincorporated areas. § 33210.

Redevelopment Team

Before embarking on the plan adoption process, the agency should determine who will be responsible for preparing the various documents and coordinating the work of the different consultants and staff members who are working on the adoption. Individual specialized tasks involved in the preparation of a redevelopment plan include the preparation of an environmental impact report, planning and surveying in connection with the various reports that document the existence of blight, financial forecasting and specialized legal counsel. These specialized tasks can either be performed by staff persons or by outside consultants. However, because these tasks are time consuming and require highly specialized knowledge, many communities prefer to hire outside consultants. Agencies should take great care to select consultants who will perform the necessary detailed research and analysis so that there will be a well documented, factual basis for the findings required to be made by the legislative body when it adopts the redevelopment plan. This has become increasingly important as courts have begun to examine the underlying documentation more carefully.

Prerequisites to Redevelopment Plan Adoption

Before a redevelopment plan may be adopted, the city or county must have a planning agency established pursuant to law or charter and a general plan conforming to the requirements of state law. §§ 33301,

33302. The community's general plan must include the following mandatory elements:

- Land use. Gov. Code § 65302(a)
- Circulation. Gov. Code § 65302(b)
- Housing. Gov. Code §§ 65302(c), 65580
- Conservation. Gov. Code § 65302(d)
- Open space. Gov. Code §§ 65302(e), 65560
- Noise element. Gov. Code § 65302(f)
- Safety element. Gov. Code § 65302(g)

One finding that the legislative body must make in the ordinance adopting the redevelopment plan is that the redevelopment plan conforms to the general plan of the community, including, but not limited to, the community's housing element (which must comply with state planning and zoning law). § 33367(d)(4). This requirement merits special attention because of case law holding invalid the adoption of zoning ordinances, subdivision approvals, and similar land use decisions where the community's general plan is incomplete or inadequate. *See, e.g., Resource Defense Fund v. County of Santa Cruz* (1982) 133 Cal. App. 3d 800, 806.

Before commencing procedures to adopt or amend a redevelopment plan, a community should undertake a thorough review of its general plan to determine that it is complete and adequate and that the proposed redevelopment plan is consistent with the general plan. If there are problems with the general plan, or proposed land uses conflict with those designated in the general plan, an amendment or update can be processed concurrently. Care must be exercised, however, in timing the adoption of a redevelopment plan or an amendment to a redevelopment plan based on a contemporaneous general plan amendment. A court decision has held that an action (in that case the approval of a development agreement) based on a finding of conformity to a contemporaneous general plan amendment was not valid because the general plan amendment was not then in effect, since the 30-day referendum period then applicable had not run. *Midway Orchards v. County of Butte* (1990) 220 Cal. App. 3d 765.

If a community is in the process of revising or updating its general plan, it may seek an extension of time, not to exceed two years, from the state Director of Planning and Research for the preparation and adoption of all or part of the general plan, except the housing element. Gov. Code § 65361. The legislative body must first hold a public hearing and make one of the findings specified in the section, identifying the supporting reasons. This section further provides that during the extension:

> The city or county is not subject to the requirement that a complete and adequate general plan be adopted, or the requirements that it be adopted within a specific period of time. Development approvals shall be

consistent with those portions of the general plan for which an extension has been granted, except as provided by the conditions imposed by the director pursuant to subdivision (d). Development approvals shall be consistent with any element or elements that have been adopted and for which an extension of time is not sought.

Gov. Code § 65361(e)

Thus, if it appears that a general plan amendment may not be completed by the time the redevelopment plan is supposed to be adopted, the provisions of Government Code section 65361 may offer some protection against this type of challenge.

Designation of Survey Area

The legislative body designates a survey area by resolution as the first planning step to determine whether a redevelopment project within that area is feasible.

The legislative body designates a survey area by resolution as the first planning step to determine whether a redevelopment project within that area is feasible. The adoption of the resolution does not require notice or a public hearing. If the legislative body so authorizes by resolution, a survey area may also be designated by resolution of either the redevelopment agency or the planning agency. § 33310. The resolution designating the survey area must contain a finding that the area requires study to determine if a redevelopment project is feasible within that area. It must also include a description of the area's boundaries.

The designation of the survey area is important because the final project area for the redevelopment plan must be within the boundaries of the survey area. (However, subsequent amendment of a survey area is relatively simple, requiring only an amendatory resolution.) The designation of a survey area by itself does not have any legal impact on properties within the survey area, and many survey areas exist for which no redevelopment plans have been adopted.

Before committing to the time and expense of adopting a redevelopment plan, many communities conduct, or hire consultants to conduct, an initial feasibility study.

Before committing to the time and expense of adopting a redevelopment plan, many communities conduct, or hire consultants to conduct, an initial feasibility study. This study can be done either prior to or after the selection of a survey area and can be used to help select the boundaries of the survey and/or project area. The focus of the study should be to make a preliminary determination of the blighting conditions within the area, the feasible land uses, the market demand for such uses, and financial feasibility.

Project Area Prerequisites and Formulation of Preliminary Plans

Project Area Prerequisites

Blight. The legal justification for use of the extraordinary public powers authorized by the Community Redevelopment Law is the elimination of blight. *Berman v. Parker* (1954) 348 U.S. 26. The elimination of blighted areas is the public purpose that has justified allowing a redevelopment agency to impose design controls, restrict uses, acquire property by eminent domain, and expend public funds. *Redevelopment Agency v. Hayes* (1954) 122 Cal. App. 2d 777; *cert. denied* (1954) 348 U.S. 897; § 33030 *et seq.* By eliminating blight, the agency is carrying out state policy. *Redevelopment Agency v. City of Berkeley* (1978) 80 Cal. App. 3d 158, 168. The condemnation of private property by a redevelopment agency for resale to a private party for redevelopment is an authorized means of carrying out this state policy. § 33037.

The characteristics of blight are defined by the state legislature. Subject to the statutory definitions and certain exceptions, blighting conditions must predominate and injuriously affect the entire project area. *Regus v. City of Baldwin Park* (1977) 70 Cal. App. 3d 968; § 33321. The concept of blight applies to the area as a whole and not necessarily to particular properties. *Berman v. Parker* (1954) 348 U.S. 26, 35. Each individual property within a redevelopment project area need not be blighted. *Id.*

The legislative definition of blight has evolved over the years, generally becoming more restrictive with the passage of time. Major redevelopment reform legislation in 1993 (AB 1290) and 2006 (SB 1206) has progressively narrowed and tightened the statutory definition of blight. SB 1206 in particular stated that the purpose of the amendment was "to focus public officials' attention and their extraordinary redevelopment powers on properties with physical and economic conditions that are so significantly degraded that they seriously harm the prospects for physical and economic development without the use of redevelopment." Taking their cue from the legislature, recent court decisions tend to impose on redevelopment agencies a greater burden of proof of the conditions constituting blight than was the case a generation ago. Redevelopment agencies should therefore exercise great care in investigating and documenting the conditions of blight within a proposed redevelopment project area or they may be faced with a judicial decision invalidating the redevelopment plan.

The legislative definition of blight is found in sections 33030 and 33031. That definition requires that:

- The redevelopment project area be predominately urbanized, as defined in section 33320.1. *See* the discussion of *Friends of Mammoth*, in this chapter.
- The redevelopment project area must be an area in which the combination of physical and economic conditions set forth below is so prevalent and so substantial that it causes

Rusted storage tanks gave way to bustling retail and residential units on Bay Street in Emeryville.

Redevelopment agencies should exercise great care in investigating and documenting the conditions of blight within a proposed redevelopment project area.

a reduction of, or lack of, proper utilization of the area to such an extent that it constitutes a serious physical and economic burden on the community that cannot reasonably be expected to be reversed or alleviated by private enterprise, or governmental action, or both, without redevelopment.

- The area is characterized by one or more of the physical conditions and one or more of the economic conditions set forth below.

Physical Blight. Subdivision (a) of section 33031 describes the physical conditions that cause blight as follows:

- Buildings in which is it unsafe or unhealthy for persons to live or work. These conditions can be caused by serious building code violations, serious dilapidation and deterioration caused by long-term neglect, construction that is vulnerable to serious damage from seismic or geologic hazards, and faulty or inadequate water or sewer utilities.

- Conditions that prevent or substantially hinder the economically viable use or capacity of buildings or lots. These conditions may be caused by buildings of substandard, defective, or obsolete design or construction given the present general plan, zoning, or other development standards.

- Adjacent or nearby incompatible land uses that prevent development of those parcels or other portions of the project area.

- The existence of subdivided lots that are in multiple ownership and where physical development has been impaired by their irregular shapes and inadequate sizes, given present general plan and zoning standards and present market conditions.

Economic Blight. Subdivision (b) of section 33031 describes the economic conditions that cause blight as follows:

- Depreciated or stagnant property values

- Impaired property values, due in significant part to hazardous wastes on property where the agency may be eligible to use its authority as specified in Article 12.5 (commencing with § 33459), discussed in chapter 6 (Environmental Issues)

- Abnormally high business vacancies, abnormally low lease rates, or an abnormally high number of abandoned buildings

- A serious lack of necessary commercial facilities that are normally found in neighborhoods, including grocery stores, drugstores and banks, and other lending institutions

- Serious residential overcrowding that has resulted in significant public health or safety problems. "Overcrowding" means exceeding the standard referenced in Article 5 (commencing with § 32) of Chapter 1 of Title 25 of the California Code of Regulations

- An excess of bars, liquor stores, or adult-oriented businesses that has resulted in significant public health, safety, or welfare problems
- A high crime rate that constitutes a serious threat to the public safety and welfare

Nonblighted properties may be included only if their inclusion is necessary for the effective redevelopment of the area of which they are a part. They may not be included for the purpose of obtaining tax-increment revenues without other substantial justification for their inclusion. § 33321; *In re Redevelopment Plan for Bunker Hill* (1964) 61 Cal. 2d 21, *appeal dism'd, cert. denied* (1964) 379 U.S. 28, 899; *Regus v. City of Baldwin Park* (1977) 70 Cal. App. 3d 968. For example, nonblighted properties in an area that contains predominantly blighted properties may be included if it is necessary for comprehensive planning and development of the area. Land does not qualify as being blighted merely because it is not being put to its optimum use or may be more valuable for other uses. *Sweetwater Valley Civic Assn. v. City of National City* (1976) 18 Cal. 3d 270. Prime agricultural land, for example, is not blighted because it lacks adequate infrastructure to service proposed industrial and recreational uses if the current infrastructure is sufficient to service the property's current use and if that use is not a serious economic or physical liability to the community. *Emmington v. Solano County Redevelopment Agency* (1987) 195 Cal. App. 3d 491. There must be evidence that the asserted blighting conditions substantially burden the *existing* uses of the area.

Nonblighted, noncontiguous areas may be included in a project area only if they are being used predominantly for either the relocation of owners or tenants from other noncontiguous areas in the same or other project areas or low- and moderate-income housing. § 33320.2.

Many judicial opinions have interpreted the meaning of the legislative definition of blight. When reviewing a city council's determination that an area is blighted, the court examines the record of proceedings to see if the finding is supported by substantial evidence. Decisions rendered prior to the legislative changes to the definition of blight in 1993 (AB 1290) and 2006 (SB 1206) remain instructive. Pre-AB 1290 and SB 1206 cases *upholding* a determination of blight include: *In Re Redevelopment Plan for Bunker Hill* (1964) 61 Cal. 2d 21, 45, *appeal dism'd, cert. denied* (1964) 379 U.S.28, 899; *Morgan v. Community Redevelopment Agency* (1991) 231 Cal. App.3d 243, *cert denied* (1992) 503 U.S. 937; *Fosselman's, Inc. v. City of Alhambra* (1986) 178 Cal. App. 3d 806; *National City Business Assoc. v. City of National City* (1983) 146 Cal. App. 3d 1060; *Fellom v. Redevelopment Agency* (1958) 157 Cal. App. 2d 243, 246, *cert. denied* (1958) 358 U.S. 56; and *Redevelopment Agency v. Hayes* (1954) 122 Cal. App. 2d 777, 783–784, 786, 797, *cert. denied* (1954) 348 U.S. 897. Cases *overturning* a city council's determination of blight include: *Sweetwater Valley Civic Assn. v. City of National City* (1976) 18 Cal. 3d 270;

Nonblighted properties may be included only if their inclusion is necessary for the effective redevelopment of the area of which they are a part.

Land does not qualify as blighted merely because it is not being put to its optimum use or may be more valuable for other uses.

Regus v. City of Baldwin Park (1977) 70 Cal. App. 3d 968; and *Emmington v. Solano County* (1987) 195 Cal. App. 3d 491, 497.

In another pre-AB 1290 case, *Gonzales v. City of Santa Ana* (1993) 12 Cal. App. 4th 1335, the court found sufficient evidence that the project area suffered from overcrowding, a substantial number of dilapidated buildings, and a crime rate higher than the citywide average. Because the evidence of dilapidation was based solely on an exterior structural survey, the court said that evidence alone would have been insufficient to support a finding of blight. It was only because there was additional evidence in the record of overcrowding and crime that the court held the evidence was sufficient. This holding in the *Gonzales* case has been reinforced by SB 1206. There the legislature amended section 33352, describing the contents of the agency's report to the legislative body, to require that the description of conditions in the project area contain "specific, quantifiable evidence" that documents both: (1) the physical and economic conditions constituting blight, and (2) that the described physical and economic conditions are so prevalent and substantial that, collectively, they seriously harm the entire project area. SB 1206 also requires the ordinance adopting a redevelopment plan to contain findings based on "clearly articulated and documented evidence." These amendments have codified the holdings of *Gonzales* and the other cases cited herein that have rejected blight findings based on mere conclusions not supported by specific, quantifiable evidence. As a result, redevelopment agencies should be careful not to rely exclusively on "windshield" surveys to support a finding that physical blighting conditions exist in a proposed project area. The preliminary report and report to the city council should contain specific, detailed, and, to the greatest extent possible, quantifiable evidence of the conditions of blight.

The preliminary report and report to the city council should contain specific, detailed, and, to the greatest extent possible, quantifiable evidence of the conditions of blight.

Since the adoption of AB 1290, a number of cases have dealt with challenges to redevelopment plan adoptions on the grounds that the project area was not blighted. Generally, these cases are consistent with cases preceding AB 1290, but "raise the bar," in that they require even more concrete evidence of conditions that the legislature defines as blight. With the passage of SB 1206, the courts can be expected to be even more demanding of specific, quantifiable evidence in support of blight findings.

In *County of Riverside v. City of Murrieta* (1998) 65 Cal. App. 4th 616, the court applied the definition of blight contained in AB 1290 for the first time and determined that the redevelopment agency had not presented substantial evidence demonstrating the existence of blight. The court found that the report to the city council offered little concrete evidence of actual conditions of blight. Instead, it merely recited the statutory language used to define blight and contained conclusory generalizations, not tangible proof of specific problems.

In *Beach-Courchesne v. City of Diamond Bar* (2000) 80 Cal. App. 4th 388, the court also considered whether substantial evidence existed to support a finding that the project area was blighted within the meaning of Community Redevelopment Law. The court concluded that the redevelopment project proposed by the defendant failed to establish blight due to a lack of substantial supporting evidence in the administrative record. The court explained that in order to establish blight, reports must discuss specific defects in specific properties and not generalized recitals of the statutory language.

To establish blight, reports must discuss specific defects in specific properties and not generalized recitals of the statutory language.

In *Friends of Mammoth v. Town of Mammoth Lakes Redevelopment Agency* (2000) 82 Cal. App. 4th 511, the Court of Appeal overturned a trial court decision upholding the adoption of a redevelopment plan on the grounds that the project area was not blighted. The court found fault with the evidence the town relied on to support the existence of both physical and economic blight. The evidence supporting physical blight was inadequate because the methodology used by the town to document building conditions was flawed. Specifically, the definitions of terms such as "deterioration" and "dilapidation" were over-broad, including conditions such as the presence of peeling paint and dry rot, making it impossible to determine whether a sufficient number of structures were affected by conditions that were sufficiently serious that they resulted in buildings that were unsafe or unhealthy for human occupancy. With respect to economic blight, the court found that it is not sufficient to show factors that *limit* a property's economic viability. The statute requires a showing of economic factors that *prevent or substantially hinder* a parcel's economic viability. The fact that a more economic use of the parcel could be made is not sufficient. The evidence must demonstrate that conditions make the *current* use uneconomic.

Graber v. City of Upland (2002) 99 Cal. App. 4th 424, reinforced the holdings in *Murrieta, Diamond Bar,* and *Mammoth Lakes* on the issue of blight. *Graber* also criticized the use of surveys of physical conditions that used categories that were not tightly defined. The court noted that under the definition used by the consultants, a building could be considered deteriorated if it had peeling paint or cracked fascia. The use of over-broad definitions such as this prevented the city council from determining whether the project area could truly be characterized as containing buildings unsafe for human occupancy due to their deteriorated and dilapidated condition. The case also held that in a redevelopment project comprised of several noncontiguous subareas, each subarea must be either blighted or necessary for effective redevelopment. In other words, combining a subarea with only physical blight and a noncontiguous subarea with only economic blight would not make the combined area blighted. Each noncontiguous subarea must contain elements of physical and economic blight or be necessary for effective redevelopment.

On the other hand, in *San Franciscans Upholding the Downtown Plan v. City and County of San Francisco* (2002) 102 Cal. App. 4th 656, the court found that there had been extensive evidence to support the finding of blight in an area that was being added to a redevelopment project area. The added area included several historic buildings that were largely vacant. The evidence included a detailed history of the area and the buildings, extensive descriptions of the obsolete and deteriorated condition of the structures, and separate but consistent analyses of the economic infeasibility of rehabilitating the buildings. *See also Evans v. City of San Jose* (2005) 128 Cal. App. 4th 1123, holding that substantial evidence supported the findings contained in the ordinance adopting the redevelopment plan that the project area was a blighted area.

Predominantly Urbanized. In addition to the requirement that a project area exhibit conditions of both physical and economic blight, a project area must also be "predominantly urbanized." This means that not less than 80 percent of all the land in the project area has been or is developed for urban uses or is an integral part of one or more areas developed for urban uses that are surrounded or substantially surrounded by parcels that have been or are developed for urban uses. § 33320.1. The ordinance adopting the plan must find that the project area is predominantly urbanized. This provision of the law is intended to prevent the adoption of project areas with large sections of vacant land; the legislature wanted to curb what it perceived to be abuses of redevelopment by communities that had adopted projects with large undeveloped parcels primarily for the significant tax increment that would result from the development of those vacant parcels.

Prior to the adoption of SB 1206 in 2006, there was an exception to the requirement that project areas be predominantly urbanized. Areas characterized by antiquated subdivisions, *e.g.*, subdivided lots of irregular form and shape and inadequate size for proper usefulness and development, were exempt from this requirement. SB 1206 repealed this exception, effective January 1, 2007. Areas characterized by antiquated subdivisions may now be included in redevelopment project areas only if they also qualify as being predominantly urbanized.

In *County of Riverside v. City of Murrieta* (1998) 65 Cal. App. 4th 616, the court addressed the definition of "predominantly urbanized" for the first time and held that the agency's proposed project area did not meet the 80 percent test. The court declined to give a judicial definition of "urban" that could be used in all situations. Factors to be evaluated in determining whether an area is urban or rural include: density, surrounding developments, proximity to or potential of becoming an incorporated area, existence of public facilities, parcel size, availability of public transit and similar characteristics. The court determined that 596 acres

In addition to the requirement that a project area exhibit conditions of both physical and economic blight, a project area must also be predominantly urbanized.

categorized as "rural-residential" and "equestrian-residential," allowing horses, other livestock, and other agricultural uses, were not urban uses under any definition. *Id.* at 620–624.

In *Friends of Mammoth v. Town of Mammoth Lakes Redevelopment Agency* (2000) 82 Cal. App. 4th 511, the Court of Appeal overturned the trial court decision upholding the adoption of a redevelopment plan on the grounds that the project area did not meet the predominantly urbanized test. The proposed project area contained a 76-acre community college site, 74 acres of which were not developed, 80 acres of a golf course and a 202-acre airport site, only a small portion of which was actually developed. The court held that an entire parcel may not be classified as "urbanized" merely because a portion of the parcel is developed. *Id.* at 542–543.

Graber v. City of Upland (2002) 99 Cal. App. 4th 424, also contained an important holding on the issue of urbanization. In this case, approximately one-half of a 380-acre noncontiguous subarea was the site of a mining operation and a municipal dump. The mining operations commenced in the early 1980s and were discontinued in 1985. Little or no investment or development had occurred on the property since then. The city claimed that the property, though essentially vacant, had been previously developed for urban uses. The court rejected this claim, saying:

> If, as *Friends of Mammoth* holds, the urban character of a property depends more on the property's location, characteristics and environs than its type of use, we should consider those characteristics based upon the status of the property at the time of the previous development. Thus, although we have been unable to find any authority discussing the issue, it seems that the question we must consider should be whether the rock mine and dump were developed for urban uses in the early 1980's. We therefore disagree with the City's argument that we must consider the current built-out condition of the City as showing the area is predominantly urban.

Id. at 438

The Metro Senior Apartments for very low-income persons was developed in conjunction with the 42-unit CityPark Townhouses in Foster City. Financing included city park in-lieu fees, tax-increment bond financing, and housing tax credits.

In *Neilson v. City of California City* (2007) 146 Cal. App. 4th 633, the city amended its redevelopment plan to add 24.4 square miles of vacant desert land to accommodate a proposed Hyundai automobile test track facility. The city determined that the added area was urbanized and blighted based on "[t]he existence of subdivided lots of irregular form and shape and inadequate size for proper usefulness and development that are in multiple ownership." *See* former § 33031(a)(4). The parcels in question were large and rectangular in shape, but lacked access to a public road and were therefore undevelopable. The city's report focused on the impracticality of development, arguing that "irregular" could be interpreted to mean not conforming to the standard of law, propriety, method, or custom. Under this definition, a lot is irregular because without access to a public street it cannot be developed. Project opponents focused on the actual physical shape and size of parcels, claiming the expansion area was not predominantly urbanized and did not meet the statutory definition of "blight."

The Court of Appeal rejected the broad interpretation of "irregular" used by the city and held that large rectangular lots do not have an "irregular form and shape" regardless of whether they lack access to a public street.

Agricultural Lands. In reaction to at least one agency's unsuccessful attempt to include thousands of acres of prime agricultural lands within a redevelopment project area, the legislature passed legislation prohibiting the inclusion of Williamson Act lands within a project area. Agricultural and open space lands that are "enforceably restricted," as defined in sections 422 and 422.5 of the Revenue and Taxation Code, may not be included within a project area. In addition, a parcel of land greater than two acres in size and used for agricultural purposes, but not enforceably restricted, may only be included in a project area if the agency makes certain findings:

- The inclusion of such land is consistent with redevelopment purposes
- The inclusion of such land will not cause the removal of adjacent land, designated for agricultural use in the community's general plan, from agricultural use
- The inclusion of such land is consistent with the community's general plan
- The inclusion of such land will result in a more contiguous pattern of development
- There is no proximate land that is not in agricultural use that is both available and suitable for inclusion within the project area, and is not already proposed to be within the project area

§ 33321.5

Housing—Relocation/Replacement/Use of 20 Percent of Tax Increment. In selecting appropriate project area boundaries, the redevelopment agency should comply with the following legal requirements:

- A redevelopment agency must locate or provide housing for project area residents displaced by the agency's activities.

- A redevelopment agency must replace in the project area or elsewhere in the community each low- and moderate-income housing unit destroyed or removed from the project area.

- Not less than 20 percent of the tax-increment funds allocated to an agency from a redevelopment project must be used by the agency (unless certain findings are made as set forth in chapter 11) either within the project area or elsewhere in the community, for the purpose of increasing, improving, or preserving the community's supply of low- and moderate-income housing.

- For plans and plan amendments adopted after 1975, at least 30 percent of all new and substantially rehabilitated dwelling units developed by an agency and at least 15 percent of all new and substantially rehabilitated dwelling units developed in the project area under the jurisdiction of an agency by public or private entities or persons other than the agency are to be available at affordable housing cost to persons and families of low- and moderate-income.

§ 33413

These inclusionary housing requirements and their exceptions should be considered in determining how much of a project area will be included for residential development. *See* chapter 11 for a more thorough discussion of inclusionary housing requirements.

Other Considerations. When selecting a project area, other factors to consider include: market demand for potential new uses, business relocation, and the financial feasibility of redevelopment. These are important because the legislative body must find that the time limitations and, if applicable, the amount of tax increment to be allocated to the agency are reasonably related to the proposed projects and to the ability of the agency to eliminate blight within the project area. The agency must also consider how specific agency projects will alleviate the identified blighting conditions.

If a project area includes residential properties, a project area committee must be formed if either a substantial number of low- or moderate-income persons live in the project area, and the plan authorizes the agency to acquire property by eminent domain on which any persons reside, or the plan contains one or more public projects that will displace a substantial number of low- or moderate-income persons. § 33385. *See* Project Area Committee, in this chapter.

Gateway Courtyard Shopping Center in Fairfield contains approximately 140,000 square feet of retail.

Upon a preliminary determination that a redevelopment project is feasible, the planning agency is charged with the responsibility for the initial designation of the project area boundaries, either on its own motion or at the request of the agency. The planning agency *must* select a project area if directed to do so by the legislative body, or upon the written petition of a majority of the property owners in the area. § 33322.

Adoption of Redevelopment Plan

Preparation of Preliminary Plan; County Fiscal Officer's Report

The planning agency is required to prepare a preliminary plan for the redevelopment of each selected project area.

The planning agency is required to prepare a preliminary plan for the redevelopment of each selected project area. Typically a brief document outlining the basic concept for redevelopment of the selected project area, the preliminary plan should describe the boundaries of the project area and contain a general statement of land uses, the layout of principal streets, population densities, building intensities, and standards proposed as the basis for the redevelopment of the project area. The preliminary plan should also show how the purposes of the Community Redevelopment Law will be attained, how the proposed redevelopment conforms to the general plan of the community, and generally describe the impact of the project on the residents of the project area and the surrounding neighborhood. § 33324.

After the preliminary plan has been prepared and accepted by the redevelopment agency, the agency then notifies all taxing agencies within the project area and the State Board of Equalization of its intent.

After the preliminary plan has been prepared and accepted by the redevelopment agency, the agency then notifies all taxing agencies within the project area and the State Board of Equalization of its intent. The agency must also notify those officials and agencies of the last equalized assessment roll it proposes to use for purposes of allocating tax-increment revenues to the agency (the "base year assessment roll"). This notification, called a Statement of Preparation, must be accompanied by a map of the project area. The map must conform to certain criteria published by the State Board of Equalization. Upon receipt of that information, the county fiscal officer and the State Board of Equalization begin preparation of a report identifying the total assessed valuation of taxable property within the project area, the affected taxing agencies, the share of tax revenues allocated to each taxing agency from the base year assessment roll, estimated first year taxes available to the agency broken down by taxing agency, and the assessed valuation of the project area for the preceding year (or, if requested by the agency, for the preceding five years). That report must be submitted to the redevelopment agency and each taxing agency within 60 days (90 days if the agency requests the assessed valuation for the preceding five years) of the date of filing with the State Board of Equalization or the date the base year assessment roll is equalized, whichever is later.

§§ 33327, 33328. If the report is not received within the time limitations set forth by statute, the agency may proceed with the adoption of the redevelopment plan.

In addition to the report required by section 33328, SB 1206 requires the county officials to prepare and deliver a new, specified report to the Department of Finance at the same time they deliver the report required by section 33328. § 33328.1. This new report must contain, in addition to the information required in the section 33328 report discussed above, projections of specified tax revenues, including projections of:

- The total amount of tax revenues that may be allocated pursuant to sections 33670 and 33670.5. § 33328.1(a)(2)
- The total amount of tax revenues that would have been allocated to each school district, county office of education, and community college district for the duration of the project area, but for sections 33670 and 33670.5. § 33328.1(a)(3)
- The total amount of tax revenues that may be allocated to each school district, county office of education, and community college district for the duration of the project area. § 33328.1(a)(4)

The report regarding schools requires the agency to request that each school district, county office of education, and community college district within the project area begin preparing the report very early in the plan adoption process. The agency must reimburse any school district, county office of education, or community college district for costs incurred by such entity in preparing the section 33328.1(b) report. § 33328.7.

Section 33328.5 provides that an agency that proposes to use one equalized assessment roll at the beginning of the adoption process, but later determines that it will be using the following year's assessment roll, must either notify the county officials to prepare a new fiscal officer's report based on the changed assessment roll or prepare the updated report itself. At least 14 days prior to the public hearing on the redevelopment plan, the agency must either prepare and deliver to each taxing agency a supplementary report analyzing the effect of the use of the different equalized assessment roll or include the information in its final report required by section 33352.

The assessment roll is equalized each year on August 20. Rev. & Tax Code § 2052. In order to use the current base year assessment roll, the ordinance adopting the redevelopment plan must become effective prior to that date. SB 1206 revised section 33378 to provide for a 90-day referendum period for ordinances adopting or amending a redevelopment plan, replacing the 30-day referendum period that had been applicable in most jurisdictions. The effect of extending the referendum period on the effective date of an ordinance adopting a redevelopment plan is an open question. However, a conservative approach would be to assume that, in order to use the current base year assessment roll, the second reading of an ordinance adopting or amending a redevelopment plan should occur no later than May 21 (90 days before the equalization date of August 20). This results in a relatively small window of time after the completion of the assessment roll data by the county assessor in the Fall to prepare the necessary plan adoption documents. Consequently, it is likely that more agencies will need to use the procedures for changing the base year assessment roll during the plan adoption process.

The State Board of Equalization has established a schedule of fees for filing and processing the documents, which the agency must pay at the time it files the statement and map. § 33328.4. In addition, the agency must reimburse the county for its costs in preparing the section 33328 and section 33328.1(a) reports. § 33328.7.

Project Area Committee

When adopting a redevelopment plan, the legislative body must call upon residents and existing community organizations in a redevelopment project area to form a project area committee (PAC) if either of the following situations exists:

- A substantial number of low- or moderate-income persons, or both, live within the project area, and the redevelopment plan as adopted will contain authority for the agency to acquire, by eminent domain, property on which anyone resides, or
- The redevelopment plan as adopted contains one or more public projects that will displace a substantial number of low- and/or moderate-income persons.

§ 33385

PAC = Project area committee

If a PAC is not to be formed, the legislative body should adopt a resolution making a finding that the formation of a PAC is not required.

If a PAC is not to be formed, the legislative body should adopt a resolution making a finding that the formation of a PAC is not required. The finding should be supported by a statement of the specific reasons why the project will not displace a substantial number of low- and/or moderate-income persons. If the formation of a PAC is not required, an agency nevertheless must either choose to form a PAC or consult with residents and community organizations before submitting the redevelopment plan to the legislative body. § 33385(f).

If a PAC will be formed, the legislative body must adopt, by resolution, a procedure for its formation that must include, but is not limited to, the following:

- Publicizing the opportunity to serve on the PAC by providing written notice by first-class mail to all residents, businesses, and community organizations, including religious institutions and other nonprofit organizations, within the project area at least 30 days prior to the formation of the committee. § 33385(b)(1)

- Conducting by the agency at least one public meeting to explain the establishment of, functions of, and opportunity to serve on the PAC. At the meeting, the agency must distribute copies of the procedure for forming the PAC, copies of sections 33347.5 and 33366, the proposed redevelopment plan or preliminary plan or pertinent portions thereof, and any other materials the agency feels would be useful. § 33385(b)(2)
- Providing published notices of all meetings, hearings, or plebiscites conducted by, or on behalf of, the agency or legislative body regarding the formation and selection of the PAC. Notices must be published at least once in a newspaper of general circulation at least 10 days prior to the hearing or, if no such newspaper exists, posted in at least three public places at least 10 days prior to the hearing. Gov. Code § 65090; § 33385
- Providing written notice to all residents, businesses, and community organizations in the project area of all meetings, hearings, or plebiscites conducted by, or on behalf of, the agency or legislative body regarding the formation and selection of the PAC; however, this requirement only applies when the agency can obtain mailing addresses at a reasonable cost. Instead of providing separate notices, the agency may provide a single notice listing all the dates, times, and locations of such meetings, hearings, or plebiscites. If an agency acts in good faith to comply with these requirements, the formation or actions of the PAC will not be invalidated. § 33385(b)(4)(A)
- Providing other forms of notice appropriate to the community in which the project area is to be established, as determined by the agency. These may include public service announcements, advertisements in foreign language publications, or flyers. § 33385(b)(5)
- Determining the number of community organizations and the method of selection, which may include election, appointment, or both. § 33385(b)(6)
- Establishing any other forms of assistance that the legislative body requires in connection with the formation of the PAC. § 33385(b)(7)

A PAC shall only include, when applicable, elected representatives of residential owner-occupants, residential tenants, business owners, and existing organizations within the project area; these members serve without compensation. Each group must be adequately represented. § 33385(c).

Each represented organization must appoint one of its members to the committee. Neither the legislative body, redevelopment agency, nor any member of either body may appoint a committee member. *Id.*

After the project area is selected (by adoption of the preliminary plan), the election of committee members must be held within 100 days.

A PAC shall only include, when applicable, elected representatives of residential owner-occupants, residential tenants, business owners, and existing organizations within the project area.

Then, after a noticed public hearing, the legislative body must adopt community-wide procedures for filing for election, publicizing an election, holding an election, and for reviewing disputed elections, filling vacated seats, and other related matters. The procedures must prohibit crossover voting among categories of residential owner-occupants, residential tenants, and business owners to ensure, for example, that a business owner cannot vote for a tenant representative. However, if the legislative body determines that the method for selecting community organizations shall include election, it must define the appropriate electorate and may authorize crossover voting in the election of community organizations. § 33385(d)(1).

The committee formation procedures also must provide that a challenge to an election or to an electoral procedure be filed with the legislative body no more than 15 calendar days after the election. The legislative body must find that all adopted procedures in the election were followed, and the procedures shall require that the validity of all challenges be determined within 30 days after the election. § 33385(d)(2).

Section 33385 specifically states that PAC meetings are subject to the Ralph M. Brown Act (Gov. Code § 54950 *et seq.*) requiring open meetings.

The PAC serves as an advisory body to the redevelopment agency.

The PAC serves as an advisory body to the redevelopment agency, which must consult with the PAC concerning policy matters that deal with the planning and provision of residential facilities for residents displaced by the project and on other policy matters affecting the residents of the project area. § 33386. The agency must continue to consult with the PAC for at least three years after the plan is adopted, subject to one year extensions by the legislative body. *Id.*

The redevelopment plan must be submitted to the PAC for review, and the PAC then prepares a report and recommendation to the legislative body.

The redevelopment plan must be submitted to the PAC for review, and the PAC then prepares a report and recommendation to the legislative body. If the PAC has recommended against the approval of the redevelopment plan, the legislative body may only adopt it by a two-thirds vote of its entire eligible and qualified members. § 33366.

The legislative body is required to provide the PAC with the necessary funds or resources for operations, including office, equipment and supplies, legal counsel, and staff. The only litigation expenses that the legislative body must fund are those related to litigation to enforce or defend the rights of the PAC. § 33388.

In *North Hollywood Project Area Committee v. City of Los Angeles* (1998) 61 Cal. App. 4th 719, the court held that section 33388 does not entitle a project area committee to choose its own legal counsel and does allow the city to provide legal services to the project area committee by offering the services of the city attorney.

FPPC = California Fair Political Practices Commission

The California Fair Political Practices Commission (FPPC) has determined that members of a PAC are "public officials," subject to the conflict of interest provisions set forth in the Political Reform Act. Gov. Code

§ 81000 *et seq.*; *Rotman* opinion (1987) 10 FPPC Ops. 1. This often results in the anomalous situation of PAC members being disqualified from participating in decisions regarding the redevelopment plan even though the Community Redevelopment Law *requires* that PAC members represent certain types of interests within the project area. Compare this opinion with the conclusion reached by the Attorney General that a PAC may advise an agency on the approval of a development agreement where several members of the PAC owned property in the project area without violating Government Code section 1090. 82 Ops. Atty. Gen. 126 (1989). For further discussion regarding conflict-of-interest issues, *see* chapter 4.

Preparation of the Preliminary Report

Upon receipt of the section 33328 report by the county fiscal officer (or after the time period for preparation has passed), the agency is required to prepare a preliminary report for all of the taxing agencies receiving property tax revenues from the project area (the affected taxing agencies). § 33344.5. This document is critical because it requires the agency to identify the types of blighting conditions in the project area as well as the scope and purpose of the redevelopment plan. The preliminary report must contain the following information:

- Reasons for the selection of the project area
- Description of the physical and economic conditions existing in the project area
- Description of the project area detailed enough to determine compliance with the rule that project areas be predominantly urbanized, including:
    - Total number of acres within the project area
    - Total number of acres characterized by the condition described in paragraph (4) of subdivision (a) of section 33031 (antiquated subdivisions)
    - Total number of acres that are in agricultural use
    - Total number of acres integral to an area developed for urban uses
    - Percentage of property within the project area that is predominantly urbanized
    - Map of the project area identifying the property described in the three preceeding items and the property not developed for urban use
- A preliminary assessment of the proposed method for financing the redevelopment of the project area, including an assessment of the economic feasibility of the project and the reasons for including a provision for the division of taxes pursuant to section 33670

Upon receipt of the section 33328 report by the county fiscal officer, the agency is required to prepare a preliminary report for all of the taxing agencies receiving property tax revenues from the project area.

in the redevelopment plan. If tax-increment financing will be used, the report should include a projection of the tax increment expected to be allocated to the agency over the life of the plan, the assumptions used in making such projections, and the costs of the proposed projects (including the funds to be set aside for low- and moderate-income housing pursuant to section 33334.2). The report should also analyze the feasibility (or infeasibility) of other types of financing, both public and private, such as capital facilities fees, assessment districts, direct developer contributions, and grants.

- Description of the specific project or projects then proposed by the agency
- Description of how the project(s) to be pursued by the agency will improve or alleviate the previously described existing project area conditions

§ 33344.5

If the project area includes agricultural lands, the preliminary report must be sent to the Department of Conservation, the county agricultural commissioner, the county farm bureau, the California Farm Bureau Federation, and agricultural entities and general farm organizations that provide a written request for notice about that particular redevelopment plan or plan amendment. *Id.*

Previously, the law did not specify the time limit within which the agency was required to send the preliminary report to the taxing agencies. SB 1382 added section 33344.6, which requires an agency to send the preliminary report at least 90 days prior to the public hearing on a proposed plan adoption. However, the agency may send the report 21 days before the hearing under any of the following circumstances:

- The redevelopment plan is proposed to be adopted pursuant to the special provisions for the redevelopment of closed military bases. § 33492 *et seq.*
- The redevelopment plan is proposed to be adopted pursuant to the Community Redevelopment Disaster Project Law. § 34000 *et seq.*
- The redevelopment plan is proposed to be amended and the amendment will not add new territory to the project area, increase the tax-increment limit, increase the bonded indebtedness limit, increase the time limit on debt incurrence or the time limit on the receipt of property taxes, or merge project areas
- The affected taxing agencies waive in writing the 90-day notice requirement

HCD = Department of Housing and Community Development

SB 1206 added the requirement that the agency deliver, not later than 45 days prior to the public hearing on a proposed plan adoption, a copy of the preliminary report and notice of the date of the public hearing to the Department of Finance and the HCD. § 33360.5(a). The

Department of Finance must then prepare an estimate of how adoption of the redevelopment plan will affect the state's general fund, including the need for school facilities. § 33360.5(b). Within 21 days of receiving this report, either the Department of Finance or the HCD may send comments regarding the proposed plan adoption to the agency and the legislative body. These comments must be considered at the public hearing on the proposed plan adoption. § 33360.5(c). If no comments are received within 21 days, the agency and the legislative body may proceed without them. *Id.* Either department may also refer their comments to the Attorney General for further action. § 33360.5(d).

Redevelopment Plan Preparation, Owner Participation Rules, Environmental Impact Report, and Report to the Legislative Body

Redevelopment Plan

A redevelopment plan functions like a charter. *County of Santa Cruz v. City of Watsonville* (1985) 177 Cal. App. 3d 831, 837. It contains the basic authority for and limits upon the redevelopment agency's activities over a long period of time. It generally does not contain detailed descriptions of specific projects. The plan must contain certain legally required provisions and should set forth, in general terms, the goals and policies of the agency for the project and the proposed redevelopment activities. The mandatory elements of a redevelopment plan are as follows:

- Legal description of the project area. § 33332
- Approximate amount of open space to be provided and street layout. § 33333(a)
- Limitations on type, size, height, number, and proposed use of buildings. § 33333(b)
- Approximate number of dwelling units. § 33333(c)
- Property to be devoted to public purposes and the nature of such purposes. § 33333(d)
- General description of the proposed method of financing, such as federal funds, city advances, and tax-increment financing. § 33334
- Limitation on the amount of bonded indebtedness that can be outstanding at any one time. § 33334.1
- Twenty percent of all tax-increment funds allocated to the redevelopment agency must be used for purposes of increasing, improving, and preserving the supply of low- and

Corona's Corporate II consists of two new 60,000 square foot office buildings and created over 400 new jobs. Private investment totaled $12.1 million and the agency's assistance totaled $100,000.

moderate-income housing, subject to certain limited exceptions. § 33334.2. For further discussion regarding this requirement, *see* chapter 11.

- Replacement housing is required to be constructed on a one-to-one basis when dwelling units housing persons and families of low- or moderate-income are destroyed or removed from the low- or moderate-income housing market as part of a redevelopment project. § 33334.5. Such replacement housing must be provided within four years of such destruction or removal.

Replacement housing is required to be constructed on a one-to-one basis when dwelling units housing persons and families of low- or moderate-income are destroyed or removed from the market as part of a redevelopment project.

- Provision for the agency to sell or lease property it acquires. § 33335
- Adequate safeguards that redevelopment will be carried out pursuant to the plan. § 33336(a)
- Provision for the retention of controls and restrictions or covenants running with the land sold or leased for private use. § 33336(b)
- Nondiscrimination provisions as a requirement for all deeds, leases, or contracts for the transfer of any land in a redevelopment project. §§ 33337, 33436
- Other covenants, conditions, and restrictions prescribed by the legislative body. § 33338
- Provision for participation by owners conditioned upon their agreeing to develop or rehabilitate their property in conformance with the redevelopment plan. §§ 33339, 33345. (While a redevelopment plan is not required to have a provision giving priority to businesses in the project area to reenter the project, the agency is required to adopt rules for owner participation and for preferences to businesses prior to the adoption of the redevelopment plan.) § 33339.5
- A list of specific public improvements (including any land) to be provided by the agency in connection with the redevelopment plan. § 33445

Pursuant to SB 53, every redevelopment plan adopted on or after January 1, 2007, must describe the agency's program to acquire real property by eminent domain.

- Pursuant to SB 53, every redevelopment plan adopted on or after January 1, 2007, must describe the agency's program to acquire real property by eminent domain. § 33342.5. If a plan was adopted prior to January 1, 2007, the legislative body was required to adopt an ordinance on or before July 1, 2007, that contains a description of the agency's program to acquire real property by eminent domain. § 33342.7

A redevelopment plan may contain the following optional provisions:

- Issuance of bonds by the agency. § 33341
- Acquisition of real property by the agency. § 33391. The redevelopment plan must contain a provision authorizing the agency to acquire property by eminent domain in order for the agency to exercise that right. § 33342

- Expenditure of money by the community. § 33343
- Actions by the community to undertake and complete any proceedings necessary to complete the project (such as street construction, vacation of public rights-of-way, etc.). § 33344
- The allocation of tax-increment revenues to the agency. § 33670

In *Franklin-McKinley School Dist. v. City of San Jose* (1991) 234 Cal. App. 3d 1599, the court noted that although the redevelopment plan did not specifically detail the information required by section 33333, the plan repeatedly referred to the city's general plan, in effect incorporating the general plan into the redevelopment plan. The court held that when taken together with the general plan, the redevelopment plan contained the information sought by that section.

Redevelopment plans are also required to contain time limits on incurring indebtedness, the duration of the land use and other provisions of the plan, the time for repaying any indebtedness with tax-increment revenue, and the time for exercising eminent domain. These time limits have been frequently amended and are very complex. There are two statutory provisions, one applying to redevelopment plans adopted on or before December 31, 1993 (§ 33333.6) and the other applying to redevelopment plans adopted on or after January 1, 1994 (§ 33333.2). Many of the limitations prescribed by these sections are the same, but there are also some important differences.

Redevelopment plans are required to contain time limits on incurring indebtedness, the duration of the land use and other provisions of the plan, the time for repaying any indebtedness with tax-increment revenue, and the time for exercising eminent domain.

Time Limit on Incurring Indebtedness

For redevelopment plans adopted on or after January 1, 1994, loans, advances and indebtedness that are to be repaid from tax increment may not be established beyond 20 years from the adoption of the redevelopment plan, except by amendment of the plan. § 33333.2(a)(1)(A). Redevelopment plans adopted prior to January 1, 1994 were subject to a similar requirement and, as originally adopted, should have contained this limitation. However, SB 211, adopted in 2001 and effective January 1, 2002, authorizes the amendment of redevelopment plans adopted prior to January 1, 1994, to eliminate the limit on the time for incurring indebtedness to be repaid from tax increment. § 33333.6(e)(2). In adopting the ordinance amending the plan, neither the city council nor the agency is required to comply with any of the provisions of the Community Redevelopment Law relating to amendment of redevelopment plans. *Id.*

If an amendment is adopted to eliminate the time limit on the establishment of loans, advances, or indebtedness, the agency must comply with section 33607.7. That section provides that if a redevelopment plan adopted prior to January 1, 1994, is amended to increase or eliminate the time limit on the establishment of loans, advances, or indebtedness, the agency must pay to each affected taxing agency either of the following:

- If there is an existing agreement with the taxing agency for the payment of a portion of the tax increment to alleviate a financial burden or detriment caused by the redevelopment project (often called a pass-through agreement),[1] the amount required by the agreement; or
- If there is no pass-through agreement, the agency must pay the affected taxing agency the amount of the AB 1290 statutory payments (§§ 33607.5(b), (c), (d) and (e)), commencing with the year in which the time limit on establishing indebtedness would have expired absent the SB 211 amendment.

SB 1206 added procedural requirements to certain redevelopment plan amendments ("SB 1206 Amendment Requirements," discussed below), including an amendment to change the time limit on the establishment of loans, advances, and indebtedness. § 33451.5(a)(3). However, the SB 1206 Amendment Requirements do not apply to an amendment to eliminate, rather than change, the time limit on the establishment of loans, advances, and indebtedness because the regular procedures for the amendment of redevelopment plans, including the making of findings of remaining blight, are not required for such an amendment pursuant to SB 211. § 33333.6(e)(2)(B).

For redevelopment plans that contain a time limit on incurring indebtedness, the time limit does not prevent the agency from incurring indebtedness to be repaid from the agency's low- and moderate-income housing fund or establishing more debt in order to fulfill the agency's housing obligations under section 33333.8(a). The time limit also does not prevent the agency from refinancing, refunding, or restructuring indebtedness after the time limit has expired as long as the indebtedness is not increased and the time during which the indebtedness is to be repaid is not extended beyond the time limit. § 33333.2(a)(1)(A).

For redevelopment plans adopted after January 1, 1994, in order to extend the time limit for incurring indebtedness, the redevelopment plan must be amended following the regular plan amendment procedures. The agency must find that significant blight remains within the project area that cannot be eliminated without establishing additional indebtedness. The amended time limitation may not exceed 30 years from the effective date of the ordinance adopting the redevelopment plan, except as necessary to comply with the agency's housing obligations under section 33333.8(a). § 33333.2(a)(1)(B).

---

1. Such agreements were formerly authorized under the provisions of section 33401. Since the adoption of AB 1290, effective January 1, 1994, redevelopment agencies may no longer enter into such agreements.

Time Limit on Effectiveness of the Redevelopment Plan

For redevelopment plans adopted on or after January 1, 1994, the redevelopment plan must contain a time limit, not to exceed 30 years from the adoption of the redevelopment plan, on the effectiveness of the redevelopment plan. After this time limit has expired, the agency has no authority to act pursuant to the redevelopment plan except to repay previously incurred indebtedness and enforce existing covenants and contracts, unless the agency has not completed its housing obligations pursuant to section 33333.8(a), in which case the agency retains the authority necessary to implement those obligations. § 33333.2(a)(2). There is no provision for the extension of this time limit by amendment, except where the agency has used funds from the project to make ERAF payments. *See* Time Limit Extensions for ERAF Contributions, below.

For redevelopment plans adopted prior to January 1, 1994, the time limit on the effectiveness of the redevelopment plan may not exceed 40 years from the adoption of the redevelopment plan or January 1, 2009, whichever is later (§ 33333.6(a)) unless the redevelopment plan is amended pursuant to section 33333.10. Section 33333.10, effective January 1, 2002, authorizes extending the time limit on the effectiveness of redevelopment plans that were adopted prior to January 1, 1994, for up to an additional ten years. In order to do so, the agency must find that significant blight remains within the project area and this blight cannot be eliminated without extending the effectiveness of the plan and receipt of tax increment. As used in section 33333.10, "significant" blight means blight that is important and of a magnitude to warrant agency assistance. § 33333.10(c). Significantly more extensive procedural steps also apply to a redevelopment plan amendment enacted pursuant to section 33333.10. §§ 33333.10(h); 33333.11. *See* Extended Consultations, below. In addition, if a redevelopment plan is amended pursuant to section 33333.10 to extend the effectiveness of the plan, subsection (g) of that section requires that the amount of tax increment paid into the agency's low- and moderate-income housing fund be increased from at least 20 percent to at least 30 percent, commencing with the first fiscal year that commences after the date of adoption of the amendment.

SB 1206 Amendment Requirements also apply to a plan amendment that changes the time limit on the effectiveness of the redevelopment plan. Not less than 45 days prior to the public hearing on the proposed plan amendment, the agency must notify the HCD and the Department of Finance of the date of the hearing and the proposed amendment. § 33451.5(b). The notice must be accompanied by a new, specified report. *Id.* The new report must contain:

For redevelopment plans adopted on or after January 1, 1994, the redevelopment plan must contain a time limit, not to exceed 30 years from the adoption of the redevelopment plan, on the effectiveness of the redevelopment plan.

- A map of the project area that identifies the portion, if any, of the project area that is no longer blighted, the portion of the project area that is blighted, and the portion of the project area that contains necessary and essential parcels for the elimination of the remaining blight. § 33451.5(c)(1).

- A description of the remaining blight. § 33451.5(c)(2)

- A description of the projects or programs proposed to eliminate any remaining blight. § 33451.5(c)(3)

- A description of how these projects or programs will improve the conditions of blight. § 33451.5(c)(4)

- The reasons why the projects or programs cannot be completed without the plan amendment. § 33451.5(c)(5)

- The proposed method of financing these programs or projects, including the amount of tax-increment revenues that is projected to be generated as a result of the proposed plan amendment, including amounts projected to be deposited into the Low and Moderate Income Housing Fund and amounts to be paid to affected taxing entities. This description must also include the sources and amounts of moneys other than tax-increment revenues available to finance these projects or programs, and the reasons that the remaining blight cannot reasonably be expected to be reversed or alleviated by private enterprise or governmental action, or both, without the use of tax-increment revenues available to the agency because of the proposed amendment. § 33451.5(c)(6)

- An amendment to the implementation plan that includes the agency's housing responsibilities under section 33490. The agency is not required to hold a separate public hearing on the implementation plan in addition to the public hearing on the redevelopment plan amendment. § 33451.5(c)(7)

- A new neighborhood impact report if required by section 33352(m). § 33451.5(c)(8)

Upon receiving the report, the Department of Finance is required to prepare an estimate of how the proposed amendment will affect the state's general fund, including a determination of whether the amendment will affect the need for school facilities. § 33451.5(d). Within 21 days of receiving the report, either the Department of Finance or the HCD may send any comments regarding the proposed plan amendment to the agency and the legislative body. These comments must be considered at the public hearing. § 33451.5(e). If no comments are received, the agency and legislative body may proceed without them. *Id.* Either the Department of Finance or HCD may also refer comments to the Attorney General for further action. § 33451.5(f).

Time Limit on Repayment of Indebtedness

For redevelopment plans adopted on or after January 1, 1994, the redevelopment plan must contain a time limit, not to exceed 45 years from the date of adoption of the plan, to repay indebtedness with tax-increment revenues. After this time limit expires, the agency may not receive tax increment, except as necessary to comply with the agency's housing obligations as set forth in section 33333.8. § 33333.2(a)(3). There is no provision for the extension of this time limit by amendment, except where the agency has used funds from the project to make ERAF payments. *See* Time Limit Extensions for ERAF Contributions, below.

For redevelopment plans adopted prior to January 1, 1994, the time limit on receipt of property taxes is ten years from the date of termination of the effectiveness of the redevelopment plan. § 33333.6(b). There are two exceptions to this rule. First, the time limit does not apply to the extent necessary for the agency to comply with its housing obligations as required by section 33333.8(a). § 33333.6(f). Second, the limit may not operate to affect the validity of any bonds, indebtedness or other obligations. § 33333.6(g).[2]

Section 33333.10, discussed above, also permits the amendment of pre-1994 redevelopment plans to increase the time limit on receiving tax increment and repaying indebtedness for an additional ten years.[3] If a redevelopment plan is so amended, in addition to increasing the housing set-aside from 20 percent to 30 percent, two other significant consequences become applicable to the redevelopment plan. First, after the time limit on the payment of indebtedness and receipt of tax increment would have taken effect but for the amendment, the agency may only expend tax-increment funds within the portion of the project area that has been identified as containing blighted parcels and parcels that are not blighted, but are necessary and essential to the elimination of blight and have been so identified in the report to the city council prepared in connection with the redevelopment plan amendment. § 33333.10(e). Second, after the time limit on the payment of indebtedness and receipt of tax increment would have taken effect but for the amendment, the use of funds from the agency's low- and moderate-income housing fund to assist moderate-income housing is severely restricted. § 33333.10(f).

---

2. Even without such a provision, legislation enacted after the issuance of bonds or other obligations may not operate to affect the validity of those bonds or obligations. *See* §§ 33641.5(b) and 33671.5.
3. For all practical purposes, it is difficult to conceive of a situation where an agency would amend the time limit on the effectiveness of the redevelopment plan without also amending the time limit on the receipt of tax increment and repayment of indebtedness, though this is theoretically possible under the statute.

ERAF = Education Revenue Augmentation Fund

Time Limit Extensions for ERAF Contributions

Agencies that are required to and have contributed tax increment to county Educational Revenue Augmentation Funds (ERAF) for fiscal years 2003–04, 2004–05, and 2005–06 are entitled to extend the time limits on redevelopment plan effectiveness and receipt of tax increment by up to one year for each year a contribution was made, provided certain conditions are satisfied. *See* §§ 33333.2(c) and (d); 33333.6(e)(2)(C) and (D). No such time limit extension was authorized for the ERAF contribution required for fiscal year 2008–09.

Special Procedures Applicable to SB 211 Amendments

SB 211 authorizes a redevelopment agency to amend a redevelopment plan adopted before December 31, 1993, to extend for up to an additional ten years the time limit on the effectiveness of the plan and/or the time limit on receiving tax increment and repaying indebtedness.

SB 211, codified as sections 33333.10 and 33333.11, authorizes a redevelopment agency to amend a redevelopment plan adopted before December 31, 1993, to extend for up to an additional ten years the time limit on the effectiveness of the plan and/or the time limit on receiving tax increment and repaying indebtedness. In order to take advantage of this opportunity, the agency must follow a number of additional procedural steps that go beyond the regular redevelopment plan amendment provisions found in section 33450 *et seq.* These additional procedural steps can be divided into two categories: prior determinations and extended consultations, as further explained below. In addition, if the redevelopment plan was adopted prior to January 1, 1976, and for that reason is not subject to the housing production requirements of section 33413(b), the redevelopment plan must be amended at the same time to make those requirements applicable (prospectively, not retroactively).

In addition, as discussed above, the SB 1206 Amendment Requirements are applicable to an amendment to extend the time limit on the effectiveness of the plan, as well as to an amendment to *change* (as opposed to eliminate) the time limit on establishing indebtedness. § 33451.5(a)(3)–(4).

Prior Determinations. Before a redevelopment agency may amend its redevelopment plan under section 33333.10, it must first adopt a resolution that makes the following findings based on substantial evidence:

- The community has adopted a housing element for its general plan that the HCD has determined pursuant to section 65585 of the Government Code to be in substantial compliance with the sections of the Government Code governing the contents of housing elements. § 33333.10(h)(1)[4]

---

4. Under the Housing Element Law, HCD's determination concerning substantial compliance is not controlling. Gov. Code § 65585. Cities are authorized to and sometimes do adopt a housing element despite the absence of a finding of substantial compliance from HCD. This situation

- During the three fiscal years prior to the year in which the amendment is adopted, the agency has not been included in the report sent by the Controller to the Attorney General pursuant to section 33080.8(b) as an agency that has a "major violation," defined as failing to file an independent audit report in substantial compliance with section 33080.1(a) or a fiscal statement that includes substantially all of the information required by section 33080.1, failure to establish the time limits required by section 33333.6, failure to establish a low- and moderate-income housing fund as required by section 33334.3 and to accrue interest to the housing fund as required by that section, failure to initiate housing on real property acquired with the proceeds of the low- and moderate-income housing fund as required by section 33334.16 or failure to adopt an implementation plan as required by section 33490. § 33333.10(h)(2).
- The HCD has issued a letter to the agency confirming that the agency has not accumulated an excess surplus in its low- and moderate-income housing fund, as defined in section 33334.12.

Extended Consultations. In addition to the usual consultations with taxing agencies and community groups required for any redevelopment plan amendment, an amendment adopted pursuant to section 33333.10 is subject to the further requirements described in section 33333.11. These additional requirements are described below:

- The redevelopment agency must give each affected taxing agency the opportunity to meet and confer. Written comments received from the taxing agencies must be included in the preliminary report and responses to those comments must be included in the final report to the city council. §§ 33333.11(c); 33333.11(h)(4)
- The preliminary report must be sent to all affected taxing agencies and the HCD at least 120 days prior to the public hearing on the plan amendment. The contents of the preliminary report must include:
  - A map of the project area identifying the portions that are: (1) blighted, (2) no longer blighted, and (3) necessary and essential for the elimination of remaining blight.
  - A description of the remaining blight.
  - A description of the programs and projects proposed to eliminate the remaining blight.

The redevelopment agency must give each affected taxing agency the opportunity to meet and confer.

presents a problem, however, if the city's redevelopment agency intends to adopt an amendment under section 33333.10, since that section explicitly requires a finding of substantial compliance. It may be necessary to process an amendment to the housing element in order to obtain HCD's finding of substantial compliance prior to adopting the amendment to the redevelopment plan.

Transforming an 81-year-old auto showroom into lofts, offices and restaurants in downtown Sacramento took technical savvy and a balancing act between historical detail and modern design.

- A description of how the projects or programs will improve the conditions of blight.
- The reasons why the projects and programs cannot be completed without extending the time limits as proposed.
- The proposed method of financing the programs or projects, including an estimate of the amount of tax increment that will be generated during the extension and sources and amounts of money other than tax increment that are available to finance the programs or projects. The method of financing should also explain why the remaining blight cannot reasonably be expected to be reversed or alleviated by private enterprise or governmental action, or both, without the use of tax increment generated during the proposed extension.
- An amendment to the agency's implementation plan.
- A neighborhood impact report. § 33333.11(e)

• At least 45 days prior to the hearing on the redevelopment plan amendment, the agency must send notice of the hearing to all affected taxing agencies, the HCD, and the Department of Finance. The notice must be accompanied by the agency's final report to the city council. § 33333.11(g)

• The final report of the agency to the city council must be adopted not less than 45 days prior to the public hearing. In addition to the usual contents, the report must contain the written responses of the agency to the concerns expressed by residents, community organizations and affected taxing agencies. § 33333.11(h)

• The amendment must be submitted to the planning commission at least 120 days prior to the public hearing. § 33333.11(f)

• The agency must obtain the advice of the project area committee, if one exists, prior to publication of notice of the public hearing and the preliminary report must be made available to the PAC at least 120 days prior to the public hearing. § 33333.11(d)

To summarize the additional procedural steps, at least 120 days prior to the public hearing, the agency must: first send the preliminary report to taxing agencies, the HCD, the Department of Finance, and the PAC, if any, and second, refer the plan amendment to the planning commission for its report and recommendation. At least 45 days prior to the public hearing the agency must also send notice of the public hearing to the affected taxing agencies, the Department of Finance, and the HCD, including with the notice a copy of the final report of the agency to the city council and the new report required by section 33451.5(c).

Time Limit on Exercise of Eminent Domain

For all redevelopment plans adopted on or after October 1, 1976, the plan must contain a limit, not exceeding 12 years, for the commencement of proceedings to acquire property by eminent domain. This time limit may only be extended by amendment of the redevelopment plan. §§ 33333.2(a)(4); 33333.4(g)(12).

Previously, it was unclear whether or not an amendment to extend eminent domain required new blight findings. In *Blue v. City of Los Angeles* (2006) 137 Cal. App. 4th 1131, the court held that an amendment to extend the power of eminent domain does require a finding that significant blight remains in the project area. SB 53 codified this holding and added the additional required finding that the blight cannot be eliminated without the use of eminent domain. §§ 33333.2(a)(4), 33333.4(a)(3).

Effect of Merger on Time Limits

If redevelopment plans having different dates of adoption are merged, the time limits are counted separately for each merged plan. § 33333.6(c). That is, the time limits for individual merged redevelopment plans are not affected by the merger and each must be separately determined.

Effect of Amendments on Time Limits

If a redevelopment plan is amended to add territory to the project area, the time limitations for the added area are calculated from the date of adoption of the amendment adding the new territory. §§ 33333.2(b); 33333.6(c)(1).

Owner Participation Rules

Section 33339 requires each redevelopment plan to provide for the participation of property owners in the redevelopment of the project area if they agree to participate in conformity with the redevelopment plan. Section 33339.5 requires an agency to extend reasonable preferences to displaced businesses to reenter in business within the redeveloped area if they meet the requirements prescribed by the plan. To implement these obligations, the agency is required to promulgate and adopt owner participation rules prior to adoption of the plan. § 33345. Owner participation rules are usually brief and general. Typically, they describe the agency's objectives for owner participation, establish priorities for selection among competing owner participants and describe the limits on owner participation. Owner participation rules are usually reviewed by the PAC, if one has been established, or, if there is no PAC, by a citizens advisory committee or whatever other group has been established to provide community involvement in the redevelopment plan. No specific time is prescribed for adoption of owner participation rules other than that it must occur prior to adoption of the redevelopment plan by the legislative body. For a discussion of owner participation rules as it relates to redevelopment plan implementation, *see* chapter 8.

Environmental Impact Report

The environmental impact report (EIR) on the redevelopment plan is included as part of the report to the legislative body (§ 33352(k)) and should describe the existing environmental conditions in the project area, assess the environmental impacts of the redevelopment plan, and recommend mitigation measures. Pub. Resources Code § 21002.1; Cal. Code Regs., tit. 14, § 15063(b)(1). The EIR is an informational document; it must describe the project, list technical and environmental characteristics, and discuss the following subjects: significant environmental effects that cannot be avoided; mitigation measures proposed to minimize the significant effects; alternatives to the project; the relationship between short-term uses and long-term productivity of the environment; significant irreversible environmental change; and any growth-inducing impact. Cal. Code Regs., tit. 14, §§ 15124, 15125, 15126. Cumulative effects should also be discussed. Cal. Code Regs., tit. 14, § 15130. Determination of whether an effect is significant is governed by the California Code of Regulations, Title 14, sections 15064 and 15065.

The California Environmental Quality Act (CEQA) (Public Resources Code § 21000 *et seq.*) and the State CEQA Guidelines (California Code of Regulations, Title 14, § 15000 *et seq.*) contain important provisions unique to redevelopment projects. Prior to September 17, 2002, Public Resources Code, section 21090 provided as follows:

> For all purposes of this division, all public and private activities or undertakings pursuant to, or in furtherance of, a redevelopment plan shall be deemed to be a single project. However, further environmental review of any public or private activity or undertaking pursuant to, or in furtherance of, a redevelopment plan shall be conducted if any of the events specified in Section 21166 have occurred.

Section 15180(b) of the State CEQA Guidelines contains a similar provision:

> An EIR on a redevelopment plan shall be treated as a program EIR with no subsequent EIRs required for individual components of the redevelopment plan unless a subsequent EIR or a supplement to an EIR would be required by Section 15162 or 15163.

Public Resources Code section 21090 was amended in 2002 by SB 649 in response to the holding in *Friends of Mammoth v. Town of*

EIR = Environmental impact report

CEQA = California Environmental Quality Act

The California Environmental Quality Act and the State CEQA Guidelines contain important provisions unique to redevelopment projects.

Mammoth Lakes Redevelopment Agency (2000) 82 Cal. App. 4th 511. In that case, the town had adopted a redevelopment plan that listed 72 separate and identified public improvements and facilities. The amount of specific information about each of these facilities varied, but the location, function, size, cost and general extent of most of the projects was identified in either the EIR or the report to the town council. Relying on section 21090, the program EIR prepared by the town did not analyze the direct or indirect environmental impacts potentially caused by the 72 development proposals. Instead, it analyzed primarily the cumulative impacts that could foreseeably occur if all of the proposed projects were actually developed, deferring detailed analysis of the 72 development proposals until they were individually brought forward for approval. The plaintiffs argued that the town had a duty to gather and analyze in the EIR as much information about the 72 development proposals as possible instead of deferring such specific review until later.

The court decided in favor of the plaintiffs, holding that the EIR was inadequate. The court based its decision in large part on the content of Public Resources Code section 21090, which then provided that all public and private activities undertaken pursuant to or in furtherance of a redevelopment plan are deemed a single project that, for CEQA purposes, is deemed approved at the time of adoption of the redevelopment plan. The court held that the effect of this provision was to exempt from further CEQA analysis individual activities implementing the redevelopment plan unless the circumstances requiring the preparation of a supplemental or subsequent EIR had occurred. The court reasoned that this feature of CEQA made program EIRs prepared for redevelopment plan adoptions different from other program EIRs because the standard for preparation of subsequent environmental documents tiering off a standard program EIR is more relaxed. Plaintiffs feared and the court agreed that to the extent information was available about the environmental impacts of these 72 projects at the time the redevelopment plan was approved, subsequent environmental analysis based on those impacts would be prohibited by section 21090.

In response to the Mammoth Lakes case, the legislature amended Public Resources Code section 21090 to read as follows:

> (a) An environmental impact report for a redevelopment plan may be a master environmental impact report,[5] program environmental impact

In response to the Mammoth Lakes case, the legislature amended Public Resources Code section 21090.

---

5. Public Resources Code section 21157 also authorizes the use of a master environmental impact report (MEIR) in connection with the adoption of a redevelopment plan. An MEIR is similar to a program environmental impact report. In the experience of the authors, MEIRs are rarely used, and most EIRs prepared in connection with redevelopment plan adoptions are program EIRs. A "project" EIR (CEQA Guidelines, § 15161) may also be used for those few redevelopment plans that are limited to a discrete development proposal about which the details are relatively well known.

report, or a project environmental impact report. Any environmental impact report for a redevelopment plan shall specify the type of environmental impact report that is prepared for the redevelopment plan.

(b) If the environmental impact report for a redevelopment plan is a project environmental impact report, all public and private activities and/or undertakings pursuant to, or in furtherance of, a redevelopment plan shall be deemed to be a single project. However, further environmental review of any public or private activity or undertaking pursuant to, or in furtherance of, a redevelopment plan for which a project environmental impact report has been certified shall be conducted if any of the events specified in Section 21166 have occurred.

Section 15180 of the State CEQA Guidelines was amended to reflect these changes to Public Resources Code section 21090.

The intent of the revisions to section 21090 was to resolve the legal conundrum in which redevelopment agencies were placed as a result of the *Mammoth Lakes* decision. Redevelopment plans tend to be quite general. (*See* the discussion of the general nature of redevelopment plans, above.) However, some provisions of redevelopment law require that a redevelopment plan contain a certain level of specificity. For example, section 33445 requires the redevelopment agency to provide for the "acquisition of property and installation or construction of *each* facility" in the redevelopment plan. Likewise, section 33344.5 requires the preliminary report to contain "a description of the specific project or projects then proposed by the agency" and a description of how the project or projects to be pursued by the agency in the project area will improve or alleviate the conditions of blight identified in the report. These provisions push the agency in the direction of providing more detailed information. Prior to *Mammoth Lakes,* redevelopment agencies tended to deal with this tension by pointing out that the EIR was a program EIR that would be supplemented with additional CEQA analysis pursuant to section 21166 as the implementation of the plan proceeded and more detailed information became available. After *Mammoth Lakes*, this approach was less viable. To the extent that the redevelopment plan or the preliminary report identified specific projects, it was required to analyze their environmental consequences in detail or risk a court's determining that the EIR was inadequate. This additional analysis could greatly increase the cost of the EIR. In the context of shrinking public revenues, this cost was not an insignificant consideration.

The effect of the changes to Public Resources Code section 21090 was to restore the flexibility that had been lost as a result of the Mammoth Lakes *case.*

The effect of the changes to Public Resources Code section 21090 was to restore the flexibility that had been lost as a result of the *Mammoth Lakes* case. EIRs prepared in connection with the adoption of a redevelopment plan may be either program or project EIRs. Only if the EIR is a project EIR will the prohibition on further environmental review contained in subsection (b) of section 21090 be applicable. If the

EIR is a program EIR, it will be subject to the same procedures and limitations as other program EIRs.

In *Citizens for Responsible Equitable Environmental Development v. City of San Diego Redevelopment Agency* (2005) 134 Cal. App. 4th 598, the plaintiffs challenged a redevelopment hotel project under CEQA, alleging that the decision that the hotel project was covered by previous EIRs was an abuse of discretion, and asserting that section 21090 required the preparation of a new project-specific EIR for the hotel project. The court rejected this argument, finding that the plain language of section 21090 does not require that an agency conduct a project specific EIR. Rather, the court held that "section 21090 *prohibits* an agency from requiring further environmental review of redevelopment plans for which a project EIR has been prepared, *unless* the circumstances specified in section 21166 exist." *Id.* at 606 (footnote omitted).

Most EIRs prepared for redevelopment plan adoptions will be program EIRs. The use of a program EIR is the initial step in what is referred to as the "tiering" of environmental impact reports. This legislatively favored procedure is described in Public Resources Code, section 21093:

> (a) The legislature finds and declares that tiering of environmental impact reports will promote construction of needed housing and other development projects by (1) streamlining regulatory procedures, (2) avoiding repetitive discussions of the same issues in successive environmental impact reports, and (3) ensuring that environmental impact reports prepared for later projects which are consistent with a previously approved policy, plan, program, or ordinance concentrate upon environmental effects which may be mitigated or avoided in connection with the decision on each later project. The Legislature further finds and declares that tiering is appropriate when it helps a public agency to focus upon the issues ripe for decision at each level of environmental review and in order to exclude duplicative analysis of environmental effects examined in previous environmental impact reports.
>
> (b) To achieve this purpose, environmental impact reports shall be tiered whenever feasible, as determined by the lead agency.

Thus, a program EIR prepared in connection with redevelopment plan adoption is usually a more general document than an EIR that might be prepared for a discrete development project. The program EIR should focus on the "cumulative" or "synergistic" impacts of the entire program. At this stage, less specific

Criminal activity was rampant in the neighborhood surrounding this warehouse, which was constructed in the early 1900s. Equity financing from the Emeryville Redevelopment Agency enabled 20 percent of the 142 units to be affordable to low- and moderate-income purchasers.

information is required about subsequent plan implementing activities than will be the case when those activities are before the public agency for decision. At that point, the agency must examine the environmental record to determine whether it adequately discloses and analyzes the environmental consequences of the specific implementing activity. If it does, then the agency may proceed with the decision on the basis of the existing environmental record. If it does not, then further environmental studies disclosing those specific impacts must first be prepared.

The environmental effects of subsequent redevelopment plan implementing activities are considered as they are proposed, and either an additional environmental document is prepared (which could be a subsequent or a supplemental EIR, a focused EIR, a mitigated negative declaration or an addendum to the EIR) or no new environmental document is required because the program EIR sufficiently described the environmental effects.

The environmental effects of subsequent redevelopment plan implementing activities are considered as they are proposed, and either an additional environmental document is prepared, or no new environmental document is required.

Subsequent or supplemental EIRs are required when:

- Substantial changes are proposed in the project requiring major revisions to the Program EIR due to the involvement of new significant environmental impacts not considered in the program EIR or a substantial increase in the severity of previously identified significant effects.

- Substantial changes occur with respect to the circumstances under which the project is undertaken requiring major revisions to the program EIR due to the involvement of new significant environmental impacts not covered in the program EIR.

- New information of substantial importance that was not known and could not have been known with the exercise of reasonable diligence at the time the program EIR was certified as complete, shows any of the following:
    - The project will have one or more significant effects not discussed in the program EIR.
    - Significant effects previously examined will be substantially more severe than shown in the program EIR.
    - Mitigation measures or alternatives previously found not to be feasible would in fact be feasible and would substantially reduce one or more significant effects of the project, but the project proponents decline to adopt the mitigation measure or alternative.
    - Mitigation measures or alternatives that are considerably different from those analyzed in the program EIR would substantially reduce one or more significant effects on the environment, but the project proponents decline to adopt the mitigation measure or alternative.

Cal. Code Regs., tit. 14, §§ 15162, 15163

Once an agency has prepared and certified an EIR, its decision that a later project is within the scope of the previous EIR is reviewed under the deferential "substantial evidence" standard. *Citizens for Responsible Equitable Environmental Development v. City of San Diego Redevelopment Agency* (2005) 134 Cal. App. 4th 598, 605.

During the plan adoption process, the agency must send a copy of the notice of preparation of the EIR to each affected taxing agency. § 33333.3. Once the draft EIR is completed and available for public review and comment, a copy must be sent to each taxing agency. *Id.* If the project area contains agricultural land, the agency must also send the draft EIR to the Department of Conservation, the county agricultural commissioner, the county farm bureau, the California Farm Bureau Federation, and agricultural entities and general farm organizations that provide a written request for notice regarding that particular redevelopment plan or plan amendment. *Id.*

After the public review period, a lead agency must evaluate the comments received and respond in writing. Whether the lead agency for purposes of CEQA is the redevelopment agency or the legislative body will vary depending on local procedure. The final EIR must be certified as having been completed in accordance with CEQA prior to the approval of the project. The final EIR must be presented to the legislative body, and the legislative body must review and consider the information contained in the final EIR before approving the project. *See City of Carmel-by-the-Sea v. Board of Supervisors* (1977) 71 Cal. App. 3d 84, 94–06.

For each significant effect identified in the EIR, the lead agency must make one or more of the following findings in writing:

- Changes or alterations have been required in, or incorporated into, the project that avoid or substantially lessen the effect on the environment.
- The lead agency lacks jurisdiction to make the change, but that another agency has such authority, and the change can and should be adopted by such other agency.
- Specific economic, legal, social, technological, or other considerations, including considerations for the provision of employment opportunities for highly trained workers, make infeasible the mitigation measures or project alternatives identified in the final EIR.

Pub. Resources Code § 21081; Cal. Code Regs., tit. 14, § 15091

These findings must be supported by substantial evidence in the record. Pub. Resources Code § 21081.5. There is also a requirement that when an agency makes the first finding, it must adopt a reporting or monitoring program designed to ensure compliance during project implementation. Pub. Resources Code § 21081.6. To ensure compliance with the mitigation measures, care should be taken to structure the program with sufficient controls and opportunities for review.

Report to the Legislative Body

The report must contain a comprehensive analysis of the scope of, basis for, and impacts of the redevelopment plan.

When submitted to the legislative body for consideration, a redevelopment plan must be accompanied by a report containing the specifically required analyses of the project. This report must contain a comprehensive analysis of the scope of, basis for, and impacts of the redevelopment plan. Some of the elements, such as the blight analysis and method of financing, will have been previously included in the preliminary report, and this report is an opportunity to expand and document those discussions. The report must contain evidence for the legislative body to consider when determining whether or not to adopt the redevelopment plan and must also include:

- Reasons for selecting the project area, a description of the specific projects proposed by the agency, and a description of how these projects will improve or alleviate the conditions of blight. § 33352(a)
- Description of the physical and economic conditions specified in section 33031 existing in the area, including specific blighting conditions and a map showing where those conditions exist. § 33352(b) SB 1206 added the requirement that the description must contain specific, quantifiable evidence documenting (1) the physical and economic conditions causing blight; and (2) that the described physical and economic conditions are so prevalent and substantial that, collectively, they seriously harm the entire project area. *Id.* This addition codified the standard that courts had already been applying to these determinations for years.
- An implementation plan describing agency goals and objectives, specific programs, including potential projects, and estimated expenditures to be made within the first five years of the plan, and a description of how these projects will improve or alleviate blighting conditions described in section 33031. § 33352(c)
- An explanation of why the elimination of blight and the redevelopment of the project area cannot reasonably be expected to be accomplished by private enterprise acting alone or by the legislative body's use of financing alternatives other than tax-increment financing. § 33352(d)
- Proposed method of financing the project. § 33352(e)
- Method for relocating persons and families. § 33352(f)
- An analysis of the preliminary plan. § 33352(g)
- The report and recommendation of the planning agency. § 33352(h)
- Summary of the project area committee meetings. § 33352(i)
- Report of the planning agency regarding acquisition of real property. § 33352(j); Gov. Code § 65402

The report must include an explanation of why the elimination of blight and the redevelopment of the project area cannot reasonably be expected to be accomplished by private enterprise acting alone.

- The EIR. § 33352(k); Pub. Resources Code § 21150
- Report of the county fiscal officer. §§ 33352(l), 33328
- Neighborhood impact report if the project area contains low- or moderate-income housing. § 33352(m)
- Analysis of the county fiscal officer's report, including a summary of the agency's consultations with affected taxing agencies. If any taxing entities have expressed written objections or concerns with the proposed project area as part of the agency's consultations with the taxing entities, the agency must include a response to those concerns and may include, at the agency's discretion, proposed or adopted mitigation measures. Mitigation measures may include amendment to the redevelopment plan with respect to the size or location of the project area, time duration, total amount of tax increment to be received by the agency or the proposed use, size, density, or location of development to be assisted by the agency, but shall not include obligations to make payments to any affected taxing entity. § 33352(n)

Public Hearings and Approval

Review by Other Bodies

Before being submitted to the legislative body, a proposed redevelopment plan must first be submitted to the planning agency and to the project area committee, if one exists. §§ 33347.5, 33346. The planning agency has 30 days after receipt of the plan to file its report and recommendation concerning the redevelopment plan and its conformity to the general plan. If it fails to do so within that time period, the planning agency is deemed to have waived its report, and the legislative body may approve the plan without the planning agency's report and recommendation. § 33347. If the planning agency, or the PAC, recommends that the project not be approved, the legislative body must approve the project by a two-thirds vote of its eligible and qualified members. § 33366.

Before being submitted to the legislative body, a proposed redevelopment plan must first be submitted to the planning agency and to the project area committee, if one exists.

Notice; Public Hearing

The Community Redevelopment Law provides that both the agency and legislative body shall conduct public hearings to approve the redevelopment plan. § 33348, 33360. However, the more typical approach in cities and counties where the members of the legislative body are also members of the agency is for the agency and legislative body to conduct a joint public hearing on the plan. § 33355.

The Community Redevelopment Law provides that both the agency and legislative body shall conduct public hearings to approve the redevelopment plan.

Pursuant to SB 1206, not later than 45 days prior to the public hearing on a proposed plan adoption, the agency must send notice of the date of the public hearing with the copy of the preliminary report to the Department of Finance and the HCD. § 33360.5(a). Within 21 days of receiving this report, either the Department of Finance or the HCD may send comments regarding the proposed plan adoption to the agency and the legislative body. These comments must be considered at the public hearing on the proposed plan adoption. § 33360.5(c). If no comments are received within 21 days, the agency and the legislative body may proceed without them. § 33360.5(c).

Notice of the hearing must be published at least once a week for four successive weeks prior to the hearing (a full 28 days must elapse from the date of the first publication of the notice to the date of the hearing). The notice must be published in a newspaper of general circulation in the community and include a legible map of the project area boundaries, a notice that the legal description of the project area is available free of charge, and a general statement of the scope and objectives of the redevelopment plan. The agency must prepare a legal description of the project area boundaries and make it available to the public free of charge. Copies of the notice must be mailed by first-class mail to the last known assessee of each parcel of land in the project area. The agency must also send notices, by first-class mail, at least 30 days prior to the hearing, to all residents and businesses within the project area. This requirement only applies if the agency can obtain the mailing addresses at a reasonable cost. Copies of the notice must also be sent to each of the taxing agencies by certified mail, return receipt requested. The agency should maintain a list of all the persons and entities to whom the notice was mailed, and a certificate or affidavit of such mailing should be prepared and entered into the record at the public hearing. § 33349.

If any property in the project area would be subject to acquisition by purchase or condemnation, the agency must send a statement to that effect to each assessee with the notice of hearing. As an alternative, the agency may attach a list or map of all properties subject to acquisition or condemnation under the plan. § 33350.

Sections 33349 and 33350 require that the description of the goals and objectives of the plan and notice of authority to acquire property by eminent domain, if any, be in nontechnical language using words with common and everyday meaning.

If the clerk of the legislative body has not received written objections prior to the public hearing, and if no written objections are presented during the hearing, the legislative body may adopt the redevelopment plan after the hearing. However, if written objections are presented, the plan may only be adopted after the objections have been considered and written findings adopted *at least one week* after the time the public hearing began. § 33364. While, technically, this may mean an ordinance may be introduced for first reading before acting upon the written objections, the better practice is to introduce the ordinance *after* the legislative body has made its findings. The legislative body must address the objections in detail and give reasons for not accepting specified objections and suggestions, using a good faith reasoned analysis in its response, supported by factual information. § 33363.

If the agency and legislative body members are not the same, the agency must recommend approval of the redevelopment plan by the legislative body. §§ 33347, 33348. Adoption of the redevelopment plan by the legislative body must be by ordinance, with explicit findings required regarding, among others, the existence of blight, necessity of condemnation, economic feasibility of the plan, adequacy of the relocation plan and the fact that the project area is predominately urbanized. § 33367. A majority vote is required to adopt the redevelopment plan unless either the planning agency or the PAC has recommended against approval. In that case, approval must be by a two-thirds vote of the entire legislative body eligible and qualified to vote. § 33366.

After the redevelopment plan and the accompanying documents have been submitted to the legislative body, and at any time prior to the adoption of the plan, the legislative body, upon the agency's recommendation without additional public hearings, may change the plan or exclude property from the project area. However, the change must first be submitted to the planning agency, which must file its report and recommendation on the proposed change within 30 days. If no report is filed within that time, the legislative body may proceed to act upon the plan without the report and recommendation of the planning agency. The legislative body must consider any proposed changes at a public hearing reopened for that limited purpose. § 33363.5.

Following the close of the public hearing (and, if written objections are received, at least one week after the public hearing began), the legislative body introduces the ordinance adopting the redevelopment plan and has its first reading. Section 33367 specifies what the ordinance adopting the redevelopment plan must contain.

SB 1206 added two requirements to this ordinance. First, all the findings and determinations of the legislative body under section 33367(c) must be based upon "clearly articulated and documented evidence." § 33367(d). Second, the legislative body must make a new finding that the implementation of the redevelopment plan will improve or alleviate the physical and economic conditions of blight in the project area. § 33367(d)(14).

The ordinance may be adopted in accordance with the legislative body's normal procedures (subject to the requirement for a two-thirds vote if either the planning commission or project area committee has recommended against approval). Note, however, that SB 1206 amended section 33378 to provide for a 90-day referendum period for all ordinances adopting or amending a redevelopment plan, extending the 30-day

If the agency and legislative body members are not the same, the agency must recommend approval of the redevelopment plan by the legislative body.

Following the close of the public hearing (and, if written objections are received, at least one week after the public hearing began), the legislative body introduces the ordinance adopting the redevelopment plan.

referendum period that had been applicable in most jurisdictions.[6] The effect of this change on the effective date of an ordinance adopting a redevelopment plan is an open question. However, a conservative approach would be to assume the ordinance is not effective until the referendum period has expired. *See, e.g., Cline v. Lewis* (1917) 175 Cal. 315; *Midway Orchards v. County of Butte* (1990) 220 Cal. App. 3d 765; *Gilmore v. Pearson* (1925) 71 Cal. App. 284.

Care should be taken in the conduct of the public hearing to create a clear and complete record of the proceedings in the event of a legal challenge to the adoption of the redevelopment plan.

Care should be taken in the conduct of the public hearing to create a clear and complete record of the proceedings in the event of a legal challenge to the adoption of the redevelopment plan. Proof of publication and certificates of mailing of the notice of the public hearing should be preserved and entered into the record. Copies of resolutions or minutes of the planning commission and PAC should be preserved and made a part of the record. A reliable method of preserving the oral testimony should be utilized, such as tape recording or use of a court reporter. Any photographs or other evidence used as part of a staff report or presentation should also be preserved.

Notifications after Plan Adoption

Once the ordinance has been adopted, a copy must be sent to the agency vested with the responsibility for implementing the plan.

Once the ordinance has been adopted, a copy must be sent to the agency vested with the responsibility for implementing the plan. § 33372. Notice of the adoption of the plan must be given by recording a statement and legal description of the project area with the county recorder. § 33373. SB 1809 requires that this notice be recorded within 60 days of the redevelopment plan adoption. § 33373(a). If the redevelopment plan contains the power of eminent domain, SB 1809 also requires the recorded statement to include:

- A prominent heading in boldface type noting that the property that is the subject of the statement is located within a redevelopment project. § 33373(b)(1)
- A general description of the provisions of the redevelopment plan that authorize the agency's use of eminent domain. § 33373(b)(2)
- A general description of any limitations on the use of the power of eminent domain contained in the redevelopment plan, including the time limit on the exercise of eminent domain required by section 33333.2. § 33373(b)(3)

For a redevelopment plan that includes the power of eminent domain that was adopted on or before December 31, 2006, the agency was required to, on or before December 31, 2007, record a revised statement with the county recorder containing all of the information required

---

6. Prior to SB 1206, the 90-day referendum period was applicable only to jurisdictions with a population over 500,000.

by SB 1809. § 33373(c). SB 1809 prohibits an agency from commencing an action in eminent domain until the statement is recorded. § 33373(d).

Notices must also be sent to the county auditor, county assessor, State Board of Equalization, and to all taxing agencies if the plan authorizes the agency to receive tax increment. §§ 33670, 33375. The legal effect of this latter notice is to establish the time for the first allocation of tax increments to the agency—the tax year beginning after the next December 1 following the transmittal of the notice. It is, therefore, good practice to send these notices by certified mail, return receipt requested, giving the agency a record of the transmittal. § 33674. Care should also be taken to ensure that the notice of determination regarding the approval of the plan required by CEQA is filed with the county clerk and posted as soon as possible after adopting the ordinance. It is the date of the posting that triggers the 30-day statute of limitations for legal challenges to the adequacy of the EIR on the plan. Cal. Code Regs., tit. 14, § 15094.

Referenda

By statute, the ordinance adopting a redevelopment plan or redevelopment plan amendment is subject to referendum. § 33365. Under SB 1206, opponents of a redevelopment plan in all cities and counties now have 90 days to gather sufficient signatures to qualify a referendum petition on the plan adoption. § 33378(b)(2). The Community Redevelopment Law states that, if the plan or plan amendment provides for tax increment to be allocated to the redevelopment agency, the language of the ballot measure must clearly state that a yes vote is a vote in favor of adoption of the redevelopment plan or amendment and a no vote is a vote against the adoption of the plan or amendment. § 33378(a).

By statute, the ordinance adopting a redevelopment plan or redevelopment plan amendment is subject to referendum.

The measure must also include in the ballot pamphlet an analysis by the county auditor/controller and, at the legislative body's option, a separate analysis by the legislative body or agency of the redevelopment plan, which will include an estimate of the potential impact on property taxes for each $10,000 of assessed valuation for taxpayers located in the project area, and an estimate of what would happen to the project area in the absence of the redevelopment project. § 33378.

Legal Actions

No action challenging the validity of a redevelopment plan or redevelopment plan amendment may be brought after 90 days from the date of the ordinance adopting the plan or amendment. §§ 33500, 33501(b). SB 1206 lengthened the time limit on such legal actions from 60 to 90 days. Any legal challenge must be in the form of a validation action pursuant to section 860 *et seq.* of the Code of Civil Procedure (§ 33501; *Community Redevelopment Agency v. Superior Court* (1967) 248 Cal. App. 2d 164; *Sibbet v. Board of Directors* (1965) 237 Cal. App. 2d 731), although

No action challenging the validity of a redevelopment plan or redevelopment plan amendment may be brought after 90 days from the date of the ordinance adopting the plan or amendment.

the validation action may be combined with other types of actions as long as it is filed within the 90-day statute of limitations (*Regus v. City of Baldwin Park* (1977) 70 Cal. App. 3d 968). *See* chapter 13 for further discussion regarding validation proceedings.

SB 1206 prohibits an action from being brought against a redevelopment agency or legislative body unless the grounds for noncompliance with the Community Redevelopment Law are presented to the agency or legislative body orally or in writing before the close of the public hearing. § 33501.2. This requirement effectively codifies prior case law holding that the doctrine of exhaustion of administrative remedies applies to challenges to both the adoption and amendment of redevelopment plans, and that failure to object to the plan adoption or amendment at the public hearing constitutes a failure to exhaust available remedies and precludes later filing a lawsuit. *Evans v. City of San Jose* (2005) 128 Cal. App. 4th 1123; *Redevelopment Agency v. Superior Court* (1991) 228 Cal. App. 3d 1487.

SB 1206 also makes the Department of Finance and the Attorney General "interested parties" in actions challenging a redevelopment plan or plan amendment. § 33501(c). Moreover, the Attorney General is granted the right to intervene in actions challenging the validity of any finding and determination that a project area is blighted. § 33501.1.

Redevelopment Plan Amendments

After adopting a redevelopment plan, the legislative body may amend the plan by ordinance. § 33450. If the proposed amendment is to add tax-increment financing to a redevelopment plan that does not include that provision, the agency must follow the same procedures and the legislative body is subject to the same restrictions set forth for the adoption of a redevelopment plan. § 33354.5. When the existing plan includes authority for the allocation of tax increment to an agency and the proposed amendment (1) adds new territory; (2) either increases the limitation on the amount of tax increment to be allocated to the agency or the time limit on the establishment of loans, advances, and indebtedness (pursuant to paragraphs (1) and (2) of subdivision (a) of section 33333.2 or paragraphs (1) and (2) of subdivision (a) of section 33333.4); (3) lengthens the period during which the redevelopment plan is effective; (4) merges project areas; or (5) adds significant additional capital improvement projects, the agency must follow the same procedures, and the legislative body is subject to the same restrictions required for adopting a redevelopment plan. § 33354.6. With the exception of an amendment to add significant capital improvement projects, each of the foregoing amendments is also subject to the SB 1206 Amendment Requirements. § 33451.5.

A PAC must be formed if an agency proposes to amend a redevelopment plan so as to:

- Allow the agency to acquire by eminent domain property on which persons reside in a project area in which a substantial number of low- and moderate-income persons live, or
- Add territory in which a substantial number of low- and moderate-income persons reside and allow the agency to acquire by eminent domain property on which persons reside in the added territory

The PAC may be composed of persons from only the added territory or from both the added area and the existing project area. § 33385.3.

If an agency amends a pre-1994 redevelopment plan to increase the amount of tax increment the agency may receive, to increase or eliminate the time for incurring debt, or to extend the duration of the plan, it is required to pay affected taxing entities, other than basic aid school districts, as follows:

- If a pass-through agreement was entered into prior to January 1, 1994 that requires payment to the taxing entity, the amounts required by that agreement.
- If there is no pass-through agreement, the same amounts required for new plans. Payments (calculated against the amount of assessed value by which the current year value exceeds an adjusted base year assessed value) shall continue until termination of the redevelopment plan. The amounts are to be allocated between educational facilities and property taxes according to the section 33607.5(a)(3) formula. In determining the applicable amount under section 33607.5, the first fiscal year shall be the first fiscal year following the one in which the adjusted base year value is determined. The adjusted base year value is the assessed value of the project area in the year in which the limitation being amended would have otherwise taken effect; or, if more than one limitation is being amended, it is the first year in which one or more of the limitations would have taken effect without the amendment.

The agency must begin making these payments according to the terms of the agreement, if applicable, or if there is no agreement, in the first fiscal year following the one in which the adjusted base year value is determined. § 33607.7.

Special provisions apply to basic aid school districts when a plan is amended (§ 33676(b)(3)), with local education agencies receiving either of the following:

- If a pass-through agreement existed prior to January 1, 1994, the agency must make payments required by that agreement.
- If there is no pass-through agreement, the percentage share of the increase in property taxes from the project area allocated among all of the affected taxing entities during the fiscal year the funds in the project area are allocated. This is derived from 80 percent of the

If a PAC must be formed, it may be composed of persons from only the added territory or from both the added area and the existing project area.

Special provisions apply to basic aid school districts when a plan is amended.

growth in assessed value that occurs within the portion of the district within the redevelopment project area. Payments begin when the amendment takes effect pursuant to subdivision (c) of section 33607.7.

The notice and hearing requirements applicable to the adoption of a plan amendment are similar to those for adopting a redevelopment plan. §§ 33451, 33452, 33453, 33454, 33455, 33458. However, the ordinance approving the amendment need only contain the findings required by section 33367 to the extent warranted by the amendment. § 33457.1. By the same token, the information contained in the report to the legislative body, which must be made available to the public prior to the public hearing, need only contain the information warranted by the proposed amendment. *Id.*

Copies of the ordinance adopting the amendment and a description of the project area must be sent to the taxing officials, taxing agencies, and the State Board of Equalization within 30 days after adopting the amendment. § 33457.

Mergers

If a community has more than one redevelopment project, the projects may be merged by amending each redevelopment plan in the manner described above. The project areas in redevelopment projects need not be contiguous. § 33486(a). In addition to the general SB 1206 Amendment Requirements, which apply to an amendment to merge project areas, SB 1206 imposed additional requirements for plan mergers. These new requirements include findings by the legislative body that significant blight remains within one of the project areas, and this blight cannot be eliminated without merging the project areas and the receipt of property taxes. *Id.*

Section 33488 provides that the agency must notify the HCD of its intention to merge the project areas at least 30 days prior to adopting ordinances that provide for the merger of redevelopment projects within a community. § 33488. This notice is in addition to, and slightly incongruous with, the SB 1206 Amendment Requirement that the agency provide notice to the HCD and the Department of Finance not less than 45 days prior to the public hearing, discussed above.

The primary advantage of merging redevelopment projects is to allow a redevelopment agency greater flexibility in the use of its tax-increment revenues. Ordinarily, the Community Redevelopment Law requires that tax increment be used to repay indebtedness incurred to carry out the project generating the tax increment. § 33670(b). When redevelopment projects are merged, tax increment allocated to the agency from a project may be used to finance agency activities anywhere in the merged project area subject to any previous financial commitments. § 33486.

Joint Exercise or Delegation of Authority to Redevelop

The Community Redevelopment Law authorizes two or more agencies within different communities to conduct their redevelopment activities jointly. In these instances, the agencies, planning agencies, and legislative bodies may either hold joint meetings and hearings, or the legislative bodies of each community, acting separately, may designate the agency of one of the communities to act as the agency for all of the interested communities. § 33210.

If one agency is designated, it must obtain the report and recommendation of the planning agency of each community on the redevelopment plan's conformance to the general plan of each community before presenting the plan to the appropriate legislative bodies for adoption. § 33211.

In addition, the legislative body of one community may delegate the redevelopment of an area within its jurisdiction to another community if the area is adjacent to that other community. The delegation must be accomplished by the adoption of an ordinance by the authorizing legislative body. The community undertaking the redevelopment activities may then proceed as though the area were within its own territorial jurisdiction. However, any redevelopment plan for that area must also be approved by an ordinance enacted by the legislative body of the authorizing community. § 33213.

The Community Redevelopment Law also specifies that a county retains jurisdiction over territory within a redevelopment project area, even if that territory is subsequently annexed to a city or included within the boundaries of a new city, unless the county transfers jurisdiction to the city pursuant to either section 33215 or section 33216. § 33214.

If all of the territory within a project area is subsequently annexed to a city or included within a new city, section 33215 provides that a city may initiate the transfer of jurisdiction (from the agency of the county to the agency of the city) if it agrees to reimburse the county for all costs it incurs in conducting the transfer. The city must also adopt two ordinances. One must declare the need for an agency to function in the city pursuant to section 33101, and the other adopts the county's redevelopment plan as it stands or with amendments, as long as the amendments do not violate agreements previously entered into by the agency of the county or the board of supervisors. § 33215. For purposes of allocating tax-increment revenues, the plan is treated as though it was adopted by the city council on the date it was originally adopted by the board of supervisors.

If all or a substantial portion of the territory is later annexed to a city or included within a new city, section 33216 provides that jurisdiction over all or a substantial portion of that territory may be transferred from the agency of the county to the agency of the city. Under these

The Community Redevelopment Law authorizes two or more agencies within different communities to conduct their redevelopment activities jointly.

The legislative body of one community may delegate the redevelopment of an area within its jurisdiction to another community if the area is adjacent to that other community.

procedures, the city and the county redevelopment agency must enter into an agreement containing the following provisions:

- All of the territory included within the project area is transferred to the agency of the city or those specific portions of the area over which each agency will have territorial jurisdiction.
- Tax increment shall be allocated to the city if the city will have territorial jurisdiction over the entire project area being transferred; or, if only a portion of the project area is being transferred, that a proportionate amount of tax increment be allocated between the city and the county agencies that is reasonably related to the relative costs of the project for each.
- Tax increment shall be used by the agency of the city to pay previously incurred indebtedness by the agency of the county if that debt was secured by a pledge of tax increment.
- If a substantial portion of the territory is transferred to the agency of the city, any amendments to the redevelopment plan proposed by either agency with respect to their portion of the project area be approved by an ordinance of the other agency.

§ 33216

In addition, the agreement may provide that:

- If a substantial portion of the territory is transferred to the agency of the city, either agency may undertake activities to implement the plan in the portion of the project area within the other agency's territorial jurisdiction.
- Any other terms that the agencies or legislative bodies mutually determine are necessary to facilitate the transfer of territorial jurisdiction and plan implementation.

§ 33216

Section 33216 governs when all or a substantial portion of a previously noncontiguous project area is annexed to a city or included within the boundaries of a new city.

Section 33216 also governs when all or a substantial portion of a previously noncontiguous project area is annexed to a city or included within the boundaries of a new city. In addition, sections 33214 through 33216 apply to transfer of a project area from a city that adopted the project area to a newly incorporated city. Section 33217 provides an incentive to the city that initially formed a project area to reach agreement with a newly incorporated city that includes a portion of the project area. These provisions were in anticipation of the possible secession of a portion of the City of Los Angeles and the formation of a new city, but they are applicable statewide.

In *Shasta Lake v. County of Shasta* (1999) 75 Cal. App. 4th 1, a newly incorporated city and city redevelopment agency filed a declaratory relief action against a county and county redevelopment agency. The relief requested a determination of conditions in a local agency formation commission resolution that approved the city's incorporation. In dispute was the property tax to be shared between the city and county and their respective agencies, and the manner of repayment for the cost of services rendered by the county. The court held that because the newly incorporated city was receiving services from the county, it was required to pay to the county the costs of supplying such services, less the tax revenues generated within the boundaries of the city for the city and city redevelopment agency.

Implementation Plans

Redevelopment agencies are required to adopt implementation plans every five years. Section 33490 provides that each agency that adopted a redevelopment plan prior to January 1, 1994, must adopt, after a public hearing, an implementation plan on or before December 31, 1994 and every 5 years thereafter. Redevelopment plans adopted on or after January 1, 1994, are required to have an initial implementation plan as part of the report to the legislative body. A new implementation plan must be adopted every five years. Pursuant to SB 1206, implementation plans must also be amended in conjunction with redevelopment plan amendments subject to the SB 1206 Amendment Requirements. § 33451.5(c)(7).

Agencies may adopt an implementation plan that includes more than one project area and hold a single hearing to adopt that implementation plan. Adoption of an implementation plan does not constitute an approval of any specific program, project, or expenditure described in the plan, and therefore an implementation plan is not a project under CEQA requiring environmental documentation. Implementation plans may be amended after a public hearing.

An agency must conduct a noticed public hearing at least once during the five-year term of the implementation plan. The hearing must be held no earlier than two years and no later than three years after adoption. One hearing may be held for two or more project areas if they are included within the same plan. § 33490.

The implementation plan must contain specific goals and objectives of the agency for the project area and specific programs and estimated expenditures proposed to be made during the next five years as well as an explanation of how these will eliminate blight within the project area and implement the low- and moderate-income housing requirements.

The plan should be viewed as a policy and program document. Amendments to section 33490 in 1994 eliminated the requirement to include specific projects and instead require "specific programs, including potential projects, and estimated expenditures proposed to be made." Thus specific sites for specific projects need not be identified.

The implementation plan is required to contain a section describing the agency's low- and moderate-income housing programs. The housing plan provisions previously contained in section 33413 have been rewritten

Redevelopment agencies are required to adopt implementation plans every five years.

The implementation plan must contain specific goals and objectives of the agency for the project area and specific programs and estimated expenditures proposed to be made during the next five years.

and are now included within section 33490. This section of the implementation plan may be adopted every five years in conjunction with either the housing element cycle or the implementation plan cycle. The housing section of the plan must contain:

- Amounts presently available and estimates of amounts that will be deposited in the Housing Fund during the next five years
- A program that estimates the number of units to be assisted from the Housing Fund during the next five years
- A description of how the housing program will implement the requirement for expenditures of money from the Low and Moderate Income Housing Fund over a 10-year period for various groups as required by section 33334.4

If section 33413 production or inclusionary requirements apply, the plan must also contain:

- Estimates of the number of units that have been developed and that will be developed by the agency and others over the life of the plan and the next ten years
- Estimates of the number of units of very low, low, and moderate income households required to be developed in order to meet the housing production requirements of section 33413(b)(2), both over the life of the plan and during the next ten years
- The number of units of very low, low, and moderate income units that have been developed that meet the housing production requirements of section 33413(b)(2)
- Estimates of the number of agency developed residential units that will be developed during the next five years, if any, that will be governed by the housing production requirements of section 33413(b)(1)
- Estimates of the number of agency developed units for very low, low, and moderate income households that will be developed by the agency during the next five years to meet the housing production requirements of section 33413(b)(1)

The housing section of the implementation plan must also contain:

- The number of housing units needed for very low income persons, low income persons, and moderate income persons as each of those needs have been indentified in the most recent determination pursuant to section 65584 of the Government Code, and the proposed amount of expenditure from the Low and Moderate Income Housing Fund for each income group during each year of the implementation plan period
- The total population of the community and the population under 65 year of age or reported in the most recent census

The housing section of the implementation plan must include a description of how the housing program will implement the requirement for expenditures of money from the Low and Moderate Income Housing Fund.

The housing section of the implementation plan must also include the number of housing units needed for very low income persons, low income persons, and moderate income persons.

- A housing program that provides a detailed schedule of actions the agency is undertaking or intends to undertake to ensure expenditure of the Low and Moderate Income Housing Fund in the proportions required by section 33333.4 (and section 33333.10, if applicable)
- For the previous implementation plan period, the amounts of Low and Moderate Income Housing Fund money utilized to assist units affordable to those income groups; the number, location, and level of affordability of units newly constructed with other locally controlled government assistance and without agency assistance and that are required to be affordable to those income groups; and the amount of Low and Moderate Income Housing fund money utilized to assist housing units available to families with children, and the number, location, and level of affordability of those units

If the implementation plan contains a project that will result in the destruction or removal of dwelling units that will have to be replaced, the implementation plan should identify proposed locations suitable for those replacement dwellings.

For a project area that is within six years of the time limit on the effectiveness of the redevelopment plan, the housing section should also address the ability of the agency to comply, prior to the expiration of that time limit, with its affordable housing obligations.

The implementation plan must also identify the fiscal year that the agency expects each of the following time limits to expire:

- Time limit for the commencement of eminent domain proceedings
- Time limit for the establishment of loans, advances, and indebtedness (if applicable)
- Time limit for the effectiveness of the redevelopment plan
- Time limit to repay indebtedness with tax increment

Community Redevelopment Disaster Project Law

Part 1.5 of the Community Redevelopment Law, section 34000 *et seq.*, includes alternative provisions for the adoption of a redevelopment project area after a disaster and can only be used in areas in which a major disaster has occurred. § 34001(b). The proposed project area must be limited to the area in which damage caused by the disaster has occurred. § 34002. Plan adoption must commence within six months and be completed 24 months after the declaration of the disaster. These alternative

An earthquake in 1989 destroyed 50 percent of the buildings in downtown Santa Cruz. Special legislation to streamline the plan adoption process provided a mechanism to assist with reconstruction.

These alternative provisions allow a redevelopment agency to adopt a redevelopment plan in a shorter period of time than is usual and without complying with some of the procedures ordinarily required.

provisions allow a redevelopment agency to adopt a redevelopment plan in a shorter period of time than is usual and without complying with some of the procedures ordinarily required for redevelopment plan adoption. A number of procedural steps are eliminated: blight findings do not have to be made, and the preparation of an EIR on the redevelopment plan can be deferred, although CEQA review on individual projects is required until the EIR on the redevelopment plan is certified. §§ 34004, 34005. Maximum time limits on the plan are shorter than normal: ten years to incur debt, ten years for plan effectiveness, and thirty years for repayment of debt. § 34004(g). After plan adoption, tax increment can only be used to repair or replace improvements within the project area that have been damaged or destroyed by the disaster. § 34007.

4

Conflicts of Interest

The Political Reform Act applies to agency members, planning commissioners, and other public officials and employees who participate in the adoption and/or amendment of redevelopment plans.

Political Reform Act

General

The provisions of the Political Reform Act (the Act) (Gov. Code § 81000 et seq.) and its implementing regulations (the FPPC Regulations) (Cal. Code Regs., tit. 2, § 18110 *et seq.*) apply to agency members, planning commissioners, and other public officials and employees who participate in the adoption and/or amendment of redevelopment plans and in redevelopment plan implementation. They also apply to members of project area committees (PACs), which, as discussed in further detail below, can often present special difficulties. (As discussed in chapter 2, a redevelopment agency must adopt its own conflict of interest code.) The Act generally requires these public officials to disclose their financial interests within 30 days of assuming office or upon adoption of a conflict of interest code and annually thereafter. These officials must disqualify themselves from participating in decisions in which they have an "economic interest," as defined in the Act and the FPPC Regulations.

California's Fair Political Practices Commission is primarily responsible for administering the provisions of the Act. In addition to adopting the Regulations, the FPPC issues advice letters, formal commission opinions and reports, and conducts enforcement proceedings.

As a practical matter, community and agency officials should determine *before a survey area is adopted* whether they have a potential conflict of interest and whether they should disqualify themselves from participating in the decisions regarding the adoption or amendment of a redevelopment plan. Once it has been determined that a conflict of interest exists, the official must disqualify himself from *all* decisions regarding the adoption of the redevelopment plan, not just the ordinance actually adopting the plan.

FPPC = California Fair Political Practices Commission

PAC = Project area committee

California's Fair Political Practices Commission is primarily responsible for administering the provisions of the Act.

87

However, once a redevelopment plan or amendment has been adopted, an official who has been disqualified from participating in plan adoption decisions *may* be able to vote on specific decisions to implement the plan if they do not affect the official's economic interests. For example, if an agency member owned commercial property in the city's downtown area and the agency was asked to approve a disposition and development agreement for a residential project a mile away, that official would be able to vote on the project approval. *See,* for example, *Scudder* Advice Letter, FPPC No. A-88-181, June 20, 1988; *Rousch* Advice Letter, FPPC No. A-88-404, December 7, 1988.

Because the penalties for violations of the Act can be severe and officials are personally liable, an official should seek legal advice if a conflict appears to exist.

The rules regarding conflicts of interest are quite complex, and the following discussion is merely intended to provide an overview of the provisions of the Act and the FPPC Regulations. In addition, decisions regarding disqualification often are heavily dependent upon the particular facts in a given situation. Because the penalties for violations of the Act can be severe and officials are personally liable, an official should seek legal advice if a conflict appears to exist.

Disclosure

Certain public officials are required under the Act to file statements of economic interests: members of city councils and boards of supervisors, planning commissioners, county counsels, city attorneys, city managers, county administrative officers, city treasurers, county treasurers, and other public officials who manage public investments. Gov. Code §§ 87200; 82019; Cal. Code Regs., tit. 2, § 18701. An official wearing two hats—one for the city or county and another for the agency—should designate both entities on his or her statement of economic interest (FPPC Form 700).

In addition, the redevelopment agency's conflict of interest code should specify those "designated employees" who also must file statements of economic interests.

In addition, the redevelopment agency's conflict of interest code should specify those "designated employees" who also must file statements of economic interests. These designated employees, who could include consultants to the redevelopment agency, are those persons who would make or participate in making decisions that could present a conflict of interest for them. Gov. Code § 87302; Cal. Code Regs., tit. 2, § 18701. Moreover, members of a PAC, if one is formed during the redevelopment plan adoption process, are considered to be "public officials" under the Act. Thus, they are subject to the Act's disclosure requirements and should be listed as "designated employees" under the agency's conflict of interest code. *Rotman* opinion, 10 FPPC Ops. 1 (1987). The practical effect of the *Rotman* opinion is to create a virtually irreconcilable tension between the requirements of the Community Redevelopment Law, which requires persons with certain types of interests to be represented on the PAC, and the conflict of interest rules as discussed later in this chapter.

In general, the official or designated employee must disclose, on his or her statement of economic interests, investments, interests in real property (excluding personal residence), sources of income over $500 and gifts over $50 held or derived from within the agency's jurisdiction, as well as business entities in which he or she holds office or a position of management. The jurisdiction for a city redevelopment agency is the entire city, while the jurisdiction for a county redevelopment agency is the unincorporated area of the county.

Disqualification

Section 87100 of the Government Code provides the following general prohibition:

> No public official at any level of state or local government shall make, participate in making, or in any way attempt to use his official position to influence a governmental decision in which he knows or has reason to know he has a financial interest.

Section 87103 of the Government Code establishes the general rule for determining if disqualification is required. That section provides that an official has a financial interest in a decision within the meaning of Government Code section 87100 if it is reasonably foreseeable that the decision will have a material financial effect, distinguishable from its effect on the public generally, on the official or a member of his or her immediate family or on a specified type of economic interest. While the rule may appear fairly straightforward, the analysis of the various economic interests often requires careful maneuvering through the FPPC Regulations that define the terms and standards to be applied. The FPPC Regulations set forth an eight-step analysis, with regulations defining each separate step. Cal. Code Regs., tit. 2, § 18700.

Making or Participating in a Decision. An official makes a governmental decision when he or she, acting within the authority of his or her office: (1) votes; (2) appoints a person; (3) obligates his agency to any course of action; (4) enters into any contractual agreement; or (5) determines not to act. Participating in the making of a decision includes negotiating with a governmental entity or person about the decision or making recommendations to the decision maker. Cal. Code Regs., tit. 2, §§ 18702.1, 18702.2. Using an official position to influence a decision occurs if the official contacts or appears before or otherwise attempts to influence any member, officer, employee, or consultant of the official's agency. Cal. Code Regs., tit. 2, § 18702.3. However, under certain circumstances, an official may make appearances in the same manner as any other member of the general public solely to represent himself on a personal interest. Cal. Code Regs., tit. 2, § 18702.4(b)(1).

Types of Economic Interests. The six types of economic interests that may cause an official to disqualify himself from participating in decisions are as follows:

- The personal finances of the official and members of his or her immediate family. Cal. Code Regs., tit. 2, § 18703.5. This includes a spouse and dependent children up to 18 years old.
- A business entity in which the public official has a direct or indirect investment worth $2,000 or more. This includes stock, partnership, or other ownership interests owned by the official or a member of his or her immediate family, or a *pro rata* share of investments of any business entity, mutual fund, or trust in which the official or family member owns—directly, indirectly, or beneficially—a ten percent or greater interest. It does not include shares in a diversified mutual fund or government bonds. Gov. Code § 82034; Cal. Code Regs., tit. 2, § 18703.1.
- Any real property in which the public official has a direct or indirect interest worth $2,000 or more. These include leasehold (except for month-to-month tenancies), beneficial, or ownership interests or options to acquire such an interest in real property within the jurisdiction of the agency, as well as a *pro rata* share of interests in real property of any business entity or trust in which the official or family member owns—directly, indirectly, or beneficially—a ten percent or greater interest. Gov. Code § 82033; Cal. Code Regs., tit. 2, §§ 18233; 18703.2.
- Any source of income aggregating $500 or more provided to, received by, or promised to the official within 12 months prior to the time when the decision is made. Income includes a community property interest in the income of a spouse, outstanding loans, and a *pro rata* share of any business entity or trust in which the official or spouse owns a ten percent or greater interest. Income does not include, among other things: loans received from a commercial lending institution to finance the official's principal residence or where the balance owed does not exceed $10,000; income from a business not doing business within the agency's jurisdiction; salary from a state, local, or federal government agency; or campaign contributions. Gov. Code § 82030. If the official owns a ten percent or greater interest in a business that conducts retail sales of goods or services, a retail customer is not a source of income if the business entity's customers constitute a significant segment of the public and the amount of income received from the customer is not distinguishable from the amount received from other customers. Gov. Code § 87103.5. There are specific reporting requirements for commission income earned by brokers, agents and salespersons. Cal. Code Regs., tit. 2, § 18703.3.
- Any business entity in which the official is a director, officer, partner, trustee, employee, or holds any position of management. Cal. Code Regs., tit. 2, § 18703.1.

Income includes a community property interest in the income of a spouse, outstanding loans, and a pro rata *share of any business entity or trust in which the official or spouse owns a ten percent or greater interest.*

- Any donor of gifts aggregating $420 or more in value received by or promised to the official within 12 months prior to the time when the decision was made. Gov. Code § 87103; Cal. Code Regs., tit. 2, § 18703.4. (But note that Government Code section 89503 prohibits local officials from accepting gifts that aggregate more than $420 from a single source in a calendar year.) The gift limit is adjusted every two years by the FPPC; the $420 limit is in effect until December 31, 2010.

Often an official will have a number of economic interests involved in one decision. Each of those interests must be analyzed in order to determine if any would require his or her disqualification from participating in a decision.

Direct or Indirect Involvement in Decision. Once the specific economic interests have been identified, there must be a determination of whether the interests are directly or indirectly involved in the decision. This is important because different materiality standards apply. A person, including a business entity, or a source of income or gifts, is directly involved if that person initiates the proceeding or is a named party or the subject of a proceeding before the public agency. Cal. Code Regs., tit. 2, § 18704.1. Real property is directly involved in a decision if it is the subject of or within 500 feet of the boundaries of the proposed decision, such as those dealing with land use, taxes or fees, public improvements and redevelopment plan adoptions. Cal. Code Regs., tit. 2, § 18704.2. An official's personal finances are directly involved if the governmental decision will have any financial effect on the official or the finances of a member of his or her immediate family. Cal. Code Regs., tit. 2, § 18704.5.

Once the specific economic interests have been identified, there must be a determination of whether the interests are directly or indirectly involved in the decision.

Reasonable Foreseeability. The element of reasonable foreseeability is met if there is a substantial likelihood that the materiality standards defined in the FPPC Regulations for a particular economic interest will be met as a result of the decision. The effect of a decision must be more than a mere possibility; however, certainty is not required. *Downey Cares v. Downey Community Development Com.* (1987) 196 Cal. App. 3d 983, 989–991; *Witt v. Morrow* (1977) 70 Cal. App. 3d 817; *In re Thorner*, 1 FPPC Ops. 198 (1975).

The effect of a decision must be more than a mere possibility; however, certainty is not required.

Materiality. In 2001, the FPPC significantly revised a host of regulations defining materiality for each type of economic interest. Cal. Code Regs., tit. 2, § 18705 *et seq.*

- *Real Property–Directly Involved.* In the context of decisions regarding the adoption of a redevelopment plan, the types of economic interest that often are directly involved in those decisions would be any interest in real property located within 500 feet of the boundaries of the survey area. Section 18704.2, subsection (a)(5) of the FPPC Regulations, California Code of Regulations, Title 2, provides that an official's real property is directly involved in a governmental decision if:

(5) The governmental decision is to designate the survey area, to select the project area, to adopt the preliminary plan, to form a project area committee, to certify the environmental document, to adopt the redevelopment plan, to add territory to the redevelopment area, or to rescind or amend any of the above decisions; and the real property in which the official has an interest, or any part of it is located within the boundaries (or the proposed boundaries) of the redevelopment area.

Furthermore, subdivision (a)(1) provides that for purposes of subdivision (a)(5), real property is located "within 500 feet of the boundaries (or proposed boundaries) of the real property which is the subject of the governmental decision" if any part of the real property is within 500 feet of the boundaries (or proposed boundaries) of the redevelopment project area. Cal. Code Regs., tit. 2, § 18704.2(a).

If the official has an interest other than a leasehold in *real property* that is within 500 feet from the boundaries of the redevelopment area in question, there is a rebuttable presumption that the financial effect of the redevelopment decisions will be material. If the official has a leasehold interest in that property, the effect of these decisions is presumed to be material unless there is proof that it is not reasonably foreseeable that the decision will affect any of the following: (1) the termination date of the lease; (2) the amount of rent; (3) the value of the lessee's right to sublease the property; (4) the legally allowable use or current use of the property by the lessee; or (5) the use or enjoyment of the property by the lessee. Cal. Code Regs., tit. 2, § 18705.2(a).

- *Real Property—Indirectly Involved.* If the official has an interest in real property that is 500 feet or more from the boundaries of the redevelopment area, the rebuttable presumption is that the effect of the decision is *not* material. That presumption can be rebutted, however, if the decision likely will affect the development potential or use of the official's property. If the interest is a leasehold, that presumption may be rebutted by proof that the circumstances make it reasonably foreseeable that the decision will: (1) change the legally allowable use of the property and the lessee has a right to sublease that property; (2) change the lessee's actual use of the real property; (3) substantially enhance or decrease the lessee's use or enjoyment of the property; (4) affect the rent by five percent during the 12 months after the decision; or (5) change the termination date of the lease. Cal. Code Regs., tit. 2, § 18705.2(b).

If the official has an interest in real property that is 500 feet or more from the boundaries of the redevelopment area, the rebuttable presumption is that the effect of the decision is not material.

- *Business Entities—Directly Involved.* If a business entity in which an official has an economic interest (whether as a stockholder, employee or officer, for example) is directly involved in a decision, materiality is presumed. There is an exception if the official's only interest in the entity is stock worth $25,000 or less, and the entity is a Fortune 500 company or is listed on or meets the listing criteria for the New York Stock Exchange. In that instance, the effect of the decision is only considered material if it meets the materiality standards for *indirectly* involved business entities for a Fortune 500 or New York Stock Exchange company, whichever is applicable. Cal. Code Regs., tit. 2, § 18705.1.

- *Business Entities—Indirectly Involved.* As would be expected, the materiality standards vary with the size of the business entity. For a Fortune 500 company, a decision is material if it will affect the entity's (1) gross revenues in a fiscal year by $10 million or more; (2) expenses in a fiscal year by $2.5 million or more; or (3) assets or liabilities by $10 million or more. For a New York Stock Exchange company, a decision is material if it will affect the entity's (1) gross revenues in a fiscal year by $500,000 or more; (2) expenses in a fiscal year by $200,000 or more; or (3) assets or liabilities by $500,000 or more. If a business entity is listed or meets the criteria for listing on NASDAQ or AMEX, a decision is material if it will affect the entity's (1) gross revenues in a fiscal year by $300,000 or more; (2) expenses in a fiscal year by $100,000 or more; or (3) assets or liabilities by $300,000 or more. For all other entities, the effect is considered material if it will affect an entity's (1) gross revenues in a fiscal year by $20,000 or more; (2) expenses in a fiscal year by $5,000 or more; or (3) assets or liabilities by $20,000 or more. Cal. Code Regs., tit. 2, § 18705.1.

  As would be expected, the materiality standards vary with the size of the business entity.

- *Source of Income—Directly Involved.* Any reasonably foreseeable financial effect on a person (which includes a business entity) who is a source of income to an official and who is directly involved in the decision is deemed material. Cal. Code Regs., tit. 2 § 18705.3(a).

- *Source of Income—Indirectly Involved.* If the source of income is a business entity, the materiality test is as set forth above for business entities that are indirectly involved. If the source of income is an individual, the materiality standard is met if the decision will affect the individual's income, investments or other tangible or intangible assets or liabilities (other than real property) by $1,000 or more. If the decision will affect that individual's real property interest, then the real property materiality standard is used. Cal. Code Regs., tit. 2, § 18705.3(b)(3)(A), (B).

  If the source of income is a business entity, the materiality test is as set forth above for business entities that are indirectly involved.

  There are also specific materiality standards if the source of income is a nonprofit entity, including a governmental entity. The materiality standards vary, depending on the amount of the entity's gross annual receipts, expenses, or assets or liabilities. Cal. Code Regs., tit. 2, § 18705.3(b)(2).

- *Personal Finances.* A decision is considered to have a material financial effect upon an official's personal finances if it is at least $250 in any 12-month period. However, this standard does not include the effect upon an official's real property interest or interest in a business entity. For those two economic interests, the specific materiality standards for real property and business entities apply. Cal. Code Regs., tit. 2, § 18705.5.

Distinguishable from the Public Generally. Another part of the analysis is whether the effect on the official's economic interest is distinguishable from the effect on the public generally. Stated another way, if the official's interest is affected in the same manner as on all members of the public or a substantial segment of the public, then disqualification would not be required. Cal. Code Regs., tit. 2, § 18707. In the *Legan* opinion, 9 FPPC Ops. 1 (1985), the FPPC stated:

> In order to be considered a significant segment of the public, we think a group usually must be large in number and heterogeneous in quality.

Legan, p. 13

Section 18707.1 of the FPPC Regulations provides that a governmental decision will affect a significant segment of the public generally in the following situations:

- *Individuals.* For decisions that affect the personal expenses, income, assets or liabilities of a public official or a member of his or her immediate family, or an individual who is a source of income or gifts to the official, the decision also affects:
  - Ten percent or more of the population in the jurisdiction of the official's agency or the district the official represents, or
  - Five thousand individuals who are residents of the jurisdiction.

  Cal. Code Regs., tit. 2, § 18707.1(b)(1)(A)

- *Real property.* For decisions that affect an official's real property interest, the decision also affects:
  - Ten percent or more of all property owners or all homeowners in the jurisdiction of the official's agency or the district the official represents, or
  - Five thousand property owners or residential property owners in the jurisdiction of the official's agency.

  Cal. Code Regs., tit. 2, § 18707.1(b)(1)(B)

- *Business entities.* For decisions that affect a business entity in which the official has an economic interest, the decision also affects two thousand or twenty-five percent of all business entities in the jurisdiction or the district the official represents, so long as the effect is on persons composed of more than a single industry, trade, or profession. For purposes of this subdivision, a nonprofit entity other than a governmental entity is treated as a business entity. Cal. Code Regs., tit. 2, § 18707.1(b)(1)(C)

- *Governmental entities.* For decisions that affect a federal, state, or local government entity in which the official has an economic interest, the decision will affect all members of the public under the jurisdiction of that governmental entity. Cal. Code Regs., tit. 2, § 18707.1(b)(1)(D)
- The decision will affect a segment of the population that does not meet any of the above tests; however, due to exceptional circumstances regarding the decision, it is determined that this segment constitutes a significant segment of the public generally. Cal. Code Regs., tit. 2, § 18707.1(b)(1)(E)

Thus, this regulation quantifies what constitutes a "significant segment" of the public and should make it somewhat easier for members of PACs and other public officials to determine if they may participate in a particular decision. If the effect on the official's economic interest is substantially the same as the effect on the economic interests of a significant segment of the public identified above, the official need not disqualify himself or herself from participating in the decision.

There are three limited refinements to the above definition that may apply to decisions on a redevelopment plan adoption or amendment. The first relates to PACs established during the plan adoption process; the second applies to small cities; the third applies specifically to certain residential properties.

Project Area Committees. In the *Rotman* opinion (10 FPPC Ops. 1 (1987)), the FPPC concluded that the "public," with respect to a PAC, consisted of those persons within the redevelopment project area.

> Accordingly, members of project area committees are required to disqualify themselves from participating in decisions which will materially affect their economic interests only if the effect of the decision will be distinguishable from the effect on all other persons in the project area or on a significant segment of the persons in the project area. For example, if persons owning businesses in the project area constitute a significant segment of the persons in the project area, project area committee members who own businesses in the project area are disqualified from participation in decisions of the project area committee only if the decision will have a material financial effect on their business which is distinguishable from other businesses in the project area.

Rotman, p. 9

PACs are required to include residential owner occupants, residential tenants, business owners, and existing organizations from the proposed project area. § 33385(c). In determining whether a PAC member has a conflict of interest, one must look at whether the decision will have a similar effect on a significant segment of the public within the project area itself. (This is a narrower focus, for example, than determining whether a city council member has a conflict. In that situation, the official's jurisdiction is the *entire city*.)

In California Attorney General Opinion No. 99-304, the Office of the Attorney General answered the question whether a PAC could provide advice to a redevelopment agency where several members of the committee owned property within the project area. The Attorney General concluded that project area property owners could serve as members of a PAC formed pursuant to section 33385 of the Community Redevelopment Law. The Opinion made clear that not only had the potential conflicting interests among members been anticipated by the legislature, the statutory framework was constructed to ensure such a result and guarantee a broad PAC perspective.

The California Attorney General has concluded that project area property owners could serve as members of a PAC formed pursuant to section 33385 of the Community Redevelopment Law.

Small Jurisdictions. The second refinement to the definition of "public generally" applies to small jurisdictions and an official's domicile (permanent residence). California Code of Regulations, title 2, section 18707.10 provides that the "public generally" exception applies if all of the following criteria are satisfied:

- The official's agency has jurisdiction over a population of 30,000 or less and covers a geographic area of ten square miles or less
- The official is required to live within the jurisdiction
- If the official has been elected, the official was elected in an at large jurisdiction
- The official's property is more than 300 feet from the boundaries of the property that is the subject of the decision
- There are at least 20 other properties under separate ownership within a 500 foot radius of the boundaries of the property that is the subject of the decision that are similar in value
- The official's principal residence is on a parcel of land not more than one-quarter of an acre in size or not larger than 125 percent of the median residential lot size in the jurisdiction

The Concord Redevelopment Agency provided financing for the construction of the Todos Santos Parking Center.

This exception does not change the general rule that would prohibit an official from participating in redevelopment plan adoption decisions if the official's home was located within the project area. However, it generally would allow an official for a small city to vote if his or her home were more than 300 feet from the boundaries of the project area.

Residential properties. If an official owns three or fewer residential property units (not including the official's principal residence), and the effect of a decision will affect 5,000 or ten percent or more of all property owners or all homeowners in the jurisdiction similarly, the "public generally" exception is met with respect to an official's real property interest.

If, however, the official owns more than three residential property units, he or she may only participate if all of the following conditions are met: (1) the decision affects the respective rights or liabilities of tenants and owners of residential properties; (2) the official has no other economic interest arising out of the ownership or rental of the residential property being analyzed; (3) the official's property is indirectly involved in the decision; (4) the decision affects at least ten percent of the residential property units in the jurisdiction or official's district; and (5) other residential property owners shall be affected in substantially the same manner as the official. Cal. Code Regs., tit. 2, § 18707.9.

Examples. The following types of situations arise frequently in the context of redevelopment plan decisions:

- An agency member is a real estate broker who has represented parties in transactions within a redevelopment project area within 12 months of the plan adoption decisions. That official is considered to have several sources of income, each of which must be analyzed to determine whether disqualification may be required. Subsection (c)(2)(B) of section 18703.3 of the FPPC Regulations provides that the broker's sources of income are:
    - The person the broker represents in the transaction
    - If the broker receives a commission from a transaction conducted by an agent working under the broker's auspices, the person represented by the agent
    - Any brokerage business entity through which the broker conducts business, and
    - Any person who receives a finders' or other referral fee for referring a party to the transaction to the broker, or who makes a referral pursuant to a contract with a broker

Cal. Code Regs., tit. 2, § 18703.3(c)(2)(B)

That section of the FPPC Regulations also defines sources of income for other persons who receive commissions, such as insurance brokers, stockbrokers, and salespersons.

This exception does not change the general rule that would prohibit an official from participating in redevelopment plan adoption decisions if the official's home was located within the project area.

- A planning commissioner who owns commercial property within a project area leased to a local business has at least two economic interests. He has an interest in real property and a source of income in his tenant. He would most likely have to disqualify himself from participating in redevelopment plan adoption decisions because the decisions would have a material financial effect on the value of his property, and the segment of the public who owns commercial property is not likely to be significant in number. In addition, if the redevelopment plan could significantly increase the number of his tenant's customers (that is, have a material financial effect on the official's source of income), disqualification could be required on those grounds as well. Cal. Code Regs., tit. 2, § 18707.4.

- The mayor owns more than $2,000 worth of stock in a locally-owned bank. That is his only economic interest in the bank. The bank owns the land on which its only building is situated, located 100 feet from the project area. The mayor has an investment in a business entity. Disqualification would likely be required if it was reasonably foreseeable that the effect of the redevelopment plan adoption decisions would have a material financial effect on the bank (by increasing the value of the bank's land and building) by the requisite amounts. Cal. Code Regs., tit. 2, § 18705.1.

Recusal

If an official has a conflict of interest and cannot participate in a decision, section 87105 requires the official to publicly identify the financial interest in detail, recuse himself or herself from voting, and leave the room until the matter is concluded.

If an official has a conflict of interest and cannot participate in a decision, Government Code section 87105 requires the official, immediately prior to the consideration of the matter, to publicly identify the financial interest in detail (excepting a personal residence address), recuse himself or herself from voting, and leave the room until the matter is concluded. The only exceptions to this requirement is if the matter is on the consent agenda, in which case the official need not leave the room; or if the official wishes to speak on the matter as a member of the general public.

Legally Required Participation— The Rule of Necessity

The Political Reform Act provides that a public official may participate in a decision to the "extent that his participation is legally required for the action or decision to be made."

The Political Reform Act provides that a public official may participate in a decision to the "extent that his participation is legally required for the action or decision to be made." The FPPC Regulations further provide that "[a] public official who has a financial interest in a decision may establish that he or she is legally required to make or to participate in the making of a governmental decision... only if there exists no alternative source of decision consistent with the purposes and terms of the statute authorizing the decision." Cal. Code Regs., tit. 2, § 18708. The Community Redevelopment Law clearly specifies that actions regarding the adoption of a plan must be taken by particular bodies. Thus, if a quorum cannot be achieved because of disqualifications based upon conflicts of interest, the body may invoke the so-called "rule of necessity" to bring back the minimum number of members necessary to have a quorum. *Hudson* opinion, 4 FPPC Ops. 13 (1978). Selecting who should be brought back may be done by drawing lots or some other random method. Cal. Code Regs., tit. 2, § 18708(c)(3).

If the rule of necessity is invoked during the plan adoption process, the same persons participate in all of the plan adoption decisions, rather than having the members with conflicts drawing lots for each individual decision. *Id.* The FPPC Regulations allow an official with a conflict of interest who is selected to participate under the rule of necessity to fully participate in the discussions and decisions in an open meeting of the agency or in closed session. *Id.* The regulation contains very specific disclosure requirements when the rule of necessity is invoked. Cal. Code Regs., tit. 2, § 18708(b)(4).

> *If the rule of necessity is invoked during the plan adoption process, it's probably a good practice to have the same persons participate in all of the plan adoption decisions, rather than drawing lots for each individual decision.*

In *Kunec v. Brea Redevelopment Agency* (1997) 55 Cal. App. 4th 511, the court held that the agency's resolution of necessity was invalid because the agency invoked the rule of necessity to allow two agency members to vote without making a full public disclosure on the record, recorded in the minutes, as to why those agency members had actual or potential conflicts of interest and without explaining why the agency had no alternative as a source of decisionmaking. The court held this disclosure was required by FPPC regulations interpreting the rule of necessity.

Section 18708 of the FPPC Regulations requires the official to disclose the existence of the conflict and the specific nature of the economic interest he or she has that gives rise to the conflict. The disclosures must include the following:

- For investments in a business entity, the name of the entity.
- For business positions, a general description of the business activity of the business entity.
- For real property, the address or location of the property, unless it is the official's principal residence, in which case that fact is disclosed.
- For income, loans, or gifts, the person or entity that is the source.

Cal. Code Regs., tit. 2, § 18708(b)

> *Section 18708 of the FPPC Regulations requires the official to disclose the existence of the conflict and the specific nature of the economic interest he or she has that gives rise to the conflict.*

In addition, either the official or another officer or employee of the agency must describe the nature of the potential conflict and the legal basis for concluding there is not an alternative source of decision-making. The disclosures must be made orally before the decision is made, and such disclosure must be entered in the minutes of the meeting or as a writing filed with the agency. Cal. Code Regs., tit. 2, § 18708.

In *Brown v. Fair Political Practices Comm.* (2000) 84 Cal. App. 4th 137 (1-A091305, Div. 2), the Court of Appeals of the First Appellate

District overruled an opinion by the Fair Political Practices Commission and held that under a newly enacted city charter, the mayor's participation in decisions concerning a redevelopment project near property owned by the mayor was "legally required" under the provisions of the Political Reform Act, and that therefore, the mayor could participate in these decisions. However, that decision focused on the specific provisions of the city's charter regarding the mayor's role.

FPPC Opinions, Advice

An official may request the FPPC either to issue a formal opinion regarding his or her duties under the Political Reform Act or to provide written advice.

An official may request the FPPC either to issue a formal opinion regarding his or her duties under the Political Reform Act or to provide written advice. Gov. Code § 83114. A commission opinion provides the official with immunity from criminal or civil penalties if the official acts in good faith upon the opinion, as long as the material facts provided to the commission are correct. However, the commission currently issues very few opinions unless new legal questions are presented or it wishes to revise a rule or policy set forth in a previous opinion.

Commission staff, upon request by the official or the official's representative, will provide written advice about *future* actions (rather than past conduct). If followed, this advice will provide the official with immunity from any enforcement proceeding by the commission itself and will be evidence of good faith conduct in any other civil or criminal proceeding, *if* the advice was requested at least 21 working days prior to the alleged violation, all relevant facts were presented to the staff, and the advice was either followed or the commission failed to provide advice in a timely manner. Gov. Code § 83114(b). Requests for advice and advice letters are public documents. Cal. Code Regs., tit. 2, § 18329(b)(6).

Informal advice may also be requested by an official or his or her representative and given either orally or in writing. However, informal advice does not provide the official with immunity from prosecution. Cal. Code Regs., tit. 2, § 18329(c).

Violations

If an official violates the provisions of the Political Reform Act, the FPPC may bring an administrative action and impose penalties of up to $5,000 per violation.

If an official violates the provisions of the Political Reform Act, the FPPC may bring an administrative action and impose penalties of up to $5,000 per violation. Gov. Code § 83116. In addition, an official may be subject to civil lawsuits (Gov. Code §§ 91005, 91005.5) and criminal prosecution if there has been a willful violation of the Political Reform Act. A fine of up to the greater of $10,000 or three times the amount the person failed to report or unlawfully contributed, expended, gave, or received may be imposed for each violation. Gov. Code § 91000. If an official is convicted of a misdemeanor, he or she cannot run for office for four years thereafter. Gov. Code § 91002. The statute of limitations for bringing civil and criminal enforcement proceedings is four years from the date of violation. Gov. Code §§ 91000(c), 91011(b).

Effect of Violations on Decisions

A governmental decision made by an official or designated employee who had a conflict of interest may, but need not, be set aside by a court. If the court determines that a violation occurred and that the official action might not otherwise have been taken or approved, the court may set aside the official action. In making its determination, the court must also consider any injury that may be suffered by innocent persons relying on the official action. Gov. Code § 91003.

A governmental decision made by an official or designated employee who had a conflict of interest may, but need not, be set aside by a court.

Community Redevelopment Law

The Community Redevelopment Law contains its own conflict-of-interest provisions, adopted prior to the adoption of the Political Reform Act. Because there is far less publicity about these provisions than those in the Political Reform Act, they are often overlooked. These provisions strictly prohibit the acquisition of real property interests, direct or indirect, by an official or employee in the project area. Because the courts have generally construed conflict of interest provisions strictly, it would be prudent for such persons to refrain from acquiring property interests once the planning agency has selected a project area. Section 33130(a) of the Community Redevelopment Law provides—

The Community Redevelopment Law contains its own conflict-of-interest provisions, adopted prior to the adoption of the Political Reform Act.

> No agency or community officer or employee who in the course of his or her duties is required to participate in the formulation of, or to approve plans or policies for, the redevelopment of a project area shall acquire any interest in any property included within a project area within the community. If any such officer or employee owns or has any direct or indirect financial interest in property included within a project area, that officer or employee shall immediately make a written disclosure of that financial interest to the agency and the legislative body and the disclosure shall be entered on the minutes of the agency and the legislative body. Failure to make the disclosure required by this subdivision constitutes misconduct in office.

There are three limited exceptions to the above prohibition.

The first exception applies to officers or employees who acquire a property interest to participate as an owner participant or who are reentering in business if the officer or employee has owned a substantially equal interest as that being acquired for the three years prior to the selection of the project area. § 33130(b).

The second exception allows an officer or employee to lease property within the project area if (1) the lease contains terms substantially equivalent to those available to other members of the public for comparable property, (2) the lease prohibits subletting at a rent greater than that in the original lease, (3) the official or employee uses the property for his or her principal business or occupation, and (4) the official or employee immediately discloses his or her leasehold interest. § 33130(c).

The third exception allows an officer or employee to acquire property for personal residential use after the agency has certified that the improvements on the property have been completed or that no work needs to be done on the property. Immediate written disclosure of the acquisition is required, and failure to disclose constitutes misconduct in office. § 33130.5.

Finally, to avoid the appearance of impropriety, the Community Redevelopment Law prohibits an agency from acquiring property from any of its members or officers except through eminent domain proceedings. § 33393.

Other Conflict-of-Interest Provisions

In addition to the Political Reform Act and the Community Redevelopment Law, other conflict of interest provisions apply to redevelopment agencies.

Government Code section 1090 *et seq.* prohibits county and city officers and employees from being financially interested in any contract made by them in their official capacity or by any body or board of which they are members. It also prohibits them from being purchasers at any sale or vendors at any purchase made by them in their official capacity. In *Thomson v. Call* (1985) 38 Cal. 3d 633, the California Supreme Court reiterated the long-standing purpose of section 1090, which was to make certain that:

> Every public officer be guided solely by the public interest, rather than by personal interest, when dealing with contracts in an official capacity. Resulting in substantial forfeiture, this remedy provides public officials with a strong incentive to avoid conflict-of-interest situations scrupulously.

Thomson v. Call, p. 650

Membership alone on a board establishes a presumption that the officer made a contract executed by the board or agency under its jurisdiction, even if the board member disqualified himself or herself from participating in any decisions regarding the contract. *Thomson v. Call*, 38 Cal. 3d 633, pp. 645, 649; *Fraser-Yamor Agency, Inc. v. County of Del Norte* (1977) 68 Cal. App. 3d 201. The prohibitions of Government Code section 1090 apply even if the contract is fair and equitable. *Thomson v. Call*, p. 649.

Government Code sections 1091 and 1091.5 provide that in certain situations an official will not be considered to be financially interested in a contract.

The penalties for a violation of Government Code section 1090 include fines of up to $1,000, imprisonment in state prison, and permanent disqualification from holding office in the state. Gov. Code § 1097. Although Government Code, section 1091 provides that a contract made in violation of these provisions is voidable by the public entity, in *Thomson v. Call* (1985) 38 Cal. 3d 633, the California Supreme Court held that the contract was void. The Court held that the official had to return any consideration paid to him *and* that the public entity was entitled to keep any benefits that it had received under the contract. *Thomson v. Call*, p. 650.

SB 1210 added a specific conflict of interest provision related to eminent domain decisions. Government Code section 1091.6 was added to prohibit an officer who is also a member of the governing body of an organization that has an interest in, or to which the public agency may transfer an interest in, property that the public agency may acquire by eminent domain from voting on any matter affecting that organization.

Some statutory provisions also prohibit local agency officers or employees from engaging in activities for compensation that are incompatible with their duties or with the duties of the agency by which they are employed unless those activities have been expressly approved by the agency or applicable "appointing power." Gov. Code § 1126. That section provides specific examples of the types of activities that may be prohibited and allows a local agency to promulgate rules establishing procedures regarding notification and application of the rules to its employees.

SB 1210 added a specific conflict of interest provision related to eminent domain decisions.

5
Property Acquisition

Introduction

Among the activities that may be undertaken by a redevelopment agency in carrying out its statutory mandate, few are more central than the acquisition and disposition of property. It is commonly, and not unreasonably, assumed that any entity in the business of disposing of property must first acquire that property. While this assumption would seem to apply logically to the activities of redevelopment agencies, this is not always the case. Agencies often progress to the approval and execution stage of a disposition and development agreement governing particular parcels of property before they have actually acquired that property. They may enter such agreements after having begun voluntary acquisition discussions with the owners of the subject parcels or may do so in contemplation of eventual acquisition by eminent domain. In either case, while the agency's agreement to dispose of property will necessarily be contingent upon its acquisition, much of the agency's planning and negotiating regarding disposition of property will go forward prior to or simultaneously with its acquisition. Consequently, this chapter should be considered in light of the discussion in chapter 8 concerning property disposition.

General Authority and Statutory Requirements

Section 33391 of the Community Redevelopment Law sets forth the principal statutory authority for the acquisition of property by a redevelopment agency, providing that:

> Within the survey area or for the purposes of redevelopment, an agency may:

(a) Purchase, lease, obtain option upon, acquire by gift, grant, bequest, devise, or otherwise, any real or personal property, any interest in property, and any improvements on it....

(b) Acquire real property by eminent domain.

§ 33391 *et seq.*

Case law does not clearly establish whether an agency may acquire property outside its territorial jurisdiction even for purposes of redevelopment.

As the language of this statutory provision makes clear, a redevelopment agency's authority to acquire property is very broad. The geographic limitations on its authority extend explicitly throughout any designated survey areas and, because of the disjunctive "or" in section 33391, also to the boundaries of the agency's territorial jurisdiction[1] when employed for purposes of redevelopment. It is not clearly established by case law whether an agency may acquire property outside its territorial jurisdiction even for purposes of redevelopment.

The agency's authority over the *types* of property interests that it may acquire and the legal vehicles it may employ to acquire those interests is limited only by:

- Express restrictions in the Community Redevelopment Law—
  - Property devoted to public use may be acquired by the agency through eminent domain, but property of a public body shall not be acquired without its consent. § 33395
  - Without the consent of an owner, an agency shall not acquire any real property on which an existing building is to be continued on its present site and in its present form and use unless the building requires structural alteration, improvement, modernization, or rehabilitation, or the site or lot on which the building is situated requires modification in size, shape, or use, or it is necessary to impose upon such property any of the standards, restrictions, and controls of the plan, and the owner fails or refuses to agree to participate in the redevelopment plan, under applicable provisions of the Community Redevelopment Law. § 33394
  - Eminent domain proceedings must be commenced, if at all, within 12 years after adoption or amendment of the redevelopment plan. §§ 33333.2, 33333.4

SB 53 requires that all redevelopment plans adopted after January 1, 2007 that contain eminent domain authority describe the agency's program to acquire real property by eminent domain.

  - SB 53 requires that all redevelopment plans adopted after January 1, 2007 that contain eminent domain authority describe the agency's program to acquire real property by eminent domain. Legislative bodies that adopted redevelopment plans before January 1, 2007 were required to adopt an ordinance

---

1. *See* section 33120, which provides that "the territorial jurisdiction of the agency of a county is the unincorporated territory in the county, and that of a city and county is the territory within its limits."

before July 1, 2007 that described the agency's eminent domain program. §§ 33342.5, 33342.7

- SB 1809 requires that the statement of proceedings filed with the county recorder after a redevelopment plan is adopted contain additional information if it authorizes the agency to use eminent domain. The statement must include specific information regarding the scope and limits of the agency's power of eminent domain. Statements for existing redevelopment plans already on file with the county recorder were to be amended to comply with this requirement on or before December 31, 2007. An agency may not commence an action in eminent domain until the required statement or amended statement is recorded. § 33373(d)

- Express restrictions in the State of California Constitution–
  - Article I, Section 19 of the California Constitution, as added by the Home Owners and Private Property Protection Act (Proposition 99) approved by the voters in June of 2008, prohibits the use of eminent domain by the state or a local government to acquire an owner-occupied, single family residence for resale to a private person

- Express limitations in the redevelopment plan (for example: a provision adopted pursuant to section 33385 or, in the interest of local political sensitivities, stating that property devoted to residential use shall not be acquired by the agency without the consent of the owner)

- Procedural requirements of the Eminent Domain Law (*see* discussion below)

- Relocation requirements imposed by state or federal law (*see* chapter 7)

- Owner participation requirements imposed by statute or by adopted rules of the agency (*see* chapter 8)

The practical constraints that apply to an agency's acquisition of property, including limitations imposed pursuant to AB 1290 upon its authority to assist certain commercial projects (§ 33426.5) and certain public facilities (§ 33445), relate largely to the purposes for which the property is acquired (the "redevelopment purpose") and the procedural steps an agency must undertake to initiate and complete the acquisition.

Contaminated Property

Property contaminated by hazardous substances is common in urban areas in California and often is a major impediment to development. The Community Redevelopment Law specifies that contaminated property can be a condition of blight used to justify the establishment of a

A brownfields site was transformed in Santa Rosa to a hotel-conference center.

project area. § 33031(b)(2). The existence of hazardous wastes often prevents or delays the disposition and development of property because of the expense of testing and remediating hazardous wastes, the difficulty in resolving existing or potential liability issues, and the difficulty in obtaining financing. More and more frequently, redevelopment agencies are being asked to intervene and assist in the cleanup of properties with hazardous wastes.

Before acquiring any property, a redevelopment agency should be certain that it understands whether hazardous wastes exist in, on, or under the property and, if so, the type and the extent of the contamination.

Before acquiring any property, a redevelopment agency should be certain that it understands whether hazardous wastes exist in, on, or under the property and, if so, the type and the extent of the contamination. This is because redevelopment agencies, like other property owners, will be held responsible for cleanup pursuant to state and federal law whether or not they caused the contamination. While they may be able to seek payment from those who did cause the contamination, those persons may not have the resources to pay for the cleanup of the site. Since the costs of both testing and cleanup can be enormous, an agency should understand the extent of the risk prior to acquiring contaminated property. *See* chapter 6, Environmental Issues, for a detailed discussion of the issues associated with acquisition and cleanup of contaminated property, including the powers afforded to redevelopment agencies by the Polanco Act.

Voluntary Sales

An agency seeking to acquire property for redevelopment under California law normally has it appraised and offers the owner its fair market value, which must be not less than the appraised value of the property.

An agency seeking to acquire property for redevelopment under California law normally has it appraised and offers the owner its fair market value, which must be not less than the appraised value of the property. Gov. Code § 7267.2(a). However, where the owner offers to sell property *for a specified price* that is less than fair market value, the agency may acquire the property for this price. In fact, one case has held that, where the public agency is not exercising its power of eminent domain, the provisions of Government Code section 7267.2 are inapplicable. *Melamed v. City of Long Beach* (1993) 15 Cal. App. 4th 70. An appraisal would still seem to be prudent in most cases to assure that the agency is not paying too much and making a gift of public funds. Where federal funds are used in acquisition, construction, or project development, federal law takes precedence over California law. Gov. Code § 7267.2(d). A more detailed discussion of precondemnation procedures is provided in Eminent Domain Procedures, page 119–132.

Under California law, a property is "offered for sale" if the owner offers it directly to the public agency for a specified price before the agency begins negotiations, or if it is offered for sale to the public at an advertised or published price set no more than six months before and still available when the public agency first contacts the landowner about possible acquisition. Gov. Code § 7267.2(e).

When a public agency acquires property, the agency must ordinarily provide relocation assistance and other payments required by law to any persons displaced (*see* chapter 7). This is not necessary where the property is offered for sale by the owner, sold at execution or foreclosure sale, or sold pursuant to court order *and* all of the following conditions are met:

- The property is occupied by the owner or is unoccupied (tenants are entitled to relocation assistance).
- The offer to sell is not induced by the redevelopment of that land or surrounding land.
- The sale price is fair market value or less, as determined by a qualified appraiser.
- Federal funding is not involved or, if it is, the agency must follow federal relocation assistance guidelines.

Gov. Code § 7277(a)

In this situation, an offer of sale is defined more narrowly than it is when determining sale price. Property must either be advertised for sale in a publication of general circulation published at least once a week or be listed with a licensed broker and published in multiple listings pursuant to section 1087 of the Civil Code. Gov. Code § 7277(a). A direct offer to the public agency likely would qualify only if the property were also offered to the general public through these means.

At the same time that it offers to purchase property that is on the market, the agency must notify the owner in writing of its plans to develop that or surrounding property and of any relocation assistance or benefits that the property owner may be foregoing. Gov. Code § 7277(b). The letter should state that "although your property has not previously been considered for redevelopment, now that it is offered for sale we would like to purchase it for this purpose." It is also good practice for the agency to obtain from the property owner an informed waiver in writing of his or her rights, if any, to relocation benefits. This may help to avoid the possibility that a property owner will later allege that the sale was induced by the redevelopment agency, which might entitle that owner to relocation assistance.

Eminent Domain

Power to Take

Generally. The right of a government to take private property for public use is a central and inherent element of sovereignty. Known as eminent domain or condemnation, this right predates the written constitutions that established the forms of government for both the United States and the State of California. In fact, the power of eminent domain is so essential to the concept of the sovereignty of general governments that our federal and state constitutions do not purport to grant to the government a right of eminent domain but merely place limitations on its exercise of that power.

The Fifth Amendment to the United States Constitution provides that "private property shall not be taken for a public use, without just compensation," a protection made applicable to the states through the Fourteenth Amendment. Further, the California Constitution, Article I, Section 19, provides that:

> Private property may be taken or damaged for public use only when just compensation, ascertained by a jury unless waived, has first been paid to, or into court for, the owner....

The two fundamental constitutional restraints on the power of eminent domain, then, are that the taking be for a "public use" and that "just compensation" be paid for the property taken.

While the government's power of eminent domain is subject only to constitutional limits, that power inures solely to the legislature and not directly to subordinate municipal governments or agencies. It is then the legislature's prerogative to determine whether to create further limitations or conditions on the use of its authority and to craft-specific procedures to permit exercise of that authority, both by the general government itself and, through the general government, by subordinate municipal governments.

The California legislature has chosen to exercise its authority through the enactment of a comprehensive statute known as the Eminent Domain Law, found in Title 7, Part III, of the Code of Civil Procedure, section 1230.010 *et seq.*

Exercise of Eminent Domain Authority by Redevelopment Agencies. In *Berman v. Parker* (1954) 348 U.S. 26, a unanimous United States Supreme Court upheld the use of eminent domain as authorized by Congress for redevelopment in the District of Columbia. The Court determined redevelopment to be a public purpose for which Congress could exercise its police power and its power of eminent domain, even as to properties within a redevelopment area that were themselves not blighted. The Court stated:

We deal, in other words, with what traditionally has been known as the police power. An attempt to define its reach or trace its outer limits is fruitless, for each case must turn on its own facts. The definition is essentially the product of legislative determinations addressed to the purposes of government, purposes neither abstractly nor historically capable of complete definition. Subject to specific constitutional limitations, when the legislature has spoken, the public interest has been declared in terms well-nigh conclusive. In such cases the legislature, not the judiciary, is the main guardian of the public needs to be served by social legislation, whether it be Congress legislating concerning the District of Columbia... or the States legislating concerning local affairs.... This principle admits of no exception merely because the power of eminent domain is involved....

Berman v. Parker, p. 32

Once the object is within the authority of Congress, the right to realize it through the exercise of eminent domain is clear. For the power of eminent domain is merely the means to the end.... Once the object is within the authority of Congress, the means by which it will be attained is also for Congress to determine. Here one of the means chosen is the use of private enterprise for redevelopment of the area. Appellants argue that this makes the project a taking from one businessman for the benefit of another businessman. But the means of executing the project are for Congress and Congress alone to determine, once the public purpose has been established.

Id. at p. 33

The decision in *Berman v. Parker* is important to redevelopment agencies and to those whose property interests are affected by the redevelopment process because it established the principle that it is the legislature that decides what constitutes a "public use." Without departing from the reasoning of *Berman,* the Court went further in *Hawaii Housing Authority v. Midkiff* (1984) 467 U.S. 229, finding that:

> The mere fact that property taken outright by eminent domain is transferred in the first instance to private beneficiaries does not condemn that taking as having only a private purpose. The Court long ago rejected any literal requirement that condemned property be put into use for the general public. "It is not essential that the entire community, nor even any considerable portion,... directly enjoy or participate in any improvement in order [for it] to constitute a public use."

Hawaii v. Midkiff, pp. 243–244

It is clear from this decision, which upheld the Hawaii Land Reform Act, that among the public purposes for which private property may be taken is for transfer to another private person for the purpose of redevelopment. This element of a redevelopment agency's power distinguishes

The decision in Berman v. Parker *is important because it established the principle that it is the legislature that decides what constitutes a "public use."*

the agency's scope of authority from that of a municipality, which generally cannot take property for reconveyance to another private party. *See* chapters 2, 8, and 11 for a further discussion of the unique powers of a redevelopment agency.

In its 5–4 decision in Kelo v. City of New London, *the Supreme Court held that economic development is a public purpose for which property may be taken under the Fifth Amendment.*

In its 5–4 decision in *Kelo v. City of New London* (2005) 545 U.S. 469, the Supreme Court held that economic development is a public purpose for which property may be taken under the Fifth Amendment. Citing longstanding deference to the legislature in this field, the Court reasoned that there is "no principled way of distinguishing economic development from other [recognized] public purposes." This affirmation of public agency authority to acquire property for economic development purposes generated widespread efforts around the country to constrain the use of eminent domain. In 2006, the voters in California rejected Proposition 90, which would have significantly limited the ability of redevelopment agencies to exercise eminent domain. In 2008 the voters again rejected a similar proposition (Proposition 98). However, Proposition 99, sponsored by the League of California Cities and the California Redevelopment Association, entitled the "Home Owners and Private Property Protection Act" was adopted. As a consequence, neither the state nor any local agency may acquire by eminent domain any owner-occupied single family dwelling where acquisition is for the purpose of conveying the property to a private party. Since a redevelopment agency enjoys no sovereign eminent domain power in its own right, but rather exercises such authority derivatively as an arm of the state, the scope of its authority is limited to that provided in state statutory law. In the case of California redevelopment agencies, such law includes both the Community Redevelopment Law and the Eminent Domain Law.

The most basic statement of the redevelopment agency's condemnation authority is contained in section 33342, which provides that redevelopment plans may "provide for the agency to acquire by gift, purchase, lease, or condemnation all or part of the real property in the project area." Further, as discussed earlier, section 33391 provides that an agency may acquire property if it is located within a survey area or if the property is acquired for "purposes of redevelopment" pursuant to an adopted redevelopment plan. In order for an agency to exercise the condemnation authority permitted by state law, then, the ordinance adopting the redevelopment plan must specifically include that authority, and the redevelopment plan must describe the agency's eminent domain program, including any limitations on the agency's authority. §§ 33367, 33342.5, 33342.7; *Anaheim Redevelopment Agency v. Dusek* (1987) 193 Cal. App. 3d 249. In general, if the plan is not challenged within the 90-day limitation period of section 33500 (*see* chapter 13), a condemnee cannot challenge the redevelopment agency's right to take. *See* § 33368; *Redevelopment Agency of the City of Chula Vista v. Rados*

In order for an agency to exercise the condemnation authority permitted by state law, the ordinance adopting the redevelopment plan must specifically include that authority, and the plan must describe the agency's eminent domain program.

Bros. (2001) 95 Cal. App. 4th 309; *Anaheim Redevelopment Agency v. Dusek* (1987) 193 Cal. App. 3d 249, 253; *Redevelopment Agency v. Del-Camp Investments, Inc.* (1974) 38 Cal. App. 3d 836. However, the 90-day limit does not apply to a challenge alleging that the plan is being illegally implemented. *See Redevelopment Agency v. Herrold* (1978) 86 Cal. App. 3d 1024, 1029.

A redevelopment agency exercising condemnation authority within a project area under an approved redevelopment plan traditionally has been afforded a strong presumption that the taking is for a valid public purpose. While this presumption still applies, recent changes in the Community Redevelopment Law and other provisions of the California Eminent Domain Law have liberalized the legal framework for challenging an agency's actions and factual determinations. Most notably, the procedures for obtaining a prejudgment order of possession now require an agency to show that (a) the agency has the right to take the property, (b) the agency has an overriding need to possess the property before a judgment for condemnation can be obtained, and (c) the agency's need outweighs the hardship the owner or occupier will suffer if the order is granted. *See* the detailed discussion under Deposit of Probable Compensation; Order for Possession in this chapter. Thus, despite the traditional presumptions in favor of the condemning agency, it is important for the agency to include in any resolution of necessity specific facts to support the finding that acquisition of the subject property will help achieve the redevelopment agency's goals, including elimination of blight. This is even more important when the agency acts, pursuant to section 33391, outside a project area because the presumption in favor of the agency's right to take is not as clear.

Recent changes in the Community Redevelopment Law and other provisions of the California Eminent Domain Law have liberalized the legal framework for challenging an agency's actions and factual determinations.

It is important for the agency to include in any resolution of necessity specific facts to support the finding that acquisition of the subject property will help achieve the redevelopment agency's goals, including elimination of blight.

Like all public agencies, a redevelopment agency must include factual findings in a resolution of necessity (*see* Eminent Domain Procedures, page 119–132). In addition, redevelopment agencies are also subject to several statutory constraints relating directly to the fundamental nature and purpose of the redevelopment process—

- Section 33333.2(a)(4) requires agencies adopting redevelopment plans that include eminent domain authority to impose a time limit—not to exceed 12 years from the adoption of the redevelopment plan—for commencement of eminent domain proceedings to acquire property within the project area. This time limit may be extended by amendment of the redevelopment plan if the agency makes findings regarding the continuing existence of blight required by sections 33333.2(a)(4)(A)–(B). *See also Blue v. City of Los Angeles* (2006) 137 Cal. App. 4th 1131, 1141 (substantially codified in §33333.2(a)).

- Section 33393 provides that an agency acquiring property from any of its members or officers must use eminent domain procedures.

PAC = Project area committee

- In the event an agency proposes to adopt a redevelopment plan containing authority to acquire residential property by eminent domain, and substantial numbers of low- or moderate-income persons reside within the project area, or the plan contains a public project that will displace a substantial number of low- or moderate-income persons, section 33385 provides that the agency must follow the procedures required for the formation of a PAC for that project area. Such procedures apply as well to plan amendments that include the grant of eminent domain authority for residential properties.

- Section 33394 limits and conditions the authority of the agency to acquire without consent of the owner "any real property on which an existing building is to be continued on its present site and in its present form and use...." An officer who is also a member of the governing body of an organization that has an interest in, or to which the agency may transfer an interest in, property that the agency may acquire by eminent domain cannot vote on any matter affecting that organization. Gov. Code §1091.6.

A significant exclusion from the section 33394 prohibition concerns owners who fail or refuse to participate in the redevelopment plan.

A significant exclusion from the section 33394 prohibition concerns owners who fail or refuse to participate in the redevelopment plan. Redevelopment plans must afford participation opportunities for owners of property in the project area (§ 33339) and must extend preferences to businesses located in the project area (§ 33339.5) (*see* pages 180–184). Conversely, section 33394 gives effect to the section 33340 requirement that plans contemplating owner participation must contain alternative provisions for redevelopment of property if the owners fail to participate. Section 33395 provides that:

> Property already devoted to a public use may be acquired by the agency through eminent domain, but property of a public body shall not be acquired without its consent.

Section 33399 creates a mechanism by which a property owner may achieve some certainty that the agency will either take action to acquire property within a specified period or will have its right to take foreclosed.

Section 33399 creates a mechanism, similar to a tender offer, by which a property owner may achieve some certainty that the agency will either take action to acquire property within a specified period or will have its right to take foreclosed. In brief, that section provides that when three years have elapsed from the date the redevelopment plan is adopted, the owners of property in the project area subject to condemnation may offer to sell that property to the agency for its fair market value. The agency then has 18 months either to acquire the property or institute an eminent domain action to acquire it. Should the agency fail to do so, the owner may institute an action for damages against the agency in inverse condemnation. Additional time limitations apply to the agency's use of the property once the property has been acquired. *See* chapter 8.

Political and Policy Concerns

While the Eminent Domain Law reflects a legislative effort to balance the prerogatives and needs of the state against the interests of individual property owners in the use and enjoyment of their property, the principal protections afforded private owners are the constitutionally-based public interest and necessity tests and the right to full and fair compensation. The Community Redevelopment Law acts as a further check to the substantial powers of a redevelopment agency over private property. By requiring extensive public review and opportunity for public input in the early stages of the redevelopment plan adoption process, the law subjects the agency to a demanding test of its plans and intentions. Moreover, through environmental review and public hearing processes, the agency is required to refine and thoroughly clarify its redevelopment goals. Finally, adopting—and often defending through litigation or referendum—an ordinance based on findings of blight and of the necessity for eminent domain is a significant political hurdle not lightly attempted and not easily cleared.

The Community Redevelopment Law acts as a further check to the substantial powers of a redevelopment agency over private property.

Precondemnation Procedures

Statutory Requirements. The eminent domain procedure comprises two distinct elements: precondemnation procedures and condemnation procedures. Condemnation procedures are covered on pages 119–132. The most important precondemnation steps are spelled out in the Government Code, section 7260 *et seq.* These sections provide that the property that is the object of the action must be appraised before the initiation of negotiations (Gov. Code § 7267.1(b)); the agency shall make every reasonable effort to acquire the property by negotiation (Gov. Code § 7267.1(a)); and the agency shall offer the owner the full amount of what the agency determines to be just compensation, which shall not be less than the agency's approved fair market value appraisal (Gov. Code § 7267.2). The offer of purchase must be accompanied by a written statement of the basis for the amount the agency has established as just compensation. Gov. Code § 7267.2. In addition, each public agency is required to adopt rules and regulations to implement payments and relocation assistance to displaced occupants or businesses. Gov. Code § 7267.8; *also see* the discussion of relocation in chapter 7. Where the subject property is owner-occupied residential property containing less than four units, the agency must provide the owner with a copy of the appraisal. Gov. Code § 7267.2(c). Providing a copy of the appraisal can be used to satisfy the requirement to provide a written statement and summary of the basis for the amount established as just compensation. *Id.* The agency must also offer to pay the reasonable cost (up to $5,000) for a property owner to obtain an independent appraisal. Code Civ. Proc. § 1263.025.

The eminent domain procedure comprises two distinct elements: precondemnation procedures and condemnation procedures.

It is often appropriate for an agency to make a preliminary survey and informal appraisal of properties in the project area it intends to acquire.

Before initiating negotiations, the agency must give the property owner or a designated representative written notice that the agency will appraise the property.

The agency must provide the owner with a written statement and summary of the basis for the amount it has established as just compensation.

It is often appropriate for an agency to make a preliminary survey and informal appraisal of properties in the project area it intends to acquire. This may be done without formal notice to property owners and need not be more extensive than a view of external appearance, a survey of recorded documents pertaining to the property, and a familiarity with sales patterns and prices in the vicinity. Information gathered in this way may be contained in an agency's internal working documents and may be useful for budgeting and planning, but would have no official or legal effect.

Before initiating negotiations, the agency must give the property owner or a designated representative written notice that the agency will appraise the property. The agency also must give the property owner an opportunity to accompany the appraiser during her or his inspection of the property. Gov. Code § 7267.1(b). The notice should state that the owner's property is within the redevelopment project area, that at the time the redevelopment plan was adopted the property owner was notified that the property was subject to acquisition pursuant to the redevelopment plan, and that the agency may acquire the owner's property in connection with the redevelopment of the area. The notice should specify that the public use contemplated for that particular parcel is "redevelopment." *See* Cal. Code Regs., tit. 25, § 6184. If the agency has not yet decided to acquire the property, but wants to consider a preliminary appraisal before making its decision, the notice should contain that information. Only one appraisal is required by law, though as a precaution, many agencies routinely undertake two appraisals.

The appraised value must be based on the highest price the property could command, not the most probable price. This is an important distinction, as an appraisal obtained in connection with a private party transaction typically determines value based on the most probable price that would be paid for the property. Prior to adopting a resolution of necessity (*see* Eminent Domain Procedures, page 119), and initiating negotiations for the acquisition of real property, the agency must make an offer to the owner of record to acquire the property for the full amount that it believes to be just compensation. Gov. Code § 7267.2. In no event may this amount be less than the appraisal of the fair market value of the property. The agency must also provide the owner with a written statement and summary of the basis for the amount it has established as just compensation. *Id.* The statement should include a general statement of the public use for which the property is to be acquired; a description of the location and extent of the property to be taken; an inventory identifying the buildings, structures, fixtures, and other improvements; and a recital of the amount of the offer and a statement that it is the full amount believed to be just compensation and is not less than the approved appraisal of the fair market value of the property. *See* Cal. Code Regs., tit. 25, § 6182(d). At the time of negotiation, the agency should also inform the owner and all tenants of the pertinent relocation benefits and payments available, the possible right to compensation for loss of goodwill, and other procedures and policies of the agency for acquisition and relocation. *See* the discussion of relocation in chapter 7.

The agency may not defer negotiations or take any action coercive in nature to compel an agreement on the price to be paid for the property. Gov. Code § 7267.5. Finally, if the acquisition of only part of the property would leave its owner with an "uneconomic remnant" the agency must offer to acquire the entire property if the owner so desires. Gov. Code § 7267.7.

In addition to the statutes relating directly to the precondemnation stage of an eminent domain action, the condemning agency must be careful to comply with environmental and planning laws. For instance, failure to comply with the California Environmental Quality Act (CEQA) may defeat—or at least postpone—the agency's power to condemn. *See City of San Jose v. Great Oaks Water Co.* (1987) 192 Cal. App. 3d 1005; *Burbank-Glendale-Pasadena Airport Authority v. Hensler* (1991) 233 Cal. App. 3d 577.

Before acquiring real property through its condemnation power, the agency must give notice to the property owner, hold a public hearing, and make certain findings pursuant to the Eminent Domain Law. The agency can avoid these procedures in a negotiated agreement to purchase, but the property owner may desire the tax advantages associated with the condemnation of the property for a public use.[2] To reconcile the objectives of both parties, a redevelopment agency may acquire property by negotiated purchase under threat of condemnation. In order to give the property owner evidence of acquisition under threat of condemnation, the agency should send him a letter indicating that the redevelopment agency is a public entity having the power of eminent domain pursuant to the California Eminent Domain Law, the Community Redevelopment Law, and the redevelopment plan, and that, if unable to acquire the property through negotiation, the agency will acquire such property through its power of eminent domain.

Acquisition Team. Once the agency decides to acquire property, it should establish a workable implementation method. Most large agencies have procedures for acquiring property, but many smaller agencies do not. Thoughtful consideration of how the process will work and who will be responsible will save the condemning agency substantial time and money.

---

2. Discussion of the income tax and property tax implications of a taking of property by eminent domain is beyond the scope of this text. *See* Matteoni & Veit, Condemnation Practice in California, Continuing Education of the Bar, for an excellent discussion and additional citations.

PRACTICE TIP

During the course of negotiations for the acquisition of property, whether such negotiations are voluntary or are related to the eminent domain process, it is typical that the agency board will wish to consult privately with its counsel and/or its negotiator. This consultation may take place in executive session provided that the agency complies with pertinent requirements of the Ralph M. Brown Act (Gov. Code § 54950 *et seq.; see* §§ 54954.5(b), 54954.5(c), 54956.8 and 54956.9), California's open meeting law.

A skilled negotiator, or right-of-way agent, can be critical to the success of a project, particularly where numerous properties must be acquired.

It is best to have one staff member lead the team that will participate in the process. Depending on the nature and scope of the project and the amount of property that needs to be acquired, the team may include not only the leader but also an appraiser, an acquisition agent, a relocation specialist, an engineer, and legal counsel.

- *Identifying the Property.* Carefully define the property necessary to the project. Prepare a legal description for each separate parcel and determine whether the acquisition will be in fee or easement. Normally someone from the public works department of the redevelopment agency's city or county prepares the necessary legal description and accompanying map. These documents must be accurate, for they will form the basis for filing an eminent domain action if the property cannot be acquired through negotiation.

- *Selecting the Appraiser.* If possible, the agency should select an appraiser familiar with eminent domain procedures who will be able to testify competently in court as to his or her opinion of the property's value. The appraiser should be familiar with all aspects of the project, especially where only a portion of an individual owner's property is being taken and the possibility of severance damages to the remainder of the property exists. The appraiser should be selected by, or at least approved by, the attorney who will be conducting the eminent domain action. Because competent appraisers sometimes make poor witnesses, it is important that the appraiser be both technically competent *and* a convincing witness.

    – The appraiser will need sufficient lead time to do the job. Good appraisers are in short supply, and many will not respond to requests for a quick turnaround.

    – Although not required, some agencies hire two appraisers to ensure the accuracy of the valuation process. The agency should determine whether it wants a full, bound appraisal report or just the appraiser's conclusions on value with specific justifying information. A full report often contains matters that are not of immediate interest to the agency (such as population characteristics of the area, growth patterns, etc.). The agency may save money by instructing the appraiser to limit the scope of the report.

- *Acquisition Agent.* A skilled negotiator, or right-of-way agent, can be critical to the success of a project, particularly where numerous properties must be acquired. The agency's direct link with the property owner is the acquisition agent, whose successful efforts will result in avoiding litigation and speeding the process. The agent should be skilled at dealing with people, particularly those who may be hostile to the project or to the idea of a forced acquisition, and should convey a positive image of the agency, keeping detailed notes of all contacts with individual property owners.

Many agencies direct the acquisition agent to personally deliver the agency's written offer of compensation so that a dialogue with the owner may commence immediately.

- *Relocation Specialist.* Where the property to be acquired is occupied, the owner or tenant will be entitled to certain relocation benefits as defined by statute. *See* the discussion of relocation in chapter 7. A person familiar with the rules and regulations should be employed to ensure that each owner receives the benefits provided by law. Ordinarily, this should be someone other than the acquisition agent since the function of acquiring the property is distinct from that of determining any relocation benefits to which the owner may be entitled.

- *Legal Counsel.* From the beginning, knowledgeable legal counsel should be part of the acquisition team. Counsel can spot specific legal or valuation problems and give necessary advice to the appraiser, acquisition agent, or relocation specialist.

    Early involvement also gives counsel an opportunity to be fully familiar with the project, the various property interests (including leasehold interests) that must be acquired, and any particular difficulties associated with individual acquisitions. Counsel can then better provide advice in response to settlement demands from owners and other problems associated with the overall acquisition program.

Depending on the complexity of the acquisition program, the team should meet frequently to discuss what each team member is doing and the program's overall progress. Each team member should keep a separate file for each parcel to be acquired, and the team leader should ensure that an overall record of the status of each property acquisition exists.

Because the acquisition of real property for redevelopment is frequently carried out through the use of funds advanced by a developer who has contracted with the agency to carry out the redevelopment, it is important that the members of the acquisition team—particularly the team leader and legal counsel—be familiar with the relevant provisions of the disposition and development (or other) agreement governing the advance and use of acquisition funds. For a more comprehensive discussion, *see* chapter 8.

Eminent Domain Procedures

The rules governing the acquisition of property in eminent domain for redevelopment projects are the same as those for any municipal acquisition of property for a public purpose. The Eminent Domain Law is found in Title 7, Part III of the Code of Civil Procedure at section 1230.010 *et seq.*

An eminent domain action must be filed in the superior court of the county in which the property is located. Its purpose is to transfer title to the property from its owner to the redevelopment agency upon payment of just compensation.

An eminent domain action must be filed in the superior court of the county in which the property is located. Its purpose is to transfer title to the property from its owner to the redevelopment agency upon payment of just compensation. Just compensation is measured by the fair market value of the property taken (severance damages), any damages to the property that is not taken, and any damage to the goodwill of a business conducted on the property. Code Civ. Proc. § 1263.010 *et seq.*

What follows is a general outline of the procedures necessary when a redevelopment agency determines that it is unable to acquire the property through direct negotiations with an owner. More detailed explanations of procedures and laws governing eminent domain are available in several treatises on the subject, including Richard G. Rypinski, *Eminent Domain: A Step-by-Step Guide to the Acquisition of Real Property* (Solano Press, 2002), and those published by the Continuing Education of the Bar.

The redevelopment agency must adopt a resolution of necessity, which requires a vote of not less than two-thirds of all the members of the board. Prior to adopting the resolution, the agency must give the property owner an opportunity to be heard.

Resolution of Necessity; Hearing; Notice. Prior to filing a suit in superior court to obtain the property and have the court award just compensation, several procedural steps are required.[3] Failure to follow these steps means that the superior court may dismiss the suit.

The redevelopment agency must adopt a resolution of necessity (Code Civ. Proc. § 1245.220), which requires a vote of not less than two-thirds of all the members of the board. Code Civ. Proc. § 1245.240. Since most agencies in California are governed by a five-member board, in most jurisdictions four affirmative votes are required. The agency has authority to adopt the resolution of necessity without the need for separate action by the legislative body. *Long Beach Community Redevelopment Agency v. Morgan* (1993) 14 Cal. App. 4th 1047.

Prior to adopting the resolution, the agency must give the property owner an opportunity to be heard. Notice is sent to the property owner whose name appears on the last equalized county tax roll, by either giving 15 days notice of a particular hearing date or giving at least 15 days in which the owner can request such a hearing. Code Civ. Proc. § 1245.235. It is usually easier to set a hearing date and give notice than to require the owner to ask for a hearing.

---

3. In addition to taking care to comply with standard procedural requirements outlined herein, agencies anticipating disposition and development of the property to be acquired must be aware of and take steps to avoid the potential problems that gave rise to the decision in *Redevelopment Agency v. Norm's Slauson* (1985) 173 Cal. App. 3d 1121. That case, discussed in detail in chapter 8, found that the agency's approval of a disposition and development agreement that required condemnation of an owner's property resulted in a violation of the owner's property and participation rights and reduced the resolution of necessity hearing to a "sham." *Norm's Slauson* was distinguished by *City of Saratoga v. Hinz* (2004) 115 Cal. App. 4th 1202 (formation of an assessment district before adopting a resolution of necessity did not irrevocably commit the city to condemn the property).

The required contents of the resolution are set out in the statute. Generally, the redevelopment agency must specify the authority for the taking, describe the property to be taken, and find all of the following:

- That the public interest and necessity require the project
- That the proposed project is planned and located in such a way as to do the greatest public good and the least public harm
- That the property to be acquired is necessary for the project
- That the property owner has been offered just compensation

Code Civ. Proc. § 1245.230

Since its actions are subject to judicial review, it is advisable that the agency keep a complete record of the proceedings. Either a tape recording or a stenographic transcript is appropriate. Agency staff should describe the project and explain why the property must be acquired. Any maps or diagrams used should be marked and made part of the record. Because the findings of a redevelopment agency contained in a resolution of necessity are quasi-legislative in character, detailed factual sub-findings are not required. *Anaheim Redevelopment Agency v. Dusek* (1987) 193 Cal. App. 3d 249. However, specific findings stating how the proposed project will facilitate redevelopment are important to enable the judge to make the findings required to grant a pre-condemnation order of possession. Over-reliance on conclusory statements that the redevelopment agency is taking the property for a valid public purpose increases the likelihood that the project will be delayed due to denial of a motion for prejudgment order of possession or a right to take challenge.

The hearing is not a public hearing in the sense that persons other than the property owner are permitted to participate. However, under the Ralph M. Brown Act, any person may speak to any item on a public agency agenda. Gov. Code § 54954.3. Consequently, persons other than the owner must be heard. It is not appropriate at the hearing to discuss the price of the property or for the agency to respond to demands for compensation.

In an interesting result, the court in the case of *City of Lake Elsinore v. Ranel Development Co.* (1998) 60 Cal. App. 4th 974, ordered not to be published at *City of Lake Elsinore v. Ranel Dev. Co.* (1998) 70 Cal. Rptr. 2d 715, Supreme Court Minute Order 04-01-1998, held that the defendant in the city's complaint in eminent domain had waived its right to object to the fact that the agency, not the city, had adopted the resolution of necessity when its answer did not allege either that the city had failed to adopt a resolution of necessity or that it had been adopted by another entity. The Court also held that Government Code sections 7267.1 through 7267.7 are "merely advisory guidelines," and the fact that the city's offer was so close to the adoption of the resolution as to preclude meaningful negotiations could not invalidate the resolution of necessity. The Court overruled the trial court's decision to dismiss the city's eminent domain action, concluded that the defendant's inverse condemnation case was superfluous and, therefore, held that an award of litigation expenses could not be made.

The Complaint. A complaint is filed in superior court, describing the property to be taken, the agency's legal authority for condemnation, and those whom the agency believes to be entitled to compensation. Code Civ. Proc. § 1250.310. Prior to filing the complaint, a litigation guarantee—listing those with a record interest in the property—should be obtained from a reputable title company. Those whose interests will be affected by the taking are properly named defendants, as are persons whom the agency believes may have unrecorded interests, such as business tenants.

Deposit of Probable Compensation; Order of Possession. If it wants to proceed with the project while the value of the land is being determined, the redevelopment agency may seek an order of prejudgment possession from the court. The order must be obtained by a motion that notifies the owner and occupants (if any) of the right to oppose the order of possession. Code Civ. Proc. § 1255.410 *et seq.* The hearing on the motion must take place at least 60 days after service of the motion on the property owner if the property is unoccupied. If the property is occupied, the hearing must take place at least 90 days after service. Ex parte proceedings to obtain an order of possession are permitted only in certain utility emergencies, but may be used to obtain possession without serving the order where the record owner cannot be located. Code Civ. Proc. §§ 1255.410(e)(1), 1255.450(e). Where the motion is opposed, the court may grant an order of possession if it finds under Code of Civil Procedure section 1255.410(d) that:

- The agency is entitled to take the property by eminent domain
- The agency has deposited probable compensation
- There is an overriding need for the agency to possess the property prior to final judgment in the case and the agency will suffer substantial hardship if prejudgment possession is not granted, and
- The hardship to the agency outweighs any hardship to the owner or occupant that would be caused by granting the order for prejudgment possession

Code of Civ. Proc. § 1255.410(d)

In order to enable the judge to make these findings, it is important that the agency include in any resolution of necessity detailed factual findings regarding the necessity of obtaining the subject property to achieve the agency's goals. The agency will likely want to commence efforts to relocate the owner or occupant in advance of bringing the motion for prejudgment possession in order to mitigate the actual and perceived hardship to the property owner or occupant and thereby increase the likelihood that the court will rule in favor of the agency. Advance consideration of relocation measures is also important because recent amendments to the Code of Civil Procedure allow the agency to take possession of the property within a shorter period following the grant of an order of prejudgment possession. Code Civ. Proc. § 1255.450(b).

The prejudgment order of possession states the date on which the agency may take possession. Except in cases of agency emergency or by agreement with the property owner, possession may be taken within 10 to 30 days from service of the order depending on whether the property is occupied and the use to which the property is devoted. *Id.* As noted above, this shortened time period on effectiveness of the order of possession suggests that the agency will want to make substantial progress on relocation prior to the hearing on the motion. The agency or court may grant extensions of time to the owner or occupant in cases of hardship.

The obvious risk in taking possession and proceeding with site work based on an order of prejudgment possession is that the property value may ultimately be determined to be an amount in excess of the agency's budget. Payment of probable compensation into the court generally freezes the date of valuing the property at the date of deposit. If no deposit is made, the date of valuing the property is either the day the complaint is filed or the day of trial if the matter is not brought to trial within one year. Code Civ. Proc. § 1263.110 *et seq.* Since it is virtually impossible to get a civil case to trial within one year in most California counties, the agency is well advised to deposit probable compensation with the court even if it does not take possession and start the project. It is important to note, however, that the statutory date of valuation may not control if the effect of that date is to deny the property owner just compensation. *City of Santa Clarita v. NTS Technical Systems* (2006) 137 Cal. App. 4th 264, 271. This analysis includes any substantial increase in the fair market value of the property between the date of valuation and the taking. *Saratoga Fire Protection Dist. v. Hackett* (2002) 97 Cal. App. 4th 895, 900.

Challenging the Right to Take. Due to recent amendments to the procedure for obtaining a prejudgment order of possession, a right to take challenge is likely to initially arise in opposition to the motion for an order of possession. Code Civ. Proc. § 1255.410(c). If such an order is not sought or is not opposed, a right to take challenge may be litigated before the court considers the issue of valuing the property. Code Civ. Proc. § 1260.110. *et seq.* In *Dina v. The People ex rel. Department of Transportation* (2007) 151 Cal. App. 4th 1029, the court held that Code of

The Hayward Redevelopment Agency assembled and cleared the site for development of the City Walk Townhouse Condominiums, adjacent to the new City Hall Plaza and within walking distance of the BART station and downtown businesses.

Civil Procedure section 1260.040 may be used to dispose of a legal issue—in that case a claim of inverse condemnation. Section 1260.040 permits the trial court, upon motion of either party, to rule on "an evidentiary or other legal issue affecting the determination of compensation." It remains to be seen whether this section may be used to summarily dispose of a right to take claim, or whether Code of Civil Procedure section 1260.110, under which a party may move the court to specially set a trial on the issue, is the sole applicable procedure.

Direct challenges to the right to take the property, including a challenge to the validity of the resolution of necessity, can be made on several statutory grounds, including a claim that the agency did not comply with applicable pre-condemnation requirements or is not taking the property for a valid public purpose.

Other challenges may include a claim that the resolution of necessity was "influenced or affected by gross abuse of discretion" or that a member of the agency board took a bribe. Code Civ. Proc. §§ 1245.255, 1245.270, 1250.360, 1250.370. A gross abuse of discretion may be shown by a lack of substantial evidence supporting the resolution of necessity. It may also be shown where at the time of the hearing on the resolution of necessity, the condemnor had irrevocably committed itself to a taking of the property regardless of the evidence presented. *Redevelopment Agency v. Norm's Slauson* (1985) 173 Cal. App. 3d 1121, 1127.

If right to take challenges have not been resolved as part of the prejudgment possession motion proceedings, the court will resolve such challenges before the determination of just compensation.

If right to take challenges have not been resolved as part of the prejudgment possession motion proceedings, the court will resolve such challenges before the determination of just compensation. In *Santa Cruz County Redevelopment Agency v. Izant* (1995) 37 Cal. App. 4th 141, the court ruled that the property owners had the right to introduce evidence at trial on their objections to the redevelopment agency's right to take even though the redevelopment agency had adopted a resolution of necessity and conclusively decided other issues. *See also City of Lincoln v. Barringer* (2002) 102 Cal. App. 4th 1211. Again, specific findings in the resolution of necessity as to the manner in which the project serves the agency's goals will assist in overcoming a right to take challenge. If the property owner withdraws the deposit of probable compensation made by the agency, the right to take challenge is waived. Code Civ. Proc. § 1255.260.

If the property owner withdraws the deposit of probable compensation made by the agency, the right to take challenge is waived.

It should be noted that two United States District Court judges in the Central District of California have permitted parties to collaterally challenge in a separate federal court action the right of a redevelopment agency to take private property. In *99 Cents Only Stores, Inc. v. Lancaster Redevelopment Agency* (C.D. Cal. 2001) 237 F. Supp. 2d 1123, the District Court issued a broad injunction against the Lancaster Redevelopment Agency and the City of Lancaster, preventing Lancaster from instituting eminent domain proceedings to condemn a leasehold interest held by 99 Cents Only Stores, Inc. so long as the purpose or effect of such proceedings was to displace 99 Cents and permit the physical expansion of another private party, Costco, onto that property. The injunction issued even where Lancaster had rescinded its resolutions of necessity, and no condemnation action was ever initiated. In an unpublished memorandum, the Ninth Circuit dismissed the appeal, finding the issues were nullified because the 99 Cents property was no longer needed.

Another District Court judge issued a preliminary injunction enjoining the Cypress Redevelopment Agency from exercising the power of eminent domain against a church, the Cottonwood Christian Center. *Cottonwood Christian Ctr. v. Cypress Redevelopment Agency* (C.D. Cal. 2002) 218 F. Supp. 2d 1203. In *Cottonwood Christian Center*, the redevelopment agency had adopted resolutions of necessity and filed an eminent domain action. The Cottonwood Christian Center then instituted the federal court action, claiming that the agency's actions interfered with its exercise of religion and violated the Religious Land Use and Institutionalized Persons Act (RLUIPA), 42 U.S.C. § 2000 *et seq*. The district court enjoined the agency's eminent domain proceedings and denied the agency's motion to dismiss finding that federal abstention was not required because the state court proceeding was brought after the federal court action commenced.

RLUIPA = Religious Land Use and Institutionalized Persons Act

Both *99 Cents Only* and *Cottonwood Christian Center* represent attempts to make an "end run" around the state condemnation procedures, based on a perception that owners may fare better in federal court than state court on challenges to the right to take. More recently, the Ninth Circuit Court of Appeals has held that a federal court must abstain from interfering in state court eminent domain proceedings under the Younger abstention doctrine even where the state court action is filed subsequent to the federal action. *M&A Gabaee v. Community Redevelopment Agency* (9th Cir. 2005) 419 F. 3d 1036, 1039, 1041–42.

Both 99 Cents Only *and* Cottonwood Christian Center *represent attempts to make an "end run" around the state condemnation procedures, based on a perception that owners may fare better in federal court than state court.*

Compensation to the Owner. The owner is compensated for the property taken as though no condemnation had occurred. The law postulates a sales transaction on the date of value between a willing seller and a knowledgeable buyer offering the highest price the property could command.

The owner is compensated for the property taken as though no condemnation had occurred.

Highest and Best Use. In determining fair market value, it is necessary to determine the highest and best use of the property. This is often the focal point of determining compensation. The owner may argue for any use that would be reasonable in the private market. Expert testimony may be given as to the probability of such use, including the probability of any necessary zoning change or other land use entitlement required to accomplish the highest and best use. It was generally assumed that the property owner had the burden of proof on the issue of the probability of a rezoning. However, in *Metropolitan Water Dist. of So. Cal. v. Campus Crusade for Christ* (2007) 41 Cal. 4th 954, the California Supreme Court held that no such burden exists. The property owner bears the burden of producing evidence that such a probability exists. Once that burden is met, neither party bears the burden of persuasion on the issue.

The owner is entitled to argue that the use to which the agency intends to put the property is the same highest and best use as would have been available in the private market (*i.e.*, a parking lot). *City of Los Angeles v. Decker* (1977) 18 Cal. 3d 860. However, this evidence must come from private market sources and not by reference to the agency project itself. The owner does not have the right to put the agency project on trial. The owner is entitled to compensation based only on the private market and not on the value of the property in the hands of the agency.

Valuation Techniques. Three standard methods are used to determine fair market value. If the land is vacant, then sales of comparable properties are used, while improved properties are valued by reference to comparable sales of similarly improved properties. For income property, the "income approach," which measures the value of the property in terms of its ability to produce income, is appropriate. The third generally accepted method is the "cost approach," which analyzes the cost to reproduce improvements on the land less depreciation. However, this method is generally regarded as the least reliable, since it is often difficult to determine what it would cost to reproduce older improvements or the amount of physical depreciation they have suffered.

In unusual situations, the court may adopt other methods of valuation that will provide adequate compensation to the owner. *See* Code Civ. Proc. § 1263.320(b).

Emeryville Redevelopment Agency v. Harcros Pigments, Inc. (2002) 101 Cal. App. 4th 1083, clarified a number of valuation issues in the context of a redevelopment project. First, the court held that evidence about the specific development plan for the property was inadmissible when there was no factual dispute about the "highest and best use" for the property, and there was no other material purpose for such evidence. In this case, the parties had agreed that the highest and best use was for a mixed commercial use. Second, the court held that the jury could not consider, and appraisal witnesses could not rely upon, a recital in a contract for the purchase of neighboring property that purported to allocate the purchase

The owner is entitled to compensation based only on the private market and not on the value of the property in the hands of the agency.

price between the portions located within Emeryville and Oakland. The court stated that the purported allocation of value was no assurance that it accurately reflected market value. Third, the court determined that evidence about the purchase price paid by the agency for neighboring properties was inadmissible to establish the value of the condemned property under the provisions of former Evidence Code section 822(a)(1).

Severance Damages. If less than the whole property is being acquired, there may be damages to the portion of property not taken. In such an instance, damages are measured by the loss in value attributable to the agency's project. Code Civ. Proc. § 1263.410 *et seq.* Severance damages may arise in a wide variety of circumstances—examples include harm done to the remainder because of the partial loss of access, reduction in the number of parking spaces for a business being conducted on the property not taken, or a decrease in the development potential of the remainder because its size and shape after construction of the agency project make it less adaptable to its highest and best use than previously.

In *Los Angeles County Metropolitan Transportation Authority v. Continental Development Corporation* (1997) 16 Cal. 4th 694, the Court held that the condemning authority's entitlement to an offset against the owner's severance damages was not limited to "special" benefits, that is, those benefits peculiar to the land in question, but could include any evidence of conditions caused by the transportation authority's project that would affect the fair market value of the remainder property.

Loss of Business Goodwill. A going business concern operating on property taken by eminent domain may suffer a loss of business goodwill by virtue of the taking. "Goodwill" is defined as "the benefits that accrue to a business as a result of its location, reputation for dependability, skill or quality, and any other circumstances resulting in probable retention of old or acquisition of new patronage." Code Civ. Proc. § 1263.510(b). An agency must compensate a business owner for loss of goodwill only when loss cannot be cured by the relocation of the business or by taking prudent steps to preserve the goodwill. Code Civ. Proc. § 1263.510(a). The Supreme Court has interpreted the statutory definition of goodwill to include the locational benefit of "cheap rent in an older building." *People ex rel. Dept. of Transportation v. Muller* (1984) 36 Cal. 3d 263, 268. In dictum, the Court hypothesized that a business owner would be "entitled to compensation for expenses reasonably incurred in an effort to prevent loss of patronage." *Id.* at 271–72. As a result of *Muller* and subsequent case law, the owner of a profitable business operating under a below market rent lease may be entitled to compensation for loss of goodwill, if the owner, in a reasonable effort to prevent loss of patronage, leases a new facility at a higher rent. In *Barthelemy v. Orange County Flood Control District* (1998) 65 Cal. App. 4th 558, 561 however, the court denied the claimants' requests for the costs of mitigating their loss of business goodwill. In that case, owners of a dairy farm purchased a relocation site before the condemning agency had commenced formal condemnation proceedings. The court reasoned that absent proof of a special and direct interference with a land owner's use of property, a claimant is not entitled to compensation for the "cloud" that arises from pre-condemnation activities by the condemning agency. *Id.* at 571 (citing *Contra Costa Water District v. Vaquero Farms, Inc.* (1997) 58 Cal. App. 4th 883). *See also Regents of University of California v. Sheily* (2004) 122 Cal. App. 4th 824, 833.

The property owner has the burden of proving goodwill damages (Code Civ. Proc. § 1263.510(a)), but she or he may use any of a variety of methods to quantify the loss. In *Muller*, the Court approved use of the "capitalization of excess earnings" method of estimating goodwill damages. *Muller, supra,* 36 Cal. 3d at 271. In a footnote, it stated, "Nothing in this opinion is intended to restrict litigants in eminent domain actions from using other valuation methods than the one employed here." *Id.* at 271, fn.7. Because the task of quantifying loss of goodwill requires a detailed analysis of the business owner's accounting records, it is typical for the condemning agency to retain the services of a business valuation appraiser or accountant. If the eminent domain case goes to trial, the valuation appraiser will be an expert witness for the agency. Therefore, the agency will need to consider, in addition to the appraiser's technical competence, his or her ability to be a convincing witness. A goodwill claim is an independent right not tied to an interest in real property. A business owner may bring an action for goodwill damages even if she or he has waived any right to compensation for loss of a leasehold interest. *See Redevelopment Agency of San Diego v. Attisha* (2005) 128 Cal. App. 4th 357, 367; *City of Vista v. Fielder* (1996) 13 Cal. 4th 612, 617 fn.1; *New Haven Unified School District v. Taco Bell Corp.* (1994) 24 Cal. App. 4th 1473, 1478–79. A business owner also may bring an inverse condemnation action for the loss of goodwill, and the provisions of the Eminent Domain Law regarding goodwill apply. *Chhour v. Community Redevelopment Agency* (1996) 46 Cal. App. 4th 273, 282.

In *Emeryville Redevelopment Agency v. Harcros Pigments, Inc.* (2002) 101 Cal. App. 4th 1083, the property owner claimed a loss of business goodwill, business fixtures, and equipment that was inconsistent with its appraisal, which was based upon a higher and better use of the property. As the court stated, "although we know of no case so stating, we have little doubt that California law incorporates the principle of 'consistent use,' *i.e.,* 'that land cannot be valued based on one use while improvements are valued based on another.'" *Id.* at 1110. Moreover, the court determined that it was the judge, not the jury, who is to determine the issue of whether the defendant is entitled to goodwill compensation. The jury only determines the amount of compensation

An 18-screen theater is part of Modesto's Tenth Street Place project that includes a joint city hall/county administration building, private office building, and public parking garage.

A business owner may bring an inverse condemnation action for the loss of goodwill, and the provisions of the Eminent Domain Law regarding goodwill apply.

if the judge finds that such entitlement exists. *Accord, City of Santa Clarita v. NTS Technical Systems* (2006) 137 Cal. App. 4th 264, 269–70.

In *Inglewood Redevelopment Agency v. Aklilu* (2007) 153 Cal. App. 4th 1095, the court addressed the issue of whether an owner whose business was taken in its entirety, but which had not been operating long enough to generate excess profits, could still recover for loss of goodwill. The court ruled in the affirmative. It held that a nascent business may not have experienced excess profits, but it may still have goodwill as defined by statute. The goodwill appraiser may then use a "cost to create" approach to value.

However, speculative testimony regarding the value of lost goodwill based on hypothetical uses, rather than actual use of the property in question, is not admissible. *Redevelopment Agency of San Diego v. Mesdaq* (2007) 154 Cal. App. 4th 1111.

For a more detailed discussion of compensation for loss of goodwill, *see* Richard G. Rypinski, *Eminent Domain: A Step-by-Step Guide to the Acquisition of Real Property* (Solano Press) and Matteoni & Veit, *Condemnation Practice in California* (Continuing Education of the Bar).

Apportioning Compensation Between Property Owner and Tenant. Though property is valued as an undivided estate, a tenant may be entitled to a portion of the eminent domain award as compensation for loss of leasehold bonus value. Leasehold bonus value represents the value to a tenant of a long-term lease that provides for a rental rate that is below current market rate rents. Ordinarily, the apportionment of compensation between a property owner/landlord and a tenant is governed by a condemnation clause in the lease. Although such clauses may appear to assign to the owner/landlord all compensation for the undivided ownership of the property, the agency should exercise caution before relying on the wording of the lease as a basis for reaching a settlement with the landlord for the full appraised value of the property. Unless the tenant has explicitly and unconditionally agreed to waive any interest in compensation or has consented to an apportionment, the agency risks paying twice if it settles with the owner/landlord. In *City of Vista v. Fielder* (1996) 13 Cal. 4th 612, 618, the City of Vista reached a settlement with the owner/landlord on the presumption that a termination clause in the lease acted as a waiver of the tenant's right to compensation. The Supreme Court held, however, that the termination clause did not deprive the tenant

Speculative testimony regarding the value of lost goodwill based on hypothetical uses, rather than actual use of the property in question, is not admissible.

Hilton Garden Inn. The Redevelopment Agency originally purchased over 80 acres of land and assisted with the development of the Solano Mall, adjacent shopping centers, the Hilton Garden Inn Hotel, and several restaurants.

of any right he might have to compensation for leasehold bonus value or the taking of his other property. Generally speaking, an agency that cannot obtain the written consent of a property owner and all tenants and other claimants to the apportionment of a settlement agreement should file an eminent domain action, invoke Code of Civil Procedure, section 1260.220(b) to interplead all claims, and leave the task of apportionment to the court. Otherwise, the agency risks paying repeatedly for the same property.

Trial. Compensation to the owner is based on the expert opinions of witnesses familiar with the valuation of real estate. When property is encumbered with a leasehold or other interest, the agency may request the court first to determine the total compensation that is due all defendants then to apportion the award among all the claimants. Code Civ Proc. § 1260.220(b).

Compensation is awarded as of the "date of value" set by statute—either the date probable compensation is deposited or, if there is no deposit, the date of trial. Under limited circumstances, a trial court may modify the date of value to protect the constitutional interests of a property owner where land prices have been escalating rapidly. *Saratoga Fire Protection Dist. v. Hackett* (2002) 97 Cal. App. 4th 895. However, that rule only applies when there has been no deposit of probable compensation. If such a deposit has been made, the Supreme Court has held that using the date of deposit as the date for ascertaining just compensation meets constitutional requirements once the trial court determines that the deposit was reasonable. *Mt. San Jacinto Community College District v. Superior Court* (2007) 40 Cal. 4th 648.

Most condemnation cases are tried before a jury. Even though they are the defendants in a condemnation action, property owners are entitled to present their evidence first. Code Civ. Proc. § 1260.210. An owner may offer an opinion of value, although most owners do not since they may lack qualifications that will impress the court or jury and are not disinterested parties. Planners, engineers, and other experts may be called as witnesses to discuss the adaptability of the property to its highest and best use, and business valuation appraisers or accountants normally place a value on goodwill. An owner's plans for the property may be shown to the jury to demonstrate how the property might be used, but such plans are illustrative only and are not conclusive on the issue of how the property is to be valued. *People ex rel. Dept. of Transportation v. Tanczos* (1996) 42 Cal. App. 4th 1215.

When the agency offers its case, it presents experts who offer an opinion of value. The opinion of value is not necessarily identical to the initial appraisal. If the agency has gained possession by the time of trial, it may have reason to further refine its opinion of a property's value. As a general rule, a reappraisal based on significant new information that has come to light after the agency has taken possession cannot be used to impeach the agency's appraiser. *In Community Redevelopment Agency v. World Wide Enterprises, Inc.* (2000) 77 Cal. App. 4th 1156 (this decision has been depublished, may not be cited, and is available only at (2000) 92 Cal. Rptr. 2d 244), a redevelopment agency brought a condemnation action against a property owner. The court ruled that the trial court did not abuse its discretion when it granted a motion *in limine* precluding the property owner from impeaching the agency's expert appraiser witness over inconsistent appraisal reports. The court clarified that though the first appraisal, made for the deposit of probable compensation ($1,020,000), and the second, issued for the just compensation trial ($810,000), differed significantly, the appraisals were not inconsistent, as the second appraisal was made after the plaintiff obtained possession of the property and conducted a more extensive investigation, finding significant asbestos and dilapidation in the building's interior. The court based its ruling on Code of Civil Procedure section 1255.060, which expressly prohibits impeachment of a witness based on appraisals made in connection with deposits of probable compensation.

Two additional issues affecting valuation must be considered. The first involves the issue of "project enhanced value." An appraiser may not take into account the project for which the property is being taken in valuing that property. However, the rise in value of a property *before* it is included in the project may be taken into consideration. This knotty doctrine was first announced in *Merced Irrigation Dist. v. Woolstenhulme* (1971) 4 Cal. 3d 478. For a more recent discussion of this thorny issue, *see City of San Diego v. Barratt-American, Inc.* (2005) 128 Cal. App. 4th 917.

An appraiser may not take into account the project for which the property is being taken in valuing that property. However, the rise in value of a property before it is included in the project may be taken into consideration.

The second involves the issue of dedication. If, in order to obtain the highest and best use of the property being acquired, an owner would have to dedicate a portion of the property for a public use (*i.e.,* for a street), then that portion of the property that must be dedicated is valued not at the "highest and best use" value, but rather in its current undeveloped state. This is known as the *Porterville* doctrine. For a recent discussion upholding this doctrine against a constitutional challenge, *see State Route 4 Bypass Authority v. Superior Ct.* (2007) 153 Cal. App. 4th 1546.

Additionally, *City of Fremont v. Fisher* (2008) 160 Cal. App. 4th 666 discusses the issue of the extent temporary severance damages are compensable due to the acquisition and use by the agency of a temporary construction easement.

Judgment and Appeal. After the jury returns its determination of the value of the property, any severance damage to the remainder, and any compensation for lost goodwill, judgment is entered by the court. The agency, which has 30 days to pay the judgment (Code Civ. Proc.

§ 1268.010), receives credit for any amounts deposited previously. Interest on the award is credited at market rates until the award is paid. Interest accrues from the earliest of the following: (1) the date of possession of the property, (2) the date on which a prejudgment order of possession authorizes the agency to take possession, or (3) the date of entry of judgment. Code Civ. Proc. §1268.310. As in any civil case, either side may appeal.

Unlike most other civil actions, the property owner is automatically entitled to court costs. Code Civ. Proc. § 1268.710. Plaintiff's court costs may include litigation expenses if the trial judge determines—on the basis of the final offer of the agency and the final demand of the owner made at least 20 days prior to trial—that, in light of the jury's verdict, the agency's offer was not reasonable and that the owner's final demand was reasonable. Code Civ. Proc. § 1250.410. Litigation expenses are defined as the "party's reasonable attorney's fees and costs, including expert witness and appraiser fees." Code Civ. Proc. §1250.410(e).

Whenever a defendant is dismissed from an eminent domain proceeding "for any reason," that defendant is entitled to litigation expenses. This is true even when the reason for the dismissal is that the defendant has sold the property and no longer has a claim to compensation! *Temple City Redevelopment Agency v. Bayside Drive Ltd. Partnership* (2007) 146 Cal. App. 4th 1555.

In *Community Redevelopment Agency v. Force Electronics* (1997) 55 Cal. App. 4th 622, the court held that a property owner is entitled to be paid the full amount for his or her property within 30 days after final judgment. If a government agency does not have the full amount, the agency must abandon the condemnation and cannot, against the will of the owner, pay the judgment over a 10-year period. The owner can either elect to receive the judgment over 10 years or get its property back. Making the owner into an involuntary lender is not the full and perfect equivalent of giving the property back to the owner. *See* Richard G. Rypinski, *Eminent Domain, A Step-by-Step Guide to the Acquisition of Real Property* (Solano Press).

Inverse Condemnation

Inverse condemnation—or "reverse condemnation"—occurs when a property owner sues a public agency for having taken property without following the procedures required by the Eminent Domain Law discussed above. There are two types of inverse condemnation.

The first occurs when the agency physically invades property and appropriates a right (for example, an agency may construct a new street without first obtaining the necessary right-of-way either by a consensual sale or in an eminent domain proceeding). Whether this action is intentional or inadvertent, the agency is held strictly liable. It must pay for the property interest taken and reimburse the owner for costs incurred to obtain recovery, including attorneys' fees.

The second type of inverse condemnation occurs from over-regulation of property—for example, a downzoning of property so that it cannot be used for any economic purpose. The "regulatory taking" issue has been before the courts on numerous occasions. In the last two decades, the United States Supreme Court has held that certain land use regulations can go beyond constitutionally permitted limits and constitute inverse condemnation. *Dolan v. City of Tigard* (1994) 512 U.S. 374; *First English Evangelical Lutheran Church v. Los Angeles County* (1987) 482 U.S. 304; *Nollan v. California Coastal Commission* (1987) 483 U.S. 825. The exact circumstances under which such a taking occurs are decided on a case-by-case basis, with a court looking at individual facts peculiar to the claim involved. While a detailed discussion of the law pertaining to regulatory takings is beyond the scope of this book, certain principles are particularly important to redevelopment agencies.

The exact circumstances under which a taking occurs are decided on a case-by-case basis, with a court looking at individual facts peculiar to the claim involved.

The mere adoption of a redevelopment plan, even if it shows the potential future acquisition of private property for a public use, does not constitute inverse condemnation. *Cambria Spring Co. v. City of Pico Rivera* (1985) 171 Cal. App. 3d 1080. Nor does the denial of a land use entitlement followed by later acquisition of the land for redevelopment purposes. *Redevelopment Agency v. Contra Costa Theatre, Inc.* (1982) 135 Cal. App. 3d 73. It has been held that a redevelopment agency's Polanco Act notice giving a property owner 60 days to present a remedial action plan, sent just prior to the redevelopment agency's filing of an eminent domain action, was not compensable precondemnation conduct. *Redevelopment Agency of San Diego v. Mesdaq* (2007) 154 Cal. App. 4th 1111.

However, when an agency either announces its intent to condemn property and then unreasonably delays the action, or takes other unreasonable action prior to condemnation, it may be liable for damages if the landowner suffers a direct loss from the agency's actions. *Klopping v. City of Whittier* (1972) 8 Cal. 3d 39; *Border Business Park, Inc. v. City of San Diego* (2006) 142 Cal. App. 4th 1538; *San Diego Metropolitan Transit Development Board v. Handlery Hotel, Inc.* (1999) 73 Cal. App. 4th 517, 529–30. What constitutes unreasonable delay or a direct and substantial impairment of property rights is a question of fact to be determined on a case-by-case basis. In order to assess whether an agency has unreasonably delayed a condemnation action, the finder of fact must determine the point at which the agency's activities shifted from the planning stage to the acquisition stage. Ordinarily, the pivotal official act marking the transition is the adoption of the resolution of necessity. Absent a formal resolution of condemnation, the public entity's conduct must have significantly invaded or appropriated the use or enjoyment of the property in order for the owner to state a claim for

When an agency either announces its intent to condemn property and then unreasonably delays the action, or takes other unreasonable action prior to condemnation, it may be liable for damages.

inverse condemnation. *Contra Costa Water District v. Vaquero Farms, Inc.* (1997) 58 Cal. App. 4th 883, 897–98.

Further, in *Border Business Park, Inc. v. City of San Diego* (2006) 142 Cal. App. 4th 1538, 1548–49, the court held that, as a matter of law, in order to prevail on a claim of inverse condemnation, the property owner must show that its property interest was injured in some way that is distinct from the general impact of the project on the surrounding area. In that case, the project proposal did not "directly and specially" affect the plaintiff. *Id.* at 1551. Therefore, the inverse condemnation claim failed. *Ibid.* An owner of property who is denied all economic and beneficial use of property proposed for redevelopment may claim that the property has been taken as a result of the denial. *Terminals Equipment Co. v. City and County of San Francisco* (1990) 221 Cal. App. 3d 234, 243. In order to perfect such a claim, the property owner must show that even after trying to meet all reasonable planning concerns of the city or county, he or she has still not been permitted to make any meaningful use of the land. *MacDonald, Sommer & Frates v. County of Yolo* (1986) 477 U.S. 340. The mere fact a land use decision causes an owner to lose potential profits, or that the land suffers a diminution of value, does not constitute an inverse condemnation claim. *Penn Central Transp. Co. v. New York City* (1978) 438 U.S. 104; *HFH, Ltd. v. Superior Court* (1975) 15 Cal. 3d 508. Before bringing an action for a regulatory taking, a property owner must exhaust administrative means to free the property from the burdensome regulation. *Hensler v. City of Glendale* (1994) 8 Cal. 4th 1, 13. Whether an action constitutes a regulatory taking is a question of law, to be determined by the court, though the question of damages is one for the jury. *Id.* at 15.

When a land use entitlement is denied for property within a redevelopment project area, substantial evidence based on valid health, safety, and welfare considerations must support the denial. It is important to develop an adequate record in these cases to avoid the possibility that a court will determine that the denial was done not to carry out valid land use principles but only to make it cheaper and easier for the redevelopment agency to acquire property for its own purposes.

Leaseholders have unsuccessfully attempted to use inverse condemnation to obtain compensation relating to the loss of tenant interests. In *Langer v. Redevelopment Agency* (1999) 71 Cal. App. 4th 998, 1010, the court held that commercial tenants whose month-to-month leases were terminated by a property owner who voluntarily relinquished property for redevelopment were not entitled to damages for inverse condemnation even though the agency had paid the tenants' relocation costs. The court made plain that acquisition of property on the open market without use of the eminent domain power does not give rise to a claim for inverse condemnation or its substantial equivalent. In *County of Ventura v. Channel Islands Marina, Inc.* (2008) 159 Cal. App. 4th 615, the court held that inverse condemnation is not an appropriate remedy for a breach of a lease.

Interim Property Management

While an agency does not have general authority to permanently manage private property, as a practical matter, agencies must often manage property the agency acquires prior to relocating occupants, demolishing buildings, and transferring the site to a developer. For this purpose, agencies are given specific authority to rent, maintain, insure, and manage property. § 33400. Consistent with this role as an interim property manager, authority is given for a reasonable period to allow the agency to sell or lease the property for redevelopment. §§ 33402, 33449.

Consistent with its role as an interim property manager, authority is given for a reasonable period to allow the agency to sell or lease the property for redevelopment.

6

Environmental Issues

Introduction: Interplay Between Redevelopment and Environmental Law

As with nearly all real estate transactions, environmental contamination issues have become increasingly significant in implementing redevelopment projects. Local, state, and federal environmental laws and regulations are complex and often impose liability upon any entity with control over a contaminated property to remediate the contamination. Fortunately, as discussed in this chapter, redevelopment agencies have certain specific tools to require remediation and provide relief from future liability, thus allowing projects to move forward.

By design, California and federal environmental laws are onerous and often unfair when applied to individual entities. This is based on the premise that "polluters" and any other entity in a position to prevent, control, or profit from the release of pollutants into the environment should bear the cost of cleanup. Under this philosophy, which guides the creation, implementation, and enforcement of environmental laws in this country, it is considered more fair to attach liability to anyone associated with the pollution, even those who acquired property long after the release of pollutants, than to have society at large bear the expense of cleanup. The leading example of this is the federal Superfund statute, discussed below, that provides for strict, retroactive, joint and several liability for any person in a broadly defined category of "owners" or "operators."

The Community Redevelopment Law, however, provides for certain exemptions from some of the harsher applications of the environmental statutes. As will be discussed in detail below, squarely seated at the intersection of redevelopment law and environmental law is the Polanco

As with nearly all real estate transactions, environmental contamination issues have become increasingly significant in implementing redevelopment projects.

By design, California and federal environmental laws are onerous and often unfair when applied to individual entities.

Redevelopment Act. A few other recently enacted pieces of state and federal legislation both expand the ability of public entities to pursue redevelopment of contaminated properties, and also limit liability that may be imposed on both public and private entities engaging in cleanup efforts.

Contaminated Property in the Redevelopment Context

Property contaminated by hazardous substances is common in urban areas in California and often is a major impediment to development.

Property contaminated by hazardous substances is common in urban areas in California and often is a major impediment to development. The Community Redevelopment Law specifies that contaminated property can be a condition of blight used to justify the establishment of a project area. § 33031(b)(2). However, the existence of hazardous wastes often prevents or delays the disposition and development of property because of the expense of testing and remediating hazardous wastes, the difficulty in resolving existing or potential liability issues, and the difficulty in obtaining financing. As a result, more and more frequently, redevelopment agencies are being asked to intervene and assist in the cleanup of properties with hazardous wastes.

Redevelopment agencies, like other property owners, will be held responsible for cleanup pursuant to state and federal law whether or not they caused the contamination.

Before acquiring any property, a redevelopment agency should be certain that it understands whether hazardous wastes exist in, on, or under the property and, if so, the type and the extent of the contamination. This is because redevelopment agencies, like other property owners, will be held responsible for cleanup pursuant to state and federal law whether or not they caused the contamination. While they may be able to seek payment from those who did cause the contamination, those persons may not have the resources to pay for the cleanup of the site. Since the costs of both testing and cleanup can be enormous, an agency should understand the extent of the risk prior to acquiring contaminated property.

Polanco Redevelopment Act of 1990

To give redevelopment agencies additional encouragement in addressing brownfield properties, in 1990 the Legislature enacted the Polanco Redevelopment Act (Polanco Act), which added sections 33459 through 33459.8. These statutory provisions allow a redevelopment agency, subject to certain restrictions, to take any actions that the agency determines are necessary to address a release of hazardous substances on, under, or from property within its project area. In return, the agency, the developer of the property, and subsequent owners receive limited immunity from further cleanup liability.

US-EPA = United States Environmental Protection Agency

The Polanco Act is the product of the Legislature's desire to promote the cleanup and reuse of contaminated urban properties, which are commonly referred to as brownfields. The United States Environmental Protection Agency (US-EPA) recently revised the definition of brownfields, as follows:

The term "brownfield site" means real property, the expansion, redevelopment, or reuse of which may be complicated by the presence or potential presence of a hazardous substance, pollutant, or contaminant. The definition of "brownfield site" is subject to many exclusions, as set forth in 42 U.S.C. § 9601(39)(B), (C) and (D).

42 U.S.C. § 9601(39)(A)

In early 2004, Cal/EPA's Department of Toxic Substances Control (DTSC) and CRA developed a prototypical Environmental Oversight Agreement (EOA) to facilitate the redevelopment of brownfields sites by redevelopment agencies. Under an EOA, DTSC can provide redevelopment agencies with technical assistance and consultation and supervise site cleanups without the agency being named a "responsible party." The EOA was designed for agencies seeking to exercise their authority under the Polanco Act.

The Polanco Act gives redevelopment agencies and the developers they work with a way out of the liability trap in which an entity that controls contaminated property through ownership or other legal means remains liable for cleaning up the contamination (and effects of the contamination on third parties) essentially forever. The Polanco Act's immunity provisions do not apply to federal claims brought either by the government or private parties pursuant to statutes like the federal Comprehensive Environmental Response, Compensation and Liability Act (CERCLA), discussed below. Nevertheless, the provisions of the Polanco Act give redevelopment agencies powerful tools to identify, investigate, remediate, and even acquire these contaminated properties without incurring the environmental liability under state and local laws that might normally accompany such actions.

The Polanco Act gives redevelopment agencies and the developers they work with a way out of the liability trap in which an entity that controls contaminated property remains liable for cleaning up the contamination essentially forever.

Cal/EPA = California Environmental Protection Agency

CERCLA = Comprehensive Environmental Response, Compensation and Liability Act

DTSC = Department of Toxic Substances Control

EOA = Environmental Oversight Agreement

Generally speaking, under the statute, a redevelopment agency has two options for pursuing cleanup of contaminated property slated for redevelopment. It may contract for cleanup itself without further interaction from the state, or it may have a certified independent contractor prepare a remedial action plan and have it approved by DTSC, the applicable regional water quality control board, or, in some cases, a local agency before beginning cleanup. If the redevelopment agency chooses the first option, it and its developers remain potentially liable for later cleanup efforts. If, on the other hand, the agency seeks and receives approval by the state or the local agency, the redevelopment agency and its successors are granted broad immunity from subsequent cleanup costs. § 33459.3.

The Polanco Act gives redevelopment agencies specific authority to both investigate and remediate contaminated property as follows:

Investigation. One very practical provision in the Polanco Act authorizes the redevelopment agency to investigate property for suspected contamination *before* it is acquired. In this regard, section 33459.1(e) provides that:

> To facilitate redevelopment planning, the agency may require the owner or operator of any site within a project area to provide the agency with all existing environmental information pertaining to the site, including the results of any Phase I or subsequent environmental assessment.... If environmental assessment information is not available, the agency may require the owner of the property to conduct an assessment in accordance with standard real estate practices for conducting phase I or phase II environmental assessments.

§ 33459.1(e)

Therefore, not only is a redevelopment agency entitled to receive existing environmental information, but it can force the owner of the property to conduct additional investigations, and turn over those results as well. On November 1, 2006, the US-EPA's New Rule for All Appropriate Inquiries went into effect simultaneously with the new standard for Phase I Environmental Site Assessments established by the American Society for Testing and Material (ASTM 1527 E-05) (collectively, the "New Rules"). The New Rules require several additional tasks and set certain new limitations and requirements. For example, the person conducting a Phase I Environmental Assessment must meet minimum educational and experience thresholds. The New Rules also now mandate, rather than suggest, interviews with historical owners or operators of the subject property. Importantly, the Phase I Environmental Assessment now has a limited shelf life where portions of it must be updated after 180 days and the entire assessment must be re-done if older than a year. An agency would be well-advised to select a professional who understands all of the new requirements and limitations prior to conducting a Phase I Assessment. A Phase II Assessment consists of soil and/or groundwater sampling if recommended in the Phase I report. A Phase II will also follow-up on any other recommendations in the Phase I Assessment.

If a redevelopment agency is interested in possibly asserting one or more of the various defenses available under CERCLA or the state superfund law (discussed later in this chapter), such as being an innocent landowner, bona fide prospective purchaser, or contiguous landowner, the agency will be required to prove it has complied with the New Rules. In addition, the same showing of compliance is required if an agency is seeking funds from the US-EPA Brownfields Grant Program.

Needless to say, many property owners, even if they suspect their property is contaminated, are loath to conduct such tests. As discussed further below, knowledge of contamination can obligate them to report the findings to a regulatory agency, and potentially trigger demands or

---

Not only is a redevelopment agency entitled to receive existing environmental information, but it can force the owner of the property to conduct additional investigations.

ASTM = American Society for Testing and Material

An agency would be well-advised to select a professional who understands all of the new requirements and limitations prior to conducting a Phase I Assessment.

orders to clean up the property. However, knowing the nature and extent of the contamination at a site is essential to the valuation of the property and its redevelopment.

Remediation. The Polanco Act allows the redevelopment agency to assume the position of an environmental regulatory agency with the power to conduct environmental remediation and then recover the cost of such work.

Notice Requirements. Prior to undertaking cleanup work on its own, a redevelopment agency is required to give a 60-day notice to the party determined by the agency to be responsible for the release. This notice is designed to give the responsible party the opportunity to undertake the work itself, which will give it greater control over the scope and cost of the work than if left up to the redevelopment agency alone. In this regard, the calculation is much like that made by responsible parties at CERCLA sites, where owners have the option of conducting the cleanup themselves or letting the government do it at the owners' expense.

Prior to undertaking cleanup work on its own, a redevelopment agency is required to give a 60-day notice to the party determined by the agency to be responsible for the release.

Recovery of Cleanup Costs. If it incurs costs for cleanup, the agency may bring a civil action against those parties responsible for the contamination. § 33459.4. The agency may recover only those costs incurred after the effective date of section 33459 *et seq.*, that is, January 1, 1991. *Torrance Redevelopment Agency v. Solvent Coating Company* (C.D. Cal. 1991) 781 F. Supp. 650, 651–652. Costs incurred prior to January 1, 1991, may be recoverable under other state law causes of action or under CERCLA. A word of caution: If there are no responsible parties with any money to pay for cleanup, the agency may well have to pay the entire cost itself. The Polanco Act provides no independent funding mechanism.

In *Redevelopment Agency of the City of San Diego v. Salvation Army* (2002) 103 Cal. App. 4th 755, the court described the Polanco Act as follows:

> By explicitly granting an agency authority over properties owned by responsible parties and participating owners, as well as expanding its authority to act when those parties fail to cooperate, the Polanco Act gives redevelopment agencies "more clout to clean up blighted properties."

Id. at 765

Before Chiron Corporation could construct its 2.2 million square foot office campus in Emeryville, the Redevelopment Agency had to oversee the cleanup of hazardous materials from the site.

The court reaffirmed that the Salvation Army was liable for the cleanup costs as a responsible party because it owned the property at the time the agency filed its eminent domain action, even though the remediation work was performed after the agency obtained possession of the property. Because the Salvation Army did not respond in a timely manner to the agency's request to submit a remedial action plan, the agency was entitled to deduct all of its remediation costs from the total amount that the parties had agreed would compensate the Salvation Army for all claims under the eminent domain cause of action. The agency's remediation costs included those incurred for soil contamination discovered after the agency took possession of the property, but prior to the final order of condemnation.

In *Redevelopment Agency of the City of San Diego v. San Diego Gas & Electric Company* (2003) 111 Cal. App. 4th 912, the court held that the Polanco Act allowed the agency to compel a responsible party through a civil action to remedy or remove hazardous substances and then to recover its costs to pursue that action. The court also held that the agency need not plead actual financial injury or damage in order to obtain such an order. The court said that, under the Polanco Act, the agency was authorized to take "any actions" necessary to remove hazardous substances from property within a project area, whether the agency owned that property or not, and nothing in the Polanco Act required the agency to show it suffered "injury" in order to compel a responsible party to remediate contaminated property within its territory.

In *City of Modesto Redevelopment Agency v. Superior Court* (2004) 119 Cal. App. 4th 28, the agency sued the manufacturers and various distributors of two dry cleaning solvents, alleging that the solvents caused risks to health and the environment, that dry cleaners customarily dumped solvent wastewater into the public sewer systems, and that dry cleaners experienced a habitual problem of chlorinated solvents leaking into the environment. The agency claimed, among other things, that it was entitled to recover cleanup costs under the Polanco Act from solvent manufacturers, distributors, and equipment manufacturers as responsible parties liable for the contamination. The Polanco Act includes as a responsible party a person defined under California Water Code section 13304(a), which is "[a]ny person...who has caused or permitted, causes or permits, or threatens to cause or permit any waste to be discharged or deposited...into the waters of the state [and who] shall upon order of the regional board, clean up the waste or abate the effects of the waste...."

Applying the law of nuisance, the court concluded that parties who take affirmative steps to assist in the unauthorized disposal of hazardous wastes can be liable under the Polanco Act.

Applying the law of nuisance, the court concluded that parties who take affirmative steps to assist in the unauthorized disposal of hazardous wastes can be liable under the Polanco Act—such as a manufacturer of equipment allegedly designed to discharge solvents into drains and sewers or persons who instructed dry cleaners to dispose of solvents improperly. However, those persons who merely placed solvents in the stream of commerce without warning of the dangers of improper disposal were not liable. *City of Modesto Redevelopment Agency v. Superior Court* (2004) 119 Cal. App. 4th 28, 43.

Environmental Agency Oversight. DTSC and the Regional Water Quality Control Boards are statutorily required to respond to redevelopment agency requests to approve cleanup guidelines and remedial action plans within a reasonable period of time. The redevelopment agency must reimburse the applicable approving agency for its cost to process and approve the remedial action plan. § 33459.3(m). Certain agencies have been amenable to negotiating the terms of reimbursement. This flexibility may extend to placing a cap on total oversight costs. In this regard, the state Regional Water Quality Control Boards have created standardized contract documents for oversight work.

Remediation of Petroleum Contamination. Unlike CERCLA, the Polanco Act includes petroleum products in its definition of "hazardous substances." Section 33459 incorporates by reference most of the terms from the state and federal Superfund laws. However, under both the state and federal Superfund laws, the definition of "hazardous waste" excludes petroleum hydrocarbons. *See* 42 U.S.C. § 9601; § 2531(a). In contrast, the Polanco Act specifically incorporates by reference the definition from the state underground storage tank law, which does include petroleum and petroleum byproducts. *See* § 33459(c).

Thus, the Polanco Act essentially creates a state-CERCLA action that includes petroleum products. The importance of this cannot be overstated. Without the Polanco Act, in these circumstances redevelopment agencies would have to rely on the slow and uncertain process of litigating liability under traditional common law theories like nuisance and trespass while at the same time receiving no guarantees that any cleanup would be final. The Polanco Act thus allows redevelopment agencies to help clean up former gas station sites, often encountered in older project areas, that may contain petroleum products and additives such as MTBE from leaking underground storage tanks.

Perhaps the most attractive attribute of the Polanco Act is the flexibility it gives redevelopment agencies. Some agencies have used it as a way to hasten cleanup of petroleum contamination by the responsible party or in conjunction with the state's Underground Storage Tank Cleanup Fund. *See* §§ 25299.50; 25299.79. Note, however, that the statutory authorization for the Underground Storage Tank Cleanup Fund will expire in 2016 unless extended by the legislature. For other agencies, the Polanco Act is a mechanism that allows the agency to clean the property at its own pace and pursue the responsible parties later. For still others, the Polanco Act has been used to give the redevelopment agency enforcement powers within the given project area.

Immunity from Liability. After the remediation has been completed in accordance with an approved plan and a certificate of completion issued by the applicable regulatory agency, the redevelopment agency and subsequent owners are immune from liability with respect only to the substance or substances covered by the approved remediation plan. The immunity extends to any employee or agent of the redevelopment agency, any person who acquires the property pursuant to an agreement with the agency or subsequently, and any lender to the property owner. These immunity provisions thus make previously undevelopable sites much more attractive to developers and their lenders, and allow the site to be used productively.

The Polanco Act essentially creates a state-CERCLA action that includes petroleum products. The importance of this cannot be overstated.

MTBE = Methyl tertiary butyl ether

For some agencies, the Polanco Act is a mechanism that allows the agency to clean the property at its own pace and pursue the responsible parties later.

Other Key Environmental Statutes

It is beyond the scope of this chapter to provide a primer on environmental law for the redevelopment practitioner. However, several environmental statutes have broad enough application that they should be considered in conjunction with any project dealing with property contaminated with hazardous substances.

Federal Superfund

CERCLA, as amended, is a federal statute that is fairly viewed as the proverbial 800-pound gorilla of environmental laws. CERCLA applies retroactive, strict, joint and several liability for responding to hazardous substance contamination on a broad array of "owners" and "operators" of property. However, CERCLA has been somewhat tamed by the liability exemption for property acquired by eminent domain, and by federal legislation that took effect in January 2002. 42 U.S.C. §§ 9601(35)(A); 9607(b)(3).

In certain cases involving eminent domain, a redevelopment agency may be exempt from CERCLA liability under the so-called "innocent landowner" provisions found at 42 U.S.C. sections 9601(35)(A) and 9607(b)(3). A redevelopment agency may qualify as an innocent landowner if it satisfies both of the following conditions: First, it must be able to show that it acquired the property at issue after the contamination occurred, and second, it must acquire the property through the exercise of eminent domain authority by purchase or condemnation. 42 U.S.C. §§ 9601(35)(A)(ii); 9607(b)(3). However, proving when hazardous substances were released on a property, and when they stopped being released, is often a difficult and highly speculative case to make.

Another exemption from CERCLA liability in the redevelopment context was recently created by an amendment designed to promote redevelopment of contaminated urban properties. By amending CERCLA (42 U.S.C. 9601 *et seq.*), the Small Business Liability Relief and Brownfields Revitalization Act (H.R. 2869, or the "Brownfield Amendments" to CERCLA) allows liability relief under CERCLA. The provisions exempt from liability certain defined "innocent purchasers," "contiguous land owners," and "bona fide purchasers." One vitally important provision to brownfields developers even allows for a liability exemption in cases where parties take title to known contaminated parcels. In all cases, however, the party seeking exemption from liability must prove that it made an "all appropriate inquiry" regarding the condition of the property. On November 1, 2006, the U.S. EPA issued its New Rule defining "all appropriate inquiry" (*see* discussion under

The Polanco Redevelopment Act of 1990—Investigation, above). The CERCLA exemptions only apply to CERCLA liability, and do not provide relief under any other state or federal statute.

In December 2004, the U.S. Supreme Court issued its decision in *Cooper Industries, Inc. v. Aviall Services, Inc.* (2004) 543 U.S. 157. The Court held that a potentially responsible person (PRP) who voluntarily cleaned up contaminated property could not sue another PRP for contribution under CERCLA's section 9613 without having first been sued under sections 9606 or 9607(a). The Court left open the question whether that PRP could sue another PRP for cost recovery under section 9607. This ruling was a departure from all previous interpretation and practice, and meant that a party wanting to engage in a voluntary cleanup was potentially unable to recover any contribution from other responsible parties under CERCLA. In 2007, the Supreme Court issued its opinion in *United States v. Atlantic Research Corp.* (2007) 551 U.S. 128, 127 S. Ct. 2331. There, the Court held that a PRP could sue another PRP for cost recovery under section 9607. A question remains, however, regarding how the settlement bar protection in section 113(f)(2) may apply to claims between PRPs under section 107.

The above discussion does not apply to property contaminated with petroleum. Petroleum and petroleum products are strictly excluded from CERCLA's liability scheme.

State Superfund

California's Carpenter-Presley-Tanner Hazardous Substance Account Act (HSAA), found at section 25300 *et seq.*, is patterned after, but not identical to, the federal CERCLA statute. The HSAA, commonly referred to as the State Superfund, authorizes lawsuits as follows:

> Any person who has incurred removal or remedial action costs in accordance with this chapter or the federal act [CERCLA] may seek contribution or indemnity from any person who is liable pursuant to this chapter....

§ 25363(e)

The HSAA defines "person" to include, among other things, "a government corporation," and "any city, county, city and county, district, commission, the state or any department, agency, or political subdivision thereof...." § 25319.

Like CERCLA, the HSAA excludes petroleum from its definition of "hazardous substances."

The CERCLA exemptions only apply to CERCLA liability, and do not provide relief under any other state or federal statute.

HSAA = Carpenter-Presley-Tanner Hazardous Substance Account Act

PRP = Potentially responsible person

In Davis, the Redevelopment Agency assisted with site acquisition, toxics remediation and relocation to enable the development of a 60,000 square foot office building leased to the U.S. Department of Agriculture.

With respect to lawsuits to recover costs spent cleaning up hazardous substances, differences between the state and federal Superfund statutes make the HSAA a poor choice when CERCLA is available.

In cleaning up parcels targeted for redevelopment, cities and counties may initiate removal and remedial actions for sites on the state Superfund list under certain circumstances. § 25351.2. Once the cleanup is completed, DTSC must reimburse the city or county and then seek cost recovery from responsible parties. However, with respect to lawsuits to recover costs spent cleaning up hazardous substances, certain differences between the state and federal Superfund statutes make the HSAA a poor choice when CERCLA is available. For example, liability under HSAA is not joint and several. Accordingly, while lawsuits based on the HSAA may be encountered less frequently than those brought pursuant to CERCLA, they still can be a viable option under the right circumstances.

AB 389—California Land Reuse and Revitalization Act

CLRRA = California Land Reuse and Revitalization Act

AB 389, or the California Land Reuse and Revitalization Act (CLRRA), is loosely modeled on the 2002 Brownfield Amendments to CERCLA (the Small Business Liability Relief and Brownfields Revitalization Act, discussed under Federal Superfund, above). § 25396.60. It provides immunity from a broad range of state environmental laws for innocent landowners, bona fide purchasers, and contiguous property owners of contaminated property. However, in order to receive and retain AB 389's liability immunity: (1) the site must qualify as an eligible site; (2) the person seeking immunity must enter into and not materially deviate from the terms of a cleanup agreement with either the DTSC or a Regional Water Quality Control Board; (3) the person must satisfy the Act's liability relief prerequisites and continuing obligations; and (4) the Act's re-opener provisions must not apply. There are specific exceptions to CLRRA's immunity protections, and it is unclear whether the immunity extends to common law claims. In addition, to be eligible, a party must prove that it conducted an "all appropriate inquiry" regarding the condition of the property. *See* discussion of the New Rules under The Polanco Redevelopment Act of 1990—Investigation, above. CLRRA is scheduled to expire on January 1, 2010, but the immunities obtained prior to that date will survive provided the parties are in compliance with the cleanup agreement.

A redevelopment agency may wish to consider CLRRA, Polanco, CERCLA, or the state superfund when contemplating a redevelopment project. Depending on the circumstances, one act may offer benefits that another does not.

A redevelopment agency may wish to consider CLRRA, Polanco, CERCLA, or the state superfund (or other applicable statutes) when contemplating a redevelopment project. Depending on the circumstances of a given project, one act may offer benefits that another does not. For example, the immunities provided under CLRRA are conferred at the time the party signs the agreement with DTSC, whereas the immunity provided under the Polanco Act attaches once the remediation is complete and the party has received a certificate of completion from the appropriate agency.

State Programs to Assist with Remediation of Contaminated Properties

DTSC has long been at the forefront of efforts to assist in the redevelopment of contaminated urban brownfields properties. Some of the current programs and initiatives run by DTSC are summarized below. However, before jumping in, close evaluation of these assistance programs is warranted in light of the specifics of a particular redevelopment project. Many of the programs are limited in scope and in a given fiscal year may or may not have sufficient funding to be of practical use.

Before jumping in, close evaluation of these assistance programs is warranted in light of the specifics of a particular redevelopment project.

Voluntary Cleanup Program

Through the Voluntary Cleanup Program (VCP), parties liable for cleanup of defined low-priority sites can contract with DTSC to provide oversight services during private party-initiated voluntary cleanup. The VCP provides mutually agreed-upon DTSC oversight in assessing or remediating low-priority, low-risk sites. When the work is completed, DTSC provides a no-further-action (NFA) letter. This sounds much rosier than the reality many VCP participants have experienced, but with careful negotiation and careful selection of the "right" site for the program, the VCP can still be a valuable tool when a responsible party wants to take up the challenge and has the financial means to do so.

ERAP = Expediated Remedial Action Program
NFA = No further action
VCP = Voluntary Cleanup Program

Expedited Remedial Action Program (ERAP or SB 923)

A pilot program to promote accelerated site remediation, ERAP is a voluntary program that provides incentives to parties liable for cleaning up a contaminated property to accelerate the work of investigating and remediating the site. The pilot nature of the program limits it to 30 sites. Moreover, the program has experienced considerable difficulty obtaining funding to provide the monetary incentives for even the limited number of sites enrolled.

CalSites Validation Program

DTSC maintains the CalSites database to track properties that may be contaminated with hazardous substances. A property listed in this database is innocent until proven guilty. However, the database can be revised to delete properties shown not to be contaminated or that were listed incorrectly, thus removing a potential stigma that would prevent redevelopment. In 1996, DTSC completed a three-year reevaluation of the database that resulted in the removal of more than 22,000 properties from the list. Property listed improperly may prove a hindrance to obtaining loans or to the parcel's overall marketability. Thus, removal from the CalSites list should be requested, if appropriate.

DTSC maintains the CalSites database to track properties that may be contaminated with hazardous substances.

Institutional Controls

Pursuant to the provisions of Health and Safety Code section 25220(f), DTSC maintains a list of institutional controls (or land use restrictions) that are recorded on property with some contamination left in place. In the contaminated property redevelopment context, these are sites that are restricted to certain uses—for example, industrial use, rather than residential—thus allowing so called risk-based closure for the industrial use. The land use restrictions are recorded to give notice to future purchasers that the use of the property is limited, unless further remediation is undertaken.

Other Statutes Applicable to Environmental Issues Affecting Redevelopment

In general, a redevelopment agency owning contaminated property, like other public and private property, is responsible for cleanup pursuant to state and federal law whether or not it caused the contamination. However, a redevelopment agency also has special rights to seek a contribution from those responsible, as discussed above. There are also provisions specifically governing liability of public agencies that own or lease property where a release or disposal of hazardous waste has occurred.

In addition to the statutes described above, the following statutes may prove helpful to the success of a redevelopment project faced with environmental issues.

Mello-Roos Community Facilities Act

The Mello-Roos Community Facilities Act Amendments of 1990 (AB 2610) created the first long-term financing options for hazardous substance cleanups on both public and private property by empowering community facilities districts to levy special taxes and issue bonds to provide funds for site cleanups. *See* Gov. Code §§ 53314.6–53314.7.

The Mello-Roos Community Facilities Act authorizes cities, counties, and special districts to levy special taxes and issue bonds for the purpose of establishing revolving funds to remediate contaminated property. At present, a community facilities district may be established to finance services relating to removal and/or remedial action for the cleanup of any hazardous substance that has been released into the environment. The district may finance the acquisition, improvement, rehabilitation, or maintenance of real or other tangible property within an estimated useful life of five years or longer through bonds secured by and payable from a special tax levied on property owners within an established district.

Importantly, the Act makes responsible parties liable to the community facilities district for cleanup costs. Thus, the district is allowed to recoup its costs through a CERCLA-like private recovery action calling for joint and several liability among responsible parties. For a broader discussion of Mello-Roos Bonds, *see* chapter 10.

Hazardous Waste Disposal on Public Land

Sections 25242 through 25242.3, entitled "Hazardous Waste Disposal on Public Land," address situations where hazardous waste has been disposed of on public property.

These sections require all public agencies to inform DTSC when any agency "knows or has reasonable cause to believe that a disposal of hazardous waste...has occurred." § 25242(a). Once it has determined that such a disposal has occurred, DTSC must notify the county in which the land is located and all residents living within 2,000 feet of the property line. DTSC must also conduct public hearings on any proposed hazardous waste management plans.

Prior to, or simultaneous with, utilizing the provisions of this article, DTSC "shall diligently pursue all feasible civil and criminal actions" against the owner of the land or other party responsible for the disposal of the hazardous waste. § 25242.2. The owner, lessee, or lessor of the contaminated land may recover the cleanup costs "from any person who was responsible for the disposal." *Id.*

Section 25242 *et seq.*, read literally, would seem to make cleanup of public property DTSC's primary responsibility. However, DTSC has never taken any steps to enforce the provisions, and no cases and no implementing regulations are published under these sections.

Proposition 65

A number of miscellaneous provisions can potentially affect an agency attempting to address contaminated property. These include section 25180.7, adopted as part of Proposition 65. Under this section, certain public employees who, in the course of their official duties, obtain information revealing the release of a hazardous substance must report it to the local Board of Supervisors within 72 hours.

Proposition 65, formally known as the Safe Drinking Water and Toxic Enforcement Act of 1986, is codified at section 25249.5 *et seq.* Generally, Proposition 65 prohibits businesses with more than 10 employees from (1) knowingly discharging chemicals into any source of drinking water, or (2) knowingly and intentionally exposing any person to a chemical known to the State of California to cause cancer or reproductive toxicity without first giving a clear and reasonable warning to that person. §§ 25249.5, 25249.6. The list of chemicals "known to the state" is maintained and updated by Cal/EPA's Office of Environmental Health Hazard Assessment (OEHHA).

The exposures for which Proposition 65 warnings are required fall into two categories: occupational exposures that occur in the workplace

> *A number of miscellaneous provisions can potentially affect an agency attempting to address contaminated property. These include section 25180.7, adopted as part of Proposition 65.*

OEHHA = Office of Environmental Health Hazard Assessment

and environmental exposures that occur simply from coming into contact with an environmental medium, such as air, water, soil, etc. Proposition 65 warning notices are only required where actual exposure takes place. The problem is that it is at best expensive, and at worst impossible, to confirm or deny exposures that exceed Proposition 65 thresholds. Thus, many businesses/property owners simply supply the Proposition 65 notices, rather than risk liability for violating the statute. The statute provides specific examples of warnings that satisfy the notification requirements.

Cleanup-Related Taxes and Fees

There is a constantly changing group of fees and taxes on the generation, use, and disposal of hazardous substances and wastes.

Finally, there is a constantly changing group of fees and taxes on the generation, use, and disposal of hazardous substances and wastes. Some apply when the hazardous waste is being generated as the result of remediation of contaminated property. *See*, for example, § 25205 *et seq.*; Rev. & Tax. Code § 43001 *et seq.*; and §§ 43800, 46001, and 50101. These fees can add up to a significant sum and should not be ignored when evaluating the cost of cleanup.

Other Environmental Laws to Consider at Specific Sites

Reporting Requirements

The applicability of the federal and California's numerous overlapping reporting requirements is often more a question of art than science.

The applicability of the federal and California's numerous overlapping reporting requirements is often more a question of art than science. In some instances, a redevelopment agency that receives notice of a release of contamination may have a reporting obligation, even if the release occurred long ago. Different statutory reporting requirements apply depending upon the nature of the contaminant (petroleum, hazardous substances, etc.), the amount (reportable quantity, etc.), and how the release occurred (from an underground storage tank, etc.).

Generally, the duty to report a release of contaminants lies with the owner or operator of the property where the release occurred.

Generally, the duty to report a release of contaminants lies with the owner or operator of the property where the release occurred. In that sense, a redevelopment agency that orders a property owner to conduct a Phase I or Phase II environmental investigation does not have a duty to file a report with the appropriate regulatory agency. (Incidentally, many inadvertent violations of reporting statutes occur when the wrong regulatory agency is notified, or if the correct agency is not notified within the statutory timeframe. Penalties can be harsh—up to $25,000 per day while the release remains unreported.)

To the extent that a redevelopment agency undertakes work at a contaminated property, and may thus be considered the "operator," competent environmental compliance counsel should be consulted about the agency's specific reporting obligations. Counsel can help agency staff and contractors identify the appropriate contacts for releases requiring immediate reporting and non-emergency situations. As with most environmental compliance issues, developing procedures and providing basic training before a crisis occurs may prevent costly violation, and, should a violation occur, will argue in favor of a reduced penalty for a good-faith effort to comply.

Local CERCLA-Like Ordinances

In 2002, the Ninth Circuit upheld a new breed of environmental ordinance that a city or county can enact to bestow CERCLA-like powers. *Fireman's Fund Insurance Company v. City of Lodi* (9th Cir. 2002) 302 F. 3d 928. One city in San Joaquin County has adopted a Municipal Environmental Response and Liability Ordinance (MERLO) that is patterned after the federal CERCLA statute. With such an ordinance, a local entity has greater control over the direction and scope of a hazardous substance cleanup within its jurisdiction.

In 2003, the U.S. District Court for the Eastern District of California concluded the city was a potentially responsible person and held that certain portions of MERLO were preempted by CERCLA to the extent they shielded the city from liability. *Fireman's Fund Ins. Co. v. City of Lodi* (E.D. Cal. 2003) 296 F. Supp. 2d 1197.

The following year, in *City of Lodi v. Randtron* (2004) 118 Cal. App. 4th 337, the Court of Appeal ruled that the city was preempted by state law from enforcing an administrative order issued under MERLO. The property owner asserted that the administrative order was void and unenforceable because the HSAA, or state superfund, preempted the local ordinance under which the order was issued. The court held that DTSC was required to prepare or approve remedial action plans for all DTSC-listed sites and to oversee the implementation of those plans. The property in question was located within a listed site. Accordingly, the city lacked authority to order any remedial action without first obtaining a judgment against the property owner to abate a public nuisance or obtaining approval from DTSC.

Toxic Substances Control Act

Where polychlorinated biphenyls (PCBs) are present, a lesser-known federal statute, the Toxic Substances Control Act (TSCA), applies. 15 U.S.C. § 2601 *et seq*. Since TSCA is a completely separate regulatory scheme from CERCLA and related statutes, care should be taken to comply with its unique provisions.

PCBs are most commonly encountered in locations where electric utility lines exist or existed and usually result from

The innovative design of a full-size grocery/drug store complex in downtown Hayward complements its commercial core. The Redevelopment Agency facilitated land assembly, relocation, and remediation of toxics on the site.

MERLO = Municipal Environmental Response and Liability Ordinance

PCB = Polychlorinated biphenyl

TSCA = Toxic Substance Control Act

Since TSCA is a completely separate regulatory scheme from CERCLA and related statutes, care should be taken to comply with its unique provisions.

transformer fires that release deadly dioxin. Where testing reveals the presence of released PCBs, cleanup should be completed in compliance with TSCA provisions.

Asbestos and Lead

When a project requires that an old structure be refurbished or demolished, the laws and regulations relating to asbestos and lead apply. Prior to any demolition activity and/or improper disposal, it is critical that screening tests are conducted and appropriate actions taken to avoid exposing workers and the public to these contaminants. If screening tests reveal the presence of lead-based paint or regulated, asbestos-containing materials (RACM), then specialized contractors must remove or encapsulate those substances before any other demolition or construction activity can proceed.

Military Base Cleanup and Reuse

Redevelopment issues regarding the closure of military bases are discussed in chapter 12. Aside from the transfer of liability and overall responsibility for cleanup, remediation of environmental contamination on a military base is fairly standard. However, a military base may also pose extraordinary environmental problems, including unexploded ordnance (UXO) and radioactive waste, which the transfer documents should address. The fact that the military is in the process of handing over some of the most desirable property in California, such as Fort Ord near Monterey, can make redevelopment economically feasible despite the additional obstacles.

Paying for Cleanup of Contaminated Property

Redevelopment Project Proponent as the Deep Pocket

Clearly one of the major factors in the success of any redevelopment-initiated environmental cleanup will be the availability of sufficient funds to conduct the work. While the Polanco Act allows a redevelopment agency to contract for the cleanup and then recover the cost from the responsible parties, there will undoubtedly be instances when recovery is unavailable. Therefore, the redevelopment agency or other project proponent may have to assist the responsible parties in identifying and obtaining funds to which they are entitled, either to reimburse the agency for the cleanup it has already conducted on behalf of the responsible parties, or to enable the responsible parties to conduct the work themselves. In this respect, the agency will need to identify various funding possibilities, including government grant and loan programs, outside the resources of the potentially responsible parties.

Responsible Parties' Insurance Policies

An entire cottage industry that locates old insurance policies belonging to current and former owners and/or operators of contaminated properties has developed, and many contaminated properties have been investigated and remediated exclusively with the proceeds from old insurance policies. In fact, it is becoming more and more common for certain types of businesses to purchase insurance that specifically covers any necessary environmental cleanup.

Many contaminated properties have been investigated and remediated exclusively with the proceeds from old insurance policies.

Policies issued prior to the 1980s often did not exclude coverage for pollution or contamination. In any case, all insurance records should be obtained and examined for potential coverage. Current California case law provides that actual litigation must be commenced to force an insurer to comply with its duty to defend and indemnify the insured in a matter of environmental contamination. However, rather than incur the additional costs of litigation, many insurance companies have extended some form of coverage.

Governmental Funding Sources

While perhaps not quite as helpful as insurance proceeds, various government funds have been set up to assist in cleanup efforts. Some of these exist more in name than in reality, due to the lack of sufficient funding.

Underground Storage Tank Cleanup Fund. One very successful program is the state's Underground Storage Tank Cleanup Fund (UST Fund). The UST Fund receives its revenue from a fee that is levied on each gallon of petroleum fuel stored in an underground tank. Authorized reimbursement commitments from the UST Fund vary from year to year, but have reached almost $240 million on an annual basis.

Authorized reimbursement commitments from the UST Fund vary from year to year, but have reached almost $240 million on an annual basis.

For the uninitiated, the rules and procedures governing access to the up to $1.5 million per UST release site can be daunting, but literally hundreds of millions of dollars have been given to former owners and operators of leaky USTs to reimburse them for cleanup. The program is currently scheduled to sunset in 2016.

CLEAN = Cleanup Loans and Environmental Assistance to Neighborhoods

UST = Underground storage tank

Cleanup Loans and Environmental Assistance to Neighborhoods Program. DTSC's Cleanup Loans and Environmental Assistance to Neighborhoods (CLEAN) Program was enacted in 2000 and can be found at section 25395.22 *et seq.* The CLEAN program is intended to establish new financial incentives to encourage property owners, developers, community groups, and local governments/redevelopment agencies to redevelop abandoned and underutilized urban properties. DTSC maintains a list of all eligible urban areas.

PEA = Preliminary Endangerment Assessment

The CLEAN program has two main components:

- *Investigating Site Contamination Program.* This program provides low-interest loans of up to $100,000 to conduct a Preliminary Endangerment Assessment (PEA). Based on the PEA, if redevelopment of the subject property is determined to be economically infeasible, then up to 75 percent of the loan can be waived.
- *Cleanup Loans.* This program provides low-interest loans of up to $2.5 million for the cleanup or removal of hazardous materials where redevelopment is likely to have a beneficial impact on a community's property values, economic vitality, and quality of life.

Unfortunately, the CLEAN Program quickly ran into a funding crisis, and whether it will accomplish its noble goal or is just another well-intentioned but underfunded government program remains to be seen. At the time of publication, DTSC was working out program administrative details.

Conclusion

While the complexity and potential liability of dealing with a contaminated property can be daunting, a number of statutes and programs are designed to assist redevelopers facing environmental issues. Early involvement of appropriate professionals can assure an adequate assessment of contamination and the development of a plan to manage the issues of liability, cost, and realistic cleanup goals in relation to a site's intended future use. With a proper recognition of the risk, a contaminated parcel should not prove to be an insurmountable obstacle to redevelopment.

Early involvement of appropriate professionals can assure an adequate assessment of contamination and the development of a plan to manage the issues of liability, cost, and realistic cleanup goals.

7

Relocation

To carry out the goals and objectives of redevelopment, redevelopment agencies may acquire, assemble, and dispose of property that may result in the displacement of residents or businesses.

To carry out the goals and objectives of redevelopment, redevelopment agencies may acquire, assemble, and dispose of property that may result in the displacement of residents or businesses. In such instances, agencies must comply with the applicable relocation law, discussed below.

History and the Law

In 1968, the U.S. Congress adopted the Federal Aid Highway Act. This was the first legislation to provide a more equitable and just system of relocation payments for both displaced tenants and property owners. However, it was the Uniform Relocation Assistance and Real Property Acquisition Policies Act of 1970 (42 U.S.C. § 4601 *et seq.*) (Federal Act) that guaranteed that all displaced persons would be entitled to certain assistance, payments, and rights. The Federal Act was adopted to establish a uniform policy with respect to the fair and equitable treatment of persons displaced; provide compensation to those persons being displaced to assist in their moving expenses and increased expenses at their new replacement dwellings; and ensure that no persons would be displaced from their dwellings until comparable decent, safe, and sanitary replacement housing was available. As amended by the Uniform Relocation Act Amendments of 1987, the Federal Act requires that the head of each federal agency adopt regulations and implement procedures consistent with Department of Transportation (DOT) regulations and procedures contained in 49 Code of Federal Regulations, section 24.1 *et seq.* (the "Federal DOT Guidelines").

In response to the Federal Act, California adopted the California Relocation Assistance Act of 1970 (Gov. Code § 7260 *et seq.*) (the State Act), requiring all state public entities that cause displacement of residents and

The Uniform Relocation Assistance and Real Property Acquisition Policies Act of 1970 guaranteed that all displaced persons would be entitled to certain assistance, payments, and rights.

DOT = Department of Transportation

businesses when carrying out their projects to provide relocation assistance and payments patterned after those provided in the Federal Act. The State Act also requires that all public entities causing displacement adopt guidelines for relocation assistance and real property acquisition consistent with the Relocation Assistance and Real Property Acquisition Guidelines adopted by the California Department of Housing and Community Development (Cal. Code Regs., tit. 25, § 6000 *et seq.*) (State Guidelines).

When redevelopment agencies use federal funds, the State Act provides that, in general, redevelopment agencies must follow the Federal Act.

When redevelopment agencies use federal funds, the State Act provides that, in general, redevelopment agencies must follow the Federal Act. However, if any provision of the State Act allows relocation benefits or assistance not covered by or in excess of the Federal Act, the State's provision shall also apply. *United Auto Workers v. Department of Transportation* (1993) 20 Cal. App. 4th 1462 held that the Federal Act's applicability cannot be used to bar a claim under the State Act, since the Federal Act establishes the minimum and not the maximum benefits for federally assisted projects. The Federal Act requires federal agencies whose programs may cause displacement to adopt relocation guidelines for those programs that are consistent with Federal DOT Guidelines.

CDBG = Community Development Block Grant

HUD = U.S. Department of Housing and Urban Development

In general, for federal projects using other than Community Development Block Grant (CDBG) funds, redevelopment agencies must follow certain provisions of the Federal DOT Guidelines. However, when displacing low- and moderate-income tenants with CDBG funds, redevelopment agencies must follow the relocation guidelines adopted by the U.S. Department of Housing and Urban Development, contained in 24 Code of Federal Regulations, Part 42 (Federal HUD Guidelines). When using federal funds, agencies should consult the specific program relocation guideline requirements to ascertain whether the Federal DOT Guidelines apply or whether the federal agency providing the funding has adopted any additional relocation guidelines or other requirements.

In addition to the State Act, redevelopment agencies are also subject to the specific relocation provisions in Article 9 of the Community Redevelopment Law.

In addition to the State Act, redevelopment agencies are also subject to the specific relocation provisions in Article 9 of the Community Redevelopment Law. § 33410 *et seq.* The Community Redevelopment Law includes provisions already required under the State Act, such as preparation of a method or plan for relocation, making payments, and providing relocation advisory assistance. In addition, Article 9 includes provisions authorizing a redevelopment agency to use any public or private funds to carry out its relocation obligations and creating within each community that has a redevelopment agency a relocation appeals board to hear complaints brought by residents being displaced.

Requirements Prior to Displacement

Prior to undertaking or participating in a project that will result in displacement of any residents or businesses, redevelopment agencies must:

- Adopt relocation rules and regulations

- Provide certain determinations and assurances
- If applicable, adopt a relocation plan

Agency Relocation Rules and Regulations

The agency must adopt rules and regulations in accordance with the State Guidelines to implement payments and administer relocation assistance under the State Act. Gov. Code § 7267.8; Cal. Code Regs., tit. 25, § 6006. Generally, an agency either adopts its community's relocation rules and regulations or adopts the State Guidelines. Whichever alternative is chosen, the agency's rules and regulations should provide that, if the State Act or State Guidelines are amended, agency rules and regulations are automatically amended to be consistent with the new amendments.

Generally, an agency either adopts its community's relocation rules and regulations or adopts the State Guidelines.

If the redevelopment agency is carrying out a federally assisted project, the agency must adopt rules and regulations consistent with the Federal Act and the applicable federal guidelines.

Prior Determinations/Assurances

Section 6010 of the State Guidelines provides that no public entity may proceed with any phase of a project or other activity that will result in the displacement of any person, business, or farm until it determines that:

- Fair and reasonable relocation payments will be provided to eligible persons. Cal. Code Regs., tit. 25, § 6010(a)(1).
- A relocation assistance program will be established. Cal. Code Regs., tit. 25, § 6010(a)(2).
- Eligible persons will be adequately informed of the assistance, benefits, policies, practices, and procedures—including grievance procedures—provided for in the State Guidelines. Cal. Code Regs., tit. 25, § 6010(a)(3).
- Based upon a recent survey and analysis of both the housing needs of persons displaced and the availability of comparable replacement housing—and considering competing demands for that housing—comparable replacement dwellings sufficient in number, size, and cost for the eligible persons who require them will be available or provided, if necessary, within a reasonable period of time prior to displacement. Cal. Code Regs., tit. 25, § 6010(a)(4).

    Note. In order to make this determination, and if a relocation plan that would contain the required survey information is not required, this survey must be initiated within 60 days following the initiation of negotiations. In addition, if 15 or more households are being displaced, the survey results must be submitted for review to local housing, development, and planning agencies and compared to other existing information on housing availability. Cal. Code Regs., tit. 25, § 6052.

- Adequate provisions have been made to provide orderly, timely, and efficient relocation of eligible persons to comparable replacement housing that is available without regard to race, color, religion, sex, marital status, or national origin with minimum hardship to those affected. Cal. Code Regs., tit. 25, § 6008(c)(3).
- If applicable, a relocation plan will be prepared.

These findings, usually made by agency resolution, must precede an acquisition of property that will result in displacement.

Under section 4630 of the Federal Act, federal agencies shall not approve any contract or agreement with, or any grant to, any state agency, including a redevelopment agency, that is receiving federal financial assistance unless the agency assures that:

- Displaced persons will receive fair and reasonable relocation payments and assistance, as provided in the Federal Act.
- Relocation assistance programs offering services described in the Federal Act shall be provided.
- Within a reasonable period of time prior to displacement, comparable replacement dwellings will be available.

A redevelopment agency generally adopts a resolution making these assurances to the applicable federal agency.

The Community Redevelopment Law also requires the legislative body to make certain findings at the time a redevelopment plan is adopted if the project may result in residential displacement. § 33367.

Relocation Plans

At the time of adoption, a proposed redevelopment plan should include a general relocation plan as part of the agency's report to the legislative body.

Sections 33411 and 33411.1 require redevelopment agencies to develop a method or plan for the relocation of residents. At the time of adoption, a proposed redevelopment plan should include a general relocation plan as part of the agency's report to the legislative body. § 33352. The relocation plan is general in nature because specifics, such as where and when displacement may occur, are usually not known at the time the redevelopment plan is adopted. The relocation plan should include the prior determinations and assurances mentioned earlier, the agency's proposed relocation assistance advisory program, and the agency's intent to carry out relocation in accordance with the State Act and State Guidelines—or, if applicable, the Federal Act and appropriate federal guidelines.

HCD = Department of Housing and Community Development

Section 6038 of the State Guidelines provides that, in the event the project will displace 15 or fewer households, the agency may complete the Model Relocation Plan offered by the Department of Housing and Community Development (HCD), rather than preparing a relocation plan for the project. Cal. Code Regs., tit. 25, § 6038. Section 6038 further provides that any displaced person or interested organization may petition HCD to review the relocation plan, and that if the implementation of the relocation plan is delayed by more than one year, the plan must be updated prior to implementation of the program. A copy of the plan must be submitted for review to the relocation committee formed for the project 30 days prior to submission to the legislative body, if such a committee is formed in an effort to encourage citizen participation.

Section 24.205(a) of the Federal DOT Guidelines requires that projects that will displace persons be planned in a manner that will minimize adverse impacts of displacement and advises that this planning may include a relocation survey or study; however, it does not specifically require a written relocation plan. 49 C.F.R. § 24.205(a).

Section 24.205(a) of the Federal DOT Guidelines requires that projects that will displace persons be planned in a manner that will minimize adverse impacts of displacement.

The Federal HUD Guidelines, which pertain only to the displacement of low- and moderate-income residential tenants as a result of CDBG activities, require agencies to adopt, make public, and certify that they are following a residential antidisplacement and relocation assistance plan in accordance with section 42.325 of the Federal HUD Guidelines. 24 C.F.R. § 42.325.

Relocation Assistance Advisory Program

Both the State Act and the Federal Act require agencies to provide a relocation assistance advisory program for persons to be displaced. The minimum requirements of the program under the State Act are contained in section 6040 of the State Guidelines (Cal. Code Regs., tit. 25, § 6040 *et seq.*) and under the Federal Act in section 24.205(c) of the Federal DOT Guidelines (49 C.F.R. § 24.205(c)). In general, however, state and federal requirements are substantially the same. Both require the relocation assistance advisory program to include measures, facilities, or services that will enable the agency to:

Both the State Act and the Federal Act require agencies to provide a relocation assistance advisory program for persons to be displaced. In general, the state and federal requirements are substantially the same.

- Determine the needs and preferences of persons to be displaced
- Provide current and continuing information on the availability, sales prices, and rentals of comparable replacement dwellings and comparable commercial properties and locations for displaced businesses
- Inform all eligible persons to be displaced of the availability of relocation benefits and assistance and eligibility requirements
- Assure eligible persons displaced from their dwellings that within a reasonable period of time prior to displacement comparable replacement housing will be available, and assist these displaced persons in obtaining and moving to comparable replacement dwellings
- Assist each eligible person displaced from a business or farm operation to obtain and become established in a suitable replacement location
- Advise displaced persons of the agency's grievance procedures and eviction policies

Guadalupe River Park winds through downtown San Jose. It includes 130 acres, 2.6 miles of trails and 27 plazas, and was jointly developed by the San Jose Redevelopment Agency, U.S. Army Corps of Engineers and Santa Clara Valley Water District.

Key Elements of a Successful Relocation Program

The key elements of a successful relocation program are to inform, assist, and make payments.

Information

The relocation program should—

- Inform persons to be displaced as early as possible of the relocation assistance and benefits for which they may be eligible and keep them informed throughout the entire process. Make sure they know the eligibility requirements for the respective payments so that they do not jeopardize their eligibility.

- Make sure all displacees receive all the required written notices described in the notices section.

- Advise them as early as possible of the agency's projected time schedule for displacement and inform them about any projected schedule changes.

- It is highly recommended that the relocation program be explained in person. The agency's representative should set up a meeting and be prepared to explain the written informational statement the displacee is required to receive. At this first meeting, the agency representative should also interview the person and obtain as much information as possible to establish the displacee's relocation needs and the types of payments for which the displacee is eligible.

The agency representative should be prepared to spend as much time as necessary at this first meeting, as it is the foundation of the relationship for the relocation process. If all goes well, by the end of the first meeting, displacees will feel they know what is going on, when and how they will be affected, how they will be assisted, and who they need to contact if they have any questions or need assistance.

In addition, the agency representative should have a good understanding of the type of replacement dwelling or business location required, including size, special features (for example, no steps, close to public transportation for residents, or rollup doors or special electrical needs for businesses), proximity to services, and the displacee's preferences as far as timing and affordability. The agency representative should also have adequate information to estimate the relocation costs to the agency.

- Assist displaced persons in completing applications for payments and benefits, and provide other services to help minimize their hardship—such as providing services to ensure nondiscrimination in the relocation process and providing information and referrals on other types of state or federal assistance that may be available

Comparable Replacement Dwelling Units

No eligible person can be required to move from a dwelling unit unless—within a reasonable time prior to displacement—a comparable replacement dwelling is made available.

A comparable replacement dwelling unit must be decent, safe, and sanitary as defined in section 6008(d) of the State Guidelines. Cal. Code Regs., tit. 25, § 6008(d). Second, it must be within the financial means of the displaced person. Rental housing is within the financial means of the displaced person if the monthly rental cost including utilities and other reasonable recurring expenses, does not exceed thirty percent of the person's average monthly income. Average monthly income means gross income, as defined in section 6008(l) of the State Guidelines, divided by 12. For displaced homeowners, a replacement dwelling is within the financial means of the displaced person if the purchase price plus related increased interest costs and other reasonable expenses (including closing costs) does not exceed the total compensation paid by the agency for the property plus any replacement housing payments made by the agency to the person. Third, the replacement dwelling must be comparable with respect to the number of rooms, habitable space, and type and quality of construction, but not be lesser in rooms or living space than necessary to accommodate the displaced person. This does not mean a strict feature-by-feature comparability; however, the replacement dwelling should have the same basic principal features as the acquired dwelling. Fourth, the replacement dwelling must not be in an area subject to unreasonable, adverse environmental conditions. Fifth, the location of the replacement dwelling generally must not be less desirable than the location of the displaced person's dwelling with respect to public utilities, facilities, services, and the displaced person's place of employment. If the displaced person wishes to stay in his or her existing neighborhood, the agency is additionally required to make every reasonable effort to relocate that person in or near his or her existing neighborhood. Sixth, the replacement dwelling must be available on the private market to the displaced person.

Required Notices to Persons Being Displaced

Within 60 days following the initiation of negotiations to acquire property, but not later than the close of escrow, and not less than 90 days in advance of requiring displacement, the agency is required to provide written information to the occupants describing the relocation benefits and assistance available, the eligibility requirements, and any other agency procedures and policies, such as the agency's eviction policy and grievance procedures. *See* Attachment A of the State Guidelines for a detailed list of the information to be provided. The information should also include the following two statements, which will fulfill the agency's requirement to advise displacees of these requirements:

- No eligible persons shall be required to move from a dwelling unless comparable replacement dwellings are available to them within a reasonable period of time prior to displacement.
- No eligible persons occupying property shall be required to move from a dwelling or to move a business or farm operation without at least 90 days' written notice from the agency requiring the displacement.

Forms of Assistance

The agency may assist displacees in the following ways:

- Locating potential new replacement dwellings or business locations and providing written notice to the displacee of each referral given. Typical sources are newspapers, rental services, and real estate offices.
- Where applicable and possible, obtaining assistance from other public agencies—for example, housing authorities for subsidized housing and the Small Business Administration for businesses.
- Obtaining moving bids and filing claims for relocation payments.
- Contacting potential landlords, real estate brokers, or other agencies or persons that may need to be assured that the displacees will be receiving monies for the purpose of paying rental expenses, such as first and last month's rent and security deposits or, for homeowner-occupants, the monies for the downpayment or purchase price.
- Inspecting replacement dwelling units immediately to make sure they are decent, safe, and sanitary. A displacee could be ineligible for relocation payments if the replacement dwelling unit does not meet this requirement.

Payments

The agency should provide relocation payments as soon as possible after the necessary claim forms have been filed, making sure that its accounting systems for relocation payments are set up for maximum expediency. Prompt payments can be essential to a displacee's ability to secure a replacement location. Landlords and real estate brokers have no obligation to hold an available house without the appropriate deposit, and displacees often need their relocation monies for the deposit.

The Agency's Relocation Representative

The agency's relocation representative should be (1) knowledgeable about the relocation benefits and assistance requirements, (2) readily available to provide assistance and answer questions, and (3) fully aware that, although employed by the agency, he or she must ensure that the displacees are aware of and receive the benefits and assistance to which they are entitled under the law. In carrying out a relocation program, the agency must follow the process and procedures set forth in the State Act and State Guidelines (or, if applicable, the Federal Act and appropriate federal guidelines). ■

Agencies must make written offers of comparable replacement housing prior to requiring displacement; section 6042(c) of the State Guidelines provides that the number of offers determined to be reasonable should be not less than three.

Agencies must make written offers of comparable replacement housing prior to requiring displacement. This requirement is fulfilled if the agency offers reasonable choices for replacement housing that are refused; section 6042(c) of the State Guidelines provides that the number of offers determined to be reasonable should be not less than three. Cal. Code Regs., tit. 25, § 6042(c).

For purposes of triggering the State Guidelines notice requirements, the "initiation of negotiations" for a public entity acquisition occurs when the acquiring entity makes its initial written offer to purchase the property. For the purposes of private acquisitions of real property that implement an agreement with a public entity, the State Guidelines define "initiation of negotiations" as the later of the date of acquisition or the date of the written agreement between the private entity and the public entity for purposes of acquiring or developing the property for the project.

Relocation Payments to Displaced Persons

In order to be eligible for any relocation payments, a person must qualify as a "displaced person," which, according to section 7260(c) of the State Act, means both of the following:

- Any person who moves from real property, or who moves his or her personal property from real property, either
  - As a direct result of a written notice of intent to acquire or the acquisition of the real property, in whole or in part, for a program or project undertaken by a public entity or by any person having an agreement with or acting on behalf of a public entity, or
  - As a direct result of the rehabilitation, demolition, or other displacing activity the public entity may prescribe under a program or project undertaken by a public entity of real property on which the person is a residential tenant (which includes residents of a residential hotel unit and residents of employee housing) or conducts a business or farm operation in any case in which the public entity determines that the displacement is permanent.
- Solely for the purposes of receiving relocation advisory assistance and moving expenses, any person who moves from real property, or moves his or her personal property from real property, either
  - As a direct result of a written notice of intent to acquire or the acquisition of other real property, in whole or in part, on which the person conducts a business or

This apartment complex in downtown San Jose includes 323 rental apartments, with 65 for very low-income households, retail space, a business center and multi-media conference room, and a two-level subterranean parking garage.

farm operation for a program or project undertaken by a public entity, or

- As a direct result of the rehabilitation, demolition or other displacing activity the public entity may prescribe under a program or project undertaken by a public entity of other real property on which the person conducts a business or farm operation in any case in which the public entity determines that the displacement is permanent.

Gov. Code § 7260 *et seq.*

A "displaced person" includes persons displaced as a result of public action where they are displaced as a result of an owner participation agreement or an acquisition carried out by a private person for or in connection with a public use where the public entity is otherwise empowered to acquire the property to carry out the public use.

A "displaced person" does not include any of the following:

- Any person in unlawful occupancy of displacement dwellings.
- Any person whose right of possession at the time of moving arose after the date the public entity acquired the real property.[1] However, this does not include persons or families of low- and moderate-income who are occupants of housing that was made available to them on a permanent basis by a public agency and who are required to move from the housing.
- Any person who has occupied the real property for the purpose of obtaining relocation assistance.
- Any person who occupies the property for a period subject to termination when the property is needed for the program or project (other than a person who was an occupant of the property at the time it was acquired).

The definitions of "displaced person" set forth in section 24.2 of the Federal DOT Guidelines, which is generally applicable when using federal funds, and section 570.606(b)(2) of the Federal HUD Guidelines, which is applicable when displacing low- or moderate-income persons for projects using federal CDBG funds, are set forth in Appendix C.

Payments for Businesses

Any business, except the lessee of a farm operation where the agency acquires the property and assumes all the terms of the lease, that meets the qualifications and eligibility requirements of a "displaced person" is entitled to relocation payments for the following:

A "displaced person" does not include any person in unlawful occupancy of displacement dwellings, or any person who has occupied the real property for the purpose of obtaining relocation assistance.

---

1. Although post-acquisition tenants are not displaced persons and are therefore not eligible for relocation assistance and benefits, it is recommended that an agency, prior to renting property to a post-acquisition tenant, obtain a written acknowledgement that the tenant is aware of the status of the property and the agency's future plans and that he or she will not be eligible for relocation assistance or payments when the agency terminates the tenancy.

- Actual moving and related expenses.
- Direct losses of tangible personal property as a result of moving or discontinuing a business (not to exceed the cost of relocating the personal property).
- Actual and reasonable expenses in searching for a replacement business, not to exceed $1,000.
- Actual and reasonable expenses necessary to reestablish a displaced farm, nonprofit organization, or small business at its new site, not to exceed $10,000. (A "small business" means a business with 500 or fewer employees.)

Although certain categories of the above payments contain limits, no limit applies to the cumulative total of the actual reasonable moving expenses.

Section 6090(i) of the State Guidelines and section 24.304 of the Federal DOT Guidelines define a business reestablishment expense and include a nonexclusive list of eligible and ineligible expenses.

Section 6090(i) of the State Guidelines and Federal DOT Guidelines section 24.304 include a list of eligible and ineligible expenses.

If the agency is satisfied that a business cannot be relocated without substantial loss of patronage—and that it is not part of a commercial enterprise having at least one other establishment not being acquired engaged in the same or similar business—the business may elect to receive an alternative payment in lieu of the actual moving and related expenses in an amount equal to the average annual net earnings of the business, but the payment shall not be less than $1,000 nor more than $20,000. "Average annual net earnings" is defined in section 6100(f) of the State Guidelines. Cal. Code Regs., tit. 25, § 6100(f). For the agency to be able to determine the amount of the payment, businesses must submit state income tax records, financial statements, and accounting records to the agency for confidential use. If the business is an outdoor advertising display, this payment is limited to the amount necessary to physically move or replace the display.

For the agency to be able to determine the amount of the payment, businesses must submit state income tax records, financial statements, and accounting records to the agency for confidential use.

Note. The revised State Guidelines state that a condition of eligibility for the alternate payment in lieu of actual moving expenses is that the business is not part of a commercial enterprise having "no more than" [sic] three other establishments not being acquired for a project and which is engaged in the same or similar business. The existing statute states that the business must not be a part of a commercial enterprise having at least one other business establishment that is not being acquired. Presumably, the statute controls.

Payments for Homeowner-Occupants

Homeowner-occupants may receive either the actual cost of their moving expenses or an alternate fixed moving expense payment.

All homeowner-occupants who qualify as displaced persons may receive either the actual cost of their moving expenses or an alternate fixed moving expense payment to be determined according to a schedule established by the redevelopment agency and consistent with the schedule approved by the Federal Highway Administration. Gov. Code § 7262(b); 49 C.F.R. § 24.302. Effective June 15, 2005, the Federal Highway Administration schedule provides for a moving expense fixed payment for tenants who do not own furniture in the amount of $400 for the first room and $65 for each additional room. For tenants or homeowner-occupants who own their furniture, the fixed moving expense payment is equal to $625 for one room, $800 for two rooms, $1,000 for three rooms, $1,175 for four rooms, $1,425 for five rooms, $1,650 for six rooms, $1,900 for seven rooms, $2,150 for eight rooms, and $225 for each additional room. This schedule is updated periodically, therefore, the payment amounts should be confirmed prior to making these payments.

The fixed moving expense payment schedule is updated periodically, therefore, the payment amounts should be confirmed prior to making these payments.

In addition, eligible homeowners who have occupied the property being acquired for not less than 180 days prior to the initiation of negotiations (the date the public entity makes the first written offer to acquire the property) shall be eligible for a replacement housing payment of up to $22,500, which shall be based on specific factors. Gov. Code § 7263; 42 U.S.C. § 4623(a).

Payments for Residential Tenants

All residential tenants who qualify as displaced persons are eligible for the same moving expenses as those for homeowner-occupants. In addition, if they have occupied the rental dwelling unit from which they are being displaced for at least 90 days prior to the initiation of negotiations, these tenants are entitled to receive a replacement housing payment of up to $5,250, which is calculated by determining the additional amount necessary to enable a person to lease or rent a comparable replacement dwelling for a period not to exceed 42 months. (The Federal HUD Guidelines compute this payment for a 60-month period.) Chapter 597 of the Statutes of 1997 revised the basis for the calculation of the replacement housing payment for tenants from 48 months to 42 months, in order to make the state requirements consistent with the requirements of the Federal Act. However, the bill making this revision included specific "grandfathering" provisions, and as a result the 48 month calculation period still applies to tenants displaced pursuant to a relocation plan submitted to HCD or a local relocation committee prior to January 1, 1998, and to tenants displaced pursuant to an acquisition process initiated prior to January 1, 1998.

Wrigley Market Place represented a joint venture between Long Beach and the Metropolitan Transportation Authority, in conjunction with a private developer, to combine neighborhood-serving retail with a park-and-ride facility for light rail commuters.

Tenants eligible for this payment may elect to apply the payment to a downpayment and other incidental expenses incurred for the purchase of a decent, safe, and sanitary replacement dwelling. Homeowner-occupants who do not meet the length of residency requirements for the replacement housing payment for homeowners may also be eligible for this payment. *See* Payments for Homeowner-Occupants, above.

Tenants residing in any rental project who are temporarily displaced for one year or less as part of a rehabilitation project shall not be eligible for permanent housing assistance (replacement housing payments) provided the following conditions are met:

- The property is a "qualified affordable housing preservation project" as defined in subparagraph (a) of section 7262.5 of the Government Code.
- The resident is offered the right to return to his or her original unit, or a comparable unit in the same complex if his or her original unit is not otherwise available due to the rehabilitation, with rent for the first 12 months after that return being the lower of: up to five percent higher than the rent at the time of displacement or up to thirty percent of household income.
- The estimated time of displacement is reasonable, and the temporary unit is not unreasonably affected by the effects of the construction, taking into consideration the ages and physical conditions of the members of the displaced household.
- All other financial benefits and services otherwise required under the State Act are provided to the residents temporarily displaced from their units, including relocation to a comparable replacement unit. Residents shall be temporarily relocated to a unit within the same complex or to a unit located reasonably near the complex if that unit is in a comparable location.

Authority to Exceed Minimum Payments

Government Code section 7272.3 authorizes a redevelopment agency to exceed the maximum relocation assistance payments established in the State Act. In these cases, an agency should adopt a policy establishing the requirements and conditions for providing excess payments so that it is clear that the payments are not arbitrary but are based on certain uniform requirements and conditions.

Government Code section 7272.3 authorizes a redevelopment agency to exceed the maximum relocation assistance payments established in the State Act.

Time Limit for Submitting Claims

Under the State Guidelines, all claims for relocation benefits must be submitted to the agency within 18 months of the date on which the claimant receives final payment for the property or the date on which the claimant moves, whichever is later (State Guidelines § 6088), unless the agency extends this period upon a proper showing of good cause. In *Bi-Rite Meat and Provisions Co. v. Redevelopment Agency of the City of Hawaiian Gardens* (2007) 156 Cal. App. 4th 1419, the Court of Appeal concluded that the term "moves," as used in section 6088 of the State Guidelines, means "moves from" real property, and upheld the agency's finding of "no good cause" to extend the filing period.

Other Major Components of the Relocation Law and Process

Grievance Procedures

Both section 6150 of the State Guidelines and section 24.10 of the Federal DOT Guidelines require a method whereby any person who feels aggrieved by a determination regarding eligibility for (or the amount of) a payment may have the public entity review the application. In the case of redevelopment agencies, the review is to be conducted by a relocation appeals board established by section 33417.5 of the Community Redevelopment Law.

Eviction Policies

Section 6058 of the State Guidelines states that upon the public entity's acquisition of property, the public entity may only evict persons for one or more of the following reasons:

- Failure to pay rent, except in those cases where failure to pay is due to the lessor's failure to keep the premises in habitable condition, is the result of harassment or retaliatory action, or is the result of discontinuation or substantial interruption of services
- Performance of a dangerous illegal act in the unit
- Material breach of the rental agreement and failure to correct breach within 30 days of notice
- Maintenance of a nuisance and failure to abate within a reasonable time following notice
- Refusal to accept one of a reasonable number of offers of replacement dwellings
- The eviction is required by state or local law and cannot be prevented by reasonable efforts on the part of the public entity

Cal. Code Regs., tit. 25, § 6058

Section 24.206 of the Federal DOT Guidelines states that eviction for cause must conform to applicable state or local law. 49 C.F.R. § 24.206.

The State Guidelines and Federal DOT Guidelines differ as to the effect eviction has on eligibility for relocation payments. Under the State Guidelines, eviction does not affect a displaced person's eligibility for relocation payments. Under the Federal DOT Guidelines, any person who occupies the real property lawfully on the date negotiations are initiated is presumed to be entitled to relocation payments unless the agency determines that:

- The person received an eviction notice prior to the initiation of negotiations and, as a result of that notice, is later evicted, or
- The person is evicted after negotiations are initiated for serious or repeated violation of material terms of the lease or occupancy agreement, and
- In either of these two situations, the eviction was not undertaken for the purpose of evading the obligation to make available the payments and other assistance set forth in the Federal DOT Guidelines.

Last Resort Housing

Both the State Guidelines and the Federal DOT Guidelines provide authority for agencies to develop or construct replacement housing or make payments in excess of the stated maximum amounts as a last resort, if comparable replacement housing will not be available when needed to carry out the project on a timely basis.

Both the State and Federal DOT Guidelines provide authority for agencies to develop or construct replacement housing or make payments in excess of the stated maximum amounts as a last resort.

Good Record Keeping

In carrying out any relocation program it is essential to have a good record of all contacts and information given to persons being displaced. Not only should the agency keep copies of every letter or notice provided, but a record of any contacts made in person or on the telephone should also be kept. In addition, the agency should have a record of every replacement referral to businesses and residents (both owners and tenants) and a record of every payment made. Agency records in sufficient detail to demonstrate compliance are evidence that it has carried out the relocation program, provided assistance, and made the payments required by the law.

Not only should the agency keep copies of every letter or notice provided, but a record of any contacts made in person or on the telephone should also be kept.

Relocation Payments Not Considered Income

Section 7269 of the State Act and section 4636 of the Federal Act both provide that relocation payments shall not be considered income for the purposes of taxes or for purposes of income or resources to any recipient of public assistance. This is to prevent a person who receives Social Security or public assistance payments from having those payments reduced by the amount received under the State Act or Federal Act.

Property "Offered for Sale" by Owner-Occupant

An agency is not required to provide relocation assistance and benefits under the State Act if it purchases property that is (1) "offered for sale," as defined in Government Code section 7277, by the owner, (2) being sold at execution or foreclosure sale, or (3) being sold as a result of a court order or under court supervision, if the following circumstances exist: (1) the property being sold is either occupied by the owner or is unoccupied; (2) the offer for sale is not induced by public entity disposition, planned condemnation, or redevelopment of surrounding lands; (3) the sale price is fair market value or less, as determined by a qualified appraiser; and (4) no federal funds are involved in the acquisition, construction, or project development.

If it is considering the purchase of property, an agency, at the time of making an offer to acquire the property, must notify the owner in writing of its plans for developing the property to be acquired or the surrounding property, and of any relocation assistance and benefits provided pursuant to the State Act that the property owner may be forgoing (due to the owner's decision to offer the property for sale prior to the agency's actual immediate or impending need of the property).

The Federal DOT Guidelines contain a similar exception to the requirement to provide relocation assistance and benefits to persons who voluntarily convey property to an agency. DOT Guidelines §§ 24.2(a)(9)(ii)(H) (definition of "displaced person"), 24.101(a)(2), and 24.101(b)(1) or (2).

Utility Relocation

Agencies are not responsible for the costs of relocating utility lines and facilities from vacated and abandoned streets in furtherance of a redevelopment project. The common law view is that a public utility accepts franchise rights in a public right-of-way subject to an implied obligation to relocate its facilities at its own expense when necessary to make way for proper governmental use of the streets. California adheres to the common law view unless the legislature has enacted a statute specifically providing for compensation. *Pacific Tel. and Tel. Co. v. Redevelopment Agency of the City of Glendale* (1978) 87 Cal. App. 3d 296.

Agencies are not responsible for the costs of relocating utility lines and facilities from vacated and abandoned streets in furtherance of a redevelopment project.

8
Property Disposition

General Rules

The corollary function to the acquisition of property by a redevelopment agency is its disposition of property for redevelopment purposes. The Community Redevelopment Law provides redevelopment agencies with broad powers concerning the disposition of real property.

Section 33430 provides that a redevelopment agency "may, within the survey area or for purposes of redevelopment, sell, lease, for a period not to exceed 99 years, exchange, subdivide, transfer, assign, pledge, encumber by mortgage, deed of trust, or otherwise, or otherwise dispose of any real or personal property or any interest in property." An agency need not undertake a public bidding process, as long as a public hearing is held prior to the sale or lease of land. § 33431. California Redevelopment Law thus empowers redevelopment agencies to negotiate directly with prospective developers for the disposition of property without undertaking any bidding or other competitive process. The authority to dispose of property without public bidding distinguishes redevelopment agencies from other public entities and affords agencies great flexibility in the developer selection process.

Redevelopment agencies are also permitted to dispose of property for less than its acquisition cost. However the agency has an obligation to secure from a redeveloper a price not less than that justified by the development opportunity, given the use, constraints, and criteria imposed by the agency. Particularly since the cost of acquisition often includes purchase of improvements that still have a useful life (although not for purposes that are consistent with the goals of the redevelopment plan) and may involve relocation costs, the price justified by the new development opportunity is often less than the acquisition cost.

Because a redevelopment agency is using public dollars to write down land for private development, public hearings are required in order to assure that agency powers are used prudently.

DIR = Department of Industrial Relations

Generally, the fair reuse value is less than the value at the highest and best use because a redevelopment agency imposes on a developer specific development conditions that are more restrictive than what would be permitted under highest and best use.

The difference between the cost to the agency and the disposition price is referred to as a "land write-down." Because a redevelopment agency is using public dollars to write down land for private development, public hearings are required—together with disclosure of the terms of the sale or lease—in order to assure that agency powers are used prudently. *Contra Costa Theatre, Inc. v. Redevelopment Agency* (1982) 131 Cal. App. 3d 860, 865. Another consideration now for agencies and developers to weigh is whether a "land write-down" will trigger the requirement that prevailing wages be paid on the project. Agencies and developers should also be aware that under current Department of Industrial Relations (DIR) rulings, a land "write-down" or transfer of property for less than "fair market price" will be deemed to constitute a "payment of public funds" triggering an obligation to pay prevailing wages. *See* Public Works Case No. 2004-035, *Santa Ana Transit Village*. For a more detailed discussion of the recent changes in prevailing wage law, see page 193–197.

Where tax-increment funds have been used, either directly or indirectly, to acquire the property, the legislature requires that the agency disclose certain information and that the agency's legislative body make certain findings before it approves the disposition of such property by sale or lease. § 33433. The legislative body must analyze the proposed transaction as to:

- Whether the consideration is not less than the fair reuse value of the property at the use and with the covenants, conditions, and criteria authorized by the sale or lease

- How the consideration compares to the fair market value of the property at its highest and best use in accordance with the redevelopment plan

In order to support the required findings, the redevelopment agency must prepare a report that describes both the "fair reuse value" and the fair market value of the property at its highest and best use in accordance with the redevelopment plan. Generally, the fair reuse value is less than the value at the highest and best use because a redevelopment agency (as the seller of the property) imposes on a developer specific development conditions, covenants, and criteria that are more restrictive than what would be permitted under highest and best use. These requirements have a negative impact, often significant, on the value of the development opportunity and, therefore, of the property.

Agency controls that affect property value can include its precise use, the scale of permitted development, the exterior design and appearance of the project, and a precise timetable for commencing and completing development. On a hypothetical property where the highest and best use (and, therefore, the highest land value) might be for a retail shopping center, the redevelopment agency may instead require that the property be used for an affordable housing project. The agency might further require expensive underground or structured parking at an additional cost not supported by the project's rents. All such requirements tend to have a negative impact on the land value.

In contrast to reuse value, highest and best use value is governed by the redevelopment plan, which usually contains only very broad limitations on the use of the property. Highest and best use is also governed by zoning, which likewise tends to be general and permits a wide variety of uses. For example, a typical property in a downtown redevelopment project might be limited to "commercial uses" under the redevelopment plan and a general commercial designation under the zoning ordinance or general plan. Under these circumstances, determining the highest and best use is a matter of identifying what specific use permitted under the general commercial designation would bring the greatest financial return given property location, market conditions, and other factors affecting value. Since these conditions are more general, highest and best use value is almost always higher than reuse value rather than lower.

Agreements providing for the sale or lease of property by a redevelopment agency must obligate purchasers and lessees to refrain from restricting the sale, rental, or use of the property on the basis of race, religion, sex, sexual orientation, marital status, nationality, familial status, source of income, or disability. § 33435. Specified covenants concerning nondiscrimination are required to be included in all deeds, leases, and contracts. § 33436. Purchasers or lessees may be obligated to use the property for the purpose designated in the redevelopment plan, begin redevelopment within a time that the agency fixes as reasonable, and comply with any other provisions that the agency believes are necessary to carry out the effective redevelopment of the project area. § 33437. Among the controls that may be imposed to assure satisfactory completion of development are covenants running with the land, the breach of which may cause the reversion of the interest conveyed. § 33438. Covenants and restrictions that impose these limitations and controls should ordinarily be incorporated into any disposition agreements (*see* Documenting the Transaction, below) and any instruments conveying an interest in property, such as a deed or a lease.

Note. Under current law, any public subsidy to a redevelopment project, including some land value write-downs, may trigger a prevailing wage requirement (discussed further on pages 193–197).

Developer Selection

Using this broad property disposition authority, redevelopment agencies have developed a variety of techniques for selecting prospective

Determining Fair Reuse Value

Establishing value at the "highest and best use" is generally more simple than determining "fair reuse" value because the conditions that govern highest and best use make it easier to collect a greater number of comparable sales. By contrast, the more specific conditions governing reuse value tend to reduce the number and quality of comparable sales that are available to inform the appraiser. Therefore, determination of fair reuse value often relies most heavily on the complex appraisal process of a "land residual" or "economic" approach to value, and transaction comparisons are used only as a cross check.

Detailed discussion of a land residual/economic approach to value is beyond the scope of this book. Greatly simplified, however, this approach defines land value as a function of the economic performance of a completed project. Assumptions must therefore be made about the costs and timing of development and maintenance, revenue that will be realized, appropriate capitalization rates, interest rates, inflation, and other factors. Clearly, this methodology is sensitive to given assumptions, since different assumptions can result in significantly different conclusions. It is critical that these appraisals be performed by a well qualified, experienced professional who can determine whether the best available comparable sales with appropriate adjustments can be used as a "reality check" on the results of the land residual-economic approach to value. ∎

Property Disposition Process

- Selection of Developer/Owner Participant
- Exclusive Negotiation Agreement
- Negotiations
- Hearings
- Reports
- Approval of DDA
- Resolutions and Findings
- Close of Escrow

A redevelopment agency is authorized to negotiate with a prospective developer without undertaking any kind of selection process.

developers. Each is appropriate for a given set of circumstances. A discussion of the various methods of developer selection follows.

Highest Bid/Auction

Although not commonly used, a redevelopment agency is, of course, authorized to dispose of property through a highest bid procedure or auction. This method of disposition is not often used because, although it may theoretically bring the highest monetary return, it provides the least flexible means for dealing with terms of payment, design, scope, and timing of development and other issues of concern to a redevelopment agency. It is generally used only for smaller parcels of property where any development consistent with zoning would be acceptable to the agency, and the agency's only concern is obtaining a fair price for the land.

There is no prescribed form or procedure for selling property in this fashion. Typically, the agency notifies the public that it will accept bids for the property either in writing or at an auction. The notice describes the general characteristics of the property, including any applicable land use controls and specific development requirements, and may also specify a minimum acceptable bid. Bidders should also be notified that the property will be sold subject to covenants contained in the redevelopment plan forbidding discrimination in the sale, lease, or occupancy of the property on the basis of race, religion, sex, sexual orientation, marital status, nationality, familial status, source of income, or disability and requiring use and development of the property in accordance with the redevelopment plan. Forms of the deed, agreement for sale, and other disposition documents should be made part of the bidder's packet, and a good faith deposit should be required of a purchaser when the bid is accepted. No public hearing is required for the disposition of property in this fashion unless tax-increment funds were used (directly or indirectly) to acquire the property, in which case the agency must prepare the report and the legislative body must hold the public hearing required by section 33433. *See* The Approval Process, pages 211–214.

Negotiation with Single Developer without Formal Selection Process

As noted above, a redevelopment agency is authorized to negotiate with a prospective developer without undertaking any kind of selection process. This procedure was more common during the early stage of redevelopment in California, when many developers were uncomfortable with participating in redevelopment projects because of the numerous problems with the old federal process. However, occasionally the sole source method is still appropriate.

Request for Qualifications

In addition to the highest bid and sole source procedures, other methods of developer selection are Request for Qualifications (RFQ), Request for Proposal (RFP), and a combined RFQ/RFP. RFQs alone as a basis for developer selection tend to be used when time is of the essence or when the agency has only been able to identify a few developers likely to be interested in and capable of meeting the agency's goals for a particular site.

Request for Proposal

RFPs require developers to respond to agency solicitations with information about program, design, and business terms as well as their qualifications and a description of their experience with similar projects. Unlike an RFQ, an RFP costs the developer and the agency more time and money to prepare and analyze. RFPs are most effective when the agency has been able to offer an extensive definition of community goals and the project's design is fairly straightforward. Where an agency has a site of moderate market strength but where two or three qualified developers have expressed interest, the agency may choose an RFP process. This procedure provides the agency with such benefits of competitive proposals as business terms, timing and quality of development, and other advantages.

Many developers resist involvement in formal requests for proposals. They tend to view them as "beauty contests" in which the cost to participate is high while the chance of being selected is low. They are less resistant to RFQs because these do not require the preparation of expensive designs, models, and drawings. One agency technique to encourage participation by developers in the RFP process is to limit their submission costs, either by specifying the materials required or by agreeing to pay a portion of the developer's submission costs.

Combined RFQ/RFP

In recent years, agencies have often used the combined RFQ/RFP process. This is particularly appropriate when the site has strong market support and a high profile in the community, and is one where multiple qualified developers either have or are likely to express interest. Since RFPs are usually costly for developers to prepare and costly in time or money or both for agencies to analyze, both parties benefit from a procedure where the RFQ component of the process is used to select only a limited number of developers to proceed to the more costly RFP stage of the two-stage selection processes.

Preparation of the RFQ/RFP. Developer selection begins with the preparation of the formal request by agency staff. This is typically a fairly involved document that describes in detail the development opportunity, including pictures or diagrams of the site, agency development objectives,

---

PRACTICE TIP

To encourage participation in the RFP process, limit developers' submission costs—either by specifying the materials required or by agreeing to pay a portion of the submission costs.

RFP = Request for Proposal

RFQ = Request for Qualifications

In recent years, agencies have often used the combined RFQ/RFP process. This is particularly appropriate when the site has strong market support and a high profile in the community.

and formal selection criteria. It calls for a detailed submission on the part of the developer, which may include architectural drawings, models, lists of development experience, and a financial statement. The agency may or may not specify minimum requirements for business terms depending on the circumstances. Similarly, it may or may not require a developer to submit proposed business terms, depending on whether or not the agency desires to negotiate these terms after initial developer selection. An exclusive negotiation agreement is commonly attached to the RFQ/RFP, with a requirement that it be executed and returned by the developer as part of the response, together with a good faith deposit. The RFQ/RFP is given the widest possible circulation in order to attract as many responses as possible.

Evaluation of the RFQ/RFP. Responses submitted by developers are typically evaluated by a panel on the basis of formal selection criteria set forth in the RFQ/RFP. The agency and its consultants need to formulate the criteria carefully, so that the ultimate selection process not only will reflect the development goals that are important to the community, but will also result in high probability of actual implementation. The panel may consist of staff, agency members, outside consultants, or a combination of these. There may be intermediate steps in which a majority of the proposals are eliminated, and the remaining developers are asked to make more detailed submittals. Ultimately, the developer is selected by formal action of the agency, and the agency and the developer enter into an exclusive negotiation agreement. Prior to making the selection, some agencies will require the short list of developers under final consideration to submit an agreement or proposal, frequently backed by a cash or letter of credit security, which binds the developer to certain project requirements and business terms, if selected.

When dealing with a formal RFQ/RFP, there are few legal requirements. The agency has broad discretion to select the proposal that it concludes is most in the public interest. *See,* for example, *Old Town Dev. Corp. v. Urban Renewal Agency* (1967) 249 Cal. App. 2d 313. Basically, the courts have required only that an agency follow whatever rules it places in the RFQ/RFP and that it fairly consider each proposal. Common problems include requests for additional time to respond and responses that differ in some material way from what was requested in the RFQ/RFP. If additional time is granted for one respondent, the agency must notify all others and offer the same extension of time. Similarly, if it decides to consider a proposal that differs materially from the description in the RFQ/RFP, the agency should offer other proposers the opportunity to modify their proposals.

Once a developer is selected, a question may arise as to whether a proposed change in the project arising out of negotiations could give rise to a successful challenge by the unsuccessful applicants. Unfortunately, there is little guidance in this area. The nature of the change as well as the latitude reserved by the agency in its RFQ/RFP will be factors in assessing the fairness and propriety of agency procedures.

Master Developers

There are both advantages and disadvantages to the use of master developers. The primary disadvantages arise out of the length of time required to "build out" the project in most master development situations, the increase in the risks and market factors that may affect the overall development, and the agency's loss of negotiating leverage after the master developer has been selected. Most master developer agreements permit redevelopment in phases over a long period of time. The master developer for a large project will negotiate to make those periods as long as possible, with as few deadlines as possible, in order to guard against negative changes in market demand, the availability and cost of financing, and similar risks.

A new office complex in Concord was developed with the assistance of tax increments from the Redevelopment Agency.

The agency, on the other hand, is usually anxious to require the developer to proceed as quickly as possible. If the agreement is not negotiated tightly with firm performance deadlines, the agency risks having the master developer wait for optimum business conditions or become preoccupied with other projects when, perhaps, development might otherwise go forward. This can result in prolonged periods of development inactivity with little or no ability to make the project move forward. A phased development with a master developer also includes the prospect that each phase will become a separate and distinct development, even though it remains coordinated as part of a larger plan, because operators, lenders, and major tenants require relief from cross-default liabilities and other restrictions. Finally, a project phased over a lengthy period of time may face changes required by market conditions, political concerns or other factors not contemplated by the parties at the time of the original agreement.

The principal advantages of using a master developer relate to the resources that the master developer brings to the transaction (both financial and creative), and overall coordination and control of development and integrated operation and management. A master developer should bring a significant financial commitment to the project. This can be essential for financing the public costs of development, such as land acquisition and clearance, as well as for its ability to attract financing

The principal advantages of using a master developer relate to the resources that the master developer brings to the transaction, and overall coordination and control of development.

Chapter 8 *Property Disposition* 177

for private improvements. The master developer may also be willing to make an extensive commitment to project planning and urban design. This relationship may offer the agency greater flexibility during the development process. Staging of construction can be more flexible, joint development economics can be maximized, and a greater variety of design alternatives can be considered.

Exclusive Negotiation Agreements

An exclusive negotiation agreement is not legally required, but both agencies and developers have found such agreements to be useful for giving structure to the negotiation process.

Once a developer has been selected, the agency and the developer may enter into an exclusive negotiation agreement. This agreement is not legally required, but both agencies and developers have found such agreements to be useful for giving structure to the negotiation process. No specific authorization for an exclusive negotiation agreement is found in the Community Redevelopment Law, but the authority for such agreements can reasonably be inferred from the agency's power to enter into contracts to carry out any of its corporate purposes. § 33125.

While no two exclusive negotiation agreements are the same, most have a number of features in common. The agreement should specifically identify the development entity. It is common for developers to create separate legal entities to undertake each separate development project. The agency should know whether it is dealing with the parent entity or one of these special development entities. If it is specially created for this project, the agency will want to know that the entity is adequately capitalized. If it is a limited liability company, the agency should know the identity of the managing member and other members.

DDA = Disposition and development agreement

A DDA provides the developer with an assurance that it can expend the money necessary to determine the project's feasibility without fear of the project being awarded to a competitor.

The agreement must specify a period of time during which the agency will negotiate *exclusively* with the developer for the purpose of concluding a binding agreement for the sale and development of certain property in the redevelopment project area (commonly referred to as a disposition and development agreement or DDA). This provides the developer with an assurance that it can expend the money necessary to determine the project's feasibility without fear of the project being awarded to a competitor. The negotiation period identified in the agreement will vary according to the size and complexity of the project. For smaller, simpler projects, a negotiation period of 90 to 120 days may be sufficient. For larger projects, negotiation periods of a year or more may be necessary. Where lengthy negotiation periods are required, the agreement should identify intermediate steps or "performance mileposts." If these performance mileposts are not achieved satisfactorily, then the agreement may be terminated prior to the expiration of the negotiation period. Agencies will often be willing to extend exclusive negotiation periods if they determine that the developer is acting diligently and in good faith.

It is standard practice to require a developer to make a good faith deposit with the agency in connection with the execution of an exclusive negotiation agreement. The size of the deposit will vary with the scope of the project and other factors. Typically, the form of the deposit may be either cash, a certified check, letter of credit, or some other form of security that can be easily converted to cash in the event of a default. The agency holds the deposit during the negotiation period and either keeps the deposit if the developer does not negotiate in good faith, returns it at the conclusion of negotiations if the developer has negotiated in good faith, or applies it to any good faith deposit requirements that may be contained in an approved DDA. Exclusive negotiation agreements may permit the agency to draw down the good faith deposit to pay for agency staff time or for the fees of attorneys or for consultants utilized in connection with the negotiations. This is particularly true where competition for the development opportunity is present.

Where the development opportunity is strong, an agency may structure the exclusive negotiation agreement in a form similar to an option agreement. The agency might require the developer to make an option or negotiating payment to the agency for the right to negotiate. Additional money would be required for extensions of the negotiation period. The option or negotiating payments are typically nonrefundable, but may be credited, in whole or in part, to the developer's land payments if negotiations are successful and a DDA is concluded.

The Granary—a dark industrial building, became an energy-efficient building with office and retail uses, and now serves as a gateway to Morgan Hill.

It is extremely important that the agency expressly reserve its discretion with respect to the approval of any agreement for the sale or other disposition of the property that may result from the negotiations. This requirement distinguishes an exclusive negotiation agreement from a private real estate option. Language such as the following should be included in all exclusive negotiation agreements:

It is extremely important that the agency expressly reserve its discretion with respect to the approval of any agreement for the sale or other disposition of the property that may result from the negotiations.

> By its execution of this Agreement, the Agency is not committing itself to or agreeing to undertake: (a) any disposition of land to the Developer; or (b) any other acts or activities requiring the subsequent independent exercise of discretion by the Agency, the City, or any agency or department thereof. This Agreement does not constitute a disposition of property or exercise of control over property by the Agency or the City and does not require a public hearing. Execution of this Agreement by the Agency is merely an agreement to enter into a period of exclusive negotiations according to the terms hereof, reserving final discretion and approval by the Agency and City as to any Disposition and Development Agreement and all proceedings and decisions in connection therewith.

An exclusive negotiation agreement should be formally approved by the agency but does not require a public hearing. No supporting environmental analysis or documentation is required under the California Environmental Quality Act as long as the agreement contains language like the foregoing that makes it clear that the agency is not committing

An exclusive negotiation agreement should be formally approved by the agency but does not require a public hearing.

Chapter 8 *Property Disposition* 179

itself to carry out a project. *See Save Tara v. City of West Hollywood* (2008) 45 Cal. 4th 116.

Owner Participation

General Rules

The Community Redevelopment Law provides that every redevelopment plan "shall provide for participation in the redevelopment of the property in the project area by the owners of all or part of such property if the owners agree to participate in the redevelopment in conformity with the redevelopment plan...." § 33339. Rules governing owner participation must be adopted by a redevelopment agency prior to the approval of a redevelopment plan. § 33345. Every redevelopment agency is required to "extend reasonable preference to persons who are engaged in business in the project area to reenter in business within the redeveloped area if they otherwise meet the requirements prescribed by the redevelopment plan." The agency is required to adopt rules for that purpose prior to the approval of a redevelopment plan. § 33339.5. Finally, every redevelopment plan that contemplates property owner participation must contain alternative provisions for redevelopment of the property if an owner fails to participate. § 33340.

Rules governing owner participation must be adopted by a redevelopment agency prior to the approval of a redevelopment plan.

Owner participation issues frequently arise because a redevelopment agency has entered into an agreement for the disposition of property before it has actually acquired the property in question, made possible by the agency's power of eminent domain.[1] This practice of contracting for the sale of land before it is acquired can, however, cause friction with property owners who, under the provisions of the Community Redevelopment Law and local redevelopment plans, must be extended opportunities to participate in redevelopment. Particularly in the process of land disposition, reasonable opportunities must be offered to owners of property in the project area to participate in redevelopment, or serious legal consequences and liabilities will follow. *See,* for example, *Redevelopment Agency v. Norm's Slauson* (1985) 173 Cal. App. 3d 1121, discussed further in The "Norm's Slauson" Problem, below.

The practice of contracting for the sale of land before it is acquired can cause friction with property owners who must be extended opportunities to participate in redevelopment.

---

1. There are a number of sound reasons for this practice. First, experience with the federal urban renewal program, which provided for property assembly prior to obtaining binding development commitments, proved unsatisfactory in many communities. Communities were often left with large areas acquired and cleared with no real prospects for redevelopment. In many cases, this unsold land inventory stood vacant for decades before redevelopers could be found to undertake feasible projects.

    Not only were public funds tied up in unsold land, but businesses and residents were displaced, taking property off the tax rolls. Second, with the withdrawal of federal support for redevelopment and restrictions on the use of tax exempt bonds for many redevelopment activities, redevelopment agencies have increasingly come to depend on developer loans and advances to finance the costs of site assembly. Even where public funds are available, agencies are reluctant to commit them for site acquisition, in priority over other uses, in the absence of an agreement with a developer.

The courts have provided some useful interpretation and elaboration of the meaning of the rather sketchy provisions of the Community Redevelopment Law pertaining to owner participation. Owner participation was first addressed by the California courts in *Fellom v. Redevelopment Agency* (1958) 157 Cal. App. 2d 243, in which the plaintiffs complained of violations of the provisions of section 33701 (now § 33339). At the time of *Fellom*, section 33745 provided that owners forfeited their participation rights "if for 30 days after the adoption of the plan, the owners fail or refuse to enter into binding agreements for participation in accordance with the plan."

The plaintiffs in *Fellom* argued that the San Francisco Redevelopment Agency's denial of participation to 90 percent of the total acreage and 97 percent of the unimproved acreage in the project area violated the owners' participation rights. The court found that such an interpretation of the statute would be inconsistent with the remainder of the Community Redevelopment Law, reasoning that:

> For instance, the express power of eminent domain would negate the necessity of participation by the owners, if the agency in its exercise of its constitutional powers acts fairly and without discrimination. Even the language of, "Every redevelopment plan shall provide for participation in the redevelopment of property in the project area by the owners of all or part of such property....," contemplates that participation be not extended to all owners of the property. This, of course, imposes upon the agency a duty of reasonableness and good faith, if they wish to make participation available to part of the owners of the property embraced in the redevelopment project.

Fellom v. Redevelopment Agency (1958) 157 Cal. App. 2d 250

The court found that the actions of the San Francisco Redevelopment Agency, which excluded most owners and distinguished between owners of improved property and unimproved property, were reasonable and therefore satisfied the law.

The California Supreme Court adopted the reasoning of *Fellom* in *In re Redevelopment Plan for Bunker Hill* (1964) 61 Cal. 2d 21. The Court summarized the owner participation claims of the plaintiff as follows:

> The final plan herein requires that prospective owner-participants qualify as being financially responsible and able to perform their owner-participation agreement with the agency. The plan further sets forth proposed uses for certain areas of the project which require the assembly of large plots of land. The requirement that the prospective owner-participant be financially responsible, when combined with the planning proposals requiring assembly of large plots of land, makes it impossible for many small property owners to participate. Therefore, it is argued, the final plan violates section 33701.

Bunker Hill, p. 59

The courts have provided some useful interpretation and elaboration of the meaning of the rather sketchy provisions of the Community Redevelopment Law pertaining to owner participation.

Rejecting this argument, the Court held:

That there is no absolute right of owner participation in the redevelopment of each separately owned parcel of land within the project area is apparent from the provisions of section 33701 itself in that it provides that as a condition thereof an owner desiring to participate must agree "to participate in the redevelopment in conformity with the redevelopment plan adopted by the legislative body for the area." "Redevelopment," as defined by section 33013 [*see* present § 33020], includes provision for "such residential, commercial, industrial, public, or other structures or spaces as may be appropriate or necessary in the interest of the general welfare."

* * *

Because the final plan necessitates assembly of large plots to carry out the proposed uses in certain areas of the project and requires prospective owner-participants to qualify as financially responsible, and thus in some cases renders it impossible for small property owners, as such, to separately participate with the same status, does not in and of itself establish a violation of section 33701.

The question with respect to the owner-participation provisions would appear to be, as stated in the Fellom case, whether the agency has fulfilled its obligation of "reasonableness and good faith." The imposition of reasonable terms and conditions upon the right to participate as the agency may deem necessary or appropriate in light of the redevelopment proposed would seem to be not only within the power but a duty of the agency and this would include such rules as would reasonably assure fulfillment of an owner-participation agreement including such matters as the establishment of financial ability. The plan restrictions as to land coverage apply equally to redevelopers as well as to owner-participants and there does not appear to be anything unfair or discriminatory in requiring that an owner-participant, as a condition of his right to participate, shall subject himself to the same restrictions that are required of an outside developer and which are reasonably necessary to achieve a successful redevelopment.

Bunker Hill, pp. 59–61

Bunker Hill has since been applied to uphold limitations on owner participation in *Sanguineti v. City Council* (1965) 231 Cal. App. 2d 813, where the redevelopment agency denied owner participation to all but three parcels in a nine-block area, and *Huntington Park Redevelopment Agency v. Duncan* (1983) 142 Cal. App. 3d 17, where the redevelopment agency exercised the power of eminent domain to take the parking lot of one business and resell it to the adjoining property owner for the expansion of his business.

It is clear from these cases that a redevelopment agency may limit owner participation opportunities but that, in doing so, the agency must act reasonably and in good faith. Certain procedures have evolved from redevelopment agency practice that provide owners with notice and reasonable opportunities to participate in redevelopment. These are summarized below.

If an agency solicits proposals for the redevelopment of a specified area, property owners within that area should be given an opportunity to submit a proposal. This is easily accomplished where there is a written request for proposals by sending each property owner a copy of the RFP. A record should be made of all those to whom the request for proposals is mailed or given. Where no written request for proposals is distributed, property owners should be notified by some other means, such as a letter explaining the agency's objectives for the area and inviting the owner to respond. Again, a record of such communications should be kept.

Before entering into an exclusive negotiation agreement with a developer, the agency should again send notices to property owners within the area that will be the subject of the agreement. The letter should notify each owner of the time and place of the meeting at which the agency intends to consider the agreement, state that the owner's property may be acquired if a disposition and development agreement is concluded with the developer, and invite the owner to submit an alternative proposal or otherwise comment. The letter should also explain that participation opportunities are not accorded as a matter of right and that the ultimate selection of a developer rests with the agency, based on such factors as development qualifications and the agency's objectives for the area. Once again, it is important to keep a record of all those to whom the letter is sent.

If an owner submits an alternative proposal, the agency should prepare a factual analysis of both proposals, containing information to enable the agency to make a selection on the basis of objective, identifiable facts. Such facts may include the development experience and financial strength of the proposers and the extent to which the different proposals would respond to the objectives of the agency in carrying out the redevelopment plan, such as job creation, enhancement of property tax revenues, increased retail activity, desired specific uses, and creating so-called "catalyst" projects, among others. As the number of experienced developers who have completed successful redevelopment projects increases, agencies find those developers acquiring property in project areas and seeking owner participation opportunities. This trend presents significant opportunities for both the agencies and the private developers. Agencies avoid the up front cost of land acquisition and may greatly simplify the developer selection process. They also have the opportunity to deal with developers who have demonstrated a commitment to the community and a familiarity with the requirements of redevelopment law and process. The developers are able to incorporate additional financial assistance into their

> **PRACTICE TIP**
>
> A redevelopment agency should always consult the owner participation rules adopted for the applicable project area and proceed in conformity with those rules in addition to procedures described in this book.

Before entering into an exclusive negotiation agreement with a developer, the agency should again send notices to property owners within the area that will be the subject of the agreement.

Obstacles to Effective Owner Participation

Participation by an owner who is not an experienced developer is difficult because of—

- Lack of mutual financial and other goals
- Lack of trust because there is no shared past experience
- Need of owner to surrender control to developer
- If hard times occur, vulnerability to bad decisions by an inexperienced owner

project budgets, and have the advantage of working with supportive agencies and city decision makers through the land and entitlement process.

A frequently asked question is whether an owner's proposal must reflect the same use and scope of development as that of the developer. For example, if a developer is proposing a regional shopping center, may an owner submit a proposal that encompasses only the property that he or she owns or that contemplates a different use? The answer is yes. The agency should consider any proposal submitted by an owner. However, the agency does have the discretion and authority to decide that what is needed to carry out the redevelopment plan is a particular kind of development and may therefore reject nonconforming proposals.

The agency should consider any proposal submitted by an owner.

The "Norm's Slauson" Problem

In 1985, the Court of Appeal rendered a decision in *Redevelopment Agency v. Norm's Slauson* (1985) 173 Cal. App. 3d 1121, that must be taken into account when undertaking property disposition. In 1980, the City of Huntington Park adopted a redevelopment plan providing for residential development in the city block that embraced the defendant's property (a restaurant). The plan, however, made no specific mention of the defendant's property. The court found that, at the time the redevelopment plan was adopted, there was nothing to indicate that the restaurant would not be permitted to continue to operate as in the past. In fact, the redevelopment agency had notified property owners that the redevelopment plan would enable the agency to help existing businesses expand or rehabilitate. Following the adoption of the redevelopment plan, the agency entered into an owner participation agreement that required the agency to acquire the parking lot of the restaurant for conveyance to a developer in connection with new residential development. Mortgage revenue bonds were sold to provide financing for the development. Subsequently, the agency initiated eminent domain proceedings to acquire the four lots constituting the restaurant's parking area.

An eight-story library to be jointly owned by the City of San Jose and California State University, San Jose, is considered a key element of the downtown revitalization program.

The court reviewed the requirements of the State Eminent Domain Law, which requires that, as a prerequisite to the exercise of eminent domain, a resolution of necessity must be adopted, after a public hearing, to satisfy three basic criteria: (1) the property is necessary for a public project; (2) the project is, in turn, necessary for a public purpose; and (3) the taking of the particular property is compatible with the greatest public good and the least private injury. The court concluded that:

Implicit in this requirement of a hearing and the adoption of a resolution of necessity is the concept that, in arriving at its decision to take, the Agency engage in a good faith and judicious consideration of the pros and cons of the issue and that the decision to take be buttressed by substantial evidence of the existence of the three basic requirements set forth in Code of Civil Procedure, section 1240.030, *supra*. (Footnote omitted.)

* * *

In the instant case, it seems clear that the hearing which led to the adoption of the resolution of necessity was a sham and the Agency's policy making board simply "rubber stamped" a predetermined result.

By the time the Agency actually conducted a hearing to determine the "necessity" for taking the property in question, it had, by virtue of its contract with the developer and issuance of revenue bonds, irrevocably committed itself to take the property in question, regardless of any evidence that might be presented at that hearing. All the while the owner had been misled, if not deceived, as to what fate was going to befall his property.

Redevelopment Agency v. Norm's Slauson, 173 Cal. App. 3d 1125–1127

Based on the foregoing conclusions, the court reasoned as follows:

As we see it, once a defendant property owner establishes by substantial evidence that the resolution of necessity was invalidly adopted and because of a gross abuse of discretion is not entitled to its ordinary conclusive effect, the burden of proving the elements for a particular taking must rest on the governmental agency. In such a case, the trial court must then determine whether the agency has made its case by a preponderance of the evidence. Appellate review of the trial court's decision is limited by the substantial evidence test.

Redevelopment Agency v. Norm's Slauson, 173 Cal. App. 3d 1128

The court upheld the judgment of the superior court denying the agency's right to condemn the four lots in question.

As previously discussed, it has been common procedure for redevelopment agencies to first negotiate and enter into DDAs with developers and then proceed with property acquisition once financing to pay the costs of acquisition is assured. Many agencies do not have the funds available to commence property acquisition in advance of the funding to be provided pursuant to the DDA (which could be public funding secured by the agency based on the development agreement or funds advanced by the developer). To undertake property acquisition without an assured source of funding could subject an agency, at the least, to costs of abandonment and, at the most, to damages in inverse condemnation. Further, it is neither prudent nor desirable in most cases to acquire specific properties in advance of having a DDA for those properties.

It has been common procedure for redevelopment agencies to first negotiate and enter into DDAs with developers and then proceed with property acquisition once financing to pay the costs of acquisition is assured.

The recommended and preferred procedure, applied by many agencies routinely since *Norm's Slauson*, has been:

- To adequately advise property owners of pending negotiations with a developer and of scheduled hearings on proposed development agreements so that the property owners are on notice of the potential acquisition of their property and have a fair opportunity to be heard and assert owner participation opportunities provided under the redevelopment plan.

- To avoid a contractual commitment to acquire property in the development agreement by, instead, conditioning the development agreement upon the adoption of a resolution of necessity that, if not adopted within a specified time, could lead to a termination of the agreement. This type of provision attempts to reserve to the agency its subsequent discretion as to whether or not to proceed with condemnation.

Under these procedures, the agency could legitimately claim that the property owner has been treated fairly and given fair notice at relevant stages in the process of the potential acquisition of the property. The problem is that the property owner in an eminent domain action may still raise the *Norm's Slauson* issues. Any order for immediate possession is clouded until those issues are resolved. Even if those issues are tried quickly by a trial court and resolved in favor of the agency, a final determination by an appellate court—including the compensation to be paid—might be years away.

Prudent developers will not proceed without an indemnification and hold harmless agreement from the agency or, as is the more common practice, without a policy of title insurance issued by a title insurance company that, in turn, would be based on an agency's indemnification agreement.

Another option is for the agency to give notice and adopt the resolution of necessity at the same time as the hearing on and approval of the DDA. A two-thirds vote is required for the resolution of necessity, thereby effectively establishing the vote requirement for the DDA. This procedure would appear to overcome the major difficulties posed by the language. However, an agency must then be prepared to file its eminent domain action within six months, meaning it must have the developer committed and the financing assured within that time. Further, before adopting the resolution of necessity and concurrently with approving the DDA, the agency would have to first comply with the law's precondemnation requirements: appraisals, offer, and an opportunity to negotiate. The agency could be at risk, if the agreement fell through, for relocation costs, costs of abandoning the condemnation action, and possible liability in inverse condemnation. In some instances, agencies have made *conditional offers* to acquire property, premised on an effective development agreement or upon securing financing, but this procedure is done reluctantly because it is so disruptive to the plans of property owners, tenants, residents, and businesses.

A third option is for the agency to undertake, when funding is available, property acquisition in advance of entering into development agreements for the property. However, while this would make the situation easier for the developer and the agency, it is usually not practical, prudent, or politically possible in many circumstances.

Negotiations

Objectives

In negotiating a disposition and development agreement, a redevelopment agency and a developer have different objectives and responsibilities. A redevelopment agency will still generally negotiate toward the following business objectives, while taking care not to exceed its risk tolerance:

- Obtaining a fair price for the land, consistent with providing the developer with a reasonable return commensurate with risks
- Deferring major financial commitments on the part of the agency until the developer is firmly bound to proceed
- Obtaining sufficient revenue from the project by way of land sale proceeds, lease rentals, tax increment, and other developer contributions and payments to make it financially feasible for the agency to undertake and pay for its obligations
- Securing maximum feasible good faith deposits or performance guarantees
- In a phased project, conditioning the ability of a developer to proceed with the more attractive portions of the project (from the developer's standpoint) on a commitment to complete the entire project

A developer, in keeping with its own risk calculation, will generally negotiate toward these objectives:

- Controlling the site early under an agreement with the agency so that it can undertake market studies, feasibility studies, and planning, and contact potential tenants
- Obtaining environmental and toxic assessments, planning approvals, and other entitlement at the earliest possible time with maximum contribution to costs by the public sector
- Minimizing the developer's front-end predevelopment costs until the project is ready to move forward
- Limiting the developer's obligation to proceed with development by conditioning it on obtaining tenant commitments and financing
- Phasing in separate project components and retaining the ability to proceed with separate parts of the project without being committed to later phases

---

Financing Considerations for Developers and Agencies

Developers should accept the contingencies of agency financing and agree to an adjustment in the business terms or participation by the agency in the financial success of a project as a condition of making the agreement. Redevelopment agencies, on the other hand, must learn to accept the uncertainties facing the developer in today's capital markets and be flexible by adjusting the terms of the agreement to help the developer obtain financing. Each development opportunity presents its own particular problems to be solved, with opportunities for a wide variety of creative public/private joint development approaches. ■

Notwithstanding the different motivations of the private and public sectors, the key issue remains the availability of financing that, in turn, is dependent upon securing credit-worthy tenants.

Notwithstanding the different motivations of the private and public sectors, the key issue remains the availability of financing that, in turn, is dependent upon securing credit-worthy tenants. Redevelopment agencies must understand the uncertainties the developer faces in today's capital markets and be flexible in order to help the developer obtain financing. Developers, in turn, should acknowledge the agency's contribution to financing and be prepared to adjust the business terms or provide for agency participation in the financial success of the project as a condition of making the agreement. Each development opportunity presents its own particular problems to be solved.

Preparation for Negotiation

Redevelopment transactions tend to be complex. The complexity arises from the difficulty of attracting tenants and capital in markets that the private sector has historically found unattractive; the problems of dealing with land that has already been developed and, in many cases, neglected or abused over a long period of time; the extra layers of procedure required when a public agency is an active participant in the development process; and so forth. At another level, redevelopment deals are politically complex. It is no small matter to use public tax dollars to uproot existing owners, residents and businesses in order to subsidize development of that same property by a private developer who may be an outsider to the community. Use of the power of eminent domain is often a very difficult step for the redevelopment agency to take. Because of this complexity, a redevelopment agency should carefully and thoughtfully prepare for negotiating a DDA.

The first step in preparing for negotiations is to clearly identify the public sector goals and policy objectives. In nearly all situations, the policy makers will not be conducting the negotiations and will rely on staff and consultants to meet with the developer and document the transaction. The redevelopment agency's negotiating team must have a clear understanding of the decision makers' objectives and priorities. Is the agency's objective to maximize the price of the land or to see certain public amenities included in the project, that may necessarily reduce land value? Does the agency require particular uses or tenants? If the agency's objectives have not been clearly defined and communicated, they may be compromised or lost in the give and take of negotiations.

The negotiating team must also have a workable method for ongoing communication with the decision makers as negotiations progress. A transaction evolves during the course of negotiations and rarely ends up looking exactly like what either the agency or the developer anticipated at the beginning of the process. Effective communication between the agency and its negotiating team is complicated by two conflicting demands—the need for confidentiality and the limitations on a

Effective Negotiations

- Clearly define objectives
- Carefully select negotiating team
- Establish effective lines of communication between negotiating team and decision makers
- Speak with one voice
- Document interim agreements

The negotiating team must have a workable method for ongoing communication with the decision makers as negotiations progress.

public agency's ability to transact business in secret. No responsible agency would consult with its negotiating team in public, where the other party could discover elements of strategy such as proposed compromises. Yet, with few exceptions, public agencies are required by California law to conduct their affairs in public session.

This conflict can be reconciled in a number of ways. First, the Brown Act, that requires that the business of a public agency be conducted openly and in public, contains an exception for real estate transactions where the agency is meeting to give instructions to its negotiator. Gov. Code § 54956.8. This provision permits an agency to meet in executive session with its negotiating team to give the team direction and to discuss the progress of negotiations. This exception is limited to discussion of the "price and terms of payment for the purchase, sale, exchange or lease" of property. *See* pages 28–29, for a discussion of the Brown Act. Moreover, where the agency must give a quick response, it may be impractical to use an executive session since many agencies meet only once or twice a month, and the logistical problems associated with calling special meetings can be formidable. For these reasons, many redevelopment agencies will appoint a special *ad hoc* subcommittee consisting of less than a quorum of the agency to meet informally with the negotiating team and provide direction. This procedure is also sanctioned by the Brown Act, although care must be taken that the subcommittee not constitute a "standing committee" whose meetings must be open to the public. Gov. Code § 54952(b); *Freedom Newspapers, Inc. v. Orange County Employees Retirement System* (1993) 6 Cal. 4th 821.

The composition of the agency's negotiating team also merits careful consideration. Generally, real estate developers have more expert knowledge of their business than do redevelopment agencies. This is particularly true for agencies in small and medium-sized cities, which often cannot afford to maintain real estate development specialists on staff. The negotiating team for a redevelopment agency should attempt to balance this disadvantage, employing, as necessary, specialized consultants and attorneys to fill the gaps in the staff's experience and expertise. Depending upon the size and complexity of the project, the team may include one or more staff members, an attorney, and a real estate/finance consultant. If the public costs of the project will be financed by tax-exempt bonds, the participation of bond counsel and underwriters at certain points in the negotiations may also be beneficial.

The Fairfield Redevelopment Agency sold the site for fair market value and financed the construction of a road. The project created 225 new jobs in the city.

Many redevelopment agencies will appoint a special ad hoc subcommittee consisting of less than a quorum of the agency to meet informally with the negotiating team and provide direction.

Members of the agency board are rarely, if ever, present at the negotiating table. There are a number of good reasons for this. First, negotiations on even a modest project can consume a great deal of time. Most agency members cannot make such a significant time commitment in addition to their other responsibilities. Secondly, there is value in "keeping the kings in their castle." An agency member's objectivity and judgment on the completed DDA is enhanced by maintaining a distance from the rough and tumble of negotiations. Finally, few agency members are willing to risk their individual prestige and reputation by personal involvement in uncertain negotiations.

Members of the agency board are rarely, if ever, present at the negotiating table.

Structuring the Negotiation Process

Entire books have been written on negotiating strategy, and this chapter does not purport to address this issue comprehensively. However, a few general guidelines have particular application to the negotiation of redevelopment transactions.

It is critical that the agency speak to the developer with one voice. If the public sector goals and policy objectives have been clearly defined, are endorsed by the policy makers and supported by the community, then misunderstandings can be kept to a minimum. It is also useful to designate one member of the agency's negotiating team as the lead negotiator, through whom all significant communication with the developer should flow. Finally, the agency should discourage the developer from making inappropriate contact with policy makers. Although it is probably not constitutionally permissible to forbid the developer to approach elected officials, policy makers should direct these contacts back to the agency's negotiating team.

It is critical that the agency speak to the developer with one voice.

It is also crucial to the success of negotiations to understand who has the authority to make commitments for both the agency and the developer. Frequently, the developer's negotiator does not have such authority and will need to seek approval from a partner, a lender, or a superior in the organization before a real commitment can be made. The same is true with the agency—a deal is not a deal until it has been approved by the agency board. With this in mind, true commitments should be made jointly and simultaneously. It is best to avoid a situation where either party gets too far ahead of the other in its commitment to the project.

It is also crucial to the success of negotiations to understand who has the authority to make commitments for both the agency and the developer.

Particularly in long and complex negotiations, interim written documentation of agreed-upon points can be useful for keeping track of the transaction and avoiding renegotiations. This can take the form of minutes of the negotiating sessions, which are circulated and approved, or interim memoranda documenting specific agreements—all subject to the understanding that no issue is final until the entire transaction has been negotiated.

Methods of Assisting Development When Necessary

Redevelopment project areas must compete with other, nonblighted areas for real estate investment capital. The playing field is not a level one, particularly in the early stages of a multiphased project. Especially in the early years of a redevelopment plan, blighted project areas are saddled with enormous handicaps, which act as a disincentive for new investment. The physical condition of the land itself is often a serious problem.

Most of these conditions arise from previous development, often under antiquated planning and building codes. Issues related to the physical condition of the property include fragmented ownership, inadequate and outdated parcelization, the need to relocate occupants and demolish improvements, deteriorating or inadequate utilities, the presence of toxic or hazardous substances, etc. All of these factors contribute to a much higher land cost in comparison to nonblighted, suburban locations.

Other factors contribute to a higher development cost in blighted areas. Often, the planning process is more complex, and therefore more time-consuming and expensive than in suburban locations. Redevelopment transactions tend to have higher visibility than ordinary real estate developments and so may be subject to manipulation by interest groups. Because of the greater time needed for activities such as planning and site preparation, redevelopment projects are also more vulnerable to changes in political climate and economic cycles. Social conditions in the area such as crime, graffiti, and homelessness may make the project less attractive to tenants and lenders.

In order to assist the private sector to overcome these numerous and significant obstacles, redevelopment agencies are given an array of powers, including:

- Assistance in relieving a developer's front-end costs by paying for feasibility and market studies, soil reports, title reports, surveys, appraisals, and architectural and engineering costs
- Using eminent domain to assemble sites for development
- Selling land at less than cost ("land write-down") or structuring ground rents consistent with the economics of the project in order to provide a developer with a reasonable development opportunity
- Reducing or eliminating front-end option and holding costs by delaying conveyance until the developer is ready to proceed
- Paying for site preparation costs, such as relocation, demolition, soil preparation, grading, and the construction of building pads
- Paying for the construction of public improvements, such as utilities, parking, streets, curbs, gutters, sidewalks, and street lighting, including, in the proper setting, shared-use facilities such as plazas, malls, and other areas used by the general public

Redevelopment project areas must compete with other, nonblighted areas for real estate investment capital. The playing field is not a level one, particularly in the early stages of a multiphased project.

Often, the planning process is more complex, and therefore more time-consuming and expensive than in suburban locations.

- Providing public financing for certain development costs through the use of tax-increment revenue, lease-revenue financing, assessment districts, and other financing techniques

The most common forms of redevelopment assistance to specific types of projects are:

- *Residential uses:* Substantial land write-down; off-site and on-site improvements; and, in appropriate cases, direct financing assistance by cash payments (in some cases rental assistance or second trust deed financing) or through the issuance of housing bonds.
- *Office uses:* Site assembly; off-site improvements only (on-site improvements paid for by developer); in weak markets, substantial land write-down.
- *Retail uses:* Substantial land write-down; off-site and on-site improvements, including parking in appropriate circumstances.
- *Hotel uses:* Land write-down; off-site and on-site improvements; construction of parking and public areas and lease to hotel (subject to limitations on exclusive use).

These traditional forms of assistance have been tempered in recent years, however, due to concerns that they may trigger prevailing wage requirements. *See* discussion on pages 193–197.

In addition to its traditional role as land merchant and constructor and/or financier of public improvements, a redevelopment agency may provide loans for commercial or residential rehabilitation, pay a portion of the assessments for a special assessment district or community facilities district, and otherwise encourage or subsidize redevelopment in a wide variety of creative ways. An agency's powers are not unlimited, however. The agency is a creature of statute, and any assistance it provides must be founded in statutorily granted powers or in powers that can be reasonably inferred from those powers.

As a result of what the legislature perceived to be an abuse of the process, redevelopment agencies are specifically prohibited from assisting certain types of development and have had one of their tools for assisting development (sales tax authority) revoked.

One of the many unintended consequences of the passage of California's Proposition 13 was to greatly increase the importance of sales tax revenues in municipal budgets. The years since 1978 have seen a pronounced shift, decreasing the significance of property taxes in municipal budgets and increasing reliance on sales taxes. At about the same time, redevelopment agencies were given the power to levy a sales tax in project areas. Initially, this sales tax authority was intended only as a supplemental source of security for property tax allocation bonds. The statutory authority was broad, however, and it was not long before some agencies were using this authority to offer large subsidies (including sales tax rebates in some cases) to users such as auto dealers and "big box" retailers who generated high sales taxes.

In some cases, redevelopment project areas were created in outlying, unblighted, or marginally blighted areas for the exclusive purpose of subsidizing these high sales tax generators. This led to spirited and sometimes harmful competition between jurisdictions for these users, each trying to outdo the other with their package of subsidies and incentives for increased sales taxes. The state Department of Finance believed (with justification) that all this activity resulted in no net benefit to the state because, in most cases, the users were either relocating from one California jurisdiction to another or were merely playing neighboring cities against one another for a new facility, which in any event would be built somewhere in the region.

In 1993, recognizing this situation as unhealthy, the California Redevelopment Association sponsored legislation, the effect of which was to revoke agencies' authority to levy sales taxes and to greatly limit their ability to assist large sales tax generators. This legislation was adopted as part of AB 1290 (Chapter 942 of the Statutes of 1993) and became effective in 1994. Except in certain narrowly defined circumstances, redevelopment agencies are now specifically prohibited from providing any form of direct assistance to either an automobile dealership on land that has not previously been developed for urban use; or a development on land of five acres or more that has not been previously developed for urban use and that will, when developed, generate sales or use taxes, unless the principal permitted use of the development is office, hotel, manufacturing, or industrial. § 33426.5. This section does not prevent an agency from assisting with the cost of public improvements that are of area wide benefit and that may incidentally benefit an auto dealer or other prohibited user.

In addition, agencies are prohibited from providing any form of financial assistance to a vehicle dealer or big box retailer, or a business entity that sells or leases land to a vehicle dealer or big box retailer, that is relocating from the territorial jurisdiction of one community to the territorial jurisdiction of another community but within the same market area. § 33426.7.

Prevailing Wage Considerations

Agencies and developers must always consider whether redevelopment agency involvement in a development project will cause the project to be a "public work," triggering prevailing

This 242-suite hotel, adjacent to Old Town and five blocks from the State Capitol, features more than 8,000 square feet of meeting space, including a business center and, at 3,050 square feet, the largest ballroom in downtown Sacramento.

Except in certain narrowly defined circumstances, redevelopment agencies are now specifically prohibited from providing any form of direct assistance to an automobile dealership on land that has not previously been developed for urban use.

Chapter 8 *Property Disposition* 193

wage requirements for an otherwise private development. In many parts of the state, prevailing wage requirements will increase labor costs significantly, and may render an otherwise viable project infeasible. Additionally, the existing definition of "public works" is relatively new due to a significant revision to Labor Code section 1720 that took effect in 2002, and there are only a few cases interpreting the application of the new definition to redevelopment projects.[2]

Labor Code section 1720 defines "public works" for prevailing wage purposes as "[c]onstruction, alteration, demolition, installation, or repair work done under contract and *paid for in whole or in part out of public funds....*" Labor Code § 1720 (emphasis added). Section 1720 defines the term "paid for in whole or in part out of public funds" to mean:

- The payment of money or its equivalent by a state or political subdivision directly to or on behalf of the public works contractor, subcontractor, or developer
- The performance of construction work by the state or political subdivision in execution of the project
- The transfer of an asset of value for less than fair market price
- Fees, costs, rents, insurance or bond premiums, loans, interest rates, or other obligations that would normally be required in the execution of the contract, that are paid, reduced, charged at less than fair market value, waived, or forgiven
- Money to be repaid on a contingent basis
- Credits applied against repayment obligations

This definition of "paid for in whole or in part out of public funds" indicates that many traditional forms of redevelopment assistance will constitute payments of public funds that will trigger prevailing wage requirements. For example, the transfer of an asset of value, such as land, to a developer for less than "fair market price" will constitute a payment of public funds triggering prevailing wage requirements. While some have argued that in the context of a land transfer, the legislature intended the term "fair market price" to include the fair reuse value of the land as defined in section 33433, the Department of Industrial Relations determined in the context of Public Works Case No. 2004-035, *Santa Ana Transit Village/City of Santa Ana,* that the fair reuse value of the property in that case did not constitute "fair market price," and the sale of property at fair reuse value triggered prevailing wages. The *Santa Ana* determination is discussed in more detail below.

2. As of the publication of this book, the only published case interpreting the new definition of "public works" is *State Building and Construction Trades Council of California v. Duncan* (2008) 162 Cal. App. 4th 289, which held that an allocation of state low-income housing tax credits does not constitute a "payment of money or the equivalent of money" by the state, or a "transfer by the state...of an asset of value for less than fair market price," and therefore low-income housing tax credits do not trigger state prevailing wage requirements.

Other typical forms of redevelopment assistance will also trigger prevailing wages under the state law. Any payments, waivers, forgiveness, or reduction of fees or costs associated with a project by an agency or city trigger prevailing wages. If a loan made by an agency is to be paid back on a contingent basis, that loan will trigger prevailing wages. If an agency offers a developer credits toward the repayment of a loan as part of an incentive program intended to encourage specific types of development, those credits will trigger prevailing wages.

There are a number of exemptions from the definition of prevailing wages listed in the law. While some of these are helpful in exempting some affordable housing projects, they are otherwise fairly limited in scope:

- Private residential projects that are built on private property are not subject to prevailing wage requirements unless the projects are built pursuant to an agreement with a state agency, redevelopment agency, or local public housing authority.
- If the state or a political subdivision requires a developer to perform work on a public work or improvement as a condition of regulatory approval, and the state or political subdivision only contributes the amount of money necessary to perform the required work, the overall project will not be considered a public work, so long as the state or political subdivision does not maintain a proprietary interest in the overall project. "Proprietary interest" is not defined.
- If the state or political subdivision reimburses a developer for costs that would normally be borne by the public, or provides a subsidy that is *de minimis* in the context of the overall project, the reimbursement or subsidy will not trigger prevailing wages. "*De minimis*" is not defined, but the DIR has found this exemption to apply in cases where a public subsidy is valued at 1.64 percent of the total project cost and less. *See, e.g.,* Public Works Case No. 2004-024, *New Mitsubishi Auto Dealership/Victorville Redevelopment Agency*; Public Works Case No. 2007-012, *Sand City Design Center/Sand City Redevelopment Agency*.
- The construction or rehabilitation of affordable housing units for low or moderate income persons is not subject to prevailing wages if that construction or rehabilitation is paid for solely with 20 percent affordable housing set-aside money or a combination of 20 percent affordable housing set-aside money and private funds.
- Self-help housing projects in which the homebuyers perform at least 500 hours of construction work are not subject to prevailing wages unless otherwise required by a public funding program.
- The rehabilitation or expansion of temporary or transitional housing for homeless persons is not subject to prevailing wages if the

Any payments, waivers, forgiveness, or reduction of fees or costs associated with a project by an agency or city trigger prevailing wages.

If the state or political subdivision reimburses a developer for costs that would normally be borne by the public, the reimbursement or subsidy will not trigger prevailing wages.

project cost is less than $25,000 and prevailing wages are not otherwise required by a public funding program.

- Mortgage assistance, downpayment assistance, and assistance provided for the rehabilitation of a single-family home will not trigger prevailing wages.

- The construction, expansion, or rehabilitation of a nonprofit facility providing emergency or transitional shelter and ancillary services and assistance to homeless adults and children will not be subject to prevailing wages, provided that prevailing wages are not otherwise required by a public funding program, and the nonprofit organization operating the facility provides at least 50 percent of the project cost from non-public sources.

- The public assistance in the project is in the form of below market interest rate loans for a project in which occupancy of at least 40 percent of the units is restricted for at least 20 years, by deed or regulatory agreement, to households earning no more than 80 percent of the area median income.

The DIR makes administrative level determinations as to whether or not a development project constitutes a "public work" subject to state prevailing wage requirements.

The DIR makes administrative level determinations as to whether or not a development project constitutes a "public work" subject to state prevailing wage requirements. In the past, the DIR maintained a list of "precedential" determinations on its website that interested parties could rely on to represent its position on whether certain forms of financing or assistance would trigger prevailing wages. However, in 2007, the DIR issued a notice declaring that it would no longer designate public works coverage determinations as "precedential." The notice states that "[t]he determinations should be considered advice letters directed to specific individuals or entities about whether a specific project or type of work is a public work subject to prevailing wage requirements." The DIR currently lists all the prevailing wage determinations on its website from 2002 to the present (www.dir.ca.gov/dlsr/PWDecision.asp). While no determinations on the present list enjoy "precedential" status, they do offer insight into how the DIR interprets the law, and the DIR continues to rely on its past determinations to support new determinations. It is important to note that DIR determinations can offer guidance to agencies and developers, but do not carry the same weight as published case law or the language of the statutes themselves.

DIR determinations can offer guidance to agencies and developers, but they do not carry the same weight as published case law or the language of the statutes themselves.

The DIR's determination in Public Works Case No. 2004-035, *Santa Ana Transit Village/City of Santa Ana* is the first determination to address the question of whether "fair reuse value" determined pursuant to Health and Safety Code section 33433 constitutes "fair market price" for purposes of determining whether prevailing wages apply to a redevelopment project. In this determination, the Santa Ana Redevelopment Agency entered into a DDA for the development of 108 live-work units. The developer acquired a portion of the development site through private sales, and the remaining portion of the site was sold by the agency to the developer. The section 33433 report prepared by the agency stated that the fair market value of the agency parcels was $2,520,000. The fair reuse value of $1,620,000 for the parcels was calculated based on the projected proceeds from the sale of the units, less the cost of acquisition of the private parcels, the estimated cost of construction, and expected profit to the developer. The DIR found that fair reuse value, as it was determined in this instance, did not constitute "fair market price," and the project was therefore subject to prevailing wages. The DIR did leave open the possibility that fair reuse value could, in some cases, be equal to "fair market price," if the purchase price for a property sold subject to redevelopment restrictions is based on an open market sale or a competitive bidding process, rather than exclusive negotiations with a single developer. The DIR upheld the Santa Ana determination on administrative appeal.

In *City of Long Beach v. Dept. of Industrial Relations* (2004) 34 Cal. 4th 942, the California Supreme Court held that assistance granted for certain "pre-construction" costs, including legal fees, insurance premiums, architectural design costs, and project management and surveying fees, did not trigger prevailing wages under the definition of "public works" in place prior to 2002, because that assistance did not constitute a payment for construction. Similarly, in *Greystone Homes, Inc. v. Cake* (2005) 135 Cal. App. 4th 1, the Court of Appeal held that contribution of (1) a single parcel of land, (2) reimbursement of property acquisition costs associated with several other parcels, and (3) payment of traffic impact fees by the Pleasant Hill Redevelopment Agency pursuant to a DDA for a housing development did not trigger prevailing wages for the project at issue because the public funds did not constitute a payment for actual construction. However, both courts explicitly noted that they were interpreting the pre-2002 definition of "public works" set forth in Labor Code section 1720, which did not include a definition of the phrase "paid for in whole or in part out of public funds." The DIR has explicitly refused to follow the holdings of the *Long Beach* and *Greystone Homes* cases in interpreting the existing definition of "public works." *See* Public Works Case No. 2005-016, *Oxnard Marketplace Shopping Center—Fry's Electronics/City of Oxnard*. Consequently, these cases are likely of limited benefit, since they do not apply the current language of Labor Code section 1720.

The DIR found that fair reuse value, as it was determined in this instance, did not constitute "fair market price," and the project was therefore subject to prevailing wages.

Before and After. *Construction of a mixed-use, mixed-income project containing 69 apartments and ground floor commercial space in Sacramento.*

Documenting the Transaction

Specialized agreements have been developed to document redevelopment transactions. These include disposition and development agreements, owner participation agreements (OPAs), and, where a long-term lease of the property from the agency is contemplated, ground leases.

Disposition and Development Agreements

A DDA is an agreement between a redevelopment agency and a devel-oper for the sale and development of property in the project area.

A DDA is an agreement between a redevelopment agency and a developer for the sale and development of property in the project area. Although the form of a DDA varies somewhat from one community to another, most of these agreements have the following common elements:

- *Sale of Land.* The agency agrees to acquire the property that is the subject of the agreement and sell it to the developer for a specified purchase price. The developer agrees to purchase the property at that purchase price. In some cases, the DDA may provide for an advance of the purchase price by the developer to assist the agency with site assembly.

OPA = Owner participation agreement

- *Development.* The developer agrees to purchase the property for development and not for speculation or landholding (§§ 33437, 33437.5). The property must be developed according to a specific scope of development that prescribes the use of the property and general design characteristics. A specific time schedule for development is included. A developer's failure to adhere to the schedule will constitute a default under the DDA that, if not cured, may result in reversion of title in the property to the agency.

- *Architectural Review.* The DDA typically establishes a procedure and schedule for the submission by the developer and review by the agency of progressively more detailed architectural plans and drawings. In this fashion, the agency maintains control over the quality of design and construction.

The DDA details the nature and extent of any agency assistance, such as the construction of public improvements and provision for public financing.

- *Agency Assistance.* The DDA details the nature and extent of any agency assistance, such as the construction of public improvements and provision for public financing.

- *Financing Provisions.* Provisions required by lenders to protect their interests are included to assure that the transaction can be financed.

- *Use Covenants.* Covenants running with the land are imposed on continued use of the property, including nondiscrimination covenants and the requirement that the property be used and maintained in accordance with the redevelopment plan.

- *Remedies.* The rights and remedies of both parties in the event of a breach of the agreement are described, and the conditions to the performance of both parties are specifically set forth.

The DDA should contain all of the terms and conditions relating to the sale and development of the property. It becomes the instrument that governs the relationship between the agency and the developer until development has been completed.

Because conditions affecting development are subject to frequent change, it often becomes necessary to revise or amend the DDA during the course of its implementation. For major projects, revising the document several times before development is completed is not uncommon. This is particularly true with respect to the schedule of performance. Both developers and redevelopment agencies must keep in mind the need to be flexible and adapt to changed conditions.

Because conditions affecting development are subject to frequent change, it often becomes necessary to revise or amend the DDA during the course of its implementation.

Owner Participation Agreements

There are two kinds of OPAs. In the first, an owner of property within the project area wishes to redevelop property that he or she owns in conjunction with adjacent property to be acquired by the agency and sold or leased to the owner. The second involves only the redevelopment of the property of the owner. The former is essentially identical to a DDA; the latter omits only those provisions pertaining to the disposition of property and adds a waiver of the agency's power of eminent domain if the owner redevelops and maintains the property in accordance with the OPA.

Ground Leases

Where a lease (rather than a sale) of the land is contemplated, the agency and the developer will enter into a ground lease of the property. A ground lease is a long-term lease (usually in excess of 55 years) containing provisions for the development and financing of the property. Each project will, of course, be different, but the length and terms of ground leases will necessitate realistic business decisions. The ground lease may be attached to a DDA or an OPA if the agency does not already own the property, or it may stand alone where the agency has title to the leased premises.

Where a lease (rather than a sale) of the land is contemplated, the agency and the developer will enter into a ground lease of the property.

Ground leases are not unique to redevelopment agencies. Private parties have used ground leases for centuries, and they have a long history of use by public agencies, primarily for dealing with activities that are ancillary to the public agency's primary statutory purpose, such as the lease of commercial space at harbors and airports. It is beyond the scope of this chapter to consider the many intricate issues involved in negotiating a ground lease, but the following discussion addresses those issues or problems that are either unique or particularly important in the context of redevelopment.

Using a ground lease in the redevelopment context has several important advantages:

- It reduces, or eliminates, the developer's up-front land cost.
- It provides a flexible way of structuring the consideration for the land that can take into account the future economic performance of the development.
- It allows an agency to more easily maintain ongoing controls over a completed project than a sale.
- When the lease term is up, the agency reclaims the land.

This last point can be significant because cities, unlike people, will have real property needs at the conclusion of a 50-year or even a 99-year lease term.

The primary disadvantages of ground leases are:

- They are cumbersome and expensive to negotiate and administer.
- They will usually increase the cost of financing the development and, in some cases, may make financing infeasible.

Structuring ground rents offers an unusually effective tool both to measure the value of the land by its economic performance and to provide a redevelopment agency with revenue participation in the success of the development. Several different kinds of rent have been used in the redevelopment context:

- *Holding Rent.* A minimum payment prior to and during the construction period.
- *Base Rent.* The basic minimum rent once construction has been completed, figured in accordance with the use of the property and anticipated economic performance. Base rents are usually adjusted periodically to account for inflation.
- *Percentage Rent.* An additional rent calculated on the basis of the volume of sales from the leased premises. This can be useful where the property is to be used for retail activity.
- *Participation Rent.* An additional rent calculated on the basis of the gross or net income of the development.

Both percentage rent and participation rent are usually calculated as overages—that is, they are paid only to the extent they exceed the base rent.

Whether the agency will subordinate its fee title to the lien of the developer's lender is an issue of primary concern. If the ground lease is unsubordinated, a foreclosing lender takes the ground lease subject to the agency's fee title interest in the property. If subordinated, a foreclosing lender obtains title to the property free and clear of any interest of the agency. All other things being equal, a redevelopment agency will prefer an unsubordinated ground lease. However, an agency may have valid reasons for subordinating its position to the developer's lender.

An unsubordinated ground lease will be more difficult and costly for the developer to finance. This in turn will affect the developer's cash flow, with the likely result of decreasing the ground rent. Without risking loss of its land, an agency may satisfy a lender by subordinating its right to receive rent, and perhaps its rights under other lease covenants, to the rights of a foreclosing lender in possession who wishes to recover all payments due and any costs incurred. A lease can be structured to protect the agency in the event a developer defaults by providing the agency with notice and an opportunity to cure the delinquency before the lender can foreclose. In any event, the decision to subordinate the agency's fee title to the developer's lender should be made only after a careful evaluation of the risks and benefits, based on the advice of experienced attorneys.

Agency Participation in Cash Flow

Redevelopment agencies have demanded and been given the right to participate with the developer in the profits of a development. There can be several justifications for agency participation in cash flow. First, there may be a disagreement between the agency and the developer about the value of the land. This disagreement is often caused by differing assumptions about the future economic performance of the project. Giving the agency a share of the cash flow is one way to resolve these kinds of disputes by tying compensation for the land to the *actual* economic performance of the project. Second, agency participation in cash flow provides a means for a community to recover other kinds of public expenditures that benefit the project but that cannot be recouped as part of the price of the land, such as parking and freeway interchanges.

The Mandela Gateway Project in Oakland converted a distressed public housing project into a 168-unit mixed-income housing project with 20,000 square feet of commercial space.

Agency participation is generally calculated on the basis of a percentage of either the gross income or net cash flow of the project. Net cash flow computations usually begin with gross income as the base and make deductions for debt service and the cost of operating and maintaining the development. Operation and maintenance deductions are often "capped" by reference to some industry standard. Some formulas provide for a preferential return to the developer. Other formulas base the agency's cash flow participation on a percentage of net operating income (before debt service) over a preferential return (for both equity and debt combined) on total development costs. Particular attention should be paid to defining terms precisely in these agreements in order to avoid misunderstandings and disputes over the subsequent computation of net cash flow. For this reason, redevelopment agencies wishing to participate should negotiate for a percentage of gross income or an easily computed method to determine net cash flow. For some projects, however, more complex formulas cannot be avoided.

Redevelopment agencies wishing to participate should negotiate for a percentage of gross income or an easily computed method to determine net cash flow.

The form of payment an agency receives to participate in cash flow varies. In the case of a sale, it can be paid as a deferred purchase price and can be secured by a deed of trust or other security device. Where the property is leased, ground rents can be structured to provide a convenient method for participating in the cash flow.

Developer Advances

In the event that a redevelopment agency does not have sufficient funds to undertake the costs of land acquisition, clearance, and relocation, it may wish to negotiate for an advance of funds from its developer prior to conveyance of the property. Where used, developer advances must be accomplished in a manner that assures the agency unconditional access to the funds before it begins to acquire land and negotiate with property owners. Funds advanced by the developer will include the advance payment of the agreed-upon purchase price, the amount of the good faith deposit, and additional funds, if any, needed to cover the agency's costs of land acquisition, including condemnation costs.

In some cases, the developer agrees that the purchase price of the property will be equal to the agency's total costs of acquisition, clearance, relocation, and related matters. In other instances, the portion of the advance that exceeds the agreed-upon purchase price is treated as a loan to be repaid, with interest, from tax increment generated by the project. It is often more cost-effective for the agency to acquire the land and deliver the property to the developer "as is," leaving demolition and site preparation costs to the developer, who can usually do the work more cheaply.

In negotiating an advance from a developer, the agency should:

- Assure access to sufficient funds to complete acquisition, clearance, and relocation of properties, once begun; this can be accomplished by requiring a cash deposit, an unconditional letter of credit, or some other form of security that is readily convertible to cash
- Protect itself against costs not recoverable from the advance of funds from the developer
- Limit its repayment obligations to tax increment received by the agency from the development of the property

Developers, on the other hand, will seek to:

- Protect themselves on cost overruns
- Assure themselves of the agency's ability to complete acquisition of the entire site
- Assure themselves of the agency's ability to repay the funds advanced that are in excess of the purchase price through a deed of trust or some other security device

The developer's lender, if involved in the advance, will want to secure repayment of its advance of funds. This will generally be through an assignment by the developer to the lender of its development rights under the DDA and may include personal guarantees from the developer to the lender. In certain situations, a developer or lender has asked for and received from the agency deeds of trust on property acquired securing repayment of the funds advanced.

The agency must preserve its ability to finance other activities in the redevelopment project, including its ability to issue tax allocation bonds or notes against the entire project area. In order to do this, the agency must be able to pledge all tax increments from the redevelopment project area, including the particular development, to the repayment of its tax allocation bonds or notes. The agency should reserve this right by agreeing that, in any such financing, it will either obtain and set aside sufficient proceeds to repay the funds advanced by the developer and the lender, or assure that there will be sufficient surplus tax increment—after first paying debt service on the bonds—to repay the agency's obligation to the developer or lender.

Subsequent Discretionary Approvals

It is common for a DDA to contemplate subsequent governmental approvals by the city or other public entities that require the independent exercise of discretion by those public entities. A good example would be a planning approval required to permit development as contemplated in the DDA. The customary way to handle these subsequent discretionary approvals is to make them conditions of performance; that is, if the subsequent discretionary approval is not given within an identified period of time (after the developer's having duly made application and otherwise acted in good faith), then the agreement may be terminated and the performance of both parties is excused.

One technique that has been used to advantage (particularly with large, complex projects with multiple subsequent discretionary approvals) is for the agency and the city (or, in the case of a county, the agency and the county) to enter into a cooperation agreement at the time the DDA is approved by the agency. Section 33220 provides that, for the purpose of aiding and cooperating in the planning, undertaking, or construction of a redevelopment project, any public body may, with or without consideration, dedicate, sell, or lease property to an agency; construct public improvements; dedicate, close, vacate, or install streets; and plan or replan, zone or rezone property, and make any legal exceptions from building regulations and ordinances.

This section further authorizes public entities to enter into agreements with an agency "respecting action to be taken pursuant to any of the powers granted by this part or any other law...." The purpose of the cooperation agreement is to obligate the public entity contractually to take those subsequent actions necessary to implement the DDA. Such agreements have been held to be enforceable (*see*, for example, *Housing Authority v. City of Los Angeles* (1952) 38 Cal. 2d 853) and may have the further effect of insulating those subsequent approvals from referendum. *See*, for

The Role of Redevelopment Agencies in Foreclosures

Foreclosures were commonplace in the 1990s, and again beginning in 2008. Generally, agencies have viewed foreclosures as an issue between a developer and a lender. Agencies usually only became involved when they were able to avoid becoming a venture partner in the strict legal sense of the word and when some overwhelming public purpose was served, such as saving the project, causing highly visible space to be leased, or protecting a significant financial interest in the project. Instances of overwhelming public purpose are rare, however, and agencies generally are well advised to let a developer and lender work out foreclosure issues. ■

The purpose of the cooperation agreement is to obligate the public entity contractually to take those subsequent actions necessary to implement the DDA.

example, *Andrews v. City of San Bernardino* (1959) 175 Cal. App. 2d 459. A city or county must be careful, however, to avoid a general fund commitment that would violate constitutional debt limitations. *See,* for example, *Starr v. City and County of San Francisco* (1977) 72 Cal. App. 3d 164.

Another technique developers prefer is for the city to enter into a statutory development agreement with the developer contemporaneously with the redevelopment agency and developer entering into a DDA. Government Code, section 65865 *et seq.* authorizes cities and counties to enter into statutory development agreements in the exercise of their planning power. A detailed discussion of statutory development agreements is beyond the scope of this chapter. Generally, however, development agreements provide a degree of certainty in the planning process by spelling out the rights of a developer to proceed with development according to planning laws, ordinances, and policies in effect at the time the agreement is entered into, subject only to the limitations and conditions in the development agreement and other statutory exceptions such as changes in federal and state laws. Many developers of complex, phased projects, and their lenders, feel that a statutory development agreement, combined with a DDA with the redevelopment agency, provides additional certainty in obtaining future discretionary approvals.

Renegotiating the Deal

As built, most major redevelopment projects in California differ substantially from what the parties to the original agreements contemplated.

As built, most major redevelopment projects in California differ substantially from what the parties to the original agreements contemplated. Often these changes improve the project. However, the ever-changing development environment requires that the initial agreement between the parties operates less as a fixed, rigid contract and more in the nature of a document establishing an ongoing working relationship between the parties.

Changes in projects usually result from responses to:
- Changed market conditions
- Requirements of major tenants and operators
- The design approval process
- Economic factors
- Changes in public financing requirements
- Shifting public priorities

It may be appropriate to reopen some issues previously compromised or given up in the original negotiations.

As these renegotiations occur, it is important for the agency to keep in mind its essential bargained-for objectives. In this context, it may be appropriate to reopen some issues previously compromised or given up in the original negotiations. Similarly, a developer requesting changes should be prepared to provide offsetting public benefits for those changes if they are favorable to the developer and unfavorable to the agency.

Lenders often present a difficult problem for the renegotiation process. Their demands are often extensive and will frequently appear onerous to the agency. The agency will want to accommodate the financing for the project without vitiating the agreement, but the time available to resolve lender requirements is often very short. The best rule of practice is to try to anticipate lender concerns and draft fair and complete lender protective provisions in the original DDA with the developer.

The best rule of practice is to try to anticipate lender concerns and draft fair and complete lender protective provisions in the original DDA with the developer.

When negotiating with lenders, the best rule is to distinguish between demands that are legitimately designed to protect the lender's interests in the event of foreclosure and those designed to sweeten the deal.

Lenders should be reasonably accommodated with respect to such matters as:

- Notice and opportunity to cure defaults
- Extensions of time to complete foreclosure proceedings
- Relief from certain affirmative obligations, provided that these will be passed on to a purchaser or assumed by the lender if it assumes the ownership and operation of the project
- Modification of certain use or quality restrictions
- The priority of project income to service the lender's debt obligation

Under a ground lease, the agency will not want to subordinate its underlying fee title interest in the land and risk losing it to a foreclosing lender, but it may be willing to subordinate certain rents to priority payments to a lender.

It is wise to resist "deal sweeteners" that create more favorable terms for the developer than those the agency negotiated. A lender will hold out for these to enhance the project's security or to protect its equity interest or percentage of cash flow. Lenders will also ask for representations and warranties, backed by legal opinions, concerning land use and zoning regulations, environmental clearances, the absence of litigation affecting the project, and the nondefault status of the developer. They may also ask for extensive representations and warranties concerning the absence of toxics on the site and other conditions. These representations and warranties carry significant financial exposure and must be examined closely and negotiated with great care.

It is wise to resist "deal sweeteners" that create more favorable terms for the developer than those the agency negotiated.

Dealing with Unforeseen Contingencies

It is important that a DDA or OPA not only anticipate and deal with the likelihood of changes but also accommodate untoward circumstances resulting from intentional acts of the parties, inadvertence, or unanticipated events. The following things can go wrong:

Significant changes in design or materials—not approved by the agency—may occur during construction. What should the agency do?

Stop construction? Order the changes to be undone? Frequently these are not practical alternatives. The best method is to prevent these changes from occurring in the first place by spelling out in the DDA:

- Clear standards for design and quality of construction and for substitute materials
- Practical design review and change-order procedures
- Effective monitoring and construction supervision

Because of market conditions, the developer may seek to reduce the quality of the project and the quality of its tenant mix (for example, by downgrading the quality of a hotel or a retail complex). If construction is already underway, this places the agency in a difficult position. To avoid this, the agency may seek to require binding commitments from major operators and tenants prior to and as a condition of closing.

The project may be adversely affected by a variety of unforeseen circumstances, such as:

- A voter initiative, such as a growth control measure
- Federal or state requirements, such as those related to the discovery of a wetlands problem
- New building regulations, such as fire safety or handicapped access requirements
- The discovery of toxics or other serious site conditions after conveyance
- Other unforeseen circumstances

To the extent that the DDA does not anticipate or provide for these circumstances, the terms of the agreement will have to be renegotiated. Solutions may be legally or politically impractical or economically infeasible, in which case the project cannot go forward.

As a result of the cyclical nature of the real estate development industry, it is not uncommon for a redevelopment agency to be asked to help rescue completed projects that have failed or are about to fail. The causes of failure can vary. Perhaps the project has not leased as anticipated, or significant cost overruns have occurred. Whatever the cause, foreclosure and/or bankruptcy now seem imminent. The developer or the lender have approached the agency to ask for further assistance. Perhaps the agency has an ongoing interest in the project in the form of some revenue participation. Depending on the extent to which the agency was initially involved, its prestige and the success of future projects may also be at risk. These projects present many new and different problems and demand different strategies and solutions.

When faced with such a problem, an agency's first step should be to determine what went wrong with the project and why. The answers to these questions will help determine whether the agency should assist the project and, if so, to what extent. Is it the kind of problem that can likely be fixed with a short-term, limited infusion of money or other assistance, or is the project doomed to failure regardless of any assistance the agency may be able to provide?

If the agency decides to rescue the project, a number of principles should be understood. First, the agency is limited to exercising statutorily authorized powers or those that may reasonably be inferred from the statutes. The Community Redevelopment Law does not authorize a redevelopment agency to become a partner to a real estate venture in the strict legal sense of the word. Assistance to a troubled project must be structured to use clearly granted powers, such as the power to purchase, sell, and lease real property. For example, a redevelopment agency is authorized to lease real property within a redevelopment project area. If a project fails to lease at projected rents, an agency could lease vacant space at the pro forma rent, and then sublease the space at market rate, thereby subsidizing the leases.

Assistance to a troubled project must be structured to use clearly granted powers, such as the power to purchase, sell, and lease real property.

Second, any form of assistance should have clearly defined limits, both in terms of time and the amount of assistance to be provided. If, despite the agency's help, the project continues to perform poorly, the agency should have the ability to "stop the bleeding" and terminate its commitment to the project. The agency should avoid at all costs uncapped commitments or liabilities. For the same reason, an agency should scrupulously avoid guaranteeing the developer's operating losses, debt service, or other unlimited financial obligations.

The agency should avoid at all costs uncapped commitments or liabilities.

Third, when taking on this kind of responsibility, the agency should demand a reasonable level of control over its operation. This could include the ability to replace a manager or to veto operational decisions that have a financial impact on the project.

Finally, when deciding whether to assist a troubled project, the agency should remember that foreclosure or bankruptcy is not the end of the world. Although unfortunate, defaults are everyday occurrences. Most projects will remain open and operating through the procedure and emerge on the other side prepared to move forward. The lender has a powerful incentive to straighten the project out as quickly as possible. While it may be difficult to refuse the developer's request or to see a project in which the agency has invested time and money foreclosed, this is often the best decision.

Effect of Initiatives, Referenda, and Local Legislative Enactments

The use of local initiatives and referenda has become increasingly popular, particularly with respect to controversial land use decisions and growth control policies. But occasionally these conflict with the provisions of redevelopment plans and transactions, like DDAs and OPAs, that implement redevelopment plans.

Generally, California courts have permitted the use of initiatives and referenda on a broad range of issues, holding that the scope of such reserved powers is to be liberally construed.

Generally, California courts have permitted the use of initiatives and referenda on a broad range of issues, holding that the scope of such reserved powers is to be liberally construed. *Pacific Rock Etc. Co. v. City of Upland* (1967) 67 Cal. 2d 666. Consistent with this general principle, their use has been sanctioned in connection with, for example, the zoning of real property (*Associated Home Builders Etc., Inc. v. City of Livermore* (1976) 18 Cal. 3d 582; *Arnel Development Co. v. City of Costa Mesa* (1980) 28 Cal. 3d 511), land use decisions relating to property in the coastal zone (*Yost v. Thomas* (1984) 36 Cal. 3d 561), and the enactment of growth limitations. *Pardee Construction Co. v. City of Camarillo* (1984) 37 Cal. 3d 465. Nevertheless, when found to have a *statewide* purpose so that the subject matter can be said to have been preempted by the state legislature, that matter is *not* a proper subject for an initiative or referendum. *Committee of Seven Thousand v. Superior Court* (1988) 45 Cal. 3d 491.[3]

Community redevelopment is deemed to be a matter of statewide concern and thus preempted by the state legislature. The Community Redevelopment Law explicitly recognizes that:

For these reasons it is declared to be the policy of the State:

* * *

(c) That the redevelopment of blighted areas and the provisions for appropriate continuing land use and construction policies in them constitute public uses and purposes for which public money may be advanced or expended and private property acquired, and are governmental functions of state concern in the interest of health, safety, and welfare of the people of the State and of the communities in which the areas exist. (§ 33037.)

Numerous cases have restricted the use of local initiative or referendum measures that attempt to limit or direct the implementation of redevelopment plans. In *Andrews v. City of San Bernardino* (1959) 175 Cal. App. 2d 459, referendum petitions had been submitted on an ordinance of the San Bernardino City Council adopting and approving a redevelopment plan. Relying on a line of cases holding that housing authorities are administrative arms of the state and are therefore not subject to control through local initiative and referendum powers (*Housing Authority v. City of Los Angeles* (1952) 38 Cal. 2d 853; *Kleiber v. City and County of San Francisco* (1941) 18 Cal. 2d

The Emeryville station mixed-use project includes office uses, housing, and an AMTRAK station. The agency assembled parcels and assisted with toxics remediation.

---

3. See also *City of Burbank v. Burbank-Glendale-Pasadena Airport Authority* (2003) 113 Cal. App. 4th 465.

718), the court held that the adoption of a redevelopment plan by a city was not a proper subject of referendum:

> Upon the formation of the Redevelopment Agency the state law thereupon and thereafter controlled the city and Redevelopment Agency, and all other acts fell within the executive or administrative functions. "Neither is functioning independently of that state law. In pursuing the state objective each is governed by the state law and neither may exercise powers not vested or recognized by that law." *Housing Authority v. City of Los Angeles,* 38 Cal. 2d 853, 862 (243 P. 2d 515). As a consequence, when operating pursuant to the Community Redevelopment Law, the same rules apply as with respect to the Housing Authority Law wherein it has been held that the city and Housing Authorities function as administrative arms of the state because they pursue a state concern and effectuate a state legislative objective. (*Andrews v. City of San Bernardino,* 175 Cal. App. 2d, p. 462.)[4]

In *Kehoe v. City of Berkeley* (1977) 67 Cal. App. 3d 666, the court examined the application within a redevelopment project area of an ordinance adopted by initiative restricting the issuance of demolition permits for residential structures. The stated purpose of the ordinance was "to deal with an emergency situation arising from current development trends in the City of Berkeley" that were resulting in the reduction in the stock of low-rent older homes. The city manager issued demolition permits for structures located within a redevelopment project area without complying with procedures set forth in the initiative ordinance. The redevelopment plan provided for the acquisition and reuse of land within the project area for commercial and light industrial development, and residential uses were prohibited. The city manager contended that "the Redevelopment Agency, as a state agency, is not subject to regulation by Berkeley ordinances, and... even if they were subject to such ordinances, the demolition permit provisions of the [initiative] are not an "applicable building ordinance" with which they must comply as a local agency within the provisions of Government Code section 53091." *Kehoe,* p. 672.

The Kehoe *court examined the application within a redevelopment project area of an ordinance adopted by initiative restricting the issuance of demolition permits for residential structures.*

The court first found that a redevelopment agency, as "an agency of the state for the local performance of governmental or proprietary function within limited boundaries," falls within the definition of a "local agency" as set forth in section 53090(a) of the Government Code and must therefore comply with all applicable building and zoning ordinances of the City of Berkeley. The court concluded, however, that the initiative was not an "applicable building ordinance" since the provisions regarding

---

4. In 1977, provisions were added to the Community Redevelopment Law that authorized a local referendum on the ordinance adopting a redevelopment plan. *See* §§ 33378, 33365, and 33450. These provisions do not authorize other forms of voter approval or disapproval, nor do they provide authority for making changes in an adopted redevelopment plan, including by initiative.

demolition permits conflicted with state statutes. The local ordinance must give way to the state statute, which is controlling.

The court found that the initiative conflicted with state statutes on several different levels:

- The initiative required a finding that demolition would not be materially detrimental to the housing needs and public interest of the affected neighborhood, which, if applied to the redevelopment agency, would require a redetermination of the policy established in the original adoption of the redevelopment plan

- Provisions of the initiative requiring an owner and/or developer to provide alternative housing for residents of structures to be demolished conflicted with the comprehensive relocation provisions of the Community Redevelopment Law set forth in Health and Safety Code sections 33410–33418

- Provisions of the initiative prescribing a finding that each structure to be demolished be a hazardous or unrepairable structure conflicted with provisions of the Community Redevelopment Law contemplating an area determination of blight

- To the extent it purported to modify or amend the redevelopment plan, the initiative conflicted with provisions of the Community Redevelopment Law governing the proper manner to amend redevelopment plans

Redevelopment Agency v. City of Berkeley (1978) 80 Cal. App. 3d 158 dealt with the adoption by initiative of an ordinance that, among other things, rezoned a portion of an adopted redevelopment project area from "Special Industrial and Manufacturing" to "Restricted Multiple Family Residential." The court found the ordinance at issue to be an improper subject of the initiative power, and stated:

> The principle is well established that the local governing body is carrying out state policy when it acts in proceedings under the Community Redevelopment Law. As the court explained in *Gibbs v. City of Napa* (1976) 59 Cal. App. 3d 148, 153 [130 Cal. Rptr. 382]: "The policy question, whether a city's redevelopment agency shall function, is of a legislative nature. But when the need for the agency to function is determined, 'all considerations of wisdom, policy and desirability connected with the functioning of a redevelopment plan [become] settled...." The agency's acts thereafter fall "within the executive or administrative functions." And case authority

The Vineyard is one of several affordable housing projects developed under Anaheim's Affordable Housing Strategic Plan.

makes it "clear that once the legislative policy is established...the administrative acts following therefrom are not subject to referendum." (Citations omitted.)

* * *

A legislative intent to preempt the field of community redevelopment is apparent.... The redevelopment of blighted areas was declared to be a governmental function of state concern, in the interest of health, safety, and welfare of the people of the state and of the communities in which the areas exist. *Redevelopment Agency v. City of Berkeley*, 80 Cal. App. 3d, pages 168–169. (Italics in text.)

The basic principle that can be derived from these cases is that the actions of the community and its redevelopment agency taken pursuant to the Community Redevelopment Law in the implementation of an adopted redevelopment plan are not subject to local initiative or referendum.

Approval Process

The Community Redevelopment Law establishes a procedure for the approval of agreements for the disposition of property. This procedure includes the preparation of various reports, holding public hearings and, in some cases, making written findings. In addition, the California Environmental Quality Act (CEQA) must be taken into account and may require the preparation of additional environmental documentation, holding public hearings, and making written findings.

CEQA = California Environmental Quality Act

Hearings, Reports and Special Findings, and Determinations

Section 33431 establishes the basic requirement that a redevelopment agency hold a public hearing prior to any sale or lease of property made without public bidding. Notice of the time and place of the hearing must be published in a newspaper of general circulation in the county in which the land is located once a week for two weeks. This provision is commonly understood to require a notice period of at least 14 days prior to the date of the hearing, beginning on the day the publication first appears and ending on the 14th day; there should be at least five days between the dates of publication of the notice. Gov. Code § 6066. No special report is mentioned in connection with this hearing. It is good practice to make a copy of the proposed agreement available for public inspection prior to the hearing and to include a statement to this effect in the notice.

Section 33431 establishes the basic requirement that a redevelopment agency hold a public hearing prior to any sale or lease of property made without public bidding.

It is good practice to make a copy of the proposed agreement available for public inspection prior to the hearing and to include a statement to this effect in the notice.

If tax-increment revenue was used directly or indirectly to acquire the property that is the subject of the sale or lease, section 33433 requires that a special report be prepared and a public hearing held by the legislative body (city council or board of supervisors). The hearing is subject to the same notice requirements set forth in section 33431.

It is common practice to hold this hearing jointly with the hearing required by section 33431. The special report must be made available to the public no later than the first date of publication of the notice of the public hearing and must contain:

- A copy of the proposed sale or lease
- A summary that specifies and describes:
  - The cost of the agreement to the agency—including land acquisition costs, clearance costs, the costs of any improvements to be provided by the agency, and the expected interest on any loans or bonds used to finance the agreement
  - The estimated value of the interest to be conveyed or leased, determined at the highest and best use permitted under the redevelopment plan
  - The estimated value of the interest to be conveyed or leased, determined at the use and with the conditions, covenants, and development costs required by the sale or lease, together with the purchase price or sum of the lease payments that the lessor will be required to make during the term of the lease
  - Why the sale or lease of property will assist in the elimination of blight, with reference to all supporting facts and materials relied upon in making this determination

If the sale price or sum of the lease payments is less than the fair market value of the interest to be conveyed or leased, determined at the highest and best use consistent with the redevelopment plan, then the report should also explain the reasons for the difference.

The requirements of section 33433 do not apply to the sale or lease of a small housing project.

The requirements of section 33433 do not apply to the sale or lease of a small housing project, which is defined in section 33013, and is, in general, a housing project of four dwelling units or less that is to be sold or leased to persons of low or moderate income. Prior to the sale or lease of a small housing project, the agency must hold a public hearing and, within 30 days of the end of the fiscal year, file a report with the legislative body containing specified information. § 33433(c).

The courts have held that the purpose of section 33433 is to ensure full disclosure of the essential terms of agency transactions, thereby ensuring accountability to the public.

The courts have held that the purpose of section 33433 is to ensure full disclosure of the essential terms of agency transactions, thereby ensuring accountability to the public. A summary that did not contain the actual purchase price but contained only a formula for deriving the purchase price was held to be legally sufficient. *Contra Costa Theatre, Inc. v. Redevelopment Agency* (1982) 131 Cal. App. 3d 860.

Section 33433 requires the sale or lease to be approved by a resolution of the legislative body. That resolution must contain findings of the legislative body that the sale or lease of the property will assist in the elimination of blight and that the consideration paid for the interest conveyed is either not less than the fair market value at its highest and best use in accordance with the redevelopment plan; or not less than the fair reuse value at the use and with the covenants, conditions, and development costs authorized by the sale or lease. The meaning of such terms as "highest and best use" and "fair reuse value" is discussed in General Rules, above.

To implement a project, an agency may pay for land or the construction of a public building, facility, or other improvement, or reimburse another public agency (such as a city or parking authority) for such costs. Section 33445 requires the consent of the legislative body, based on determinations by the legislative body that:

- The public improvements will benefit the project area or the immediate neighborhood in which the project is located
- That no other reasonable means to finance the improvements is available to the community[5]
- That payment of funds for the acquisition of land or the cost of buildings or facilities will assist in eliminating one or more conditions of blight in the project area and that the project is consistent with the implementation plan.

These findings are frequently made in connection with the approval of a DDA or OPA.

If the DDA calls for an agency to use its authority under section 33445 to construct or pay for the construction of publicly owned buildings (other than parking facilities) from tax-increment revenues, it must also hold a hearing and prepare a report pursuant to section 33679. *See* the discussion of the contents of this report in chapter 9, Basic Powers.

If the DDA requires an agency to install or construct streets, utilities, parks, playgrounds, or other public improvements that the developer would otherwise be required to provide, the agency should first obtain the consent of the legislative body. In giving its consent, the legislative body must make a finding that providing these improvements is necessary to accomplish the purposes of the redevelopment plan. § 33421.1.

If the DDA or OPA will lead to the destruction or removal of dwelling units from the low- and moderate-income housing market, the agency must adopt a replacement housing plan at least thirty days prior to approving the agreement. The replacement housing plan must include:

- The general location of the replacement housing
- Identification of an adequate means of financing the replacement housing

To implement a project, an agency may pay for land or the construction of a public building, facility, or other improvement, or reimburse another public agency (such as a city or parking authority) for such costs.

If the DDA requires an agency to install or construct public improvements that the developer would otherwise be required to provide, the agency should first obtain the consent of the legislative body.

---

5. Where the agency will be paying for the cost of a facility owned by a public entity other than the legislative body, this finding should be made by the public agency that will own the facility. *See* the discussion of *Meaney v. Sacramento Housing and Redevelopment Agency* (1993) 13 Cal. App. 4th 566, in chapter 9, pp. 220–222.

- A finding that the replacement housing does not require voter approval under Article XXXIV of the Constitution or that this approval has been obtained
- The number of replacement units to be constructed; and
- A timetable for developing or rehabilitating the replacement housing

§ 33413.5

CEQA

The disposition of property by a redevelopment agency will be considered a discretionary action subject to the provisions of CEQA unless a statutory or categorical exemption applies.

The disposition of property by a redevelopment agency will be considered a discretionary action subject to the provisions of CEQA unless a statutory or categorical exemption applies. *See* Cal. Code Regs., tit. 14, §§ 15260 *et seq.*, 15300 *et seq.* Ordinarily, CEQA compliance will be required prior to approval of a DDA or other property disposition, and an agency may not condition its approval on subsequent CEQA compliance. *Save Tara v. City of West Hollywood* (2008) 45 Cal. 4th 116.

Due to the nature of the redevelopment process and, in particular, the general nature of a redevelopment plan, CEQA recognizes redevelopment as a special case.[6] Public Resources Code section 21090 states that:

(a) An environmental impact report for a redevelopment plan may be a master environmental impact report, program environmental impact report, or a project environmental impact report. Any environmental impact report for a redevelopment plan shall specify the type of environmental impact report that is prepared for the redevelopment plan.

(b) If the environmental impact report for a redevelopment plan is a project environmental impact report, all public and private activities or undertakings pursuant to, or in furtherance of, a redevelopment plan shall be deemed to be a single project. However, further environmental review of any public or private activity or undertaking pursuant to, or in furtherance of, a redevelopment plan for which a project environmental impact report has been certified shall be conducted if any of the events specified in Section 21166 have occurred.

EIR = Environmental impact report

If the EIR on the redevelopment plan was a program EIR, then a subsequent EIR or a supplement to the EIR may be required.

If the EIR on the redevelopment plan was a program EIR, then a subsequent EIR or a supplement to the EIR may be required.

The State CEQA Guidelines describe the use of a program EIR in connection with subsequent activities implementing the program (such as a DDA) in the following terms:

(c) Use with Later Activities. Subsequent activities in the program must be examined in the light of the program EIR to determine whether an additional environmental document must be prepared.

---

6. *See* the detailed discussion of Public Resources Code section 21090 in chapter 3

(1) If a later activity would have effects that were not examined in the program EIR, a new initial study would need to be prepared leading to either an EIR or a negative declaration.

(2) If the agency finds that pursuant to section 15162, no new effects could occur or no new mitigation measures would be required, the agency can approve the activity as being within the scope of the project covered by the program EIR, and no new environmental document would be required.

(3) An agency shall incorporate feasible mitigation measures and alternatives developed in the program EIR into subsequent actions in the program.

Cal. Code Regs., tit. 14, § 15168

Chapter 4.5 to CEQA, entitled "Streamlined Environmental Review," describes a tiered environmental review process that certain kinds of projects may follow, including "[p]ublic and private projects pursuant to, or in furtherance of, a redevelopment plan." The "streamlined" procedure described (which is nothing more than a form of tiering already authorized under Public Resources Code, sections 21068.5 and 21093) is indistinguishable from the environmental review process that redevelopment agencies have followed for many years under the State CEQA Guidelines, involving the preparation of a "Program EIR" (CEQA Guidelines §§ 15168 and 15180) for the adoption of a redevelopment plan and subsequent or supplemental EIRs, as necessary, for subsequent redevelopment plan implementing activities such as property dispositions. For a more thorough discussion of tiering, see *Guide to the California Environmental Quality Act* (Solano Press, 2006, 11th edition, chapter 13, p. 603.)

When undertaking the disposition of land, a redevelopment agency should first examine the program or master EIR prepared for the redevelopment project and any supplemental or subsequent EIRs to determine the extent to which the development of the property has been analyzed in existing environmental documents. An initial study should then be prepared to determine whether the proposed disposition will have additional significant effects on the environment. The initial study should contain the elements described in section 15063(d) of the State CEQA Guidelines. In *League for Protection of Oakland's Architectural and Historic Resources v. City of Oakland* (1997) 52 Cal. App. 4th 896, the court held that the demolition of a building that is a presumptively historical resource cannot be approved without the preparation of an EIR.

If the initial study determines that the proposed action will not have a significant effect on the environment, then a negative declaration can be prepared.

If the initial study concludes that the proposed action will involve significant environmental impacts, but that these impacts are clearly mitigated

When undertaking the disposition of land, a redevelopment agency should first examine the program or master EIR prepared for the redevelopment project and any supplemental or subsequent EIRs.

to a point where no significant environmental effects will occur, then a mitigated negative declaration should be prepared. If it concludes that the proposed action will involve new significant environmental impacts or new information or data of substantial importance not considered in the previous EIRs, then a subsequent EIR should be prepared.

If the initial study concludes that the proposed action will involve new significant environmental impacts or new information or data of substantial importance, but that only minor changes are necessary to make the previous EIR adequate, then a supplement to the EIR should be prepared for that purpose. If the initial study concludes that the environmental impacts of the proposed disposition of property are essentially the same as those in the previous EIRs and that no additional information or data requires that previous EIRs need to be supplemented, then the agency (and the legislative body, if applicable) should adopt a resolution finding as follows:

- No substantial changes are proposed in the redevelopment project or with respect to the circumstances under which the project is to be undertaken that require major revisions to the EIR(s) previously adopted for the project due to the involvement of new significant environmental impacts not covered in such previous EIR(s)
- No subsequent EIR or supplement to the EIR is necessary or required
- The proposed disposition of property will have no significant effect on the environment, except as identified and considered in the previous EIR(s)

Prior to approving the DDA, the agency (and the legislative body, if applicable) should also make the findings required by section 15091 of the State CEQA Guidelines.

Prior to approving the DDA, the agency (and the legislative body, if applicable) should also make the findings required by section 15091 of the State CEQA Guidelines. If significant environmental impacts remain unmitigated, then the agency (and the legislative body, if applicable) should adopt a statement of overriding considerations pursuant to sections 15092 and 15093 of the State CEQA Guidelines. After the approval of a DDA, the agency should file a notice of determination pursuant to section 15094 of the State CEQA Guidelines.

9 Public Improvements

Basic Powers

Background

A traditional objective of redevelopment has been the replacement of inadequate public infrastructure and the provision of new public improvements and facilities to serve the project area. Under the original federal loan and grant programs, the costs of public improvements and public facilities, such as public buildings and parking structures, when financed locally, served as the matching local contributions required for federal funding. As redevelopment in California has become self-sustaining without dependence on federal funding, the variety of public improvements and facilities, and the means by which they are provided, has expanded to meet the changing funding mechanisms and project requirements.

Largely due to Proposition 13, the ability of an agency to construct and pay for public improvements and public buildings within a project area assumed greater importance for cities and counties facing pressures on their own general fund capital improvements budgets. Responding to criticisms that some redevelopment projects were little more than public improvements programs to circumvent the limitations of Proposition 13, the legislature in AB 1290 eliminated inadequate public improvements as evidence of blight. Further, an agency now is required to show that the provision of public improvements will help eliminate blight. Agencies cannot use tax increments to build city halls or county administration buildings and, with certain limited exceptions, cannot assist automobile dealerships or big box retailers. These restrictions are discussed below.

A traditional objective of redevelopment has been the replacement of inadequate public infrastructure and the provision of new public improvements and facilities to serve the project area.

As redevelopment in California has become self-sustaining without dependence on federal funding, the variety of public improvements and facilities, and the means by which they are provided, has expanded.

An agency now is required to show that the provision of public improvements will help eliminate blight.

Redwood City's Courthouse Square serves as the City's "outdoor living room" in the heart of downtown.

Inadequate Public Improvements Not Blight Criteria; Must Be Linked to Elimination of Blight

Prior to January 1, 1994, one of the basic criteria for blight in a project area was the existence of inadequate public improvements, public facilities, open spaces, and utilities that could not be remedied by private or governmental action without redevelopment. (§ 33032(c), repealed by Stats. 1993, c. 942 (AB 1290), § 5.) For plans adopted after January 1, 1994, AB 1290 eliminated the category of inadequate public improvements as a condition for a finding of blight. § 33031. However, the current law retains inadequate public improvements or inadequate water or sewer utilities as part of the broader definition of redevelopment so that an agency could document these problems and use its authority to construct necessary public improvements. § 33030(c).

Redevelopment, therefore, continues to be defined to include provision for open-space uses—such as streets and other public grounds; space around public or private buildings, structures, and improvements; and the improvement of public or private recreation areas and other public grounds. § 33021(b). Cities, counties, and other public bodies are specifically authorized to aid and cooperate with redevelopment agencies to cause park, playground, recreational, community, educational, water, sewer, or drainage facilities—or any other works that they are otherwise empowered to undertake—to be furnished adjacent to or in connection with redevelopment projects. § 33220(b). Cities, counties, and other public bodies are also expressly authorized to aid and cooperate with redevelopment agencies to furnish, dedicate, close, vacate, pave, install, grade, plan, or replan streets, roads, roadways, alleys, sidewalks, or other places that they are otherwise empowered to undertake. § 33220(c).

Off-Site Public Improvements

Section 33421 of the Community Redevelopment Law authorizes a redevelopment agency to acquire and develop property as building sites and to cause, provide for, or undertake—or make provision with other agencies for—the installation or construction of streets, utilities, parks, playgrounds, and other public improvements necessary in the project area for carrying out the redevelopment plan. The consent of the legislative body (the city council or county board of supervisors) is required for the agency to develop a site for industrial or commercial use so as to provide streets, sidewalks, utilities, or other improvements that an owner or operator of the site would otherwise be obliged to provide. In giving its consent, the legislative body must make a finding that providing such improvements is necessary to effectuate the purposes of the redevelopment plan. § 33421.1.

Land and Public Buildings and Facilities; Section 33445 Findings

Section 33445 of the Community Redevelopment Law authorizes a redevelopment agency, with the consent of the legislative body, to pay all or part of the value of the land for—and the cost of the installation and construction of—any building, facility, structure, or other improvement that is publicly owned either within or without the project area, if the legislative body determines all of the following:

- The buildings, facilities, structures, or other improvements are of benefit to the project area or the immediate neighborhood in which the project is located, whether or not the improvement is within another project area or, in the case of a project area in which substantially all of the land is publicly owned, the improvement is of benefit to an adjacent redevelopment project area.

- No other reasonable means of financing such buildings, facilities, structures, or other improvements is available to the community.

- The payment of funds for the acquisition of land or the cost of buildings, facilities, structures, or other improvements will assist in the elimination of one or more blighting conditions inside the project area or provide housing for low- or moderate-income persons, and is consistent with the implementation plan.

Those determinations by the agency and legislative body are deemed final and conclusive.

To carry out its authority under section 33445, a redevelopment agency may enter into a contract with the community or any other public corporation providing land or the cost of installing or constructing public improvements for the purpose of reimbursing the community or corporation for all or a part of the costs incurred by periodic payments over time. § 33445(c). Where the land has been or will be acquired by—or the cost of the installation and construction of the public improvement has been paid for by—a parking authority, joint powers entity, or other public corporation, and the improvement has been or will be leased to the community, the redevelopment agency is authorized to enter into a reimbursement

In giving its consent, the legislative body must make a finding that providing such improvements is necessary to effectuate the purposes of the redevelopment plan.

The "Our Hands" sculpture in front of Chico's Municipal Center, was funded by the Redevelopment Agency.

agreement with the community. § 33445(e). These contracts and agreements constitute an indebtedness of the agency for which tax increments, as well as other available funds, may be pledged. § 33445(d).

Notwithstanding the "final and conclusive" nature of the determinations the legislative body makes under section 33445, they may be insufficient if the building or facility in question is to be owned by a public agency other than the community. In *Meaney v. Sacramento Housing and Redevelopment Agency* (1993) 13 Cal. App. 4th 566, the First District Court of Appeal issued an opinion (after a rehearing on its opinion first published in 11 Cal. App. 4th 410) setting forth the procedures to be followed when a redevelopment agency pays for the costs of public improvements to be owned by another public agency.

The redevelopment agency in *Meaney*—pursuant to an agreement with the county that relied on section 33445—agreed to set aside tax increments in an amount the county would have received in property taxes from the project area to "assist the County in financing the costs for plans and specifications and construction for a new County courthouse and other Agency approved County public facilities consistent with the Redevelopment Plan." This agreement was challenged by the county superintendent of schools and school districts.

On procedural aspects, the court ruled that the action was reviewable under section 33445 and not under section 33401, the then-existing provision providing pass-through authority. The court then held that the action was not a validation proceeding under section 33501, which deals with the adoption of redevelopment plans and the issuance of bonds by an agency, but could be maintained as a validation action under Government Code section 53511, which deals with the validity of bonds, warrants, contracts, obligations, or other evidence of local agency indebtedness.

Turning to substantive issues, particularly the language in section 33445 that determinations under that section are final and conclusive, the court held that section 33445 determinations are clearly equivalent to findings of fact and are legislative findings. Therefore, the provision that the determinations were final and conclusive means that the evidentiary basis for the findings is beyond the reach of judicial scrutiny; the courts may not inquire whether the findings are supported by substantial evidence or by any evidence at all in the administrative record. This conclusion, however, does not preclude judicial review of the procedures that the redevelopment agency and local legislative body followed in making the determinations.

The court then concluded that the county, not the city, should have made the determination—required by section 33445—that no other reasonable means of financing the building was available to the community. "Here the City must make a determination on the benefit to the

Notwithstanding the "final and conclusive" nature of the determinations the legislative body makes under section 33445, they may be insufficient if the building or facility in question is to be owned by a public agency other than the community.

project area and the County must make the required finding on the unavailability of other means of financing." (*Meaney*, 13 Cal. App. 4th, p. 581.) The court also questioned the adequacy of the city's determination because it was not specific: "A determination that an unidentified form of financing constitutes the only 'reasonable means' of financing a County building is plainly meaningless; it cannot serve any useful function in guiding and limiting the use of tax-increment financing for public facilities. Since it does not serve the intended purposes of the statutory requirement, it may fail to qualify as a determination of fact demanded by section 33445." *Meaney*, 13 Cal. App. 4th, p. 581.

Another aspect of the *Meaney* decision dealt with the city's contention that the section 33445 determinations the city made were not reviewable because the action was not filed within 60 days following their adoption as required by the validation statutes, Code of Civil Procedure sections 860 and 869. The city council made its section 33445 determinations on July 17, 1990. The agreement with the county was dated October 10, 1990, and the action by the schools was filed on November 7, 1990. The court dismissed this contention, noting that the city conceded that the complaint was filed within 60 days after adopting the agreement, and held that "where the proceeding pertaining directly to a challenged action extends beyond the sixty-day period of limitations, the court may review the entire record of the proceeding in adjudicating the validity of the action." *Meaney*, 13 Cal. App. 4th, p. 583. (Compare *Graydon v. Pasadena Redevelopment Agency* (1980) 104 Cal. App. 3d 631, 639–642, to the effect that contracts are deemed in existence upon their authorization, notwithstanding their subsequent execution, citing Code of Civil Procedure, section 864.)

Roseville has set aside space in its downtown redevelopment corridor for public art.

The California Supreme Court denied review of the decision. The *Meaney* case must be consulted whenever section 33445 authority is being used to pay for the costs of public improvements for a public agency other than the community. Following *Meaney*, the determination under section 33445 that "no other reasonable means of financing such buildings, facilities, structures, or other improvements is available to the community" should be made first by the legislative body or governing board of the public agency for whom the improvement is being developed. That determination, together with supporting information, should then be included in the record for the legislative body of the community making the other section 33445 findings. A cautious approach suggests that the legislative body should make all three of the findings under

The Meaney *case must be consulted whenever section 33445 authority is being used to pay for the costs of public improvements for a public agency other than the community.*

section 33445, relying in part on its own determination and in part on the earlier determination the public agency made that no other reasonable means of financing was available.

Other Requirements and Limitations

Redevelopment Plan Requirements. For redevelopment plans and amendments to plans that add territory to a project area adopted after October 1, 1976, the acquisition of property and the installation or construction of each facility must be provided for in the redevelopment plan. § 33445(b).

Implementation Plan Requirements. For redevelopment projects adopted on or after January 1, 1994, the agency's report to the city council must include an implementation plan setting forth programs to improve or alleviate the blighting conditions. § 33352(c). The implementation plan must be updated every five years thereafter. For projects existing on January 1, 1994, an implementation plan must have been adopted before December 31, 1994, and updated every five years thereafter. § 33490.

Normal Maintenance and Operations Not Authorized. A redevelopment agency is not authorized to pay for the normal maintenance or operations of buildings, facilities, structures, or other improvements that are publicly owned. Normal maintenance or operations does not include the construction, expansion, addition to or reconstruction of buildings, facilities, structures, or other improvements that are publicly owned or are otherwise undertaken pursuant to section 33445. § 33445(b).

Public Hearing Required; Use of Tax Increments for Public Buildings Other Than Parking Facilities. Before an agency commits to use tax increments for land and installation and construction of any publicly-owned building other than parking facilities, the legislative body must hold a public hearing—notice of which must be published for at least two successive weeks—and make available a public summary that includes:

- Estimates of the amount of such taxes proposed to be used to pay for the land and construction of any publicly-owned building, including interest payments
- The facts supporting the determinations required to be made by the legislative body pursuant to section 33445
- A statement of the redevelopment purpose for which such taxes are being used to pay for the land and construction of such publicly-owned building

§ 33679

For redevelopment projects adopted on or after January 1, 1994, the agency's report to the city council must include an implementation plan setting forth programs to improve or alleviate the blighting conditions.

By leveraging its resources with federal and state funding, the Davis Redevelopment Agency was able to complete the Putah Creek Bike Undercrossing, thereby linking parts of the city otherwise separated by a freeway and railroad tracks.

Primary Benefit to Project Area Required for Use of Tax Increments. Section 33678 contains a further limitation on the use of tax increments by an agency to pay for improvements. This section was enacted to clarify that tax-increment funds allocated to a redevelopment agency are not subject to the expenditure limitations on "proceeds of taxes" under Article XIIIB of the California Constitution (the so-called "Gann Limit"). To be exempt from the Gann Limit under section 33678, tax increments must be used for redevelopment activity, which the section defines as meeting certain criteria, including *primary* benefit to the project area. This requirement contrasts with the finding required under section 33445, which is one of benefit (but not necessarily primary benefit) to the project area. The primary benefit requirement of section 33678 acts to preclude a redevelopment agency from spending tax-increment revenues for many community facilities of general community benefit such as water and sewer treatment plants, central police stations, and other facilities that provide a broader community benefit and do not *primarily* benefit the project area.

Prohibition on Payment for Certain Services. Section 33678 also prohibits an agency from using tax increments to pay for employee or contractual services of any local governmental agency unless those services are directly related to redevelopment activity.

Other Specific Projects Authorized

Section 33445 also contains special provisions authorizing redevelopment agencies in a county with a population exceeding 4,000,000 to aid in the design, location, construction, operation, and maintenance of transportation, collection, and distribution systems and related peripheral parking structures and facilities.

Other Community Redevelopment Law provisions expand the basic authority conferred under sections 33421 and 33445. Section 33445.5 authorizes special amendments to a redevelopment plan adopted prior to January 1, 1984, to add significant additional capital improvement projects to alleviate or eliminate school overcrowding. Section 33445.6 similarly authorizes special amendments to a redevelopment plan adopted prior to January 1, 1977, to add significant additional capital improvements to alleviate or eliminate the financial burden or detriment the plan's implementation causes a fire district.

Section 33446 authorizes a redevelopment agency to build and lease school buildings to a school district, with title to vest in the school district upon termination of the lease. Section 33448 authorizes a redevelopment agency in a county with a population exceeding 4,000,000 or a city with a population of more than 500,000—with the consent of the board of supervisors or city council—to acquire, construct, and finance through the issuance of bonds or otherwise—whether within or without a project area—a transportation, collection, and distribution system and peripheral parking structures and facilities, including sites for those purposes, to serve the project area and surrounding areas, upon a determination by resolution of the agency and legislative body that this improvement is of benefit to the project area.

Air Rights Sites

Section 33440 authorizes an agency to construct foundations, platforms, and other similar structural forms necessary for providing or utilizing air rights.

Section 33440 authorizes an agency to construct foundations, platforms, and other similar structural forms necessary for providing or utilizing air rights sites for buildings to be used for residential, commercial, industrial, or other uses contemplated by the redevelopment plan. § 33440.

Buildings for Residential, Commercial, Industrial, and Other Use

Except as otherwise specifically authorized by the Community Redevelopment Law, in the sections above and in provisions relating to relocation and low-cost housing, a redevelopment agency is not authorized to construct any of the buildings for residential, commercial, industrial, or other use contemplated by the redevelopment plan. § 33440.

Specific Applications

Typical Infrastructure Improvements

Corona's $5 million investment in streetscape improvements along North Main Street acted as a catalyst for revitalization of the area.

The usual infrastructure for a redevelopment project area—streets, curbs, gutters, sidewalks, street lighting, utilities, landscaping, and open space, including the acquisition of rights-of-way—is provided by the community pursuant to requirements, specifications, and procedures for public works. If it is going to bear all or a portion of the costs of land or public improvements, the redevelopment agency will agree to do so by means of a reimbursement agreement setting forth terms and sources of repayment to the city. Alternatively, an agency may do these public improvements directly and dedicate them to the community upon completion.

The community or agency may also form an assessment district or a Mello-Roos Community Facilities District to provide infrastructure and other public improvements authorized under the relevant enabling act, with costs borne as special assessments—in the case of assessment districts—and special taxes—in the case of Mello-Roos districts—levied against benefited private lands and developments. A redevelopment agency may agree to participate in the payment of such costs, usually pursuant to an agreement with property owners or developers (*see* chapter 10, Financing).

In all cases where the agency is directly or indirectly paying for the costs of public improvements, the procedures, findings, and limitations discussed on pages 217–222 are applicable. It is particularly important to a developer relying on an agreement by a redevelopment agency to pay all or part of the costs of public improvements to ascertain that the agency has sufficient authority to do so, has completed all relevant agreements, followed requisite procedures, and made any applicable findings.

The California Attorney General has opined that a redevelopment agency had no authority to reimburse a landowner for property assessments paid to construct a flood control project where former agency members told the landowner they would vote to reimburse him for all or some portion of the assessments from surplus funds that might come into the possession of the landowner if the landowner would not protest the project's construction. 69 Ops. Cal. Atty. Gen. 147 (1986).

Parking Facilities; Public Buildings Other Than City Halls, County Administration Buildings

A major breakthrough in retail redevelopment in California occurred in the early 1970s when techniques were developed for regional shopping center projects in Hawthorne and Glendale to provide public parking facilities integrated in both construction and management with private downtown shopping centers. This breakthrough helped induce major department stores to return to the inner cities in new regional downtown shopping centers developed in redevelopment project areas.

Typically, a redevelopment agency acquires the site for the shopping center, sometimes with full or partial advances of funds from the developer, and the city's parking authority then issues bonds to acquire the site and construct parking facilities. The parking facilities are leased to the city, with lease payments from the city to the parking authority providing the source of payments on the bonds. The agency enters into a reimbursement agreement to pay or reimburse the city the amount of its lease payments and other costs from tax increments generated by the project.

The city, in turn, subleases the parking facilities to the developer for operation and management as public parking in conjunction with the operation and management of the shopping

It is particularly important to a developer relying on an agreement by an agency to pay the costs of public improvements to ascertain that the agency has sufficient authority to do so, has completed all relevant agreements, followed requisite procedures, and made any applicable findings.

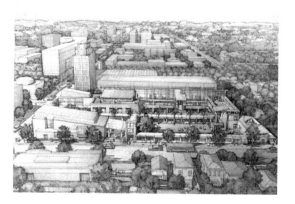

The San Jose Redevelopment Agency teamed with the San Jose Unified School District to construct a new, expanded elementary school on an old school site.

center and subjects the parking facilities, with certain specific provisions, to the reciprocal easement agreement governing the shopping center and entered into between the developer and the major department stores. The agency and the city must make appropriate section 33445 findings in connection with entering into the development agreement with the developer.

Variations of these techniques have been used by communities and redevelopment agencies to provide for other public improvements in connection with mixed-use projects. Throughout California, public convention center facilities have been developed and operated in conjunction with private hotel developments. Also, redevelopment agencies have paid for or developed public meeting facilities and public areas in private hotels for joint operation with the hotel facilities. Again, the procedures, findings, and limitations discussed in chapter 8 are applicable, and special restrictions govern the use of tax-increment funds.

Throughout California, public convention center facilities have been developed and operated in conjunction with private hotel developments.

City Halls, County Administration Buildings

Section 33445 prohibits, with certain limited exceptions, an agency from paying for the construction or rehabilitation of a building that will be used as a city hall or county administration building.

Section 33445 prohibits, with certain limited exceptions, an agency from paying for, either directly or indirectly with tax-increment funds, the construction, including land acquisition, related site clearance and design costs, or rehabilitation of a building that is, or will be used as, a city hall or county administration building. The limited exceptions allow an agency to:

- Allocate tax-increment funds for this purpose during the 1988–89 fiscal year and each fiscal year thereafter in order to comply with federal and state seismic safety and accessibility standards
- Use tax-increment funds for the purpose of rehabilitating or replacing a city hall that was seriously damaged during an earthquake declared by the President of the United States to be a natural disaster
- Use the proceeds of bonds, notes, certificates of participation, or other indebtedness that was issued prior to January 1, 1994, for the purpose of constructing or rehabilitating a city hall, as evidenced by documents approved at the time of the issuance of the indebtedness

§ 33445(g)

Assistance to Certain Automobile Dealerships and Retail Projects Prohibited

Under provisions added by AB 1290, redevelopment agencies are prohibited from providing any form of direct assistance to:

- Automobile dealerships that will be or are on a parcel of land not previously developed for urban uses. § 33426.5(a).
- Development that is or will be on a parcel of land of five acres or more not previously developed for urban use and that will, when

developed, generate sales taxes, unless the principal permitted use of the development is office, hotel, manufacturing, or industrial. A parcel is deemed to include land on an adjacent or nearby parcel on which a use exists (for example, parking) that is necessary for the legal development of the parcel. § 33426.5(b).

The above restrictions do not apply to projects for which, prior to January 1, 1994, the agency either owned the land or entered into an enforceable agreement for the purchase of the land or purchase of an interest in the land, including, but not limited to, a lease or an agreement containing covenants affecting real property requiring that the land be developed. § 33426.5.

These restrictions do not apply to projects for which, prior to January 1, 1994, the agency either owned the land or entered into an enforceable agreement for the purchase of the land.

Assistance for Relocation of Automobile Dealerships and Big Box Retailers Prohibited

Redevelopment agencies are also prohibited from providing financial assistance to vehicle dealers or big box retailers that relocate from the territorial jurisdiction of one community to the territorial jurisdiction of another community but within the same market area. § 33426.7. This restriction was originally enacted in 1999 in an effort to cut back on competition between communities for auto dealerships and big box retailers, both of which generate substantial sales tax revenues.

As originally adopted, section 33426.7 did allow redevelopment agencies to provide financial assistance to dealerships and retailers relocating within the same market area, provided that the community to which the retailer or dealership was relocating offered a contract for the even division of sales tax for 10 fiscal years to the community from which the retailer or dealership was relocating. In 2003, SB 114 amended section 33426.7 to eliminate agencies' authority to provide financial assistance to vehicle dealers or big box retailers within the same market area. The requirements of section 33426.7 do not apply to financial assistance provided by an agency pursuant to a lease, contract, agreement, or other enforceable written instrument if the applicable agreement was entered into prior to December 31, 1999. In *City of Carson v. City of La Mirada* (2004) 125 Cal. App. 4th 532, the court affirmed that the restrictions set forth in section 33426.7 apply to any store of greater than 75,000 square feet of gross buildable area that will generate sales or use tax.

"Breaking Down the Orange Curtain" is one of Brea's 145 pieces of public art in its redevelopment project areas.

Public Works Contracting Requirements

Public improvements undertaken or paid for by redevelopment agencies are subject to the provisions of Public Contract Code sections 20688.1 through 20688.4. Generally, any demolition, site work, and construction by a redevelopment agency in excess of $5,000 must be bid competitively.

The program for revitalization of the K Street District in Sacramento has resulted in the opening of the Esquire Plaza Office Tower and the IMAX Theater. The installation of capital improvements within the K Street District will assist in further increasing retail activity.

Work for less than that amount may be contracted without competitive bidding, and in contracting for such work the agency may give priority to residents of the project area and to persons displaced from the project area as a result of redevelopment activities. Pub. Contract Code § 20688.2.

Section 20688.3 also provides that to the greatest extent feasible, opportunities for training and employment arising from any contract for work shall be given to lower-income residents of the project area. An agency in a community with a population of less than 1,000 and with a secured assessed valuation of not more than $30,000,000, as shown on the 1978–79 assessment roll, may obligate lessees and purchasers of property acquired in a redevelopment project—and owners of property improved as part of a redevelopment project—to give preference to project area residents for training and employment in businesses to be conducted on the property. Such a requirement must reflect mutually agreed upon terms and conditions. Pub. Contract Code § 20688.3.

Bonds for performance, labor, and materials required for agency work must be filed with the agency by the successful bidder. Pub. Contract Code § 20688.4.

The Community Redevelopment Law provides that, to the greatest extent feasible, contracts for any work to be performed in connection with a redevelopment project should be awarded to business concerns located in, or owned in substantial part by persons residing in, the project area. § 33422.1. In contracts exceeding $100,000, the agency may also require opportunities for the employment of project area residents in a specified percentage of each craft or type of worker needed. § 33422.3.

The agency must require contractors performing work for the agency to pay prevailing wages. §§ 33423–33426.

Developer Construction of "Integrally-Related" Public Improvements

Where the public improvements are so interwoven by design and construction requirements that it is infeasible and impractical for a public agency to construct them separately according to competitive bid requirements, the agency may enter into a contract with the developer for their design and construction as part of the developer's project. This is an exception to the requirement that public work be bid competitively. Examples include public parking facilities under downtown shopping centers, public convention and meeting room facilities integrated into hotel developments, and public facilities such as plazas, open space, and museums that are integrated into private mixed-use developments.

In *Graydon v. Pasadena Redevelopment Agency* (1980) 104 Cal. App. 3d 631, a lawsuit was brought by a taxpayer to invalidate a contract for construction of a public parking garage and to compel the contract to be competitively bid. The agency had entered into an agreement with a developer for a privately owned downtown regional shopping center, to be constructed in an air rights parcel directly over a publicly owned and constructed subterranean parking garage. In reality, the shopping center and parking garage were a single structure utilizing the same foundations and structural elements, with interconnecting stairways, escalators, etc., and the agency was financing its obligations by issuing tax allocation bonds.

Because the public and private improvements were integrated, the agency awarded the construction contract for the public parking garage to the developer's contractor without competitive bidding, despite the fact that redevelopment law requires competitive bidding for any construction contract over $5,000.

The significance of this case is twofold. First, the court held that the action was barred by the 60-day statute of limitations contained in Code of Civil Procedure section 860, a section that in the past had been only applied to bonds and other financial obligations. The court held that this contract was so tied up with the agency's method of financing the garage and the bonds that had been issued for that purpose that the short statute of limitations should apply. Evidence was presented that the delay caused by bidding the contract competitively would have set back construction by nearly a year, thereby endangering the flow of tax increment that secured the bonds.

Second, the court indicated—although this was not the basis for its decision dismissing the lawsuit—that in a case with integrated overlapping public and private improvements, the contract need not be competitively bid. This aspect of the case has great importance for large mixed-use projects because of their integrated nature.

When an agency judges that developer construction of public improvements should be exempt from competitive bidding requirements, it is essential that the agency make determinations—based on analyses, as was done in the *Graydon* case—that the public improvements are so interwoven with the developer's improvements that they cannot be done practically by separate contract and that competitive bidding would result in greater public costs.

For these integrated projects, the parties should also always consider the possibility that the payment of prevailing wages may be triggered. Please see the discussion under Prevailing Wage Considerations in chapter 8.

When an agency judges that developer construction of public improvements should be exempt from bidding requirements, it is essential that the agency make determinations—based on analyses—that competitive bidding would result in greater public costs.

10

Financing

Agency Revenues

Tax-Increment Financing

Background. Article XIII, section 19, of the California Constitution, presently Article XVI, Section 16, was adopted as a constitutional amendment by the voters in 1952 to authorize the use of property tax increments for paying the indebtedness of redevelopment agencies. Article XIII, Section 19, also ratified and validated the provisions of the Community Redevelopment Law, as amended in 1951, relating to the use of taxes to finance redevelopment projects. These validation provisions were omitted in the general constitutional revision approved by the voters in 1974 when Article XIII, Section 19, became Article XVI, section 16, but references to them may still be helpful with some questions concerning historic redevelopment financing authority.

Using property tax increments to finance redevelopment was a totally new and innovative idea that is now the primary financing tool in California for paying the public costs of redevelopment activities. Based on the California experience, tax-increment financing has been adopted by more than 35 states throughout the country.

The rationale of the 1952 revisions to the California Constitution was to relieve taxpayers of the costs of redevelopment by making projects self-supporting, that is that these projects would be paid for with the increase in property taxes generated within the project areas. A response to the consistent refusal of the voters to authorize general obligation bonds to finance community redevelopment, tax-increment financing was designed to take advantage of federal urban renewal programs, which required local government to fund a percentage of the project costs.

Using property tax increments to finance redevelopment was a totally new and innovative idea that is now the primary financing tool in California for paying the public costs of redevelopment activities.

The California Constitution was amendmended by the voters in 1952 to authorize the use of property tax increments for paying the indebtedness of redevelopment agencies.

The rationale of the 1952 revisions to the California Constitution was to relieve taxpayers of the costs of redevelopment by making projects self-supporting.

Property tax-increment financing is based on the assumption that a revitalized project area will generate more property taxes than were being produced before redevelopment.

Property tax-increment financing is based on the assumption that a revitalized project area will generate more property taxes than were being produced before redevelopment. The California Supreme Court has described tax-increment financing as follows:

> In essence this section provides that if, after a redevelopment project has been approved, the *assessed valuation of taxable property* in the project increases, the taxes levied on such property in the project area are divided between the taxing agency and the redevelopment agency. The taxing agency receives the same amount of money it would have realized under the assessed valuation existing at the time the project was approved, while the additional money resulting from the rise in assessed valuation is placed in a special fund for repayment of indebtedness incurred in financing the project.

Redevelopment Agency v. County of San Bernardino (1978) 21 Cal. 3d 255, 259 (italics in original)

The authority found in Article XVI, Section 16, has been implemented by the legislature in section 33670 *et seq.* These sections state that any redevelopment plan may contain a provision for the allocation of taxes between the taxing agencies and the redevelopment agency so that (1) each year the taxing agencies receive that portion of the taxes produced from the total assessed value of taxable property in the redevelopment project "as shown upon the assessment roll used in connection with the taxation of such property by such taxing agency, last equalized prior to the effective date of such ordinance [approving the redevelopment plan]"; and (2) the redevelopment agency each year receives that portion of the levied taxes in excess of the amount that shall be deposited into a special fund of the redevelopment agency "to pay the principal of and interest on loans, monies advanced to, or indebtedness (whether funded, refunded, assumed, or otherwise) incurred by such redevelopment agency to finance or refinance, in whole or in part, such redevelopment project."

Public art enhances the Bridgecourt Apartments in Emeryville. In addition to providing a grant, the Redevelopment Agency issued bonds to help finance the affordable units.

This authority permits redevelopment agencies to receive—for payment of indebtedness—all of the property taxes levied on behalf of all the taxing agencies, such as the city, county, school district, and special districts, that are generated in a project area on increases in assessed values of property over the assessed values that existed on the day the redevelopment plan was adopted. Further, redevelopment agencies can pledge these future property tax increments to repay bonds or other borrowings.

The California courts have consistently interpreted and applied Article XVI, Section 16, in favor of its redevelopment financing objectives. In 1964, in one of the first major redevelopment decisions involving the Bunker Hill Project in the City of Los Angeles, the California Supreme Court ruled that Article XVI, Section 16, provides for the allocation of taxes to a redevelopment agency, and the consent of other taxing agencies is not required. *In re Redevelopment Plan for Bunker Hill* (1964) 61 Cal. 2d 21, 73.

In 1978, in the leading case of *Redevelopment Agency v. County of San Bernardino* (1978) 21 Cal. 3d 255, the California Supreme Court interpreted Article XVI, Section 16, to mean that when property on the tax roll at the time of project formation subsequently became tax-exempt by being devoted to public use under the redevelopment plan, the lower assessed value of that property was not to be considered when allocating taxes to taxing agencies under subsection (a) of section 33670. The Supreme Court concluded:

> To summarize, we have attempted to set forth the reasonable and accepted interpretation of the Constitution's language "assessed value of the taxable property in the redevelopment project" when project property is acquired by a tax-exempt agency. We think "taxable property" means property currently taxable; we believe that the assessed value of the taxable property should be redetermined so that the loss of the revenue resulting from the acquisition should be divided proportionately between the redevelopment agency special fund and the taxing agencies. In so doing we not only follow the interpretation of the Attorney General and the courts; we apply a practical and common sense approach, eschewing the reversal of decisions which would result in the destruction of the security of many millions of dollars of outstanding tax allocation bonds.

Redevelopment Agency v. County of San Bernardino, p. 267.

The result in this case, sometimes overlooked by redevelopment agencies, is an important one, particularly where a significant portion of a project area will be redeveloped for new public uses, including public buildings, parking facilities, open space, and recreational uses.

In 1992, section 33677.5 was added, which requires that a county auditor only offset excess amounts of property tax revenues allocated to a redevelopment project against the revenues of that same project and not against the property tax revenues of another project undertaken by the same redevelopment agency.

To clear up confusion with respect to the correct property tax allocation method, the legislature amended section 96.6 of the California Revenue and Taxation Code in 1999. The amendment established that the proper tax accounting method when allocating property tax-increment revenues in a redevelopment project is to compute the increase in property taxes minus any decrease in property taxes. The bill stated it was declaratory of existing law.

In *Redevelopment Agency v. County of Los Angeles* (1999) 75 Cal. App. 4th 68, the Court of Appeal held that the base assessment roll utilized for purposes of tax-increment financing was the roll last equalized before the effective date of the redevelopment plan, even though subsequent

The proper tax accounting method when allocating property tax-increment revenues in a redevelopment project is to compute the increase in property taxes minus any decrease in property taxes.

assessment appeals for the tax roll year in question resulted in a reduction of base roll assessed values.

In addition, in a 1999 opinion to Senator Rainey, the Legislative Counsel of California concluded that for purposes of using tax-increment financing for redevelopment plans, a statute may not authorize a redevelopment agency to use a property tax assessment roll different from the assessment roll last equalized prior to the effective date of the ordinance adopting a redevelopment plan. In answering a second related question, Legislative Counsel further concluded that a bill authorizing a redevelopment agency to use 50 percent of the existing base year as a base year for calculating property tax-increment revenues would conflict with Section 16 of Article XVI of the California Constitution in which the "last equalized" rule is outlined. (Opinion No. 23767, Oct. 27, 1999.)

Tax increment includes escape assessments and taxes on possessory interests.

Tax increment includes escape assessments. In *Community Redevelopment Agency of Oxnard v. County of Ventura* (2007) 152 Cal. App. 4th 1470, the Court of Appeal granted a writ of mandate to compel the county auditor to include escape assessments in its calculation of the allocation of tax increment, holding that section 33670(b) does not limit the taxes allocated to the agency to those derived from the last equalized assessment roll referenced in section 33670(a).

Tax increment also includes taxes on possessory interests. Section 33673 requires that property leased by a redevelopment agency in a redevelopment project to any person or persons for redevelopment is to be assessed and taxed in the same manner as privately owned property and that the lease or contract shall provide that lessee shall pay taxes upon the assessed value of the entire property and not merely the assessed value of the leasehold interest. Section 33673.1 requires notice (with a memorandum of lease and a map) to the local assessor within 30 days whenever the agency leases property in a redevelopment project to any person or persons for redevelopment.

Section 33673.1 requires notice (with a memorandum of lease and a map) to the local assessor within 30 days whenever the agency leases property in a redevelopment project to any person or persons for redevelopment.

In *City of Dinuba v. County of Tulare* (2007) 137 Cal. App. 4th 1387, the county had incorrectly computed the amount of tax increment to which the redevelopment agency was entitled. The agency sued to recover the correct amounts, but the county claimed immunity from suit under Government Code section 860.2. The California Supreme Court held that the county was not immune from liability for its miscalculation of tax increment, and the agency was entitled to enforce payment of the correct amount.

In *Graber v. City of Upland* (2002) 99 Cal. App. 4th 424, the Court of Appeal held that the detachment of a portion of an existing redevelopment project area and its reattachment to a new redevelopment project area specifically in order to obtain new base year values that would reflect the decline in assessed values was for an improper purpose that conflicts with the Community Redevelopment Law.

Limitations upon Receipt. Several constitutional and statutory provisions have limited the ability of redevelopment agencies to receive all tax increments generated from a project area.

First, Article XVI, section 16, was amended by the voters in 1988 to provide that tax revenues produced by a tax rate increase—approved by the voters of a taxing entity to pay bonded indebtedness for the purpose of acquiring or improving real property—shall be allocated to the taxing entity and not to the redevelopment agency.

Second, section 33676 was amended to authorize taxing entities to receive tax revenues produced by the inflationary increase allowed under Article XIIIA of the California Constitution, the so-called "two percent" increase. Although this authority has been revoked for plans adopted on or after January 1, 1994, taxing entities entitled to this amount prior to the change in law continue to be eligible to receive the "two percent."

For redevelopment plans adopted prior to January 1, 1994, the Court of Appeal in *Santa Ana Unified School District v. Orange County Development Agency* (2001) 90 Cal. App. 4th 404, construed the language of section 33676, as amended in 1984, as a legislative mandate for the "two percent" payment to a school district (as contrasted to other taxing agencies), which the district could not waive by its failure to timely make an election under that section. However, in this case the court ordered payment of the "two percent" revenues only from the date of the school district's late election and not retroactive to the adoption of the redevelopment plan. This case presents some unanswered questions for agencies with pre-1994 redevelopment plans where school districts did not file timely elections to receive the "two percent" increase or where there were pass-through agreements between agencies and school districts.

Third, in 1990, legislation was enacted allowing counties to collect from local governmental entities that levy property taxes a proportionate share of the costs of assessing, collecting, and allocating property taxes. Rev. & Tax. Code § 97. A number of redevelopment agencies contested the statute's application to redevelopment agencies because, in addition to other issues, the original legislation did not consider them to be local governmental agencies. In *Arcadia Redevelopment Agency v. Ikemoto* (1991) 233 Cal. App. 3d 24, this challenge was rejected and the statute was upheld. However, the California Supreme Court granted a petition for review and in December 1992 remanded the case to the Court of Appeal directing the court to vacate its decision and to reconsider its ruling in light of the adoption of Chapter 697, Statutes of 1992, which specifically applied property tax administration charges to redevelopment agencies.

In June 1993, the Court of Appeal upheld the right of the legislature to impose a proportionate share of the costs of assessing, collecting, and allocating property taxes upon redevelopment agencies. *Arcadia Redevelopment Agency v. Ikemoto* (1993) 16 Cal. App. 4th 444. The court held that Article XVI, section 16 of the California Constitution does not prevent the legislature from altering how taxes are levied and collected on property within a redevelopment project area in a manner consistent with how they are levied and collected on other property. *Arcadia Redevelopment Agency v. Ikemoto* at p. 452. The court also held that the legislature intended Revenue and Taxation Code section 97 to apply to redevelopment agencies commencing in the 1990–91 fiscal year, even though they were not specifically included until Chapter 697 amended Revenue and Taxation Code section 97.5 in 1992. It is, therefore, clear that redevelopment agencies are required to pay their share of the county's costs of administering property taxes commencing with the 1990–91 fiscal year.

Fourth, for various fiscal years, the legislature has enacted bills that have required agencies to make payments to a countywide Education Revenue Augmentation Fund, or ERAF. *See* page 249–250.

Fifth, as described below, AB 1290 (Chapter 942, Statutes of 1993) requires agencies that adopt project areas or add territory to project areas on or after January 1, 1994, to make specified payments to affected taxing entities throughout the life of the redevelopment plan.

Payments to Taxing Entities

Assembly Bill 1290 abolished the authority of agencies (under former section 33401) to enter into so-called "pass-through agreements" with taxing entities whereby the agency agreed to pay an affected taxing agency a portion of the tax increment it received in order to alleviate any fiscal burden or detriment caused by the redevelopment plan. (However, section 33607.8 still permits a redevelopment agency to make payments from tax-increment funds to an affected taxing entity that is a state water supply contractor under certain conditions.) AB 1290 also eliminated the time-consuming fiscal review committee process, thereby shortening the normal adoption process by two to three months. Another significant change was the amendment of section 33676 to eliminate the election by taxing agencies to receive the portion of taxes that are, or otherwise would be, calculated annually pursuant to subdivision (f) of section 110.1 of the Revenue and Taxation Code (the so-called "two percent inflation allocation").

In their stead is section 33607.5, which establishes a specific schedule of payments to be made by agencies to affected taxing entities. Affected taxing entities are defined in section 33353.2 as

It is clear that redevelopment agencies are required to pay their share of the county's costs of administering property taxes commencing with the 1990–91 fiscal year.

Tenth Street Place in downtown Modesto included financing from a joint powers agency formed by the City of Modesto and Stanislaus County, as well as from the Modesto Redevelopment Agency and a private developer.

any governmental taxing agency that levied a property tax within the project area in the fiscal year prior to the year in which the report establishing the base year assessed value is prepared pursuant to section 33328. Section 33607.5 applies to redevelopment plans adopted on or after January 1, 1994 (and territory added by subsequent amendments thereto) and amendments to pre-1994 plans adding territory (although the section applies only to the added territory). It specifically states that all amounts calculated pursuant to that section shall be calculated *after* the agency deducts the amount of tax increments deposited into its low- and moderate-income housing fund, pursuant to sections 33334.2, 33334.3, and 33334.6.

Section 33607.5 applies to redevelopment plans adopted on or after January 1, 1994 and amendments to pre-1994 plans adding territory.

Payments made under section 33607.5 are to be allocated among the affected taxing entities in proportion to the percentage share of property taxes each affected taxing entity receives *during the fiscal year the funds are allocated.* (In other words, if the percentage shares of the taxing entities are changed in any given year, the payments are adjusted in accordance with the changes in percentage.) In addition, the agency's payments to an affected taxing entity are reduced by any amount the agency has paid, directly or indirectly, for, or in connection with, a public facility owned or leased by that affected taxing entity, except any amounts paid pursuant to a pre-1994 pass-through agreement or any amounts that are unrelated to the specific project area or amendment governed by section 33607.5. § 33607.5(a)(2). For example, if an agency has paid for the construction of a school facility pursuant to sections 33445 or 33446, the construction costs are to be deducted from the payments to be made to the benefited school district pursuant to section 33607.5.

Payments made under section 33607.5 are to be allocated among the affected taxing entities in proportion to the percentage share of property taxes each affected taxing entity receives during the fiscal year the funds are allocated.

The amounts to be paid to the affected taxing entities, except basic aid school districts, are as follows:

- From the first fiscal year in which the agency receives tax increments until the last fiscal year in which the agency receives increments, 25 percent of the tax increments received by the agency after deducting the amount required to be deposited in the Low and Moderate Income Housing Fund.
- From the eleventh fiscal year in which the agency receives tax increments until the last fiscal year in which the agency receives increments (in addition to the amounts paid under the preceding paragraph, and after deducting the amount allocated to the Low and Moderate Income Housing Fund), 21 percent of the portion of tax increments received by the agency, which is calculated by applying the tax rate against the amount of assessed value by which the current year assessed value exceeds the first adjusted base year assessed value. The first adjusted base year assessed value is the value of the project area in the tenth fiscal year in which the agency receives tax increment.

- From the thirty-first fiscal year in which the agency receives tax increments until the last fiscal year in which it receives increments (in addition to the amounts paid under the preceding two paragraphs and after deducting the amount allocated to the Low and Moderate Income Housing Fund), 14 percent of the portion of tax increments the agency receives, which is calculated by applying the tax rate against the amount of assessed value by which the current year assessed value exceeds the second adjusted base year value. The second adjusted base year assessed value is the value of the project area in the thirtieth fiscal year in which the agency receives tax increments.

The additional payments that begin in the eleventh and thirty-first years described above are calculated against artificially created base years so that in the year the increased payment begins, the amount of tax increment received by an agency and available for its use will not be lower than the amount received during the prior year. This mechanism was designed to assist agencies in selling bonds by assuring a consistent flow of tax-increment revenue.

The community that has adopted the redevelopment plan may elect to receive an amount equal to its proportionate share of the first level of tax-increment payments, but it may not share in the increases paid to other affected taxing entities commencing in the eleventh and thirty-first fiscal years. Section 33607.5 also contains special provisions regarding the treatment of payments made to school districts, community college districts, county offices of education and special education, as follows:

- School Districts—43.3 percent of the annual payments will be considered to be property taxes, and 56.7 percent will not be considered to be property taxes and will be available for educational facilities.
- Community College Districts—47.5 percent of the annual payments will be considered to be property taxes, and 52.5 percent will not be considered to be property taxes and will be available for educational facilities.
- County Offices of Education—19 percent of the annual payments will be considered to be property taxes, and 81 percent will not be considered to be property taxes and shall be available for educational facilities.
- Special Education—19 percent of the annual payments shall be considered to be property taxes, and 81 percent shall not be considered to be property taxes and will be available for educational facilities.

These percentages represent compromises reached between school districts and the State Department of Finance. The amounts considered property taxes constitute amounts saved by the state because each

Section 33607.5 contains special provisions regarding the treatment of payments made to school districts, community college districts, and county offices of education and special education.

property tax dollar received by a school district reduces the amount required to be paid to the school district by the state.

School districts, community college districts, and county offices of education receiving payments pursuant to section 33607.5 for educational facilities must spend the money at schools that are within the project area, attended by students from the project area, attended by students generated by projects that are assisted directly by the agency, or determined by a local education agency to be of benefit to the project area. § 33607.5(a)(5).

An agency may subordinate its payments to the taxing entities to loans, bonds, or other indebtedness (except loans or advances from the community) upon obtaining the approval of the affected taxing entities. The agency must provide the taxing entity with substantial evidence that it will have sufficient funds to pay both the debt service and the payments required by section 33607.5 when due. The affected taxing entity must approve or disapprove the agency's request for subordination within 45 days. It may only disapprove the request if it finds, based upon substantial evidence, that the agency will not be able to pay the debt service and the amount required to be paid to the taxing entity. If it does not act within 45 days, the taxing entity will be deemed to have approved the request, and such approval will be final and conclusive. § 33607.5(e)(3).

Section 33607.5 specifically provides that the purpose of the payments to the taxing entities is to alleviate the financial burden or detriment that the affected taxing entities may incur as a result of the redevelopment plan. It also provides that such payments are the *exclusive* payments *required* to be made by a redevelopment agency to a taxing entity during the life of the plan. Moreover, the section states that an agency shall not be required, either directly or indirectly—in order to mitigate a significant environmental effect or as part of any settlement agreement or judgment brought in any action to challenge the validity of a redevelopment plan—to make any other payments to affected taxing entities or to pay for public facilities that will be owned or leased to an affected taxing entity. § 33607.5(f)(2). This language was included in an attempt to prevent taxing entities, and school districts in particular, from continuing to threaten litigation in order to extract additional money from redevelopment agencies.

Under section 33676(b), "basic aid" school districts (those districts that only receive a basic or constitutionally required payment from the state) receive special consideration. These districts shall receive annually their percentage share of the property taxes from the project area allocated among all of the affected taxing entities during the fiscal year the funds are allocated, increased by an amount equal to the lesser of the following:

An agency may subordinate its payments to the taxing entities to loans, bonds, or other indebtedness upon obtaining the approval of the affected taxing entities.

Section 33607.5 specifically provides that the purpose of the payments to the taxing entities is to alleviate the financial burden or detriment that the affected taxing entities may incur as a result of the redevelopment plan.

Under section 33676(b), "basic aid" school districts receive special consideration.

- The percentage growth in assessed value that occurs throughout the district, excluding the portion of the district within the redevelopment project area
- Eighty percent of the growth in assessed value occurring within the portion of the district within the redevelopment project area

These payments do not apply to a redevelopment plan if the median household income in the community is less than 80 percent of the median household income in the county in which the redevelopment project area is located, the preliminary plan was adopted on or before September 1, 1993, and the redevelopment plan was adopted on or before August 1, 1994.

Section 33676 authorizes an agency to subtract from any payments made under that section the amount of property taxes that a basic aid district receives pursuant to any payments received as an affected taxing entity under section 33607.5 in order to ensure that a basic aid school district does not receive double payments. It is not clear whether the auditor-controller or agency makes the payments or if the payments are considered tax increment and, therefore, counted in determining the agency's housing set-aside obligation.

Section 33607.7 contains special provisions that apply to an amendment to a redevelopment plan adopted prior to January 1, 1994, that increases the limitation on the amount of tax increment to be allocated to a redevelopment agency or that increases or eliminates the time limit on establishing indebtedness pursuant to subsections 33333.6(a)(1) and (a)(2). If section 33607.7 applies, the agency must begin making payments to affected taxing agencies pursuant to section 33607.5 calculated against the amount of assessed value by which the current year assessed value exceeds an adjusted base year assessed value.

Section 33607.8 was amended to provide an exception to the rule that redevelopment agencies can no longer make pass-through payments by allowing redevelopment agencies to make payments under certain conditions to an affected taxing entity that is a state water supply contractor.

In 2007, the State Controller's office, at the behest of the Legislative Analyst's office, undertook a review of statutory pass-through payments to schools by redevelopment agencies under sections 33607.5 and 33607.7. Based on its review of the annual Controller's reports on redevelopment activity, the Legislative Analyst believed that the state was not receiving the full benefit of those pass-through payments. The Controller's investigation, published in May 2008, confirmed a combination of

The historic art deco Alameda Theatre had severely deteriorated, as shown below. The theatre was completely rehabilitated and a new parking structure and multi-screen theatre were developed as part of the redevelopment project.

miscalculated and misreported redevelopment pass-through payments to schools by counties, redevelopment agencies, and school districts, resulting in an additional burden on the State's General Fund obligations to schools of $33.8 million in fiscal year 2005–06 and $29.4 million in 2006–07. This led to inclusion in a budget trailer bill (AB 1389) for the 2008–09 fiscal year of a requirement for redevelopment agencies to conduct a five-year "look-back" of their statutory pass-through payments and to reconcile their calculations with their county auditor. § 33684. Due to late passage of the budget and unrealistic deadlines and ambiguities in the sections of the Community Redevelopment Law prescribing the statutory pass-through payments, this section has led to much confusion and numerous disputes over the calculation of these payments. At this writing, the California Redevelopment Association is engaged in discussions with the Controller, counties, and other stakeholders that will hopefully lead to clarifying legislation in 2009.

Section 33684 has led to much confusion and numerous disputes over the calculation of pass-through payments.

Indebtedness. Two basic requirements must be met before a redevelopment agency can receive tax-increment funds. The first is that the redevelopment plan must expressly provide for tax-increment financing. The second is that a redevelopment agency must incur loans, advances, or other indebtedness when carrying out the redevelopment plan.

A redevelopment agency may enter into a variety of different types of indebtedness. Among those currently used, the following five categories are most prevalent in California.

Direct Bonded Debt—Tax Allocation Bonds. These are bonds issued by the redevelopment agency and secured solely and directly by the pledge of tax increments from the redevelopment project. These tax allocation bonds are typically secured by a first pledge of the tax increments from the project—that is, the bonds are usually not subordinated. These bonds are not an obligation of the community that established the agency and the project area.

Section 33334.1 provides: "If the [redevelopment] plan authorizes the issuance of bonds to be repaid in whole or in part from the allocation of taxes pursuant to Section 33670, the plan shall establish a limit on the amount of bonded indebtedness which can be outstanding at one time without an amendment to the plan." In *Fontana Redevelopment Agency v. Torres* (2007) 153 Cal. App. 4th 902, the Court of Appeal ruled that proposed tax allocation bonds sought to be validated by the agency to repay indebtedness incurred under an owner participation agreement could not be validated because the bonds would exceed the redevelopment plan limitation on bonded indebtedness. In that case, both the redevelopment plan limitation and the owner participation agreement characterized the indebtedness incurred under the owner participation agreement as "bonded indebtedness." The Court of Appeal held that,

Indebtedness

A redevelopment agency may enter into a variety of different types of indebtedness.

- Direct bonded debt—tax allocation bonds
- Repayment debt—contracts
- Reimbursement debt—obligations an agency incurs under section 33445
- Expenses an agency incurs for operation, administration, and overhead
- Contingent or contractual obligations

This development in Sacramento's Del Paso Heights redevelopment project area houses 26,000 square feet of commercial retail and offices for the Urban League's programs, including a workforce training center, classrooms, and a drop-in daycare center.

notwithstanding language in the owner participation agreement distinguishing indebtedness subject to the plan limitation from indebtedness not subject to the plan limitation, both tax allocation bonds and the owner participation debt were subject to the limitation in the redevelopment plan, and together they exceeded that limitation. A close reading of the court's opinion (*Id.* at pp. 911–913) shows that the result in this case turned on the express language used in the redevelopment plan and the owner participation agreement; therefore it should not be construed as interpreting the application of section 33334.1 in other cases where the language of the redevelopment plan limitation is limited to "bonded indebtedness which can be outstanding at one time...." The court also stated that another reason not to validate the proposed bonds was that the bond proposal, which pledged 100 percent of the tax increment for bond debt service, failed to comply with section 33334.2 (requiring deposits of 20 percent of the tax increment into the agency's low and moderate income housing fund) as that section existed at the time the bonds were authorized. *Id.* at p. 914.

Repayment Debt—Contracts. A redevelopment agency may agree under contract to repay loans of money and advances from any of the following public and private sources:

- City or county government
- Developers
- Short-term private financing—that is, short-term loans from banks or other lending institutions
- Property owners and owner participants
- Other governmental agencies—for example, state or county governments advancing money to the agency for a project of particular benefit to them

Repayment debt should be set forth in a contract between the agency and the firm, person, or entity advancing the funds. It is important for the contract to spell out the interest, if any, to be paid by the agency.

This repayment debt should be set forth in a contract between the agency and the firm, person, or entity advancing the funds. It is important for the contract to spell out the interest, if any, to be paid by the agency. In the event the agency intends to issue tax allocation bonds, the contract should specifically state that the agency's obligation to repay the loan or advance from tax increments is or will be subordinate to its pledge of tax increments for tax allocation bonds or other long-term indebtedness the agency incurs to carry out the project and to provide for subordinate debt repayment. This is particularly true for loans between the agency and its city or county.

In *County of Solano v. Vallejo Redevelopment Agency* (1999) 75 Cal. App. 4th 1262, a case involving a pre-1994 pass-through agreement, a county and a nonprofit neighborhood improvement association representing residents of a blighted area brought, *inter alia*, breach of contract and unjust enrichment claims against a redevelopment agency and city, respectively. The court found that the agency anticipatorily breached its contract with the county when it used funds ($3.2 million) earmarked for infrastructure and capital improvements within the blighted area to retire school bonds. Additionally, the court ruled that the agency's anticipatory breach excused the county from fulfilling any of the conditions precedent or concurrent in the contract.

Reimbursement Debt—Obligations Incurred by an Agency under Section 33445. Utilities, parking garages, public buildings, public facilities, and other structures—often acquired or paid for by the community or other public agencies—may be financed directly or by lease revenue bonds or other debt instruments. Section 33445 permits the redevelopment agency to pay this cost if the agency and legislative body find that doing so will benefit the project, that no other reasonable means of financing is available, and that the project will assist in the elimination of blight. This indebtedness is most commonly incurred when another public agency (such as a parking authority or joint powers authority) constructs a public facility (such as a building or parking structure) that is financed by issuing lease revenue bonds or certificates of lease participation secured by a city lease. The redevelopment agency can enter into a reimbursement agreement with a public agency permitting reimbursement for a public agency's payments under the lease from project area tax increments. If the agency intends to issue tax allocation bonds or incur other direct long-term indebtedness secured by tax increments, its obligation under the reimbursement agreement should be made specifically subordinate to any pledge of tax increments for tax allocation bonds or other direct long-term indebtedness to allow maximum flexibility in structuring agency debt in the future. Special findings and procedures required under sections 33445 and 33679 must be followed for the reimbursement agreement to be valid.

Expenses Incurred by the Agency for Operation, Administration, and Overhead. While a redevelopment agency may pay for its administration and operation expenses from a variety of sources, to receive tax increments for these expenses the agency must incur indebtedness. This makes redevelopment agencies different from other public entities and influences how they operate and how they account for those operations. One common method to establish debt for this purpose is for the city or county to annually lend the agency funds for operation, administration, and project overhead. The agency in turn pledges the tax increments from each project to repay these sums, with or without interest as specified. The transactions between the agency and the city or county must be formalized by a contract, with the pledge of tax increments specifically subordinated to the agency's pledge of tax increments for tax allocation bonds or other long-term indebtedness incurred to carry out the project. Special statutory procedures for a redevelopment agency administrative fund (§ 33610 *et seq.*) and its revolving fund (§ 33620 *et seq.*) may also be applicable.

Contingent or Contractual Obligations. These are obligations incurred under agreements with public agencies and private developers such as:

- Contractual obligations to acquire land or perform other acts in furtherance of a redevelopment project
- Agreements to acquire, install, construct, or otherwise provide public facilities and public improvements
- Contractual obligations under reciprocal easement agreements covering both public and private property
- Payments to school districts or other governmental agencies to alleviate economic hardships caused by a redevelopment project

Where possible, the agency's obligations should be limited to the remaining available tax increment after retiring any other indebtedness.

These should be represented by contracts between the redevelopment agency and other parties to the agreement on whose behalf the agency is undertaking the contingent or contractual obligation. Where possible, the agency's obligations should be limited to the remaining available tax increment after retiring any other indebtedness.

Each of these forms of indebtedness obligate the redevelopment agency to enter into a written contract to pay that, if breached, could subject the agency to some form of legal liability. This means that the obligation must be reasonably definite and not illusory, but not that it must have all the earmarks of a commercial loan. It is perfectly legitimate, for example, to condition the obligation to repay upon the existence of sufficient unencumbered tax increment, which means that the repayment period is indefinite. However, one should be able to determine the total principal amount of the indebtedness, whether interest is to be charged on the principal, and, if so, how much.

Statements of Indebtedness

In 1977, the Community Redevelopment Law was amended to require redevelopment agencies to file an annual statement of indebtedness.

In 1977, the Community Redevelopment Law was amended to require redevelopment agencies to file an annual statement of indebtedness with the county auditor or other county officer responsible for the payment of taxes to the various taxing agencies not later than October 1 of each year. § 33675. The State Controller is directed to provide a standard form for its statement of indebtedness.

AB 1290 amended section 33375 to make clear that an agency can list on its statement any indebtedness incurred prior to the October 1 date for filing the statement of indebtedness. Statements of indebtedness must now contain the date on which each loan, advance, or indebtedness was incurred or entered into; the principal amount, term, purpose, and interest rate of each advance, loan, or indebtedness; the outstanding balance and amount due or to be paid by the agency of each loan, advance, or indebtedness; the principal and interest due for that fiscal year; and the total amount of principal and interest remaining for each loan, advance, or indebtedness. In addition, agencies are required to file a reconciliation statement. § 33675(b). The statements of indebtedness must include a list of available revenue at the end of the prior fiscal year that is based on the reconciliation statement. § 33675(c)(1)(D).

The Lincoln Redevelopment Agency provided low-interest financing to rehabilitate a commercial building in the historic downtown area.

The reconciliation statement must contain the following:

- A list of the debt on the previous year's statement of indebtedness
- Debt not listed on the previous year's statement of indebtedness but entered into during the previous year and paid from tax increment
- For each debt listed above, the total amount of principal and interest remaining to be paid, any addition to the debt during the previous year, and any amount paid during the year from both tax increment or other sources
- Available revenues from both tax increment and other sources

§ 33675(d)

This information will allow the income, expenditures, and available revenues of the agency to be tracked from year to year.

Most importantly, the county auditor is directed to allocate to the agency the annual tax increment but not more than the amount of the total indebtedness *less* the available revenue. § 33675(g). To receive the total available tax increment, agencies must pay much more attention to making certain that sufficient debt is established. In addition, it is not possible for agencies to claim the same debt for several years or save it without paying the debt. However, note that using the reconciliation statement, tax increment could be spent on an obligation incurred and discharged in the period between the filing of two statements of indebtedness.

The statement of indebtedness establishes the *prima facie* evidence of the agency's indebtedness. If the county auditor disputes the amount, the auditor may request more information and, if the amount is still in dispute, may withhold the

To receive the total available tax increment, agencies must pay much more attention to making certain that sufficient debt is established.

disputed amount from the agency's allocation. If an amount is withheld, the auditor must bring a declaratory relief action in court in order to resolve the issue not later than 90 days after the auditor apprises the agency of its final determination. The issue in any such action shall involve only the amount of the indebtedness and not its validity. § 33675(h).

In practice, county auditors may attempt to question the agency's evidence of indebtedness or require additional supporting information. In *Marek v. Napa Community Redevelopment Agency* (1988) 46 Cal. 3d 1070, the county auditor disputed the agency's claim to tax increment in order to implement a disposition and development agreement with a private developer. The Supreme Court held that the auditor's function is limited to determining the amount of the indebtedness and does not extend to challenging the validity of any contract or debt instrument entered into by the agency. *Marek,* at pp. 1086–1087.

Two questions with regard to the sufficiency of indebtedness have frequently arisen. The first is whether the agency can draw down tax increments in order to build up funds for future projects. In order for this to be a proper claim against tax increments, it must be converted to one of the types of indebtedness listed above. An example of a contract that could create indebtedness for this purpose would be a public works agreement obligating the city to carry out specified public improvements for the benefit of the project—to the extent that the agency made funds available to the city and to the extent that the city had sufficient funds on hand for particular projects. Under this contract, the agency would agree to pay to the city annually a specified amount of tax increments until the city had sufficient funds to proceed with the public works projects covered by the agreement.

In the *Marek* case, the auditor argued for a narrow interpretation of "indebtedness," asserting that an agency's claim of tax increments for projected expenditures to carry out a disposition and development agreement did not constitute indebtedness because no certain sum was owed to a specific creditor by a date certain at a prescribed interest rate. The agency's obligations, argued the auditor, were a "proposed," not an "actual" indebtedness. *Marek,* 46 Cal. 3d, at p. 1080.

The Supreme Court rejected such a narrow interpretation in the context of redevelopment tax-increment provisions and applied a broad interpretation to the term "indebtedness:"

> Since redevelopment agencies are statutorily empowered to enter into binding contracts to complete redevelopment projects, the term "indebtedness" must be interpreted in a way that will enable those agencies to perform their contractual obligations. In this light, we think it clear that "indebtedness" was meant to include all redevelopment agency obligations, whether pursuant to an executory contract, a performed contract, or to repay principal and interest on bonds and loans.

To [ensure] its ability to perform its obligations, a redevelopment agency is entitled to all tax increment funds as they become available, until its "loans, advances and indebtedness, if any, and interest thereon have been paid...."

Marek, 46 Cal. 3d, at p. 1082

The Court also held that "it is only when the Agency's total indebtedness has been paid that tax-increment revenues are to be paid to the other taxing entities.... Until that time the county auditor is required to pay all available tax-increment funds up to the amount of the agency's indebtedness to the redevelopment agency...." *Marek,* 46 Cal. 3d, at p. 1086.

Redevelopment agencies, therefore, should list the total of all their contractual indebtedness on their annual statements of indebtedness, not just the contract or debt payments due in any one year. Under the *Marek* case, the agency is entitled to claim all tax increments available to it until the total of its indebtedness has been paid or tax-increment funds received are sufficient to pay the indebtedness when it comes due.

A second question is raised by the requirement that, unless certain exceptions apply, an agency must spend 20 percent of the tax increments to improve and increase the supply of low- and moderate-income housing. § 33334.2. Under AB 1290, an agency's 20 percent set-aside requirement is a debt of the agency that can be claimed on a statement of indebtedness. Once an agency receives tax increment and puts the money into its Low and Moderate Income Housing Fund, that tax increment cannot be considered available revenue. This prevents the Housing Fund from ever being considered "available" to pay non-housing debts.

Receipt by Agency. Tax-increment funds are allocated to redevelopment agencies by the county auditor or other appropriate county official at the same time as property taxes are allocated to the taxing entities. § 33675(g). The number and timing of the allocations differ from county to county, with some counties making a payment in December and one or two more payments in the spring, while other counties allocate property taxes throughout the year following their collection.

Section 33672.5 requires the county auditor or other official responsible for the allocation of tax revenues to prepare, upon written request of a redevelopment agency, an annual statement including specified information regarding calculations the county official made with respect to that redevelopment agency. Upon an agency's written request, the county auditor shall assist the agency by specifying the gross amount of tax-increment revenue allocated to the agency as well as any payments to other taxing entities. Redevelopment agencies are required to reimburse counties for reasonable and actual costs incurred to prepare this annual statement.

Section 33672.7 requires the county auditor to prepare, prior to August 15 of each year, a statement for each project area that shows the amount of tax increment distributed for the prior fiscal year and the amount of "pass-through" and statutorily required payments made to taxing entities.

Limitations upon Use. The agency may receive tax-increment funds only if its redevelopment plan contains the necessary authority and only to the extent that the agency has debt, which must be reported annually. Once an agency receives tax increments, certain limitations apply to the expenditure of those funds. These limits were modified by AB 1290.

First, the funds must be spent for redevelopment activities. After the passage by the voters of Proposition 4, adding Article XIIIB to the California Constitution requiring governmental entities to adopt spending limits, the state legislature enacted section 33678, which exempted tax increments from these limits if the following requirements are met:

- The funds must be used for the redevelopment purposes defined in sections 33020 and 33021.
- The expenditures must primarily benefit the project area.
- The funds cannot be used for the purpose of paying for employee or contractual services of any local governmental agency unless the services are directly related to defined redevelopment purposes.

AB 1290 both expanded these purposes by granting agencies new authority to make certain kinds of expenditures (*see* page 247) and limited agencies' authority by prohibiting direct assistance to certain kinds of development on land not previously developed for urban use. *See* pages 250–252.

Second, all redevelopment plans are required to contain certain limits that affect the receipt of tax increments and, therefore, the financing capacities of individual agencies. All plans, regardless of when adopted, must contain time limits on the authority of the agency to implement the plan and receipt of tax increment to repay indebtedness. These time periods cannot exceed the limits established by state law. *See* chapter 3. Plans adopted prior to January 1, 1994, must also contain a limit on the total amount of tax increment allocated to the agency. § 33333.4.

Third, tax increments cannot be used to pay for the normal maintenance or operations of buildings, facilities, structures, or other improvements that are publicly owned, nor can they be used to pay for the construction of city halls or county administration buildings. § 33445. SB 1206 (2006 legislative session) amended the provisions of section 33445(g) to explicitly prohibit the use of tax increment for construction or related costs, including land acquisition, site clearance, and design costs, for a city hall or county hall of administration.

Fourth, before tax increments can be used for off-site work of a kind normally provided by a private developer, the legislative body must make a finding that this public assistance is necessary to achieve the redevelopment of the area. § 33421.1.

Fifth, before an agency may pay the costs of land and buildings or facilities of another public agency from tax increments, the legislative body is required to make findings that the project will benefit the redevelopment area, that no other means of financing is reasonably available to the community, and that the expenditure will assist in the elimination of one or more blighting conditions and is consistent with the implementation plan. § 33445. In addition, for redevelopment plans adopted after October 1, 1976, the redevelopment plan must provide for acquisition of property and installation or construction of each facility.

Sixth, before tax increments to finance public buildings other than parking structures can be approved, the legislative body must hold a public hearing and make the following information available for public review:

- Estimates of the amount of tax increments used to acquire the land and construct the building
- Facts supporting the findings required to be made by section 33445
- The redevelopment purpose for which tax increments are being used

§ 33679

The purpose of this addition and the public hearing required by section 33679 is to prevent a community from acting to avoid the restrictions in Article XIIIB by transferring to tax-increment funding capital improvements or public services of general community benefit. *See also* chapter 9, Public Improvements.

ERAF = Education Revenue Augmentation Fund

Payments to Educational Revenue Augmentation Fund (ERAF). During weak economic periods, the legislature has used funds from local governmental entities, including redevelopment agencies, to help balance the state budget. This first occurred in the 1992 and 1993 sessions, then again in 2002–03, 2004–05, 2005–06, and 2008–09. This has been, in large part, a result of the inability of the legislature to address certain structural problems in the financing of state and local government. As part of its solution, the legislature established the Educational Revenue Augmentation Fund in each county and directed local government entities, including redevelopment agencies, to transfer a portion of the property taxes to this fund to be allocated to schools throughout the county. This new income reduced the amount of state aid to the schools.

The California Redevelopment Association initiated a challenge to the 2008–09 ERAF transfer in December 2008, claiming that ERAF transfers violate the provisions of Article XVI, section 16 requiring tax

During weak economic periods, the legislature has used funds from local governmental entities, including redevelopment agencies, to help balance the state budget.

The clear intent of section 33685 and previous ERAF transfers was to help balance the state's budget by reducing the state's Proposition 98 obligations to fund education.

The Community Redevelopment Agency in Palmdale purchased the property and installed the infrastructure for the 120-acre Fairway Business Park. Its $28.1 million investment resulted in $200 million in private development and generated more than 1,000 jobs.

increment to be paid into a special redevelopment agency fund to repay indebtedness incurred by the agency to carry out the redevelopment project. The clear intent of section 33685 and previous ERAF transfers was to help balance the state's budget by reducing the state's Proposition 98 obligations to fund education—not a redevelopment purpose. The litigation also challenges ERAF transfers on the grounds that they constitute an unconstitutional impairment of the contracts between redevelopment agencies and the holders of tax allocation bonds and other obligations. This case is not expected to be finally decided until 2010.

Miscellaneous Expenditure Authority. Because their authority to assist development projects is limited, except for assistance to housing for low- and moderate-income persons, redevelopment agencies typically attempt to assist development through their broad authority to acquire and dispose of real property and to pay for public improvements. Some other provisions include:

- Specific authority for agencies to establish a program to provide loans to owners or tenants for the rehabilitation of commercial buildings or structures within a project area. § 33444.5

- Authority for agencies, as part of a development agreement for the development or rehabilitation of an industrial or manufacturing use, to assist with the financing of facilities or capital equipment, such as pollution control devices. Prior to approving such an agreement, the agency must hold a public hearing and find that the assistance is necessary for the economic feasibility of the project and that financing cannot be obtained on economically feasible terms in the private market. § 33444.6

- Authority to remove graffiti from public or private property upon the making of a specific finding. § 33420.2

Sales and Use Tax Financing

In 1981, the legislature authorized a redevelopment agency to impose a sales and use tax of one percent or less on retail sales and use of personal property if the redevelopment agency operates in a community that will give credit against its own sales and use tax for taxes paid to the redevelopment agency. The constitutionality of this law was upheld by the California Supreme Court in *Huntington Park Redevelopment Agency v. Martin* (1985) 38 Cal. 3d 100. This authority was typically used to rebate to developers portions of the sales tax received from high sales tax producing developments such as big box retail and auto malls.

In response to concerns in the legislature that efforts by some redevelopment agencies were directed more toward assisting development that produced sales tax for cities' general funds than toward assisting development for the elimination of blight, AB 1290 ended the authority of redevelopment agencies to receive and use sales taxes. First, the authority of a redevelopment agency in Revenue and Taxation Code sections 7200.1 and 7202.6 to enact a sales tax ordinance and receive sales tax revenues was eliminated. This ended an agency's ability to rebate sales taxes to projects that produce these taxes. The legislature also eliminated an agency's authority in section 33641 to sell bonds using sales tax revenue as security.

AB 1290 clearly protected an agency's ability to fulfill obligations incurred prior to January 1, 1994, where, for example, sales tax revenues had been pledged to pay debt service on bonds or an agency had pledged sales tax revenues pursuant to a development agreement entered into before that date. Agencies were authorized to receive sales tax revenues pursuant to an ordinance enacted prior to January 1, 1994 for the limited purpose of paying obligations entered into prior to January 1, 1994.

Second, redevelopment agencies are prohibited from providing any form of direct assistance to:

- Automobile dealerships that will be or are on a parcel of land not previously developed for urban use. Projects entered into prior to January 1, 1994, are grandfathered. § 33426.5(a). Assistance to automobile dealerships on vacant land is prohibited because there was rarely a connection between the project, a financial gap and the elimination of blight.

- Section 53084 of the Government Code and section 33426.7 of the Health and Safety Code were added to prohibit redevelopment agencies, cities, and counties from giving any financial assistance to an automobile dealership or big box retailer that relocates from one city or county to another city or county within the same market area. The legislation defines important terms such as market area, big box retailer, financial assistance, and relocating. Transactions concluded prior to January 1, 2000, are not affected by this prohibition, which was intended to be prospective.

- In *City of Carson v. City of La Mirada* (2004) 125 Cal. App. 4th 532, the court adopted a broad interpretation of this section in order to implement the intent of the legislature to limit competition among jurisdictions for sales tax revenues. The court found that a large office products warehouse facility that does not accept orders from the general public and that services its customers primarily through

The Gallo Center for the Arts was built with the help of a number of financing sources, one of which was agency funds that assisted with landscaping around the exterior.

Bill Wood Photography, courtesy Gallo Center for the Arts, Modesto, California

A redevelopment agency may not provide any form of assistance for the acquisition, construction, improvement, rehabilitation, or replacement of property that is to be used for gambling or gaming or any kind.

purchase orders taken by telephone, facsimile, mail, and through the internet was nevertheless a "big box retailer" because it met the two statutory criteria: (1) physical size (greater than 75,000 square feet of gross buildable area), and (2) the ability to generate sales tax revenue.

- Development that is or will be on a parcel of land of five acres or more that has not been previously developed for urban use and that will, when developed, generate sales taxes, unless the principal permitted use of the development is office, hotel, manufacturing, or industrial. A parcel is deemed to include land on an adjacent or nearby parcel on which a use exists (for example, parking) that is necessary for the legal development of the parcel. Projects entered into prior to January 1, 1994, are grandfathered. § 33426.5(b). Assistance to projects on five acres or more of vacant land is prohibited because assistance was being given to large volume retailers on large parcels of vacant land, and the connection between these projects and the elimination of blight was difficult to determine.

A superior court has ruled that an agreement by a redevelopment agency to assist a Wal-Mart store on a site that exceeded five acres of undeveloped land violates the prohibition in section 33426.5(b). *Bozek and Gonzales v. Redevelopment Agency of the City of Chula Vista*, No. 684525 (San Diego Co. Sup. Ct., 1995).

Third, a redevelopment agency may not provide any form of assistance, either directly or indirectly, for the acquisition, construction, improvement, rehabilitation, or replacement of property that is to be used for gambling or gaming or any kind. An agency may acquire property used for gambling for the purpose of selling the property for other uses if the property is acquired for fair market value. § 33426.5.

In *Hesperia Citizens for Responsible Development v. City of Hesperia* (2007) 151 Cal. App. 4th 653, the Court of Appeal considered the application of this limitation to an agreement entered into by the city and its redevelopment agency with an Indian Tribe whereby the city agreed to provide municipal services to a proposed casino for the costs of which it would be compensated by the Tribe. The Court of Appeal held that the agency did not violate section 33426.5 by merely being a party to the agreement because the agency was not (and could not) provide the services that the city was providing, stating "there is nothing in section 33426.5 that suggests that redevelopment agencies cannot be parties to contracts in which other governmental entities provide assistance to gaming entities." 151 Cal. App. 4th at p. 663.

Sections 55704.5 and 55707 of the Government Code were amended in 1999 to authorize revenue sharing contracts between counties, counties and cities, and cities, allocating local sales and use tax revenues between them. The contract must be proposed in an ordinance or resolution of the governing body of each jurisdiction that is a party to the revenue sharing contract, and receive a two-thirds vote from each governing body to which it is submitted. Additionally, the contract must be submitted at a general or direct primary election and receive a majority of all votes cast by qualified voters of each local agency that is a party to the contract. These statutes implement Article XIII, Section 29 of the California Constitution enacted in 1998.

Transient Occupancy Tax Financing

Many California cities levy a transient occupancy tax on hotel rooms ranging from six to ten percent of the room charge. In 1987, the legislature enacted legislation similar to the sales and use tax financing provisions that authorize a city to transfer authority to its redevelopment agency to levy such a tax and pledge future proceeds for repayment of agency bonds or other indebtedness. Rev. & Tax. Code § 7280.5. Unlike sales and use tax, this authority has not been repealed and remains a viable tool to assist hotel development.[1] The impacts on the general fund and the analysis of the Gann limitation is the same as for sales and use tax financing.

Land Sale Proceeds and Lease Revenues

A redevelopment agency frequently receives money from the sale and lease of property it owns. As a general rule, this money may be deposited in the agency's general fund and used for authorized redevelopment purposes within its jurisdiction even if the property was originally acquired with tax-increment revenues. 63 Ops. Cal. Atty. Gen. 509 (1980).

Whether these proceeds are further restricted depends upon the source of the funds used to acquire the property. Proceeds from property originally acquired with funds from the agency's redevelopment revolving fund must be deposited in that fund. § 33624. When it receives proceeds from property acquired with funds from the Low and Moderate Income Housing Fund, the agency should check the provisions of section 33334.3, subdivision (b) to determine whether the proceeds must be deposited in the Low and Moderate Income Housing Fund.

---

1. Some question remains as to the application of Proposition 218 (requiring voter approval of new taxes) to a transient occupancy tax levied by a redevelopment agency under Revenue & Taxation Code section 7280.5. There are no published appellate decisions on this subject. In the opinion of the authors, Proposition 218 should not apply because there is no net increase in the tax. Any transient occupancy taxes levied by the agency must be offset by a reduction in transient occupancy taxes levied by the legislative body.

Revenues from Governmental Agencies

Community Funds

After an agency has been established and is authorized to transact business (by enacting the procedural documents described in chapter 2, Agency Activation), the legislative body of the community may lend or grant the agency working capital for administrative and start-up costs and land acquisition. § 33610. The community may also appropriate all or part of the amounts necessary for public facilities serving the project where tax increments and other funds are insufficient to assist all desired development. If structured as a loan, the agency would generally repay the debt from tax increments after repaying other indebtedness incurred to carry out the project.

Any public body, including the community, is specifically authorized to assist in the planning and implementation of redevelopment projects, with or without consideration, by conveying or purchasing property, providing public improvements, planning and zoning, and purchasing the agency's bonds. These activities may also constitute an indebtedness by the agency payable from tax increments if appropriate agreements are entered into with the cooperating public bodies. § 33220.

State

Except for establishing various programs to assist and help finance the construction of housing for persons of low and moderate income and the allocation of certain funds for planning for economic development, the State of California has not directly supported or taken an active role in redevelopment. Planning grants for small cities are available from the State Department of Housing and Community Development (HCD) and can be used in certain instances to assist in paying the costs of determining the feasibility of a redevelopment project area. The Department of Housing and Community Development administers a number of loan and grant programs, including a Homeownership Assistance Program, a Self-Help Housing Program, a Rental Housing Construction Program, and the state Community Development Block Grant (CDBG) Program (which includes planning grants to assess the feasibility of economic development and housing projects). In addition, in 2006 the voters approved Proposition 1C, a bond measure aimed at providing $2.85 billion in funds for projects that would assist the development of infill housing, including funds for associated infrastructure and parks.

Redwood City's Courthouse Square provides dining opportunities to downtown and theater visitors.

Except for establishing various programs to assist low and moderate income housing and the allocation of certain funds for planning for economic development, the State of California has not directly supported or taken an active role in redevelopment.

CDBG = Community Development Block Grant

HCD = Department of Housing and Community Development

In December 2008, those funds were temporarily suspended, pending resolution of the 2008–09 state budget crisis.

In addition, the California Housing Finance Agency (CHFA), established in 1975, has a variety of programs to assist in the financing of housing, including the Home Purchase Assistance Program, the Matching Down Payment Program, and the CHFA Resale Program.

Loans are also available from the California Infrastructure and Economic Development bank for eligible activities. *See* www.ibank.ca.gov.

Federal

Federal funding of redevelopment activities has continued to decrease steadily. Over the last decade, programs for both housing and commercial redevelopment have either been eliminated or suffered reduced funding. This has made reliance on tax-increment financing increasingly important. A few of the authorized federal programs for both commercial and housing developments are listed below, but, even though authorized, these programs can be underfunded or may not be receiving new applications for funds because of reduced appropriations. However, there is a possibility that federal funding opportunities may increase if Congress is able to enact a federal economic stimulus package in 2009.

Community Development Block Grants. This program began in 1975, replacing a number of specific aid programs to allow local communities broader discretion to administer federal community development funds. Eligible activities include acquisition and disposition of property, clearance and demolition, relocation, public facilities, and historic preservation. The funds that must be targeted to specific areas to benefit low- and moderate-income persons or eliminate slums and blight, have been allocated, in part, to support activities of redevelopment agencies and local development corporations.

Section 108(a) Loan Guarantee Program. Section 108 is the loan guarantee provision of the Community Development Block Grant program. It provides communities with front-end financing for large-scale community and economic development projects that cannot be financed from annual grants.

Urban Mass Transit Program. The Urban Mass Transit Administration of the Department of Transportation has participated in redevelopment projects by funding transit-related facilities, such as transit malls and transit stations.

Economic Stimulus Bill(s). One or more economic stimulus bills passed by Congress in 2009 or later years may contain funding authorization for various infrastructure, economic development, and housing

---

Federal Funding Available

- Community Development Block Grants
- Section 108(a) Loan Guarantee Program
- Urban Mass Transit Program
- Economic Stimulus Bill(s)
- Other Sources
  - Section 8–Lower Income Rental Assistance
  - Section 202–Housing for the Elderly and Handicapped
  - Mortgage insurance programs
  - Rehabilitation loans
  - Farmers Home Administration Programs

CHFA = California Housing Finance Agency

Section 108 is the loan guarantee provision of the Community Development Block Grant program.

Financing Team Definitions

Bond Counsel

A legal counsel with recognized expertise in state and federal law concerning the issuance of public debt. Bond counsel oversees the agency's proceedings in issuing debt and provides legal opinions as to these procedures and the taxability or tax-exempt nature of the bonds.

Financial Advisors

Consultants retained to advise the agency on the structure of the financing, the marketing of the securities, and, in the case of a negotiated sale, the interest rate and other terms of sale.

Underwriter

The firm that enters into a contract with the agency to purchase the bonds, either after a public bid or through a negotiated private placement.

Fiscal Agency/Trustee

Normally, a financial institution that receives principal and interest payments on behalf of the bond holders and acts on their behalf following issuance of the bonds.

Fiscal Consultant

A specialized consultant familiar with assessment and tax collection procedure, who provides independent analysis and projections of project tax increment.

---

programs to be implemented at the local level. As this book went to press, details of these bills were still being worked on by Congress.

Other Sources of Federal Funds. Other sources of federal assistance that target and give leverage to local community redevelopment programs include HUD housing programs, the section 312 commercial rehabilitation loan program, and loan guarantees and loan programs of the Small Business Administration. Federal tax laws have encouraged private investment in the rehabilitation of housing, older commercial structures, and historic buildings through tax credits and accelerated depreciation. In addition, a number of programs are directed exclusively toward the provision of housing for low- and moderate-income persons, including:

- *Section 8–Lower Income Rental Assistance.* Rent subsidies provided by federal funds are used to make up the difference between the amount low- and very low-income families are required to contribute based on their family income and the fair market rent for the unit as determined by HUD. Eligible tenants must pay the highest of either 30 percent of adjusted income, 10 percent of gross income, or the portion of welfare assistance designed to meet housing costs. There is also a Moderate Rehabilitation Program and an Existing Housing Certificate Program under section 8.
- *Section 202–Housing for the Elderly and Handicapped.* This program provides long-term direct loans to eligible, private nonprofit sponsors to finance rental or cooperative housing, including facilities for dining and health care facilities for the elderly or handicapped.
- *Mortgage Insurance Programs.* Used in conjunction with a variety of programs, the insurance by HUD of lenders against loss on mortgage loans is used to reduce the costs of financing a housing project.
- *Rehabilitation Loans.* CDBG and section 312 programs provide funds for below market rate loans that can be used to rehabilitate residential and nonresidential property.
- *Farmers Home Administration Programs.* The Farmers Home Administration offers a variety of loan and grant programs to assist in the provision of housing and economic development in rural areas.

Borrowing by the Agency

Redevelopment agencies are specifically authorized to borrow money by a variety of methods, including, but not limited to, the issuance of bonds. §§ 33601, 33640. Together with the ability to acquire property to be used for private development, this ability to borrow funds, particularly against a pledge of tax increments, is a unique power, and, in California, is only available to redevelopment agencies. It is an important power because project costs for redevelopment—such as land acquisition, relocation, and the provision of public improvements like public parking facilities—are often in excess of the annual funds available to an agency, require the agency to invest funds prior to beginning construction and long before receiving any revenue from the project.

Section 8855 of the Government Code establishing the California Debt and Investment Advisory Commission requires that the issuer of any new local government (or state) debt issue submit a report of final sale and a copy of the final official statement to the commission not later than 45 days after the signing of a bond purchase contract, in the case of a private placement, or the acceptance of a bid, in a competitive offering.

Prior to borrowing funds or financing projects, agencies should carefully review all the available financing options and consider a variety of factors to determine which alternative will best achieve its immediate and long-term goals. It is critically important for the agency to obtain competent and responsible advice to assist in this process by selecting, as needed, financial advisors, underwriters, and bond counsel who will prepare and present options to meet the agency's goals at the least possible cost. Among the factors the agency should consider are:

- The cost it incurs to raise funds
- The security for repayment and the relationship between the security and the cost of borrowing
- The risk incurred by issuing the debt
- The effect on the agency's or community's credit rating
- The effect on its cash flow and the agency's ability to fund future projects not paid for out of the proceeds of the borrowing
- The impact on the agency's ability to raise additional debt in the future
- Whether the borrowing can and should be tax-exempt or taxable, whether a competitive sale is required or a negotiated sale can take place, and whether the issue will be rated or unrated
- Whether the agency should issue its own debt or borrow funds from a lender or developer

Finally, it is also important to be aware of the various financing alternatives when negotiating agreements with developers so that the agency can structure its obligations to be financed most efficiently.

Tax Exemption

Until the Federal Tax Reform Act of 1986 was enacted, redevelopment agencies routinely issued bonds, usually tax allocation bonds, and used the proceeds to acquire property and convey it to a developer at less than fair market value. The interest on these bonds was exempt from both state and federal income taxes. The Tax Reform Act of 1986 greatly affects the ability of redevelopment agencies to issue tax-exempt debt. For example, the new restrictions prevent agencies in most circumstances

Real Estate Recession and Tax Allocation Bonds

Historically, California tax allocation bonds, properly underwritten, have received strong market acceptance as a relatively safe investment. Real estate values in the 1970s and 1980s grew at rates substantially higher than the inflation rate, and new development and property transfers caused tax increment growth rates in double digits.

The real estate correction beginning in 1990, however, substantially reduced property tax growth rates for most redevelopment agencies and, for some, reduced property tax allocations. While few, if any, California tax allocation bonds defaulted, the experience resulted in higher underwriting standards being applied by rating agencies and insurance companies.

Projects most at risk of reduced tax increment included urban downtown projects that saw substantial office building and/or hotel development in the mid and late 1980s, small-scale project areas with condominium and single family home developments, which occurred in the late 1980s, and single development projects also developed in the late 1980s. Less at risk were older, diverse project areas whose development occurred in the 1970s and early 1980s.

from using the proceeds of tax-exempt bonds to acquire property and convey it to a developer at less than the agency's cost if more than 10 percent of the bond proceeds are used for this purpose. Oddly enough, in certain circumstances, if land acquired with the proceeds of tax-exempt bonds is given to a developer at no cost, the tax-exempt status may not be affected. Since other restrictions are also important to redevelopment agencies, an introduction to these provisions follows.

Because these provisions and implementing regulations are highly technical and complex, agencies should seek help from bond counsel, financial consultants, and underwriters as early as possible to determine whether tax-exempt financing is feasible or economical, and whether it will accomplish the objectives of the agency.

Tax Allocation Bonds

Tax allocation bonds are secured solely by the pledge of tax increments generated by the growth in assessed value from within the project area and are not a debt of the community or the general taxpayer. Since they are limited obligations payable only from tax increments from the project area, investment grade ratings will typically be available only if the amount of bonds being sold is supported by currently generated tax increment. Binding commitments for new developments are typically not sufficient to allow bonds secured by the future increment from being marketed. This makes it difficult for an agency to borrow funds for a project that is the source of the bond repayment. Tax-increment financing of redevelopment typically funds land acquisition only when the tax increment from the project area is flowing and the bonds are not dependent on the proposed development for financing.

Off-site public improvements were provided by the Paso Robles Redevelopment Agency in connection with the development of a multi-screen theater and retail complex across from the City's historic park.

Because an agency must allocate 20 percent of its annual tax increment received to the Low and Moderate Income Housing Fund, this amount is not available to pay debt service on bonds, the proceeds of which are used on nonhousing projects. An agency can either sell bonds using 80 percent of the annual tax increments as security and deposit 20 percent of the tax increment in the Housing Fund; or it can sell a larger bond issue, pledge 100 percent of the tax increments to pay the debt service, and deposit 20 percent of the bond proceeds into the Housing Fund. Before making this choice, the agency should carefully consider the kinds of housing projects it intends to undertake and determine whether the proceeds of tax-exempt bonds can be used for those purposes. In other words, an agency must weigh the advantages of leveraging 20 percent of the funds against the disadvantages of the restrictions on the use of the proceeds of tax-exempt bonds by private persons. *See* pages 257–258 and 263–266 for a discussion of tax exemption; *see also* chapter 11 for discussion of *Craig v. Poway* (1994) 28 Cal. App. 4th 319.

As a general rule, annual tax-increment revenues available to pay debt service on the bonds should be approximately 120 to 125 percent of the maximum annual debt service when tax increment is the only source of revenue pledged for repayment. As a method of borrowing more money than could be supported by the annual tax increments existing at the time of the bond sale, the use of "escrow bonds" has developed when there is very strong evidence that annual tax increments will increase in the future. These bonds are sold in a higher amount than current annual tax increment supports. The proceeds of the bond issue that can be supported by the amount of tax increment available when the bond issue is sold can be used by the agency for redevelopment activities. The remainder is kept in an "escrow account" and is available only when the annual tax increment increases to enable the agency to make higher debt service payments. If tax increments increase as anticipated, the entire bond proceeds are made available to the agency within a relatively few number of years; if they do not, the proceeds of the bond issue not allocated to the agency are used to pay the bond holders. By selling escrow bonds, the agency avoids the very high costs of selling two or more smaller bond issues within a two- or three-year period.

The interest rate on tax allocation bonds will depend on whether or not the bond is tax-exempt, the market, and the rating, if any. This, in turn, will depend on whether or not the issue is insured, the amount of coverage, and the strength, diversity of land uses, and number of developments within the project area. Under state law, the maximum interest rate that can be earned is 12 percent with a discount not to exceed five percent.

The interest rate on tax allocation bonds will depend on whether or not the bond is tax-exempt, the market, and the rating, if any.

The proceeds available to an agency for project activities are reduced by bond costs and issuance conditions, which include requirements for funded reserves. Annual tax increments, including coverage requirements, must usually equal 1.2 to 1.3 times annual debt service, reducing the available proceeds by 25 to 30 percent.

Lease Revenue Bonds

Lease revenue bonds have been used in redevelopment project areas to finance public buildings and parking facilities. Their most common use has been to finance the costs of land assembly, clearance, and improvement of parking facilities. They have been structured to provide that the agency issues the bonds, assembles the site, constructs the parking improvements, and leases the parking facilities to the community at an rent equal to the debt service for the bonds. A developer may agree to sublease the parking facilities from the community at a negotiated rent and usually agrees to operate and maintain the parking facilities at the

The most common use of lease revenue bonds has been to finance the costs of land assembly, clearance, and improvement of parking facilities.

Layering of Financial Resources

To overcome the scarcity of private capital to finance real estate projects, agencies and developers have had to creatively mix and layer a wide range of resources. An example is a multifamily residential project financed by the following sources of funds:

- Developer equity
- Private construction loan
- Tax-exempt mortgage revenue bonds, two series
- Private credit enhancement of the mortgage revenue bonds
- Mello-Roos bonds
- Tax allocation bonds
- Low and Moderate Income Housing funds
- Public credit enhancement
- Public subordinated land loan
- Transit agency grants
- Syndication of federal income tax credits

The resulting project was the development of 320 apartment units, of which 20 percent were reserved as affordable units.

---

developer's cost. The security for the bonds is a general fund obligation of the community to annually budget and make the lease payments. In addition, the redevelopment agency may reimburse the community from tax increments for a portion of the lease payments to cover any amounts not covered by the developer's payments.

The advantages of this kind of financing are that, since the obligation of the community to make lease payments is secured by the general fund, the interest rate is lower, it is not considered a general indebtedness requiring voter approval, tax increment used to reimburse the community for lease payments may be leveraged without a coverage requirement and the bonds may be tax-exempt if the parking facilities are open to the public and other conditions are met.

The principal disadvantage is that, because they are publicly financed, the parking facilities have to be made available to the general public on a nonexclusive basis if the bond issue is to be tax-exempt under federal law. Exclusive reservation of parking for tenants of an office building, for example, is often not possible. Since the passage of the Tax Reform Act of 1986, further restrictions apply for interest on these bonds to be tax-exempt. In addition, securing approval for a lease revenue bond may be difficult politically because the general fund of the community is the ultimate security for the bonds. Finally, the approval is subject to referendum.

Certificates of Participation (Lease Participation)

Public entities often use certificates of participation to finance public improvements, including public buildings. Under this financing method, a corporation formed specifically for this purpose agrees to construct the improvements and to lease the building to the community or the agency. Against the security of this lease, certificates of participation are sold to investors, and the proceeds from their sale are used to finance the public improvements. The lease payments made by the community or the agency are equal to the debt service on the certificates. When the certificates are paid off, title to the improvements vests in the community or agency.

In many respects, a certificate of participation is similar to a lease revenue bond, but the limitation on interest rates does not apply. Like a lease revenue bond, an agency may reimburse the community or public body making the lease payments from tax-increment funds.

Assessment District Bonds

On-site and off-site public improvements may be financed using benefit assessment districts. Issued by the community, the bonds are secured by a lien on the properties benefited, and the property owners make all or part of the debt service by paying assessments (for example, Municipal

Improvement Act of 1913; Streets and Highways Code § 10000 *et seq.*). Tax increments may also be used to pay part of the assessment, relieving the developer or the private property owners of a portion of the cost.

Assessment district financing can be advantageous to both the agency and the developer because the bonds are tax-exempt; and, since the property is the security for the bonds, a lower interest rate can often be obtained than, for example, on tax-increment bonds. In addition, an assessment district bond can often be issued soon after an agreement is negotiated and approved and the property is acquired by the developer, because the security for the bond—the property—is in place.

Tax-increment revenues, on the other hand, may take years to increase to a point that makes issuing a bond economically feasible. An assessment district bond, as opposed to a tax-increment bond, shifts the risk that the project is developed and the tax revenues flow to the developer, regardless of any reimbursement agreement with the agency, because the developer and subsequent owners of the property are required to pay the assessment or tax.

Mello-Roos Bonds

The Mello-Roos Community Facilities District Act of 1982 provides communities with another method for financing the construction of public improvements and facilities. Gov. Code § 53311 *et seq.* Communities may sell bonds secured by and payable from an annual special tax levied on property owners within an established district. Mello-Roos Districts can finance improvements that are of more general benefit to properties within the district, such as schools and libraries, as well as improvements traditionally financed by assessment districts. Approval of a special tax by two-thirds of either the landowners or registered voters within the district is required.

Tax-increment financing can be combined with Mello-Roos District financing by either having the agency use tax increments to pay a portion of the taxes that would otherwise be paid by property owners, or the agency may issue tax allocation bonds and contribute the proceeds to assist payment of the public facilities, thereby reducing the amount required by the Mello-Roos District. Mello-Roos District Bonds have advantages to the agency similar to those described previously for assessment district bonds. They may be able to be sold immediately, the interest rate may be lower than a rate on a tax allocation bond, and the ultimate risk is shifted to the developer or property owner. *See* Marks-Roos Local Bond Pooling Act of 1985, Gov. Code, § 6584 *et seq.*

Residential Mortgage Revenue Bonds

While the type and kind of mortgage revenue bonds for residential purposes has been limited by the Tax Reform Act of 1986, it is still possible

Assessment district financing can be advantageous to both the agency and the developer because the bonds are tax-exempt, and because a lower interest rate can often be obtained than, for example, on tax-increment bonds.

Mello-Roos Districts can finance improvements that are of more general benefit to properties within the district, such as schools and libraries, as well as improvements traditionally financed by assessment districts.

to issue tax-exempt mortgage revenue bonds for both single-family and multifamily residential projects. Section 33750 *et seq.* authorizes redevelopment agencies to issue bonds to finance residential construction. Section 33740 *et seq.* authorizes redevelopment agencies to issue bonds to provide funds to loan to nonprofit organizations for the purpose of acquiring multifamily rental housing. This authority was amended in 1994 to allow agencies to also finance the acquisition of mobile home parks.

Section 33763.5 was added in 1997 to require that all loans made by an agency must be made according to a regulation adopted by the agency that contains standards, qualifications, and criteria for the making of loans. It is not clear whether the author intended to limit the applicability of this section by placing it in Chapter 8 of the Community Redevelopment Law, governing residential mortgage revenue bonds.

Borrowing from Developers

The developer or project proponent can be a source of funding to the redevelopment agency. Depending on interest rates, the availability of funds, and the strength of the developer, he or she may be able to obtain working capital or long-term financing as easily and as cheaply as the agency. Some institutions or projects that anticipate including users who self-finance their projects, such as some big box retailers, may have access to capital. Developers have assisted agencies in obtaining funds in various ways, some of which are discussed below.

Developer Advances

A developer can advance funds to the agency for any redevelopment purpose, including preliminary studies and agency administrative costs.

A developer can advance funds to the agency for any redevelopment purpose, including preliminary studies and agency administrative costs. Generally the developer will be repaid only if the project proceeds. The developer can also advance all or part of the funds needed for land acquisition, relocation, and site preparation. The developer could be repaid out of the tax increments generated by its development in excess of increments needed to repay other indebtedness. If the project does not proceed, the developer can be repaid out of the proceeds of the sale of the acquired land to another developer or from other project area revenues. Where the development problem is solely one of site assembly, developers have advanced and absorbed all agency costs to acquire the site.

Land Sale Proceeds

The purchase price paid by the developer for property sold or leased to it by the agency may be used by the agency to fund redevelopment activities.

The purchase price paid by the developer for property sold or leased to it by the agency may be used by the agency to fund redevelopment activities, including activities benefiting the particular development for which the property is sold. Generally, the purchase price for a site is paid by a developer at the time that title is conveyed by the redevelopment agency. In certain cases, the purchase price has been paid in advance to provide the agency with necessary working capital to acquire or prepare the site for development. Where the development problem has been site assembly, rather than the cost of land, developers have advanced and paid all agency costs to acquire the site. For a more detailed discussion of property disposition, chapter 8.

In Lieu Guarantee of Tax Increment

The ability of a redevelopment agency to incur financial obligations for a specific development may be based on a projection that the development will produce a certain amount of tax increments by a definite time. To induce the agency to proceed with its part of the activities—such as paying for the costs of public facilities to serve the development—a developer may agree to guarantee to the agency, by making an in lieu payment, the receipt of the development's tax increments in the amount and by the time projected. While not difficult to construct legally, these kinds of agreements are often hard to enforce from a practical point of view. Security for obligations such as these often presents a problem since the implicit assumption may be that the project is not complete or is not performing to expectations.

Public Purpose or Governmental Bonds

In general, the interest on bonds will be tax-exempt if used for public or governmental purposes and will be taxable if they are "private activity bonds" unless—even though the bonds are "private activity bonds"—they meet the criteria for "qualified bonds." Therefore, if the proceeds are used entirely for public purposes, such as the construction of publicly owned infrastructure, the bonds will be tax-exempt. If, however, the proceeds of the bonds are used in a way that meets the tests for "private activity bonds," they will not be tax-exempt unless the tests for "qualified bonds" are met.

They are considered "private activity bonds" if one of the following is true—

- They meet both the private business use test and the private security or payment test.
- They meet the private loan financing test.

Private Business Use Test and Private Security or Payment Test. This two-pronged test is similar to the test found under prior tax law with respect to industrial development bonds. Both parts of the test must be satisfied for an obligation to become a private activity bond.

The private business use test is satisfied if more than ten percent of the bond proceeds is used directly or indirectly in the business of a person other than a governmental entity (for this purpose, the federal government is considered to be a private individual).

Where the development problem has been site assembly, rather than the cost of land, developers have advanced and paid all agency costs to acquire the site.

If the proceeds are used entirely for public purposes, such as the construction of publicly owned infrastructure, the bonds will be tax-exempt.

The private security or payment test is satisfied if more than ten percent of the principal or interest on the bonds is directly or indirectly secured by any interest in property used or to be used in a trade or business or by any interest in payments made with respect to such property, or is to be derived from payments made with respect to property or borrowed money used or to be used in a private business.

In addition, although it allows up to ten percent of governmental bond proceeds to be used in a private business without causing the bonds to become private activity bonds, the 1986 Internal Revenue Code places a five percent limit on the amount of the proceeds that may be used by non-governmental persons for a use "unrelated" to the financed governmental project.

Under this related-use test, bonds are considered to be private activity bonds if:

- More than five percent of the proceeds is used in the business of a nongovernmental person and that use is not related to the governmental facilities also being financed with the bonds, and
- More than ten percent of the payments made with respect to the unrelated business use is made directly or indirectly by that person.

Additionally, even if the private use facility is related to the governmental facility, disproportionate unrelated business use will also count against the five percent use test.

Private Loan Financing Test. Bonds are private activity bonds if more than five percent of the proceeds is loaned directly or indirectly to nongovernmental persons. The concept of a loan is very broad and appears to include the use of tax allocation bond proceeds, for example, to acquire land that would be subsequently resold for less than fair market value on an installment basis to a developer if more than five percent was used for this purpose.

Private Activity Bonds

To be issued on a tax-exempt basis, private activity bonds must be on a permitted list and must meet certain additional requirements of the 1986 Internal Revenue Code. Unless specifically exempted, all private activity bonds are subject to a new unified state volume cap, a more restrictive 95 percent test on the use of proceeds for certain qualifying purposes, and arbitrage rebate requirements.

Use of Proceeds and Costs of Issuance. Generally, at least 95 percent of the proceeds of a private activity bond issue must be spent for its qualifying purpose.

Volume Cap. The 1986 Tax Reform Act replaced all prior volume caps with a new unified volume cap on the amount of private activity bonds each state may issue annually. Currently, the annual volume limit is the greater of $50 per resident or $150 million.

Tax Allocation Bonds—Tax-Exempt or Taxable

Tax allocation bonds may be either tax-exempt or taxable. They may be tax-exempt because they are public purpose or governmental bonds or because, even though they meet the private activity bond tests, they are "qualified redevelopment bonds."

Public Purpose or Governmental Tax Allocation Bonds. Tax allocation bonds will qualify as public purpose or governmental bonds if the private business use test, the private security or payment test, the related use requirement, and the private loan bond limitation are not met. For example, bond proceeds will not be considered to be used in a private business if they are used to finance public improvements—such as streets, curbs, gutters, sidewalks, water and wastewater facilities, and the like. The ownership and operation of these facilities must be with a public entity. The enormous advantage of obtaining tax-exempt status as a public purpose or governmental bond is that the agency is not forced to attempt to structure a bond issue to meet the artificial and impractical constraints that are necessary to gain tax-exempt status as a "qualified redevelopment bond."

Tax allocation bonds will qualify as public purpose or governmental bonds if the private business use test, the private security or payment test, the related use requirement, and the private loan bond limitation are not met.

Qualified Redevelopment Bonds. A tax allocation bond issue that fails to qualify as a public purpose or governmental bond may still qualify for tax-exempt treatment if such bonds are "qualified redevelopment bonds," a category of tax-exempt bonds created under the 1986 Internal Revenue Code but rarely utilized. A qualified redevelopment bond is one meeting all of the following requirements:

- It is issued pursuant to a state law authorizing tax-increment financing in accordance with a redevelopment plan adopted by the agency prior to issuing the bonds.
- At least 95 percent of the net proceeds (bond proceeds less reserve funds) of the issue is used for one or more redevelopment purposes in a designated blighted area.
- Any increase in real property tax revenues for such an area is reserved exclusively to the extent necessary for debt service on the bonds.

A tax allocation bond issue that fails to qualify as a public purpose or governmental bond may still qualify for tax-exempt treatment if such bonds are "qualified redevelopment bonds."

While the above definition appears to describe many tax-increment financings in California, the 1986 Internal Revenue Code—by virtue of unrealistically restrictive definitions of "redevelopment purposes" and "blighted area"—will make it very difficult for California jurisdictions to issue qualified redevelopment bonds.

Qualified redevelopment bonds may be used for specified redevelopment purposes, which are limited to:

- Acquiring property by a governmental agency with the power of eminent domain in a designated blighted area if the real property is to be transferred to persons other than governmental units for fair market value determined by including covenants and restrictions relating to the use of the real property
- Clearing and preparation of land for redevelopment
- Rehabilitating real property in designated blighted areas
- Relocating occupants of structures on acquired real property

This restrictive notion of redevelopment may preclude "write-downs" of land or the use of bond proceeds outside a project area. Additionally, while an issuer may obtain insurance or a letter of credit for a bond issue, the use of a developer guarantee or developer reimbursement of a letter of credit seems to be prohibited. Further, owners and users of real property in a project area may not be assessed special charges or fees not charged other persons for comparable property in the same jurisdiction. For these reasons, less than a handful of "qualified redevelopment bonds" have been issued across the country since they were authorized in 1986.

Taxable Tax Allocation Bonds. If it does not qualify for tax exemption as either a governmental or a private activity bond, a tax allocation bond can still be issued as a taxable instrument. The obvious drawback is the higher interest rate. However, if the issue is properly structured, interest on these bonds will still be exempt from California income tax.

If the issue is properly structured, interest on taxable bonds will still be exempt from California income tax.

11

Housing

> *The need for housing for low-income persons and families and the problems caused by slums were common reasons advanced by those who advocated the adoption of a redevelopment law in California.*

Introduction

For more than half a century, interest in using redevelopment powers primarily for downtown commercial rejuvenation and growth has been balanced against the impact of this commercial growth on housing for low-income persons and families. This tension, described in the summary of federal involvement in chapter 1, has also existed during the evolution of the Community Redevelopment Law in California. The need for housing for low-income persons and families and the problems caused by slums were common reasons advanced by those who advocated the adoption of a redevelopment law in California.

While the definition of "blight" has always identified substandard housing as a cause of social problems (Gov. Code §§ 33031, 33035), the physical elimination of slums also resulted in the elimination of housing for low-income persons and families in early redevelopment efforts. Cities whose civic leaders were convinced that the basic economic life of the community depended upon increasing the number of jobs and revitalizing the central business district often directed the limited funds available toward these goals. Using tax-increment financing instead of federal funds did little to change this emphasis, in part because low- and moderate-income housing projects did not generate as much tax increment, or other types of tax revenues, as that produced by commercial growth. In fact, several large cities with older redevelopment programs are now able to devote large amounts of tax increments to housing for low- and moderate-income persons and families, as a result of the tax increment produced by the commercial growth encouraged by redevelopment activities over the past several decades.

> *While the definition of "blight" has always identified substandard housing as a cause of social problems, the physical elimination of slums also resulted in the elimination of housing for low-income persons and families in early redevelopment efforts.*

Redevelopment agencies have produced ever-increasing numbers of low- and moderate-income housing during the last several decades.

While early urban renewal and redevelopment projects, especially those directed to the elimination of slum areas, undoubtedly had an adverse effect on the supply of housing, particularly for low and very low-income persons and families, concern that redevelopment projects in California have consistently resulted in diminishing the supply of housing is not supported by the evidence. Instead, what is demonstrated is that redevelopment agencies during the last several decades have produced ever-increasing numbers of low- and moderate-income housing.

In 1977, a report by Ralph Andersen and Associates found that, as of early 1976, 29,504 housing units had been eliminated within redevelopment project areas, 26,084 housing units had been constructed within project areas, and 3,853 housing units had been rehabilitated within project areas.[1] Approximately 80 percent of all the housing units eliminated occurred in ten older central city projects involving federal funding.[2] In most of the other project areas throughout the state, redevelopment had little, if any, impact on housing.

In 1984, in a report prepared for the California Debt Advisory Commission, Ralph Andersen and Associates again surveyed the impact of redevelopment on low- and moderate-income housing.[3] The report found that redevelopment projects had produced a net increase in the supply of housing, although very low-income units suffered a net loss: 12,335 low-income units had been destroyed by redevelopment projects, while 26,769 had been constructed, for a net gain of 14,461 low-income units. Similarly, for market-rate and more expensive housing, 3,139 units had been destroyed, while 19,611 had been constructed, for a net gain of 16,472 housing units. For very low-income units, 11,957 units had been destroyed and 6,062 had been constructed, for a net loss of 5,895 units. By 1984, redevelopment agencies or redevelopment projects resulted in at least 25,000 more housing units constructed than destroyed.

In more recent years, redevelopment agency contributions to development of affordable housing have increased dramatically, with agencies assisting significantly larger numbers of housing units each year.

In more recent years, redevelopment agency contributions to development of affordable housing have increased dramatically, with agencies assisting significantly larger numbers of housing units each year. Agency investment in affordable housing has increased to the point that agency low- and moderate-income housing funds are considered the largest single source of funds that are steadily available to increase, improve, and preserve affordable housing in California.[4] Each year the California

---

1. Ralph Andersen and Associates, *Redevelopment and Tax Increment Financing, Housing Supplement*, Sacramento (1977).
2. *Id.*, p. 25.
3. California Debt Advisory Commission, *Use of Redevelopment and Tax Increment Financing* (1984).
4. Department of Housing and Community Development, *Redevelopment Housing Activities in California*, Fiscal Year 2005–2006, Sacramento (2007), p. iii.

Department of Housing and Community Development (HCD) compiles and publishes information submitted by redevelopment agencies relating to their housing activities. This report evidences the increasing contribution to affordable housing made by redevelopment agencies throughout the state.

For the 1992–93 fiscal year, the department reported that redevelopment agencies throughout the state had expended approximately $374.2 million on housing for persons and families of low and moderate income. A total of 7,801 units (3,379 new and 4,422 rehabilitated) were completed and added to the housing stock through redevelopment efforts. With the removal of 537 units, redevelopment agencies' activities resulted in a net increase of 7,264 housing units during 1992–93. Of these units, 51 percent were for very low-income persons and families, 37 percent were for low-income persons and families, and 12 percent were for moderate-income persons and families.[5]

In the 2000–2001 fiscal year, affordable housing expenditures were up to $695 million, $96 million over the previous fiscal year.[6] Agencies assisted 20,686 households, most of which were for very low income (45 percent) or low-income (34 percent). In addition, 2,638 new units were constructed (403 more than the previous year) and 3189 were rehabilitated (up by 1,786 units) to fulfill inclusionary housing obligations.[7] Agencies acquired 517 affordability covenants, a decrease of 680 units from fiscal year 1999–2000.[8]

By the 2005–06 fiscal year, affordable housing expenditures had increased to $1.1 billion, $94 million more than the previous fiscal year. Redevelopment agencies assisted 16,255 households, including 5,688 very low- and 5,822 low-income households. This assistance led to the construction of 4,146 new units, substantial rehabilitation of 944 units, and the purchase of long term affordability covenants for 249 multifamily units.[9]

As the use of tax-increment financing increased in the 1970s, the California legislature, in response to concerns expressed by housing advocates, passed legislation in 1975 and 1976 requiring

HCD = California Department of Housing and Community Development

The First-Time Homebuyers Program in Tulare assists low-income households qualify for primary financing by providing downpayment assistance.

By the 2005–06 fiscal year, affordable housing expenditures had increased to $1.1 billion, $94 million more than the previous fiscal year.

---

5. Department of Housing and Community Development, *Redevelopment Housing Activities in California*, Fiscal Year 1992–93, Sacramento (1994), p. 1.
6. Department of Housing and Community Development, *Redevelopment Housing Activities in California*, Fiscal Year 2000–2001, Sacramento (2002), p. 2.
7. *Id.*, at p. 14.
8. *Id.*, at p. 13.
9. Department of Housing and Community Development, *Redevelopment Housing Activities in California*, Fiscal Year 2005–2006, Sacramento (2007), p. 4.

that the authority and financing powers of redevelopment agencies be used both to protect and increase the supply of housing for low- and moderate-income persons and families by requiring that a portion of tax increments be devoted to low- and moderate-income housing; that agencies replace housing for low- and moderate-income persons and families that is destroyed by agencies; and that a certain percentage of housing constructed within a project area be affordable to persons and families of low and moderate income. In addition, redevelopment agencies have been given broad authority to provide housing for low- and moderate-income persons and families.

In recent years, as the legislature has given increasing attention to the ongoing need for affordable housing throughout the state, the debate between representatives of redevelopment agencies and housing advocates has focused less on the goals of providing and supporting affordable housing, about which there is substantial agreement, and more on the best means to achieve these goals. Redevelopment agencies—arguing for flexibility both with regard to the methods of obtaining low- and moderate-income housing and its location—have stated that they can produce more units if not required to produce them within project areas with high land values. Housing advocates have emphasized the desirability of constructing more new units and have been reluctant to modify the inclusionary and housing production requirements.

Both the authority granted to agencies to construct, rehabilitate, and acquire housing for low- and moderate-income persons and families and the requirements imposed by the legislature for such housing are described in the remainder of this chapter.

The "20 Percent Set-Aside" Requirement

The most important provision relating to housing was imposed by the legislature in 1976. This is the requirement that, in redevelopment project areas adopted after 1976, 20 percent of the tax increments generated from the project area must be used by the agency to increase, improve, and preserve the community's supply of affordable housing for persons and families of low and moderate income. § 33334.2(a). *See Craig v. Poway* (1994) 28 Cal. App. 4th 319, holding that "improve" means something different than "increase." *See also* the discussion of retroactive application of the 20 percent set-aside requirement to plans adopted prior to 1977, on page 276.

In the small City of Anderson (pop. 16,000), the agency provided money to pay for critical pre-development costs and helped leverage additional funding sources for the 58-unit Seasons at Los Robles housing project.

In redevelopment project areas adopted after 1976, 20 percent of the tax increments generated from the project area must be used by the agency to increase, improve, preserve the community's supply of affordable housing.

This 20 percent set-aside requirement is important as stated by a report released in 2002 by HCD:

> For Fiscal Year 2000–2001, agencies reported a 15 percent increase in deposits of $798 million to the Low-Mod fund and spent $695 million representing an increase of 16 percent more than last year. Agencies reported total fund equity of $1.9 billion. Agencies Low-Mod funds continue to comprise the largest single source of funds available for the development, improvement, and maintenance of affordable housing. As a result, agencies have a leadership role in responding to the need for more affordable housing to address California's worsening housing crisis.[10]

The importance of the housing fund continues as agency contributions grow larger each year. In fiscal year 2005–2006, agencies reported annual deposits in excess of $1.5 billion. By that time, agency housing funds had accumulated total fund equity in excess of $3.5 billion, demonstrating that redevelopment agency housing fund money is and will continue to be a key source of funding for affordable housing.[11] The basic 20 percent set-aside requirement has since been imposed upon project areas established prior to 1977. There are slight variations for merged project areas and for areas added to project areas, as described below.

In *Redevelopment Agency v. Commission on State Mandates* (1997) 55 Cal. App. 4th 976, the court upheld the determination by the California Commission on State Mandates that redevelopment agencies cannot claim that the requirement to transfer a portion of tax increments to the housing fund is a state mandate under Article XIII B and that the state should reimburse the agency for these transferred funds. The court held that because of the nature of tax-increment financing, redevelopment agencies are not subject to appropriations limitations, do not expend "proceeds of taxes," and do not raise "general revenues for the local entity." Moreover, the state is not transferring to the agency the cost of a state program.

In 1993, the Attorney General opined that, when implementing the requirement to allocate 20 percent of tax increments to the housing fund, the 20 percent is to be calculated against the total annual amount of tax increment received by the redevelopment agency—including amounts transferred to affected taxing entities pursuant to a pass-through agreement as permitted prior to 1994 and amounts used to construct school facilities under section 33446. However, property tax revenues allocated to taxing entities pursuant to section 33676 are not to be included in determining the amount required for low- and moderate-income housing. 76 Ops. Cal. Atty. Gen. 137 (1993)

---

10. Department of Housing and Community Development, *Redevelopment Housing Activities in California*, Fiscal Year 2000–2001, Sacramento (2002), p. 1.

11. Department of Housing and Community Development, *Redevelopment Housing Activities in California*, Fiscal Year 2005–2006, Sacramento (2007), p. 1.

The opinion addresses the method an agency must use to calculate its allocation to the housing fund—either based on the "gross" amount of tax increments received by an agency, including amounts owed under pass-through agreements entered into prior to 1994, or paid to taxing entities pursuant to section 33607.5 or 33607.7, or based on the "net" amount actually available to the agency after amounts owed to taxing entities had been deducted. Stating that the calculation should be against the "gross" amount of tax increments received by an agency, the Attorney General's opinion is consistent with the plain reading of the statutes.

An action to compel an agency to deposit the required 20 percent of tax increments into its housing fund may be brought within 10 years following an alleged failure to deposit the proper amount into that fund. If the court finds that the agency has deposited less than the required amount into its housing fund, or has improperly spent money from its housing fund, the agency will be required to repay the funds, with interest. § 33334.2(j). Section 33334.2, subdivision (j) was adopted in response to *Hogar v. Community Development Commission* (2003) 110 Cal. App. 4th 1288, which applied a three-year statute of limitation in a case where the redevelopment agency had been depositing 20 percent of its net (rather than gross) tax increment into its housing set-aside fund from the time the plan had been adopted.

Project Areas Established After 1976

For project areas established after 1976, and areas added by amendment to a project area after 1976, unless a specified finding is made, 20 percent of the tax increments allocated to the agency each year from the project area or added area must be used by the agency to increase, improve, and preserve the supply of affordable housing for persons and families of low or moderate income. § 33334.2. The tax increments must be placed in a housing fund until used, along with any interest earned and repayments to the housing fund. § 33334.3.

Agencies with more than one project area may satisfy the 20 percent requirement by allocating less than 20 percent in any one year in one project area if the difference between the amount allocated and the 20 percent required is instead allocated to the housing fund from tax-increment revenues from another project area. § 33334.3(i). The total amount required to be allocated by the agency for low- and moderate-income housing would not change. This allows agencies with strong project areas to assist weaker areas by allowing more monies to be used in the weaker area for commercial development. It will enable agencies to take advantage of a particular development opportunity by devoting all the tax increment from the project area to that development for one or more years and make the housing contribution from another project area.

Exceptions

An agency may exempt itself from this 20 percent set-aside requirement if it makes one of the two following findings annually by resolution:

- That no need exists in the community to improve, increase or preserve the supply of low- and moderate-income housing and that this finding is consistent with the general plan housing element, including the community's regional housing needs assessment. § 33334.2(a)(1)

- That a stated percentage less than 20 percent is sufficient to meet the community's housing needs and that this finding is consistent with the community's general plan housing element, including the community's regional housing needs assessment. § 33334.2(a)(2)

The agency can only make these findings if the housing element of the community's general plan supports this conclusion. In addition, the finding must be consistent with the planning commission's annual report to the legislative body required by Government Code section 65400 subdivision (b), which includes the status of the community's progress in meeting its regional housing needs. Finally, in order to make either of these findings, the housing element must be current, submitted to HCD in a timely fashion, and must comply with the law.

Prior to June 30, 1993, agencies could make a third finding in order to exempt themselves from the 20 percent requirement:

- That the community is making a substantial effort consisting of direct financial contributions of local funds to meet its existing and projected housing needs for persons and families of very low, low, and moderate income, including its share of the regional housing needs, as identified in the housing element of the community's general plan, and that this effort is equivalent in impact to the use of tax increments otherwise required to be set aside for low- and moderate-income housing. § 33334.2(a)(3)(A)

The authority to make this finding expired on June 30, 1993, unless the agency can show it entered into a specific contractual obligation—for example, the sale of bonds with the specific intention of making this finding in the future in order to provide sufficient revenues to pay off the indebtedness.

Findings made pursuant to section 33334.2 subdivision (a) are required to be sent to HCD. § 33334.2(b). If a challenge to a finding is filed in court, the burden is on the agency to establish that the finding is supported by substantial evidence. § 33334.2 subdivision (c).

These exceptions are very rarely used. In fiscal year 2005–2006, HCD reported that only three agencies statewide claimed exemptions to the 20 percent set-aside requirement pursuant to Section 33334.2(a). The total amount exempted by all three agencies was $309,276, as compared

The agency can only make these findings if the housing element of the community's general plan supports this conclusion. In addition, the finding must be consistent with the planning commission's annual report to the legislative body.

to the nearly $1.5 billion deposited into housing funds state-wide that fiscal year.[12] Virtually all agencies devote 20 percent of their annual tax-increment revenues for the purpose of improving, increasing, and preserving low- and moderate-income housing.

"Excess Surplus"

In an attempt to ensure that agencies will spend the monies placed in the housing fund, and not accumulate large surpluses in their housing funds, the legislature enacted a statute that attempts to balance the agency's need to accumulate funds in order to develop or assist a housing project with the state's interest to assure that agencies with a properly established housing fund make efforts to develop affordable housing as required by the law.

"Excess surplus" means an unexpended and unencumbered amount in the housing fund that exceeds the greater of $1 million or the total amount deposited in the housing fund during the preceding four years.

"Excess surplus" means an unexpended and unencumbered amount in the housing fund that exceeds the greater of $1 million or the total amount deposited in the housing fund during the preceding four years.

Agencies are required to either—

- Spend or encumber the excess surplus funds or transfer the funds to a housing authority within one year from the date the funds become excess surplus, or
- Spend or encumber the excess surplus funds within two additional years.

If it has not spent or encumbered the excess surplus funds within three years from the date the funds become excess surplus, the agency is prohibited from encumbering any additional funds or spending any monies from any source—except that it may pay certain specified obligations, if any, that were incurred prior to three years from the date the monies became excess surplus and an amount for agency operations and administration that may not exceed 75 percent of the amount spent for these purposes the preceding year. This prohibition continues until the agency has spent or encumbered the excess surplus plus an amount equal to 50 percent of the excess surplus that remains at the end of the three-year period.

Agencies can either transfer excess surplus funds within one year of their becoming excess surplus or make a commitment to spend or encumber the funds within an additional two years.

In other words, agencies can either transfer excess surplus funds within one year of their becoming excess surplus or make a commitment to spend or encumber the funds within an additional two years. If it makes this commitment but does not spend or encumber the funds within the two- year period, the agency is then prohibited from continuing to exercise its normal authority. This is the so-called "death penalty" provision.

Section 33334.12 prohibits communities to which an agency has transferred excess surplus funds from disapproving a low- or moderate-

---

12. Department of Housing and Community Development, *Redevelopment Housing Activities in California,* Fiscal Year 2005–2006, Sacramento (2007), p. 2.

income housing project funded by excess surplus funds if the project is consistent with applicable building codes and the land use designation specified in any element of the general plan as it existed on the date the application was deemed complete. A local agency may, however, require compliance with local development standards and policies appropriate to and consistent with meeting the qualified objectives relative to the development of housing, as required in the community's housing element.

Excess surplus does not include the unspent portion of proceeds from bonds, other indebtedness, and related income. The legislature has directed HCD to appoint an advisory committee consisting of affordable housing advocates, representatives of the California Redevelopment Association, the California Society of Certified Public Accountants, the Controller, and other qualified persons and families to periodically develop and revise the excess surplus calculation mentioned above. § 33334.12.

Excess surplus does not include the unspent portion of proceeds from bonds, other indebtedness, and related income.

Use of Housing Fund Monies

Considering the broad range of powers specifically granted agencies in the expenditure of housing fund monies, the authority granted elsewhere in the law to assist housing for low- and moderate-income persons and families, and the strong statements of public policy, agencies have great discretion in determining how to spend monies from the housing fund—as long as the monies are used to increase, improve, and preserve the supply of low- and moderate-income housing. §§ 33070, 33071, 33334.2, 33449.

The agency may spend monies from the housing fund either within or outside the project area, but use outside the project area is permitted only if the agency and legislative body find that this will benefit the project area. § 33334.2(g).

The agency may raise funds for housing projects by borrowing money and using housing fund monies as security. § 33334.2(e)(9). Tax allocation bonds can be sold with a pledge of the entire annual tax increment for debt service, including the 20 percent monies normally placed in the housing fund, in which case 20 percent of the bond proceeds must be placed in the housing fund. Since the expenditure of bond proceeds to assist housing projects may not meet the requirements of the federal Tax Reform Act of 1986 for tax-exempt bonds, careful analysis is required before determining whether or not to raise monies for housing by selling bonds to be paid

The Paso Robles Redevelopment Agency provided assistance to a nonprofit housing developer for this senior low-income housing project.

The agency should carefully consider, with the assistance of bond counsel, whether bonds secured by housing fund monies should be tax-exempt or taxable.

otherwise placed in the housing fund. In addition, the agency should carefully consider, with the assistance of bond counsel, whether bonds secured by housing fund monies should be tax-exempt or taxable. This is because the ways in which tax-exempt bond proceeds can be used on particular housing projects either may be limited or precluded because of the other financing sources for such projects, such as federal Low-Income Housing Tax Credits.

In *Craig v. Poway* (1994) 28 Cal. App. 4th 319, the California Court of Appeal held that if 100 percent of the tax increment is pledged to pay debt service, the agency must deposit both 20 percent of the bond proceeds and 20 percent of the annual tax increment in the housing fund and pay the debt service on the portion of the bond proceeds in the housing fund with the tax increments deposited in the housing fund.

In the *Craig* case, the agency had deposited 20 percent of the bond proceeds in the housing fund in lieu of depositing 20 percent of the annual tax increments in the housing fund. The court held that this was insufficient because over the life of the bond payments, the tax increments from the project could be expected to increase, and 20 percent of the annual tax increments could be more than the debt service on the portion of the bonds deposited in the housing fund. The court stated that the housing fund should be treated in the same manner as the agency's general fund. The total bond proceeds should be split 20/80 between the two agency funds, as should the annual tax increments, so that as tax increments increase beyond the amount needed to pay debt service, this increase will be deposited in the appropriate fund.

Redevelopment agencies have extremely broad powers in expending monies from the housing fund to assist low- and moderate-income housing.

Redevelopment agencies have extremely broad powers in expending monies from the housing fund to assist low- and moderate-income housing. § 33334.2(e). While prohibited from constructing commercial or industrial buildings to be used for private purposes, agencies are specifically authorized to construct buildings or structures for the purpose of improving or increasing the supply of housing for low- and moderate-income persons and families. §§ 33334.2(e), 33440.

In addition, agencies may spend housing fund monies to acquire land, donate the land, acquire and rehabilitate buildings, provide subsidies in certain circumstances, maintain the community's supply of mobile homes, and preserve the availability of affordable units for lower-income persons and families when existing subsidies terminate. § 33334.2(e).

Agencies may also pay for on-site or off-site improvements made to the land, but only if (1) the improvements are part of new construction or rehabilitation of affordable housing units for low- or moderate-income persons that are directly benefited by the improvements, and are a reasonable and fundamental component of the housing units, and (2) the agency requires that the units remain available at an affordable housing cost to persons and families of very low, low, or moderate income, and are occupied by these persons and families, for the time periods required under redevelopment law, as discussed in detail below under "Maintaining Affordability." § 33334.2(e)(2)(A). If the newly constructed or rehabilitated housing units benefitted by the improvements are part of a larger project, the agency may only pay a portion of the total cost of the onsite or offsite improvement. The agency contribution to the improvements cannot be greater than the affordable units' proportionate share of the total cost of the improvements. § 33334.2(e)(2)(B).

Targeted Expenditures of Housing Fund Monies

Section 33334.4 requires that over the ten-year duration of an implementation plan, as specified in section 33490(a)(2)(A)(iii) and discussed below, the agency is to spend monies from the housing fund for low- and very low-income persons and families in at least the same proportion as the number of units needed for each of those two groups bears to the total units needed for moderate, low- and very low-income persons and families as determined within the community's housing element pursuant to section 65584 of the Government Code. Agencies can meet their threshold requirements for low-income expenditures with either very low- and low-income units; moderate-income thresholds can be satisfied with either low or moderate-income units. Agencies may count units (except for units developed pursuant to a replacement housing obligation under state or federal law) toward each income category that are newly constructed over the ten-year duration of the implementation plan and have been assisted with "locally controlled" government assistance, even if there is no agency assistance, so long as the units are required to be affordable to, and occupied by, persons and families of the income category and contain the required covenants recorded against the unit. § 33334.4(a).

Half of Richmond's Metro Walk townhouse complex are affordable.

CDBG = Community Development Block Grant

The term "locally controlled" is defined in section 33334.4 to mean government assistance where the community or other local government entity has the discretion and the authority to determine the recipient and the amount of the assistance, whether or not the source of the funds or other assistance is from the state or federal government. Examples of locally controlled government assistance include, but are not limited to, Community Development Block Grant (CDBG) Program (42 U.S.C. Sec. 5301 and following) funds allocated to a city or county, Home Investment Partnership Program (42 U.S.C.

The term "locally controlled" means government assistance where the community or other local government entity has the discretion and the authority to determine the recipient and the amount of the assistance.

Sec. 12721 and following) funds allocated to a city or county, fees or funds received by a city or county pursuant to a city or county authorized program, and the waiver or deferral of city or other charges. § 33334.4(d).

In addition, each agency is to expend, over the ten-year duration of the implementation plan, money in the housing fund for housing available to all persons regardless of age in at least the same proportion as the number of low-income households with a member under age 65 bears to the total number of low-income households of the community, as reported in the most recent census of the United States Census Bureau. § 33334.4(b). Section 33334.4, subdivision (b) was amended by SB 527 to clarify, as stated above, that housing fund expenditures for non-senior housing would be in proportion to the number of non-senior households in the community, rather than the total non-senior population of the community.

The requirements of section 33334.4 may be extended an additional five years beyond the ten-year duration of an implementation plan, if the Agency deposits an aggregate that is less than two million dollars into the housing fund over the first five years of the ten-year period of the implementation plan. § 33334.4(c). Thus, in this circumstance, the agency would have 15 years to satisfy the requirements of section 33334.4.

Implementation of "Targeting" Requirements

All implementation plans are now required to contain a description of how the housing program will implement the requirements of section 33334.4.

All implementation plans are now required to contain a description of how the housing program will implement the requirements of section 33334.4. § 33490(a)(2)(A)(iv).

For project areas to which the inclusionary housing requirements of subdivision (b) of section 33413 apply,[13] the ten-year period within which section 33334.4 is required to be implemented shall be the same ten-year period within which subdivision (b) of section 33413 is required to be implemented. In order to allow these two ten-year time periods to coincide for the first period, the time to implement the requirement of section 33334.4 shall be extended two years, and all project areas in existence on or before December 31, 1993 shall implement the requirements of section 33334.4 on or before December 31, 2014, and each ten years after that.

For project areas to which subdivision (b) of section 33413 does not apply, the requirements of section 33334.4 shall be implemented on or before December 31, 2014, and every ten years thereafter. § 33490(a)(2)(A)(iii).

---

13. Section 33413(b) applies to all plans adopted or areas added on or after January 1, 1976, and any pre-1976 plans that have been extended pursuant to section 33333.10. § 33413(d)(1).

Limitations of Housing Fund Monies

Housing fund monies are not to be used to the extent that other reasonable means of private or commercial financing of new or substantially rehabilitated units at the same level of affordability and quality are reasonably available to the agency or the owner of the units. When housing fund monies will exceed 50 percent of the cost of producing the units, agencies are required to find, based on substantial evidence and prior to approval of expenditures from the housing fund, that housing fund monies are necessary because the agency or owner of the units has made a good faith attempt but been unable to obtain commercial or private means of financing the units at the same level of affordability and quality. § 33334.3(j).

Section 33334.16 requires agencies to commence actions leading to the development of property acquired with monies from the housing fund within five years after acquiring the property. If these actions—such as entering into an agreement for the development of the property—have not commenced during the five-year period, the agency may extend the period during which it may retain the property for an additional five years. If development has not begun prior to the end of this extension, the agency is required to sell the property and deposit the proceeds in the housing fund.

Section 33334.16 requires agencies to commence actions leading to the development of property acquired with monies from the housing fund within five years after acquiring the property.

Use of Housing Funds Outside the Community

Except as authorized by two statutes that are very limited in their scope, redevelopment agencies do not have the authority to spend monies from the housing fund outside the community that established the agency. Since some agencies do not want to assist low- and moderate-income housing and others would welcome increased revenues to do so, and because neither the housing nor the job market is restricted by community boundaries, it has been suggested that agencies should be authorized to transfer monies from their housing funds to nearby communities or agencies that are willing to use them. Opponents of this idea believe that communities that avail themselves of the benefits of redevelopment, especially to attract commercial development, should not be allowed to escape the obligation to provide their share of low- and moderate-income housing. Section 33334.17, which was added in 1992, and expired on January 1, 2001, reflected this divergence of views because while it purported to authorize expenditures outside the community it was, as a practical matter, impossible to implement.

Except as authorized by two statutes that are very limited in their scope, redevelopment agencies do not have the authority to spend monies from the housing fund outside the community that established the agency.

Section 33334.25 was added to allow contiguous agencies within adjoining cities that are within a single metropolitan statistical area to create a joint powers agency in order to pool their housing funds. The legislation contains a number of limitations including but not limited to the following:

- Each participating community shall have met, in its current or previous housing element cycle, 50 percent or more of its share of the region's affordable housing needs.
- The pooled funds must be encumbered within two years.
- The funds may not be used for planning and administrative costs, offsite improvements, or fees.
- HCD must determine that each project is in compliance with the statute.

§ 33334.25(c)–(d)

Affordability

Housing fund monies must be used to increase, improve, and preserve housing available to moderate income, lower income, very low income, and extremely low income persons and families.

Housing fund monies must be used to increase, improve, and preserve housing available to moderate-income, lower-income, very low-income, and extremely low-income persons and families at an affordable cost or affordable rent, as appropriate. § 33334.2(a). The income levels for extremely low, very low, lower and moderate income households are established periodically by HUD pursuant to Section 8 of the United States Housing Act of 1937. The definitions of affordable cost and affordable rent are complex and are found in sections 50052.5 and 50053, and in the implementing regulations. Cal. Code Regs., tit. 25, § 6910 *et seq.* In very general terms, affordable housing cost means:

- Owner-occupied housing
  - Assistance from the agency received prior to 1991
    Lower-income households—25 percent of gross income
  - Assistance from the agency received after 1991
    Extremely low-income households—30 percent x 30 percent of area median income
    Very low-income households—30 percent x 50 percent of area median income
    Lower-income households—30 percent x 60 percent of area median income
    Moderate-income households—35 percent x 110 percent of area median income

For purchasers, housing costs include principal and interest on a mortgage, property taxes and assessments, fire and casualty insurance, property maintenance and repairs, allowance for utilities and homeowner association fees.

- Rental housing
  - Assistance from the agency received prior to 1991
    Lower-income households—25 percent of gross income

- Assistance from the agency received after 1991

    Extremely low-income households—30 percent x 30 percent of area median income

    Very low-income households—30 percent x 50 percent of area median income

    Lower-income households—30 percent x 60 percent of area median income

    Moderate-income households—30 percent x 110 percent of area median income

For renters, the components for determining affordability include rent, allowance for utilities, fees or service charges assessed by the lessor and charged to all tenants, and possessory interest, taxes, or other fees charged by a party other than the lessor.

All of the amounts are adjusted for family size.

Maintaining Affordability

Redevelopment agencies have always had the responsibility to assure that, when agency monies are spent to make the cost of housing affordable to low- and moderate-income persons and families, the agency's objectives are met and the public funds are not a "gift."

In order to assure that the goal of providing affordable housing is met, all new or substantially rehabilitated housing units developed or otherwise assisted with housing fund monies must remain available at affordable housing cost to, and are occupied by, persons and families of moderate, low, very low, and extremely low income, for the longest feasible time, but for not less than:

- Fifty-five years for rental units (however, the agency may replace these units with other affordable units that are provided prior to displacement of any residents of the existing units and are not developed with monies from the housing fund). § 33334.3(f)(1)(A)

- Forty-five years for owner-occupied units (however, the agency may permit sales of the units at market rates pursuant to an adopted program, such as an equity sharing program, that protects the agency's investment). § 33334.3(f)(1)(B)

- Fifteen years for mutual self-help housing units. However, the agency may allow the sale of a mutual self-help unit for market price prior to the end of the 15 year term provided that the agency protects its investment through an

Sycamore Street Commons includes a mix of one- to four-bedroom apartments, a subsidized childcare center, community room, play areas, and laundry rooms. The complex was designed to blend in with the historic character of downtown Santa Cruz.

adopted program, such as an equity share program, and ensures through a recorded instrument (such as a regulatory agreement or deed of trust) that if the unit is sold any time after expiration of the 15 year period and prior to 45 years after recording of the restriction, the agency will, at a minimum, recover the original principal provided to assist the unit. "Mutual self-help housing unit" is defined as an owner-occupied housing unit for which persons and families of very low and low income contribute no fewer than 500 hours of their own labor in individual or group efforts toward the provision of the unit they will occupy. § 33334.3(f)(1)(C)

The agency is required to record a covenant or restriction, which runs with the land, for each parcel or housing unit subject to these affordability restrictions.

The agency is required to record a covenant or restriction, which runs with the land, for each parcel or housing unit subject to these restrictions. § 33334.3(e). These covenants may be subordinated to liens of lenders, if specific conditions are met. § 33334.14.

The agency is also required to record a separate document called the "Notice of Affordability Restrictions on Transfer of Property" with the title set forth in 14-point type or larger. The notice must be recorded within 30 days after the date of recordation of the affordability covenant or restriction. It must include (1) a recitation of the affordability covenant or restriction, including the name of the document containing the covenant or restriction and recording information if available; (2) the date the covenant or restriction expires; (3) the street address of the property including, if applicable, the unit number; (4) the assessor's parcel number; and (5) the legal description for the property. § 33334.3(f)(3)(B).

The covenant or restriction recorded against the property is enforceable against the property owner or any successor in interest by (1) the agency, (2) the community, (3) a resident of a restricted unit, (4) a residents' association with members residing in restricted units, (5) a former resident of a restricted unit who last resided in that unit, (6) an applicant for a restricted unit if the applicant is of low or moderate income, is able and willing to occupy the unit, and was denied occupancy of the unit due to an alleged breach of the restriction, or (7) a person on an affordable housing waiting list who is of low or moderate income and who is able and willing to occupy a restricted unit. §33334.3(f)(7).

The requirement that a covenant be placed on property assisted with monies from the housing fund raises a number of legal and practical questions that should be considered.

The requirement that a covenant be placed on property assisted with monies from the housing fund raises a number of legal and practical questions that should be considered prior to reaching final agreement on the structure or type of assistance being provided.

Will the housing units be new or substantially rehabilitated units? Are they being developed or otherwise assisted with monies from the housing fund? Will prospective owners or tenants accept these restrictions considering the amount of assistance they are receiving? Will lenders accept these restrictions, and will subordination be required and possible? Do these restrictions conflict with maintenance of affordability requirements imposed by other financing programs being used for the project?

These issues usually can be resolved, but early consideration is important.

Plans Adopted Prior to 1977

In 1984, the legislature retroactively applied the basic 20 percent requirement to project areas established prior to 1977. Starting in the 1985–86 fiscal year, agencies were required to use 20 percent of the tax increments from project areas established before 1977 to improve and increase the housing supply for persons and families of low- and moderate-income. Agencies may exempt themselves or decrease the percentage used for this purpose by making one or more of the same findings available to agencies that have established project areas since 1977. § 33334.6.

In 1984, the legislature retroactively applied the basic 20 percent requirement to project areas established prior to 1977.

In addition—and in recognition of the fact that retroactive application of this requirement would be difficult or impossible for those agencies that had already committed their future stream of tax increments to existing debt or previously adopted programs and projects—the legislature enacted special provisions allowing agencies to phase in this requirement. Agencies were authorized to adopt, prior to September 1, 1986, a statement of existing obligations and a statement of existing programs. To provide for the payment of existing obligations, agencies are allowed to deposit less than 20 percent of the annual tax increments in the housing fund.

If an agency deposits less than 20 percent of the annual tax increments in the housing fund pursuant to the exceptions in section 33334.6, a deficit is created in the housing fund and the agency is required to adopt a plan to eliminate the deficit in subsequent years. § 33334.6(g). Thus, the ability to deposit less than 20 percent in the housing fund defers the basic obligation but does not eliminate or reduce it, unlike the exceptions based on the findings in section 33334.2. If the elimination of the deficit requires an increase in the total amount of tax increment the agency is authorized to receive or a modification of the other limits required by section 33333.4, agencies are granted special authority to amend these limits to enable the agency to eliminate the deficit.

Dilapidated and crime-ridden Ellsworth Court in Fairfield was replaced with attractive for-sale affordable housing.

Nothing in the law prevents agencies from spending more than 20 percent of the annual tax increments to increase, improve, and preserve the supply of housing for low- and moderate-income persons and families. However, if the agency uses its non-housing tax increments for affordable housing activities, it should continue to characterize those non-housing funds as such, rather than transferring them into the housing fund. Using the non-housing funds for affordable housing projects gives the agency greater flexibility in negotiating the type of developments being assisted, without being restricted by the rules associated with the use of the 20 percent set-aside funds.

Laws governing the use and expenditure of monies in the housing fund are the same regardless of when the project area was adopted.

Merger of Project Areas

Project areas that are merged pursuant to section 33485 *et seq.* are subject to the basic requirement that 20 percent of the annual tax increments be placed in the housing fund regardless of when the project areas were originally adopted. § 33487.

If, prior to the merger, an agency has incurred debt to be repaid from tax increments from one of the project areas that have been merged, the agency may deposit less than the 20 percent in the housing fund if all or a portion of these funds are needed to pay the service on this debt. If the agency deposits less than 20 percent in the housing fund in any fiscal year, a deficit in the housing fund is created. Unlike the requirement for project areas adopted prior to 1977, the agency is required to eliminate the deficit as soon as possible and prior to incurring new debt for anything other than low- and moderate-income housing. § 33487(d). In merged project areas, agencies cannot eliminate or reduce the 20 percent requirement by making the findings in section 33334.2.

The uses for which monies in the housing fund may be expended are defined as the acquisition and improvement to land; the acquisition, rehabilitation, or construction of structures; and the provision of subsidies.

The uses for which monies in the housing fund may be expended are defined as the acquisition and improvement to land; the acquisition, rehabilitation, or construction of structures; and the provision of subsidies. § 33487. While this gives an agency broad authority, it is not as complete as the authority granted to agencies in project areas that have not been merged. Whether this list is meant to be limiting, or exactly what purpose this separate grant of authority serves, is not clear.

Units assisted by the agency with housing fund monies are to remain available to, and occupied by, persons and families of very low-, low-, or moderate-income for the longest feasible time period, but not less than 55 years for rental units and 45 years for owner-occupied units.

If monies deposited in the housing fund have not been committed for a use authorized by section 33487 within six years after having been deposited, the agency is required to offer the monies to the housing authority with jurisdiction in the community, if a housing authority has been activated. This is also more stringent than the excess surplus provisions governing project areas not merged.

Redevelopment Inclusionary Housing Requirements

In addition to the requirement that agencies spend a portion of tax increments to increase, improve, and preserve the supply of housing for low- and moderate-income persons and families, the Community Redevelopment Law contains inclusionary and production housing requirements. § 33413(b). Agencies should be aware of these, not only in implementing an adopted redevelopment plan but also in the planning stages of a proposed project area.

In project areas adopted, and areas added by amendment to a redevelopment plan, after 1975, section 33413 subdivision (b)(2)(i) requires that at least 15 percent of all new and substantially rehabilitated dwelling units developed within the project area under the jurisdiction of an agency by public or private entities or persons other than a redevelopment agency shall be available at affordable housing cost to persons and families of low or moderate income and shall be occupied by these persons and families (the "15 percent requirement"). In addition, not less that 40 percent of these dwelling units required to be available at affordable housing cost to persons and families of low or moderate income shall be available at affordable housing cost to very low-income households and shall be occupied by these persons and families. The 15 percent requirement does not apply to each housing project. Instead, the agency has the discretion to determine how the requirements are to be applied.

The inclusionary housing requirements also apply to those pre-1976 redevelopment plans whose time limits have been extended pursuant to section 33333.10. In this instance, the inclusionary housing requirements apply only after the ordinance adopting such extension becomes effective. § 33413(d)(1).

On or after January 1, 2002, "substantially rehabilitated dwelling units" means all units substantially rehabilitated with agency assistance. § 33413(b)(2)(A)(iii). Prior to January 1, 2002, "substantially rehabilitated dwelling units" meant substantially rehabilitated multi-family rented dwelling units with three or more units regardless of whether there was redevelopment agency assistance, or substantially rehabilitated, with agency assistance, single-family dwelling units with one or two units. *Id.* In addition, "substantial rehabilitation" means rehabilitation, the value of which constitutes 25 percent of the after rehabilitation value of the dwelling, inclusive of the land value. § 33413(b)(2)(A)(iv).

Dwelling units developed pursuant to the 15 percent requirement are to remain available at affordable housing cost to and occupied by very low-, low-, and moderate-income persons and families for the longest feasible time, but for not less than 55 years for rental units and 45 years for owner-occupied units. § 33413(c). Mutual self-help units subject to 15-year

The Chico Redevelopment Agency provided a grant to the Butte County Housing Authority for the construction of this senior housing project.

The inclusionary housing requirements also apply to those pre-1976 redevelopment plans whose time limits have been extended pursuant to section 33333.10.

"Substantial rehabilitation" means rehabilitation, the value of which constitutes 25 percent of the after rehabilitation value of the dwelling, inclusive of the land value.

affordability restrictions can also be counted toward the 15 percent requirement, but each unit is only counted toward one-third of a unit when calculating the 15 percent requirement. Owner-occupied units and mutual self-help housing units may be sold before the expiration of the affordability period for a price above the "affordable housing cost" pursuant to an agency program that protects the agency's investment (such as an equity sharing program). In such instance, the agency must deposit the proceeds into its housing fund and ensure that an equal number of affordable units at the same income level has been provided within three years of the sale. § 33413(c)(2). Covenants running with the land are to be recorded implementing these provisions. § 33413(c)(2).

These inclusionary housing requirements have not been well understood or universally implemented since their adoption. To address this problem, the legislature amended section 33413 to require that each agency to which these requirements apply adopt, as part of the implementation plan required by section 33490, a plan demonstrating how the agency will comply with the inclusionary requirements and ensuring that they will be met every ten years. § 33413(b)(4). The implementation plan must be reviewed every five years in conjunction with either the implementation plan cycle or the housing element update cycle.

When planning a project area and determining the amount of land to be included for residential development, these requirements should be considered. *If relatively large amounts of land are included for residential growth, methods for assuring compliance with the 15 percent requirement, including the maintenance of the affordability of these units, must be created.* This may include cooperative efforts by the community in using its regulatory authority and housing fund monies. If property suitable for low- and moderate-income housing is not included within the project area, the legislative body must find that the provision of low- and moderate-income housing outside the project area will benefit the project area prior to adopting the redevelopment plan. § 33334.2(g). If relatively little property is included within the project area, then the agency will have fewer alternatives.

In addition to the mandate to adopt a plan, agencies must satisfy these inclusionary requirements every ten years. If they do not, the agency must meet the requirements on an annual basis until the requirements for the ten-year period are met. Furthermore, the agency must meet these requirements prior to termination of a redevelopment project area, as discussed below in Completion of Housing Obligations.

Inclusionary Implementation Methods

In addition to the new construction and substantial rehabilitation of dwelling units within a redevelopment project area, a redevelopment agency may satisfy its inclusionary housing obligations by other means.

These alternatives are the two-for-one alternative; the aggregation of units between redevelopment project areas; and the purchase of affordability covenants.

Two-for-One Alternative

Instead of providing units within a redevelopment project area, a redevelopment agency may meet its inclusionary housing requirement by causing to be available, by regulation or agreement, at a cost affordable to persons and families of low- and moderate- income, or to very low-income households, as applicable, two units outside a redevelopment project area for each housing unit that otherwise would have to be available inside the redevelopment project area. § 33413(b)(2)(A)(ii).

Instead of providing units within a redevelopment project area, an agency may meet its inclusionary housing requirement by causing to be available two units outside a project area for each housing unit that otherwise would have to be available inside the project area.

Aggregation between Project Areas

Redevelopment agencies are permitted to aggregate new or substantially rehabilitated dwelling units in one or more project areas to meet the inclusionary housing requirement if the agency finds, based on substantial evidence, after a public hearing, that the aggregation will not cause or exacerbate racial, ethnic, or economic segregation. § 33413(b)(2)(A)(v).

Purchase of Affordability Covenants

A redevelopment agency may also acquire long-term affordability covenants on multifamily units that restrict the cost of renting or purchasing those units that either: (1) are not presently available at affordable cost to persons and families of low- or very low-income households, as applicable; or (2) are units that are presently at affordable housing cost to this same group of persons or families, but are units that the agency finds, based on substantial evidence, after a public hearing, cannot reasonably be expected to remain affordable to this same group of persons or families. § 33413(b)(2)(B).

The restoration of the historic Mondo Building in downtown Merced has served as a catalyst for job creation and new commercial and housing development.

In order to count toward the agency's inclusionary requirement, the long-term affordability covenants acquired by the redevelopment agency shall require that the units be maintained at affordable housing cost to, and occupied by, persons and families of low and very low income, for the longest feasible time, but not less than 55 years for rental units and 45 years for owner-occupied units and the affordability covenants must be recorded and run with the property. § 33413(b)(2)(C).

The purchase or acquisition of long-term affordability covenants cannot be used to satisfy more than 50 percent of the dwelling units required to be made affordable pursuant to section 33413(b). Not less than 50 percent of these units made available through the purchase or acquisition of long-term affordability covenants must be affordable to very low-income households. § 33413(b)(2)(C).

Sale of Owner-Occupied Units

The law authorizes agencies to permit the sales of owner-occupied units prior to the end of the 45 year affordability period and mutual self-help units prior to the end of the 15 year affordability period if the agency's investment of monies from the housing fund is protected by an adopted program—such as an equity sharing program—that allows the agency and the owner to share in the proceeds of the sale, based on the length of the occupancy. Funds received by the agency are to be deposited into the housing fund. This authority to allow sales at a price in excess of that permitted by the affordability covenant is conditioned on the agency expending funds to make affordable an equal number of housing units at the same income level as the number of units sold within three years from the date of the sale of each affordable unit. § 33413(c)(2).

Production Housing Requirements

In addition to the 15 percent requirement that applies within a redevelopment project area, section 33413(b)(1) also requires redevelopment agencies that develop, i.e. construct and own, housing units to ensure that at least 30 percent of those units must be available at affordable housing cost to persons of low or moderate income and shall be occupied by these persons and families, regardless of where these units are constructed. Not less than 50 percent of these dwelling units required to be available at affordable cost to persons and families of low or moderate income shall be available at affordable housing cost to, and occupied by, very low-income households. This provision is rarely applicable as nearly all housing that is assisted by redevelopment agencies is developed and owned by private or nonprofit entities.

Of the 100 units in this multi-family housing complex in Thousand Oaks, 42 are for very low-income households.

Replacement Housing Requirements

Housing Unit Replacement

To respond to concerns that redevelopment projects were destroying residential units housing persons and families of low and moderate income, the legislature enacted statutes requiring that agencies construct housing to replace each unit destroyed or removed.

In project areas adopted, or areas added by amendment, after 1975—when residential units housing persons and families of low or moderate income are destroyed or removed from the market as part of a specific project that is subject to a written agreement with, or receives financial assistance from, the agency—the agency must rehabilitate or construct an equal number of replacement dwelling units within the jurisdiction of the agency within four years of the destruction or removal. If the units are destroyed or removed after January 1, 2002, 100 percent of the replacement units must be affordable to the same income level (very low, low or moderate) as the persons and families displaced from the destroyed or removed units. § 33413(a). For any units destroyed or removed between September 1, 1989 and December 31, 2001, only 75 percent of the replacement units must be affordable to the same income level as the persons and families displaced from such destroyed or removed units. In project areas adopted, or areas added by amendment, prior to 1976, the provisions requiring the replacement of destroyed housing units apply to units destroyed or removed from the low- and moderate-income housing market on or after January 1, 1996. § 33413(d)(1).

If the units are destroyed or removed after January 1, 2002, 100 percent of the replacement units must be affordable to the same income level as the persons and families displaced from the destroyed or removed units.

The replacement housing units are to remain available at affordable housing cost to persons and families of very low, low, and moderate income, and occupied by those persons and families, for the longest feasible time, but for not less than 55 years for rental units and 45 years for homeownership units. § 33413(c).

Priority in renting or buying housing developed as part of a redevelopment project is to be given to those persons and families displaced by a redevelopment agency regardless of whether the units are inside or outside of a project area. Additionally, since January 1, 2002, redevelopment law requires that a redevelopment agency must keep a list of those persons and families displaced from a destroyed or removed unit and may establish reasonable rules to determine the priority for such persons and families. § 33411.3.

Priority in renting or buying housing developed as part of a redevelopment project is to be given to those persons and families displaced by a redevelopment agency regardless of whether the units are inside or outside of a project area.

Replacement Housing Plan

Section 33413.5 requires an agency to adopt a replacement housing plan not less than 30 days prior to executing an agreement for the acquisition, sale or lease, or development of property that would lead to the destruction or removal of dwelling units from the low- and moderate-income housing market. For a reasonable time prior to its adoption, the agency is required to make the proposed replacement housing plan available to the public, the project area committee, and other public agencies. A housing unit that is required to be replaced pursuant to section 33413 may not be destroyed or removed from the housing market until the agency has adopted the replacement housing plan.

The replacement housing plan must include:

- The general location of the replacement housing to be rehabilitated, developed, or constructed
- An adequate means of financing the replacement housing
- A finding that approval by the voters under Article XXXIV is not required prior to development of the replacement housing
- The number of replacement dwelling units for low- or moderate-income persons and families
- The timetable for meeting the replacement housing plan's relocation, rehabilitation, and replacement housing objectives

§ 33413.5

Federal: CDBG Special Requirements

If an agency demolishes or converts to another use low- or moderate-income dwelling units that are occupied or could be occupied using CDBG funds, the agency must also comply with the replacement housing requirements contained in the "Barney Frank" provisions of the Federal HUD Guidelines. 24 C.F.R. § 570.606(c), 24 C.F.R. § 42.375. The principal differences between these requirements and the replacement housing requirements under the Community Redevelopment Law are: replacement must be completed within three years instead of four years; the duration of affordability is ten years instead of 45 or 55 years depending on whether the unit is owner-occupied or rented; and information and a plan for providing the replacement housing must be submitted to the HUD field office.

When provisions within the Community Redevelopment Law and the Federal HUD Guidelines conflict, an agency should follow the more onerous provision.

When demolishing or converting a low- or moderate-income dwelling unit with CDBG funds, an agency should review the replacement housing requirements under both the Community Redevelopment Law and the Federal HUD Guidelines to make sure it complies with both. When provisions conflict, an agency should follow the more onerous provision.

Completion of Housing Obligations

Section 33333.8 makes the requirement to complete affordable housing obligations explicit.

Since the various housing obligations under the Community Redevelopment Law are requirements, the implication has always been that agencies must complete these affordable housing obligations prior to terminating a project area or the agency itself. Section 33333.8 makes the requirement to complete affordable housing obligations explicit. Section 33333.8 requires every redevelopment agency to comply with and fulfill its affordable housing obligations with regard to the provision of affordable housing prior to the time limit on the effectiveness of the redevelopment plan established pursuant to sections 33333.2, 33333.6 and 33333.10.

A legislative body cannot adopt an ordinance terminating a redevelopment project area if the agency has not satisfied the affordable housing obligations, which include the following, found at section 33333.8(a)(1):

(a) make deposits to and expenditures from the housing fund pursuant to sections 33334.2, 33334.3, 33334.4, 33334.6, 33487, 33492.16 and other similar and related statutes;

(b) eliminate project deficits pursuant to sections 33334.6, 33492.16 and other similar and related statutes;

(c) expend or transfer excess surplus funds pursuant to section 33334.12 and other similar and related statutes;

(d) provide relocation assistance pursuant to section 33410 *et seq.*, section 7260 of the Government Code or other applicable relocation laws;

(e) provide replacement housing pursuant to section 33413, section 33410 *et seq.*, and other similar and related statutes; and

(f) provide inclusionary housing pursuant to section 33413 and other similar and related statutes and ordinances.

If, on the date of the time limit of effectiveness of the redevelopment plan or the time limit on repayment of indebtedness, an agency has not complied with these housing obligations, then the particular time limit that has expired is suspended, and the agency must use all tax-increment funds not pledged to repay indebtedness to comply with the housing obligation. § 33333.8(b)–(c).

If, on the date of the time limit on the repayment of indebtedness, the agency has complied with these housing obligations and still has monies remaining in the housing fund, the agency shall transfer the remaining monies to a housing fund for a different project area within the agency's jurisdiction, if one exists, or if a different project area does not exist, the agency shall either transfer the remaining monies to a special fund of the community or to the community or county housing authority. The community or county housing authority to which the remaining monies are transferred is subject to the same restrictions that are applicable to the housing fund. § 33333.8(d).

If a redevelopment plan contains a limit on the total amount of tax-increment funds that may be received and if that limit is reached prior to the agency complying with these housing obligations, the tax-increment limit is suspended and the agency must use tax-increment funds until the agency has fully complied with its housing obligations. § 33333.8(e). *See also* §§ 33333.6, 33333.10.

If an agency fails to comply with its obligations pursuant to section 33333.8, then any person may seek judicial relief and the court is authorized to mandate the fulfillment of these obligations. § 33333.8(f).

Special Provisions for Time Limit Extension Amendment

Sections 33333.10 and 33333.11 authorize the amendment of a redevelopment plan to extend plan effectiveness or receipt of tax increment in certain limited circumstances.

As discussed in more detail in chapter 3, sections 33333.10 and 33333.11 authorize the amendment of a redevelopment plan to extend plan effectiveness or receipt of tax increment in certain limited circumstances. After the adoption of the amendment pursuant to these sections, except for funds deposited in the housing fund, the agency must spend tax-increment funds only within the portion of the project area that has been identified as the area containing blighted parcels and necessary and essential parcels. § 33333.10(e).

Expenditures from Housing Fund

After the date limiting receipt of tax increment has been amended, agencies shall only spend monies from the housing fund for the purpose of assisting affordable housing for persons and families of low, very low, or extremely low income.

After the date limiting receipt of tax increment has been amended, agencies shall only spend monies from the housing fund for the purpose of assisting affordable housing for persons and families of low, very low, or extremely low income, as defined in sections 50079.5, 50093, 50105, and 50106. § 33333.10(f)(1). An agency that has adopted an amendment pursuant to these sections may use monies from the housing fund for persons and families of moderate income as defined in section 50093, provided, however, this amount shall not exceed, in a five-year period, the amount of monies from the housing fund that are used for persons and families of extremely low income, as defined in section 50106. In no case shall the amount expended for housing for persons and families of moderate income exceed 15 percent of the annual amount deposited in the housing fund during a five year period; and the number of housing units affordable to moderate-income persons shall not exceed the number of housing units affordable to extremely low-income persons.

From the start of the first fiscal year after the date of adoption of the amendment and until the date that the time limit on tax increment would have taken effect but for the amendment, an agency may use monies from the housing fund for moderate-income persons and families as defined in section 50093. § 33333.10(f)(2). However, this amount shall not exceed, in a five-year period period, 15 percent of the amount of monies deposited in the housing fund during that five-year period; and shall only be used to assist housing projects in which no less than 49 percent of the units are affordable to and occupied by persons and families of low, very low, or extremely low income.

Deposits into Housing Fund

Beginning with the year following amendment pursuant to these sections, an agency shall deposit not less than 30 percent of the tax increment from the project area into the housing fund. § 33333.10(g)(1). An agency adopting an amendment may deposit less than 30 percent of tax increment, but not less than 20 percent in any fiscal year, if the agency finds that the difference between the amount deposited and the amount required by section 33333.10(g)(1) is necessary to make principal and interest payments during that fiscal year on bonds sold by the agency to finance or refinance the redevelopment project prior to six months before the date of the adoption of the amendment pursuant to section 33333.10(a). § 33333.10(g)(2). This exception will only apply to bonds that are refinanced, refunded, or restructured after the adoption of the amendment if (1) the net proceeds were used to refinance the original bonds, (2) there is no increase in the amount of principal at the time of refinancing, restructuring, or refunding, and (3) the new term for repayment of the bonds does not exceed the original term. *Id.* No later than 120 days prior to depositing less than the amount required by section 33333.10(g)(1) into the housing fund, the agency shall adopt, after a noticed public hearing, a resolution with specific findings that the reduction is necessary to make payments on the bonds, and that include specific information related to the payment of the bonds. § 33333.10(g)(3).

The Fairfield Redevelopment Agency targeted a high crime residential area, and working with a nonprofit housing developer, assembled several properties for rehabilitation as one multi-family housing project.

Additionally, if the agency sells bonds after the date of a time limit extension amendment, the agency may elect to subordinate up to 16 2/3 percent of the annual 30 percent housing fund deposit obligation to those new bonds. If the agency does subordinate that portion of the deposit into the housing fund, then in any year that the agency has insufficient tax-increment revenue available to pay debt service on the bonds to which the funds from the housing fund are subordinated, the agency may deposit less than the full 100 percent of its annual 30 percent housing fund obligation but only to the extent necessary to pay that debt service and in no event is less than 83 1/3 percent of the amount required to be deposited into the housing fund for that year. § 33333.10(g)(4). The difference between the amount that is actually deposited in the housing fund and the full 30 percent housing fund deposit obligation shall constitute a deficit in the housing fund subject to repayment. § 33333.10(g)(5). Any new tax-increment funds not required to make bond debt service under section 33333.10(g)(2) or (4) must be used to reduce or eliminate the deficit prior to entering into any new contracts, commitments, or indebtedness. § 33333.10(g)(5).

The difference between the amount that is actually deposited in the housing fund and the full 30 percent housing fund deposit obligation shall constitute a deficit in the housing fund subject to repayment.

Plans Adopted Prior to 1976

Each redevelopment plan that has been adopted prior to January 1, 1976, that is amended pursuant to section 33333.10, subdivision (a), shall also be amended at the same time to include the inclusionary and housing production requirements of section 33413 subdivision (b).

Additional Housing Authority

In addition to the major provisions both requiring agencies to assist in the development of housing for low- and moderate-income persons and families and granting them the authority to implement these requirements, several other statutes can be used as authority for agency housing programs and projects. A number of the declarations of policy adopted by the legislature emphasize the importance of providing decent housing, including section 33070. Sections 33071 and 33334.6 state that a fundamental purpose of redevelopment is to expand the supply of low- and moderate-income housing.

Section 33320.2 provides that an unblighted, noncontiguous area is to be conclusively deemed necessary for effective redevelopment and thus eligible for inclusion within a project area if it is being used predominantly for low- and moderate-income housing. Section 33449 gives agencies broad authority both within and outside project areas to provide housing for persons and families of low or moderate income by acquiring land, donating land, improving sites, constructing or rehabilitating structures, and providing subsidies. This authority may be useful when other than housing fund monies are being used.

Section 33741 gives agencies the authority to issue tax-exempt bonds, the proceeds of which can be loaned to nonprofits to finance the acquisition, construction, rehabilitation, refinancing, or development of multifamily rental housing, including mobile home parks.

Article XXXIV

Article XXXIV of the California Constitution provides that a low-rent housing project shall not be developed, constructed, or acquired by any state public body until the voters of the city or county approve the project at an election. For Article XXXIV to apply, the project must be a low-rent housing project developed, constructed, or acquired by a state public body. A redevelopment agency is a state public body as defined in Article XXXIV. Therefore, in determining whether agency involvement with a particular housing project will require an Article XXXIV election, careful consideration of the other two elements is important.

Article XXXIV contains a very general definition of a "low-rent housing project" and does not define "developed, constructed, or acquired." To clarify ambiguities regarding its applicability, legislation was enacted that defined these two key terms and, in doing so, exempted a variety of housing projects from these definitions and, therefore, the requirement of voter approval. § 37000 *et seq.*

The term "low-rent housing project" does not include development projects that meet one of the following criteria:

- Privately owned housing, receiving no *ad valorem* property tax exemption not fully reimbursed to all taxing entities, and not more than 49 percent of the dwellings, apartments, or other living accommodations of this development occupied by persons and families of low-income
- Privately owned housing, not exempt from *ad valorem* taxation by reason of any public ownership, and not financed with direct long-term financing from a public body
- Intended for owner occupancy, which may include cooperative or condominium ownership, rather than for rental occupancy
- Newly constructed, privately owned, one-to-four family dwellings not located on adjoining sites
- Existing dwelling units leased by the state public body from the private owner of these dwelling units
- Consisting of the rehabilitation, reconstruction, improvement or addition to, or replacement of dwelling units of a previously existing low-rent housing project

The California Supreme Court has approved these exemptions. *California Housing Finance Agency v. Patitucci* (1978) 22 Cal. 3d 171.

Since the *Patitucci* case, the legislature added another project that is exempt from the definition of low-rent housing project:

- The development consists of acquisition, rehabilitation, reconstruction, or improvement of rental housing units that prior to the development were subject to a contract for federal or state public assistance for the purpose of providing affordable housing for low-income households and the development maintains or enters into similar federal or state assistance.

The terms "develop, construct, or acquire" are defined in section 37001.5 and case law. In *California Housing Finance Agency v. Elliott* (1976) 17 Cal. 3d 575, the California Supreme Court reviewed the role of the California Housing Finance Agency (CHFA) in projects developed by private developers and local public entities with the proceeds of revenue bonds issued by CHFA. The Court determined that CHFA was "developing," within the meaning of Article XXXIV, because of CHFA's extensive involvement, and that local elections were, therefore, required.

In *Redevelopment Agency v. Shepard* (1977) 75 Cal. App. 3d 453, the court followed *California Housing Finance Agency v. Elliott* in holding that the sale by an agency of bonds for residential construction loans with additional agency involvement in shaping and defining the project constituted developing, constructing, or acquiring within the

The terms "develop, construct, or acquire" are defined in section 37001.5 and case law.

CHFA = California Housing Finance Agency

meaning of Article XXXIV. However, the court concluded that an election was not necessary because, since there was no income test for loan eligibility or occupancy or agency authority to fix rental rates, it was not possible to determine whether the occupants would be "persons of low income."

Section 37001.5 excludes the following activities from the definition of "develop, construct, or acquire" as used in Section 1 of Article XXXIV:

- The agency provides financing to a private owner of existing housing secured by a deed of trust or other security instrument, or the agency acquires a development with the intent to convey the property to another entity.
- The agency acquires or makes improvements to land that will be conveyed to a private owner prior to development as a low-rent housing project provided that
    - The development is not subject to an exemption from property taxes by reason of public ownership for more than five years, or
    - Any loss in property taxes by affected taxing entities beyond five years is fully reimbursed to the affected taxing entities.
- The agency leases existing dwelling units from a private owner provided the lease does not result in a decrease in property tax revenues.
- The agency provides assistance to the private owner or occupant of existing housing.
- The agency provides assistance to a low-rent housing project and monitors construction or rehabilitation of the project and compliance with conditions of the assistance to the extent of
    - Carrying out routine governmental functions
    - Performing conventional activities of a lender
    - Imposing constitutionally mandated or statutorily authorized conditions of the assistance.
- The agency provides assistance to a development before it becomes a low-rent housing project without intending or expecting that it will become a low-rent housing project.

An appellate court has not approved these definitions.

The decision as to whether the provisions of Article XXXIV apply to a particular housing project depends upon a close analysis of the nature of the project, the provisions of Article XXXIV, the statutes, and the cases.

The decision as to whether the provisions of Article XXXIV apply to a particular housing project depends upon a close analysis of the nature of the project, including ownership, financing, governmental review, public assistance, and income of tenants, the provisions of Article XXXIV, the statutes, and the cases. This analysis should take place at the time the degree of agency involvement with the project is being developed so that a determination can be made as to whether an election is necessary.

Since Article XXXIV was approved in 1950, most local public agencies have sought voter approval of ballot measures stating the maximum number of dwelling units a public agency may develop, construct, or acquire, but not describing the location or design of the units, the source of the project's funding, or the specific time the project will be developed. If approved, this maximum number of units can be applied to specific housing projects that are subsequently proposed. This practice of receiving general authorization instead of approval for each specific project was recently challenged. While the California Supreme Court initially determined that general authorization did not comply with Article XXXIV provisions, in a revised opinion the Court held that voter approval of a ballot measure stating the maximum number of dwelling units is sufficient to provide Article XXXIV authorization. *Davis v. City of Berkeley* (1990) 51 Cal. 3d 227.

Reporting and Monitoring Requirements

As part of its interest in understanding the effect of redevelopment on housing for low- and moderate-income persons and families, and in response to requests by housing advocates who are interested in assessing not only the statewide impacts but in having certain information collected in a central location to assist in the filing of lawsuits, the legislature has required agencies to report annually to the state certain information regarding housing, to file certain findings with the HCD, and to monitor housing projects assisted by the agency.

Reporting

As part of the annual report prepared by the agency and sent to the state, section 33080.1 subdivision (c) requires that the agency describe its activities affecting housing and displacement. Specific information with regard to displacement, housing units destroyed, and housing units constructed is required. § 33080.4. Agencies may also have to report the amount of excess surplus in the housing fund. § 33080.7.

In order to assist in determining compliance with the excess surplus provisions of the Community Redevelopment Law, agencies must report the following:

- The number of housing units for low- and moderate-income persons and families to be constructed under the terms of an executed agreement. These figures may only be reported on units that encumber agency funds for a period of two years from the execution of the agreement. § 33080.4(a)(10)
- The date and amount of deposits and withdrawals to and from the housing fund. § 33080.4(a)(11)

As part of the annual report prepared by the agency and sent to the state, section 33080.1 subdivision (c) requires that the agency describe its activities affecting housing and displacement.

Agencies must report the number of low- and moderate-income housing units to be constructed under the terms of an executed agreement.

Findings Sent to HCD

Within ten days after making a finding under either section 33334.2 subdivision (a) or 33334.6, which authorizes depositing less than 20 percent of the annual tax increments in the housing fund, a copy of the finding and supporting evidence are to be sent to HCD.

Monitoring and Affordability Database

Section 33418 requires agencies to monitor, on an ongoing basis, any housing affordable to persons and families of low or moderate income developed or otherwise made available pursuant to the provisions of the Community Redevelopment Law.

Section 33418 requires agencies to monitor, on an ongoing basis, any housing affordable to persons and families of low or moderate income developed or otherwise made available pursuant to the provisions of the Community Redevelopment Law. As part of its monitoring, agencies are to require owners or managers of housing governed by the provisions of this section to submit annual reports to the agency including certain specified information regarding, if applicable, rental rates, income, family size, and change of ownership.

The database must be made available on the internet and updated on an annual basis.

The agency must use the information received to compile and maintain a database of affordable units assisted with money from the low- and moderate-income housing fund or otherwise counted toward the agency's inclusionary requirements under section 33413. The database must be made available on the internet and updated on an annual basis. It must include, for each owner-occupied or rental unit, the street address and assessor's parcel number of the property, the number of bedrooms for each unit, the year in which construction or substantial rehabilitation of the unit was completed, the date of recordation and document number of the affordability covenants or restrictions recorded against each unit, the date on which those covenants or restrictions expire, and for owner-occupied units that have changes ownership during the reporting year, the date and document number of the new affordability covenants against the property. The database shall not include any properties used to confidentially house victims of domestic violence. § 33418(c).

12

Closed Military Bases

> *At both the federal and state levels special approaches have been adopted to facilitate the reuse and redevelopment of closed military bases to productive use consistent with local planning and code requirements.*

The reuse and redevelopment of closed military bases is particularly complex and difficult, involving among other problems the remediation of hazardous waste prior to federal transfer of land and buildings and, after transfer, the replacement and renovation or demolition of utilities, infrastructure and buildings that were exempt under federal ownership from, and do not comply with, local codes. At both the federal and state levels special approaches have been adopted to facilitate the reuse and redevelopment of closed military bases to productive reuse consistent with local planning and code requirements.

Adoption of Redevelopment Plans

Chapter 4.5 of the Community Redevelopment Law establishes an alternative plan adoption procedure specifically for communities with military bases that have been designated for closure or realignment. § 33492 *et seq.* Cities and counties may enter into a joint powers agreement for the purpose of adopting a project area.

This chapter was significantly amended by the legislature in 1996 so that it provides certain distinct advantages over the normal plan adoption procedures contained in AB 1290.

First, unlike other project areas, a blighted area for a military base plan is one that includes two or more of the conditions listed in section 33492.11, such as:

- Buildings in which it is unsafe or unhealthy for persons to live or work.
- Factors that prevent or substantially hinder the economically viable reuse or capacity of buildings or areas. This condition can be caused by such conditions as substandard design, buildings that are too

> *Chapter 4.5 of the Community Redevelopment Law establishes an alternative plan adoption procedure specifically for communities with military bases that have been designated for closure or realignment.*

large or too small given present standards and market conditions, age, obsolescence, deterioration, dilapidation, or other physical conditions that could prevent the highest and best uses of the property. This condition can also be caused by buildings that will have to be demolished or buildings or areas with inadequate parking.

- Incompatible uses.
- Buildings on land that when subdivided, or when infrastructure is installed, will not comply with community subdivision, zoning, or planning regulations.
- Properties currently served by substandard infrastructure.
- Buildings that when built did not conform to the then effective building, plumbing, mechanical, or electrical codes adopted by the community.
- Land that contains materials or facilities, including, but not limited to, materials for aircraft landing pads and runways, that will have to be removed.

Second, the agency does not have to make the payments to other taxing entities as required by section 33607.5 until after it has received $100,000 in tax increments. §§ 33492.9, 33492.15.

Third, the agency does not need to prepare an environmental impact report (EIR) prior to the adoption of the redevelopment plan if it finds, at a noticed public hearing, that there is a need to adopt a plan at the earliest possible time. If it makes such a finding, an EIR must be certified within 18 months after the effective date of the ordinance adopting the redevelopment plan. If, based on the EIR, it is necessary to amend the redevelopment plan to mitigate any impacts, the agency shall amend the plan. If a court determines that the EIR is inadequate, the agency shall not undertake additional projects under the redevelopment plan until an adequate environmental document has been certified. However, the redevelopment plan is still valid. In addition, until an EIR is certified for the redevelopment plan, individual projects are subject to the normal California Environmental Quality Act (CEQA) requirements.

Section 21083.8.1 of the Public Resources Code was added to the California Environmental Quality Act to amend the EIR requirements as they apply to reuse plans for closed military bases and, subject to certain requirements, allows agencies to analyze significant impacts in the context of the physical conditions that were in effect at the time the decision for closure or realignment became final as opposed to existing conditions at the time of preparation of the EIR. Sections 21083.6 and 21083.7 and CEQA Guidelines provide for the coordination of an EIR under CEQA with the use of an environmental impact statement prepared under the National Environmental Policy Act of 1969.

CEQA = California Environmental Quality Act

EIR = Environmental impact report

The agency does not need to prepare an EIR prior to the adoption of the redevelopment plan if it finds, at a noticed public hearing, that there is a need to adopt a plan at the earliest possible time.

Section 21083.8.1 of the Public Resources Code was added to CEQA to amend the EIR requirements as they apply to reuse plans for closed military bases.

Fourth, certain documents need only be as complete as the currently available information permits, such as the report of the county taxing officials, the preliminary report, and the report to the legislative body. § 33492.20.

Finally, an agency may defer, for up to five years, its obligation to deposit 20 percent of its tax increments into its Low and Moderate Income Housing Fund if the legislative body annually finds that the funds are necessary for the effective redevelopment of base projects and long term tax generation, and that the vacancy rate for housing affordable to lower income households within the jurisdiction of the members of the agency is greater than four percent. The deferred amounts must be paid into the Low and Moderate Income Housing Fund no later than the end of the twentieth fiscal year after plan adoption. If the indebtedness is not eliminated by that time, the county auditor-controller must withhold that amount from the agency's tax increments and deposit it into a separate Low and Moderate Income Housing Fund for the agency's use. § 33492.16.

The deferred amounts must be paid into the Low and Moderate Income Housing Fund no later than the end of the twentieth fiscal year after plan adoption.

An agency may include territory outside a military base as part of the project area, but all the territory outside the military base must satisfy the normal plan adoption requirements for blight and be predominantly urbanized. In addition, an agency may not defer its obligation to deposit 20 percent of the tax increments generated from property located outside the military base. §§ 33492.3, 33492.10, 33492.11, 33492.16.

However, unlike other plans adopted on or after January 1, 1994, a redevelopment plan adopted pursuant to this chapter must contain a cap on the amount of tax increments an agency is authorized to receive over the life of the plan. § 33492.13.

Street improvements in downtown Vallejo will enhance the waterfront and provide easier access to the former Mare Island Naval Shipyard.

Several communities that have closed military bases designated for closure have also obtained specific legislation in chapter 4.5 governing their particular bases, or dealing with circumstances unique to the redevelopment of their particular bases.

The Military Base Reuse Authority Act (Gov. Code § 67800 *et seq.*) authorizes cities and counties to establish military base reuse authorities for the preparation of a local reuse plan for the military base and provides procedures for local general plans and zoning to be brought into conformity with the adopted reuse plan. Special legislation has also been adopted creating special reuse authorities such as the Fort Ord Reuse Authority Act (Gov. Code § 67650 *et seq.*) establishing the Fort Ord Reuse Authority, which is governed by a 13-member Board consisting of representatives of the County of Monterey and eight cities; and the

Treasure Island Conversion Act of 1997 (Chapter 898, Statutes of 1997) creating the Treasure Island Development Authority and establishing its authority for the reuse and redevelopment of the Treasure Island Naval Station and the administration of related state tidelands trust properties.

In *Save Our NTC, Inc. v. City of San Diego* (2003) 105 Cal. App. 4th 285, the Court of Appeal held that a Reuse Plan adopted pursuant to federal base closure statutes was not subject to a voter initiative imposing a height limitation on new construction, adopted prior to the transfer of the base to the city, that was inconsistent with the Reuse Plan as approved by the Defense Department and Department of Housing and Urban Development. The Court of Appeal stated:

> Pursuant to the federal and state statutory schemes governing reuse planning and transfer of military base properties, the federal government's transfer of the surplus NTC property to the City did not trigger the application of all existing zoning ordinances to the property, but instead only those that were consistent with the reuse plan approved by the Defense Department and HUD. As SONTC readily admits, the Proposition D height limitation is not consistent with the reuse plan; accordingly, the limitation did not apply to the base property, regardless of whether the voters would have intended for it to apply to property acquired by the City after its adoption.

Id. at p. 295

Pursuant to the California Military Recovery Areas Act, enacted in 1993, (Chapter 12.97, commencing with section 7105 of the Government Code) the State Department of Housing and Community Development is authorized to approve the designation of a limited number of Local Military Base Recovery Areas (LAMBRAs) for all or portions of closed military bases in order to attract reinvestment and re-employ workers. A LAMBRA provides tax incentives similar to Enterprise Zones and is binding for a period of eight years. LAMBRAs have been designated for Castle Air Force Base, George Air Force Base, Mare Island Naval Shipyard, Mather Field/McClellan Air Force Base, Norton Air Force Base, Alameda Naval Air Station, Tustin Marine Corps Air Station, and San Diego NTC Liberty Island.

Integration with BRAC Disposal Process

Traditionally, the General Services Administration (GSA) of the United States Government handled the disposal of excess or surplus federal property pursuant to the Federal Property and Administrative Services Act of 1949 (40 U.S.C. § 471 *et seq.*), as amended. The common method employed by GSA for disposition of excess property not needed by other federal, state or local governmental agencies was the sale by public bid.

A LAMBRA provides tax incentives similar to Enterprise Zones and is binding for a period of eight years.

GSA = General Services Administration

LAMBRA = Local Military Base Recovery Area

Public bid sales by GSA of excess military property (such as the auction sale of the Army portion of Hamilton Air Force Base in the City of Novato in the 1980's) presented special problems for local communities because the reuse of the property was not planned and bidders would tend to bid speculative prices for the property in anticipation of being able to apply for and receive land use designations and entitlements that would permit an economically feasible development of the property. The subsequent planning process frequently became very contentious and the speculative land price and other financial burdens of development hindered timely and appropriate reuse of the former military property.

This process changed dramatically in the early 1990's for military bases closed pursuant to the Defense Base Closure and Realignment Act of 1990 (Public Law 101-510, Title XXIX, 10 U.S.C. § 2687) as amended and implemented by succeeding legislation, and implementing regulations of the Department of Defense (32 C.F.R. Parts 174 and 175) (Base Closure and Realignment Act) pursuant to the recommendation of the Base Realignment and Closure Commission (BRAC). The Base Closure and Realignment Act established procedures for the disposal by the Department of Defense, acting through the appropriate military department, of excess military property under the BRAC process. The 1994 "Pryor Amendment" implemented the provisions of the 1994 Base Closure Community Assistance Act, an attempt to revitalize communities impacted by military base closures and speed the recovery of those impacted communities. The following is intended to illustrate the integration of the BRAC process into local reuse planning and redevelopment but is not intended to be all-inclusive, and particular attention to the applicable federal and state statutes, regulations and policies, as well as local planning and redevelopment laws and policies, is required for each particular instance of a BRAC military base closure.

The Base Closure and Realignment Act established procedures for the disposal by the Department of Defense of excess military property under the BRAC process.

BRAC = Base Realignment and Closure Commission

LRA = Local reuse authority

Establishment of Local Reuse Authority

A local reuse authority (LRA) is established pursuant to applicable state law (*e.g.*, Gov. Code § 67800 *et seq.*) or pursuant to special state legislation (*e.g.*, Gov. Code § 67650 *et seq.*; Chapter 898, Statutes of 1997).

Preparation and Adoption of a Reuse Plan

As authorized by federal BRAC legislation, including the Pryor Amendment, the LRA engages in a comprehensive planning process with all stakeholders in the community, including homeless interests, to prepare and adopt a Reuse Plan. The Reuse Plan must be approved by the Department of Housing and Urban Development for compliance with the McKinney Homeless Assistance Act. To be effective as a local planning

As authorized by federal BRAC legislation the LRA engages in a comprehensive planning process with all stakeholders in the community to prepare and adopt a Reuse Plan.

EDC = Economic development conveyance

EIS = Environmental impact statement

NEPA = National Environmental Policy Act

PBC = Public benefit conveyances

ROD = Record of decision

Originally built in 1934, these historic hangars at Hamilton Field in Novato are being renovated for office uses.

document, the Reuse Plan must subsequently be adopted and incorporated into the general plan and zoning requirements of the local community.

Federal EIS; EIS/EIR

Pursuant to the National Environmental Policy Act (NEPA), an environmental impact statement (EIS) is prepared based on the intended disposition of the closed military base. The preparation of an EIS may be combined with the preparation of an EIR under CEQA for the reuse of the closed military base and/or the Reuse Plan provided that the document satisfies the requirements of both CEQA and NEPA (note the "base line" conditions authorized by Public Resources Code, § 21083.8.1). Based on the EIS, the federal government will file a record of decision (ROD) which will include subsequent environmental actions to be undertaken.

Disposition Procedures

The Department of Defense, acting through the relevant military department, after first screening to determine whether the property should be transferred to the Department of Defense or other federal agencies, will undertake to dispose of the excess military property under one or more of the following methods:

- *Public Benefit Conveyances (PBC).* Under the base closure process, state and local government agencies as well as nonprofit institutions that serve a public purpose, including homeless providers under the McKinney Homeless Assistance Act, can receive property at no cost or at a discounted price for public and public related uses; with conflicting requests resolved by the LRA with the federal government. A PBC conveyance will be sponsored by a federal agency and will include restrictions on use.

- *Economic Development Conveyance (EDC).* Section 2905 subsection (b) (4) of the Base Closure and Realignment Act created a new conveyance mechanism allowing LRAs to request and negotiate for the transfer of excess military base property for economic development purposes (*e.g.*, job creation). EDCs can be on negotiated terms to achieve the economic development purposes of the conveyance. Also, pending the final disposition of property and provided the use is consistent with the ROD and NEPA requirements, the secretary of the applicable military department is authorized to enter into an interim lease of the property—lease in furtherance of conveyance (LIFOC)—and permit subletting, upon a determination that the LIFOC will facilitate state or local economic adjustment efforts (10 U.S.C. § 2687(f)(1)). The secretary also may accept consideration that is less than fair market value upon a determination that a public interest will be served as a result of the lease and that the fair market value of the lease is either unobtainable or not compatible with such public benefit. 10 U.S.C. § 2687(f)(2).

- *Negotiated Sale to Local Government or LRA (Negotiated Sale).* Under certain circumstances where a PBC or EDC is not authorized but a public purpose will nonetheless be served (such as the development of affordable housing), a local government or LRA may request a negotiated sale of excess military property pursuant to 40 U.S.C. section 484(e)(3)(H) as implemented by 41 CFR Part 101-47.304-9(a)(4), based on a public purpose to be served under the Reuse Plan. A negotiated sale will be at appraised fair market value and will comply with other procedures applicable to GSA sales of excess federal property. The appraised value of the property based on its intended reuse under the Reuse Plan and other terms of conveyance, including recapture of "excess profits" will frequently involve extended discussions with officials of GSA and the disposing military department and may or may not be successfully concluded.

- *Competitive Sale.* When no other disposal method is available or deemed appropriate, the property may be sold at a public bid sale to the highest qualified bidder (a "competitive sale"). 40 U.S.C. § 484(a)(1)–(2). In recent years, this has been a preferred method of disposition in established urban market areas. *See* Trends in Enhancing Value, below.

ESCA = Environmental Services Cooperative Agreement

ETCA = Early Transfer Cooperative Agreement

EUL = Enhanced use leasing

LIFOC = Lease in furtherance of conveyance

When no other disposal method is available or deemed appropriate, the property may be sold at a public bid sale to the highest qualified bidder.

Trends in Enhancing Value

In recent years, particularly since BRAC 2005, the Department of Defense has focused on ways to enhance the value of existing and surplus assets of all branches of the military services. Among the methods being used are competitive sale of surplus military lands under a bid process to qualified bidders. Two notable examples of this process in California are MCAS-City of Tustin and MCAS El Toro-City of Irvine. There is also a greater use of Early Transfer Cooperative Agreements (ETCAs), sometimes referred to as Environmental Services Cooperative Agreements (ESCAs) for the early transfer of surplus military lands pending environmental remediation in order to facilitate the efforts of private redevelopment on those lands. *See* Early Transfer Pending Remediation; Covenant Deferral, below.

Existing military assets that can be appropriately leased for private operation and investment are the subject of "enhanced use leasing" (EUL)

In recent years, particularly since BRAC 2005, the Department of Defense has focused on ways to enhance the value of existing and surplus assets of all branches of the military services.

CERCLA = Comprehensive Environmental Response, Compensation and Liability Act

The Hamilton Amphitheater Park, created on the site of a closed military base, includes a renovated 950-seat amphitheater, children's play area, gazebo, and picnic area. The amphitheater, originally constructed in 1935, is listed on the National Register of Historic Places.

at fair market value rent or in kind consideration (such as upgrading or new construction) to produce on-going proceeds or benefits for enhancement of existing military facilities. 10 U.S.C. § 2667. Finally, EUL partnerships among military bases and local communities and the private sector are being utilized to privatize military base housing and utilities, employ alternate energy resources to meet goals of energy conservation and efficiency, enhance historic resources, improve municipal services, and coordinate adjacent land use planning and development in order to better serve and enhance existing military bases.

Environmental Cleanup Prior to Transfer

The United States, through its appropriate military department, is responsible for the remediation of hazardous substances on the property to be transferred pursuant to the provisions of the Comprehensive Environmental Response, Compensation and Liability Act. 42 U.S.C. §§ 9601 *et seq.*, 9620(a)(2) (CERCLA). Deeds for the transfer of the property must contain:

- Notifications of the type and quantity of any hazardous substances known to have been stored, released or disposed of on the property, the time at which such storage, release or disposal took place and a description of the remedial action taken, if any
- A covenant warranting that all remedial action necessary to protect human health and the environment with respect to any such substance remaining on the property prior to the date of such transfer, and that any additional remedial action found necessary after the date of such transfer, shall be conducted by the United States
- A clause granting the United States access to the property in any case in which remedial action or corrective action is found necessary after transfer

42 U.S.C. § 9620(h)(3)(A)

Pursuant to section 330 of the National Defense Authorization Act for Fiscal Year 1993 (Public Law 102-484), as amended, and subject to certain exceptions and conditions stated therein, the Secretary of Defense shall hold harmless, defend and indemnify in full State or political subdivision grantees or any other person or entity that acquires ownership or control of any military installation (or portion thereof) that is closed pursuant to a base closure law, including any successor, assignee, transferee, lender, or lessee of any such persons or entities, from and against any suit, claim, demand or action, liability, judgment, cost or other fee arising out of any claim for personal injury or property damage (including death, illness, or loss) that results from, or is in any manner predicated upon, the release or threatened release of any hazardous substance, pollutant, contaminant, petroleum or petroleum derivative from or on the property, including subsurface soils, groundwater and surface waters, as a result of Department of Defense activities at the former military installation (or portion thereof). In *Richmond American Homes of Colorado, Inc. v. U.S.* (2007) 75 Fed. Cl. 376, the U.S. Court of Federal Claims ruled that environmental costs incurred by developers are the responsibility of the federal government under section 330. In the facts of this case, a homebuilder discovered asbestos-containing material in the soil after acquiring the property from the local reuse authority, which purchased the property from the U.S. Air Force. Pursuant to compliance advisories issued by the State of Colorado, the homebuilder incurred investigation and remediation costs in excess of $9 million and submitted a claim for reimbursement under section 330. The Air Force refused on the grounds that section 330 required a third party claim for personal injury or damages against the homebuilder. The Court of Federal claims applied an expansive construction of the word "claim" and ruled that the state compliance advisories were sufficient to support the homebuilder's claim for reimbursement. Caution is advised in relying upon either section 330 or the covenants under CERCLA, and environmental insurance is recommended for local reuse authorities and their developers when accepting the transfer of military base property. At Fort Ord in Monterey County, for example, the Fort Ord Reuse Authority (FORA) negotiated a $100 million base-wide policy of environmental insurance for coverage allocated to local entities and their developers.

BCT = BRAC cleanup team

DTSC = Department of Toxic Substances Control

FORA = Fort Ord Reuse Authority

FOST = Finding of suitability to transfer

RAB = Restoration advisory board

To facilitate the environmental cleanup, a BRAC Cleanup Team (BCT) is established to coordinate between federal and state regulatory agencies, and a Restoration Advisory Board (RAB) is established to provide a forum for exchange of information among the federal government, regulatory agencies, and stakeholders.

To facilitate the environmental cleanup, a BRAC Cleanup Team is established to coordinate between federal and state regulatory agencies.

Transfer of the property will be authorized by the preparation of a Finding of Suitability to Transfer (FOST) prepared by the appropriate United States department and circulated for public review and comment.

It is important to note that local governments and private owners/developers anticipating the transfer of surplus military property will be subject to all applicable laws and regulations governing hazardous substances once the property is transferred to them. Disputes may arise between the federal cleanup standards and the standards that will be applied by state regulatory agencies including the Department of Toxic Substances Control of the California Environmental Protection Agency (DTSC) and a

> RWQCB = Regional Water Quality Control Board

It is important to thoroughly review and analyze the environmental condition and remediation of the property prior to transfer by the federal government.

Regional Water Quality Control Board (RWQCB) following transfer of the property that, if not resolved prior to transfer by an agreement with DTSC or an order by the RWQCB, can delay the transfer of the property or subject the local government and/or private owner/developer to unanticipated remediation costs or use restrictions following transfer. It is important therefore to thoroughly review and analyze the environmental condition and remediation of the property, in consultations with the appropriate state regulatory agencies, prior to transfer by the federal government, and to appropriately condition any transfer agreements upon the completion of environmental remediation to state standards governing the intended use of the property or, where appropriate, to adjust the economic terms of the conveyance in consideration of any additional remediation that may be required to comply with state standards.

Early Transfer Pending Remediation; Covenant Deferral

Section 9620 subsection (h)(3)(C) of title 42 of the United States Code authorizes the early transfer of property pending remediation.

Section 9620 subsection (h)(3)(C) of title 42 of the United States Code authorizes the early transfer of property pending remediation and the deferral of the covenant under section 9620 subsection (h)(3)(A)(ii)(I) under the following requirements and conditions:

> (i) In general
>
> The Administrator, with the concurrence of the Governor of the State in which the facility is located (in the case of real property at a Federal facility that is listed on the National Priorities List), or the Governor of the State in which the facility is located (in the case of real property at a Federal facility not listed on the National Priorities List) may defer the requirement of subparagraph (A)(ii)(I) with respect to the property if the Administrator or the Governor, as the case may be, determines that the property is suitable for transfer, based on a finding that—
>
>> (I) the property is suitable for transfer for the use intended by the transferee, and the intended use is consistent with protection of human health and the environment;
>>
>> (II) the deed or other agreement proposed to govern the transfer between the United States and the transferee of the property contains the assurances set forth in clause (ii);
>>
>> (III) the Federal agency requesting deferral has provided notice, by publication in a newspaper of general circulation in the vicinity of the property, of the proposed transfer and of the opportunity for the public to submit, within a period of not less than 30 days after the date of the notice, written comments on the suitability of the property for transfer; and
>>
>> (IV) the deferral and the transfer of the property will not substantially delay any necessary response action at the property.

(ii) Response action assurances

With regard to a release or threatened release of a hazardous substance for which a Federal agency is potentially responsible under this section, the deed or other agreement proposed to govern the transfer shall contain assurances that—

(I) provide for any necessary restrictions on the use of the property to ensure the protection of human health and the environment;

(II) provide that there will be restrictions on use necessary to ensure that required remedial investigations, response action, and oversight activities will not be disrupted;

(III) provide that all necessary response action will be taken and identify the schedules for investigation and completion of all necessary response action as approved by the appropriate regulatory agency; and

(IV) provide that the Federal agency responsible for the property subject to transfer will submit a budget request to the Director of the Office of Management and Budget that adequately addresses schedules for investigation and completion of all necessary response action, subject to congressional authorizations and appropriations.

(iii) Warranty

When all response action necessary to protect human health and the environment with respect to any substance remaining on the property on the date of transfer has been taken, the United States shall execute and deliver to the transferee an appropriate document containing a warranty that all such response action has been taken, and the making of the warranty shall be considered to satisfy the requirement of subparagraph (A)(ii)(I).

EETP = Eastern Early Transfer Parcel

The Eastern Early Transfer Parcel (EETP) in Mare Island Naval Shipyard in Vallejo is believed to be the first large closed military facility to be transferred, in large part, to a local government pursuant to these early transfer provisions. In that case, the City of Vallejo and the United States Navy entered into an Environmental Services Cooperative Agreement pursuant to which the Navy agreed to pay in a series of yearly installments the costs of certain defined environmental investigation, analysis and remediation of the EETP to be undertaken by the City, in compliance with requirements of federal and state regulatory agencies including a Consent Agreement with DTSC, with the Navy retaining responsibility for certain defined conditions not assumed by the City. The Navy covenanted to issue its CERCLA warranty upon certification of completion of remediation. The City, in turn, passed these remediation responsibilities on to its master developer who contracted with an experienced and qualified environmental engineering firm to perform

The Eastern Early Transfer Parcel in Mare Island Naval Shipyard in Vallejo is believed to be the first large closed military facility to be transferred, in large part, to a local government pursuant to early transfer provisions.

ADC = Association of Defense Communities

FOSET = Finding of suitability for early transfer

MEC = Munitions and explosives of concern

A good way to keep current with the latest trends and policies affecting disposal, cleanup, and enhancement of military base property is to participate in the periodic meetings of the Association of Defense Communities.

the obligations, with a cost-cap policy and environmental liability insurance policy protecting the respective interests of the parties.

The early transfer of this portion of Mare Island was completed in March, 2002, based on a Finding of Suitability for Early Transfer (FOSET) and the Governor's approval of the CERCLA covenant deferral, has significantly expedited the reuse and redevelopment of the EETP because the cleanup was conducted in satisfaction of state requirements and the master developer will be able to phase and coordinate the work of remediation with its redevelopment of the EETP.

In 2007 the Army and the Fort Ord Reuse Authority negotiated and entered into an ESCA for Army funding of remediation of MEC (munitions and explosives of concern) on approximately 3,340 acres at Fort Ord in Monterey County where there was potential for MEC to exist in the soils, with the Army retaining responsibility for soil and groundwater cleanup of all other hazardous materials.

Given the financial pressures on the military and the desire of local communities and developers to work with the military to expedite the reuse and redevelopment of closed military bases, the early transfer for remediation promises to be the tool of increasing use and sophistication.

A good way to keep current with the latest trends and policies affecting disposal, cleanup, and enhancement of military base property is to participate in the periodic meetings of the Association of Defense Communities (ADC). These meetings bring together local community officials, private sector developers, contractors and consultants, and Department of Defense and military officials with programs designed to highlight best practices and focus on effective methods for military base reuse and enhancement.

13

Validation Litigation

A redevelopment agency is a separate and distinct legal entity from the city or county in which it functions and may sue and be sued, and is subject to much the same sort of litigation as any other public entity.

Introduction

A redevelopment agency is a separate and distinct legal entity from the city or county in which it functions and may sue and be sued. § 33125. As such, it is subject to much the same sort of litigation as any other public entity. This chapter is not meant to explore those litigation issues, common to all public entities. However, litigation challenging the adoption or amendment of redevelopment plans under the validation statutes contained in Code of Civil Procedure sections 860 through 870, is sufficiently distinct and important to merit separate treatment.

Redevelopment Plan Adoption/Amendment Litigation

Statute of Limitation

Effective January 1, 2007, the time period for action attacking the validity of any redevelopment plan or amendment, or any of the findings or determinations made by the agency or legislative body related thereto, was extended from 60 to 90 days. The same law also made clear that actions to challenge the validity of other agency and legislative determinations made in connection with implementing a redevelopment plan may also be brought within 90 days of such findings and determinations being made. SB 1206, enacted in 2006, rewrote section 33500 to read as follows:

Effective January 1, 2007, the time period for action attacking the validity of any redevelopment plan or amendment was extended from 60 to 90 days.

> (a) Notwithstanding any other provision of law, including section 33501, an action may be brought to review the validity of the adoption or amendment of a redevelopment plan at any time within 90 days after the date of the adoption of the ordinance adopting or amending the plan.

(b) Notwithstanding any other provision of law, including section 33501, an action may be brought to review the validity of any findings or determinations by the agency or the legislative body at any time within 90 days after the date on which the agency or the legislative body made those findings or determinations.

The date of adoption of the ordinance is the date of its passage, or second reading, and not the effective date of the ordinance.

The date of adoption of the ordinance is the date of its passage, or second reading, and not the effective date of the ordinance. *Gleason v. City of Santa Monica* (1962) 207 Cal. App. 2d 458. By statute, therefore, there is now a 90-day window during which the validity of a redevelopment plan or amendment can be challenged. In other words, actions filed prior to the passage of the ordinance adopting or amending the redevelopment plan are premature, and those filed after the 90-day period are too late.

The reach of section 33500 is broad. It covers all of the findings and determinations made by the legislative body in connection with the adoption of the redevelopment plan, including the findings that the project area is blighted, that the adoption and carrying out of the plan is economically sound and feasible, and that the condemnation of real property is necessary to the execution of the redevelopment plan. Thus, this section has been held to bar an attack by a property owner that the condemnation of his property by a redevelopment agency was not for a public use. *Redevelopment Agency v. Del-Camp Investments, Inc.* (1974) 38 Cal. App. 3d 836. Section 33500 has also been held to bar actions filed after the 60-day period even where the plaintiff alleged the fraudulent intent of the members of the city council in adopting the redevelopment plan. *Plunkett v. City of Lakewood* (1975) 44 Cal. App. 3d 344. On the other hand, section 33500 will not bar an action challenging the alleged illegal implementation of a redevelopment plan. *Redevelopment Agency v. Herrold* (1978) 86 Cal. App. 3d 1024.

Section 33500 has been held to bar an attack by a property owner that the condemnation of his property by a redevelopment agency was not for a public use.

Validation Procedures

Section 33501(a) provides that—

An action may be brought pursuant to Chapter 9 (commencing with section 860) of Title 10 of Part 2 of the Code of Civil Procedure to determine the validity of bonds and the redevelopment plan to be financed or refinanced, in whole or in part, by the bonds, or to determine the validity of a redevelopment plan not financed by bonds, including without limiting the generality of the foregoing, the legality and validity of all proceedings theretofore taken for or in any way connected with the establishment of the agency, its authority to transact business and exercise its powers, the designation of the survey area, the selection of the project area, the formulation of the preliminary plan, the validity of the finding and determination that the project area is predominantly urbanized, and the validity of the adoption of the redevelopment or renewal plan, and also including the legality and validity of all proceedings theretofore taken and (as provided in the bond resolution) proposed to be taken for the authorization, issuance, sale, and delivery of the bonds and for the payment of the principal thereof and interest thereon.

The meaning of this section should not be misunderstood. Although it is described in terms of authorizing a particular type of action, in fact, due to the contents of Code of Civil Procedure section 860 *et seq.*, this section operates as a limitation, requiring any action attacking the adoption or amendment of a redevelopment plan to be brought pursuant to the special validation procedures.

A validation action under section 33501 may not be brought unless the specific objections were presented, either orally or in writing, to the agency or the legislative body before the close of the required public hearing, and the person bringing the challenge objected to the adoption of the plan or amendment before the close of that public hearing. § 33501.2. These requirements do not apply to the Attorney General, nor do they apply if there was no public hearing or other opportunity for members of the public to object, or if the proper noticing procedures were not followed. *Id.*

Subsection (c) provides that both the Attorney General and the Department of Finance are considered to be interested parties in any action challenging the validity of an ordinance adopting or amending a redevelopment plan. The Attorney General has the right to intervene in any action challenging the blight findings for any plan or plan amendment and may seek a court's permission to intervene in any other validation proceeding brought under section 33501. This provision supersedes the holding in *Green v. Community Redevelopment Agency* (1979) 96 Cal. App. 3d 491, as to the Attorney General only.

The plaintiff filing any validation action challenging blight findings must serve a copy of the complaint, within three days of filing it with the court, upon the Attorney General. Copies of all pleadings and briefs in such an action must also be served upon the Attorney General. Moreover, no relief, temporary or permanent, can be granted to any party unless the court has proof that this requirement has been satisfied. A court may allow service upon the Attorney General beyond the three-day period, if such late service will not prejudice the Attorney General's ability to review and possibly participate in the action. § 33501.3.

Another change prohibits any agency or legislative body from allowing or requiring a property owner or real party in interest from indemnifying the agency or legislative body against validation actions challenging the adoption or amendment of a redevelopment plan as a condition of such adoption or amendment. § 33501.7.

Code of Civil Procedure, sections 860 through 870 were first enacted in 1961 to give public entities a simple, uniform, *in rem* procedure for

A validation action under section 33501 may not be brought unless the specific objections were presented to the agency or the legislative body before the close of the required public hearing.

The Attorney General has the right to intervene in any action challenging the blight findings for any plan or plan amendment and may seek a court's permission to intervene in any other validation proceeding brought under section 33501.

determining the validity of bonds or assessments or the legality of the entity's existence. *City of Ontario v. Superior Court* (1970) 2 Cal. 3d 335, 340. The validating procedure contained in those sections applies only when it is made applicable by another statute (such as Health and Safety Code § 33501) authorizing the particular matter to be brought pursuant to Code of Civil Procedure section 860 *et seq.*

In *Katz v. Campbell Union High School District* (2006) 144 Cal. App. 4th 1024, the Court of Appeal held that the procedural requirements of the validation procedures are to be strictly construed. In this case, the summons published by plaintiff was fatally defective in two respects. First, it failed to state a specific date by which responses were due; the court held that it was insufficient that the date was calculable from the language of the summons. In addition, the language of the summons did not provide the full amount of time required for interested persons to respond, which is "10 or more days after the completion of publication of the summons." Code Civ. Proc. § 861.1 The court said "completion of publication" of the summons occurs on the 21st day after the first date of publication of the summons. Finally, the court said that the plaintiff had shown no good cause for publishing a defective summons since the law in this area has long been settled.

An action is initiated in a validation proceeding by filing a complaint and obtaining leave of the court to publish a special summons directed to "all persons interested in the matter of [specifying the matter]." Code Civ. Proc. § 861.1. The summons is published once a week for three successive weeks in a newspaper of general circulation designated by the court, published in the county where the action is pending. Code Civ. Proc. § 861. The summons must identify a date by which any interested persons must appear and answer the complaint, which must be ten days or more after completion of publication of the summons. Publication of summons is the means of giving the court *in rem* jurisdiction, that is, making it possible for the court to issue a judgment that is binding upon all persons, whether or not they are parties to the action, and to all issues that could have been adjudicated, whether or not they were actually adjudicated. Code Civ. Proc. § 870. *In rem* jurisdiction is necessary to assure developers, lenders, bondholders, and others that the redevelopment plan, which is the legal foundation for all subsequent redevelopment activity, including issuance of bonds, is not subject to legal challenge.

Such an action may be brought by the redevelopment agency (Code Civ. Proc. § 860) or by any other interested party with standing to challenge the redevelopment plan adoption. Code Civ. Proc. § 863. If the action is commenced by a party other than the agency, the summons must also be directed to the redevelopment agency, and the plaintiff must complete publication of the summons and file proof to that effect with the court within 60 days of filing the complaint. Code Civ. Proc.

§ 863. Service on the redevelopment agency is accomplished in the same manner as with a normal service of summons. It is common practice to also include the legislative body of the city or county as a defendant in an action to challenge the adoption of a redevelopment plan since it is the legislative body that makes the required findings and adopts the ordinance approving the redevelopment plan.

As a practical matter, it is rare for a legislative body or redevelopment agency to file a validation action on its own redevelopment plan, since the combined effect of Code of Civil Procedure, section 863 and Health and Safety Code, section 33501 is to effectively validate the plan if no action is begun within 60 days (now 90 days) of adoption. As Justice Mosk stated in *City of Ontario v. Superior Court* (1970) 2 Cal. 3d 335, 341–342:

> The practical consequence of this statutory scheme should be clearly recognized: an agency may indirectly but effectively "validate" its action *by doing nothing to validate it;* unless an "interested person" brings an action of his own under section 863 within the 60-day period, the agency's action will become immune from attack whether it is legally valid or not. (Italics in original.)

Code of Civil Procedure, section 869 provides that "No contest except by the public agency or its officer or agent of any thing or matter under this chapter shall be made other than within the time and the manner herein specified." Since the adoption of Health and Safety Code, section 33501, the courts have uniformly held that the validation procedures contained in Code of Civil Procedure, sections 860 through 870 provide the *exclusive* format for challenging the validity of a redevelopment plan. In both *Community Redevelopment Agency v. Superior Court* (1967) 248 Cal. App. 2d 164 and *Sibbet v. Board of Directors* (1965) 237 Cal. App. 2d 731, the courts explicitly determined that the validating statutes applied to redevelopment plan adoptions and that the courts lacked jurisdiction over the matter when the plaintiffs failed to strictly comply with provisions relating to publication of summons—

> [T]he procedure for testing the validity of the Hoover Redevelopment Plan was controlled by sections 860 to 870, as expressly provided in section 33501, Health and Safety Code....

Community Redevelopment Agency v. Superior Court, 248 Cal. App.2d, at p. 173

> Such taxpayer suits are controlled, procedurally, by sections 860 to 870 of the Code of Civil Procedure, sections added to the code in 1961 to regulate the procedure for testing the validity of community redevelopment projects.

Sibbet v. Board of Directors, 237 Cal. App. 2d, at p. 732

In *County of Riverside v. Superior Court* (1997) 54 Cal. App. 4th 443, the court held that a published summons in a validation action must specify the precise date by which interested persons must respond. In seeking to invalidate the county's redevelopment plan pursuant to Code of Civil Procedure, section 863, plaintiff's published summons had informed its readers that they had 30 days in which to respond but did not specify a precise date. The court stated that Code of Civil Procedure, section 861.1 provides that the summons in a reverse validation action requires a response by a date specified in the summons. Since published notice in a validation action is the primary means of notice to members of the public, there is a reasonable expectation that potentially concerned parties will observe the notice and consider whether or not to take action.

Since published notice in a validation action is the primary means of notice to members of the public, there is a reasonable expectation that potentially concerned parties will observe the notice and consider whether or not to take action.

In *Green v. Community Redevelopment Agency* (1979) 96 Cal. App. 3d 491, appellant sought to intervene in a validation action challenging a redevelopment plan adoption after the time for answering the published summons had expired. Holding that the intervention was untimely, the court stated—

> These code sections [Code Civ. Proc. §§ 860–870]... provide in unambiguous language the procedures by which "any" interested persons and "all" interested persons come before the court to challenge a redevelopment project or plan.
>
> The purpose of these sections was to provide an exclusive method for bringing "interested persons" into the action, rendering section 387 of the Code of Civil Procedure both superfluous and inconsistent with the purpose of section 860 *et seq.*, Code of Civil Procedure.

Green v. Community Redevelopment Agency at p. 500

The second sentence of Code of Civil Procedure, section 869 provides that "The availability to any public agency, including any local agency, or to its officers or agents, of the remedy provided by this chapter, shall not be construed to preclude the use by such public agency or its officers or agents, of mandamus or any other remedy to determine the validity of any thing or matter." This provision has been held to mean only that traditional means long used by public agencies to validate their acts, such as the use of writs of mandate, have not been superseded by the validation statute. It does not mean that a public agency plaintiff in an action challenging the adoption of a redevelopment plan may bring an action in a manner other than as prescribed in Code of Civil Procedure section 860 *et seq. Millbrae School Dist. v. Superior Court* (1989) 209 Cal. App. 3d 1494.

The validation procedures apply to redevelopment actions other than the adoption or amendment of a redevelopment plan, but the statute for filing the redevelopment actions is 90 days rather 60 days.

The validation procedures apply to redevelopment actions other than the adoption or amendment of a redevelopment plan, but the statute for filing the redevelopment actions is 90 days, rather than the 60 days applicable to other actions filed under Code of Civil Procedure section 860 *et seq.* Government Code section 53511 makes the validation statutes applicable to the "bonds, warrants, contracts, obligations, or evidences of indebtedness" of a local agency. In *Graydon v. Pasadena*

Redevelopment Agency (1980) 104 Cal. App. 3d 631, an action challenging the validity of a contract of a redevelopment agency for the construction of a parking garage was held to be governed by Code of Civil Procedure section 860 and was dismissed for failure to file the action within 60 days of approval of the contract. The court held that the contract (which was negotiated rather than competitively bid) was an integral part of the method of financing the public costs of the redevelopment project, and the lack of a prompt validating procedure could impair the agency's ability to carry out its financial obligations and statutory purposes.

The California Supreme Court, in *Marek v. Napa Community Redevelopment Agency* (1988) 46 Cal. 3d 1070, has held that a disposition and development agreement obligating the redevelopment agency to bear certain costs constituted an "indebtedness" of the agency for purposes of allowing the agency to claim tax increments. Thus, it seems reasonable that if a contract such as the one in *Graydon* is covered by Code of Civil Procedure section 860, actions challenging other contracts of a redevelopment agency that implement the financing of a redevelopment project may also be governed by the validation procedures.

However, in *Kaatz v. City of Seaside* (2006) 143 Cal. App. 4th 13, the Court of Appeal significantly limited the type of contracts encompassed by Government Code section 53511 and the validation procedures. The City of Seaside had entered into a land disposition agreement with a developer that required it to convey to the developer, in back-to-back escrows, a portion of the former Fort Ord military base being conveyed to the city by the federal government. The plaintiff alleged, among other things, that the purchase price for the developer was less than fair market value and that the city had not offered the property to other public agencies for possible development as affordable housing, as required by law. The city and developer filed a motion to dismiss the complaint on the grounds that the land disposition agreement was a contract within the meaning of Government Code section 53511, and that plaintiff had not filed a validation action within the 60-day statute of limitation.

The Court of Appeal disagreed. It held that, "[r]ather than authorizing proceedings to validate any public agency contract—or even any contract constituting a financial obligation of a public agency—the 'contracts' under Government Code section 53511 are only those that are in the nature of, or directly relate to a public agency's bonds, warrants or other evidences of indebtedness." The Court of Appeal distinguished the facts in *Kaatz* from those in *Graydon v. Pasadena Redevelopment Agency* (1980) 104 Cal. App. 3rd 631, saying that, in the earlier case, the agency had issued tax allocation bonds to help finance part of the project being challenged. The *Kaatz* case has significant implications for redevelopment agencies, which typically enter into disposition and development agreements to sell property to developers, often at less

> *In* Kaatz v. City of Seaside, *the Court of Appeal significantly limited the type of contracts encompassed by Government Code section 53511 and the validation procedures.*

than fair market value, in order to stimulate private development activity in a redevelopment project area.

In *Bernardi v. City Council* (1997) 54 Cal. App. 4th 426, the Court of Appeal ruled that the trial court was correct in determining that it lacked jurisdiction to modify a stipulated judgment validating a redevelopment plan because the validation action was an action *in rem*. The stipulated judgment contained a section stating that the judgment was "binding and conclusive" and also placed limits on the total amount of tax-increment funds the agency could receive and the time in which the agency could repay debt.

In *Friedland v. City of Long Beach* (1998) 62 Cal. App. 4th 835, the Court of Appeal held that when a redevelopment agency obtained a validation judgment under Code of Civil Procedure, section 860 *et seq.* upholding the agency's pledge of certain revenues to guarantee repayment of bonds issued by a nonprofit organization, taxpayers could not maintain a taxpayer suit to contest this guarantee after the period to appeal the validation action had expired.

In *Coachella Valley Mosquito and Vector Control Dist. v. City of Indio* (2002) 101 Cal. App. 4th 12, the City of Indio had adopted an amendment to its redevelopment plan that added territory. The plan amendment was challenged by the local water district by a validation action and a summons was published. The Mosquito District answered the complaint and also filed a cross-complaint. However, because the summons published by the water district was defective, the original validation action was dismissed. Despite the dismissal of the underlying validation action, the Mosquito District claimed that the trial court nonetheless retained jurisdiction over its cross-complaint. The Court of Appeal disagreed, holding that the trial court never acquired jurisdiction over the cross-complaints because it never obtained jurisdiction over the underlying validation action.

In *Fontana Redevelopment Agency v. Torres* (2007) 153 Cal. App. 4th 902, the Court of Appeal ruled that a settlement agreement entered into between the Department of Housing and Community Development and a redevelopment agency to resolve audit disputes was not the type of contract that could be validated under Government Code section 53511 in a validation proceeding, narrowly construing the term "contracts" under section 53511. Other than the language in the contract itself that the HCD audit impaired the agency's ability to issue bonds and undertake financial obligations, the court said there was no evidence in the record of such impairment. *Id.* at pp. 910–911.

Standard of Review

The standard of review in an action challenging the adoption or amendment of a redevelopment plan is the "substantial evidence test." *In Re*

Redevelopment Plan For Bunker Hill (1964) 61 Cal. 2d 21. This means that the court will review the record of proceedings before the agency and legislative body to determine whether the findings contained in the ordinance adopting the redevelopment plan are supported by substantial evidence in the record, and whether the agency and the legislative body proceeded in the manner required by the Community Redevelopment Law. The court does not reweigh the evidence or substitute its judgment for that of the legislative body. In addition, the court is directed to ignore irregularities in the proceedings that do not affect the substantial rights of parties. Code Civ. Proc. § 866; *Babcock v. Community Redevelopment Agency* (1957) 148 Cal. App. 2d 38.

Thus, it is of paramount importance to make a complete, logical, and well organized record before the legislative body and to preserve that record in a form that can be readily utilized in the event of litigation. The report to the legislative body required by section 33352 is the single most critical element of this record. It should contain all of the factual data needed to support the finding of the legislative body that the project area is a blighted area as well as facts supporting all the other findings required to be contained in the ordinance adopting the redevelopment plan. § 33367(d). The report to the legislative body must contain facts, not mere recitations of legal conclusions. *Regus v. City of Baldwin Park* (1977) 70 Cal. App. 3d 968.

In order to create a clear record, many redevelopment agencies find it useful to employ a procedural outline or "script" for the public hearing on the adoption of the redevelopment plan. Care should be taken to include in the record of the public hearing all documents, testimony, and other evidence (including photographs or slides) that the legislative body will rely on to make its findings. This material should then be preserved intact so that it can be readily located and reproduced in the event of litigation challenging the redevelopment plan.

The stainless steel "Soaring Star" sculpture was funded by the Redevelopment Agency in Chico.

In order to create a clear record, many redevelopment agencies find it useful to employ a procedural outline or "script" for the public hearing on the adoption of the redevelopment plan.

Limitations on Plaintiffs: Exhaustion of Administrative Remedies and Standing to Sue

Two cases have helped define the minimum qualifications of a plaintiff in an action challenging the adoption or amendment of a redevelopment plan. *Redevelopment Agency v. Superior Court* (1991) 228 Cal. App. 3d 1487 holds that the judicial doctrine of exhaustion of administrative remedies applies to a plaintiff in an action challenging the validity of a redevelopment plan. In that case, the redevelopment agency argued that plaintiff had not exhausted his administrative remedies because he had failed to participate in the statutory hearing process required by law before a redevelopment plan is adopted. The court held that a prospective plaintiff must participate in those hearings, or he cannot maintain an action challenging the validity of the redevelopment plan.

The second case, *Torres v. City of Yorba Linda* (1993) 13 Cal. App. 4th 1035, examines what facts a plaintiff must allege in order to have standing to sue. The judicially established doctrine of standing requires that a plaintiff allege facts that, if true, would demonstrate that the plaintiff has suffered or is threatened with a direct, immediate injury. It is based on the notion that the courts will not adjudicate an action unless a real case or controversy exists. Courts are not to be used to decide abstract questions of law but to adjudicate real controversies between parties who have a genuine personal stake in the outcome.

In *Torres*, the undisputed facts were that the plaintiffs did not reside or own property in the city that had adopted the redevelopment plan. Plaintiffs attempted to establish their standing to sue on two independent theories. First, they alleged that they resided and owned property in Orange County (the county in which Yorba Linda is located) and were eligible to receive a number of health and social services funded wholly or in part by the county. They claimed that the redevelopment plan would result in the diversion of property taxes from the county to the redevelopment agency and that this diversion would decrease the funds available to the county for social services. Rejecting this contention, the court held that (1) tax-increment revenues are generated by the project area's renovation, and consequently, without a redevelopment project, it is doubtful local taxing agencies would receive increased property taxes; and (2) the fiscal review committee process established by law protects affected taxing agencies (and, indirectly, county residents) by requiring a redevelopment agency to evaluate the fiscal impact of the project on other taxing agencies and mitigate that impact where appropriate. In this case, the record showed that an agreement had been entered into between the redevelopment agency and the county to mitigate the fiscal impact of the redevelopment project. [While the fiscal review committee process no longer exists, it was replaced by the requirement that agencies pay a portion of their tax increment to affected taxing entities under section 33607.5 to mitigate fiscal impact.]

Secondly, plaintiffs attempted to establish their standing to sue as taxpayers, either by having paid property taxes in the county or by having paid a sales tax in the City of Yorba Linda. The court held that plaintiffs' allegation that they paid a property tax in the county was insufficient to distinguish them from most other county residents. The allegation that plaintiffs had paid a sales tax in the City was also insufficient since a sales tax is a tax on the retailer, not the consumer.

By narrowly construing the term "interested person" as it is used in Code of Civil Procedure, section 863, Torres has placed significant limits on the class of persons who are eligible plaintiffs in an action challenging the adoption or amendment of a redevelopment plan.

In *Boelts v. City of Lake Forest* (2005) 127 Cal. App. 4th 116, the Court of Appeal held that an amendment of a redevelopment plan to add eminent domain authority for the agency required a new finding that the project area was blighted. The court emphasized that its holding was limited to the specific facts of the case, when the agency had specifically determined in adopting the original plan that it could achieve its objectives without eminent domain, and when the amendment clearly established new objectives such that eminent domain would be needed.

Subsequently, in *Blue v. City of Los Angeles* (2006) 137 Cal. App. 4th 1131, the Court of Appeal held that an amendment to extend an agency's power of eminent domain required new findings that the project area remains blighted. (As a practical matter, for any plan amendment adopted after January 1, 2007 to extend an agency's eminent domain authority, an agency must find, based on substantial evidence that significant blight remains in the project area and that it cannot be eliminated without the use of eminent domain.) §§ 33333.2(a)(4), 33333.4(a)(3), 33333.4(g)(2).

Another case, *Evans v. City of San Jose* (2005) 128 Cal. App. 4th 1123, reiterated the principle that a plaintiff must exhaust his or her administrative remedies in order to challenge a plan adoption. In this case, the plaintiff, who owned property within a proposed redevelopment project area, merely signed a petition objecting to the proposed plan but did not participate in any other way prior to the close of the public hearing. No other person raised any objections regarding the blight findings that the agency and city council made. Because no one, including plaintiff, had raised any objections regarding blight prior to the close of the hearing, the agency did not have an opportunity to address them prior to judicial review. The Court of Appeal made it clear that, under the doctrine of exhaustion of administrative remedies, any objections were required to be "sufficiently specific" so as to allow the agency the opportunity to evaluate and respond to them. This requirement is now codified at section 33501.2.

Validating Acts

The California legislature has recognized that there must be a degree of certainty in the actions of public agencies for citizens to be able to rely on those actions. Therefore, at each legislative session, general statutes are enacted to validate specified actions of public agencies. While they may not insulate a public agency from particular challenges brought pursuant to other provisions of law, these validating statutes should be consulted as to their applicability to challenges based on procedural errors or irregularities on the part of the public agency.

Limitations on Plaintiffs: Appeal of Validation Actions

Section 870, subsection (b) reduces the time normally permitted to file a notice of appeal from a judgment in a validation action to 30 days after notice of entry of judgment, or 30 days after entry of judgment if there is no answering party.

Code of Civil Procedure, section 870, subsection (b) reduces the time normally permitted to file a notice of appeal from a judgment in a validation action to 30 days after notice of entry of judgment, or 30 days after entry of judgment if there is no answering party. This 30-day time period is applicable to appealable orders as well as judgments in validation actions. *Planning and Conservation League v. Dept. of Water Resources* (1998) 17 Cal. 4th 264. If there is no answering party, only issues related to the jurisdiction of the court to enter a judgment may be raised on appeal.

Restrictions on Filing Legal Actions

In 1994, section 33515 was enacted by Chapter 326 as an urgency measure to limit the authority of redevelopment agencies to file a legal action in two circumstances:

- Against a public agency that does not have jurisdiction to conduct its governmental activities within the jurisdiction of the redevelopment agency
- When the subject matter of the action involves real property outside the jurisdiction of the redevelopment agency

These restrictions do not preclude redevelopment agencies from defending themselves against any action or filing an action to interpret or enforce a written agreement. These restrictions should not interfere with the ability of redevelopment agencies to file or defend against legal actions relating to their normal activities.

14
Conclusion

Redevelopment in California under the Community Redevelopment Law has played a major role in the development of California since the end of World War II.

Redevelopment in California under the Community Redevelopment Law has played a major role in the development of California since the end of World War II. Terrible slums have been eradicated in many of our major cities, and the downtowns of a number of cities have been entirely rebuilt with the aid of redevelopment. Redevelopment has generated new employment opportunities and has stimulated new commercial, industrial, residential, and public development in areas that would have otherwise declined or remained stagnant. It has generated a growing and major source of funding for housing for persons of low and moderate income.

Redevelopment has generated new employment opportunities and has stimulated new commercial, industrial, residential, and public development in areas that would have otherwise declined or remained stagnant.

Many of the ideas developed through this experience have been adopted in other areas of the country. Tax-increment financing, development techniques, public-private partnerships, integrated mixed-use public and private developments, and resourceful and innovative locally financed housing programs have all been copied in other regions of the country and by the federal government.

Redevelopment has always been controversial. It gives agencies powerful tools—public financing, the power of eminent domain, and the ability both to sell property to private developers and to assist those developers to make dramatic physical changes in highly visible areas of the community. Often the large amounts of both public and private funds involved in a specific redevelopment project make it the source of public scrutiny and debate. Agencies' attempts to provide affordable housing for low- and moderate-income persons can also generate opposition. Redevelopment nearly always involves change, often major change, and this too can generate controversy. Thus, decisions made by locally elected officials in their capacity as members of a redevelopment agency are often among the most important and controversial decisions they will be asked to make during their tenure in office. Because it has worked well in most communities, redevelopment is taken seriously by elected officials, staff, and citizens, both those who support particular projects and those who oppose them.

Due in part to its success, the controversial nature of the process, and its complexity, redevelopment will continue to be carefully scrutinized both in the communities in which it is being used and at the state level, where the authority for the process is derived and which indirectly provides a part of the financial support. Recently, because of term limits, an increasing number of legislators have served on city councils and county boards of supervisors and are aware of how redevelopment works in their communities. Legislators with this practical kind of experience are generally more skeptical of the kind of ideological or theoretical attacks on the entire process that have characterized some prior debates. In addition, AB 1290 has been successful in reducing the antagonism between local government entities brought about by the redevelopment plan adoption process.

South Hamilton Park, originally two ballfields used by the military at Hamilton Field in Novato, was renovated for use throughout the Little League season. The adjacent community play area was developed by a local group of residents without any public funding.

Redevelopment legislation has continued to evolve since AB 1290 was enacted in 1993. In 2001, the Legislature adopted major legislation to deal with two major areas: affordable housing and time limits for project areas. The 2001 legislation (SB 211) reaffirmed the Legislature's commitment to affordable housing and gave notice that only those project areas that are truly in need of redevelopment tools will be allowed to continue beyond the time limits imposed in AB 1290. In 2006, the Legislature adopted SB 1206, which narrowed the statutory definitions of blight and required that agencies more carefully document the evidence of blight.

There are significant challenges for redevelopment agencies in the coming years. The need for affordable housing will increase as will, for a while, the amount of tax increment devoted to housing. But affordable housing by itself does not create the tax increment to support itself nor does it contribute to a community's general fund, which must grow to support new residents. What will happen to this source of funds for affordable housing, the largest housing program authorized by the state, when the AB 1290 time limits start requiring the termination of project areas?

Affordable housing by itself does not create the tax increment to support itself nor does it contribute to a community's general fund, which must grow to support new residents.

In addition, how will redevelopment be used in cities whose centers have been transformed with the assistance of redevelopment and the powerful real estate markets of the late 1990s?

Continued redevelopment of these areas, although in a more refined manner, is likely. To continue as vital and productive centers, these areas will need continued cooperation between the private sector and public sector. But it is likely that redevelopment will continue to evolve. The use of redevelopment authority to revitalize residential neighborhoods, often the first ring of development surrounding the commercial core, may expand. With the improvement of many downtowns, the attention of elected officials may now be drawn to the adjoining neighborhoods and new ways developed to use the resources of the newly redeveloped core to assist those who live nearby.

Innovative design and landscaping create an inviting pedestrian walkway in Pleasant Hill.

More importantly, however, is that the success of redevelopment has made it a target from another front. For five of the fiscal years between 2002–2003 and 2008–2009, the state has required that redevelopment agencies shift hundreds of millions of dollars, thereby helping the state balance its budget by reducing state aid to schools. The unprecedented $40 billion projected state budget deficit engendered suggestions that these shifts should be made permanent. In the face of this threat, the California Redevelopment Association, in a class action lawsuit on behalf of all redevelopment agencies, has challenged the 2008–2009 ERAF shift as violating the California Constitution. The outcome of this challenge likely will not be determined until 2010. The impact of such shifts, if allowed to continue, coupled with the requirement that agencies fulfill their affordable housing obligations within certain time frames, the restrictions placed on the types of assistance that agencies can provide for private development, and the current economic downturn will present unprecedented challenges to redevelopment practice.

ERAF = Education Revenue Augmentation Fund

In addition, to the extent that redevelopment agencies cannot contribute the amounts specified by the Legislature, financially-strapped cities or counties will be required to make up the difference, as has been required in the past. This situation highlights the tensions between the policies and goals established by the state that local agencies are required to implement, and the uncertainty of the fiscal resources that will be allocated to local agencies to do so.

The past success of redevelopment in California has been due to its flexibility, which has encouraged creativity and provided tools for communities of all sizes throughout the state. Redevelopment has relied upon a locally generated source of revenue, which in turn depends upon the success of both the public and private sectors. Ensuring that agencies continue to have flexibility is critical because large parts of the state, particularly in the Central Valley, have not enjoyed the growth of many of the urban coastal areas. In these inland areas, as well as areas throughout the state, stabilizing the local economy and increasing the number of jobs remain the most important goals of many communities. Moreover, the increased accountability now required of agencies regarding their activities will help assure the state (and the public) that the specified public policies are being implemented. However, the greatest challenge in the coming years will be to see if the state can enact structural reforms that will help stabilize the financing mechanisms for both local and state government, thus avoiding future significant revenue shifts.

The increased accountability now required of agencies regarding their activities will help assure the state and the public that the specified public policies are being implemented.

Appendices

Appendix A

Community Redevelopment Law of the State of California

Health and Safety Code Section 33000 *et seq.*

Effective January 1, 2009

Appendix A

Community Redevelopment Law of the State of California

Health and Safety Code Section 33000 *et seq.*

Effective January 1, 2009

PART 1
Community Redevelopment Law

Chapter 1. GENERAL

Article 1
General Definitions

33000 Community Redevelopment Law

This part may be cited as the Community Redevelopment Law.

33001 Construction of Community Redevelopment Law

The definitions and general provisions contained in this article govern the construction of this part, unless the context otherwise requires.

33002 *Community* defined

"Community" means a city, county, city and county, or Indian tribe, band, or group which is incorporated or which otherwise exercises some local governmental powers.

33003 *Agency* defined

"Agency" means a redevelopment agency created by this part or its predecessor, or a legislative body which has elected to exercise the powers granted to an agency by this part.

33004 *Public body* defined

"Public body" means the State, or any city, county, district, authority, or any other subdivision or public body of the State.

33005 *State* defined

"State" includes any state agency or instrumentality.

33006 Federal government defined

"Federal government" means the United States or any of its agencies or instrumentalities.

33007 Legislative body defined

"Legislative body" means the city council, board of supervisors, or other legislative body of the community.

33007.5 Limited-equity housing cooperative defined

"Limited-equity housing cooperative" means a corporation organized on a cooperative basis which meets all of the following requirements:

(a) The corporation is any of the following:

(1) Organized as a nonprofit public benefit corporation pursuant to Part 2 (commencing with Section 5110) of Division 2 of Title 1 of the Corporations Code.

(2) Holds title to real property as the beneficiary of a trust providing for distribution for public or charitable purposes upon termination of the trust.

(3) Holds title to real property subject to conditions which will result in reversion to a public or charitable entity upon dissolution of the corporation.

(4) Holds a leasehold interest, of at least 20 years' duration, conditioned on the corporation's continued qualification under this section, and providing for reversion to a public entity or charitable corporation.

(b) The articles of incorporation or bylaws require the purchase and sale of the stock or membership interest of resident owners who cease to be permanent residents, at no more than a transfer value determined as provided in the articles or bylaws, and which shall not exceed the aggregate of the following:

(1) The consideration paid for the membership or shares by the first occupant of the unit involved, as shown on the books of the corporation.

(2) The value, as determined by the board of directors of the corporation, of any improvements installed at the expense of the member with the prior approval of the board of directors.

(3) Accumulated interest, or an inflation allowance at a rate which may be based on a cost-of-living index, an income index, or market-interest index. Any increment pursuant to this paragraph shall not exceed a 10 percent annual increase on the consideration paid for the membership or share by the first occupant of the unit involved.

(c) The articles of incorporation or bylaws require the board of directors to sell the stock or membership interest purchased as provided in subdivision (b), to new member-occupants or resident shareholders at a price which does not exceed the "transfer value" paid for the unit.

(d) The "corporate equity," which is defined as the excess of the current fair marketed value of the corporation's real property over the sum of the current transfer values of all shares or membership interests, reduced by the principal balance of outstanding encumbrances upon the corporate real property as a whole, shall be applied as follows:

(1) So long as any such encumbrance remains outstanding, the corporate equity shall not be used for distribution to members, but only for the following purposes, and only to the extent authorized by the board, subject to the provisions and limitations of the articles of incorporation and bylaws:

(A) For the benefit of the corporation or the improvement of the real property.

(B) For expansion of the corporation by acquisition of additional real property.

(C) For public benefit or charitable purposes.

(2) Upon sale of the property, dissolution of the corporation, or occurrence of a condition requiring termination of the trust or reversion of title to the real property, the corporate equity is required by the articles, bylaws, or trust or title conditions to be paid out, or title to the property transferred, subject to outstanding encumbrances and liens, for the transfer value of membership interests or shares, for use for a public or charitable purpose.

(e) Amendment of the bylaws and articles of incorporation requires the affirmative vote of at least two-thirds of the resident-owner members or shareholders.

33008 Planning commission defined

"Planning commission" means a planning agency established pursuant to law or charter.

33009 *Obligee* defined

"Obligee" includes any bondholder, his trustee, any lessor demising to the agency property used in connection with a project area or any assignee of all or part of his interest, and the federal government when it is a party to any contract with the agency.

33010 Redevelopment project defined

"Redevelopment project" means any undertaking of an agency pursuant to this part.

33011 *Department* defined

"Department" means the Department of Housing and Community Development.

33011.2 *Director* defined

"Director" means the Director of Housing and Community Development.

33013 Small housing project defined

"Small housing project" means real property containing or proposed to contain a separate residential structure having not more than four dwelling units and which is owned by an agency and proposed to be conveyed to persons and families of low or moderate income or to private parties pursuant to an agreement with an agency to develop or maintain the residential structure which is proposed to be restricted by a recorded instrument for the use and occupancy of persons and families of low or moderate income for a period of not less than 30 years, or to the term otherwise provided by law, and which meets either of the following criteria:

(a) The real property is owned by an agency and one or more of the dwelling units therein are proposed to be restricted for the use and occupancy of persons or families to whom the agency is obligated to provide relocation assistance under Chapter 16 (commencing with Section 7260) of Division 7 of Title 1 of the Government Code or for persons and families of low or moderate income.

(b) The real property is owned by the agency and is proposed to be conveyed to persons and families of low or moderate income or developed for rental by private parties (nonprofit or otherwise) pursuant to an agreement with the redevelopment agency.

Article 2
Redevelopment

33020 *Redevelopment* defined

(a) "Redevelopment" means the planning, development, replanning, redesign, clearance, reconstruction, or rehabilitation, or any combination of these, of all or part of a survey area, and the provision of those residential, commercial, industrial, public, or other structures or spaces as may be appropriate or necessary in the interest of the general welfare, including recreational and other facilities incidental or appurtenant to them and payments to school and community college districts in the fiscal years specified in Sections 33681, 33681.5, 33681.7, 33681.9, and 33681.12.

33021 Public and private improvements; open space; replanning

Redevelopment includes:

(a) The alteration, improvement, modernization, reconstruction, or rehabilitation, or any combination of these, of existing structures in a project area.

(b) Provision for open-space types of use, such as streets and other public grounds and space around buildings, and public or private buildings, structures and improvements, and improvements of public or private recreation areas and other public grounds.

(c) The replanning or redesign or original development of undeveloped areas as to which either of the following conditions exist.

(1) The areas are stagnant or improperly utilized because of defective or inadequate street layout, faulty lot layout in relation to size, shape, accessibility, or usefulness, or for other causes.

(2) The areas require replanning and land assembly for reclamation or development in the interest of the general welfare because of widely scattered ownership, tax delinquency, or other reasons.

33021.1 Emergency shelters for homeless persons

In a city and county, redevelopment includes improving, increasing, or preserving emergency shelters for homeless persons or households. These shelters may be located within or outside of established redevelopment project areas. Notwithstanding any other provision of law, only redevelopment funds other than those available pursuant to Section 33334.3 may be used to finance these activities.

33022 Continuance of existing buildings and uses

Redevelopment does not exclude the continuance of existing buildings or uses whose demolition and rebuilding or change of use are not deemed essential to the redevelopment and rehabilitation of the area.

Article 3
Declaration of State Policy—
Blighted Areas

33030 Blighted areas defined

(a) It is found and declared that there exist in many communities blighted areas that constitute physical and economic liabilities, requiring redevelopment in the interest of the health, safety, and general welfare of the people of these communities and of the state.

(b) A blighted area is one that contains both of the following:

(1) An area that is predominantly urbanized, as that term is defined in Section 33320.1, and is an area in which the combination of conditions set forth in Section 33031 is so prevalent and so substantial that it causes a reduction of, or lack of, proper

utilization of the area to such an extent that it constitutes a serious physical and economic burden on the community that cannot reasonably be expected to be reversed or alleviated by private enterprise or governmental action, or both, without redevelopment.

(2) An area that is characterized by one or more conditions set forth in any paragraph of subdivision (a) of Section 33031 and one or more conditions set forth in any paragraph of subdivision (b) of Section 33031.

(c) A blighted area that contains the conditions described in subdivision (b) may also be characterized by the existence of inadequate public improvements or inadequate water or sewer utilities.

33031 Physical and economic blight

(a) This subdivision describes physical conditions that cause blight:

(1) Buildings in which it is unsafe or unhealthy for persons to live or work. These conditions may be caused by serious building code violations, serious dilapidation and deterioration caused by long-term neglect, construction that is vulnerable to serious damage from seismic or geologic hazards, and faulty or inadequate water or sewer utilities.

(2) Conditions that prevent or substantially hinder the viable use or capacity of buildings or lots. These conditions may be caused by buildings of substandard, defective, or obsolete design or construction given the present general plan, zoning, or other development standards.

(3) Adjacent or nearby incompatible land uses that prevent the development of those parcels or other portions of the project area.

(4) The existence of subdivided lots that are in multiple ownership and whose physical development has been impaired by their irregular shapes and inadequate sizes, given present general plan and zoning standards and present market conditions.

(b) This subdivision describes economic conditions that cause blight:

(1) Depreciated or stagnant property values.

(2) Impaired property values, due in significant part, to hazardous wastes on property where the agency may be eligible to use its authority as specified in Article 12.5 (commencing with Section 33459).

(3) Abnormally high business vacancies, abnormally low lease rates, or an abnormally high number of abandoned buildings.

(4) A serious lack of necessary commercial facilities that are normally found in neighborhoods, including grocery stores, drug stores, and banks and other lending institutions.

(5) Serious residential overcrowding that has resulted in significant public health or safety problems. As used in this paragraph, "overcrowding" means exceeding the standard referenced in Article 5 (commencing with Section 32) of Chapter 1 of Title 25 of the California Code of Regulations.

(6) An excess of bars, liquor stores, or adult-oriented businesses that has resulted in significant public health, safety, or welfare problems.

(7) A high crime rate that constitutes a serious threat to the public safety and welfare.

33035 Legislative findings and declarations

It is further found and declared that:

(a) The existence of blighted areas characterized by any or all of such conditions constitutes a serious and growing menace which is condemned as injurious and inimical to the public health, safety, and welfare of the people of the communities in which they exist and of the people of the State.

(b) Such blighted areas present difficulties and handicaps which are beyond remedy and control solely by regulatory processes in the exercise of police power.

(c) They contribute substantially and increasingly to the problems of, and necessitate excessive and disproportionate expenditures for, crime prevention, correction, prosecution, and punishment, the treatment of juvenile delinquency, the preservation of the public health and safety, and the maintaining of adequate police, fire, and accident protection and other public services and facilities.

(d) This menace is becoming increasingly direct and substantial in its significance and effect.

(e) The benefits which will result from the remedying of such conditions and the redevelopment of blighted areas will accrue to all the inhabitants and property owners of the communities in which they exist.

33036 Legislative findings and declarations

It is further found and declared that:

(a) Such conditions of blight tend to further obsolescence, deterioration, and disuse because of the lack of incentive to the individual landowner and his inability to improve, modernize, or rehabilitate his property while the condition of the neighboring properties remains unchanged.

(b) As a consequence the process of deterioration of a blighted area frequently cannot be halted or corrected except by redeveloping the entire area, or substantial portions of it.

(c) Such conditions of blight are chiefly found in areas subdivided into small parcels, held in divided and widely scattered ownerships, frequently under defective titles, and in many such instances the private assembly of the land in blighted areas for redevelopment is so difficult and costly that it is uneconomic and as a practical matter impossible for owners to undertake because of lack of the legal power and excessive costs.

(d) The remedying of such conditions may require the public acquisition at fair prices of adequate areas, the clearance of the areas through demolition of existing obsolete, inadequate, unsafe, and insanitary buildings, and the redevelopment of the areas suffering from such conditions under proper supervision, with appropriate planning, and continuing land use and construction policies.

33037 Public policy

For these reasons it is declared to be the policy of the State:

(a) To protect and promote the sound development and redevelopment of blighted areas and the general welfare of the inhabitants of the communities in which they exist by remedying such injurious conditions through the employment of all appropriate means.

(b) That whenever the redevelopment of blighted areas cannot be accomplished by private enterprise alone, without public participation and assistance in the acquisition of land, in planning and in the financing of land assembly, in the work of clearance, and in the making of improvements necessary therefor, it is in the public interest to employ the power of eminent domain, to advance or expend public funds for these purposes, and to provide a means by which blighted areas may be redeveloped or rehabilitated.

(c) That the redevelopment of blighted areas and the provisions for appropriate continuing land use and construction policies in them constitute public uses and purposes for which public money may be advanced or expended and private property acquired, and are governmental functions of state concern in the interest of health, safety, and welfare of the people of the State and of the communities in which the areas exist.

(d) That the necessity in the public interest for the provisions of this part is declared to be a matter of legislative determination.

33038 Temporary wartime housing projects

It is found and declared that blighted areas may include housing areas constructed as temporary government-owned wartime housing projects, and that such areas may be characterized by one or more of the conditions enumerated in Sections 33031 to 33034, inclusive.

33039 Public policy

The Legislature of the State of California recognizes that among the principal causes of slum and blighted residential areas are the following factors:

(a) Inadequate enforcement of health, building, and safety laws.

(b) The fact that the limited financial resources of many human beings who inhabit them make only this type of housing available to such persons.

(c) Racial discrimination against persons of certain groups in seeking housing.

(d) The neglect of absentee landlords.

It is, therefore, declared to be the public policy of this State that, in order to cope with the problems of the rehabilitation of slum or blighted areas, these factors shall be taken into consideration in any rehabilitation or redevelopment program. It is further declared to be the public policy of this State that such rehabilitation or redevelopment programs shall not be undertaken and operated in such a manner as to exchange new slums for old slums or as to congest individuals from one slum to another slum.

Article 4
Declaration of State Policy—
Antidiscrimination

33050 Prohibition against discrimination

(a) It is hereby declared to be the policy of the state that in undertaking community redevelopment projects under this part there shall be no discrimination because of any basis listed in subdivision (a) or (d) of Section 12955 of the Government Code, as those bases are defined in Sections 12926, 12926.1, subdivision (m) and paragraph (1) of subdivision (p) of Section 12955, and Section 12955.2 of the Government Code.

(b) Notwithstanding subdivision (a), with respect to familial status, subdivision (a) shall not be construed to apply to housing for older persons, as defined in Section 12955.9 of the Government Code. With respect to familial status, nothing in subdivision (a) shall be construed to affect Sections 51.2, 51.3, 51.4, 51.10, 51.11, and 799.5 of the Civil Code, relating to housing for senior citizens. Subdivision (d) of Section 51 and Section 1360 of the Civil Code and subdivisions (n), (o), and (p) of Section 12955 of the Government Code shall apply to subdivision (a).

33051 Prohibition against discrimination on basis of sexual orientation: City and County of San Francisco

If the legislative body of the City and County of San Francisco adopts, or has adopted, an ordinance which prohibits discrimination on the basis of sexual orientation, it may require the agency to prohibit discrimination on that basis. In this case, the agency shall implement Sections 33435, 33436, and 33724 as if the discrimination prohibited by the legislative body were also prohibited by Section 33050.

Article 5
Further Declaration of State Policy

33070 Importance of housing and employment opportunities

The Legislature finds and declares that decent housing and genuine employment opportunities for all the people of this state are vital to the state's future peace and prosperity, for all of the following reasons:

(a) Hazardous, congested, and insanitary housing debilitates occupants' health to the point of impairing motivation and achievement.

(b) Lack of employment opportunity creates despair and frustration which may precipitate violence.

(c) Unfit housing and lack of employment opportunity depend on each other to perpetuate a system of dependency and hopelessness which drains the state of its valuable financial and human resources.

33071 Expansion of housing and employment opportunities

The Legislature further finds and declares that a fundamental purpose of redevelopment is to expand the supply of low- and moderate-income housing, to expand employment opportunities for jobless, underemployed, and low-income persons, and to provide an environment for the social, economic, and psychological growth and well-being of all citizens.

Article 6
Reporting Requirement

33080 Annual report: preparation and filing

(a) Every redevelopment agency shall file with the Controller within six months of the end of the agency's fiscal year a copy of the report required by Section 33080.1. In addition, each redevelopment agency shall file with the department a copy of the audit report required by subdivision (a) of Section 33080.1. The reports shall be made in the time, format, and manner prescribed by the Controller after consultation with the department.

(b) The redevelopment agency shall provide a copy of the report required by Section 33080.1, upon the written request of any person, or any taxing agency. If the report does not include detailed information regarding administrative costs, professional services, or other expenditures, the person or taxing agency may request, and the redevelopment agency shall provide, that information. The person or taxing agency shall reimburse the redevelopment agency for all actual and reasonable costs incurred in connection with the provision of the requested information.

33080.1 Annual report: submission to legislative body

Every redevelopment agency shall submit the final report of any audit undertaken by any other local, state, or federal government entity to its legislative body within 30 days of receipt of that audit report. In addition, every redevelopment agency shall present an annual report to its legislative body within six months of the end of the agency's fiscal year. The annual report shall contain all of the following:

(a) (1) An independent financial audit report for the previous fiscal year. "Audit report" means an examination of, and opinion on, the financial statements of the agency which present the results of the operations and financial position of the agency, including all financial activities with moneys required to be held in a separate Low and Moderate Income Housing Fund pursuant to Section 33334.3. This audit shall be conducted by a certified public accountant or public accountant, licensed by the State of California, in accordance with Government Auditing Standards adopted by the Comptroller General of the United States. The audit report shall meet, at a minimum, the audit guidelines prescribed by the Controller's office pursuant to Section 33080.3 and also include a report on the agency's compliance with laws, regulations, and administrative requirements governing activities of the agency, and a calculation of the excess surplus in the Low and Moderate Income Housing Fund as defined in subdivision (g) of Section 33334.12.

(2) However, the legislative body may elect to omit from inclusion in the audit report any distinct activity of the agency that is funded exclusively by the federal government and that is subject to audit by the federal government.

(b) A fiscal statement for the previous fiscal year that contains the information required pursuant to Section 33080.5.

(c) A description of the agency's activities in the previous fiscal year affecting housing and displacement that contains the information required by Sections 33080.4 and 33080.7.

(d) A description of the agency's progress, including specific actions and expenditures, in alleviating blight in the previous fiscal year.

(e) A list of, and status report on, all loans made by the redevelopment agency that are fifty thousand dollars ($50,000) or more, that in the previous fiscal year were in default, or not in compliance with the terms of the loan approved by the redevelopment agency.

(f) A description of the total number and nature of the properties that the agency owns and those properties the agency has acquired in the previous fiscal year.

(g) A list of the fiscal years that the agency expects each of the following time limits to expire:

(1) The time limit for the commencement for eminent domain proceedings to acquire property within the project area.

(2) The time limit for the establishment of loans, advances, and indebtedness to finance the redevelopment project.

(3) The time limit for the effectiveness of the redevelopment plan.

(4) The time limit to repay indebtedness with the proceeds of property taxes.

(h) Any other information that the agency believes useful to explain its programs, including, but not limited to, the number of jobs created and lost in the previous fiscal year as a result of its activities.

33080.2 Annual report: review by legislative body

(a) When the agency presents the annual report to the legislative body pursuant to Section 33080.1, the agency shall inform the legislative body of any major violations of this part based on the independent financial audit report. The agency shall inform the legislative body that the failure to correct a major violation of this part may result in the filing of an action by the Attorney General pursuant to Section 33080.8.

(b) The legislative body shall review any report submitted pursuant to Section 33080.1 and take any action it deems appropriate on that report no later than the first meeting of the legislative body occurring more than 21 days from the receipt of the report.

33080.3 Annual report: compliance audit

The Controller shall develop and periodically revise the guidelines for the content of the report required by Section 33080.1. The Controller shall appoint an advisory committee to advise in the development of the guidelines. The advisory committee shall include representatives from among those persons nominated by the department, the Legislative Analyst, the California Society of Certified Public Accountants, the California Redevelopment Association, and any other authorities in the field that the Controller deems necessary and appropriate.

33080.4 Annual report: housing and displacement

(a) For the purposes of compliance with subdivision (c) of Section 33080.1, the description of the agency's activities shall contain the following information regardless of whether each activity is funded exclusively by the state or federal government, for each project area and for the agency overall:

(1) Pursuant to Section 33413, the total number of nonelderly and elderly households, including separate subtotals of the numbers of very low income households, other lower income households, and persons and families of moderate income, that were displaced or moved from their dwelling units as part of a redevelopment project of the agency during the previous fiscal year.

(2) Pursuant to Section 33413.5, the total number of nonelderly and elderly households, including separate subtotals of the numbers of very low income households, other lower income households, and persons and families of moderate income, that the agency estimates will be displaced or will move from their dwellings as part of a redevelopment project of the agency during the present fiscal year and the date of adoption of a replacement housing plan for each project area subject to Section 33413.5.

(3) The total number of dwelling units housing very low income households, other lower income households, and persons and families of moderate income, respectively, which have been destroyed or removed from the low- or moderate-income housing market during the previous fiscal year as part of a redevelopment project of the agency, specifying the number of those units which are not subject to Section 33413.

(4) The total numbers of agency-assisted dwelling units which were constructed, rehabilitated, acquired, or subsidized during the previous fiscal year for occupancy at an affordable housing cost by elderly persons and families, but only if the units are restricted by agreement or ordinance for occupancy by the elderly, and by very low income households, other lower income households, and persons and families of moderate income, respectively, specifying those units which are not currently so occupied, those units which have replaced units destroyed or removed pursuant to subdivision (a) of Section 33413, and the length of time any agency-assisted units are required to remain available at affordable costs.

(5) The total numbers of new or rehabilitated units subject to paragraph (2) of subdivision (b) of Section 33413, including separate subtotals of the number originally affordable to and currently occupied by, elderly persons and families, but only if the units are restricted by agreement or ordinance for occupancy by the elderly, and by very low income households, other lower income households, and persons and families of moderate income, respectively, and the length of time these units are required to remain available at affordable costs.

(6) The status and use of the Low and Moderate Income Housing Fund created pursuant to Section 33334.3, including information on the use of this fund for very low income households, other lower income households, and persons and families of moderate income, respectively. If the Low and Moderate Income Housing Fund is used to subsidize the cost of onsite or offsite improvements, then the description of the agency's activities shall include the number of housing units affordable to persons and families of low or moderate income which have been directly benefited by the onsite or offsite improvements.

(7) A compilation of the annual reports obtained by the agency under Section 33418 including identification of the number of units occupied by persons and families of moderate income, other lower income households, and very low income households, respectively, and identification of projects in violation of this part or any agreements in relation to affordable units.

(8) The total amount of funds expended for planning and general administrative costs as defined in subdivisions (d) and (e) of Section 33334.3.

(9) Any other information which the agency believes useful to explain its housing programs, including, but not limited to, housing for persons and families of other than low and moderate income.

(10) The total number of dwelling units for very low income households, other lower income households, and persons and families of moderate income to be constructed under the terms of an executed agreement or contract and the name and execution date of the agreement or contract. These units may only be reported for a period of two years from the execution date of the agreement or contract.

(11) The date and amount of all deposits and withdrawals of moneys deposited to and withdrawn from the Low and Moderate Income Housing Fund.

(b) As used in this section:

(1) "Elderly," has the same meaning as specified in Section 50067.

(2) "Persons and families of moderate income," has the same meaning as specified in subdivision (b) of Section 50093.

(3) "Other lower income households," has the same meaning as "lower income households" as specified in Section 50079.5, exclusive of very low income households.

(4) "Persons and families of low or moderate income," has the same meaning as specified in Section 50093.

(5) "Very low income households," has the same meaning as specified in Section 50105.

(c) Costs associated with preparing the report required by this section may be paid with moneys from the Low and Moderate Income Housing Fund.

33080.5 Annual report: fiscal statement

For the purposes of compliance with subdivision (b) of Section 33080.1, the fiscal statement shall contain the following information:

(a) The amount of outstanding indebtedness of the agency and each project area.

(b) The amount of tax increment property tax revenues generated in the agency and in each project area.

(c) The amount of tax increment revenues paid to, or spent on behalf of, a taxing agency, other than a school or community college district, pursuant to subdivision (b) of Section 33401 or Section 33676. Moneys expended on behalf of a taxing agency shall be itemized per each individual capital improvement.

(d) The financial transactions report required pursuant to Section 53891 of the Government Code.

(e) The amount allocated to school or community college districts pursuant to each of the following provisions: (1) Section 33401; (2) Section 33445; (3) Section 33445.5; (4) paragraph (2) of subdivision (a) of Section 33676; and (5) Section 33681.

(f) The amount of existing indebtedness, as defined in Section 33682, and the total amount of payments required to be paid on existing indebtedness for that fiscal year.

(g) Any other fiscal information which the agency believes useful to describe its programs.

33080.6 Report of Department of Housing and Community Development

On or before May 1 of each year, the department shall compile and publish reports of the activities of redevelopment agencies for the previous fiscal year, based on the information reported pursuant to subdivision (c) of Section 33080.1 and reporting the types of findings made by agencies pursuant to paragraph (1), (2), or (3) of subdivision (a) of Section 33334.2, including the date of the findings. The department's compilation shall also report on the project area mergers reported pursuant to Section 33488. The department shall publish this information for each project area of each redevelopment agency. These reports may also contain the biennial review of relocation assistance required by Section 50460. The first report published pursuant to this section shall be for the 1984–85 fiscal year. For fiscal year 1987–88 and succeeding fiscal years, the report shall contain a list of those project areas which are not subject to the requirements of Section 33413.

The department shall send a copy of the executive summary of its report to each redevelopment agency for which information was reported pursuant to Section 33080.1 for the fiscal year covered by the report. The department shall send a copy of its report to each redevelopment agency that requests a copy.

33080.7 Annual report: excess surplus in housing fund

For purposes of compliance with subdivision (c) of Section 33080.1 and in addition to the requirements of Section 33080.4, the description of the agency's activities shall identify the amount of excess surplus, as defined in Section 33334.10, which has accumulated in the agency's Low and Moderate Income Housing Fund. Of the total excess surplus, the description shall also identify the amount that has accrued to the Low and Moderate Income Housing Fund during each fiscal year. This component of the annual report shall also include any plan required to be reported by subdivision (c) of Section 33334.10.

33080.8 Annual report: major violations

(a) On or before April 1 of each year, the Controller shall compile a list of agencies that appear to have major audit violations as defined in this section, based on the independent financial audit reports filed with the Controller pursuant to Section 33080.

(b) On or before June 1 of each year, for each major audit violation of each agency identified pursuant to subdivision (a), the Controller shall determine if the agency has corrected the major audit violation. Before making this determination, the Controller shall consult with each affected agency. In making this determination, the Controller may request and shall receive the prompt assistance of public officials and public agencies, including, but not limited to, the affected agencies, counties, and cities. If the Controller determines that an agency has not corrected the major audit violation, the Controller shall send a list of those agencies, their major violations, all relevant documents, and the affidavits required pursuant to subdivision (d) to the Attorney General for action pursuant to this section.

(c) For each agency that the Controller refers to the Attorney General pursuant to subdivision (b), the Controller shall notify the agency and the legislative body that the agency was on the list sent to the Attorney General. The Controller's notice shall inform the agency and the legislative body of the duties imposed by Section 33080.2.

(d) Within 45 days of receiving the referral from the Controller pursuant to subdivision (b), the Attorney General shall determine whether to file an action to compel the agency's compliance with this part. Any action filed pursuant to this section shall be commenced in the County of Sacramento. The time limit for the Attorney General to make this determination is directory and not mandatory. Any action shall be accompanied by an affidavit or affidavits, to be provided by the Controller with the referral, setting forth facts that demonstrate a likelihood of success on the merits of the claim that the agency has a major audit violation. The affidavit shall also certify that the agency and the legislative body were informed not less than 10 days prior to the date on which the action was filed. The agency shall file a response to any action filed by the Attorney General pursuant to this section within 15 days of service.

(e) (1) On the earliest day that the business of the court will permit, but not later than 45 days after the filing of an action pursuant to this section, the court shall conduct a hearing to determine if good cause exists for believing that the agency has a major audit violation and has not corrected that violation.

(2) If the court determines that no good cause exists or that the agency had a major audit violation but corrected the major audit violation, the court shall dismiss the action.

(3) If the court determines that there is good cause for believing that the agency has a major audit violation and has not corrected that major audit violation, the court shall immediately issue an order that prohibits the agency from doing any of the following:

(A) Encumbering any funds or expending any money derived from any source except to pay the obligations designated in subparagraphs (A) to (G), inclusive, of paragraph (1) of subdivision (e) of Section 33334.12.

(B) Adopting a redevelopment plan.

(C) Amending a redevelopment plan except to correct the major audit violation that is the subject of the action.

(D) Issuing, selling, offering for sale, or delivering any bonds or any other evidence of indebtedness.

(E) Incurring any indebtedness.

(f) In a case that is subject to paragraph (3) of subdivision (e), the court shall also set a hearing on the matter within 60 days.

(g) If, on the basis of that subsequent hearing, the court determines that the agency has a major audit violation and has not corrected that violation, the court shall order the agency to comply with this part within 30 days, and order the agency to forfeit to the state no more than:

(1) Two thousand dollars ($2,000) in the case of a community redevelopment agency with a total revenue, in the prior year, of less than one hundred thousand dollars ($100,000) as reported in the Controller's annual financial reports.

(2) Five thousand dollars ($5,000) in the case of a community redevelopment agency with a total revenue, in the prior year, of at least one hundred thousand dollars ($100,000) but less than two hundred fifty thousand dollars ($250,000) as reported in the Controller's annual financial reports.

(3) Ten thousand dollars ($10,000) in the case of a community redevelopment agency with a total revenue, in the prior year, of at least two hundred fifty thousand dollars ($250,000) as reported in the Controller's annual financial reports.

(h) The order issued by the court pursuant to paragraph (3) of subdivision (e) shall continue in effect until the court determines that the agency has corrected the major audit violation. If the court determines that the agency has corrected the major audit violation, the court may dissolve its order issued pursuant to paragraph (3) of subdivision (e) at any time.

(i) An action filed pursuant to this section to compel an agency to comply with this part is in addition to any other remedy, and is not an exclusive means to compel compliance.

(j) As used in this section, "major audit violation" means that, for the fiscal year in question, an agency did not:

(1) File an independent financial audit report that substantially conforms with the requirements of subdivision (a) of Section 33080.1.

(2) File a fiscal statement that includes substantially all of the information required by Section 33080.5.

(3) Establish time limits, as required by Section 33333.6.

(4) Deposit all required tax increment revenues directly into the Low and Moderate Income Housing Fund upon receipt, as required by Sections 33334.3, 33334.6, 33487, or 33492.16.

(5) Establish a Low and Moderate Income Housing Fund, as required by subdivision (a) of Section 33334.3.

(6) Accrue interest earned by the Low and Moderate Income Housing Fund to that fund, as required by subdivision (b) of Section 33334.3.

(7) Determine that the planning and administrative costs charged to the Low and Moderate Income Housing Fund are necessary for the production, improvement, or preservation of low- and moderate-income housing, as required by subdivision (d) of Section 33334.3.

(8) Initiate development of housing on real property acquired using moneys from the Low and Moderate Income Housing Fund or sell the property, as required by Section 33334.16.

(9) Adopt an implementation plan, as required by Section 33490.

Chapter 2. REDEVELOPMENT AGENCIES

Article 1
Creation of Agencies

33100 Existence in each community

There is in each community a public body, corporate and politic, known as the redevelopment agency of the community.

33101 Ordinance declaring need for redevelopment agency

An agency which, on September 15, 1961, was not authorized to transact any business or exercise any powers by a resolution adopted prior to such date, shall not transact any business or exercise any powers under this part unless, by ordinance, the legislative body declares that there is need for an agency to function in the community. The ordinance of the legislative body declaring that there is need for an agency to function in the community shall be subject to referendum as prescribed by law for a county or a city ordinance.

33102 Filing of ordinance

The agency shall cause a certified copy of the ordinance to be filed in the office of the county clerk.

33103 Validity of establishment and authority of agency

In any proceeding involving the validity or enforcement of, or relating to, any contract by an agency, the agency is conclusively deemed to have been established and authorized to transact business and exercise its powers upon proof of the filing with the Secretary of State of such an ordinance.

33103.5 Validity of establishment and authority of agency: City of Crescent City

Any ordinance of a legislative body heretofore adopted declaring the need for an agency to function in Crescent City is hereby validated, and in any proceeding involving the validity of, or enforcement of, or relating to, any contract by such an agency, the agency is conclusively deemed to have been established and authorized to transact business and exercise its powers upon proof that a copy of such ordinance has been filed with the Secretary of State.

Notwithstanding Section 33101, any such ordinance adopted as an emergency ordinance is not subject to referendum.

33104 Validity of establishment and authority of agencies transacting business before September 15, 1961

Agencies which transacted business and exercised powers prior to September 15, 1961, shall, in any proceeding involving the validity of, or enforcement of, or relating to, any contract by an agency, be conclusively deemed to have been established and authorized to transact business and exercise its powers upon proof of the adoption of a resolution adopted pursuant to the provisions of this part which were in effect prior to September 15, 1961, or upon proof that a copy of such resolution has been filed with the Secretary of State.

33105 Validity of establishment and authority of reactivated agency

In any case where an agency was activated in a community by a resolution adopted pursuant to Section 33101 prior to January 1, 1951, and where thereafter and prior to January 1, 1951, the legislative body of the community purported to dissolve the agency under circumstances where Section 33140 was not applicable, and where as a result of such purported dissolution the agency was inactive for a period of at least 10 years, and where subsequent to January 1, 1962, the legislative body of the community adopted an ordinance pursuant to Section 33101 declaring that there is need for an agency to function in the community, which ordinance was not suspended by referendum, and where subsequent to the adoption of such ordinance new members of the agency were appointed pursuant to Section 33110, such agency is a valid and existing agency with full power to transact any business and exercise its powers and the members appointed subsequent to the adoption of such ordinance are the legally appointed and existing members of the agency, each for the term designated in his appointment. For the purpose of applying Section 33140 to such agency, the two-year period referred to in that section shall be measured from the date of adoption of such ordinance.

Article 2
Appointment, Compensation, and Removal of Agency Members

33110 Appointment

When the legislative body adopts an ordinance declaring the need for an agency, the mayor or chairman of the board of supervisors, with the approval of the legislative body, shall appoint five persons, who are resident electors of the community, and may include tenants of a public housing authority created pursuant to Part 2 (commencing with Section 34200) of this division, as members of the agency. The legislative body may, either at the time of the adoption of the ordinance declaring the need for an agency or at any time thereafter, adopt an ordinance increasing to seven the number of members to be appointed to the agency. Upon the exercise of such option by the legislative body, the membership of the agency shall remain at seven.

33111 Qualifications

A member may not be an elective officer or an employee of the community, but, notwithstanding any other law, he may be a member, commissioner, or employee of any other agency or authority of, or created for, the community.

33112 Terms of office

Three of the members first appointed shall be designated to serve the terms of one, two, and three years, respectively, from the date of their appointments and two shall be designated to serve for terms of four years from the date of their appointments. If and when the membership of the agency is increased to seven, one of the additional members shall be appointed to a term, or unexpired portion thereof, which is concurrent with the term then held by the member originally appointed for a term of three years or by his successor, and the other additional member shall be appointed to a term, or unexpired portion thereof, which is concurrent with the term then held by the member originally appointed for a term of two years or by his successor. Their successors shall be appointed for four-year terms. Vacancies occurring during a term shall be filled for the unexpired term. A member shall hold office until his successor has been appointed and has qualified.

33113 Chairman

The appointing officer shall designate the first chairman from among the members. When there is a vacancy in such office, the agency shall elect a chairman from among its members. Unless otherwise prescribed by the legislative body, the term of office as chairman is for the calendar year, or for that portion remaining after he is designated or elected.

33114 Compensation

Members shall receive their actual and necessary expenses, including traveling expenses incurred in the discharge of their duties. They may receive such other compensation as the legislative body prescribes.

33114.5 Compensation when legislative body is agency

Notwithstanding any other provision of law, whenever the legislative body of a city having a population of less than 200,000 or the legislative body of a county declares itself to be the agency pursuant to Section 33200, the compensation provided for in Section 33114 shall not exceed thirty dollars ($30) per member for each meeting of the agency attended by the member. No member shall receive compensation for attending more than four meetings of the agency during any calendar month. In addition, members shall receive their actual and necessary expenses incurred in the discharge of their duties.

33115 Removal from office

For inefficiency, neglect of duty, or misconduct in office, a member may be removed by the appointing officer, but only after he has been given a copy of the charges at least 10 days prior to a public hearing on them and has had an opportunity to be heard in person or by counsel. If a member is removed, a record of the proceedings and the charges and findings shall be filed in the office of the clerk of the community.

Article 3
Nature, Jurisdiction, and General Powers of Agencies

33120 Territorial jurisdiction

The territorial jurisdiction of the agency of a county is the unincorporated territory in the county, and that of a city or city and county is the territory within its limits.

33121 Powers vested in members

The powers of each agency are vested in the members in office.

33121.5 Delegation of obligation to decide

When a decision, determination, or other action by the agency or legislative body is required by this part, neither the agency nor the legislative body shall delegate the obligation to decide, determine, or act to another entity unless a provision of this part specifically provides for that delegation.

33122 Powers prescribed by Community Redevelopment Law

Each redevelopment agency exercises governmental functions and has the powers prescribed in this part.

33123 Public function of community

Each agency is performing a public function of the community.

33125 General powers

An agency may:

(a) Sue and be sued.

(b) Have a seal.

(c) Make and execute contracts and other instruments necessary or convenient to the exercise of its powers.

(d) Make, amend, and repeal bylaws and regulations not inconsistent with, and to carry into effect, the powers and purposes of this part.

33125.5 Record of proceedings

An agency shall keep a record of the proceedings of its meetings and those records shall be open to examination by the public to the extent required by law.

33126 Employment of personnel

(a) An agency may select, appoint, and employ such permanent and temporary officers, agents, counsel, and employees as it requires, and determine their qualifications, duties, benefits, and compensation, subject only to the conditions and restrictions imposed by the legislative body on the expenditure or encumbrance of the budgetary funds appropriated to the community redevelopment agency administrative fund. To the greatest extent feasible, the opportunities for training and employment arising from a redevelopment project planning and execution shall be given to lower income residents of the project area. The agency shall adopt personnel rules and regulations applicable to all employees. Such rules shall contain procedures affecting conflicts of interest, use of funds, personnel procedures on hiring and firing including removal of personnel for inefficiency, neglect of duties, or misconduct in office. Such rules and regulations shall be of public record.

(b) An agency may contract with the Department of Housing and Community Development, or any other agency, for the furnishing by the department, or agency, of any necessary staff services associated with or required by redevelopment and which could be performed by the staff of an agency.

33127 Office and administrative expenses

An agency may:

(a) Obtain, hire, purchase, or rent office space, equipment, supplies, insurance, or services.

(b) Authorize and pay the travel expenses of agency members, officers, agents, counsel, and employees on agency business.

33128 Access to community services and facilities

For the purposes of the agency, it shall have access to the services and facilities of the planning commission, the city engineer, and other departments and offices of the community.

33129 Administrative fund

The grant of money appropriated by the legislative body of the community to the community redevelopment agency administrative fund is not to be construed as making the agency a department of the community or placing the officers, agents, counsel, and employees under civil service of the community.

33130 Conflicts of interest; exceptions

(a) No agency or community officer or employee who in the course of his or her duties is required to participate in the formulation of, or to approve plans or policies for, the redevelopment of a project area shall acquire any interest in any property included within a project area within the community. If any such officer or employee owns or has any direct or indirect financial interest in property included within a project area, that officer or employee shall immediately make a written disclosure of that financial interest to the agency and the legislative body and the disclosure shall be entered on the minutes of the agency and the legislative body. Failure to make the disclosure required by this subdivision constitutes misconduct in office.

(b) Subdivision (a) does not prohibit any agency or community officer or employee from acquiring an interest in property within the project area for the purpose of participating as an owner or reentering into business pursuant to this part if that officer or employee has owned a substantially equal interest as that being acquired for the three years immediately preceding the selection of the project area.

(c) A rental agreement or lease of property which meets all of the following conditions is not an interest in property for purposes of subdivision (a):

(1) The rental or lease agreement contains terms that are substantially equivalent to the terms of a rental or lease agreement available to any member of the general public for comparable property in the project area.

(2) The rental or lease agreement includes a provision which prohibits any subletting, sublease, or other assignment at a rate in excess of the rate in the original rental or lease agreement.

(3) The property which is subject to the rental or lease agreement is used in the pursuit of the principal business, occupation, or profession of the officer or employee.

(4) The agency or community officer or employee who obtains the rental or lease agreement immediately makes a written disclosure of that fact to the agency and the legislative body.

33130.5 Conflicts of interest; exceptions

Notwithstanding any other provisions of law, an officer, employee, consultant, or agent of the agency or community, for personal residential use, may purchase or lease property within a project area after the agency has certified that the improvements to be constructed or the work to be done on the property to be purchased or leased have been completed, or has certified that no improvements need to be constructed or that no work needs to be done on the property. Any such officer or employee who purchases or leases such property shall immediately make a written disclosure to the agency and the legislative body, which disclosure shall be entered on the minutes of the agency. Any such officer or employee shall thereafter be disqualified from voting on any matters directly affecting such a purchase, lease, or residency. Failure to so disclose constitutes misconduct in office.

33131 Redevelopment activities

An agency may:

(a) From time to time prepare and carry out plans for the improvement, rehabilitation, and redevelopment of blighted areas.

(b) Disseminate redevelopment information.

(c) Prepare applications for various federal programs and grants relating to housing and community development and plan and carry out such programs within authority otherwise granted by this part, at the request of the legislative body.

33132 Financial assistance

The agency may accept financial assistance from public or private sources as authorized by Chapter 6 (commencing with Section 33600) or any other provision in this part.

33133 Other assistance

The agency may accept any other assistance from the state or federal government or any public or private source for any redevelopment project within its area of operation or for the agency's activities, powers, and duties.

33134 Insurance

Within the survey area or for purposes of redevelopment an agency may insure or provide for the insurance of any operations of the agency against risks or hazards.

33135 Relocation and other assistance

Upon request from and at the expense of any public body, an agency may, outside any survey area, with the approval of the legislative body, provide (1) relocation assistance to persons displaced by governmental action, and (2) aid and assistance to property owners in connection with rehabilitation loans and grants.

33136 Insurance premiums: lower income housing

An agency may finance the cost of premiums necessary for the provision of insurance during the construction or rehabilitation of properties that are administered by governmental entities or nonprofit organizations to provide housing for lower income households, as defined in Section 50079.5, including rental properties, emergency shelters, transitional housing, or special residential care facilities.

Article 4
Suspension and Dissolution of Agencies

33140 Ordinance declaring no need for agency after 2 years inactivity; suspension of powers

If an agency has not redeveloped or acquired land for, or commenced the redevelopment of, a project, or entered into contracts for redevelopment within two years after the adoption of an ordinance pursuant to Section 33101, or, in the case of an agency authorized to transact business and exercise powers by resolution adopted pursuant to the provisions of Section 33101 that were in effect prior to the adoption of that resolution, the legislative body may by ordinance declare that there is no further need for the agency. A legislative body shall not adopt an ordinance declaring that there is no further need for the agency if, in one or more project areas, the agency has not complied with subdivision (a) of Section 33333.8. Upon the adoption of the ordinance the offices of the agency members are vacated and the capacity of the agency to transact business or exercise any powers is suspended until the legislative body adopts an ordinance declaring the need for the agency to function.

33141 Ordinance declaring no need for agency after motion of legislative body or recommendation of agency; conditions

Upon the motion of the legislative body or upon recommendation of the agency, the legislative body of the community may, by ordinance, order the deactivation of an agency by declaring that there is no need for an agency to function in the community, if the agency has no outstanding bonded indebtedness, no other unpaid loans, indebtedness, or advances, and no legally binding contractual obligations with persons or entities other than the community, unless the community assumes the bonded indebtedness, unpaid loans, indebtedness, and advances, and legally binding contractual obligations. A legislative body shall not adopt an ordinance declaring that there is no need for the agency, if in one or more project areas, the agency has not complied with subdivision (a) of Section 33333.8. An ordinance of a legislative body declaring there is no need for an agency to function in the community shall be subject to referendum as prescribed by law for the ordinances of the legislative body.

33142 Filing of ordinance

The legislative body of the community shall file with the Secretary of State a certified copy of any ordinance suspending or dissolving an agency pursuant to Section 33140 or 33141.

Chapter 3. OTHER ENTITIES UNDERTAKING OR ASSISTING REDEVELOPMENT

Article 1
Legislative Body as the Agency

33200 Ordinance declaring legislative body as agency

(a) As an alternative to the appointment of five members of the agency, the legislative body may, at the time of the adoption of an ordinance pursuant to Section 33101 or 33140 of this part, or at any time thereafter by adoption of an ordinance, declare itself to be the agency; in which case, all the rights, powers, duties, privileges and immunities, vested by this part in an agency, except as otherwise provided in this article, shall be vested in the legislative body of the community. If a member of the legislative body of a city or county does not wish to serve on the agency, the members may so notify the legislative body of the city or county, and the legislative body of the city or county shall appoint a replacement who is an elector of the city or county to serve out the term of the replaced member.

However, in any community in San Bernardino County which is a charter city, the adoption of any order or resolution by the legislative body acting as the agency shall be governed by the same procedures as are set forth in the provisions of the charter, and the mayor shall be the chairperson of the agency, having the same power and authority in the conduct of the agency and the meetings of the legislative body acting as the agency, that the mayor has in the conduct of the affairs of the city.

As part of the legislative body's ordinance declaring itself to be the redevelopment agency pursuant to this subdivision, the legislative body shall make findings that the action shall serve the public interest and promote the public safety and welfare in an effective manner.

(b) In the event an appointive agency has been designated and has been in existence for at least three years, the legislative body shall not adopt an ordinance declaring itself to be the agency without first conducting a public hearing on the proposed ordinance.

Notice of the public hearing required by this subdivision shall be published not less than once during the 10 calendar days immediately prior to the hearing in a newspaper of general circulation, printed and published in the community, or if there is none, in a newspaper selected by the legislative body. The notice of hearing shall include a general statement of the procedure and effect of the legislative body's declaring itself to be the agency. Copies of the notice shall be posted throughout the affected project area or areas at least 10 calendar days prior to the hearing. The legislative body shall also mail by first-class mail copies of the notice at least 10 calendar days prior to the hearing, to all persons who have expressed to the agency or the legislative body an interest in receiving information on redevelopment activities.

The legislative body shall cause the preparation of any report or reports or proposals, as are necessary to substantiate and explain the determination that the legislative body shall declare itself the redevelopment agency, to be presented at the public hearing.

As part of the legislative body's ordinance declaring itself to be the redevelopment agency pursuant to this subdivision, the legislative body shall make findings that (1) the action will serve the public interest and promote the public safety and welfare in a more effective manner than the current organization, and (2) there has been full public disclosure of all reports and proposals relating to the legislative body's intent to declare itself the redevelopment agency.

33201 Community redevelopment commission: creation

(a) A legislative body which has declared itself to be the agency pursuant to Section 33200 may by ordinance create a community redevelopment commission. The ordinance shall establish the number of members of the commission, but not less than seven, their terms of office, and the method of their appointment and removal.

(b) (1) No member of the commission shall acquire any interest in any property included within a project area. Any member who owns or has any direct or indirect financial interest in any property within a project area shall immediately make a written disclosure of that interest to the legislative body.

(2) A rental agreement or lease of property which meets all of the following conditions is not an interest in property for purposes of paragraph (1):

(A) The rental or lease agreement contains terms that are substantially equivalent to the terms of a rental or lease agreement available to any member of the general public for comparable property in the project area.

(B) The rental or lease agreement includes a provision which prohibits any subletting, sublease, or other assignment at a rate in excess of the rate in the original rental or lease agreement.

(C) The property which is subject to the rental or lease agreement is used in the pursuit of the principal business, occupation, or profession of the member of the commission.

(D) The member of the commission who obtains the rental or lease agreement immediately makes a written disclosure of that fact to the commission and the legislative body.

33202 Community redevelopment commission: functions

If a community redevelopment commission is created as provided in Section 33201, its functions shall be to prepare a redevelopment plan for each project area, hold and conduct hearings thereon, adopt and submit such plan, together with a report, to the legislative body, pursuant to all of the provisions, requirements and procedures of Article 4 (commencing with Section 33330) of Chapter 4 of this part; and the agency, in such case, shall not be required to perform such functions. The legislative body may additionally delegate any of its functions as the governing body of the agency to the community redevelopment commission.

33203 Legislative body no longer to function as agency; appointment of resident electors

A legislative body which has declared itself to be the agency pursuant to Section 33200 may at any time by resolution determine that it shall no longer function as an agency, in which event, the mayor or chairman of the board of supervisors with the approval of the legislative body shall appoint five or seven resident electors of the community as members of the agency, and, upon such appointment, the community redevelopment commission, if any, shall no longer function.

33204 Charter cities

A chartered city may enact its own procedural ordinance and exercise the powers granted by this part.

33205 Delegation of authority

An agency is authorized to delegate to a community any of the powers or functions of the agency with respect to the planning or undertaking of a redevelopment project in the area in which such community is authorized to act, and such community is hereby authorized to carry out or perform such powers or functions for the agency.

33206 Contracts for staff services

Notwithstanding any other provision of law, a legislative body, at the time of the adoption of an ordinance pursuant to Section 33101 or 33140, and pursuant to a resolution authorizing such an action, may contract with the Department of Housing and Community Development, or any other agency or housing authority, for the furnishing by the department, agency, or housing authority of any necessary staff services associated with or required by redevelopment and which could be performed by the staff of an agency. In such a case the legislative body shall be vested with all of the rights, powers, duties, and privileges and immunities vested by this part in an agency.

Article 2
Joint Exercise or Delegation of Power to Redevelop

33210 Joint exercise of powers

Two or more agencies within two or more communities may jointly exercise the powers granted under this part. In such case the agencies, the planning commissions, and the legislative bodies may hold joint hearings and meetings, or the legislative bodies of the communities acting separately may each designate the agency of one of the communities to act as the agency for all of the interested communities.

33210.5 Applicable only to the City of San Leandro and County of Alameda; Joint exercise of powers

(a) As used in this section, the following terms have the following meanings:

(1) "Joint Redevelopment Plan" means the Redevelopment Plan for the Alameda County-City of San Leandro Redevelopment Project, adopted pursuant to this part by the City of San Leandro by ordinance dated July 12, 1993, as amended.

(2) "Joint Project Area" means the redevelopment project area established by the Joint Redevelopment Plan, which includes territory within both the City of San Leandro and the unincorporated territory of the County of Alameda.

(b) The Legislature finds and declares all of the following:

(1) Pursuant to Section 33213, the Board of Supervisors of the County of Alameda has authorized the redevelopment of the portion of the Joint Project Area within its territorial limits by the San Leandro Redevelopment Agency pursuant to the Joint Redevelopment Plan.

(2) Since adoption of the Joint Redevelopment Plan, the San Leandro Redevelopment Agency has exercised powers granted in this part in the entire Joint Project Area.

(c) By ordinance, the legislative bodies of the City of San Leandro and the County of Alameda may designate the Alameda County Redevelopment Agency to exercise exclusively any of the powers granted under this part, including, but not limited to, the power of eminent domain, within that portion of the Joint Project Area within the unincorporated territory of the County of Alameda.

(d) Notwithstanding subdivision (c), by ordinance, the legislative bodies of the City of San Leandro and the County of Alameda may further declare that insofar as it is necessary or convenient for the San Leandro Redevelopment Agency to continue to exercise certain specified powers granted under this part within or for the portion of the Joint Project Area within the unincorporated territory of the County of Alameda, including, but not limited to, those relating to the receipt of tax increment revenue, the San Leandro Redevelopment Agency shall continue to exercise those powers.

(e) For the purposes of this part, the legislative body of the community with respect to actions taken by the San Leandro Redevelopment Agency pursuant to the Joint Redevelopment Plan shall mean the City Council of the City of San Leandro, and the legislative body of the community with respect to actions taken by the Alameda County Redevelopment Agency pursuant to the Joint Redevelopment Plan shall mean the Board of Supervisors of the County of Alameda.

(f) No action taken in accordance with and in furtherance of this section shall affect the calculation of tax increment revenue to be allocated pursuant to Section 33670 or Section 33676 in effect at the time of the adoption of the Joint Redevelopment Plan or the validity of any agreement entered into by the San Leandro Redevelopment Agency with an affected taxing entity pursuant to Section 33401 in effect at the time of execution of that agreement.

(g) The legislative body of the County of Alameda may amend, by ordinance, the Joint Redevelopment Plan without any further action of the legislative body, redevelopment agency, or planning commission of the City of San Leandro. Any amendment adopted pursuant to this subdivision shall affect only property within that portion of the Joint Project Area within the unincorporated territory of Alameda County and shall otherwise be processed in accordance with the applicable procedures and requirements of this part for such an amendment.

(h) The legislative body of the City of San Leandro may amend, by ordinance, the Joint Redevelopment Plan without any further action of the legislative body, redevelopment agency, or planning commission of the County of Alameda. Any amendment adopted pursuant to this subdivision shall affect only property within that portion of the Joint Project Area within the City of San Leandro and shall otherwise be prepared and processed in accordance with the applicable procedures and requirements of this part for such an amendment.

(i) The legislative body of the City of San Leandro and the legislative body of the County of Alameda shall not take any action pursuant to this section until the San Leandro Redevelopment Agency files with the Controller a corrected report required by Section 33080.1 for the 1999-2000 fiscal year.

33211 Reports of planning commissions

If one agency is designated, it shall obtain the report and recommendation of the planning commission of each community on the redevelopment plan and its conformity to the general plan of each community before presenting the redevelopment plan to the respective legislative bodies for adoption.

33212 Cooperation between agency and planning commissions

The designated agency and each planning commission shall cooperate in formulating redevelopment plans.

33213 Authorization for redevelopment by another community

By ordinance the legislative body of a community may authorize the redevelopment of an area within its territorial limits by another community if such area is contiguous to such other community. The ordinance shall designate the community to undertake such redevelopment. The community so authorized may undertake the redevelopment of such area in all respects as if the area was within its territorial limits and its legislative body, agency, and planning commission shall have all the rights, powers, and privileges with respect to such area as if it was within the territorial limits of the community so authorized. Neither the legislative body, agency nor planning commission of the community so authorizing shall be required to comply with any requirements of this part except as set forth in this section. Any redevelopment plan for such area shall be approved by ordinance enacted by the legislative body of the community so authorizing.

33214 Territorial jurisdiction

(a) Notwithstanding Section 33120, the territorial jurisdiction of an agency in the county shall include all of the unincorporated territory that was included in a project area selected pursuant to Section 33322 or 34004 even if that territory is subsequently annexed to a city or included within the boundaries of a new city, unless territorial jurisdiction over the project area is transferred from a county to a city pursuant to Section 33215, 33216, or 33217.

(b) Notwithstanding Section 33120, the territorial jurisdiction of an agency in a city shall include all of the territory within the limits of the city that was included in a project area selected pursuant to Section 33322 or 34004 even if that territory is subsequently annexed to another city or included within the boundaries of a new city, unless territorial jurisdiction over the project area is transferred to the other city pursuant to Section 33215, 33216 or 33217.

33214.5 Definitions

As used in Sections 33215 and 33216:

(a) "Creating agency" means the community redevelopment agency that created the project area that is to be transferred pursuant to Section 33215 or 33216.

(b) "Receiving agency" means the community redevelopment agency that will acquire jurisdiction over a project area pursuant to Section 33215 or 33216.

33215 Transfer of territorial jurisdiction to agency of city; procedure; effective date; effect; agreements to facilitate transfer

(a) If all of the territory included within a project area, including any noncontiguous territory within the project area, selected pursuant to Section 33322 or 34004 is subsequently annexed to a city or included within the boundaries of a new city, the territorial jurisdiction of the creating agency over all of the territory in that project area may be transferred from the creating agency to a receiving agency pursuant to this section.

(b) The legislative body of the community of the receiving agency, in which the territory described in subdivision (a) is located, may unilaterally transfer the territorial jurisdiction described in subdivision (a) if that legislative body agrees to reimburse the community of the creating agency for all costs incurred by the community of the creating agency in conducting the transfer and adopts, or has adopted, both of the following ordinances:

(1) An ordinance pursuant to Section 33101 declaring the need for an agency to function in the city.

(2) An ordinance adopting the same redevelopment plan for the project area that was previously adopted by the legislative body of the creating agency or an ordinance adopting that redevelopment plan, with amendments. However, no amendment to a redevelopment plan may be adopted if the amendment would violate any agreement entered into by the creating agency or its legislative body, as determined by thzt legislative body, prior to the effective date of the transfer of territorial jurisdiction, as determined pursuant to subdivision (c).

(c) The effective date of the transfer of territorial jurisdiction is the first day of the fiscal year that begins following the effective date of the later enacted of the ordinances adopted pursuant to subdivision (b).

(d) The transfer of territorial jurisdiction shall have all of the following effects on and after the effective date of the transfer of territorial jurisdiction, as determined pursuant to subdivision (c):

(1) The receiving agency and its legislative body shall have all of the rights, powers, and responsibilities provided by this part with respect to the project area and the redevelopment plan for that project area.

(2) The debts and any other obligations of the creating agency or its legislative body in connection with the project area or the redevelopment plan for that project area shall be assumed by the receiving agency.

(3) For the purposes of this part, including Section 33670, the redevelopment plan for the project area for which territorial

jurisdiction is transferred from the creating agency to the receiving agency pursuant to this section shall be considered to have been adopted by the legislative body of the receiving agency on the date the redevelopment plan was originally adopted by the legislative body of the creating agency.

(e) The creating agency, the receiving agency, and their respective legislative bodies may enter into any agreements which those entities mutually determine to be necessary or desirable to facilitate the transfer of territorial jurisdiction provided for by this section.

33216 Transfer of territorial jurisdiction to agency of city; agreement and adoption of ordinances; contents of agreement; effective date; rights, powers, debts and obligations

(a) If all, or a substantial portion, of the territory included within a project area selected pursuant to Section 33322 or 34004 is subsequently annexed to a city or included within the boundaries of a new city, the territorial jurisdiction of the creating agency over all, or a substantial portion, of the territory in that project area may be transferred from the creating agency to the receiving agency pursuant to this section. If all, or a substantial portion, of the noncontiguous territory of a project area of a creating agency is subsequently annexed to a city or included within the boundaries of a new city, the jurisdiction of the creating agency over all, or a substantial portion, of the noncontiguous territory may be transferred to the receiving agency pursuant to this section.

(b) The transfer of territorial jurisdiction described in subdivision (a) is not effective unless all of the following occur:

(1) The creating agency and the receiving agency enter into the agreement described in subdivision (c), and their respective legislative bodies both adopt a resolution approving that agreement.

(2) The legislative body of the receiving agency adopts, or has adopted, both of the following ordinances:

(A) An ordinance pursuant to Section 33101 declaring the need for an agency to function in the city.

(B) An ordinance adopting the same redevelopment plan for the project area that was previously adopted by the legislative body of the creating agency.

(c) The agreement required to be entered into between the creating agency and the receiving agency pursuant to paragraph (1) of subdivision (b) shall contain all of the provisions described in paragraphs (1), (2), (3), and (4), and may contain the provisions described in paragraphs (5) and (6):

(1) A provision specifying that all of the territory included within the project area is transferred from the creating agency to the receiving agency, or a provision specifying the portions of the project area over which each agency will have territorial jurisdiction.

(2) (A) If all of the territory included within the project area is transferred from the creating agency to the receiving agency, a provision for the allocation of all of the taxes payable from the project area pursuant to subdivision (b) of Section 33670 to the receiving agency.

(B) If a substantial portion of the territory included within the project area is transferred from the creating agency to the receiving agency, a provision for the allocation of taxes payable from the project area pursuant to subdivision (b) of Section 33670 between the receiving agency and the creating agency. That allocation of taxes shall be reasonably related to the costs that the community of the creating agency and the community of the receiving agency expect to incur in carrying out the redevelopment plan and the outstanding indebtedness that the creating agency has incurred in carrying out the redevelopment plan. That indebtedness shall include repayment of expenditures to, or on behalf of, the redevelopment project area from other resources or borrowing of the creating agency. That allocation of taxes may differ from the allocation that would have been made if the portion of the project area under the territorial jurisdiction of the creating agency and the portion of the project area under the territorial jurisdiction of the receiving agency had been separate project areas at the time of adoption of the redevelopment plan by the legislative body of the creating agency.

(3) A requirement that all taxes payable from the project area pursuant to subdivision (b) of Section 33670 that are allocated to the receiving agency, as required by subparagraph (B) of paragraph (2), shall be available if necessary to pay any indebtedness incurred by the creating agency prior to the effective date of the transfer of jurisdiction in connection with the project area and the redevelopment plan if that indebtedness was secured by the taxes payable from the project area pursuant to subdivision (b) of Section 33670.

(4) If a substantial portion of the territory included within the project area is transferred from the creating agency to the receiving agency, a requirement that any amendment to the redevelopment plan for that portion of the territory of the project area under the jurisdiction of the creating agency shall, in addition to any other requirements under this part, be approved by an ordinance adopted by the legislative body of the receiving agency, and that any amendment to the redevelopment plan for that portion of the territory of the project area under the jurisdiction of the receiving agency shall, in addition to any other requirements under this part, be approved by an ordinance adopted by the legislative body of the creating agency.

(5) If a substantial portion of the territory included within the project area is transferred from the creating agency to the receiving agency, a provision permitting the creating agency to undertake activities to implement the redevelopment plan in portions of the project area under the territorial jurisdiction of the receiving agency or for the receiving agency to undertake activities to implement the redevelopment plan in portions of the project area under the territorial jurisdiction of the creating agency.

(6) Any other terms and conditions that the creating agency, the receiving agency, or their respective legislative bodies mutually determine to be necessary or desirable to facilitate the transfer of territorial jurisdiction over all, or a substantial portion, of the project area and the implementation of the redevelopment plan.

(d) The effective date of the transfer of territorial jurisdiction is the first day of the fiscal year that begins following the effective date of the resolution adopted pursuant to paragraph (1) of subdivision (b), or the effective date of the later enacted of the ordinances adopted pursuant to paragraph (2) of subdivision (b), whichever date is later.

(e) On and after the effective date of the transfer of territorial jurisdiction:

(1) Except as otherwise provided by the agreement entered into pursuant to paragraph (1) of subdivision (b), the receiving

agency and its legislative body shall have all of the rights, powers, and responsibilities provided by this part with respect to all, or the portion, of the project area for which the territorial jurisdiction has been transferred to the receiving agency and with respect to all, or the portion, of the redevelopment plan for all, or that portion, of the project area.

(2) The debts and any other obligations of the creating agency or its legislative body in connection with the project area, or a substantial portion of the project area transferred to the receiving agency, as the case may be, or the redevelopment plan for that project area, or portion of the project area, shall be assumed by the receiving agency.

(3) For the purposes of this part, including Section 33670, the redevelopment plan for all, or a substantial portion of the project area for which territorial jurisdiction is transferred from the creating agency to the receiving agency pursuant to this section shall be considered to have been adopted by the legislative body of the receiving agency on the date the redevelopment plan was originally adopted by the legislative body of the creating agency.

33216.1 Transfer of territorial jurisdiction: County of Orange to city agency

(a) The Legislature finds and declares all of the following:

(1) The Orange County Board of Supervisors established the Neighborhood Development and Preservation Project on June 28, 1988.

(2) The Orange County Neighborhood Development and Preservation Project consists of 13 independent areas either within the territorial jurisdiction of incorporated cities or the sphere of influence of existing cities.

(3) The County of Orange and affected cities are in agreement that the territorial jurisdiction for the Neighborhood Development and Preservation Project areas for those areas presently within the boundaries of an incorporated city, and areas which upon their annexation or inclusion otherwise are included within the boundaries of an incorporated city should be transferred to the appropriate city.

(b) If any portion, including a subarea of the Orange County Neighborhood Development and Preservation Project, of the territory is currently within the boundaries of a city, or is subsequently annexed to a city or otherwise included within the boundaries of a city, the territorial jurisdiction of the agency of the county over that portion including a subarea of the project area, of the territory in the Orange County Neighborhood Development and Preservation Project may be transferred from the agency of the county to the agency of the city pursuant to Section 33216, except as provided below:

(1) If any portion, including a subarea of the Orange County Neighborhood Development and Preservation Project is transferred from the agency of the county to the agency of the city pursuant to this subdivision, the city ordinance adopting the same redevelopment plan as adopted by the board of supervisors may include an amendment to the plan. Any public notice required to amend the plan shall apply only to the portion, including a subarea, jurisdictionally transferred to the agency of the city.

(2) Notwithstanding paragraph (4) of subdivision (c) of Section 33216, any amendment adopted by the agency of the city shall not require the approval of the board of supervisors, unless that amendment would violate any agreement entered into by the agency of the county or the board of supervisors, as determined by the board of supervisors, prior to the effective date of the transfer of territorial jurisdiction.

33216.5 Transfer of territorial jurisdiction: County of Shasta to City of Shasta Lake

(a) The Legislature finds and declares all of the following:

(1) The City of Shasta Lake, which is located in the County of Shasta, was incorporated on July 2, 1993.

(2) The Shasta Dam Area Redevelopment Project, which was established in July 1991, is located within the City of Shasta Lake.

(3) The City of Shasta Lake and the County of Shasta are in agreement that territorial jurisdiction for the Shasta Dam Area Redevelopment Project should be transferred from the redevelopment agency of the County of Shasta to the redevelopment agency of the City of Shasta Lake. Pursuant to subdivision (b) of Section 33215, the city council has adopted an ordinance declaring the need for an agency to function in the city.

(4) Under subdivision (c) of Section 33215, however, the transfer of jurisdiction for the Shasta Dam Area Redevelopment Project cannot become effective until the first day of the first fiscal year beginning after the adoption of the later of the required ordinances.

(5) Because the City of Shasta Lake was incorporated on the second day of the current fiscal year, the city is uniquely burdened by the requirement of existing law, which delays until July 1, 1994, the effectiveness of the agreement to transfer the redevelopment project from the agency of the county to the agency of the city.

(6) Therefore, to effectuate the purposes of the Community Redevelopment Law, the transfer of the territorial jurisdiction for the Shasta Dam Area Redevelopment Project from the redevelopment agency of the County of Shasta to the redevelopment agency of the City of Shasta Lake should be authorized forthwith.

(b) Notwithstanding Section 33215 or any other provision of law, territorial jurisdiction for the Shasta Dam Area Redevelopment Project is hereby transferred, as of the effective date of the act that adds this section, from the redevelopment agency of the County of Shasta to the redevelopment agency of the City of Shasta Lake under the terms and conditions agreed upon by the city and county.

33217 Territorial jurisdiction: New city

If a portion of a city containing a portion of a redevelopment project area is incorporated as a new city, and the new city establishes an agency to be the receiving agency for that portion of the project area, the creating agency and the receiving agency shall have six months from the date of the establishment of that receiving agency to enter into an agreement pursuant to Section 33216. If that agreement is not entered into within that six-month period, the creating agency shall not thereafter expend any money pursuant to this part or Part 1.5 (commencing with Section 34000) within the project area, except to repay existing indebtedness, until those agencies have entered into that agreement. That indebtedness shall include outstanding bonded indebtedness, existing agreements, contracts, leases, and expenditures made to, or on behalf of, the project area from other resources or borrowings of the creating agency.

Article 3
Aid, Assistance and Co-operation

33220 Aid and cooperation of public bodies

For the purpose of aiding and co-operating in the planning, undertaking, construction, or operation of redevelopment projects located within the area in which it is authorized to act, any public body, upon the terms and with or without consideration as it determines, may:

(a) Dedicate, sell, convey, or lease any of its property to a redevelopment agency.

(b) Cause parks, playgrounds, recreational, community, educational, water, sewer or drainage facilities, or any other works which it is otherwise empowered to undertake, to be furnished adjacent to or in connection with redevelopment projects.

(c) Furnish, dedicate, close, vacate, pave, install, grade, regrade, plan, or replan streets, roads, roadways, alleys, sidewalks, or other places which it is otherwise empowered to undertake.

(d) Plan or replan, zone or rezone any part of such area and make any legal exceptions from building regulations and ordinances.

(e) Enter into agreements with the federal government, an agency, or any other public body respecting action to be taken pursuant to any of the powers granted by this part or any other law; such agreements may extend over any period, notwithstanding any law to the contrary.

(f) Purchase or legally invest in any of the bonds of an agency and exercise all of the rights of any holder of such bonds.

(g) Purchase and buy or otherwise acquire land in a project area from an agency for redevelopment in accordance with the plan, and in connection therewith, is hereby authorized to become obligated in accordance with Section 33437 except that subdivision (b) of Section 33437 shall apply to a public body only to the extent that it is authorized (and funds have been made available) to make the redevelopment improvements or structures required.

33221 Bond purchases

The bonds and obligations issued by an agency also may be purchased, invested in, or used for security as authorized in Section 33663.

Chapter 4. REDEVELOPMENT PROCEDURES AND ACTIVITIES

Article 1
Community Prerequisites

33300 Compliance with requirements of article

Before any area is designated for redevelopment, the community authorized to undertake such development shall comply with the requirements of this article.

33301 Planning agency

The community shall have a planning agency established pursuant to law or charter.

33302 General plan

The community shall have a general plan which complies with Article 5 (commencing with Section 65300) of Chapter 3 of Division 1 of Title 7 of the Government Code, and which includes, but is not limited to, a housing element that substantially complies with state law.

Article 2
Designation of Survey Area

33310 Resolution designating survey area

Survey areas may be designated by resolution of the legislative body, or the legislative body may by resolution authorize the designation of survey areas by resolution of the planning commission or by resolution of the members of the agency.

33311 Request for designation of survey area

Any person, group, association or corporation may in writing, request the legislative body (or the planning commission or the agency if they are authorized by the legislative body to designate survey areas) to designate a survey area or areas for project study purposes, and may submit with their request plans showing the proposed redevelopment of such areas or any part or parts thereof.

33312 Contents of resolution designating survey area

The resolution designating a survey area or areas shall contain the following:

(a) A finding that the area requires study to determine if a redevelopment project or projects within said area are feasible;

(b) A description of the boundaries of the area designated.

Article 3
Selection of Project Area and Formulation of Preliminary Plans

33320.1 Project area defined

(a) "Project area" means, except as provided in Section 33320.2, 33320.3, 33320.4, or 33492.3, a predominantly urbanized area of a community that is a blighted area, the redevelopment of which is necessary to effectuate the public purposes declared in this part, and that is selected by the planning commission pursuant to Section 33322.

(b) As used in this section, "predominantly urbanized" means that not less than 80 percent of the land in the project area is either of the following:

(1) Has been or is developed for urban uses.

(2) Is an integral part of one or more areas developed for urban uses that are surrounded or substantially surrounded by parcels that have been or are developed for urban uses. Parcels separated by only an improved right-of-way shall be deemed adjacent for the purpose of this subdivision. Parcels that are not blighted shall not be included in the project area for the purpose of obtaining the allocation of taxes from the area pursuant to Section 33670 without other substantial justification for their inclusion.

(c) For the purposes of this section, a parcel of property as shown on the official maps of the county assessor is developed if that parcel is developed in a manner that is consistent with zoning standards or is otherwise permitted under law.

(d) The requirement that a project be predominantly urbanized shall apply only to a project area for which a final redevelopment plan is adopted on or after January 1, 1984, or to an area that is added to a project area by an amendment to a redevelopment plan, which amendment is adopted on or after January 1, 1984.

33320.2 Contiguous or noncontiguous areas; limitation on eminent domain

(a) The area included within a project and a project area may be either contiguous or noncontiguous. All noncontiguous areas of a project area shall be either blighted or necessary for effective redevelopment. An unblighted, noncontiguous area shall be conclusively deemed necessary for effective redevelopment if that area is being used predominantly for:

(1) The relocation of owners or tenants from other noncontiguous areas in the same project area or from other project areas in the community.

(2) The construction and rehabilitation of low- or moderate-income housing.

(b) An unblighted, noncontiguous area shall be deemed not necessary for effective redevelopment if that area is included for the purpose of obtaining the allocation of taxes from such area pursuant to Section 33670 without other substantial justification for its inclusion.

(c) The redevelopment agency shall not use the power of eminent domain for acquisition of property, other than vacant land, in noncontiguous, unblighted areas.

33320.3 Contiguous or noncontiguous areas: City of Victorville

(a) The area included within a project and a project area may be either contiguous or noncontiguous. All noncontiguous areas of a project area shall be either blighted or necessary for effective redevelopment. An unblighted, noncontiguous area within the City of Victorville which is a part of a freeway interchange project that is included in the State Transportation Improvement Program, as adopted by the California Transportation Commission in June 1984, and an unblighted area contiguous to that freeway interchange project east of Armagosa, north of Seneca Road, west of Seventh Street, and South of Plaza Drive and Mohave Drive, excluding any subdivided and developed area, shall be conclusively deemed necessary for effective redevelopment and may be included within a noncontiguous project area by the redevelopment agency in the City of Victorville.

(b) The redevelopment agency shall not use the power of eminent domain for acquisition of property, other than vacant land, in noncontiguous, unblighted areas.

(c) This section shall only apply to a redevelopment project area and the redevelopment agency within the City of Victorville.

33320.4 Unblighted territory contiguous to existing project areas: City of Sanger

(a) The unblighted territory that is described in paragraphs (1) and (2) is contiguous to an existing redevelopment project area within the City of Sanger, California. If all of that unblighted territory is annexed to the City of Sanger, the planning agency within the City of Sanger may, with the approval of the redevelopment agency, include that territory in a proposed project area, or the redevelopment agency may amend the redevelopment plan to include that territory within an existing contiguous project area, if the planning agency or the redevelopment agency, as the case may be, determines that the inclusion of that territory is necessary for effective redevelopment of the project area. If either, or both, of those determinations are made, the territory shall be conclusively presumed necessary for effective redevelopment within the proposed or existing project area. Any actions taken by the planning agency or redevelopment agency in accordance with this section shall comply with all of the other requirements of this part.

(1) All that portion of Fresno County, California, within the City of Sanger in Sections 26 and 25, Township 14 South, Range 22 East, Mount Diablo Base and Meridian, according to the United States Government Township Plat thereof, described as follows:

Beginning at the southwest corner of the northwest quarter of Section 26; thence along the existing city limits line of Sanger as follows, N. 89 47' E., a distance of 2638.53 feet to the southeast corner of the northwest quarter of Section 26; thence N. 0 03' W., along the west line of the northeast quarter of that Section, a distance of 345.52 feet to the northerly right-of-way line of the Garfield Ditch; thence northeasterly along northerly right-of-way line, a distance of 913.00 feet, a little more or less, to a point on the westerly right-of-way line of the Centerville and Kingsburg Canal; thence along the easterly right-of-way line of the Centerville and Kingsburg Canal as follows: N. 09 52'28" E., 708.50 feet; N. 09 26'40" E., 297.07 feet; N. 07 14'16" E., 549.23 feet; and N. 09 15'10" E., a distance of 539.47 feet to a point on a line 30.00 feet south of the north line of the northeast quarter of Section 26; thence leaving the westerly right-of-way line, N. 89 43' E., along that line 30.00 feet south of and parallel with the north line of the northeast quarter of Section 26 and the easterly prolongation thereof, a distance of 1860.41 feet; thence S. 0 14' E., 1151.07 feet; thence S. 73 01' W., 357.58 feet; thence S. 55 46' W., 985.00 feet; thence S. 40 46' W., 218.00 feet; thence S. 24 31' W., 364.00 feet; thence N. 75 44' W., 312.87 feet to a point on the west line of the southeast quarter of the northeast quarter of Section 26; thence S. 0 17'12" E., along said west line, 413.31 feet to the southwest corner thereof; thence S. 0 16'28" E., along the west line of the northeast quarter of the southeast quarter of Section 26, 1332.38 feet to the southwest corner thereof; thence leaving the existing city limits line of Sanger, N. 89 06'46" W., along the north line of the south half of the southeast quarter of Section 26, 592.10 feet to the northeast corner of that parcel of land conveyed to Archie Mekealian and Verlene Mekealian by deed dated February 23, 1944, and recorded in Book 2157 at Page 119, Fresno County records, with the corner being 742.00 feet east of the northwest corner of the south half of the southeast quarter of Section 26; thence S. 4 36'52" W., along the east line to the parcel, 1330.31 feet to the southeast corner thereof and to a point on the south line of the southeast quarter of Section 26; thence N. 88 44'19" W., along the south line, 619.00 feet, more or less to the southwest corner of the southeast quarter of Section 26; thence S. 89 51'20" W., along the south line of the southwest quarter of Section 26, 2639.90 feet to the southwest corner thereof; thence north, along the west line of the southwest quarter of Section 26, 2643.60 feet to the northwest corner thereof and the point of beginning. This territory contains a little more or less than 316.58 acres.

(2) All that portion of Fresno County, California, within the City of Sanger, in the northeast quarter of Section 15 in Township 14 South, Range 22 East, Mount Diablo Base and Meridian, according to the United States Government Township Plat thereof, described as follows:

Commencing at the northeast corner of the northeast quarter of the northeast quarter of Section 15, thence southerly along the east line of the northeast quarter of Section 15 992.05 feet to the existing city limits line of Sanger, then continuing south along the east line of the northeast quarter of Section 15 475.01 feet, that being contiguous with the existing city limit of Sanger, for a total of 1467.06 feet, thence westerly, along a line 1180.15 feet 15, 880.90 feet, more or less to the easterly right-of-way line of the Southern Pacific Railroad Company's right-of-way; thence leaving the existing city limits line of Sanger, northwesterly, along the easterly right-of-way line of the railroad as the same is shown on the Map of Mountain View Addition to Sanger, recorded February 18, 1891, in Book 4 of Plats, Page 66, Fresno County Records, to the point of intersection with the north line of the northeast quarter of Section 15; thence easterly along the north line, 2191.00 feet to the point of commencement. This territory contains a little more or less than 50.13 acres.

(b) The conclusive presumption that the unblighted territory described in subdivision (a) is necessary for effective redevelopment applies only to territory within the City of Sanger.

33320.8 Exception to prohibited inclusion within project area of certain agricultural and open space lands

(a) The territory that is described in subdivision (b) shall not be subject to the requirements of subdivision (b) of Section 33321.5.

(b) All lands not enforceably restricted within the Counties of Riverside and San Bernardino, within the spheres of influence of the Cities of Chino and Ontario as of January 1, 1996, according to the United States Government Township Plat thereof, described as follows:

(1) That portion of Township 2 South, Range 7 West, San Bernardino Meridian, in the County of San Bernardino, State of California, described as follows:

Beginning at the center line intersection of Euclid Avenue and Riverside Drive, said intersection being on the existing city limits of Ontario; thence east along said city limits line and continuing along said line, following all of its various courses to the intersection of Riverside Drive with the San Bernardino County line; thence leaving said city limits line south and southwesterly along said county line to the north line of Section 27, said Township 2 South, Range 7 West; thence west along said north line, being also the center line of Remington Avenue, to the center line of Carpenter Avenue; thence north along said center line to the center line of Merrill Avenue; thence west along said center line to the east line of Grove Avenue; thence north along said east line to the north line of Merrill Avenue; thence west along said north line and its prolongation to the center line of Euclid Avenue; thence north along said center line to the Point of Beginning.

(2) Those portions of Townships 2 and 3 South, Ranges 7 and 8 West, San Bernardino Meridian, in the County of San Bernardino, State of California, described as follows:

Beginning at the intersection of the center line of Merrill Avenue with the east line of Grove Avenue; thence east along said center line of Merrill Avenue to the center line of Carpenter Avenue; thence south along said center line to the north line of Government Lot 1 of Section 27, said Township 2 South, Range 7 West, said point being also on the center line of Remington Avenue; thence east along said center line to the San Bernardino County line; thence southwesterly, southerly and westerly along said county line to the center line of State Highway 71 being also on the existing city limits line of Chino Hills; thence northwesterly along said center line and city limits line to the southwesterly prolongation of the center line of Pine Avenue; thence easterly along said prolongation and center line to the center line of Chino Creek; thence southeasterly along said center line to the west line of Section 6, said Township 3 South, Range 7 West; thence north along said west line and the west line of Section 31, said Township 2 South, Range 7 West, to the center line of Pine Avenue; thence westerly along said center line to the center line of El Prado Road, formerly Central Avenue; thence northwesterly along said center line to the center line of Kimball Avenue, said point being on the existing city limits of Chino; thence east along said city limits line and continuing along said city limits, following all of its various courses to the center line intersection of Kimball Avenue and vacated Campus Avenue; thence leaving said city limits line east along said center line of Kimball Avenue to the center line of Grove Avenue; thence north along said center line to the center line of Remington Avenue, vacated; thence east along said vacated center line to the east line of Grove Avenue; thence north along said last line to the Point of Beginning.

(3) Those portions of Sections 6, 7, 18, 19, 30, and 31, Township 2 South, Range 6 West, San Bernardino Meridian; Sections 23, 24, 25, 26, 27, 34, 35, and 36, Township 2 South, Range 7 West, San Bernardino Meridian; and Sections 2, 3, and 10, Township 3 South, Range 7 West, San Bernardino Meridian, within the unincorporated area of the County of Riverside.

33320.51 Base year for redevelopment plans of joint powers agency in County of San Bernardino

(a) Any redevelopment plan, or any amendment to an existing redevelopment plan adopted on or after July 1, 1993, that is subject to Section 33320.5, may utilize as the base year either the year it was adopted or the 1994–95 fiscal year, at the option of the adopting agency, as referenced by a duly adopted ordinance of the governing board. If the governing board adopts the 1994–95 fiscal year as the base year, that designation shall remain in effect only until the time that the county assessor certifies that assessed values for the redevelopment project area equal or exceed the assessed value in the initial base year. When that certification is made by the county assessor, the base year shall revert to the initial base year at the time of plan adoption.

(b) To the extent any adjustment in the base year pursuant to this section creates a negative fiscal impact on the state, the governing board shall, on or before the expiration of five years from the date of the adjustment of the base year pursuant to this section, remit to the State Controller the total amount of increased aid to schools received from the state as a result of the adjustment in the base year as determined by the Department of Finance in consultation with the governing board.

33321 Project area: properties included

A project area need not be restricted to buildings, improvements, or lands which are detrimental or inimical to the public health, safety, or welfare, but may consist of an area in which such conditions predominate and injuriously affect the entire area. A project area may include lands, buildings, or improvements which are not detrimental to the public health, safety or welfare, but whose inclusion is found necessary for the effective redevelopment of the area of which they are a part. Each such area included under this section shall be necessary for effective redevelopment and shall not be included for the purpose of obtaining the allocation of tax increment revenue from such area pursuant to Section 33670 without other substantial justification for its inclusion.

33321.5 Prohibited inclusion within project area of certain agricultural and open space lands

(a) Agricultural land and open-space land that is enforceably restricted shall not be included within a project area.

(b) A parcel of land that is larger than two acres and is in agricultural use, but that is not enforceably restricted, shall not be included within a project area unless the agency makes each of the following findings, based upon substantial evidence in the record:

(1) The inclusion of the land in the project area is consistent with the purposes of this part.

(2) The inclusion of the land in the project area will not cause the removal of adjacent land, designated for agricultural use in the community's general plan, from agricultural use.

(3) The inclusion of the land within the project area is consistent with the community's general plan.

(4) The inclusion of the land in the project area will result in a more contiguous pattern of development.

(5) There is no proximate land that is not in agricultural use, that is both available and suitable for inclusion within the project area, and is not already proposed to be within the project area.

(c) As used in this section the following definitions apply:

(1) "Agricultural use" has the same meaning as that term is defined in subdivision (b) of Section 51201 of the Government Code.

(2) "Enforceably restricted" has the same meaning as that term is defined in Sections 422 and 422.5 of the Revenue and Taxation Code.

(3) "Suitable" has the same meaning as that term is defined in subdivision (c) of Section 51282 of the Government Code.

(d) The provisions of subdivision (b) shall not apply to the territory described in Section 33320.8.

33322 Project area: selection of boundaries and formulation of preliminary plan

The planning commission may select one or more project areas comprised of all or part of any survey area, on its own motion, or at the request of the agency. The planning commission shall select one or more project areas comprised of all or part of any survey area, at the direction of the legislative body, or upon the written petition of the owners in fee of the majority in area of a proposed project area, excluding publicly owned areas or areas dedicated to a public use.

The planning commission shall formulate a preliminary plan for the redevelopment of each selected project area.

33323 Cooperation between agency and planning commission

The agency and planning commission shall cooperate in the selection of project areas and in the preparation of the preliminary plan.

33324 Preliminary plan: contents

A preliminary plan need not be detailed and is sufficient if it:

(a) Describes the boundaries of the project area.

(b) Contains a general statement of the land uses, layout of principal streets, population densities and building intensities, and standards proposed as the basis for the redevelopment of the project area.

(c) Shows how the purposes of this part would be attained by redevelopment.

(d) Shows that the proposed redevelopment is consistent with the community's general plan.

(e) Describes, generally, the impact of the project upon the area's residents and upon the surrounding neighborhood.

33325 Preliminary plan: submission to agency

The planning commission shall submit the preliminary plan for each project area to the agency.

33326 Project area: change of boundaries

Prior to publication of notice of the agency public hearing, the planning commission may change the boundaries of a project area with the approval of the agency.

33327 Statement of preparation of redevelopment plan

After receipt of any preliminary redevelopment plan pursuant to Section 33325, the agency shall transmit to the county auditor and county assessor of the county in which the proposed project is located, or to the officer or officers performing the functions of the auditor or assessor for any taxing agencies which, in levying or collecting its taxes, do not use the county assessment roll or do not collect its taxes through the county, to the legislative or governing bodies of local agencies which receive a portion of the property tax levied pursuant to Part 0.5 (commencing with Section 50) of the Revenue and Taxation Code and to the State Board of Equalization:

(a) A description of the boundaries of the project area.

(b) A statement that a plan for the redevelopment of the area is being prepared.

(c) A map indicating the boundaries of the project area.

In addition, the agency may include a listing, by tax rate area, of all parcels within the boundaries of the project area and the value used for each parcel on the secured property tax roll.

Thereafter, if the boundaries of the proposed project are changed, the agency shall notify the taxing officials and the State Board of Equalization within 30 days by transmitting a description and map indicating each boundary change made. The State Board of Equalization shall prescribe the format of the description of boundaries and statements, and the form, size, contents, and number of copies of the map required to be transmitted pursuant to this section.

33328 Report of county taxing officials; consultations with taxing entities

When it transmits the map of the project area to the county officials, taxing agencies, and the State Board of Equalization pursuant to Section 33327, the redevelopment agency shall also advise those officials and agencies of the last equalized assessment roll it proposes to use for the allocation of taxes that will comply with Sections 33670 and 33670.5. That roll shall be known and referred to as the base year assessment roll. The county officials charged with the responsibility of allocating taxes under Sections 33670 and 33670.5 shall prepare and deliver to the redevelopment agency and each of the taxing agencies, a report which shall include all of the following:

(a) The total assessed valuation of all taxable property within the project area as shown on the base year assessment roll.

(b) The identifications of each taxing agency levying taxes in the project area.

(c) The amount of tax revenue to be derived by each taxing agency from the base year assessment roll from the project area, including state subventions for homeowners, business inventory, and similar subventions.

(d) For each taxing agency, its total ad valorem tax revenues from all property within its boundaries, whether inside or outside the project area.

(e) The estimated first year taxes available to the redevelopment agency, if any, based upon information submitted by the redevelopment agency, broken down by taxing agencies.

(f) The assessed valuation of the project area for the preceding year, or, if requested by the redevelopment agency, for the preceding five years, except for state assessed property on the board roll. However, in preparing this information, the requirements of Section 33670.5 shall be observed. The assessed value shall be reported by block if the property is divided by blocks, or by any other geographical area as may be agreed upon by the agency and county officials.

The report shall be prepared and delivered to the redevelopment agency and each of the taxing agencies within 60 days of the date of filing by the redevelopment agency with the State Board of Equalization or as otherwise agreed upon by the agency and the State Board of Equalization, unless the redevelopment agency requests the assessed valuation for the preceding five years, in which case the report shall be prepared and delivered within 90 days. If the proposed base year assessment roll has not yet been equalized at the time of the receipt of that advice, then the report shall be prepared and delivered within 60 days, or other period, otherwise agreed upon, by the agency and the State Board of Equalization, from the date set forth in Section 2052 of the Revenue and Taxation Code, unless the agency requests the assessed valuation for the preceding five years, in which case, the report shall be prepared and delivered within 90 days.

If the filing does not comply with the requirements of Section 33327, the State Board of Equalization or the official of the taxing agency entitled to receive those documents shall notify the filing agency within 10 days, stating the manner in which the filing of documents does not comply with this section. If no notice is given it shall be conclusively presumed that the agency has complied with the provisions of this section.

If the report is not received within the time prescribed by this section, the redevelopment agency may proceed with the adoption of the redevelopment plan. The county officials may transmit a partial report, and any final report or additional information, if received by the agency prior to the close of the public hearing on the redevelopment plan, shall become part of the record of the public hearing.

The State Board of Equalization and officials of all taxing agencies shall provide the county officials preparing the report with all information necessary for its preparation. All data and information upon which the report is based shall be available to the agency to the extent permitted by law.

Prior to the publication of notice of the legislative body's public hearing on the plan, the agency shall consult with each taxing agency which levies taxes, or for which taxes are levied, on property in the project area with respect to the plan and to the allocation of taxes pursuant to Section 33670.

33328.1 Report of county taxing officials; content

(a) When the county officials charged with the responsibility of allocating taxes pursuant to Sections 33670 and 33670.5 deliver the report required pursuant to Section 33328, they shall also prepare and deliver to the Department of Finance, in the form and manner prescribed by the department, a report that includes all of the following:

(1) The information specified in subdivisions (a), (b), and (c) of Section 33328.

(2) A projection of the total amount of tax revenues that may be allocated pursuant to Sections 33670 and 33670.5 for the duration of the project area.

(3) A projection of the amount of tax revenues that would have been allocated to each school district, county office of education, and community college district for the duration of the project area, but for the allocation of tax revenues pursuant to Sections 33670 and 33670.5.

(4) A projection of the amount of tax revenues that may be allocated to each school district, county office of education, and community college district pursuant to Sections 33401, 33607.5, 33607.7, and 33676 for the duration of the project area.

(b) When the redevelopment agency transmits the map of the project area pursuant to Section 33327, the agency shall also prepare and deliver to the Department of Finance, in the form and manner prescribed by the department, a report that includes all of the following:

(1) A projection of any change in the number of residents, including, but not limited to, the number of schoolage children, within the project area for the duration of the project area.

(2) A projection prepared by each school district, county office of education, and community college district within the project area of any change in the need for school facilities within the project area for the duration of the project area.

33328.3 Statement of preparation and report by county taxing officials for change of project area boundaries

If the boundaries of an existing project area for which the redevelopment plan contains a provision for the division of taxes as permitted by Section 33670 are changed pursuant to Article 4 (commencing with Section 33330), the redevelopment agency shall notify the county officials by transmitting to them, the legislative or governing bodies of the taxing agencies, and to the State Board of Equalization, the information required by Section 33327 indicating the areas to be added or detached. Within 60 days from the date of filing or a period as otherwise agreed to by the agency and the State Board of Equalization, the county officials shall prepare and submit to the redevelopment agency and the taxing agencies a report containing the information required under Section 33328, with respect to those areas to be added to or detached from the project area.

If a filing does not comply with the requirements of this section, the State Board of Equalization or the official of the taxing agency entitled to receive those documents shall notify the filing agency within 10 days, stating the manner in which the filing of documents does not comply with this section. If no notice is given, it shall be conclusively presumed that the agency has complied with the provisions of this section.

33328.4 State Board of Equalization fees

The State Board of Equalization shall establish a schedule of fees for filing and processing the statements and maps which are required to be filed with the State Board of Equalization pursuant to Section 33327, 33328.3, 33328.5, 33375, or 33457. This schedule shall not include any fee which exceeds the reasonably anticipated cost to the State Board of Equalization of performing the work to which the fee relates. The agency forwarding the statement and map pursuant to Section 33327, 33328.3, 33328.5, 33375, or 33457 shall accompany the statement and map with the necessary fee.

33328.5 Change in base year assessment roll

(a) If a redevelopment agency proposes to use the equalized assessment roll for the year following the equalized assessment roll which the redevelopment agency advised it would use pursuant to Section 33328, the redevelopment agency shall, prior to the adoption of the redevelopment plan using that different equalized assessment roll, either notify the county officials, taxing agencies, and the State Board of Equalization of the change in the equalized assessment roll that it proposes to use for the allocation of taxes pursuant to Section 33670 or prepare a report containing the information specified in subdivisions (a), (b), (c), (d), (e), and (f) of Section 33328.

(b) Upon receipt of a notice pursuant to subdivision (a), the county officials charged with the responsibility of allocating taxes under Section 33670 and 33670.5 shall prepare and deliver to the redevelopment agency a report containing the information specified in subdivisions (a), (b), (c), (d), (e), and (f) of Section 33328. The report shall be prepared and delivered within the time periods specified in Section 33328 for reports prepared pursuant to that section. If a redevelopment agency gives the notice specified in subdivision (a), the redevelopment plan specified in the notice shall not be adopted until the time period for delivery of the report has expired.

(c) At least 14 days prior to the public hearing on the redevelopment plan for which the redevelopment agency proposes to use a different equalized assessment roll, the redevelopment agency shall prepare and deliver to each taxing agency a supplementary report analyzing the effect of the use of the different equalized assessment roll which shall include those subjects required by subdivisions (b), (e), and (n) of Section 33352. In lieu of a supplementary report, a redevelopment agency may include in the report required to be prepared pursuant to Section 33352, the information required to be included in the supplementary report.

(d) A redevelopment agency shall not be required to prepare a subsequent preliminary report specified in Section 33344.5, unless the report prepared pursuant to subdivision (b) states that the total assessed value in the project area is less than the total assessed value in the project area contained in the original report prepared pursuant to Section 33328, in which case a new preliminary report shall be prepared.

(e) The use of a different assessment roll pursuant to this section shall meet the requirements of Section 16 of Article XVI of the California Constitution.

(f) This section shall only apply to redevelopment plans adopted on or after January 1, 1993. The Legislature finds and declares that the enactment of this section shall not be deemed to invalidate or limit the adoption of redevelopment plans pursuant to a different procedure prior to January 1, 1993.

33328.7 Reimbursement of county or school district costs

Any costs incurred by a county, a school district, a county office of education, or a community college district, in preparing a report pursuant to Section 33328, 33328.1, 33328.3, or 33328.5 shall be reimbursed by the redevelopment agency which filed for the report as provided in those sections. In the event a final redevelopment plan is adopted for all or a portion of the project area concerning which the report is prepared, the agency may charge and account for the reimbursed costs as a cost of the redevelopment project. Otherwise these costs shall be accounted for as general administrative expenses of the agency.

Article 4
Preparation and Adoption of Redevelopment Plans by the Agency

33330 Preparation and approval

Each agency shall prepare or cause to be prepared, and approve, a redevelopment plan for each project area and for that purpose may hold hearings and conduct examinations, investigations, and other negotiations. The agency shall consult with the planning commission of the community and with the project area committee, if applicable, in preparing a redevelopment plan.

33331 Conformity to general plan

Every redevelopment plan shall be consistent with the community's general plan.

33332 Legal description; preliminary plan as basis

Every redevelopment plan shall contain a legal description of the boundaries of the project area and shall be based upon the preliminary plan.

33333 Open space; street layout; building restrictions; dwelling units; property for public use

Every redevelopment plan shall show by diagram and in general terms:

(a) The approximate amount of open space to be provided and street layout.

(b) Limitations on type, size, height, number, and proposed use of buildings.

(c) The approximate number of dwelling units.

(d) The property to be devoted to public purposes and the nature of such purposes.

33333.2 Limitations on incurring and repaying indebtedness, duration of plan and use of eminent domain

(a) A redevelopment plan containing the provisions set forth in Section 33670 shall contain all of the following limitations. A redevelopment plan that does not contain the provisions set forth in Section 33670 shall contain the limitations in paragraph (4):

(1) (A) A time limit on the establishing of loans, advances, and indebtedness to be paid with the proceeds of property taxes received pursuant to Section 33670 to finance in whole or in part the redevelopment project, which may not exceed 20 years from the adoption of the redevelopment plan, except by amendment of the redevelopment plan as authorized by subparagraph (B). This limit, however, shall not prevent agencies from incurring debt to be paid from the Low and Moderate Income Housing Fund or establishing more debt in order to fulfill the agency's housing obligations under subdivision (a) of Section 33333.8. The loans,

advances, or indebtedness may be repaid over a period of time longer than this time limit as provided in this section. No loans, advances, or indebtedness to be repaid from the allocation of taxes shall be established or incurred by the agency beyond this time limitation. This limit shall not prevent agencies from refinancing, refunding, or restructuring indebtedness after the time limit if the indebtedness is not increased and the time during which the indebtedness is to be repaid is not extended beyond the time limit to repay indebtedness required by this section.

(B) The time limitation established by subparagraph (A) may be extended only by amendment of the redevelopment plan after the agency finds, based on substantial evidence, that (i) significant blight remains within the project area; and (ii) this blight cannot be eliminated without the establishment of additional debt. However, this amended time limitation may not exceed 30 years from the effective date of the ordinance adopting the redevelopment plan, except as necessary to comply with subdivision (a) of Section 33333.8.

(2) A time limit, not to exceed 30 years from the adoption of the redevelopment plan, on the effectiveness of the redevelopment plan. After the time limit on the effectiveness of the redevelopment plan, the agency shall have no authority to act pursuant to the redevelopment plan except to pay previously incurred indebtedness and to enforce existing covenants or contracts, unless the agency has not completed its housing obligations pursuant to subdivision (a) of Section 33333.8, in which case the agency shall retain its authority to implement requirements under subdivision (a) of Section 33333.8, including its ability to incur and pay indebtedness for this purpose, and shall use this authority to complete these housing obligations as soon as is reasonably possible.

(3) A time limit, not to exceed 45 years from the adoption of the redevelopment plan, to repay indebtedness with the proceeds of property taxes received pursuant to Section 33670. After the time limit established pursuant to this paragraph, an agency may not receive property taxes pursuant to Section 33670, except as necessary to comply with subdivision (a) of Section 33333.8.

(4) A time limit, not to exceed 12 years from the adoption of the redevelopment plan, for commencement of eminent domain proceedings to acquire property within the project area. This time limitation may be extended only by amendment of the redevelopment plan after the agency finds, based on substantial evidence, both of the following:

(A) That significant blight remains within the project area.

(B) That this blight cannot be eliminated without the use of eminent domain.

(b) If a redevelopment plan is amended to add territory, the amendment shall contain the time limits required by this section.

(c) When an agency is required to make a payment pursuant to Section 33681.9, the legislative body may amend the redevelopment plan to extend the time limits required pursuant to paragraphs (2) and (3) of subdivision (a) by one year by adoption of an ordinance. In adopting this ordinance, neither the legislative body nor the agency is required to comply with Section 33354.6, Article 12 (commencing with Section 33450), or any other provision of this part relating to the amendment of redevelopment plans.

(d) When an agency is required pursuant to Section 33681.12 to make a payment to the county auditor for deposit in the county's Educational Revenue Augmentation Fund created pursuant to Article 3 (commencing with Section 97) of Chapter 6 of Part 0.5 of Division 1 of the Revenue and Taxation Code, the legislative body may amend the redevelopment plan to extend the time limits required pursuant to paragraphs (2) and (3) of subdivision (a) by the following:

(1) One year for each year in which a payment is made, if the time limit for the effectiveness of the redevelopment plan established pursuant to paragraph (2) of subdivision (a) is 10 years or less from the last day of the fiscal year in which that payment is made.

(2) One year for each year in which a payment is made, if both of the following apply:

(A) The time limit for the effectiveness of the redevelopment plan established pursuant to paragraph (2) of subdivision (a) is more than 10 years but less than 20 years from the last day of the fiscal year in which a payment is made.

(B) The legislative body determines in the ordinance adopting the amendment that, with respect to the project, all of the following apply:

(i) The agency is in compliance with the requirements of Section 33334.2 or 33334.6, as applicable.

(ii) The agency has adopted an implementation plan in accordance with the requirements of Section 33490.

(iii) The agency is in compliance with subdivisions (a) and (b) of Section 33413, to the extent applicable.

(iv) The agency is not subject to sanctions pursuant to subdivision (e) of Section 33334.12 for failure to expend, encumber, or disburse an excess surplus.

(3) This subdivision shall not apply to any redevelopment plan if the time limits for the effectiveness of the redevelopment plan established pursuant to paragraph (2) of subdivision (a) is more than 20 years after the last day of the fiscal year in which a payment is made.

(4) The legislative body by ordinance may adopt the amendments provided for under this subdivision following a public hearing. Notice of the public hearing shall be mailed to the governing body of each of the affected taxing entities at least 30 days prior to the hearing. Notice shall also be published in a newspaper of general circulation in the community at least once, not less than 10 days prior to the date of the public hearing. The ordinance shall contain a finding of the legislative body that funds used to make a payment to the county's Educational Revenue Augmentation Fund pursuant to Section 33681.12 would otherwise have been used to pay the costs of projects and activities necessary to carry out the goals and objectives of the redevelopment plan. In adopting an ordinance pursuant to this subdivision, neither the legislative body nor the agency is required to comply with Section 33354.6, Article 12 (commencing with Section 33450), or any other provision of this part.

(e) This section shall apply only to redevelopment projects for which a final redevelopment plan is adopted pursuant to Article 5 (commencing with Section 33360) on or after January 1, 1994, and to amendments that add territory and that are adopted on or after January 1, 1994.

33333.3 Environmental information to affected taxing agencies

(a) The redevelopment agency shall send a notice of preparation and a copy of a draft environmental impact report to each affected taxing entity, as defined in Section 33353.2, prepared in accordance with the provisions of the California Environmental Quality Act (Division 13 (commencing with Section 21000) of the Public Resources Code) and regulations adopted pursuant thereto.

(b) If the project area contains land in agricultural use, as defined in subdivision (b) of Section 51201 of the Government Code, the redevelopment agency shall also send a copy of the draft environmental impact report to the Department of Conservation, the county agricultural commissioner, the county farm bureau, the California Farm Bureau Federation, and agricultural entities and general farm organizations that provide a written request for notice. A separate written request for notice shall be required for each proposed redevelopment plan or amendment that adds territory. A written request for notice applicable to one redevelopment plan or amendment shall not be effective for a subsequent plan or amendment.

33333.4 Limitations on tax increments, incurring indebtedness and use of eminent domain: retrospective application

(a) Every legislative body that adopted a final redevelopment plan prior to October 1, 1976, that contains the provisions set forth in Section 33670 but does not contain all of the limitations required by Section 33333.2, shall adopt an ordinance on or before December 31, 1986, that contains all of the following:

(1) A limitation on the number of dollars of taxes that may be divided and allocated to the redevelopment agency pursuant to the plan, including any amendments to the plan. Taxes shall not be divided and shall not be allocated to the redevelopment agency beyond that limitation, except as necessary to comply with subdivision (a) of Section 33333.8.

(2) A time limit on the establishing of loans, advances, and indebtedness to finance in whole, or in part, the redevelopment project. No loans, advances, or indebtedness to be repaid from the allocation of taxes shall be established or incurred by the agency beyond the time limitation, except as necessary to comply with subdivision (a) of Section 33333.8.

(3) A time limit, not to exceed 12 years, for commencement of eminent domain proceedings to acquire property within the project area. This time limitation may be extended only by amendment of the redevelopment plan after the agency finds, based on substantial evidence, both of the following:

(A) That significant blight remains within the project area.

(B) That this blight cannot be eliminated without the use of eminent domain.

(b) The limitations established in the ordinance adopted pursuant to this section shall apply to the redevelopment plan as if the redevelopment plan had been amended to include those limitations. However, in adopting the ordinance, neither the legislative body nor the agency is required to comply with Article 12 (commencing with Section 33450) or any other provision of this part relating to the amendment of redevelopment plans.

(c) The limitations established in the ordinance adopted pursuant to this section shall not be applied to limit allocation of taxes to an agency to the extent required to eliminate project deficits created under subdivision (g) of Section 33334.6 in accordance with the plan adopted pursuant thereto for the purpose of eliminating the deficit or to comply with subdivision (a) of Section 33333.8. In the event of a conflict between these limitations and the obligations under Section 33334.6 or subdivision (a) of Section 33333.8, the legislative body shall amend the ordinance adopted pursuant to this section to modify the limitations to the extent necessary to permit compliance with the plan adopted pursuant to subdivision (g) of Section 33334.6, to permit compliance with subdivision (a) of Section 33333.8, and to allow full expenditure of moneys in the agency's Low and Moderate Income Housing Fund in accordance with Section 33334.3. The procedure for amending the ordinance pursuant to this subdivision shall be the same as for adopting the ordinance under subdivision (b).

(d) This section shall not be construed to allow the impairment of any obligation or indebtedness incurred by the legislative body or the agency pursuant to this part.

(e) In any litigation to challenge or attack any ordinance adopted pursuant to this section, the court shall sustain the actions of the legislative body and the agency unless the court finds those actions were arbitrary or capricious. The Legislature finds and declares that this is necessary because redevelopment agencies with project areas established prior to October 1, 1976, have incurred existing obligations and indebtedness and have adopted projects, programs, and activities with the authority to receive and pledge the entire allocation of taxes authorized by Section 33670 and that it is necessary to protect against the possible impairment of existing obligations and indebtedness and to allow the completion of adopted projects and programs.

(f) The ordinance adopted by the legislative body in compliance with this section does not relieve any agency of its obligations under Section 33333.8, 33334.2, 33334.3, Article 9 (commencing with Section 33410), or any other requirement contained in this part.

(g) A redevelopment plan adopted on or after October 1, 1976, and prior to January 1, 1994, containing the provisions set forth in Section 33670, shall also contain:

(1) A limitation on the number of dollars of taxes that may be divided and allocated to the agency pursuant to the plan, including any amendments to the plan. Taxes shall not be divided and shall not be allocated to the agency beyond this limitation, except pursuant to amendment of the redevelopment plan, or as necessary to comply with subdivision (a) of Section 33333.8.

(2) A time limit, not to exceed 12 years, for commencement of eminent domain proceedings to acquire property within the project area. This time limitation may be extended only by amendment of the redevelopment plan after the agency finds, based on substantial evidence, both of the following:

(A) That significant blight remains within the project area.

(B) That this blight cannot be eliminated without the use of eminent domain.

33333.5 Redevelopment: City of South Gate

(a) With respect to the adoption of the redevelopment plan for an area of the City of South Gate with the approximate boundaries east of Atlantic Boulevard, south of Wood Avenue, north of Aldrich Road, and west of the Los Angeles River, the agency shall be exempt from the provisions of Sections 33322 to 33327, inclusive, and Section 33330 related to the addition of new territory to existing project areas.

(b) Notwithstanding any other exemption granted by this section, the City of South Gate shall, prior to adoption of a redevelopment plan, conduct at least two public meetings on the proposed plan for South Gate residents and property owners. The City of South Gate shall also cause to be organized a citizens' advisory committee comprised of residents and property owners of the project, which shall advise the agency on development strategy and plans and other matters that may affect the residents of the project area. The citizens' advisory committee shall remain in existence for at least three years.

(c) The adoption of a redevelopment plan pursuant to this section is limited to a plan that adds land into an existing redevelopment plan and does not involve a change of any general plan or zoning ordinance or grant any variance. Any change in zoning, a general plan, or a variance relating to the additional redevelopment plan area shall be subject to all applicable requirements of law.

(d) Nothing in this section shall preclude the City of South Gate or its redevelopment agency from using a prior environmental impact report prepared for the site, referenced in subdivision (a), pursuant to Section 15153 of Title 14 of the California Code of Regulations.

33333.6 Limitations on incurring and repaying indebtedness and duration of plan: retrospective application

The limitations of this section shall apply to every redevelopment plan adopted on or before December 31, 1993.

(a) The effectiveness of every redevelopment plan to which this section applies shall terminate at a date that shall not exceed 40 years from the adoption of the redevelopment plan or January 1, 2009, whichever is later. After the time limit on the effectiveness of the redevelopment plan, the agency shall have no authority to act pursuant to the redevelopment plan except to pay previously incurred indebtedness, to comply with Section 33333.8 and to enforce existing covenants, contracts, or other obligations.

(b) Except as provided in subdivisions (f) and (g), a redevelopment agency may not pay indebtedness or receive property taxes pursuant to Section 33670 after 10 years from the termination of the effectiveness of the redevelopment plan pursuant to subdivision (a).

(c) (1) If plans that had different dates of adoption were merged on or before December 31, 1993, the time limitations required by this section shall be counted individually for each merged plan from the date of the adoption of each plan. If an amendment to a redevelopment plan added territory to the project area on or before December 31, 1993, the time limitations required by this section shall commence, with respect to the redevelopment plan, from the date of the adoption of the redevelopment plan, and, with respect to the added territory, from the date of the adoption of the amendment.

(2) If plans that had different dates of adoption are merged on or after January 1, 1994, the time limitations required by this section shall be counted individually for each merged plan from the date of the adoption of each plan.

(d) (1) Unless a redevelopment plan adopted prior to January 1, 1994, contains all of the limitations required by this section and each of these limitations does not exceed the applicable time limits established by this section, the legislative body, acting by ordinance on or before December 31, 1994, shall amend every redevelopment plan adopted prior to January 1, 1994, either to amend an existing time limit that exceeds the applicable time limit established by this section or to establish time limits that do not exceed the provisions of subdivision (b) or (c).

(2) The limitations established in the ordinance adopted pursuant to this section shall apply to the redevelopment plan as if the redevelopment plan had been amended to include those limitations. However, in adopting the ordinance required by this section, neither the legislative body nor the agency is required to comply with Article 12 (commencing with Section 33450) or any other provision of this part relating to the amendment of redevelopment plans.

(e) (1) If a redevelopment plan adopted prior to January 1, 1994, contains one or more limitations required by this section, and the limitation does not exceed the applicable time limit required by this section, this section shall not be construed to require an amendment of this limitation.

(2) (A) A redevelopment plan adopted prior to January 1, 1994, that has a limitation shorter than the terms provided in this section may be amended by a legislative body by adoption of an ordinance on or after January 1, 1999, but on or before December 31, 1999, to extend the limitation, provided that the plan as so amended does not exceed the terms provided in this section. In adopting an ordinance pursuant to this subparagraph, neither the legislative body nor the agency is required to comply with Section 33354.6, Article 12 (commencing with Section 33450), or any other provision of this part relating to the amendment of redevelopment plans.

(B) On or after January 1, 2002, a redevelopment plan may be amended by a legislative body by adoption of an ordinance to eliminate the time limit on the establishment of loans, advances, and indebtedness required by this section prior to January 1, 2002. In adopting an ordinance pursuant to this subparagraph, neither the legislative body nor the agency is required to comply with Section 33354.6, Article 12 (commencing with Section 33450) or any other provision of this part relating to the amendment of redevelopment plans, except that the agency shall make the payment to affected taxing entities required by Section 33607.7.

(C) When an agency is required to make a payment pursuant to Section 33681.9, the legislative body may amend the redevelopment plan to extend the time limits required pursuant to subdivisions (a) and (b) by one year by adoption of an ordinance. In adopting an ordinance pursuant to this subparagraph, neither the legislative body nor the agency is required to comply with Section 33354.6, Article 12 (commencing with Section 33450), or any other provision of this part relating to the amendment of redevelopment plans, including, but not limited to, the requirement to make the payment to affected taxing entities required by Section 33607.7.

(D) When an agency is required pursuant to Section 33681.12 to make a payment to the county auditor for deposit in the county's Educational Revenue Augmentation Fund created pursuant to Article 3 (commencing with Section 97) of Chapter 6 of Part 0.5 of Division 1 of the Revenue and Taxation Code, the legislative body may amend the redevelopment plan to extend the time limits required pursuant to subdivisions (a) and (b) by the following:

(i) One year for each year in which a payment is made, if the time limit for the effectiveness of the redevelopment plan established pursuant to subdivision (a) is 10 years or less from the last day of the fiscal year in which a payment is made.

(ii) One year for each year in which a payment is made, if both of the following apply:

(I) The time limit for the effectiveness of the redevelopment plan established pursuant to subdivision (a) is more than 10 years but less than 20 years from the last day of the fiscal year in which a payment is made.

(II) The legislative body determines in the ordinance adopting the amendment that, with respect to the project, the agency is in compliance with Section 33334.2 or 33334.6, as applicable, has adopted an implementation plan in accordance with the requirements of Section 33490, is in compliance with subdivisions (a) and (b) of Section 33413, to the extent applicable, and is not subject to sanctions pursuant to subdivision (e) of Section 33334.12 for failure to expend, encumber, or disburse an excess surplus.

(iii) This subparagraph shall not apply to any redevelopment plan if the time limit for the effectiveness of the redevelopment plan established pursuant to subdivision (a) is more than 20 years after the last day of the fiscal year in which a payment is made.

(3) (A) The legislative body by ordinance may adopt the amendments provided for under this paragraph following a public hearing. Notice of the public hearing shall be mailed to the governing body of each affected taxing entity at least 30 days prior to the public hearing and published in a newspaper of general circulation in the community at least once, not less than 10 days prior to the date of the public hearing. The ordinance shall contain a finding of the legislative body that funds used to make a payment to the county's Educational Revenue Augmentation Fund pursuant to Section 33681.12 would otherwise have been used to pay the costs of projects and activities necessary to carry out the goals and objectives of the redevelopment plan. In adopting an ordinance pursuant to this paragraph, neither the legislative body nor the agency is required to comply with Section 33354.6, Article 12 (commencing with Section 33450), or any other provision of this part relating to the amendment of redevelopment plans.

(B) The time limit on the establishment of loans, advances, and indebtedness shall be deemed suspended and of no force or effect but only for the purpose of issuing bonds or other indebtedness the proceeds of which are used to make the payments required by Section 33681.12 if the following apply:

(i) The time limit on the establishment of loans, advances, and indebtedness required by this section prior to January 1, 2002, has expired and has not been eliminated pursuant to subparagraph (B).

(ii) The agency is required to make a payment pursuant to Section 33681.12.

(iii) The agency determines that in order to make the payment required by Section 33681.12, it is necessary to issue bonds or incur other indebtedness.

(iv) The proceeds of the bonds issued or indebtedness incurred are used solely for the purpose of making the payments required by Section 33681.12 and related costs.

The suspension of the time limit on the establishment of loans, advances, and indebtedness pursuant to this subparagraph shall not require the agency to make the payment to affected taxing entities required by Section 33607.7.

(4) (A) A time limit on the establishing of loans, advances, and indebtedness to be paid with the proceeds of property taxes received pursuant to Section 33670 to finance in whole or in part the redevelopment project shall not prevent an agency from incurring debt to be paid from the agency's Low and Moderate Income Housing Fund or establishing more debt in order to fulfill the agency's affordable housing obligations, as defined in paragraph (1) of subdivision (a) of Section 33333.8.

(B) A redevelopment plan may be amended by a legislative body to provide that there shall be no time limit on the establishment of loans, advances, and indebtedness paid from the agency's Low and Moderate Income Housing Fund or establishing more debt in order to fulfill the agency's affordable housing obligations, as defined in paragraph (1) of subdivision (a) of Section 33333.8. In adopting an ordinance pursuant to this subparagraph, neither the legislative body nor the agency is required to comply with Section 33345.6, Article 12 (commencing with Section 33450), or any other provision of this part relating to the amendment of redevelopment plans, and the agency shall not make the payment to affected taxing entities required by Section 33607.7.

(f) The limitations established in the ordinance adopted pursuant to this section shall not be applied to limit the allocation of taxes to an agency to the extent required to comply with Section 33333.8. In the event of a conflict between these limitations and the obligations under Section 33333.8, the limitations established in the ordinance shall be suspended pursuant to Section 33333.8.

(g) (1) This section does not effect the validity of any bond, indebtedness, or other obligation, including any mitigation agreement entered into pursuant to Section 33401, authorized by the legislative body, or the agency pursuant to this part, prior to January 1, 1994

(2) This section does not affect the right of an agency to receive property taxes, pursuant to Section 33670, to pay the bond, indebtedness, or other obligation.

(3) This section does not affect the right of an agency to receive property taxes pursuant to Section 33670 to pay refunding bonds issued to refinance, refund, or restructure indebtedness authorized prior to January 1, 1994, if the last maturity date of these refunding bonds is not later than the last maturity date of the refunded indebtedness and the sum of the total net interest cost to maturity on the refunding bonds plus the principal amount of the refunding bonds is less than the sum of the total net interest cost to maturity on the refunded indebtedness plus the principal amount of the refunded indebtedness.

(h) A redevelopment agency shall not pay indebtedness or receive property taxes pursuant to Section 33670, with respect to a redevelopment plan adopted prior to January 1, 1994, after the date identified in subdivision (b) or the date identified in the redevelopment plan, whichever is earlier, except as provided in paragraph (2) of subdivision (e), in subdivision (g), or in Section 33333.8.

(i) The Legislature finds and declares that the amendments made to this section by Chapter 942 of the Statutes of 1993 are intended to add limitations to the law on and after January 1, 1994, and are not intended to change or express legislative intent with respect to the law prior to that date. It is not the intent of the Legislature to affect the merits of any litigation regarding the ability of a redevelopment agency to sell bonds for a term that exceeds the limit of a redevelopment plan pursuant to law that existed prior to January 1, 1994.

(j) If a redevelopment plan is amended to add territory, the amendment shall contain the time limits required by Section 33333.2.

33333.7 Redevelopment Plans: San Francisco

(a) Notwithstanding the time limits in paragraph (1) of subdivision (a) of Section 33333.6, as that paragraph (1) read on December 31, 2001, the Redevelopment Agency of the City and County of San Francisco may, subject to the approval of the Board of

Supervisors of the City and County of San Francisco, retain its ability to incur indebtedness exclusively for Low and Moderate Income Housing Fund activities eligible under Sections 33334.2 and 33334.3 until January 1, 2014, or until the agency replaces all of the housing units demolished prior to the enactment of the replacement housing obligations in Chapter 970 of the Statutes of 1975, whichever occurs earlier. The ability of the agency to receive tax increment revenues to repay indebtedness incurred for these Low and Moderate Income Housing Fund activities may be extended until no later than January 1, 2044. Nothing in this paragraph shall be construed to extend a plan's effectiveness, except to incur additional indebtedness for Low and Moderate Income Housing Fund activities, to pay previously incurred indebtedness, and to enforce existing covenants, contracts, or other obligations.

(b) Annual revenues shall not exceed the amount necessary to fund the Low and Moderate Income Housing Fund activities of the agency. The agency shall neither collect nor spend more than 10 percent for the planning and administrative costs authorized pursuant to subdivision (e) of Section 33334.3. Revenues received under this paragraph shall not exceed the amount of tax increment received and allocated to the agency pursuant to the plan, as it has been amended, less the amount necessary to pay prior outstanding indebtedness, and less the amount of the project area's property tax revenue that school entities are entitled to receive pursuant to Chapter 3 (commencing with Section 75) and Chapter 6 (commencing with Section 95) of Part 0.5 of Division 1 of the Revenue and Taxation Code if the plan had not been amended. Additionally, revenues collected under this paragraph are subject to the payments to affected taxing entities pursuant to Section 33607.

(c) The activities conducted with revenues received under this paragraph shall be consistent with the policies and objectives of the community's housing element, as reviewed and approved by the department, and shall address the unmet housing needs of very low, low- and moderate-income households. The activities shall also be consistent with the community's most recently approved consolidated and annual action plans submitted to the United States Department of Housing and Urban Development, and if the director deems it necessary, the annual action plans shall be submitted to the department on an annual basis. No less than 50 percent of the revenues received shall be devoted to assisting in the development of housing that is affordable to very low income households.

(d) The agency shall not incur any indebtedness pursuant to this paragraph until the director certifies, after consulting with the agency, the net difference between the number of housing units affordable to persons and families of low and moderate income that the agency destroyed or removed prior to January 1, 1976, and the number of housing units affordable to persons and families of low and moderate income that the agency rehabilitated, developed, or constructed, or caused to be rehabilitated, developed, or constructed within the project areas adopted prior to January 1, 1976.

(e) The agency shall not incur any indebtedness pursuant to this paragraph unless the director of the department certifies annually, prior to the creation of indebtedness, all of the following:

(1) The community has a current housing element that substantially complies with the requirements of Article 10.6 (commencing with Section 65580) of Chapter 3 of Division 1 of Title 7 of the Government Code.

(2) The community's housing element indicates an unmet need for Low and Moderate Income Housing Fund activities.

(3) The agency's most recent independent financial audit report prepared pursuant to Section 33080.1 reports acceptable findings and no major violations of this part.

(4) The agency has complied with subdivision (a) of Section 33334.2.

(5) The agency has met the requirements of this part with respect to the provision of dwelling units for persons and families of low or moderate income, including, but not limited to, the requirements of Section 33413.

33333.8 Redevelopment plans; affordable housing compliance; time limit

(a) Every redevelopment agency shall comply with and fulfill its obligations with regard to the provision of affordable housing as required by this part prior to the time limit on the effectiveness of the redevelopment plan established pursuant to Sections 33333.2, 33333.6, and 33333.10, and before the agency exceeds a limit on the number of dollars of taxes that may be divided and allocated to the redevelopment agency if required by Section 33333.4 or the limit on the number of dollars of taxes in a redevelopment plan. A legislative body may not adopt an ordinance terminating a redevelopment project area if the agency has not complied with its affordable housing obligations. Notwithstanding any other provision of law, this section shall apply to each redevelopment agency and each redevelopment project area established or merged pursuant to this part and Part 1.5 (commencing with Section 34000), including project areas authorized pursuant to this chapter and each individual project area that is authorized pursuant to any other provision of law.

(1) The affordable housing obligations specified in subdivision (a) shall include all of the following:

(A) The obligation to make deposits to and expenditures from the Low and Moderate Income Housing Fund pursuant to Sections 33334.2, 33334.3, 33334.4, 33334.6, 33487, 33492.16, and other similar and related statutes.

(B) The obligation to eliminate project deficits pursuant to Sections 33334.6, 33487, 33492.16, and other similar and related statutes.

(C) The obligation to expend or transfer excess surplus funds pursuant to Section 33334.12 and other similar and related statutes.

(D) The obligation to provide relocation assistance pursuant to Article 9 (commencing with Section 33410), Section 7260 of the Government Code, or other applicable relocation laws.

(E) The obligation to provide replacement housing pursuant to subdivision (a) of Section 33413, Article 9 (commencing with Section 33410), and other similar and related statutes.

(F) The obligation to provide inclusionary housing pursuant to Section 33413 and other similar and related statutes and ordinances.

(2) A redevelopment agency shall not adopt an ordinance terminating a redevelopment project area if the agency has not complied with these obligations.

(b) If, on the date of the time limit on the effectiveness of the redevelopment plan, a redevelopment agency has not complied with subdivision (a), the time limit on the effectiveness of the redevelopment plan, and, if necessary, the time limit for repayment of indebtedness, shall be suspended until the agency has complied with subdivision (a). In addition, the agency shall receive and use all tax increment funds that are not pledged to repay indebtedness until the agency has fully complied with its obligations.

(c) If, on the date of the time limit on the repayment of indebtedness, the agency has not complied with subdivision (a), the time limit on the repayment of indebtedness shall be suspended until the agency has complied with subdivision (a). In addition, the agency shall receive and use tax increment funds until the agency has fully complied with its obligations.

(d) If, on the date of the time limit on the repayment of indebtedness, the agency has complied with its obligations under subdivision (a) and has moneys remaining in the Low and Moderate Income Housing Fund, the agency shall transfer the remaining moneys to a low and moderate income housing fund or account for a different project area within the agency's jurisdiction, if one exists, or if a different project area does not exist, the agency shall either transfer the remaining moneys to a special fund of the community or to the community or county housing authority. The community, community housing authority, or county housing authority to which the remaining moneys are transferred shall utilize the moneys for the purposes of, and subject to the same restrictions that are applicable to, the redevelopment agency under this part.

(e) If a redevelopment plan provides a limit on the total amount of tax increment funds that may be received by a redevelopment agency for any project area, and if that limit is reached prior to the agency complying with its obligations pursuant to subdivision (a), that limit is suspended until the agency has complied with subdivision (a) and the agency shall receive and use tax increment funds until the agency has fully complied with its obligations.

(f) If an agency fails to comply with its obligations pursuant to this section, any person may seek judicial relief. The court shall require the agency to take all steps necessary to comply with those obligations, including, as necessary, the adoption of ordinances, to incur debt, to obtain tax increments, to expend tax increments, and to enter into contracts as necessary to meet its housing obligations under this part.

33333.10 Amendment of redevelopment plans; extension of time limitations

(a) (1) Notwithstanding the time limits in subdivisions (a) and (b) of Section 33333.6, an agency that adopted a redevelopment plan on or before December 31, 1993, may, pursuant to this section, amend that plan to extend the time limit on effectiveness of the plan for up to 10 additional years beyond the limit allowed by subdivision (a) of Section 33333.6.

(2) In addition, the agency may, pursuant to this section, amend that plan to extend the time limit on the payment of indebtedness and receipt of property taxes to be not more than 10 years from the termination of the effectiveness of the redevelopment plan as that time limit has been amended pursuant to paragraph (1).

(b) A redevelopment plan may be amended pursuant to subdivision (a) only after the agency finds, based on substantial evidence, that both of the following conditions exist:

(1) Significant blight remains within the project area.

(2) This blight cannot be eliminated without extending the effectiveness of the plan and the receipt of property taxes.

(c) As used in this section:

(1) "Blight" has the same meaning as that term is given in Section 33030.

(2) "Significant" means important and of a magnitude to warrant agency assistance.

(3) "Necessary and essential parcels" means parcels that are not blighted but are so necessary and essential to the elimination of the blight that these parcels should be included within the portion of the project area in which tax increment funds may be spent. "Necessary and essential parcels" are (A) parcels that are adjacent to one or more blighted parcels that are to be assembled in order to create a parcel of adequate size given present standards and market conditions, and (B) parcels that are adjacent or near parcels that are blighted on which it is necessary to construct a public improvement to eliminate the blight.

(d) For purposes of this section, significant blight can exist in a project area even though blight is not prevalent in a project area. The report submitted to the legislative body pursuant to Section 33352 shall identify on a map the portion of the project area in which significant blight remains.

(e) After the limit on the payment of indebtedness and receipt of property taxes that would have taken effect but for the amendment pursuant to this section, except for funds deposited in the Low and Moderate Income Housing Fund pursuant to Section 33334.2 or 33334.6, the agency shall spend tax increment funds only within the portion of the project area that has been identified in the report adopted pursuant to Section 33352 as the area containing blighted parcels and necessary and essential parcels. Except as otherwise limited by subdivisions (f) and (g), agencies may continue to spend funds deposited in the Low and Moderate Income Housing Fund in accordance with this division.

(f) (1) Except as otherwise provided in this subdivision, after the limit on the payment of indebtedness and receipt of property taxes that would have taken effect, but for the amendment pursuant to this section, agencies shall only spend moneys from the Low and Moderate Income Housing Fund for the purpose of increasing, improving, and preserving the community's supply of housing at affordable housing cost to persons and families of low, very low, or extremely low income, as defined in Sections 50079.5, 50093, 50105, and 50106. During this period, an agency that has adopted an amendment pursuant to subdivision (a) may use moneys from the Low and Moderate Income Housing Fund for the purpose of increasing, improving, and preserving housing at affordable housing cost to persons and families of moderate income as defined in Section 50093. However, this amount shall not exceed, in a five-year period, the amount of moneys from the Low and Moderate Income Housing Fund that are used to increase, improve, and preserve housing at affordable housing cost to persons and families of extremely low income, as defined in Section 50106. In no case shall the amount expended for housing for persons and families of moderate income exceed 15 percent of the annual amount deposited in the Low and Moderate Income Housing Fund during a five-year period and the number of housing units affordable to moderate income persons shall not exceed the number of housing units affordable to extremely low income persons.

(2) Commencing with the first fiscal year that commences after the date of the adoption of an amendment pursuant to subdivision (a) and until the limit on the payment of indebtedness and receipt of property taxes that would have taken effect but for the amendment pursuant to this section, an agency that has adopted an amendment pursuant to subdivision (a) may use moneys from the Low and Moderate Income Housing Fund for the purpose of increasing, improving, and preserving housing at affordable housing cost to persons and families of moderate income as defined in Section 50093. However, this amount shall not exceed, in a five-year period, 15 percent of the amount of moneys

deposited in the Low and Moderate Income Housing Fund during that five-year period and shall only be used to assist housing projects in which no less than 49 percent of the units are affordable to and occupied by persons and families of low, very low, or extremely low income. An agency may spend an additional amount of moneys in the same or other housing projects to assist housing units affordable to and occupied by moderate-income persons. However, this amount shall not exceed the lesser of: the amount of moneys spent to increase, improve, and preserve housing at affordable housing cost to persons and families of extremely low income as defined in Section 50106, or 5 percent of the moneys deposited in the Low and Moderate Income Housing Fund during that five-year period.

(g) (1) Except as provided in paragraph (2) or (3), commencing with the first fiscal year that commences after the date of adoption of an amendment pursuant to subdivision (a), not less than 30 percent of all taxes that are allocated to the agency pursuant to Section 33670 from the redevelopment project area so amended shall be deposited into that project's Low and Moderate Income Housing Fund for the purposes specified in subdivision (f).

(2) In any fiscal year, the agency may deposit less than the amount required by paragraph (1), but not less than the amount required by Section 33334.2 or 33334.6, into the Low and Moderate Income Housing Fund if the agency finds that the difference between the amount deposited and the amount required by paragraph (1) is necessary to make principal and interest payments during that fiscal year on bonds sold by the agency to finance or refinance the redevelopment project prior to six months before the date of adoption of the amendment pursuant to subdivision (a). Bonds sold by the agency prior to six months before the date of the adoption of the amendment pursuant to subdivision (a) may only be refinanced, refunded, or restructured after the date of the amendment pursuant to subdivision (a). However, for purposes of this section, bonds refinanced, refunded, or restructured after the date of the amendment pursuant to subdivision (a) may only be treated as if sold on the date the original bonds were sold if (A) the net proceeds were used to refinance the original bonds, (B) there is no increase in the amount of principal at the time of refinancing, restructuring, or refunding, and (C) the time during which the refinanced indebtedness is to be repaid does not exceed the date on which the existing indebtedness would have been repaid.

(3) No later than 120 days prior to depositing less than the amount required by paragraph (1) into the Low and Moderate Income Housing Fund, the agency shall adopt, by resolution after a noticed public hearing, a finding that the difference between the amount allocated and the amount required by paragraph (1) is necessary to make payments on bonds sold by the agency to finance or refinance the redevelopment project and identified in the preliminary report adopted pursuant to paragraph (9) of subdivision (e) of Section 33333.11, and specifying the amount of principal remaining on the bonds, the amount of annual payments, and the date on which the indebtedness will be repaid. Notice of the time and place of the public hearing shall be published in a newspaper of general circulation once a week for at least two successive weeks prior to the public hearing. The agency shall make available to the public the proposed resolution no later than the time of the publication of the first notice of the public hearing. A copy of the resolution shall be transmitted to the Department of Housing and Community Development within 10 days after adoption.

(4) Notwithstanding paragraph (1), an agency that sells bonds on or after the date of adoption of an amendment pursuant to subdivision (a), the repayment of which is to be made from taxes allocated to the agency pursuant to Section 33670 from the project so amended, may elect to subordinate up to 16 2/3 percent of its annual 30-percent Low and Moderate Income Housing Fund deposit obligation to the payment of debt service on the bonds. If the agency makes that election and in any year the agency has insufficient tax-increment revenue available to pay debt service on the bonds to which the funds from the Low and Moderate Income Housing Fund are subordinated, the agency may deposit less than the full 100 percent of its annual 30-percent Low and Moderate Income Housing Fund obligation but only to the extent necessary to pay that debt service and in no event shall less than 83 1/3 percent of that obligation be deposited into the Low and Moderate Income Housing Fund for that year. The difference between the amount that is actually deposited in the Low and Moderate Income Housing Fund and the full 100 percent of the agency's 30-percent Low and Moderate Income Housing Fund deposit obligation shall constitute a deficit in the Low and Moderate Income Housing Fund subject to repayment pursuant to paragraph (5).

(5) If, pursuant to paragraph (2) or (4), the agency deposits less than 30 percent of the taxes allocated to the agency pursuant to Section 33670 in any fiscal year in the Low and Moderate Income Housing Fund, the amount equal to the difference between 30 percent of the taxes allocated to the agency pursuant to Section 33670 for each affected redevelopment project area and the amount actually deposited in the Low and Moderate Income Housing Fund for that fiscal year shall be established as a deficit in the Low and Moderate Income Housing Fund. Any new tax increment funds not encumbered pursuant to paragraph (2) or (4) shall be utilized to reduce or eliminate the deficit prior to entering into any new contracts, commitments or indebtedness. The obligations imposed by this section are hereby declared to be an indebtedness of the redevelopment project to which they relate, payable from taxes allocated to the agency pursuant to Section 33670 and, notwithstanding any other provision of law, shall constitute an indebtedness of the agency with respect to the redevelopment project, and the agency shall continue to receive allocations of taxes pursuant to Section 33670 until the deficit is paid in full.

(h) An agency may not amend its redevelopment plan pursuant to this section unless the agency first adopts a resolution that finds, based on substantial evidence, all of the following:

(1) The community has adopted a housing element that the department has determined pursuant to Section 65585 of the Government Code to be in substantial compliance with the requirements of Article 10.6 (commencing with Section 65580) of Chapter 3 of Division 1 of Title 7 of the Government Code, or if applicable, an eligible city or county within the jurisdiction of the San Diego Association of Governments has adopted a self-certification of compliance with its adopted housing element pursuant to Section 65585.1 of the Government Code.

(2) During the three fiscal years prior to the year in which the amendment is adopted, the agency has not been included in the report sent by the Controller to the Attorney General pursuant to subdivision (b) of Section 33080.8 as an agency that has a "major violation" pursuant to Section 33080.8.

(3) After a written request by the agency and provision of the information requested by the department, the department has issued a letter to the agency, confirming that the agency has not

accumulated an excess surplus in its Low and Moderate Income Housing Fund. As used in this section, "excess surplus" has the same meaning as that term is defined in Section 33334.12. The department shall develop a methodology to collect information required by this section. Information requested by the department shall include a certification by the agency's independent auditor on the status of excess surplus and submittal of data for the department to verify the status of excess surplus. The independent auditor shall make the required certification based on the Controller's office guidelines which shall include the methodology prescribed by the department pursuant to subparagraph (D) of paragraph (3) of subdivision (g) of Section 33334.12. If the department does not respond to the written request of the agency for this determination within 90 days after receipt of the written request, compliance with this requirement shall be deemed confirmed.

(i) Each redevelopment plan that has been adopted prior to January 1, 1976, that is amended pursuant to subdivision (a) shall also be amended at the same time to make subdivision (b) of Section 33413 applicable to the redevelopment plan in accordance with paragraph (1) of subdivision (d) of Section 33413.

(j) The amendment to the redevelopment plan authorized pursuant to this section shall be made by ordinance pursuant to Article 12 (commencing with Section 33450). The ordinance shall be subject to referendum as prescribed by law for ordinances of the legislative body.

(k) This section shall not apply to a project area that retains its eligibility to incur indebtedness and receive tax increment revenues pursuant to Section 33333.7.

(l) The limitations established in the ordinance adopted pursuant to this section shall not be applied to limit allocation of taxes to an agency to the extent required to comply with Section 33333.8. In the event of a conflict between these limitations and the obligations under Section 33333.8, the limitation established in the ordinance shall be suspended pursuant to Section 33333.8.

33333.11 Amendment of redevelopment plans; community participation; participation by other entities

(a) In order to adopt an amendment pursuant to Section 33333.10, the redevelopment agency shall also comply with the procedures in this section.

(b) Before adopting an amendment of the plan, the agency shall hold a public hearing on the proposed amendment. The notice of the public hearing shall comply with Section 33452.

(c) Prior to the publication of the notice of the public hearing on the proposed amendment, the agency shall consult with each affected taxing agency with respect to the proposed amendment. At a minimum, the agency shall give each affected taxing agency the opportunity to meet with representatives of the agency for the purpose of discussing the effect of the proposed amendment upon the affected taxing agency and shall notify each affected taxing agency that any written comments from the affected taxing agency will be included in the report to the legislative body.

(d) Prior to the publication of the notice of the public hearing on the proposed amendment, the agency shall consult with and obtain the advice of members of a project area committee, if a project area committee exists, and residents and community organizations and provide to those persons and organizations, including the project area committee, if any, the amendment prior to the agency's submitting the amendment to the legislative body. In addition, the preliminary report prepared pursuant to subdivision (e) shall be made available at no cost to the project area committee, if one exists, and residents and community organizations not later than 120 days prior to holding a public hearing on the proposed amendment.

(e) No later than 120 days prior to holding a public hearing on the proposed amendment, the agency shall send to each affected taxing entity, as defined in Section 33353.2, the Department of Finance, and the Department of Housing and Community Development, a preliminary report that contains all of the following:

(1) A map of the project area that identifies the portion, if any, of the project area that is no longer blighted and the portion of the project area that is blighted and the portion of the project area that contains necessary and essential parcels for the elimination of the remaining blight.

(2) A description of the remaining blight.

(3) A description of the projects or programs proposed to eliminate the remaining blight.

(4) A description of how the project or programs will improve the conditions of blight.

(5) The reasons why the projects or programs cannot be completed without extending the time limits on the effectiveness of the plan and receipt of tax increment revenues.

(6) The proposed method of financing these programs or projects. This description shall include the amount of tax increment revenues that is projected to be generated during the period of the extension, including amounts projected to be deposited into the Low and Moderate Income Housing Fund and amounts to be paid to affected taxing entities. This description shall also include sources and amounts of moneys other than tax increment revenues that are available to finance these projects or programs. This description shall also include the reasons that the remaining blight cannot reasonably be expected to be reversed or alleviated by private enterprise or governmental action, or both, without the use of the tax increment revenues available to the agency because of the proposed amendment.

(7) An amendment to the agency's implementation plan that includes, but is not limited to, the agency's housing responsibilities pursuant to Section 33490. However, the agency shall not be required to hold a separate public hearing on the implementation plan pursuant to subdivision (d) of Section 33490 in addition to the public hearing on the amendment to the redevelopment plan.

(8) A new neighborhood impact report if required by subdivision (m) of Section 33352.

(9) A description of each bond sold by the agency to finance or refinance the redevelopment project prior to six months before the date of adoption of the proposed amendment, and listing for each bond the amount of remaining principal, the annual payments, and the date that the bond will be paid in full.

(f) No later than 120 days prior to holding a public hearing on the proposed amendment, the agency shall send the proposed amendment to the planning commission. If the planning commission does not report upon the amendment within 30 days after its submission by the agency, the planning commission shall be deemed to have waived its report and recommendations concerning the amendment.

(g) No later than 45 days prior to the public hearing on the proposed amendment by the agency or the joint public hearing of the agency and the legislative body, the agency shall notify each affected taxing entity, the Department of Finance, the Department of Housing and Community Development, and each individual and organization that submitted comments on the preliminary report by certified mail of the public hearing, the date of the public hearing, and the proposed amendment. This notice shall be accompanied by the report required to be prepared pursuant to subdivision (h).

(h) No later than 45 days prior to the public hearing on the proposed amendment by the agency or the joint public hearing by the agency and the legislative body, the agency shall adopt a report to the legislative body containing all of the following:

(1) All of the information required to be contained in the preliminary report prepared pursuant to subdivision (e).

(2) The report and recommendation of the planning commission.

(3) A negative declaration, environmental impact report or other document that is required in order to comply with the California Environmental Quality Act (Division 13 (commencing with Section 21000) of the Public Resources Code.

(4) A summary of the consultations with the affected taxing entities. If any of the affected taxing entities, a project area committee, if any, residents, or community organizations have expressed written objections or concerns with the proposed amendment as part of these consultations, the agency shall include a response to these concerns.

(5) A summary of the consultation with residents and community organizations, including the project area committee, if any.

(i) After receiving the recommendation of the agency on the proposed amendment, and not sooner than 30 days after the submission of changes to the planning commission, the legislative body shall hold a public hearing on the proposed amendment. The notice of the public hearing shall comply with Section 33452.

(j) As an alternative to the separate public hearing required by subdivision (i), the agency and the legislative body, with the consent of both, may hold a joint public hearing on the proposed amendment. Notice of this public hearing shall comply with Section 33452. When a joint public hearing is held and the legislative body is also the agency, the legislative body may adopt the amended plan with no actions required of the agency. If, after the public hearing, the legislative body determines that the amendment to the plan is necessary or desirable, the legislative body shall adopt an ordinance amending the ordinance adopting the plan thus amended. The ordinance adopting the amendment shall contain findings that both (1) significant blight remains within the project area, and (2) the blight cannot be eliminated without the extension of the effectiveness of the plan and receipt of tax increment revenues.

(k) If an affected taxing entity, the Department of Finance, or the Department of Housing and Community Development believes that significant remaining blight does not exist within the portion of the project area designated as blighted in the report to the legislative body regarding a proposed amendment to be adopted pursuant to Section 33333.10, the affected taxing entity, the Department of Finance, or the Department of Housing and Community Development may request the Attorney General to participate in the amendment process. The affected taxing entity, the Department of Finance, or the Department of Housing and Community Development shall request this participation within 21 days after receipt of the notice of the public hearing sent pursuant to subdivision (g). The Attorney General shall determine whether or not to participate in the amendment process. The Attorney General may consult with and request the assistance of departments of the state and any other persons or groups that are interested or that have expertise in redevelopment. The Attorney General may participate in the amendment process by requesting additional information from the agency, conducting his or her own review of the project area, meeting with the agency and any affected taxing entity, submitting evidence for consideration at the public hearing, or presenting oral evidence at the public hearing. No later than five days prior to the public hearing on the proposed amendment, the Attorney General shall notify each affected taxing agency, each department that has requested the Attorney General to review the proposed amendment, and the redevelopment agency with regard to whether the Attorney General will participate in the amendment process and, if so, how he or she will participate, on their behalf.

(l) The Attorney General may bring a civil action pursuant to Section 33501 to determine the validity of an amendment adopted pursuant to Section 33333.10. The Department of Finance and the Department of Housing and Community Development shall be considered interested persons for the purposes of protecting the interests of the state pursuant to Section 863 of the Code of Civil Procedure in any action brought with regard to the validity of an ordinance adopting a proposed amendment pursuant to Section 33333.10. Either department may request the Attorney General to bring an action pursuant to Section 33501 to determine the validity of an amendment adopted pursuant to Section 33333.10. Actions brought pursuant to this subdivision are in addition to any other actions that may be brought by the Attorney General or other persons.

33334 Method of financing

Every redevelopment plan shall describe generally the proposed method of financing the redevelopment of the project area.

33334.1 Limitation on bonded indebtedness

If the plan authorizes the issuance of bonds to be repaid in whole or in part from the allocation of taxes pursuant to Section 33670, the plan shall establish a limit on the amount of bonded indebtedness which can be outstanding at one time without an amendment of the plan. This section shall apply only to redevelopment plans adopted on or after October 1, 1976.

33334.2 Low and moderate income housing set aside: purposes; findings

(a) Not less than 20 percent of all taxes that are allocated to the agency pursuant to Section 33670 shall be used by the agency for the purposes of increasing, improving, and preserving the community's supply of low- and moderate-income housing available at affordable housing cost, as defined by Section 50052.5, to persons and families of low or moderate income, as defined in Section 50093, lower income households, as defined by Section 50079.5, very low income households, as defined in Section 50105, and extremely low income households, as defined by Section 50106, that is occupied by these persons and families, unless one of the following findings is made annually by resolution:

(1) (A) That no need exists in the community to improve, increase, or preserve the supply of low- and moderate-income housing, including housing for very low income households in a manner that would benefit the project area and that this finding is consistent with the housing element of the community's general plan required by Article 10.6 (commencing with Section 65580) of Chapter 3 of Division 1 of Title 7 of the Government

Code, including its share of the regional housing needs of very low income households and persons and families of low or moderate income.

(B) This finding shall only be made if the housing element of the community's general plan demonstrates that the community does not have a need to improve, increase, or preserve the supply of low and moderate income housing available at affordable housing cost to persons and families of low- or moderate-income and to very low income households. This finding shall only be made if it is consistent with the planning agency's annual report to the legislative body on implementation of the housing element required by subdivision (b) of Section 65400 of the Government Code. No agency of a charter city shall make this finding unless the planning agency submits the report pursuant to subdivision (b) of Section 65400 of the Government Code. This finding shall not take effect until the agency has complied with subdivision (b) of this section.

(2) (A) That some stated percentage less than 20 percent of the taxes that are allocated to the agency pursuant to Section 33670 is sufficient to meet the housing needs of the community, including its share of the regional housing needs of persons and families of low- or moderate-income and very low income households, and that this finding is consistent with the housing element of the community's general plan required by Article 10.6 (commencing with Section 65580) of Chapter 3 of Division 1 of Title 7 of the Government Code.

(B) This finding shall only be made if the housing element of the community's general plan demonstrates that a percentage of less than 20 percent will be sufficient to meet the community's need to improve, increase, or preserve the supply of low- and moderate-income housing available at affordable housing cost to persons and families of low or moderate income and to very low income households. This finding shall only be made if it is consistent with the planning agency's annual report to the legislative body on implementation of the housing element required by subdivision (b) of Section 65400 of the Government Code. No agency of a charter city shall make this finding unless the planning agency submits the report pursuant to subdivision (b) of Section 65400 of the Government Code. This finding shall not take effect until the agency has complied with subdivision (b) of this section.

(C) For purposes of making the findings specified in this paragraph and paragraph (1), the housing element of the general plan of a city, county, or city and county shall be current, and shall have been determined by the department pursuant to Section 65585 to be in substantial compliance with Article 10.6 (commencing with Section 65580) of Chapter 3 of Division 1 of Title 7 of the Government Code.

(3) (A) That the community is making a substantial effort to meet its existing and projected housing needs, including its share of the regional housing needs, with respect to persons and families of low and moderate income, particularly very low income households as identified in the housing element of the community's general plan required by Article 10.6 (commencing with Section 65580) of Chapter 3 of Division 1 of Title 7 of the Government Code, and that this effort, consisting of direct financial contributions of local funds used to increase and improve the supply of housing affordable to, and occupied by, persons and families of low or moderate income and very low income households, is equivalent in impact to the funds otherwise required to be set aside pursuant to this section. In addition to any other local funds, these direct financial contributions may include federal or state grants paid directly to a community and that the community has the discretion of using for the purposes for which moneys in the Low and Moderate Income Housing Fund may be used. The legislative body shall consider the need that can be reasonably foreseen because of displacement of persons and families of low or moderate income or very low income households from within, or adjacent to, the project area, because of increased employment opportunities, or because of any other direct or indirect result of implementation of the redevelopment plan. No finding under this subdivision may be made until the community has provided or ensured the availability of replacement dwelling units as defined in Section 33411.2 and until it has complied with Article 9 (commencing with Section 33410).

(B) In making the determination that other financial contributions are equivalent in impact pursuant to this subdivision, the agency shall include only those financial contributions that are directly related to programs or activities authorized under subdivision (e).

(C) The authority for making the finding specified in this paragraph shall expire on June 30, 1993, except that the expiration shall not be deemed to impair contractual obligations to bondholders or private entities incurred prior to May 1, 1991, and made in reliance on the provisions of this paragraph. Agencies that make this finding after June 30, 1993, shall show evidence that the agency entered into the specific contractual obligation with the specific intention of making a finding under this paragraph in order to provide sufficient revenues to pay off the indebtedness.

(b) Within 10 days following the making of a finding under either paragraph (1) or (2) of subdivision (a), the agency shall send the Department of Housing and Community Development a copy of the finding, including the factual information supporting the finding and other factual information in the housing element that demonstrates that either (1) the community does not need to increase, improve, or preserve the supply of housing for low- and moderate-income households, including very low income households, or (2) a percentage less than 20 percent will be sufficient to meet the community's need to improve, increase, and preserve the supply of housing for low- and moderate-income households, including very low income households. Within 10 days following the making of a finding under paragraph (3) of subdivision (a), the agency shall send the Department of Housing and Community Development a copy of the finding, including the factual information supporting the finding that the community is making a substantial effort to meet its existing and projected housing needs. Agencies that make this finding after June 30, 1993, shall also submit evidence to the department of its contractual obligations with bondholders or private entities incurred prior to May 1, 1991, and made in reliance on this finding.

(c) In any litigation to challenge or attack a finding made under paragraph (1), (2), or (3) of subdivision (a), the burden shall be upon the agency to establish that the finding is supported by substantial evidence in light of the entire record before the agency. If an agency is determined by a court to have knowingly misrepresented any material facts regarding the community's share of its regional housing need for low- and moderate-income housing, including very low income households, or the community's production record in meeting its share of the regional housing need pursuant to the report required by subdivision (b) of Section 65400 of the Government Code, the agency shall be liable for all court costs and plaintiff's attorney's fees, and shall be required to allocate not less than 25 percent of the agency's tax increment revenues to its Low and Moderate Income Housing Fund in each year thereafter.

(d) Nothing in this section shall be construed as relieving any other public entity or entity with the power of eminent domain of any legal obligations for replacement or relocation housing arising out of its activities.

(e) In carrying out the purposes of this section, the agency may exercise any or all of its powers for the construction, rehabilitation, or preservation of affordable housing for extremely low, very low, low-, and moderate-income persons or families, including the following:

(1) Acquire real property or building sites subject to Section 33334.16.

(2) (A) Improve real property or building sites with onsite or offsite improvements, but only if both (i) the improvements are part of the new construction or rehabilitation of affordable housing units for low- or moderate-income persons that are directly benefited by the improvements, and are a reasonable and fundamental component of the housing units, and (ii) the agency requires that the units remain available at affordable housing cost to, and occupied by, persons and families of extremely low, very low, low, or moderate income for the same time period and in the same manner as provided in subdivision (c) and paragraph (2) of subdivision (f) of Section 33334.3.

(B) If the newly constructed or rehabilitated housing units are part of a larger project and the agency improves or pays for onsite or offsite improvements pursuant to the authority in this subdivision, the agency shall pay only a portion of the total cost of the onsite or offsite improvement. The maximum percentage of the total cost of the improvement paid for by the agency shall be determined by dividing the number of housing units that are affordable to low- or moderate-income persons by the total number of housing units, if the project is a housing project, or by dividing the cost of the affordable housing units by the total cost of the project, if the project is not a housing project.

(3) Donate real property to private or public persons or entities.

(4) Finance insurance premiums pursuant to Section 33136.

(5) Construct buildings or structures.

(6) Acquire buildings or structures.

(7) Rehabilitate buildings or structures.

(8) Provide subsidies to, or for the benefit of, extremely low income households, as defined by Section 50106, very low income households, as defined by Section 50105, lower income households, as defined by Section 50079.5, or persons and families of low or moderate income, as defined by Section 50093, to the extent those households cannot obtain housing at affordable costs on the open market. Housing units available on the open market are those units developed without direct government subsidies.

(9) Develop plans, pay principal and interest on bonds, loans, advances, or other indebtedness, or pay financing or carrying charges.

(10) Maintain the community's supply of mobilehomes.

(11) Preserve the availability to lower income households of affordable housing units in housing developments that are assisted or subsidized by public entities and that are threatened with imminent conversion to market rates.

(f) The agency may use these funds to meet, in whole or in part, the replacement housing provisions in Section 33413. However, nothing in this section shall be construed as limiting in any way the requirements of that section.

(g) (1) The agency may use these funds inside or outside the project area. The agency may only use these funds outside the project area upon a resolution of the agency and the legislative body that the use will be of benefit to the project. The determination by the agency and the legislative body shall be final and conclusive as to the issue of benefit to the project area. The Legislature finds and declares that the provision of replacement housing pursuant to Section 33413 is always of benefit to a project. Unless the legislative body finds, before the redevelopment plan is adopted, that the provision of low- and moderate-income housing outside the project area will be of benefit to the project, the project area shall include property suitable for low-and moderate-income housing.

(2) (A) The Contra Costa County Redevelopment Agency may use these funds anywhere within the unincorporated territory, or within the incorporated limits of the City of Walnut Creek on sites contiguous to the Pleasant Hill BART Station Area Redevelopment Project area. The agency may only use these funds outside the project area upon a resolution of the agency and board of supervisors determining that the use will be of benefit to the project area. In addition, the agency may use these funds within the incorporated limits of the City of Walnut Creek only if the agency and the board of supervisors find all of the following:

(i) Both the County of Contra Costa and the City of Walnut Creek have adopted and are implementing complete and current housing elements of their general plans that the Department of Housing and Community Development has determined to be in compliance with the requirements of Article 10.6 (commencing with Section 65580) of Chapter 3 of Division 1 of Title 7 of the Government Code.

(ii) The development to be funded shall not result in any residential displacement from the site where the development is to be built.

(iii) The development to be funded shall not be constructed in an area that currently has more than 50 percent of its population comprised of racial minorities or low-income families.

(iv) The development to be funded shall allow construction of affordable housing closer to a rapid transit station than could be constructed in the unincorporated territory outside the Pleasant Hill BART Station Area Redevelopment Project.

(B) If the agency uses these funds within the incorporated limits of the City of Walnut Creek, all of the following requirements shall apply:

(i) The funds shall be used only for the acquisition of land for, and the design and construction of, the development of housing containing units affordable to, and occupied by, low- and moderate-income persons.

(ii) If less than all the units in the development are affordable to, and occupied by, low- or moderate-income persons, any agency assistance shall not exceed the amount needed to make the housing affordable to, and occupied by, low- or moderate-income persons.

(iii) The units in the development that are affordable to, and occupied by, low- or moderate-income persons shall remain affordable for a period of at least 55 years.

(iv) The agency and the City of Walnut Creek shall determine, if applicable, whether Article XXXIV of the California Constitution permits the development.

(h) The Legislature finds and declares that expenditures or obligations incurred by the agency pursuant to this section shall constitute an indebtedness of the project.

(i) This section shall only apply to taxes allocated to a redevelopment agency for which a final redevelopment plan is adopted on or after January 1, 1977, or for any area that is added to a project by an amendment to a redevelopment plan, which amendment is adopted on or after the effective date of this section. An agency may, by resolution, elect to make all or part of the requirements of this section applicable to any redevelopment project for which a redevelopment plan was adopted prior to January 1, 1977, subject to any indebtedness incurred prior to the election.

(j) (1) (A) An action to compel compliance with the requirement of Section 33334.3 to deposit not less than 20 percent of all taxes that are allocated to the agency pursuant to Section 33670 in the Low and Moderate Income Housing Fund shall be commenced within 10 years of the alleged violation. A cause of action for a violation accrues on the last day of the fiscal year in which the funds were required to be deposited in the Low and Moderate Income Housing Fund.

(B) An action to compel compliance with the requirement of this section or Section 33334.6 that money deposited in the Low and Moderate Income Housing Fund be used by the agency for purposes of increasing, improving, and preserving the community's supply of low- and moderate-income housing available at affordable housing cost shall be commenced within 10 years of the alleged violation. A cause of action for a violation accrues on the date of the actual expenditure of the funds.

(C) An agency found to have deposited less into the Low and Moderate Income Housing Fund than mandated by Section 33334.3 or to have spent money from the Low and Moderate Income Housing Fund for purposes other than increasing, improving, and preserving the community's supply of low- and moderate-income housing, as mandated, by this section or Section 33334.6 shall repay the funds with interest in one lump sum pursuant to Section 970.4 or 970.5 of the Government Code or may do either of the following:

(i) Petition the court under Section 970.6 for repayment in installments.

(ii) Repay the portion of the judgment due to the Low and Moderate Income Housing Fund in equal installments over a period of five years following the judgment.

(2) Repayment shall not be made from the funds required to be set aside or used for low-and moderate-income housing pursuant to this section.

(3) Notwithstanding clauses (i) and (ii) of subparagraph (C) of paragraph (1), all costs, including reasonable attorney's fees if included in the judgment, are due and shall be paid upon entry of judgment or order.

(4) Except as otherwise provided in this subdivision, Chapter 2 (commencing with Section 970) of Part 5 of Division 3.6 of Title 1 of the Government Code for the enforcement of a judgment against a local public entity applies to a judgment against a local public entity that violates this section.

(5) This subdivision applies to actions filed on and after January 1, 2006.

(6) The limitations period specified in subparagraphs (A) and (B) of paragraph (1) does not apply to a cause of action brought pursuant to Chapter 9 (commencing with Section 860) of Title 10 of Part 2 of the Code of Civil Procedure.

33334.2a Low and moderate income housing funds: Orange County Development Agency

(a) The Orange County Development Agency may use the funds described in Section 33334.2 anywhere within the unincorporated territory, or within the incorporated limits of any city within the County of Orange. The agency may only use these funds outside the project area upon a resolution of the agency and board of supervisors determining that the use will be of benefit to the project area. In addition, the agency may use these funds within the incorporated limits of a city only if the agency and the board of supervisors find all of the following:

(1) Both the County of Orange and the city have adopted and are implementing complete and current housing elements of their general plans that the department has determined to be in compliance with the requirements of Article 10.6 (commencing with Section 65580) of Chapter 3 of Division 1 of Title 7 of the Government Code.

(2) The development to be funded shall not result in any residential displacement from the site where the development is to be built.

(3) The development to be funded shall be a rental housing development containing units affordable to lower income households or very low income households, as defined in Sections 50079.5 and 50105.

(4) The development is in an area with a need for additional affordable housing.

(5) If applicable, Article XXXIV of the California Constitution permits the development.

(6) The city in which the development is to be constructed has certified to the agency that the city's redevelopment agency, if one exists, is not subject to sanctions pursuant to subdivision (e) of Section 33334.12 for failure to expend or encumber a housing fund excess surplus.

(b) If the agency uses these funds within the incorporated limits of a city, all of the following requirements shall apply:

(1) The funds shall be used only for the acquisition of land for, and the design and construction of, housing containing units affordable to lower income households or very low income households, as defined in Sections 50079.5 and 50105, or for the acquisition or rehabilitation of publicly assisted rental housing that is threatened with conversion to market rates.

(2) If less than all the units in the development are affordable to lower income households or very low income households, any agency assistance shall not exceed the amount needed to make the housing affordable to lower income households and very low income households.

(3) The units in the development that are affordable to lower income households or very low income households shall remain affordable for a period of at least 55 years. Compliance with this requirement shall be ensured by the execution and recordation of covenants and restrictions that, notwithstanding any other provision of law, shall run with the land.

(4) No development shall be located in a census tract where more than 50 percent of its population is very low income.

(5) Assisted developments shall be located on sites suitable for multifamily housing near public transportation.

(6) Developed units shall not be treated as meeting the regional housing needs allocation under both the city's and county's housing elements.

(7) The funds shall be used only for developments for which the city in which the development will be constructed has approved the agency's use of funds for the development or has granted land use approvals for the development.

(8) The aggregate number of units assisted by the county over each five-year period shall include at least 10 percent that are affordable to households earning 30 percent or less of the area median income, and at least 40 percent that are affordable to very low income households.

(c) The Orange County Development Agency shall make diligent efforts to obtain the development of low- and moderate-income housing in unincorporated areas, including in developing areas of the county.

33334.3 Low and moderate income housing fund

(a) The funds that are required by Section 33334.2 or 33334.6 to be used for the purposes of increasing, improving, and preserving the community's supply of low- and moderate-income housing shall be held in a separate Low and Moderate Income Housing Fund until used.

(b) Any interest earned by the Low and Moderate Income Housing Fund and any repayments or other income to the agency for loans, advances, or grants, of any kind from the Low and Moderate Income Housing Fund, shall accrue to and be deposited in, the fund and may only be used in the manner prescribed for the Low and Moderate Income Housing Fund.

(c) The moneys in the Low and Moderate Income Housing Fund shall be used to increase, improve, and preserve the supply of low- and moderate-income housing within the territorial jurisdiction of the agency.

(d) It is the intent of the Legislature that the Low and Moderate Income Housing Fund be used to the maximum extent possible to defray the costs of production, improvement, and preservation of low- and moderate-income housing and that the amount of money spent for planning and general administrative activities associated with the development, improvement, and preservation of that housing not be disproportionate to the amount actually spent for the costs of production, improvement, or preservation of that housing. The agency shall determine annually that the planning and administrative expenses are necessary for the production, improvement, or preservation of low- and moderate-income housing.

(e) (1) Planning and general administrative costs which may be paid with moneys from the Low and Moderate Income Housing Fund are those expenses incurred by the agency which are directly related to the programs and activities authorized under subdivision (e) of Section 33334.2 and are limited to the following:

(A) Costs incurred for salaries, wages, and related costs of the agency's staff or for services provided through interagency agreements, and agreements with contractors, including usual indirect costs related thereto.

(B) Costs incurred by a nonprofit corporation which are not directly attributable to a specific project.

(2) Legal, architectural, and engineering costs and other salaries, wages, and costs directly related to the planning and execution of a specific project that are authorized under subdivision (e) of Section 33334.2 and that are incurred by a nonprofit housing sponsor are not planning and administrative costs for the purposes of this section, but are instead project costs.

(f) (1) The requirements of this subdivision apply to all new or substantially rehabilitated housing units developed or otherwise assisted, with moneys from the Low and Moderate Income Housing Fund, pursuant to an agreement approved by an agency on or after January 1, 1988. Except to the extent that a longer period of time may be required by other provisions of law, the agency shall require that housing units subject to this subdivision shall remain available at affordable housing cost to, and occupied by, persons and families of low or moderate income and very low income and extremely low income households for the longest feasible time, but for not less than the following periods of time:

(A) Fifty-five years for rental units. However, the agency may replace rental units with equally affordable and comparable rental units in another location within the community if (i) the replacement units are available for occupancy prior to the displacement of any persons and families of low or moderate income residing in the units to be replaced and (ii) the comparable replacement units are not developed with moneys from the Low and Moderate Income Housing Fund.

(B) Forty-five years for owner-occupied units. However, the agency may permit sales of owner-occupied units prior to the expiration of the 45-year period for a price in excess of that otherwise permitted under this subdivision pursuant to an adopted program which protects the agency's investment of moneys from the Low and Moderate Income Housing Fund, including, but not limited to, an equity sharing program which establishes a schedule of equity sharing that permits retention by the seller of a portion of those excess proceeds based on the length of occupancy. The remainder of the excess proceeds of the sale shall be allocated to the agency and deposited in the Low and Moderate Income Housing Fund. Only the units originally assisted by the agency shall be counted towards the agency's obligations under Section 33413.

(C) Fifteen years for mutual self-help housing units that are occupied by and affordable to very low and low-income households. However, the agency may permit sales of mutual self-help housing units prior to expiration of the 15- year period for a price in excess of that otherwise permitted under this subdivision pursuant to an adopted program that (i) protects the agency's investment of moneys from the Low and Moderate Income Housing Fund, including, but not limited to, an equity sharing program that establishes a schedule of equity sharing that permits retention by the seller of a portion of those excess proceeds based on the length of occupancy; and (ii) ensures through a recorded regulatory agreement, deed of trust, or similar recorded instrument that if a mutual self-help housing unit is sold at any time after expiration of the 15-year period and prior to 45 years after the date of recording of the covenants or restrictions required pursuant to paragraph (2), the agency recovers, at a minimum, its original principal from the Low and Moderate Income Housing Fund from the proceeds of the sale and deposits those funds into the Low and Moderate Income Housing Fund. The remainder of the excess proceeds of the sale not retained by the seller shall be allocated to the agency and deposited in the Low and Moderate Income Housing Fund. For the purposes of this subparagraph, "mutual self-help housing unit" means an owner-occupied housing unit for which persons and families of very low and low income contribute no fewer than 500 hours of their own labor in individual or group efforts to provide a decent, safe, and sanitary ownership housing unit for themselves, their families, and others authorized to occupy that unit. Nothing in this subparagraph precludes the agency and the developer of the mutual self-help housing units from agreeing to 45-year deed restrictions.

(2) If land on which those dwelling units are located is deleted from the project area, the agency shall continue to require that those units remain affordable as specified in this subdivision.

(3) The agency shall require the recording in the office of the county recorder of the following documents:

(A) The covenants or restrictions implementing this subdivision for each parcel or unit of real property subject to this subdivision. The agency shall obtain and maintain a copy of the recorded covenants or restrictions for not less than the life of the covenant or restriction.

(B) For all new or substantially rehabilitated units developed or otherwise assisted with moneys from the Low and Moderate Income Housing Fund on or after January 1, 2008, a separate document called "Notice of Affordability Restrictions on Transfer of Property," set forth in 14-point type or larger. This document shall contain all of the following information:

(i) A recitation of the affordability covenants or restrictions. If the document recorded under this subparagraph is recorded concurrently with the covenants or restrictions recorded under subparagraph (A), the recitation of the affordability covenants or restrictions shall also reference the concurrently recorded document. If the document recorded under this subparagraph is not recorded concurrently with the covenants or restrictions recorded under subparagraph (A), the recitation of the affordability covenants or restrictions shall also reference the recorder's identification number of the document recorded under subparagraph (A).

(ii) The date the covenants or restrictions expire.

(iii) The street address of the property, including, if applicable, the unit number.

(iv) The assessor's parcel number for the property.

(v) The legal description of the property.

(4) The agency shall require the recording of the document required under subparagraph (B) of paragraph (3) not more than 30 days after the date of recordation of the covenants or restrictions required under subparagraph (A) of paragraph (3).

(5) The county recorder shall index the documents required to be recorded under paragraph (3) by the agency and current owner.

(6) Notwithstanding Section 27383 of the Government Code, a county recorder may charge all authorized recording fees to any party, including a public agency, for recording the document specified in subparagraph (B) of paragraph (3).

(7) Notwithstanding any other provision of law, the covenants or restrictions implementing this subdivision shall run with the land and shall be enforceable against any owner who violates a covenant or restriction and each successor in interest who continues the violation, by any of the following:

(A) The agency.

(B) The community, as defined in Section 33002.

(C) A resident of a unit subject to this subdivision.

(D) A residents' association with members who reside in units subject to this subdivision.

(E) A former resident of a unit subject to this subdivision who last resided in that unit.

(F) An applicant seeking to enforce the covenants or restrictions for a particular unit that is subject to this subdivision, if the applicant conforms to all of the following:

(i) Is of low or moderate income, as defined in Section 50093.

(ii) Is able and willing to occupy that particular unit.

(iii) Was denied occupancy of that particular unit due to an alleged breach of a covenant or restriction implementing this subdivision.

(G) A person on an affordable housing waiting list who is of low or moderate income, as defined in Section 50093, and who is able and willing to occupy a unit subject to this subdivision.

(8) A dwelling unit shall not be counted as satisfying the affordable housing requirements of this part, unless covenants for that dwelling unit are recorded in compliance with subparagraph (A) of paragraph (3).

(9) Failure to comply with the requirements of subparagraph (B) of paragraph (3) shall not invalidate any covenants or restrictions recorded pursuant to subparagraph (A) of paragraph 3.

(g) "Housing," as used in this section, includes residential hotels, as defined in subdivision (k) of Section 37912. The definitions of "lower income households," "very low income households," and "extremely low income households" in Sections 50079.5, 50105, and 50106 shall apply to this section. "Longest feasible time," as used in this section, includes, but is not limited to, unlimited duration.

(h) "Increasing, improving, and preserving the community's supply of low- and moderate-income housing," as used in this section and in Section 33334.2, includes the preservation of rental housing units assisted by federal, state, or local government on the condition that units remain affordable to, and occupied by, low- and moderate-income households, including extremely low and very low income households, for the longest feasible time, but not less than 55 years, beyond the date the subsidies and use restrictions could be terminated and the assisted housing units converted to market rate rentals. In preserving these units the agency shall require that the units remain affordable to, and occupied by, persons and families of low- and moderate-income and extremely low and very low income households for the longest feasible time but not less than 55 years. However, the agency may replace rental units with equally affordable and comparable rental units in another location within the community if (1) the replacement units in another location are available for occupancy prior to the displacement of any persons and families of low or moderate income residing in the units to be replaced and (2) the comparable replacement units are not developed with moneys from the Low and Moderate Income Housing Fund.

(i) Agencies that have more than one project area may satisfy the requirements of Sections 33334.2 and 33334.6 and of this section by allocating, in any fiscal year, less than 20 percent in one project area, if the difference between the amount allocated and the 20 percent required is instead allocated, in that same fiscal year, to the Low and Moderate Income Housing Fund from tax increment revenues from other project areas. Prior to allocating funds pursuant to this subdivision, the agency shall make the finding required by subdivision (g) of Section 33334.2.

(j) Funds from the Low and Moderate Income Housing Fund shall not be used to the extent that other reasonable means of private or commercial financing of the new or substantially rehabilitated units at the same level of affordability and quantity are reasonably available to the agency or to the owner of the units. Prior to the expenditure of funds from the Low and Moderate Income

Housing Fund for new or substantially rehabilitated housing units, where those funds will exceed 50 percent of the cost of producing the units, the agency shall find, based on substantial evidence, that the use of the funds is necessary because the agency or owner of the units has made a good faith attempt but been unable to obtain commercial or private means of financing the units at the same level of affordability and quantity.

33334.4 Public policy for expenditure of housing funds

(a) Except as specified in subdivision (d), each agency shall expend, over each 10-year period of the implementation plan, as specified in clause (iii) of subparagraph (A) of paragraph (2) of subdivision (a) of Section 33490, the moneys in the Low and Moderate Income Housing Fund to assist housing for persons of low income and housing for persons of very low income in at least the same proportion as the total number of housing units needed for each of those income groups bears to the total number of units needed for persons of moderate, low and very low income within the community, as those needs have been determined for the community pursuant to Section 65584 of the Government Code. In determining compliance with this obligation, the agency may adjust the proportion by subtracting from the need identified for each income category, the number of units for persons of that income category that are newly constructed over the duration of the implementation plan with other locally controlled government assistance and without agency assistance and that are required to be affordable to, and occupied by, persons of the income category for at least 55 years for rental housing and 45 years for ownership housing, except that in making an adjustment the agency may not subtract units developed pursuant to a replacement housing obligation under state or federal law.

(b) Each agency shall expend over the duration of each redevelopment implementation plan, the moneys in the Low and Moderate Income Housing Fund to assist housing that is available to all persons regardless of age in at least the same proportion as the number of low-income households with a member under age 65 years bears to the total number of low-income households of the community as reported in the most recent census of the United States Census Bureau.

(c) An agency that has deposited in the Low and Moderate Income Housing Fund over the first five years of the period of an implementation plan an aggregate that is less than two million dollars ($2,000,000) shall have an extra five years to meet the requirements of this section.

(d) For the purposes of this section, "locally controlled" means government assistance where the community or other local government entity has the discretion and the authority to determine the recipient and the amount of the assistance, whether or not the source of the funds or other assistance is from the state or federal government. Examples of locally controlled government assistance include, but are not limited to, Community Development Block Grant Program (42 U.S.C. Sec. 5301 and following) funds allocated to a city or county, Home Investment Partnership Program (42 U.S.C. Sec. 12721 and following) funds allocated to a city or county, fees or funds received by a city or county pursuant to a city or county authorized program, and the waiver or deferral of city or other charges.

33334.5 Replacement housing

Every redevelopment plan adopted or amended to expand the project area after January 1, 1977, shall contain a provision that whenever dwelling units housing persons and families of low or moderate income are destroyed or removed from the low- and moderate-income housing market as part of a redevelopment project, the agency shall, within four years of such destruction or removal, rehabilitate, develop, or construct, or cause to be rehabilitated, developed, or constructed, for rental or sale to persons and families of low or moderate income an equal number of replacement dwelling units at affordable housing costs, as defined by Section 50052.5, within the project area or within the territorial jurisdiction of the agency. in accordance with all of the provisions of Sections 33413 and 33413.5.

33334.6 Low and moderate income housing set aside: retrospective application; purposes; findings

(a) The Legislature finds and declares that the provision of housing is itself a fundamental purpose of the Community Redevelopment Law and that a generally inadequate statewide supply of decent, safe, and sanitary housing affordable to persons and families of low or moderate income, as defined by Section 50093, threatens the accomplishment of the primary purposes of the Community Redevelopment Law, including job creation, attracting new private investments, and creating physical, economic, social, and environmental conditions to remove and prevent the recurrence of blight. The Legislature further finds and declares that the provision and improvement of affordable housing, as provided by Section 33334.2, outside of redevelopment project areas can be of direct benefit to those projects in assisting the accomplishment of project objectives whether or not those redevelopment projects provide for housing within the project area. The Legislature finds and determines that the provision of affordable housing by redevelopment agencies and the use of taxes allocated to the agency pursuant to subdivision (b) of Section 33670 is of statewide benefit and of particular benefit and assistance to all local governmental agencies in the areas where the housing is provided.

(b) This section is applicable to all project areas, or portions of project areas, which are not subject to Section 33334.2, except that a project area, or portion of a project area, for which a resolution was adopted pursuant to subdivision (i) of Section 33334.2 is subject to this section. Project areas subject to this section which are merged are subject to the requirements of both this section and Section 33487. The deposit of taxes into the Low and Moderate Income Housing Fund in compliance with either this section or Section 33487 shall satisfy the requirements of both sections in the year those taxes are deposited.

(c) Except as otherwise permitted by subdivisions (d) and (e), not less than 20 percent of the taxes allocated to the agency pursuant to Section 33670 from project areas specified in subdivision (b) for the 1985-86 fiscal year and each succeeding fiscal year shall be deposited into the Low and Moderate Income Housing Fund established pursuant to Section 33334.3 and used for the purposes set forth in Section 33334.2, unless the agency, by resolution, makes one of the findings described in paragraphs (1) to (3), inclusive, of subdivision (a) of Section 33334.2, except that the authority to make the finding specified in paragraph (3) of subdivision (a) of that section shall expire as specified in that paragraph. Subdivisions (b) and (c) of Section 33334.2 apply if an agency makes any of those findings.

(d) In any fiscal year, the agency may deposit less than the amount required by subdivision (c) into the Low and Moderate Income Housing Fund if the agency finds that the difference between the amount deposited and the amount required by subdivision (c) is necessary to make payments under existing obligations of amounts due or required to be committed, set aside, or reserved by the agency during that fiscal year and which are used by the agency for that purpose. For purposes of this section, "existing obligations" means the principal of, and interest on, loans, moneys advanced to, or indebtedness (whether funded, refunded, assumed, or otherwise) incurred by the agency to finance or refinance, in whole or in part, any redevelopment project existing on, and created prior to January 1, 1986, and contained on the statement of existing obligations adopted pursuant to subdivision (f). Obligations incurred on or after January 1, 1986, shall be deemed existing obligations for purposes of this section if the net proceeds are used to refinance existing obligations contained on the statement.

(e) In each fiscal year prior to July 1, 1996, the agency may deposit less than the amount required by subdivisions (c) and (d) into the Low and Moderate Income Housing Fund if the agency finds that the deposit of less than the amount required by those subdivisions is necessary in order to provide for the orderly and timely completion of public and private projects, programs, or activities approved by the agency prior to January 1, 1986, which are contained on the statement of existing programs adopted pursuant to subdivision (f). Approval of these projects, programs, and activities means approval by the agency of written documents which demonstrate an intent to implement a specific project, program, or activity and is not limited to final approval of a specific project, program, or activity.

(f) Any agency which deposits less than the amount required by subdivision (c) into the Low and Moderate Income Housing Fund pursuant to subdivision (d) or (e) shall adopt prior to September 1, 1986, by resolution, after a noticed public hearing, a statement of existing obligations or a statement of existing programs, or both.

(1) The agency shall prepare and submit the proposed statement to the legislative body and to the Department of Housing and Community Development prior to giving notice of the public hearing. Notice of the time and place of the public hearing shall be transmitted to the Department of Housing and Community Development at least 15 days prior to the public hearing and notice of the time and place of the public hearing shall be published in a newspaper of general circulation in the community once a week for at least two successive weeks prior to the public hearing. The legislative body shall maintain a record of the public hearing.

(2) A copy of the resolution adopted by the agency, together with any amendments to the statement of the agency, shall be transmitted to the Department of Housing and Community Development within 10 days following adoption of the resolution by the agency.

(3) A statement of existing obligations shall describe each existing obligation and, based upon the best available information, as determined by the agency, list the total amount of the existing obligation, the annual payments required to be made by the agency pursuant to the existing obligation, and the date the existing obligation will be discharged in full.

(4) A statement of existing programs shall list the specific public and private projects, programs, or activities approved prior to January 1, 1986, which are necessary for the orderly completion of the redevelopment plan as it existed on January 1, 1986.

No project, program, or activity shall be included on the statement of existing programs unless written evidence of the existence and approval of the project, program, or activity prior to January 1, 1986, is attached to the statement of existing programs.

(g) If, pursuant to subdivision (d) or (e), the agency deposits less than 20 percent of the taxes allocated to the agency pursuant to Section 33670 in the 1985–86 fiscal year or any subsequent fiscal year in the Low and Moderate Income Housing Fund, the amount equal to the difference between 20 percent of the taxes allocated to the agency pursuant to Section 33670 for each affected project and the amount deposited that year shall constitute a deficit of the project. The agency shall adopt a plan to eliminate the deficit in subsequent years as determined by the agency.

(h) The obligations imposed by this section, including deficits, if any, created under this section, are hereby declared to be an indebtedness of the redevelopment project to which they relate, payable from taxes allocated to the agency pursuant to Section 33670, and shall constitute an indebtedness of the agency with respect to the redevelopment project until paid in full.

(i) In any litigation to challenge or attack a statement of existing obligations, the decision by the agency after the public hearing to include an existing obligation on the statement of existing obligations, or the decision by the agency after the public hearing to include a project, program, or activity on the statement of existing programs, the court shall uphold the action of the agency unless the court finds that the agency has abused its discretion. The Legislature finds and declares that this standard of review is necessary in order to protect against the possible impairment of existing obligations, programs, and activities because agencies with project areas adopted prior to January 1, 1977, have incurred existing obligations and have adopted projects, programs, and activities with the authority to receive and pledge the entire allocation of funds authorized by Section 33670.

33334.7 Low and moderate income housing programs: priority consideration for assistance

Programs to assist or develop low- and moderate-income housing pursuant to Sections 33334.2, 33334.3, 33334.6, 33413, and 33449 shall be entitled to priority consideration for assistance in housing programs administered by the California Housing Finance Agency, the Department of Housing and Community Development, and other state agencies and departments, if those agencies or departments determine that the housing is otherwise eligible for assistance under a particular program.

33334.8 Multifamily rental housing: notice requirements

The same notice requirements as specified in Section 65863.10 of the Government Code shall apply to multifamily rental housing that receives financial assistance pursuant to Sections 33334.2, 33334.3, and 33334.6.

33334.9 Low and moderate income housing set aside: credit for certain assistance

Notwithstanding Sections 33334.2 and 33334.3, assistance provided by an agency to preserve the availability to lower income households of affordable housing units which are assisted or subsidized by public entities and which are threatened with imminent conversion to market rates may be credited and offset against an agency's obligations under Section 33334.2.

33334.10 Low and moderate income housing fund: excess surplus; plan for expenditure

(a) Except as otherwise provided in this subdivision, not later than six months following the close of any fiscal year of an agency in which excess surplus accumulates in the agency's Low and Moderate Income Housing Fund, the agency may adopt a plan pursuant to this section for expenditure of all moneys in the Low and Moderate Income Housing Fund within five years from the end of that fiscal year. The plan may be general and need not be site-specific, but shall include objectives respecting the number and type of housing to be assisted, identification of the entities, which will administer the plan, alternative means of ensuring the affordability of housing units for the longest feasible time, as specified in subdivision (e) of Section 33334.3 the income groups to be assisted, and a schedule by fiscal year for expenditure of the excess surplus.

(b) The agency shall separately account for each excess surplus either as part of or in addition to a Low and Moderate Income Housing Fund.

(c) If the agency develops a plan for expenditure of excess surplus or other moneys in the Low and Moderate Income Housing Fund, a copy of that plan and any amendments thereto shall be included in the agency's annual report required by Article 6 (commencing with Section 33080).

33334.12 Low and moderate income housing fund: transfer of excess surplus after 1 year

(a) (1) Upon failure of the agency to expend or encumber excess surplus in the Low and Moderate Income Housing Fund within one year from the date the moneys become excess surplus, as defined in paragraph (1) of subdivision (g), the agency shall do either of the following:

(A) Disburse voluntarily its excess surplus to the county housing authority or to another public agency exercising housing development powers within the territorial jurisdiction of the agency in accordance with subdivision (b).

(B) Expend or encumber its excess surplus within two additional years.

(2) If an agency, after three years has elapsed from the date that the moneys become excess surplus, has not expended or encumbered its excess surplus, the agency shall be subject to sanctions pursuant to subdivision (e), until the agency has expended or encumbered its excess surplus plus an additional amount, equal to 50 percent of the amount of the excess surplus that remains at the end of the three-year period. The additional expenditure shall not be from the agency's Low and Moderate Income Housing Fund, but shall be used in a manner that meets all requirements for expenditures from that fund.

(b) The housing authority or other public agency to which the money is transferred shall utilize the moneys for the purposes of, and subject to the same restrictions that are applicable to, the redevelopment agency under this part, and for that purpose may exercise all of the powers of a housing authority under Part 2 (commencing with Section 34200) to an extent not inconsistent with these limitations.

(c) Notwithstanding Section 34209 or any other provision of law, for the purpose of accepting a transfer of, and using, moneys pursuant to this section, the housing authority of a county or other public agency may exercise its powers within the territorial jurisdiction of a city redevelopment agency located in that county.

(d) The amount of excess surplus that shall be transferred to the housing authority or other public agency because of a failure of the redevelopment agency to expend or encumber excess surplus within one year shall be the amount of the excess surplus that is not so expended or encumbered. The housing authority or other public agency to which the moneys are transferred shall expend or encumber these moneys for authorized purposes not later than three years after the date these moneys were transferred from the Low and Moderate Income Housing Fund.

(e) (1) Until a time when the agency has expended or encumbered excess surplus moneys pursuant to subdivision (a), the agency shall be prohibited from encumbering any funds or expending any moneys derived from any source, except that the agency may encumber funds and expend moneys to pay the following obligations, if any, that were incurred by the agency prior to three years from the date the moneys became excess surplus:

(A) Bonds, notes, interim certificates, debentures, or other obligations issued by an agency, whether funded, refunded, assumed, or otherwise, pursuant to Article 5 (commencing with Section 33640).

(B) Loans or moneys advanced to the agency, including, but not limited to, loans from federal, state, or local agencies, or a private entity.

(C) Contractual obligations which, if breached, could subject the agency to damages or other liabilities or remedies.

(D) Obligations incurred pursuant to Section 33445.

(E) Indebtedness incurred pursuant to Section 33334.2 or 33334.6.

(F) Obligations incurred pursuant to Section 33401.

(G) An amount, to be expended for the operation and administration of the agency, that may not exceed 75 percent of the amount spent for those purposes in the preceding fiscal year.

(2) This subdivision shall not be construed to prohibit the expenditure of excess surplus funds or other funds to meet the requirement in paragraph (2) of subdivision (a) that the agency spend or encumber excess surplus funds, plus an amount equal to 50 percent of excess surplus, prior to spending or encumbering funds for any other purpose.

(f) Nothing in this section shall be construed to limit any authority a redevelopment agency may have under other provisions of this part to contract with a housing authority for increasing or improving the community's supply of low- and moderate-income housing.

(g) For purposes of this section:

(1) "Excess surplus" means any unexpended and unencumbered amount in an agency's Low and Moderate Income Housing Fund that exceeds the greater of one million dollars ($1,000,000) or the aggregate amount deposited into the Low and Moderate Income Housing Fund pursuant to Sections 33334.2 and 33334.6 during the agency's preceding four fiscal years. The first fiscal year to be included in this computation is the 1989–90 fiscal year, and the first date on which an excess surplus may exist is July 1, 1994.

(2) Moneys shall be deemed encumbered if committed pursuant to a legally enforceable contract or agreement for expenditure for purposes specified in Section 33334.2 or 33334.3.

(3) (A) For purposes of determining whether an excess surplus exists, it is the intent of the Legislature to give credit to

agencies which convey land for less than fair market value, on which low- and moderate-income housing is built or is to be built if at least 49 percent of the units developed on the land are available at affordable housing cost to lower income households for at least the time specified in subdivision (e) of Section 33334.3, and otherwise comply with all of the provisions of this division applicable to expenditures of moneys from a low- and moderate-income housing fund established pursuant to Section 33334.3. Therefore, for the sole purpose of determining the amount, if any, of an excess surplus, an agency may make the following calculation: if an agency sells, leases, or grants land acquired with moneys from the Low and Moderate Income Housing Fund, established pursuant to Section 33334.3, for an amount which is below fair market value, and if at least 49 percent of the units constructed or rehabilitated on the land are affordable to lower income households, as defined in Section 50079.5, the difference between the fair market value of the land and the amount the agency receives may be subtracted from the amount of moneys in an agency's Low and Moderate Income Housing Fund.

(B) If taxes that are deposited in the Low and Moderate Income Housing Fund are used as security for bonds or other indebtedness, the proceeds of the bonds or other indebtedness, and income and expenditures related to those proceeds, shall not be counted in determining whether an excess surplus exists. The unspent portion of the proceeds of bonds or other indebtedness, and income related thereto, shall be excluded from the calculation of the unexpended and unencumbered amount in the Low and Moderate Income Housing Fund when determining whether an excess surplus exists.

(C) Nothing in this subdivision shall be construed to restrict the authority of an agency provided in any other provision of this part to expend funds from the Low and Moderate Income Housing Fund.

(D) The department shall develop and periodically revise the methodology to be used in the calculation of excess surplus as required by this section. The director shall appoint an advisory committee to advise in the development of this methodology. The advisory committee shall include department staff, affordable housing advocates, and representatives of the California Redevelopment Association, the California Society of Certified Public Accountants, the Controller, and any other authorities or persons interested in the field that the director deems necessary and appropriate.

(h) Communities in which an agency has disbursed excess surplus funds pursuant to this section shall not disapprove a low- or moderate-income housing project funded in whole or in part by the excess surplus funds if the project is consistent with applicable building codes and the land use designation specified in any element of the general plan as it existed on the date the application was deemed complete. A local agency may require compliance with local development standards and policies appropriate to and consistent with meeting the quantified objectives relative to the development of housing, as required in housing elements of the community pursuant to subdivision (b) of Section 65583 of the Government Code.

(i) Notwithstanding subdivision (a), any agency that has funds that become excess surplus on July 1, 1994, shall have, pursuant to subdivision (a), until January 1, 1995, to decide to transfer the funds to a housing authority or other public agency, or until January 1, 1997, to expend or encumber those funds, or face sanctions pursuant to subdivision (e).

33334.13 Assistance to mortgagors: area median income defined; limitations

(a) Notwithstanding Sections 50079.5, 50093, and 50105, for purposes of providing assistance to mortgagors participating in a homeownership residential mortgage revenue bond program pursuant to Section 33750, or a home financing program pursuant to Section 52020, or a California Housing Finance Agency home financing program, "area median income" means the highest of the following:

(1) Statewide median household income.
(2) Countywide median household income.
(3) Median family income for the area, as determined by the United States Department of Housing and Urban Development with respect to either a standard metropolitan statistical area or an area outside of a standard metropolitan statistical area.

Nothing in Section 50093 shall prevent the agency from adopting separate family size adjustment factors or programmatic definitions of income to qualify households, persons, and families for the programs of the agency.

(b) To the extent that any portion of the Low and Moderate Income Housing Fund is expended to provide assistance to mortgagors participating in programs whose income exceeds that of persons and families of low or moderate income, as defined in Section 50093, the agency shall, within two years, expend or enter into a legally enforceable agreement to expend twice that sum exclusively to increase and improve the community's supply of housing available at affordable housing cost, as defined in Section 50052.5, to lower income households, as defined in Section 50079.5, of which at least 50 percent shall be very low income households, as defined in Section 50105.

(c) In addition to the requirements of subdivision (c) of Section 33413, the agency shall require that the lower and very low income dwelling units developed pursuant to this subdivision remain available at affordable housing cost to lower and very low income households for at least 30 years, except as to dwelling units developed with the assistance of federal or state subsidy programs which terminate in a shorter period and cannot be extended or renewed.

(d) The agency shall include within the report required by Section 33080 information with respect to compliance by the agency with the requirements of this subdivision.

33334.14 Low and moderate income housing affordability restrictions: subordination

(a) The covenants or restrictions imposed by the agency pursuant to subdivision (e) of Section 33334.3 may be subordinated under any of the following alternatives:

(1) To a lien, encumbrance, or regulatory agreement under a federal or state program when a federal or state agency is providing financing, refinancing, or other assistance to the housing units or parcels, if the federal or state agency refuses to consent to the seniority of the agency's covenant or restriction on the basis that it is required to maintain its lien, encumbrance, or regulatory agreement or restrictions due to statutory or regulatory requirements, adopted or approved policies, or other guidelines pertaining to the financing, refinancing, or other assistance of the housing units or parcels.

(2) To a lien, encumbrance, or regulatory agreement of a lender other than the agency or from a bond issuance providing

financing, refinancing, or other assistance of owner-occupied units or parcels where the agency makes a finding that an economically feasible alternative method of financing, refinancing, or assisting the units or parcels on substantially comparable terms and conditions, but without subordination, is not reasonably available.

(3) To an existing lien, encumbrance, or regulatory agreement of a lender other than the agency or from a bond issuance providing financing, refinancing, or other assistance of rental units, where the agency's funds are utilized for rehabilitation of the rental units.

(4) To a lien, encumbrance, or regulatory agreement of a lender other than the agency or from a bond issuance providing financing, refinancing, or other assistance of rental units or parcels where the agency makes a finding that an economically feasible alternative method of financing, refinancing, or assisting the units or parcels on substantially comparable terms and conditions, but without subordination, is not reasonably available, and where the agency obtains written commitments reasonably designed to protect the agency's investment in the event of default, including, but not limited to, any of the following:

(A) A right of the agency to cure a default on the loan.

(B) A right of the agency to negotiate with the lender after notice of default from the lender.

(C) An agreement that if prior to foreclosure of the loan, the agency takes title to the property and cures the default on the loan, the lender will not exercise any right it may have to accelerate the loan by reason of the transfer of title to the agency.

(D) A right of the agency to purchase property from the owner at any time after a default on the loan.

(b) Notwithstanding the definition of "construction and rehabilitation" in subdivision (a) of Section 33487, an agency that has merged redevelopment projects pursuant to Article 16 (commencing with Section 33485) of Chapter 4, and that is required to deposit taxes into the Low and Moderate Income Housing Fund pursuant to subdivision (a) of Section 33487, may use any of the funds for the purposes and in the manner permitted by Sections 33334.2 and 33334.3. Nothing in this subdivision shall allow an agency with merged project areas pursuant to Article 16 (commencing with Section 33485) to utilize the provisions of paragraph (1), (2), or (3) of subdivision (a) of Section 33334.2 so as to avoid or reduce its obligations to deposit taxes from merged project areas into the Low and Moderate Income Housing Fund.

33334.15 Low and moderate income housing: subsidies

Subsidies provided pursuant to paragraph (8) of subdivision (e) of Section 33334.2 may include payment of a portion of the principal and interest on bonds issued by a public agency to finance housing for persons and families specified in that paragraph if the agency ensures by contract that the benefit of the subsidy will be passed on to those persons and families in the form of lower housing costs.

33334.16 Low and moderate income housing fund: time limit for development of real property acquired

For each interest in real property acquired using moneys from the Low and Moderate Income Housing Fund, the agency shall, within five years from the date it first acquires the property interest for the development of housing affordable to persons and families of low and moderate income, initiate activities consistent with the development of the property for that purpose. These activities may include, but are not limited to, zoning changes or agreements entered into for the development and disposition of the property. If these activities have not been initiated within this period, the legislative body may, by resolution, extend the period during which the agency may retain the property for one additional period not to exceed five years. The resolution of extension shall affirm the intention of the legislative body that the property be used for the development of housing affordable to persons and families of low and moderate income. In the event that physical development of the property for this purpose has not begun by the end of the extended period, or if the agency does not comply with this requirement, the property shall be sold and the moneys from the sale, less reimbursement to the agency for the cost of the sale, shall be deposited in the agency's Low and Moderate Income Housing Fund.

33334.19 Low and moderate income set aside: use within transit village plan

(a) Notwithstanding Section 33670 or any other provision of this division, an agency may increase, improve, and preserve the supply of low- and moderate-income housing located within a transit village plan adopted pursuant to the Transit Village Development Planning Act of 1994, Article 8.5 (commencing with Section 65460) of Chapter 3 of Division 1 of Title 7 of the Government Code, and is within its territorial limits but outside of a project area. In the event that the agency seeks to comply with any of its obligations under Section 33413 under a transit village plan, it shall provide two units outside of a project area, both of which shall be at the same level of affordability as, and otherwise comply with, all requirements pertaining to the unit that would otherwise have been available inside a project area.

(b) To implement subdivision (a), an agency may increase, improve, and preserve the supply of low- and moderate-income housing which is located within a transit village plan with funds from the Low and Moderate Income Housing Fund. In using these funds, the agency shall comply with all requirements of the Community Redevelopment Law (Division 24 (commencing with Section 33000) of the Health and Safety Code).

(c) To implement subdivision (a), notwithstanding subdivision (a) of Section 33670, an agency may determine the location and character of any residential construction which is located within a transit village plan and which is to be financed pursuant to Chapter 8 (commencing with Section 33750) and may make mortgage or construction loans to participating parties through qualified mortgage lenders, or purchase mortgage or construction loans without premium made by qualified mortgage lenders to participating parties, for financing residential construction of multifamily rental units located within a transit village plan.

(d) Expenditures from the Low and Moderate Income Housing Fund pursuant to this section shall be deemed to be part of the agency's redevelopment plans, as if those redevelopment plans had been amended to include those expenditures, and the agency is not required to comply with Article 12 (commencing with Section 33450). The Legislature hereby deems those expenditures to benefit the agency's project areas.

33334.22 Housing assistance: Santa Cruz County

(a) The Legislature finds and declares that in order to avoid serious economic hardships and accompanying blight, it is necessary to enact this section for the purpose of providing housing assistance to very low, lower, and moderate-income households. This section applies to any redevelopment agency located within Santa Cruz County, the Contra Costa County Redevelopment Agency, and the Monterey County Redevelopment Agency.

(b) Notwithstanding Section 50052.5, any redevelopment agency to which this section applies may make assistance available from its low- and moderate-income housing fund directly to a home buyer for the purchase of an owner-occupied home, and for purposes of that assistance and this section, "affordable housing cost" shall not exceed the following:

(1) For very low income households, the product of 40 percent times 50 percent of the area median income adjusted for family size appropriate for the unit.

(2) For lower income households whose gross incomes exceed the maximum income for very low income households and do not exceed 70 percent of the area median income adjusted for family size, the product of 40 percent times 70 percent of the area median income adjusted for family size appropriate for the unit. In addition, for any lower income household that has a gross income that equals or exceeds 70 percent of the area median income adjusted for family size, it shall be optional for any state or local funding agency to require that the affordable housing cost not exceed 40 percent of the gross income of the household.

(3) For moderate income households, affordable housing cost shall not exceed the product of 40 percent times 110 percent of the area median income adjusted for family size appropriate for the unit. In addition, for any moderate-income household that has a gross income that exceeds 110 percent of the area median income adjusted for family size, it shall be optional for any state or local funding agency to require that affordable housing cost not exceed 40 percent of the gross income of the household.

(c) Any agency that provides assistance pursuant to this section shall include in the annual report to the Controller, pursuant to Sections 33080 and 33080.1, all of the following information:

(1) The sales price of homes purchased with assistance from the agency's Low and Moderate Income Housing Fund for each year the program has been in operation.

(2) The sales price of homes purchased and rehabilitated with assistance from the agency's Low and Moderate Income Housing Fund for each year the program has been in operation.

(3) The incomes, and percentage of income paid for housing costs, of all households that purchased, and that purchased and rehabilitated, homes with assistance from the agency's Low and Moderate Income Housing Fund for each year the program has been in operation.

(d) Except as provided in subdivision (b), all provisions of Section 50052.5, including any definitions, requirements, standards, and regulations adopted to implement those provisions, shall apply to this section.

(e) This section shall remain in effect only until January 1, 2013, and as of that date is repealed, unless a later enacted statute, that is enacted before January 1, 2013, deletes or extends that date.

33334.25 Joint Powers Authority; conditions; legislative intent

(a) The Legislature finds and declares all of the following:

(1) The transfer of funds to a joint powers authority and the use of pooled funds within the housing market area of the participating agencies for the purpose of providing affordable housing is of benefit to the project area producing the tax increment.

(2) The cost and availability of land, geophysical and environmental limitations, community patterns, and the lack of financing make the availability of affordable housing more difficult in some communities.

(3) The cooperation of local agencies and the use of pooled funds will result in more resources than would otherwise be available for affordable housing.

(b) Notwithstanding any other provision of law, contiguous agencies located within adjoining cities within a single Metropolitan Statistical Area (MSA) may create and participate in a joint powers authority for the purpose of pooling their low- and moderate-income housing funds for affordable housing uses. Agencies may transfer a portion of their housing funds to a joint powers authority for use by the joint powers authority pursuant to this section. The joint powers authority may determine the kinds of housing projects or activities to be assisted, consistent with this section. The joint powers authority may loan, grant, or advance transferred housing funds from participating agencies to a receiving entity for any eligible housing development within the participating agency's jurisdiction, subject to the requirements of this section. In addition, the agreement may authorize the joint powers authority to issue bonds and to use the pooled funds to leverage other funds to assist eligible developments, including loans from private institutions and assistance provided by other governmental agencies.

(c) Each of the following conditions shall be met and described in a mutually binding agreement between the joint powers authority and each participating agency:

(1) The community of each participating agency shall have adopted up-to-date housing elements pursuant to Article 10.6 (commencing with Section 66580) of Division 1 of Title 7 of the Government Code, and the housing elements have been determined to be in compliance with the law by the Department of Housing and Community Development.

(2) The community of each participating agency shall have met, in its current or previous housing element cycle, 50 percent or more of its share of the region's affordable housing needs, as defined in Section 65584 of the Government Code, in the very low and lower income categories of income groups defined in Section 50025.5.

(3) Each participating agency shall hold, at least 45 days prior to the transfer of funds to the joint powers authority, a public hearing, after providing notice pursuant to Section 6062 of the Government Code to solicit public comments on the draft agreement.

(4) No housing funds shall be transferred from a project area that has an indebtedness to its low- and moderate-income housing fund pursuant to Section 33334.6.

(5) No housing funds shall be transferred from an agency that has not met its need for replacement housing pursuant to Section 33413, unless the agency has encumbered and contractually committed sufficient funds to meet those requirements.

(6) Pooled funds shall be used within the participating agencies' jurisdictions.

(7) The agreement shall require compliance by the joint powers authority with the provisions of this section.

(8) The joint powers authority shall ensure that the funds it receives are used in accordance with the requirements of this section.

(9) Funds transferred by an agency to a joint powers authority pursuant to this section shall be expended or encumbered

by the joint powers authority for the purposes of this section within two years of the transfer. Transferred funds not so expended or encumbered by the joint powers authority within two years after the transfer shall be returned to the original agency and shall be deemed excess surplus funds as provided in, and subject to, the requirements of Sections 33334.10 and 33334.12. Excess surplus funds held by an agency may not be transferred to a joint powers authority.

(10) The joint powers authority shall prepare and submit an annual report to the department that documents the amount of housing funds received and expended or allocated for specific housing assistance activities consistent with Section 33080.4.

(d) Each of the following conditions shall be met and described in a mutually binding contract between the joint powers authority and a receiving entity:

(1) Pooled housing funds may only be used to pay for the direct costs of constructing, substantially rehabilitating, or preserving the affordability of housing units that are affordable to very low or low income households. Units assisted with pooled funds shall remain available at affordable housing costs in accordance with subdivision (f) of Section 33334.3.

(2) Except as provided in this section, pooled housing funds may not be used in any way that is inconsistent with the requirements of Section 33334.3. Pooled housing funds may not be used to pay for planning and administrative costs, offsite improvements associated with a housing project, or fees or exactions levied solely for development projects constructed, substantially rehabilitated, or preserved with pooled funds. The receiving entity shall be subject to the same replacement requirements provided in Section 33413 and any relocation requirements applicable pursuant to Section 7260 of the Government Code.

(3) The joint powers authority shall make findings, based on substantial evidence on the record, that each proposed use of pooled funds will not exacerbate racial or economic segregation.

(4) The Department of Housing and Community Development has evaluated each proposed use of pooled funds to construct, substantially rehabilitate, or preserve the affordability of housing and determined that the proposed use is in compliance with this section. In considering whether a proposed use of funds will exacerbate racial or economic segregation, the department shall consider all of the following:

(A) The record of participating jurisdictions in meeting their share of the regional need for low and very low income households allocated to the jurisdiction pursuant to Section 65584 of the Government Code.

(B) The distance of the proposed housing from a redevelopment area from which pooled funds originated.

(C) The income and ethnicity of the residents of the census tract from which the pooled funds originated and in which the housing will be located.

(D) The housing need and availability of sufficient site for housing within jurisdictions from which pooled funds originated.

(e) As used in this section, the following terms shall apply:

(1) "Housing funds" mean funds in or from the low- and moderate-income housing fund established by an agency pursuant to Section 33334.3.

(2) "Joint powers authority" means a joint powers authority created pursuant to Chapter 5 (commencing with Section 6500) of Division 7 of Title 1 of the Government Code for the purposes of receiving and using housing funds pursuant to this section.

(3) "Receiving entity" means any person, partnership, joint venture, corporation, governmental body, or other organization receiving housing funds from a joint powers authority for the purpose of providing housing pursuant to this section.

(f) On or after January 1, 2008, no participating agency shall create a new joint powers authority or transfer funds to an existing joint powers authority pursuant to this section, unless a later enacted statute, which is enacted before January 1, 2008, deletes or extends that date.

(g) This section shall remain in effect only until January 1, 2010, and as of that date is repealed, unless a later enacted statute, that is enacted on or before January 1, 2010, deletes or extends that date.

33334.28 Public policy for expenditure of housing funds—City of Covina

(a) Until January 1, 2012, subdivision (b) of Section 33334.4 shall not apply to the Redevelopment Agency of the City of Covina insofar as it exceeds the authorized ratio due exclusively to the use of Low and Moderate Income Housing Fund moneys to continue to provide rental subsidies to households with members over the age of 65 years if those rental subsidies were initially provided to these households prior to January 1, 2002.

(b) This section shall remain in effect only until January 1, 2012, and as of that date is repealed, unless a later enacted statute, that is enacted before January 1, 2012, deletes or extends that date.

33334.29 Public policy for expenditure of housing funds—City of Redding

(a) Notwithstanding Sections 33334.2, 33334.3, and 33334.6, the redevelopment agency of the City of Redding, of the County of Shasta, or of any other city located within the County of Shasta, may borrow and use up to two million three hundred thousand dollars ($2,300,000) from its Low and Moderate Income Housing Fund to provide financial assistance for the acquisition of property for a veterans home within the territorial jurisdiction of the agency of the City of Redding. As used in this section, "veterans' home" shall mean a veterans' home authorized pursuant to Division 5 (commencing with Section 1010) of the Military and Veterans Code.

(b) Funds borrowed pursuant to subdivision (a) shall be repaid within 15 years from the date they are loaned, with interest at the rate earned from time to time on funds deposited in the State of California Local Agency Investment Fund. The indebtedness created pursuant to this section shall not be considered to meet the requirements imposed by Section 33333.8, and the agency shall comply in full with that section. If a redevelopment agency described in subdivision (a) is required to remit an amount of tax increment funds to the county auditor for deposit in the county's Educational Revenue Augmentation Fund, created pursuant to Article 3 (commencing with Section 97) of Chapter 6 of Part 0.5 of Division 1 of the Revenue and Taxation Code, then the time limit on repayment of the funds borrowed pursuant to this section shall be suspended for one year after the funds are remitted to the county auditor. In addition, the agency shall receive and use tax increment funds to pay the loan described in subdivision (a) until the funds borrowed pursuant to subdivision (a) have been fully repaid. The agency may not incur any obligation with respect to loans, advance of money, or indebtedness, or whether funded, refunded, assumed or otherwise, that would impair or delay its ability or capacity to repay the funds loaned pursuant to this section; except that the agency may incur indebtedness against non-Low and Moderate Income Housing Fund moneys if the proceeds of the indebtedness will be used to repay the funds borrowed pursuant to this section.

33334.30 Public policy for expenditure of housing funds– County of San Mateo

(a) The Legislature finds and declares all of the following:

(1) The transfer of funds to a joint powers authority and the use of pooled funds within the housing market area of the County of San Mateo, within one-third of a mile of the Peninsula Corridor Joint Powers Authority right-of-way, on property provided by the San Mateo County Transit Authority for the purpose of providing affordable housing that is of benefit to the project area producing the tax increment.

(2) The cooperation of local agencies and the use of pooled funds result in more resources than would otherwise be available for affordable housing.

(b) Notwithstanding any other provision of law, an agency of a community within San Mateo County that has a housing element certified by the Department of Housing and Community Development and has met 40 percent of its very low and low-income housing needs may create and participate in a joint powers authority for the purpose of pooling low- and moderate-income housing funds for affordable housing uses pursuant to this section. No participating agency may transfer in any fiscal year more than 25 percent of the tax increment that is deposited into the Low and Moderate Income Housing Fund to a joint powers authority for use by the joint powers authority pursuant to this section. The joint powers authority may determine the kinds of housing projects or activities to be assisted, consistent with this section. The joint powers authority may loan, grant, or advance transferred housing funds from participating agencies to a receiving entity for any eligible housing development within the territorial jurisdiction of a participating agency in San Mateo County on property provided by the San Mateo County Transit District, the San Mateo County Transportation Authority, or the Peninsula Corridor Joint Powers Authority and located within one-half of a mile of the San Mateo County Transit District, the San Mateo County Transportation Authority or the Peninsula Corridor Joint Powers Authority right-of-way, subject to the requirements of this section. In addition, the agreement may authorize the joint powers authority to issue bonds and to use the pooled funds to leverage other funds to assist eligible developments, including loans from private institutions and assistance provided by other governmental agencies.

(c) Each of the following conditions shall be met and described in a mutually binding agreement between the joint powers authority and each participating agency:

(1) The community of each participating agency shall have adopted an up-to-date housing element pursuant to Article 10.6 (commencing with Section 65580) of Division 1 of Title 7 of the Government Code, that has been determined to be in substantial compliance with the law by the Department of Housing and Community Development.

(2) The community of each participating agency shall have met, in its current or previous housing element cycle, 40 percent or more of its share of the region's affordable housing needs, as defined in Section 65584 of the Government Code, in each of the very low and lower income categories of income groups defined in Section 50025.5.

(3) Each participating agency shall hold, at least 45 days prior to the transfer of funds to the joint powers authority, a public hearing, after providing notice pursuant to Section 6062 of the Government Code to solicit public comments on the draft agreement.

(4) No housing funds shall be transferred from a project area that has indebtedness to its Low and Moderate Income Housing Fund pursuant to Section 33334.6.

(5) No housing funds shall be transferred from an agency that has not met its need for replacement housing pursuant to Section 33413, unless the agency has encumbered and contractually committed sufficient funds to meet those requirements.

(6) Pooled funds shall be used within the territorial jurisdiction of a participating agency within the County of San Mateo, within one-half of a mile of the San Mateo County Transit District, the San Mateo County Transportation Authority, or the Peninsula Corridor Joint Powers Authority right-of-way on property provided by any of these entities.

(7) The agreement shall require compliance by the joint powers authority with the provisions of this section.

(8) The joint powers authority shall ensure that the funds it receives are used in accordance with this section.

(9) Funds transferred by an agency to a joint powers authority pursuant to this section shall be expended or encumbered by the joint powers authority for the purposes of this section within two years of the transfer. Transferred funds not so expended or encumbered by the joint powers authority within two years after the transfer shall be returned to the original agency and shall be deemed excess surplus funds as provided in, and subject to, the requirements of Sections 33334.10 and 33334.12. Excess surplus funds held by an agency may not be transferred to a joint powers authority.

(10) The joint powers authority shall prepare and submit an annual report to the department that documents the amount of housing funds received and expended or allocated for specific housing assistance activities consistent with Section 33080.4.

(d) Each of the following conditions shall be met and described in a mutually binding contract between the joint powers authority and a receiving entity:

(1) Pooled housing funds may only be used to pay for the direct costs of constructing, substantially rehabilitating, or preserving the affordability of housing units that are affordable to very low or low-income households. Units assisted with pooled funds shall remain available at affordable housing costs in accordance with subdivision (f) of Section 33334.3.

(2) Except as provided in this section, pooled housing funds may not be used in any way that is inconsistent with the requirements of Section 33334.3. Pooled housing funds may not be used to pay for planning and administrative costs, offsite improvements associated with a housing project, or fees or exactions levied solely for development projects constructed, substantially rehabilitated, or preserved with pooled funds. The receiving entity shall be subject to the same replacement requirements provided in Section 33413 and any relocation requirements applicable pursuant to Section 7260 of the Government Code.

(3) Pooled housing funds may not be used to construct a development in a census tract that currently has more than 50 percent of its population comprised of racial minorities or low-income families.

(4) The Department of Housing and Community Development has evaluated each proposed use of pooled funds to construct,

substantially rehabilitate, or preserve the affordability of housing and determined that the proposed use is in compliance with this section. In considering whether a proposed use of funds will exacerbate racial or economic segregation, the department shall consider all of the following:

(A) The record of participating jurisdictions in meeting their share of the regional need for very low and low-income households allocated to the jurisdiction pursuant to Section 65584 of the Government Code.

(B) The distance of the proposed housing from a redevelopment area from which pooled funds originated.

(C) The income and ethnicity of the residents of the census tract from which the pooled funds originated and in which the housing will be located.

(D) The housing need and availability of sufficient sites for housing within jurisdictions from which pooled funds originated.

(e) As used in this section, the following terms shall apply:

(1) "Housing funds" mean funds in or from the low- and moderate-income housing fund established by an agency pursuant to Section 33334.3.

(2) "Joint powers authority" means a joint powers authority created pursuant to Chapter 5 (commencing with Section 6500) of Division 7 of Title 1 of the Government Code for the purposes of receiving and using housing funds pursuant to this section.

(3) "Receiving entity" means any person, partnership, joint venture, corporation, governmental body, or other organization receiving housing funds from a joint powers authority for the purpose of providing housing pursuant to this section.

(f) On or after January 1, 2009, no participating agency shall create a new joint powers authority or transfer funds to an existing joint powers authority pursuant to this section, unless a later enacted statute, which is enacted before January 1, 2009, deletes or extends that date.

(g) This section shall remain in effect only until January 1, 2010, and as of that date is repealed, unless a later enacted statute, that is enacted on or before January 1, 2010, deletes or extends that date.

33335 Redevelopment plan to provide for lease or sale of real property

Every redevelopment plan shall provide for the agency to lease or sell all real property acquired by it in any project area, except property conveyed by it to the community.

33336 Redevelopment plan to provide safeguards and controls for proper redevelopment

Every redevelopment plan shall:

(a) Contain adequate safeguards that the work of redevelopment will be carried out pursuant to the plan;

(b) Provide for the retention of controls and the establishment of any restrictions or covenants running with land sold or leased for private use for such periods of time and under such conditions as the legislative body deems necessary to effectuate the purposes of this part. The establishment of such controls is a public purpose under the provisions of this part.

33337 Redevelopment plan to provide that instruments of transfer must contain nondiscrimination clauses

Every redevelopment plan shall contain a provision requiring that all deeds, leases, or contracts for the sale, lease, sublease, or other transfer of any land in a redevelopment project shall contain the nondiscrimination clauses prescribed in Section 33436.

33338 Redevelopment plan to provide other covenants, conditions and restrictions

Every redevelopment plan shall contain other covenants, conditions, and restrictions which the legislative body prescribes.

33339 Redevelopment plan to provide for owner participation

Every redevelopment plan shall provide for participation in the redevelopment of property in the project area by the owners of all or part of such property if the owners agree to participate in the redevelopment in conformity with the redevelopment plan adopted by the legislative body for the area.

33339.5 Redevelopment plan to provide for business reentry

Every redevelopment agency shall extend reasonable preference to persons who are engaged in business in the project area to reenter in business within the redeveloped area if they otherwise meet the requirements prescribed by the redevelopment plan.

With respect to each redevelopment project, each agency shall, within a reasonable time before its approval of the redevelopment plan adopt and make available for public inspection rules to implement the operation of this section in connection with the plan.

33340 Redevelopment plan to provide alternatives on failure of owner participation

Every redevelopment plan which contemplates property owner participation in the redevelopment of the project area shall contain alternative provisions for redevelopment of the property if the owners fail to participate in the redevelopment as agreed.

33341 Redevelopment plan may provide authority to issue bonds

Redevelopment plans may provide for the agency to issue bonds and expend the proceeds from their sale in carrying out the redevelopment plan. If such an issuance is provided for, the redevelopment plan shall also contain adequate provision for the payment of principal and interest when they become due and payable.

33342 Redevelopment plan may provide authority to acquire real property

Redevelopment plans may provide for the agency to acquire by gift, purchase, lease, or condemnation all or part of the real property in the project area.

33342.5 Redevelopment plan shall describe agency's eminent domain program–Plans adopted on or after January 1, 2007

(a) A redevelopment plan adopted on or after January 1, 2007, shall describe the agency's program to acquire real property by eminent domain.

(b) The plan may prohibit the agency from acquiring by eminent domain specified types of real property, including, but not limited to, owner-occupied residences, single-family residences, or any residential property. The plan may prohibit the agency from acquiring by eminent domain real property in specified locations within the project area.

(c) An agency's program to acquire real property by eminent domain may be changed only by amending the redevelopment plan pursuant to Article 12 (commencing with Section 33450).

33342.7 Redevelopment plan shall describe agency's eminent domain program–plans adopted prior to January 1, 2007

(a) A legislative body that adopted a final redevelopment plan before January 1, 2007, shall adopt an ordinance on or before July 1, 2007, that contains a description of the agency's program to acquire real property by eminent domain. The plan may prohibit the agency from acquiring by eminent domain specified types of real property, including, but not limited to, owner-occupied residences, single-family residences, or any residential property. The plan may prohibit the agency from acquiring by eminent domain real property in specified locations within the project area.

(b) An agency's program to acquire real property by eminent domain may be changed only by amending the redevelopment plan, pursuant to Article 12 (commencing with Section 33450).

33343 Redevelopment plan may provide for community expenditures

Redevelopment plans may provide for the expenditure of money by the community.

33344 Redevelopment plan may provide for community undertakings

Redevelopment plans may provide for the community to undertake and complete any proceedings necessary to carry out the project.

33344.5 Preliminary report to affected taxing entities

After receiving the report prepared pursuant to Section 33328, or after the time period for preparation of that report has passed, a redevelopment agency that includes a provision for the division of taxes pursuant to Section 33670 in the redevelopment plan shall prepare and send to each affected taxing entity, as defined in Section 33353.2, no later than the date specified in Section 33344.6, a preliminary report which shall contain all of the following:

(a) The reasons for the selection of the project area.

(b) A description of the physical and economic conditions existing in the project area.

(c) A description of the project area which is sufficiently detailed for a determination as to whether the project area is predominantly urbanized. The description shall include at least the following information, which shall be based upon the terms described and defined in Section 33320.1:

(1) The total number of acres within the project area.

(2) The total number of acres that is characterized by the condition described in paragraph (4) of subdivision (a) of Section 33031.

(3) The total number of acres that are in agricultural use. "Agricultural use" shall have the same meaning as that term is defined in subdivision (b) of Section 51201 of the Government Code.

(4) The total number of acres that is an integral part of an area developed for urban uses.

(5) The percent of property within the project area that is predominantly urbanized.

(6) A map of the project area that identifies the property described in paragraphs (2), (3), and (4), and the property not developed for an urban use.

(d) A preliminary assessment of the proposed method of financing the redevelopment of the project area, including an assessment of the economic feasibility of the project and the reasons for including a provision for the division of taxes pursuant to Section 33670 in the redevelopment plan.

(e) A description of the specific project or projects then proposed by the agency.

(f) A description of how the project or projects to be pursued by the agency in the project area will improve or alleviate the conditions described in subdivision (b).

(g) If the project area contains lands that are in agricultural use, the preliminary report shall be sent to the Department of Conservation, the county agricultural commissioner, the county farm bureau, the California Farm Bureau Federation, and agricultural entities and general farm organizations that provide a written request for notice. A separate written request for notice shall be required for each proposed redevelopment plan or amendment that adds territory. A written request for notice applicable to one redevelopment plan or amendment shall not be effective for a subsequent plan or amendment.

33344.6 Preliminary Report to affected taxing entities— Time limit to transmit

A redevelopment agency that is required to prepare a preliminary report pursuant to Section 33344.5 shall send the preliminary report no later than 90 days before the date set for a public hearing held pursuant to Section 33355 or 33360. However, notwithstanding this requirement, the redevelopment agency may send the report no later than 21 days before the hearing held pursuant to Section 33355 or 33360 if any one of the following conditions is met:

(a) The redevelopment plan is proposed to be adopted pursuant to Chapter 4.5 (commencing with Section 33492).

(b) The redevelopment plan is proposed to be adopted pursuant to the Community Redevelopment Disaster Project Law (Part 1.5 (commencing with Section 34000)).

(c) The redevelopment plan is proposed to be amended and the amendment will not do any of the following:

(1) Add new territory to the project area.

(2) Increase the limitation on the number of dollars of property taxes that may be divided and allocated to the agency pursuant to Section 33670.

(3) Increase the limitation on the amount of the bonded indebtedness that can be outstanding at one time.

(4) Increase the time limit on the establishing of loans, advances, and indebtedness to be paid with the proceeds of property taxes received pursuant to Section 33670.

(5) Increase the time limit on the receipt of property taxes by the agency pursuant to Section 33670.

(6) Merge project areas.

(d) The agency has previously provided affected taxing agencies with the preliminary report and proposes to change the base year assessment roll pursuant to Section 33328.5.

(e) The affected taxing entities waive, in writing, the 90-day notice requirement.

33345 Owner participation rules

With respect to each redevelopment project, each agency shall, within a reasonable time before its approval of the redevelopment plan adopt and make available for public inspection rules to implement the operation of owner participation in connection with the plan.

33346 Report of planning commission

Before the redevelopment plan of each project area is submitted to the legislative body, it shall be submitted to the planning commission for its report and recommendation concerning the redevelopment plan and its conformity to the general plan adopted by the planning commission or the legislative body. The planning commission may recommend for or against the approval of the redevelopment plan.

33347 Time for report of planning commission

Within 30 days after a redevelopment plan is submitted to it for consideration, the planning commission shall make and file its report and recommendation with the agency. If the planning commission does not report upon the redevelopment plan within 30 days after its submission by the agency, the planning commission shall be deemed to have waived its report and recommendations concerning the plan and the agency may thereafter approve the plan without the report and recommendations of the planning commission.

33347.5 Report of project area committee

If there exists within the project area a project area committee, the redevelopment plan shall be submitted to such committee before it is submitted to the legislative body. The committee may, if it chooses, prepare a report and recommendation for submission to the legislative body.

33348 Public hearing by agency

Before the approval of a redevelopment plan by the agency, the agency shall conduct a public hearing on it.

33349 Notice of public hearing by agency

(a) The agency shall publish notice of the hearing not less than once a week for four successive weeks prior to the hearing. The notice shall be published in a newspaper of general circulation, printed and published in the community, or if there is none, in a newspaper selected by the agency. The notice of hearing shall include a legible map of the boundaries of the area or areas designated in the proposed redevelopment plan and a general statement of the scope and objectives of the plan in nontechnical language and in a clear and coherent manner using words with common and everyday meaning.

The agency shall prepare a legal description of the boundaries of the area or areas designated in the proposed redevelopment plan and make this legal description available to the public for inspection during the agency's normal business hours. The notice of the hearing shall state that a copy of the legal description of the boundaries is available upon request, free of charge.

(b) Copies of the notices published pursuant to this section shall be mailed, by first-class mail, to the last known assessee of each parcel of land in the area designated in the redevelopment plan, at his or her last known address as shown on the last equalized assessment roll of the county; or where a city assesses, levies, and collects its own taxes, as shown on the last equalized assessment roll of the city; or to the owner of each parcel of land within the boundaries of the area or areas designated in the proposed redevelopment plan, as shown on the records of the county recorder 30 days prior to the date the notice is published.

(c) (1) Notice shall also be provided, by first-class mail, to all residents and businesses within the project area at least 30 days prior to the hearing.

(2) The mailed notice requirement of this subdivision shall only apply when mailing addresses to all individuals and businesses, or to all occupants, are obtainable by the agency at a reasonable cost. The notice shall be mailed by first-class mail, but may be addressed to "occupant." If the agency has acted in good faith to comply with the notice requirements of this subdivision, the failure of the agency to provide the required notice to residents or businesses unknown to the agency or whose addresses cannot be obtained at a reasonable cost, shall not, in and of itself, invalidate a redevelopment plan or amendment to a redevelopment plan.

(d) Copies of the notices published pursuant to this section shall also be mailed to the governing body of each of the taxing agencies that levies taxes upon any property in the project area designated in the proposed redevelopment plan. Notices sent pursuant to this subdivision shall be mailed by certified mail, return receipt requested.

33349.5 Notice and public hearing by Redevelopment Agency of the City of Crescent City

Notwithstanding Sections 33349 and 33361, the notice provided for in such sections applicable to the Redevelopment Agency of the City of Crescent City need be published only once, at least ten days prior to the hearing in question. The notice of the hearing by the agency on the redevelopment plan may be published at the same time as the notice of the hearing by the legislative body on the redevelopment plan, and both hearings may be held on the same day.

Notwithstanding Section 33500, no action attacking or otherwise questioning the validity of any redevelopment plan, or the adoption or approval of such plan, or any of the findings or determinations of the Redevelopment Agency of the City of Crescent City or the legislative body in connection with such plan shall be brought prior to the adoption of the redevelopment plan nor at any time after the lapse of thirty days from and after the date of adoption of the ordinance adopting the plan.

33350 Statements regarding acquisition by purchase or condemnation

Each assessee whose property would be subject to acquisition by purchase or condemnation under the plan shall be sent a statement in nontechnical language and in a clear and coherent manner using words with common and everyday meaning, to that effect attached to his notice of the hearing. Alternatively, a list or map of all properties which would be subject to acquisition by purchase or condemnation under the plan may be mailed to assessees with the notices of hearing.

33350.5 Exclusion of land from proposed project area

After publication of notice of agency public hearing and prior to approval of the redevelopment plan by the agency, an agency may exclude land from a project area after receipt of a report and recommendation from the planning commission. Within 30 days after a change is submitted to it for consideration, the planning commission shall submit its report and recommendation to the agency. If the planning commission does not report upon the change within 30 days after its submission by the agency, the planning commission shall be deemed to have waived its report and recommendation concerning the change, and the agency may proceed to exclude the land from the project area without the report and recommendation of the planning commission.

33351 Submission of redevelopment plan to legislative body

Upon the preparation and approval of a redevelopment plan the agency shall submit it to the legislative body.

33352 Report of agency to legislative body

Every redevelopment plan submitted by the agency to the legislative body shall be accompanied by a report containing all of the following:

(a) The reasons for the selection of the project area, a description of the specific projects then proposed by the agency, a description of how these projects will improve or alleviate the conditions described in subdivision (b).

(b) A description of the physical and economic conditions specified in Section 33031 that exist in the area that cause the project area to be blighted. The description shall include a list of the physical and economic conditions described in Section 33031 that exist within the project area and a map showing where in the project the conditions exist. The description shall contain specific, quantifiable evidence that documents both of the following:

(1) The physical and economic conditions specified in Section 33031.

(2) That the described physical and economic conditions are so prevalent and substantial that, collectively, they seriously harm the entire project area.

(c) An implementation plan that describes specific goals and objectives of the agency, specific projects then proposed by the agency, including a program of actions and expenditures proposed to be made within the first five years of the plan, and a description of how these projects will improve or alleviate the conditions described in Section 33031.

(d) An explanation of why the elimination of blight and the redevelopment of the project area cannot reasonably be expected to be accomplished by private enterprise acting alone or by the legislative body's use of financing alternatives other than tax increment financing.

(e) The proposed method of financing the redevelopment of the project area in sufficient detail so that the legislative body may determine the economic feasibility of the plan.

(f) A method or plan for the relocation of families and persons to be temporarily or permanently displaced from housing facilities in the project area, which method or plan shall include the provision required by Section 33411.1 that no persons or families of low and moderate income shall be displaced unless and until there is a suitable housing unit available and ready for occupancy by the displaced person or family at rents comparable to those at the time of their displacement.

(g) An analysis of the preliminary plan.

(h) The report and recommendations of the planning commission.

(i) The summary referred to in Section 33387.

(j) The report required by Section 65402 of the Government Code.

(k) The report required by Section 21151 of the Public Resources Code.

(l) The report of the county fiscal officer as required by Section 33328.

(m) If the project area contains low- or moderate-income housing, a neighborhood impact report which describes in detail the impact of the project upon the residents of the project area and the surrounding areas, in terms of relocation, traffic circulation, environmental quality, availability of community facilities and services, effect on school population and quality of education, property assessments and taxes, and other matters affecting the physical and social quality of the neighborhood. The neighborhood impact report shall also include all of the following:

(1) The number of dwelling units housing persons and families of low or moderate income expected to be destroyed or removed from the low- and moderate-income housing market as part of a redevelopment project.

(2) The number of persons and families of low or moderate income expected to be displaced by the project.

(3) The general location of housing to be rehabilitated, developed, or constructed pursuant to Section 33413.

(4) The number of dwelling units housing persons and families of low or moderate income planned for construction or rehabilitation, other than replacement housing.

(5) The projected means of financing the proposed dwelling units for housing persons and families of low and moderate income planned for construction or rehabilitation.

(6) A projected timetable for meeting the plan's relocation, rehabilitation, and replacement housing objectives.

(n) (1) An analysis by the agency of the report submitted by the county as required by Section 33328, which shall include a summary of the consultation of the agency, or attempts to consult by the agency, with each of the affected taxing entities as required by Section 33328. If any of the affected taxing entities have expressed written objections or concerns with the proposed project area as part of these consultations, the agency shall include a response to these concerns, additional information, if any, and, at the discretion of the agency, proposed or adopted mitigation measures.

(2) As used in this subdivision:

(A) "Mitigation measures" may include the amendment of the redevelopment plan with respect to the size or location of the project area, time duration, total amount of tax increment to be received by the agency, or the proposed use, size, density, or location of development to be assisted by the agency.

(B) "Mitigation measures" shall not include obligations to make payments to any affected taxing entity.

33353.2 Affected taxing entity defined

"Affected taxing entity" means any governmental taxing agency that levies a property tax on all or any portion of the property located in the adopted project area in the fiscal year prior to the fiscal year in which the report prepared pursuant to Section 33328 is issued or in any fiscal year after the date the redevelopment plan is adopted. To the extent that a new governmental taxing agency wholly or partially replaces the geographic jurisdiction of a preexisting governmental taxing agency, the new taxing agency shall be an "affected taxing entity" and the preexisting taxing agency shall no longer be an "affected taxing entity."

33354.5 Redevelopment plan amendment adding tax increment authority

Where an agency proposes to amend a redevelopment plan which does not utilize tax increment financing to include a tax allocation provision, the agency shall follow the same procedure and the legislative body is subject to the same restrictions as provided for in this article for the adoption of a plan.

33354.6 Redevelopment plan amendment adding new territory, increasing financing limits, extending duration, merging areas or adding capital projects

(a) When an agency proposes to amend a redevelopment plan which utilizes tax increment financing to add new territory to the project area, to increase either the limitation on the number of dollars to be allocated to the redevelopment agency or the time limit on the establishing of loans, advances, and indebtedness established pursuant to paragraphs (1) and (2) of subdivision (a) of Section 33333.2 or pursuant to paragraphs (1) and (2) of subdivision (a) of Section 33333.4, to lengthen the period during which the redevelopment plan is effective, to merge project areas, or to add significant additional capital improvement projects, as determined by the agency, the agency shall follow the same procedure, and the legislative body is subject to the same restrictions as provided for in this article for the adoption of a plan.

(b) When an agency proposes to increase the limitation on the number of dollars to be allocated to the redevelopment agency, it shall describe and identify, in the report required by Section 33352, the remaining blight within the project area, identify the portion, if any, that is no longer blighted, the projects that are required to be completed to eradicate the remaining blight and the relationship between the costs of those projects and the amount of increase in the limitation on the number of dollars to be allocated to the agency. The ordinance adopting the amendment shall contain findings that both (1) significant blight remains with the project area and (2) the blight cannot be eliminated without the establishment of additional debt and the increase in the limitation on the number of dollars to be allocated to the redevelopment agency.

Article 4.5
Alternative Procedures for a Joint Public Hearing by the Agency and the Legislative Body

33355 Authority to hold joint public hearing

As an alternative to the separate public hearings required by Sections 33348 and 33360 of this part, the agency and the legislative body, with the consent of both, may hold a joint public hearing on a redevelopment plan. The presiding officer of the legislative body shall preside over such joint public hearing.

33356 Procedure prior to joint public hearing

Prior to such joint public hearing, the agency shall submit the plan to the planning commission by the same procedure as is provided in Section 33346, and to the legislative body. The submission of the plan to the legislative body shall be accompanied by the report required by Section 33352. Notice of the joint public hearing shall conform to all requirements prescribed by Sections 33349, 33350, and 33361. The joint public hearing shall thereafter proceed by the same requirements as are provided in Sections 33360, 33362, 33363, and 33363.5.

33357 Action by agency after joint public hearing

After the close of the joint public hearing, the agency may proceed to approve the plan and submit its approval together with any recommendations for changes to the legislative body. If the agency desires to recommend any changes in the plan, such changes shall be submitted to the planning commission for its report and recommendation by the same procedure as is provided in Sections 33346 and 33347.

33358 Action by legislative body after joint public hearing

After receipt of the approval and any recommendations for changes as well as the report and recommendation of the planning commission of the recommended changes, the legislative body may proceed to act upon the plan pursuant to Sections 33363.5 to 33375, inclusive.

33359 Action by legislative body which is also agency after joint public hearing

When a joint public hearing is held where the legislative body is also the agency, action to approve and adopt the plan need be taken only by the legislative body. At the conclusion of the joint public hearing on the plan, the legislative body may proceed to adopt the plan pursuant to Sections 33363.5 to 33375, inclusive, with no further actions necessary by the agency, even as to the recommendations required of the agency by Section 33363.5.

Article 5
Procedure for Adoption of Redevelopment Plans by the Legislative Body

33360 Public hearing by legislative body

The legislative body at a public hearing shall consider the redevelopment plan submitted by the agency. The legislative body may adjourn the hearing from time to time.

33360.5 Delivery of report to the Department of Finance and Department of Housing and Community Development prior to public hearing by legislative body

(a) No later than 45 days prior to the public hearing on a proposed plan adoption by an agency or the joint public hearing of the agency and the legislative body, the agency shall deliver a copy of the preliminary report and notice of the date of the public hearing to the Department of Finance and the Department of Housing and Community Development by first-class mail.

(b) Upon receiving the report, the Department of Finance shall prepare an estimate of how the proposed plan adoption will affect the General Fund. The Department of Finance shall determine whether the adoption will affect the need for school facilities.

(c) Within 21 days of the receipt of the report, the Department of Finance or the Department of Housing and Community

Development may send any comments regarding the proposed plan adoption in writing to the agency and the legislative body. The agency and the legislative body shall consider these comments, if any, at the public hearing on the proposed plan adoption. If these comments are not available within the prescribed time limit, the agency and the legislative body may proceed without them.

(d) The Department of Finance or the Department of Housing and Community Development may also send their comments regarding the proposed plan adoption to the Attorney General for further action pursuant to Chapter 5 (commencing with Section 33501).

33361   Notice of public hearing by legislative body

Notice of the public hearing shall be given by publication not less than once a week for four successive weeks in a newspaper of general circulation published in the county in which the land lies. The notice shall:

(a) Describe specifically the boundaries of the proposed redevelopment project area; and

(b) State the day, hour and place when and where any and all persons having any objections to the proposed redevelopment plan or who deny the existence of blight in the proposed project area, or the regularity of any of the prior proceedings, may appear before the legislative body and show cause why the proposed plan should not be adopted.

33362   Written objections to redevelopment plan

At any time not later than the hour set for hearing objections to the proposed redevelopment plan, any person may file in writing with the clerk of the legislative body a statement of his objections to the proposed plan.

33363   Written findings in response to written objections

At the hour set in the notice required by Section 33361 for hearing objections, the legislative body shall proceed to hear all written and oral objections. Before adopting the redevelopment plan the legislative body shall evaluate the report of the agency, the report and recommendation of the project area committee, and all evidence and testimony for and against the adoption of the plan and shall make written findings in response to each written objection of an affected property owner or taxing entity. The legislative body shall respond in writing to the written objections received before or at the noticed hearing, including any extensions thereof, and may additionally respond to written objections that are received after the hearing. The written responses shall describe the disposition of the issues raised. The legislative body shall address the written objections in detail, giving reasons for not accepting specified objections and suggestions. The legislative body shall include a good-faith, reasoned analysis in its response and, for this purpose, conclusionary statements unsupported by factual information shall not suffice.

33363.5   Changes to redevelopment plan or project boundaries by legislative body

After the redevelopment plan and accompanying documents have been submitted by the agency to the legislative body and at any time prior to the adoption of the plan, the legislative body upon the recommendation of the agency, without additional agency public hearings, may change such plan, or change the boundaries of the project area to exclude land from the project area, after receipt of a report and recommendation from the planning commission concerning such changes. The planning commission may recommend for or against the changes. Within 30 days after a change is submitted to it for consideration the planning commission shall make and file its report and recommendation with the legislative body. If the planning commission does not report upon the change within 30 days after its submission by the legislative body, the planning commission shall be deemed to have waived its report and recommendation concerning the change and the legislative body may proceed to act upon the plan without the report and recommendation of the planning commission. The legislative body shall consider any proposed changes at a public hearing reopened for that limited purpose.

33364   Adoption of redevelopment plan by legislative body delayed where written objections are received

If no objections in writing have been delivered to the clerk of the legislative body prior to the hour set for the hearing thereon, and if no written objections are presented during the hearing thereon, the legislative body may proceed to adopt the plan at the time set for hearing thereon. If any written objections are delivered or presented, as specified in this article, the legislative body may adopt the plan only after consideration of the objections, and adoption of written findings in response thereto, pursuant to Section 33363 at a subsequent date not less than one week after the time the hearing on objections is commenced pursuant to Section 33363.

33365   Adoption of redevelopment plan by ordinance subject to referendum

The legislative body by ordinance may adopt the redevelopment plan as the official redevelopment plan for the project area.

Except as otherwise provided in Section 33378, the ordinance adopting the redevelopment plan shall be subject to referendum as prescribed by law for the ordinances of the legislative body.

33366   Vote required to adopt redevelopment plan

If the planning commission or the project area committee has recommended against the approval of the redevelopment plan, the legislative body may adopt such plan by a two-thirds vote of its entire membership eligible and qualified to vote on such plan. If the planning commission or the project area committee has recommended approval or failed to make any recommendation within the time allowed, the legislative body may adopt the redevelopment plan by a majority vote of the entire membership eligible and qualified to vote on such plan.

33367   Contents of ordinance adopting redevelopment plan

The ordinance shall contain all of the following:

(a) The purposes and intent of the legislative body with respect to the project area.

(b) The plan incorporated by reference.

(c) A designation of the approved plan as the official redevelopment plan of the project area.

(d) The findings and determinations of the legislative body, which shall be based on clearly articulated and documented evidence, that:

(1) The project area is a blighted area, the redevelopment of which is necessary to effectuate the public purposes declared in this part.

(2) The redevelopment plan would redevelop the area in conformity with this part and in the interests of the public peace, health, safety, and welfare.

(3) The adoption and carrying out of the redevelopment plan is economically sound and feasible.

(4) The redevelopment plan is consistent with the general plan of the community, including, but not limited to, the community's housing element, which substantially complies with the requirements of Article 10.6 (commencing with Section 65580) of Chapter 3 of Division 1 of Title 7 of the Government Code.

(5) The carrying out of the redevelopment plan would promote the public peace, health, safety, and welfare of the community and would effectuate the purposes and policy of this part.

(6) The condemnation of real property, if provided for in the redevelopment plan, is necessary to the execution of the redevelopment plan and adequate provisions have been made for payment for property to be acquired as provided by law.

(7) The agency has a feasible method or plan for the relocation of families and persons displaced from the project area, if the redevelopment plan may result in the temporary or permanent displacement of any occupants of housing facilities in the project area.

(8) (A) There are, or shall be provided, in the project area or in other areas not generally less desirable in regard to public utilities and public and commercial facilities and at rents or prices within the financial means of the families and persons displaced from the project area, decent, safe, and sanitary dwellings equal in number to the number of and available to the displaced families and persons and reasonably accessible to their places of employment.

(B) Families and persons shall not be displaced prior to the adoption of a relocation plan pursuant to Sections 33411 and 33411.1. Dwelling units housing persons and families of low or moderate income shall not be removed or destroyed prior to the adoption of a replacement housing plan pursuant to Sections 33334.5, 33413, and 33413.5.

(9) All noncontiguous areas of a project area are either blighted or necessary for effective redevelopment and are not included for the purpose of obtaining the allocation of taxes from the area pursuant to Section 33670 without other substantial justification for their inclusion.

(10) Inclusion of any lands, buildings, or improvements which are not detrimental to the public health, safety, or welfare is necessary for the effective redevelopment of the area of which they are a part; that any area included is necessary for effective redevelopment and is not included for the purpose of obtaining the allocation of tax increment revenues from the area pursuant to Section 33670 without other substantial justification for its inclusion.

(11) The elimination of blight and the redevelopment of the project area could not be reasonably expected to be accomplished by private enterprise acting alone without the aid and assistance of the agency.

(12) The project area is predominantly urbanized, as defined by subdivision (b) of Section 33320.1.

(13) The time limitation and, if applicable, the limitation on the number of dollars to be allocated to the agency that are contained in the plan are reasonably related to the proposed projects to be implemented in the project area and to the ability of the agency to eliminate blight within the project area.

(14) The implementation of the redevelopment plan will improve or alleviate the physical and economic conditions of blight in the project area, as described in the report prepared pursuant to Section 33352.

(e) A statement that the legislative body is satisfied that permanent housing facilities will be available within three years from the time occupants of the project area are displaced and that, pending the development of the facilities, there will be available to the displaced occupants adequate temporary housing facilities at rents comparable to those in the community at the time of their displacement.

33368 Conclusive presumption of blight

The decision of the legislative body shall be final and conclusive, and it shall thereafter be conclusively presumed that the project area is a blighted area as defined by Section 33031 and that all prior proceedings have been duly and regularly taken.

This section shall not apply in any action questioning the validity of any redevelopment plan, or the adoption or approval of a redevelopment plan, or any of the findings or determinations of the agency or the legislative body in connection with a redevelopment plan brought pursuant to Section 33501 within the time limits prescribed by Section 33500.

33369 Legislative body to provide for community expenditures

If the plan provides for the expenditure of any money by the community, the legislative body shall provide for such expenditure at the time of or in connection with the approval of the plan.

33370 Legislative body to provide for community undertakings

The legislative body at the time of, or in connection with, the adoption of the plan, shall declare its intention to undertake and complete any proceedings necessary to be carried out by the community under the provisions of the plan.

33371 Legislative body may require agency to obtain approval for certain contracts

Before entering into any or certain types of contracts in connection with the redevelopment plan, the legislative body may require the agency to submit such contracts to the legislative body and obtain its approval.

33372 Agency vested with responsibility to carry out redevelopment plan

Upon the filing of the ordinance adopting the redevelopment plan with the clerk or other appropriate officer of the legislative body, a copy of the ordinance shall be sent to the agency, and the agency is vested with the responsibility for carrying out the plan.

33373 Recordation of project area description and statement of redevelopment proceedings

(a) Not later than 60 days after the adoption of the redevelopment plan by the legislative body there shall be recorded with the county recorder of the county in which the project area is situated a description of the land within the project area and a statement that proceedings for the redevelopment of the project area have been instituted under this part.

(b) If the redevelopment plan authorizes the agency to acquire property by eminent domain, the statement required pursuant to subdivision (a) shall contain the following:

(1) A prominent heading in boldface type noting that the property that is the subject of the statement is located within a redevelopment project.

(2) A general description of the provisions of the redevelopment plan that authorize the use of the power of eminent domain by the agency.

(3) A general description of any limitations on the use of the power of eminent domain contained in the redevelopment plan, including, without limitation, the time limit required by Section 33333.2.

(c) For a redevelopment plan adopted on or before December 31, 2006, that authorizes the acquisition of property by eminent domain, the agency shall, on or before December 31, 2007, cause a revised statement to be recorded with the county recorder of the county in which the project area is located containing all of the information required by subdivisions (a) and (b).

(d) An agency shall not commence an action in eminent domain until the statement required by this section is recorded with the county recorder of the county in which the project area is located.

(e) Additional recordation of documents may be effected pursuant to Section 27295 of the Government Code.

33374 Building department to notify applicants

After the adoption of a redevelopment plan for a project area by the legislative body, all applicants for building permits in the area for a period of two years thereafter shall be advised by the building department of the community that the site for which a building permit is sought for the construction of buildings or for other improvements is within a redevelopment project area.

33375 Transmittal of redevelopment plan adoption documents to taxing officials and entities

After the adoption by the legislative body of a redevelopment plan that contains the provision permitted by Section 33670, the clerk of the community shall transmit a copy of the description and statement recorded pursuant to Section 33373, a copy of the ordinance adopting the plan, and a map or plat indicating the boundaries of the project area to the auditor and assessor of the county in which the project is located; to the officer or officers performing the functions of auditor or assessor for any taxing agencies which, in levying or collecting its taxes, do not use the county assessment roll or do not collect its taxes through the county; to the governing body of each of the taxing agencies which levies taxes upon any property in the project area; and to the State Board of Equalization.

Those documents shall be transmitted within 30 days following the adoption of the redevelopment plan. The legal effect of those transmittals shall be as set forth in Section 33674.

33376 Emergency ordinance for Crescent City disaster area

Any ordinance adopted pursuant to this article adopting a redevelopment plan for the Crescent City disaster area, may be adopted as an emergency ordinance and shall not be subject to referendum.

Article 5.5
Referendums

33378 Referendum measures

(a) With respect to any ordinance that is subject to referendum pursuant to Sections 33365 and 33450, the language of the statement of the ballot measure shall set forth with clarity and in language understandable to the average person that a "Yes" vote is a vote in favor of adoption or amendment of the redevelopment plan and a "No" vote is a vote against the adoption or amendment of the redevelopment plan.

(b) (1) Notwithstanding any other provision of law, including the charter of any city or city and county, referendum petitions circulated in cities or counties over 500,000 in population shall bear valid signatures numbering not less than 10 percent of the total votes cast within the city or county for Governor at the last gubernatorial election.

(2) Notwithstanding any other provision of law, including the charter of any city or city and county, or Section 9242 of the Elections Code, the referendum petitions of all cities and counties submitted to the clerk of the legislative body within 90 days of the adoption of an ordinance subject to referendum under this act.

(c) With respect to any ordinance that is subject to referendum pursuant to Sections 33365 and 33450 and either provides for tax-increment financing pursuant to Section 33670 or expands a project area that is subject to tax-increment financing, the referendum measure shall include, in the ballot pamphlet, an analysis by the county auditor-controller and, at the option of the legislative body, a separate analysis by the agency, of the redevelopment plan or amendment that will include both of the following:

(1) An estimate of the potential impact on property taxes per each ten thousand dollars ($10,000) of assessed valuation for taxpayers located in the city or county, as the case may be, outside the redevelopment project area during the life of the redevelopment project.

(2) An estimate of what would happen to the project area in the absence of the redevelopment project or in the absence of the proposed amendment to the plan.

33378.5 Exemption for certain charter cities until January 1, 1983

The provisions of this part establishing a right of referendum shall not be applicable to a charter city in the County of Los Angeles containing a population of 1,000 or less until January 1, 1983.

Article 6
Owner Participation

33380 Owner participation to be permitted

An agency shall permit owner participation in the redevelopment of property in the project area in conformity with the redevelopment plan adopted by the legislative body for the area.

33381 Alternatives on failure of owner participation

If the redevelopment plan adopted provides for participation in the redevelopment of property in the area by the owners of such property, and the owners fail or refuse to enter into a binding agreement for participation in accordance with the rules adopted by the agency pursuant to Section 33339, the alternative provisions provided for in Section 33340 become effective as the official redevelopment plan of the project area.

Article 6.5
Project Area Committee

33385 Formation of project area committee

(a) The legislative body of a city or county shall call upon the residents and existing community organizations in a redevelopment project area to form a project area committee in either of the following situations:

(1) A substantial number of low-income persons or moderate-income persons, or both, reside within the project area, and the redevelopment plan as adopted will contain authority for the agency to acquire, by eminent domain, property on which any persons reside.

(2) The redevelopment plan as adopted contains one or more public projects that will displace a substantial number of low-income persons or moderate-income persons, or both.

(b) The legislative body shall, by resolution, adopt a procedure pursuant to this section for the formation of the project area committee. The procedure shall include, but not be limited to, all of the following:

(1) Publicizing the opportunity to serve on the project area committee, by providing written notice by first-class mail to all residents, businesses, and community organizations, including religious institutions and other nonprofit organizations, within the project area at least 30 days prior to the formation of the project area committee.

(2) The agency shall conduct a minimum of one public meeting to explain the establishment of, functions of, and opportunity to serve on, the project area committee. At the public meeting, the agency shall distribute copies of this article, copies of Sections 33347.5 and 33366, copies of the procedure adopted pursuant to this subdivision, copies of the redevelopment plan or preliminary plan or the pertinent portions thereof, and any other materials the agency determines would be useful.

(3) Providing published notice of all meetings, hearings, or plebiscites conducted by, or on behalf of, the agency or legislative body relative to the formation and selection of the project area committee in the same manner as specified in subdivision (a) of Section 65090 of the Government Code.

(4) (A) Providing written notice to all residents, businesses, and community organizations in the project area of all meetings, hearings, or plebiscites conducted by, or on behalf of, the agency or legislative body relative to the formation and selection of the project area committee. This mailed notice requirement shall only apply when mailing addresses to all individuals and businesses, or to all occupants, are obtainable by the agency at a reasonable cost. The notice shall be mailed by first-class mail, but may be addressed to "occupant." In lieu of providing separate notice for each meeting, hearing, or plebiscite, the agency may provide a single notice pursuant to this paragraph stating all dates, times, and locations of any meetings, hearings, and plebiscites relative to the formation and selection of the project area committee.

(B) If the agency has acted in good faith to comply with the notice requirements of this paragraph, the failure of the agency to provide the required notice to residents or businesses unknown to the agency or whose addresses cannot be obtained at a reasonable cost, shall not, in and of itself, invalidate the formation or actions of the project area committee.

(5) Providing other forms of notice appropriate to the community in which the project area is to be established, as determined by the agency. Notice provided pursuant to this paragraph may include public service announcements, advertisements in foreign-language publications, or flyers.

(6) The number of community organizations and the method of selection, which may include election, appointment, or both.

(7) Any other forms of assistance which the legislative body requires in connection with the formation of the project area committee.

(c) The project area committee shall only include, when applicable, elected representatives of residential owner occupants, residential tenants, business owners, and existing organizations within the project area. Each group shall be adequately represented. Each organization represented pursuant to this subdivision shall appoint one of its members to the project area committee. No project area committee member may be appointed by the legislative body or the redevelopment agency or any member of either body. The members of the committee shall serve without compensation.

(d) (1) The election of a representative project area committee shall be held in each project area within 100 days after the project area is selected. The legislative body shall adopt, after a duly noticed public hearing, communitywide procedures for filing for election, publicizing an election, holding an election, and for reviewing disputed elections, filling vacated seats, and other matters related to the electoral process. These procedures shall prohibit crossover voting between categories of residential owner occupants, residential tenants, and business owners to ensure, for example, that a business owner cannot vote for a tenant representative. However, if the legislative body determines that the method of selection of community organizations shall include election pursuant to subdivision (b), the legislative body shall determine the appropriate electorate and may authorize crossover voting in the election of community organizations.

(2) The procedures adopted pursuant to this subdivision shall provide that a challenge to an election or to an electoral procedure shall be filed with the legislative body no more than 15 calendar days after the election. The legislative body shall adopt a finding that all adopted procedures of the legislative body were followed in the election. The procedures shall require that the validity of all challenges be determined within 30 days following the date of the election.

(e) For project areas selected prior to March 7, 1973, the legislative body may, but shall not be required to, call upon the residents and existing community organizations to form a project area committee.

(f) If the project does not contain a substantial number of low- and moderate-income individuals, the agency shall either call upon the residents and existing community organizations to form a project area committee or the agency shall consult with, and obtain the advice of, residents and community organizations as provided for project area committees in Section 33386 and provide those persons and organizations with the redevelopment plan prior to submitting it to the legislative body.

(g) Nothing contained in this section shall prevent an agency, or the legislative body of any city or county, from creating any other committee for a project area. However, these committees shall not be merged into the project area committee subsequent to the formation thereof, and a member of any of these other committees shall not be entitled to vote in meetings of the project area committee, unless he or she is also a member of the project area committee.

(h) The meeting of a project area committee shall be subject to the Ralph M. Brown Act (Chapter 9 (commencing with Section 54950) of Division 2 of Title 5 of the Government Code).

(i) The agency may charge fees to persons purchasing or leasing property from the agency in the project area and to persons participating in redevelopment of the project area under an owner participation agreement to defray any cost to the agency or legislative body in implementing this section.

(j) The amendments made to this section by the act that adds this subdivision shall be applicable only to a redevelopment plan that is adopted or amended on or after the effective date of the act that adds this subdivision.

33385.3 Formation of project area committee for redevelopment plan amendments adding eminent domain or new territory

(a) If a project area committee does not exist, and the agency proposes to amend a redevelopment plan, the agency shall establish a project area committee pursuant to Section 33385 if the proposed amendment to a redevelopment plan would do either of the following:

(1) Grant the authority to the agency to acquire by eminent domain property on which persons reside in a project area in which a substantial number of low- and moderate-income persons reside.

(2) Add territory in which a substantial number of low- and moderate-income persons reside and grant the authority to the agency to acquire by eminent domain property on which persons reside in the added territory. The project area committee may be composed of persons from only the added territory or both the added area and the existing project area.

(b) Once a project area committee is formed, the requirements of Section 33385.5, except for project area committee expansion, shall be followed.

33385.5 Consideration of redevelopment plan amendments by project area committee; expansion of membership for new territory

The agency shall forward copies of the proposed amendment to the redevelopment plan to the project area committee, if one exists, at least 30 days before the hearing of the legislative body, required in Section 33454.

Where the proposed amendment would enlarge the project area, the redevelopment agency shall call upon the project area committee to expand its membership to include additional members on the project area committee in compliance with Section 33385. Such expansion of membership shall be submitted to the legislative body within 30 days for the body's approval within 60 days to assure that the project area committee is representative. The legislative body shall not hold the public hearing, required by Section 33454, until the enlarged project area committee has had at least 30 days to consider the proposed amendment.

The committee, if it chooses, may prepare a report and recommendations for submission to the legislative body. If the project area committee opposes the adoption of the proposed amendment, the legislative body may only adopt the amendment by a two-thirds vote of its entire membership eligible and qualified to vote on such amendments.

33386 Role of project area committee to consult with and advise agency

The redevelopment agency through its staff, consultants, and agency members shall, upon the direction of and approval of the legislative body consult with, and obtain the advice of, the project area committee concerning those policy matters which deal with the planning and provision of residential facilities or replacement housing for those to be displaced by project activities. The agency shall also consult with the committee on other policy matters which affect the residents of the project area. The provisions of this section shall apply throughout the period of preparation of the redevelopment plan and for a three-year period after the adoption of the redevelopment plan, subject to one-year extensions by the legislative body.

33387 Agency to maintain record of proceedings of project area committee

Minutes of all the meetings of the redevelopment agency with the project area committee, which meetings shall be open and public, together with a record of all information presented to the project area committee by the redevelopment agency or by the project area committee for the redevelopment agency for the purpose of carrying out the provisions of this article shall be maintained by the redevelopment agency. Such minutes and record shall be open to public inspection and a summary of such record shall be included in the report to the legislative body, submitted by the agency pursuant to Section 33352.

33388 Allocation of operating funds to project area committee

(a) Upon recommendation of the project area committee, funds as determined necessary by the legislative body for the operation of the project area committee shall be allocated to the committee by the legislative body. This allocation shall include funds or equivalent resources for a committee office, equipment and supplies, legal counsel, and adequate staff for the purposes set forth in Section 33386.

(b) No funds allocated under this section shall be used for any litigation, other than litigation to enforce or defend the rights of the project area committee under this part.

Article 7
Property Acquisition

33390 Real property defined

"Real property" means:

(a) Land, including land under water and waterfront property.

(b) Buildings, structures, fixtures, and improvements on the land.

(c) Any property appurtenant to or used in connection with the land.

(d) Every estate, interest, privilege, easement, franchise, and right in land, including rights-of-way, terms for years, and liens, charges, or encumbrances by way of judgment, mortgage, or otherwise and the indebtedness secured by such liens.

33391 Methods of acquiring property

Within the survey area or for purposes of redevelopment an agency may:

(a) Purchase, lease, obtain option upon, acquire by gift, grant, bequest, devise, or otherwise, any real or personal property, any interest in property, and any improvements on it, including repurchase of developed property previously owned by the agency.

(b) Acquire real property by eminent domain.

33392 Acquisition after formulation of preliminary plan and before adoption of redevelopment plan

Notwithstanding any other provision of this part, an agency with the approval of the legislative body of the community may acquire, by negotiation or other means, real property in a project area at any time after formulation of the preliminary plan for the area by the planning commission, and prior to the adoption of the redevelopment plan by the legislative body of the community, provided, however, that an agency may not exercise the power of eminent domain in connection with that acquisition prior to adoption of the redevelopment plan.

33393 Acquisition from members or officers

An agency shall not acquire from any of its members or officers any property or interest in property except through eminent domain proceedings.

33394 Consent of owner required

Without the consent of an owner, an agency shall not acquire any real property on which an existing building is to be continued on its present site and in its present form and use unless such building requires structural alteration, improvement, modernization or rehabilitation, or the site or lot on which the building is situated requires modification in size, shape or use or it is necessary to impose upon such property any of the standards, restrictions and controls of the plan and the owner fails or refuses to agree to participate in the redevelopment plan pursuant to Sections 33339, 33345, 33380 and 33381.

33395 Consent of public body required

Property already devoted to a public use may be acquired by the agency through eminent domain, but property of a public body shall not be acquired without its consent.

33396 Acquisition/disposition of surplus property

An agency at the request of the legislative body of the community may accept a conveyance of real property (located either within or outside a survey area) owned by a public entity and declared surplus by the public entity, or owned by a private entity.

The agency may dispose of such property to private persons or to public or private entities, by sale or long-term lease for development. All or any part of the funds derived from the sale or lease of such property may at the discretion of the legislative body of the community be paid to the community, or to the public entity from which any such property was acquired.

33397 Effect of acquisition on existing covenants, conditions or restrictions

(a) Any covenants, conditions, or restrictions existing on any real property within a project area prior to the time the agency acquires title to such property, which covenants, conditions, or restrictions restrict or purport to restrict the use of, or building upon, such real property, shall be void and unenforceable as to the agency and any other subsequent owners, tenants, lessees, easement holders, mortgagees, trustees, beneficiaries under a deed of trust, or any other persons or entities acquiring an interest in such real property from such time as title to the real property is acquired by an agency whether acquisition is by gift, purchase, eminent domain, or otherwise.

(b) Thirty days prior to the acquisition of real property other than by eminent domain, the agency shall provide notice of such acquisition and the provisions of this section to holders of interests which would be made void and unenforceable pursuant to this section as follows:

(1) The agency shall publish notice once in a newspaper of general circulation in the community in which the agency is functioning.

(2) The agency shall mail notice to holders of such interests if such holders appear of record 60 days prior to the date of acquisition.

The agency may accept any release by written instrument from the holder of any such interest or may commence action to acquire such interest after the date of acquisition of the real property.

(c) This section shall not apply to covenants, conditions or restrictions imposed by a redevelopment plan or by an agency pursuant to a redevelopment plan. This section also shall not apply to covenants, conditions or restrictions where an agency in writing expressly acquires or holds property subject to such covenants, conditions, or restrictions.

This section shall not limit or preclude any rights of reversion of owners, assignees, or beneficiaries of such covenants, conditions, or restrictions limiting the use of land in gifts of land to cities, counties, or other governmental entities. This section shall not limit or preclude the rights of owners or assignees of any land benefited by any covenants, conditions, or restrictions to recover damages against the agency if under law such owner or assignee has any right to damages. No right to damages shall exist against any purchaser from the agency or his successors or assigns, or any other persons or entities.

33398 Applicability of inverse condemnation provisions

Section 1245.260 of the Code of Civil Procedure shall not apply to any resolution or ordinance adopting, approving, amending, or approving the amendment of a redevelopment project or plan. Section 1245.260 of the Code of Civil Procedure shall apply to a resolution adopted by a redevelopment agency pursuant to Section 1245.220 of the Code of Civil Procedure with respect to a particular parcel or parcels of real property.

33399 Inverse condemnation or mandate action by owner

(a) If a public entity has adopted a redevelopment plan but has not commenced an eminent domain proceeding to acquire any particular parcel of property subject to eminent domain thereunder within three years after the date of adoption of the plan, the owner or owners of the entire fee at any time thereafter may offer in writing to sell the property to the agency for its fair market value. If the agency does not, within 18 months from the date of receipt of the original offer, acquire or institute eminent domain proceedings to acquire the property, the property owner or owners may file an action against the agency in inverse condemnation to recover damages from the agency for any interference with the possession and use of the real property resulting from the plan, provided that this section shall not be construed as establishing or creating a presumption to any right to damages or relief solely by reason of the failure of the agency to acquire the property within the time set forth in this section.

(b) No claim need be presented against a public entity under Part 3 (commencing with Section 900) of Division 3.6 of Title 1 of the Government Code as a prerequisite to commencement or maintenance of an action under subdivision (a), but any such action shall be commenced within one year and six months after the expiration of the 18 months period.

(c) A public entity may commence an eminent domain proceeding or designate the property to be exempt from eminent domain under the plan at any time before the property owner commences an action under this section. If the public entity commences an eminent domain proceeding or designates the property to be exempt from acquisition by eminent domain before the property owner commences an action under this section, the property owner may not thereafter bring an action under this section.

(d) After a property owner has commenced an action under this section, the public entity may declare the property to be exempt from acquisition by eminent domain and abandon the taking of the property only under the same circumstances and subject to the same conditions and consequences as abandonment of an eminent domain proceeding.

(e) Commencement of an action under this section does not affect any authority a public entity may have to commence an eminent domain proceeding, take possession of the property pursuant to Article 3 (commencing with Section 1255.410) of Chapter 6 of Title 7 of the Code of Civil Procedure, or abandon the eminent domain proceeding.

(f) In lieu of bringing an action under subdivision (a) or if the limitations period provided in subdivision (b) has run, the property owner may obtain a writ of mandate to compel the public entity, within such time as the court deems appropriate, to declare the property acquisition exempt or to commence an eminent domain proceeding to acquire the property.

(g) A declaration that property is exempt from acquisition by eminent domain shall be by resolution and shall be recordable. It shall exempt the property from eminent domain under the redevelopment plan, and the redevelopment agency shall have no power of eminent domain as to the property unless the redevelopment plan is thereafter amended to expressly make the property subject to acquisition by eminent domain.

(h) With respect to redevelopment projects for which a final redevelopment plan has been adopted prior to January 1, 1977, the three-year period provided for in subdivision (a) shall begin as of January 1, 1977.

Article 8
Property Management

33400 Insurance, rental, maintenance, etc.

Within the survey area or for purposes of redevelopment an agency may:

(a) Insure or provide for the insurance of any real or personal property of the agency against risks or hazards.

(b) Rent, maintain, manage, operate, repair, and clear such real property.

33401 Payments in lieu of taxes

The agency may in any year during which it owns property in a redevelopment project that is tax exempt pay directly to any city, county, city and county, district, including, but not limited to, a school district, or other public corporation for whose benefit a tax would have been levied upon the property had it not been exempt, an amount of money in lieu of taxes that may not exceed the amount of money the public entity would have received if the property had not been tax exempt.

33402 Rental property: time for resale

Except as provided in Article 9 (commencing with Section 33410), this part does not authorize an agency to own or operate rental property acquired and rehabilitated in prospect of resale beyond a reasonable period necessary to effect such resale.

Article 9
Relocation of Persons Displaced by Projects

33410 Federal aid; public or private funds

A redevelopment agency may, in order to facilitate the rehousing of families and single persons who are displaced from their homes in a project area, utilize the aids made available through federal urban renewal, redevelopment and housing legislation and may use funds derived from any public or private source to carry out the purposes of this section.

33411 Relocation plan

The agency shall prepare a feasible method or plan for relocation of all of the following:

(a) Families and persons to be temporarily or permanently displaced from housing facilities in the project area.

(b) Nonprofit local community institutions to be temporarily or permanently displaced from facilities actually used for institutional purposes in the project area.

33411.1 Comparable dwelling units required

The legislative body shall insure that such method or plan of the agency for the relocation of families or single persons to be displaced by a project shall provide that no persons or families of low and moderate income shall be displaced unless and until there is a suitable housing unit available and ready for occupancy by such displaced person or family at rents comparable to those at the time of their displacement. Such housing units shall be suitable to the needs of such displaced persons or families and must be decent, safe, sanitary, and otherwise standard dwelling. The agency shall not displace such person or family until such housing units are available and ready for occupancy.

33411.2 Definitions

As used in this article:

(a) "Affordable housing cost" has the same meaning as specified in Section 50052.5.

(b) "Persons and families of low or moderate income" has the same meaning as specified in Section 50093.

(c) "Replacement dwelling unit" means a dwelling unit developed or constructed pursuant to Section 33413 in replacement of a dwelling unit destroyed or removed from the low- and moderate-income housing market by an agency and which is decent, safe, and sanitary and contains at least the same number of bedrooms and other living areas as the dwelling unit destroyed or removed by the agency.

(d) "Very low income households" has the same meaning as specified in Section 50105.

33411.3 Priority for affordable housing units to displacees

Whenever all or any portion of a redevelopment project is developed with low- or moderate-income housing units and whenever any low-or moderate-income housing units are developed with any agency assistance or pursuant to Section 33413, the agency shall require by contract or other appropriate means that the housing be made available for rent or purchase to the persons and families of low or moderate income displaced by the redevelopment project. Those persons and families shall be given priority in renting or buying that housing. However, failure to give that priority shall not affect the validity of title to real property. The agency shall keep a list of persons and families of low and moderate income displaced by the redevelopment project who are to be given priority, and may establish reasonable rules for determining the order or priority on the list.

33411.4 Last resort housing

If insufficient suitable housing units are available in the community for low- and moderate-income persons and families to be displaced from a redevelopment project area, the legislative body shall assure that sufficient land be made available for suitable housing for rental or purchase by low- and moderate-income persons and families. If insufficient suitable housing units are available in the community for use by such persons and families of low and moderate income displaced by the redevelopment project, the redevelopment agency may, to the extent of that deficiency, direct or cause the development, rehabilitation or construction of housing units within the community, both inside and outside of redevelopment project areas.

33412 Temporary and permanent housing facilities

Permanent housing facilities shall be made available within three years from the time occupants are displaced and that pending the development of such facilities there will be available to such displaced occupants adequate temporary housing facilities at rents comparable to those in the community at the time of their displacement.

33413 Replacement housing; inclusionary requirements

(a) Whenever dwelling units housing persons and families of low or moderate income are destroyed or removed from the low- and moderate-income housing market as part of a redevelopment project that is subject to a written agreement with the agency or where financial assistance has been provided by the agency, the agency shall, within four years of the destruction or removal, rehabilitate, develop, or construct, or cause to be rehabilitated, developed, or constructed, for rental or sale to persons and families of low or moderate income, an equal number of replacement dwelling units that have an equal or greater number of bedrooms as those destroyed or removed units at affordable housing costs within the territorial jurisdiction of the agency. When dwelling units are destroyed or removed after September 1, 1989, 75 percent of the replacement dwelling units shall replace dwelling units available at affordable housing cost in the same or a lower income level of very low income households, lower income households, and persons and families of low and moderate income, as the persons displaced from those destroyed or removed units. When dwelling units are destroyed or removed on or after January 1, 2002, 100 percent of the replacement dwelling units shall be available at affordable housing cost to persons in the same or a lower income category (low, very low, or moderate), as the persons displaced from those destroyed or removed units.

(b) (1) Prior to the time limit on the effectiveness of the redevelopment plan established pursuant to Sections 33333.2, 33333.6, and 33333.10 at least 30 percent of all new and substantially rehabilitated dwelling units developed by an agency shall be available at affordable housing cost to, and occupied by, persons and families of low or moderate income. Not less than 50 percent of the dwelling units required to be available at affordable housing cost to, and occupied by, persons and families of low or moderate income shall be available at affordable housing cost to, and occupied by, very low income households.

(2) (A) (i) Prior to the time limit on the effectiveness of the redevelopment plan established pursuant to Sections 33333.2, 33333.6, and 33333.10 at least 15 percent of all new and substantially rehabilitated dwelling units developed within a project area under the jurisdiction of an agency by public or private entities or persons other than the agency shall be available at affordable housing cost to, and occupied by, persons and families of low or moderate income. Not less than 40 percent of the dwelling units required to be available at affordable housing cost to, and occupied by, persons and families of low or moderate income shall be available at affordable housing cost to, and occupied by, very low income households.

(ii) To satisfy this paragraph, in whole or in part, the agency may cause, by regulation or agreement, to be available, at affordable housing cost, to, and occupied by, persons and families of low or moderate income or to very low income households, as applicable, two units outside a project area for each unit that otherwise would have been required to be available inside a project area.

(iii) On or after January 1, 2002, as used in this paragraph and in paragraph (1), "substantially rehabilitated dwelling units" means all units substantially rehabilitated, with agency assistance. Prior to January 1, 2002, "substantially rehabilitated dwelling units" shall mean substantially rehabilitated multifamily rented dwelling units with three or more units regardless of whether there is agency assistance, or substantially rehabilitated, with agency assistance, single-family dwelling units with one or two units.

(iv) As used in this paragraph and in paragraph (1), "substantial rehabilitation" means rehabilitation, the value of which constitutes 25 percent of the after rehabilitation value of the dwelling, inclusive of the land value.

(v) To satisfy this paragraph, the agency may aggregate new or substantially rehabilitated dwelling units in one or more project areas, if the agency finds, based on substantial evidence, after a public hearing, that the aggregation will not cause or exacerbate racial, ethnic, or economic segregation.

(B) To satisfy the requirements of paragraph (1) and subparagraph (A), the agency may purchase, or otherwise acquire or cause by regulation or agreement the purchase or other acquisition of, long-term affordability covenants on multifamily units that restrict the cost of renting or purchasing those units that either: (i) are not presently available at affordable housing cost to persons and families of low or very low income households, as applicable; or (ii) are units that are presently available at affordable housing cost to this same group of persons or families, but are units that the agency finds, based upon substantial evidence, after a public hearing, cannot reasonably be expected to remain affordable to this same group of persons or families.

(C) To satisfy the requirements of paragraph (1) and subparagraph (A), the long-term affordability covenants purchased or otherwise acquired pursuant to subparagraph (B) shall be required to be maintained on dwelling units at affordable housing cost to, and occupied by, persons and families of low or very low income, for the longest feasible time but not less than 55 years for rental units and 45 years for owner-occupied units. Not more than 50 percent of the units made available pursuant to paragraph (1) and subparagraph (A) may be assisted through the purchase or acquisition of long-term affordability covenants pursuant to subparagraph (B). Not less than 50 percent of the units made available through the purchase or acquisition of long-term affordability covenants pursuant to subparagraph (B) shall be available at affordable housing cost to, and occupied by, very low income households.

(D) To satisfy the requirements of paragraph (1) and subparagraph (A), each mutual self-help housing unit, as defined in subparagraph (C) of paragraph (1) of subdivision (f) of Section 33334.3, that is subject to a 15-year deed restriction shall count as one-third of a unit.

(3) The requirements of this subdivision shall apply independently of the requirements of subdivision (a). The requirements of this subdivision shall apply, in the aggregate, to housing made available pursuant to paragraphs (1) and (2), respectively, and not to each individual case of rehabilitation, development, or construction of dwelling units, unless an agency determines otherwise.

(4) Each redevelopment agency, as part of the implementation plan required by Section 33490, shall adopt a plan to comply with the requirements of this subdivision for each project area. The plan shall be consistent with, and may be included within, the community's housing element. The plan shall be reviewed and, if necessary, amended at least every five years in conjunction with either the housing element cycle or the plan implementation cycle. The plan shall ensure that the requirements of this subdivision are met every 10 years. If the requirements of this subdivision are not met by the end of each 10-year period, the agency shall meet these goals on an annual basis until the requirements for the 10-year period are met. If the agency has exceeded the requirements within the 10-year period, the agency may count the units that exceed the requirement in order to meet the requirements during the next 10-year period. The plan shall contain the contents required by paragraphs (2), (3) and (4) of subdivision (a) of Section 33490.

(c) (1) The agency shall require that the aggregate number of replacement dwelling units and other dwelling units rehabilitated, developed, constructed, or price restricted pursuant to subdivision (a) or (b) remain available at affordable housing cost to, and occupied by, persons and families of low-income, moderate-income, and very low income households, respectively, for the longest feasible time, but for not less than 55 years for rental units, 45 years for home ownership units, and 15 years for mutual self-help housing units, as defined in subparagraph (C) of paragraph (1) of subdivision (f) of Section 33334.3, except as set forth in paragraph (2). Nothing in this paragraph precludes the agency and the developer of the mutual self-help housing units from agreeing to 45-year deed restrictions.

(2) Notwithstanding paragraph (1), the agency may permit sales of owner-occupied units prior to the expiration of the 45-year period, and mutual self-help housing units prior to the expiration of the 15-year period, established by the agency for a price in excess of that otherwise permitted under this subdivision pursuant to an adopted program that protects the agency's investment of moneys from the Low and Moderate Income Housing Fund, including, but not limited to, an equity sharing program that establishes a schedule of equity sharing that permits retention by the seller of a portion of those excess proceeds, based on the length of occupancy. The remainder of the excess proceeds of the sale shall be allocated to the agency, and deposited into the Low and Moderate Income Housing Fund. The agency shall, within three years from the date of sale pursuant to this paragraph of each home ownership or mutual self-help housing unit subject to a 45-year deed restriction, and every third mutual self-help housing unit subject to a 15-year deed restriction, expend funds to make affordable an equal number of units at the same or lowest income level as the unit or units sold pursuant to this paragraph, for a period not less than the duration of the original deed restrictions. Only the units originally assisted by the agency shall be counted towards the agency's obligations under Section 33413.

(3) The requirements of this section shall be made enforceable in the same manner as provided in paragraph (7) of subdivision (f) of Section 33334.3.

(4) If land on which the dwelling units required by this section are located is deleted from the project area, the agency shall continue to require that those units remain affordable as specified in this subdivision.

(5) For each unit counted towards the requirements of subdivisions (a) and (b), the agency shall require the recording in the office of the county recorder of covenants or restrictions that ensure compliance with this subdivision.

With respect to covenants or restrictions that are recorded on or after January 1, 2008, the agency shall comply with the requirements of paragraphs (3) and (4) of subdivision (f) of Section 33334.3.

(d) (1) This section applies only to redevelopment projects for which a final redevelopment plan is adopted pursuant to Article 5 (commencing with Section 33360) on or after January 1, 1976, and to areas that are added to a project area by amendment to a final redevelopment plan adopted on or after January 1, 1976. In addition, subdivision (a) shall apply to any other redevelopment project with respect to dwelling units destroyed or removed from the low- and moderate-income housing market on or after January 1, 1996, irrespective of the date of adoption of a final redevelopment plan or an amendment to a final redevelopment plan adding areas to a project area. Additionally, any agency may, by resolution, elect to make all or part of the requirements of this section applicable to any redevelopment project of the agency for which the final redevelopment plan was adopted prior to January 1, 1976. In addition, subdivision (b) shall apply to redevelopment plans adopted prior to January 1, 1976, for which an amendment is adopted pursuant to Section 33333.10, except that subdivision (b) shall apply to those redevelopment plans prospectively only so that the requirements of subdivision (b) shall apply only to new and substantially rehabilitated dwelling units for which the building permits are issued on or after the date that the ordinance adopting the amendment pursuant to Section 33333.10 becomes effective.

(2) An agency may, by resolution, elect to require that whenever dwelling units housing persons or families of low or moderate income are destroyed or removed from the low- and moderate-income housing market as part of a redevelopment project, the agency shall replace each dwelling unit with up to three replacement dwelling units pursuant to subdivision (a).

(e) Except as otherwise authorized by law, this section does not authorize an agency to operate a rental housing development beyond the period reasonably necessary to sell or lease the housing development.

(f) Notwithstanding subdivision (a), the agency may replace destroyed or removed dwelling units with a fewer number of replacement dwelling units if the replacement dwelling units meet both of the following criteria:

(1) The total number of bedrooms in the replacement dwelling units equals or exceeds the number of bedrooms in the destroyed or removed units. Destroyed or removed units having one or no bedroom are deemed for this purpose to have one bedroom.

(2) The replacement units are affordable to and occupied by the same income level of households as the destroyed or removed units.

(g) "Longest feasible time," as used in this section, includes, but is not limited to, unlimited duration.

33413.1 Replacement Housing; Inclusionary Requirements—Eden Redevelopment Project Area, County of Alameda Redevelopment Agency

(a) For only the Mt. Eden Sub-Area of the Eden Redevelopment Project Area, the Redevelopment Agency of the County of Alameda may count, towards satisfaction of the housing production requirements of subdivision (b) of Section 33413, the construction of units outside the project area but within the City of Hayward if all of the following conditions are met:

(1) The units shall be available at affordable housing cost to, and occupied by, persons and families of very low or low income.

(2) The units shall comply with subdivision (c) of Section 33413, except that the requirements of that subdivision shall be deemed satisfied if the recorded covenants or restrictions are enforceable by the City of Hayward.

(3) The units shall be located on a parcel or parcels immediately contiguous to the Mt. Eden Sub-Area of the Eden Redevelopment Project Area.

(4) The Redevelopment Agency of the City of Hayward shall provide to the Redevelopment Agency of the County of Alameda written consent to the measures taken pursuant to this section and shall not count any units credited to the Redevelopment Agency of Alameda County pursuant to this section towards its own production or replacement requirements under Section 33413.

(b) The Redevelopment Agency of the County of Alameda shall cause to be made available, at affordable housing cost to, and occupied by, persons and families of very low, low-, or moderate-income households, as applicable, two units outside the project area for each unit that otherwise would have been required to be available inside the project area as required by clause (ii) of subparagraph (A) of paragraph (2) of subdivision (b) of Section 33413.

(c) This section does not apply to a housing unit for which construction commences on or after January 1, 2012.

33413.5 Replacement housing plan

Not less than 30 days prior to the execution of an agreement for acquisition of real property, or the execution of an agreement for the disposition and development of property, or the execution of an owner participation agreement, which agreement would lead to the destruction or removal of dwelling units from the low- and moderate-income housing market, the agency shall adopt by resolution a replacement housing plan. For a reasonable time prior to adopting a replacement housing plan by resolution, the agency shall make available a draft of the proposed replacement housing plan for review and comment by the project area committee, other public agencies, and the general public.

The replacement housing plan shall include (1) the general location of housing to be rehabilitated, developed, or constructed pursuant to Section 33413, (2) an adequate means of financing such rehabilitation, development, or construction, (3) a finding that the replacement housing does not require the approval of the voters pursuant to Article XXXIV of the California Constitution, or that such approval has been obtained, (4) the number of dwelling units housing persons and families of low or moderate income planned for construction or rehabilitation, and (5) the timetable for meeting the plan's relocation, rehabilitation, and replacement housing objectives. A dwelling unit whose replacement is required by Section 33413 but for which no replacement housing plan has been prepared, shall not be destroyed or removed from the low- and moderate-income housing market until the agency has by resolution adopted a replacement housing plan.

Nothing in this section shall prevent an agency from destroying or removing from the low- and moderate-income housing market a dwelling unit which the agency owns and which is an immediate danger to health and safety. The agency shall, as soon as practicable, adopt by resolution a replacement housing plan with respect to such dwelling unit.

33413.7 Limited equity housing cooperatives

An agency causing the rehabilitation, development, or construction of replacement dwelling units, other than single-family residences, pursuant to Section 33413 or Section 33464, or pursuant to a replacement housing plan as required by Section 33413.5, or pursuant to provisions of a redevelopment plan required by Section 33334.5, primarily for persons of low income, as defined in Section 50093, shall give preference to those developments which are proposed to be organized as limited-equity housing cooperatives, when so requested by a project area committee established pursuant to Section 33385, provided such project is achievable in an efficient and timely manner.

Such limited-equity housing cooperatives shall, in addition to the provisions of Section 33007.5, be organized so that the consideration paid for memberships or shares by the first occupants following construction or acquisition by the corporation, including the principal amount of obligations incurred to finance the share or membership purchase, does not exceed 3 percent of the development cost or acquisition cost, or of the fair market value appraisal by the permanent lender, whichever is greater.

33414 Rehousing bureau

An agency may operate a rehousing bureau to assist site occupants in obtaining adequate temporary or permanent housing. It may incur any necessary expenses for this purpose.

33415 Relocation assistance and payments

An agency shall provide relocation assistance and shall make all of the payments required by Chapter 16 (commencing with Section 7260) of Division 7 of Title 1 of the Government Code, including the making of such payments financed by the federal government.

This section shall not be construed to limit any other authority which an agency may have to make other relocation assistance payments, or to make any relocation assistance payment in an amount which exceeds the maximum amount for such payment authorized by Chapter 16 (commencing with Section 7260) of Division 7 of Title 1 of the Government Code.

33416 Disposition of surplus real property for housing

In order to facilitate the rehousing of families and single persons displaced by any governmental action, an agency, at the request of the legislative body of the community, may dispose of the real property acquired under the provisions of Section 33396, by sale or long-term lease, for use as, or development of, housing for such displaced persons.

33417 Relocation plans: review by Department of Housing and Community Development

Plans prepared pursuant to Section 33411 shall be provided to the Department of Housing and Community Development upon request to be reviewed by the department.

33417.5 Relocation appeals board

There is in each city, county, or city and county having an agency a relocation appeals board composed of five members appointed by the mayor of the city or by the chairman of the board of supervisors of the county, subject to the approval of the legislative body. Each board shall promptly hear all complaints brought by residents of the various project areas relating to relocation and shall determine if the redevelopment agency has complied with the provisions of this chapter and, where applicable, federal regulations. The board shall, after a public hearing, transmit its findings and recommendations to the agency. The members of the relocation appeals board shall serve without compensation, but each of the members shall be reimbursed for his necessary expenses incurred in performance of his duties, as determined by the legislative body.

33418 Monitoring of affordable housing

(a) An agency shall monitor, on an ongoing basis, any housing affordable to persons and families of low or moderate income developed or otherwise made available pursuant to any provisions of this part. As part of this monitoring, an agency shall require owners or managers of the housing to submit an annual report to the agency. The annual reports shall include for each rental unit the rental rate and the income and family size of the occupants, and for each owner-occupied unit whether there was a change in ownership from the prior year and, if so, the income and family size of the new owners. The income information required by this section shall be supplied by the tenant in a certified statement on a form provided by the agency.

(b) The data specified in subdivision (a) shall be obtained by the agency from owners and managers of the housing specified therein and current data shall be included in any reports required by law to be submitted to the Department of Housing and Community Development or the Controller. The information on income and family size that is required to be reported by the owner or manager shall be supplied by the tenant and shall be the only information on income or family size that the owner or manager shall be required to submit on his or her annual report to the agency.

(c) (1) The agency shall compile and maintain a database of existing, new and substantially rehabilitated, housing units developed or otherwise assisted with moneys from the Low and Moderate Income Housing Fund, or otherwise counted towards the requirements of subdivision (a) or (b) of Section 33413. The database shall be made available to the public on the Internet and updated on an annual basis. The database shall require all of the following information for each owner-occupied unit or rental unit, or for each group of units, if more than one unit is subject to the same covenant:

(A) The street address and assessor's parcel number of the property.

(B) The size of each unit, measured by the number of bedrooms.

(C) The year in which the construction or substantial rehabilitation of the unit was completed.

(D) The date of recordation and document number of the affordability covenants or restrictions required under subdivision (f) of Section 33334.3.

(E) The date on which the covenants or restrictions expire.

(F) For owner-occupied units that have changed ownership during the reporting year, as described in subdivision (a), the date and document number of the new affordability covenants or other documents recorded to assure that the affordability restriction is enforceable and continues to run with the land.

(2) Notwithstanding subparagraphs (A) and (D) of paragraph (1), the database shall omit any property used to confidentially house victims of domestic violence.

(3) Upon establishment of a database under this section, the agency shall provide reasonable notice to the community regarding the existence of the database.

(d) The agency shall adequately fund its monitoring activities as needed to insure compliance of applicable laws and agreements in relation to affordable units. For purposes of defraying the cost of complying with the requirements of this section and the changes in reporting requirements of Section 33080.4 enacted by the act enacting this section, an agency may establish and impose fees upon owners of properties monitored pursuant to this section.

Article 10
Demolition, Clearance, Project Improvements and Site Preparation

33420 Clearance

An agency may clear or move buildings, structures, or other improvements from any real property acquired.

33420.1 Building rehabilitation or alteration

Within a project area, for any project undertaken by an agency for building rehabilitation or alteration in construction, an agency may take those actions which the agency determines necessary and which is consistent with local, state, and federal law, to provide for seismic retrofits as follows:

(a) For unreinforced masonry buildings, to meet the requirements of Chapter 1 of the Appendix of the Uniform Code for Building Conservation of the International Conference of Building Officials.

(b) For any buildings that qualify as "historical property" under Section 37602, to meet the requirements of the State Historical Building Code (Part 2.7 (commencing with Section 18950) of Division 13).

(c) For buildings other than unreinforced masonry buildings and historical properties, to meet the requirements of the most current edition of the Uniform Building Code of the International Conference of Building Officials.

If an agency undertakes seismic retrofits and proposes to add new territory to the project area, to increase either the limitation on the number of dollars to be allocated to the redevelopment agency or the time limit on the establishing of loans, advances, and indebtedness established pursuant to paragraphs (1) and (2) of Section 33333.2, to lengthen the period during which the redevelopment plan is effective, to merge project areas, or to add significant additional capital improvement projects, as determined by the agency, the agency shall amend its redevelopment plan and follow the same procedure, and the legislative body is subject to the same restrictions, as provided for in Article 4 (commencing with Section 33330) for the adoption of a plan.

33420.2 Graffiti eradication

Within a project area, an agency may take any actions that the agency determines are necessary to remove graffiti from public or private property upon making a finding that, because of the magnitude and severity of the graffiti within the project area, the action is necessary to effectuate the purposes of the redevelopment plan, and that the action will assist with the elimination of blight, as defined in Section 33031.

33421 Development of building sites

An agency may develop as a building site any real property owned or acquired by it. In connection with such development it may cause, provide or undertake or make provision with other agencies for the installation, or construction of streets, utilities, parks, playgrounds and other public improvements necessary for carrying out in the project area the redevelopment plan.

33421.1 Development of building sites for industrial or commercial use; consent by legislative body

Without the prior consent of the legislative body, the agency may not use its authority under Section 33421 to develop a site for industrial or commercial use so as to provide streets, sidewalks, utilities, or other improvements which an owner or operator of the site would otherwise be obliged to provide.

In giving consent, the legislative body shall make a finding that the provision of such improvements is necessary to effectuate the purposes of the redevelopment plan.

33422.1 Preference for award of contracts to project area businesses

To the greatest extent feasible, contracts for work to be performed in connection with any redevelopment project shall be awarded to business concerns which are located in, or owned in the substantial part by persons residing in, the project area.

33422.3 Preference for employment of project area residents

To insure training and employment opportunities for lower-income project area residents, the agency may specify in the call for bids for any contract over one hundred thousand dollars ($100,000) for work to be performed in connection with any redevelopment project that project area residents, if available, shall be employed for a specified percentage of each craft or type of workmen needed to execute the contract or work.

33423 Notice of prevailing wages in call for bids

Before awarding any contract for such work to be done in a project, the agency shall ascertain the general prevailing rate of per diem wages in the locality in which the work is to be performed, for each craft or type of workman needed to execute the contract or work, and shall specify in the call for bids for the contract and in the contract such rate and the general prevailing rate for regular holiday and overtime work in the locality, for each craft or type of workman needed to execute the contract.

33424 Payment of prevailing wages required

The contractor to whom the contract is awarded and any subcontractor under him shall pay not less than the specified prevailing rate of wages to all workmen employed in the execution of the contract.

33425 Penalty for noncompliance with prevailing wage requirements

As a penalty to the agency which awarded the contract, the contractor shall forfeit ten dollars ($10) for each calendar day or portion thereof for each workman paid less than the stipulated prevailing rates for any public work done under the contract by him or by any subcontractor under him. A stipulation to this effect shall be included in the contract.

33426 Record of wage payments

Each contractor and subcontractor shall keep an accurate record showing the name, occupation, and actual per diem wages paid to each workman employed by him in connection with the work. The record shall be kept open at all reasonable hours to the inspection of the agency.

33426.5 Limitations on agency assistance: automobile dealerships/ undeveloped acreage

Notwithstanding the provisions of Sections 33391, 33430, 33433, and 33445, or any other provision of this part, an agency shall not provide any form of direct assistance to:

(a) An automobile dealership which will be or is on a parcel of land which has not previously been developed for urban use, unless, prior to the effective date of the act that adds this section, the agency either owns the land or has entered into an enforceable agreement, for the purchase of the land or of an interest in the land, including, but not limited to, a lease or an agreement containing covenants affecting real property, that requires the land to be developed and used as an automobile dealership.

(b) (1) A development that will be or is on a parcel of land of five acres or more which has not previously been developed for urban use and that will, when developed, generate sales or use tax pursuant to Part 1.5 (commencing with Section 7200) of Division 2 of the Revenue and Taxation Code, unless the principal permitted use of the development is office, hotel, manufacturing, or industrial, or unless, prior to the effective date of the act that adds this section, the agency either owns the land or has entered into an enforceable agreement, for the purchase of the land or of an interest in the land, including, but not limited to, a lease or an agreement containing covenants affecting real property, that requires the land to be developed.

(2) For the purposes of this subdivision, a parcel shall include land on an adjacent or nearby parcel on which a use exists that is necessary for the legal development of the parcel.

(c) A development or business, either directly or indirectly, for the acquisition, construction, improvement, rehabilitation, or replacement of property that is or would be used for gambling or gaming of any kind whatsoever including, but not limited to, casinos, gaming clubs, bingo operations, or any facility wherein banked or percentage games, any form of gambling device, or lotteries, other than the California State Lottery, are or will be played.

(d) The prohibition in subdivision (c) is not intended to prohibit a redevelopment agency from acquiring property on or in which an existing gambling enterprise is located, for the purpose of selling or leasing the property for uses other than gambling, provided that the agency acquires the property for fair market value.

(e) This section shall not be construed to apply to agency assistance in the construction of public improvements that serve all or a portion of a project area and that are not required to be constructed as a condition of approval of a development described in subdivision (a), (b), or (c), or to prohibit assistance in the construction of public improvements that are being constructed for a development that is not described in subdivision (a), (b), or (c).

33426.7 Limitations on agency assistance: automobile dealerships or big box retailers relocating from one community to another within same market area

(a) Notwithstanding any other provision of this part, a redevelopment agency shall not provide any form of financial assistance to a vehicle dealer or big box retailer, or a business entity that sells or leases land to a vehicle dealer or big box retailer, that is relocating from the territorial jurisdiction of one community to the territorial jurisdiction of another community but within the same market area.

(b) As used in this section:

(1) "Big box retailer" means a store of greater than 75,000 square feet of gross buildable area that will generate sales or use tax pursuant to the Bradley-Burns Uniform Local Sales and Use Tax Law (Part 1.5 (commencing with Section 7200) of Division 2 of the Revenue and Taxation Code).

(2) "Community" and "territorial jurisdiction" have the meanings specified in Sections 33002 and 33120, respectively.

(3) "Financial assistance" includes, but is not limited to, any of the following:

(A) Any appropriation of public funds, including loans, grants, or subsidies or the payment for or construction of parking improvements.

(B) Any tax incentive, including tax exemptions, rebates, reductions, or moratoria of a tax, including any rebate or payment based upon the amount of sales tax generated from the vehicle dealer or big box retailer.

(C) The sale or lease of real property at a cost that is less than fair market value.

(D) Payment for, forgiveness of, or reduction of fees.

(4) (A) "Market area" means a geographical area that is described in independent and recognized commercial trade literature, recognized and established business or manufacturing policies or practices, or publications of recognized independent research organizations as being an area that is large enough to support the location of the specific vehicle dealer or the specific big box retailer that is relocating.

(B) With respect to a vehicle dealer, a "market area" shall not extend further than 40 miles, as measured by the most reasonable route on roads between two points, starting from the location from which the vehicle dealer is relocating and ending at the location to which the vehicle dealer is relocating.

(C) With respect to a big box retailer, a "market area" shall not extend further than 25 miles, as measured by the most reasonable route on roads between two points, starting from the location from which the big box retailer is relocating and ending at the location to which the big box retailer is relocating.

(5) "Relocating" means the closing of a vehicle dealer or big box retailer in one location and the opening of a vehicle dealer or big box retailer in another location within a 365-day period when a person or business entity has an ownership interest in both the vehicle dealer or big box retailer that has closed or will close and the one that is opening. "Relocating" does not mean and shall not include the closing of a vehicle dealer or big box retailer because the vehicle dealer or big box retailer has been or will be acquired or has been or will be closed as a result of the use of eminent domain.

(6) "Vehicle dealer" means a retailer that is also a dealer as defined by Section 285 of the Vehicle Code.

(c) This section does not apply to agency assistance in the construction of public improvements that serve all or a portion of a project area and that are not required to be constructed as a condition of approval of the vehicle dealer or big box retailer. This section also does not prohibit assistance in the construction of public improvements that are being constructed for a development other than the vehicle dealer or big box retailer.

(d) This section shall not apply to any financial assistance provided by a redevelopment agency pursuant to a lease, contract, agreement, or other enforceable written instrument entered into between the redevelopment agency and a vehicle dealer, big box retailer, or a business entity that sells or leases land to a vehicle dealer or big box retailer, if the lease, contract, agreement, or other enforceable written instrument was entered into prior to December 31, 1999.

Article 11
Property Disposition, Rehabilitation and Development

33430 Disposition of property

An agency may, within the survey area or for purposes of redevelopment, sell, lease, for a period not to exceed 99 years, exchange, subdivide, transfer, assign, pledge, encumber by mortgage, deed of trust, or otherwise, or otherwise dispose of any real or personal property or any interest in property.

33431 Lease or sale without public bidding

Any lease or sale made pursuant to Section 33430 may be made without public bidding but only after a public hearing, notice of which shall be given by publication for not less than once a week for two weeks in a newspaper of general circulation published in the county in which the land lies.

33432 Property required to be leased or sold

Except as provided in Article 9 (commencing with Section 33410) of this part, an agency shall lease or sell all real property acquired by it in any project area, except property conveyed by it to the community or any other public body. Any such lease or sale shall be conditioned on the redevelopment and use of the property in conformity with the redevelopment plan.

33433 Sale or lease of property acquired with tax increment funds; approval by legislative body after public hearing

(a) (1) Except as provided in subdivision (c), before any property of the agency acquired in whole or in part, directly or indirectly, with tax increment moneys is sold or leased for development pursuant to the redevelopment plan, the sale or lease shall first be approved by the legislative body by resolution after public hearing. Notice of the time and place of the hearing shall be published in a newspaper of general circulation in the community at least once per week for at least two successive weeks, as specified in Section 6066 of the Government Code, prior to the hearing.

(2) The agency shall make available, for public inspection and copying at a cost not to exceed the cost of duplication, a report no later than the time of publication of the first notice of the hearing mandated by this section. This report shall contain both of the following:

(A) A copy of the proposed sale or lease.

(B) A summary which describes and specifies all of the following:

(i) The cost of the agreement to the agency, including land acquisition costs, clearance costs, relocation costs, the costs of any improvements to be provided by the agency, plus the expected interest on any loans or bonds to finance the agreements.

(ii) The estimated value of the interest to be conveyed or leased, determined at the highest and best uses permitted under the plan.

(iii) The estimated value of the interest to be conveyed or leased, determined at the use and with the conditions, covenants, and development costs required by the sale or lease. The purchase price or present value of the lease payments which the lessor will be required to make during the term of the lease. If the sale price or total rental amount is less than the fair market value of the interest to be conveyed or leased, determined at the highest and best use consistent with the redevelopment plan, then the agency shall provide as part of the summary an explanation of the reasons for the difference.

(iv) An explanation of why the sale or lease of the property will assist in the elimination of blight, with reference to all supporting facts and materials relied upon in making this explanation.

(v) The report shall be made available to the public no later than the time of publication of the first notice of the hearing mandated by this section.

(b) The resolution approving the lease or sale shall be adopted by a majority vote unless the legislative body has provided by ordinance for a two-thirds vote for that purpose and shall contain a finding that the sale or lease of the property will assist in the elimination of blight or provide housing for low- or moderate-income persons, and is consistent with the implementation plan adopted pursuant to Section 33490. The resolution shall also contain one of the following findings:

(1) The consideration is not less than the fair market value at its highest and best use in accordance with the plan.

(2) The consideration is not less than the fair reuse value at the use and with the covenants and conditions and development costs authorized by the sale or lease.

(c) (1) Subdivisions (a) and (b) shall not apply to the sale or lease of a small housing project, as defined in Section 33013, if the legislative body adopts a resolution that authorizes the agency to sell or lease a small housing project pursuant to this subdivision. The agency may sell or lease a small housing project pursuant to this subdivision if, prior to the sale or lease, the agency holds a public hearing pursuant to Section 33431. Any agency that has sold or leased a small housing project pursuant to this subdivision shall, within 30 days after the end of the agency's fiscal year in which the sale or lease occurred, file a report with the legislative body which discloses the name of the buyer, the legal description or street address of the property, the date of the sale or lease, the consideration for which the property was sold or leased by the agency to the buyer or lessee, and the date on which the agency held its public hearing for the sale or lease, pursuant to Section 33431.

(2) As used in this subdivision and Section 33413, "persons and families of low- and moderate-income" has the same meaning as that term is defined in Section 50093.

33434 Approval of sale or lease of property acquired from revolving redevelopment fund

If any property acquired in whole or in part from the redevelopment revolving fund is to be sold or leased by the agency, the sale or lease shall be first approved by the legislative body by resolution adopted after public hearing. Notice of the time and place of the hearing shall be published once in the official newspaper of the community at least one week prior to the hearing. The resolution shall be adopted by a majority vote unless the legislative body has provided by ordinance for a two-thirds vote for such purpose.

33435 Obligation to refrain from discrimination

(a) Agencies shall obligate lessees and purchasers of real property acquired in redevelopment projects and owners of property improved as a part of a redevelopment project to refrain from restricting the rental, sale, or lease of the property on any basis listed in subdivision (a) or (d) of Section 12955 of the Government Code, as those bases are defined in Sections 12926, 12926.1, subdivision (m) and paragraph (1) of subdivision (p) of Section 12955, and Section 12955.2 of the Government Code. All deeds, leases, or contracts for the sale, lease, sublease, or other transfer of any land in a redevelopment project shall contain or be subject to the nondiscrimination or nonsegregation clauses hereafter prescribed.

(b) Notwithstanding subdivision (a), with respect to familial status, subdivision (a) shall not be construed to apply to housing for older persons, as defined in Section 12955.9 of the Government Code. With respect to familial status, nothing in subdivision (a) shall be construed to affect Sections 51.2, 51.3, 51.4,

51.10, 51.11, and 799.5 of the Civil Code, relating to housing for senior citizens. Subdivision (d) of Section 51 and Section 1360 of the Civil Code and subdivisions (n), (o), and (p) of Section 12955 of the Government Code shall apply to subdivision (a).

33436 Nondiscrimination and nonsegregation clauses

Express provisions shall be included in all deeds, leases and contracts that the agency proposes to enter into with respect to the sale, lease, sublease, transfer, use, occupancy, tenure, or enjoyment of any land in a redevelopment project in substantially the following form:

(a) (1) In deeds the following language shall appear — "The grantee herein covenants by and for himself or herself, his or her heirs, executors, administrators, and assigns, and all persons claiming under or through them, that there shall be no discrimination against or segregation of, any person or group of persons on account of any basis listed in subdivision (a) or (d) of Section 12955 of the Government Code, as those bases are defined in Sections 12926, 12926.1, subdivision (m) and paragraph (1) of subdivision (p) of Section 12955, and Section 12955.2 of the Government Code, in the sale, lease, sublease, transfer, use, occupancy, tenure, or enjoyment of the premises herein conveyed, nor shall the grantee or any person claiming under or through him or her, establish or permit any practice or practices of discrimination or segregation with reference to the selection, location, number, use or occupancy of tenants, lessees, subtenants, sublessees, or vendees in the premises herein conveyed. The foregoing covenants shall run with the land."

(2) Notwithstanding paragraph (1), with respect to familial status, paragraph (1) shall not be construed to apply to housing for older persons, as defined in Section 12955.9 of the Government Code. With respect to familial status, nothing in paragraph (1) shall be construed to affect Sections 51.2, 51.3, 51.4, 51.10, 51.11, and 799.5 of the Civil Code, relating to housing for senior citizens. Subdivision (d) of Section 51 and Section 1360 of the Civil Code and subdivisions (n), (o), and (p) of Section 12955 of the Government Code shall apply to paragraph (1).

(b) (1) In leases the following language shall appear — "The lessee herein covenants by and for himself or herself, his or her heirs, executors, administrators, and assigns, and all persons claiming under or through him or her, and this lease is made and accepted upon and subject to the following conditions:

That there shall be no discrimination against or segregation of any person or group of persons, on account of any basis listed in subdivision (a) or (d) of Section 12955 of the Government Code, as those bases are defined in Sections 12926, 12926.1, subdivision (m) and paragraph (1) of subdivision (p) of Section 12955, and Section 12955.2 of the Government Code, in the leasing, subleasing, transferring, use, occupancy, tenure, or enjoyment of the premises herein leased nor shall the lessee himself or herself, or any person claiming under or through him or her, establish or permit any such practice or practices of discrimination or segregation with reference to the selection, location, number, use, or occupancy, of tenants, lessees, sublessees, subtenants, or vendees in the premises herein leased."

(2) Notwithstanding paragraph (1), with respect to familial status, paragraph (1) shall not be construed to apply to housing for older persons, as defined in Section 12955.9 of the Government Code. With respect to familial status, nothing in paragraph (1) shall be construed to affect Sections 51.2, 51.3, 51.4, 51.10, 51.11, and 799.5 of the Civil Code, relating to housing for senior citizens. Subdivision (d) of Section 51 and Section 1360 of the Civil Code and subdivisions (n), (o), and (p) of Section 12955 of the Government Code shall apply to paragraph (1).

(c) In contracts entered into by the agency relating to the sale, transfer, or leasing of land or any interest therein acquired by the agency within any survey area or redevelopment project the foregoing provisions in substantially the forms set forth shall be included and the contracts shall further provide that the foregoing provisions shall be binding upon and shall obligate the contracting party or parties and any subcontracting party or parties, or other transferees under the instrument.

33437 Obligations of lessees or purchasers

An agency shall obligate lessees or purchasers of property acquired in a redevelopment project to:

(a) Use the property for the purpose designated in the redevelopment plans.

(b) Begin the redevelopment of the project area within a period of time which the agency fixes as reasonable.

(c) Comply with the covenants, conditions, or restrictions that the agency deems necessary to prevent speculation or excess profittaking in undeveloped land, including right of reverter to the agency. Covenants, conditions, and restrictions imposed by an agency may provide for the reasonable protection of lenders.

(d) Comply with other conditions which the agency deems necessary to carry out the purposes of this part.

33437.5 Property not to be the subject of real estate speculation

It is the intent of the Legislature that property acquired from a redevelopment agency pursuant to a redevelopment plan not be the subject of real estate speculation.

33438 Covenants and conditions running with land

The agency may provide in the contract that any of the obligations of the purchaser are covenants or conditions running with the land, the breach of which shall cause the fee to revert to the agency.

33439 Controls, restrictions and covenants running with land

The agency shall retain controls and establish restrictions or covenants running with land sold or leased for private use for such periods of time and under such conditions as are provided in the redevelopment plan. The establishment of such controls is a public purpose under the provisions of this part.

33440 Construction of buildings

Except as provided in Article 9 (commencing with Section 33410), this part does not authorize an agency to construct any of the buildings for residential, commercial, industrial, or other use contemplated by the redevelopment plan, except that, in addition to its powers under Section 33445, an agency may construct foundations, platforms, and other like structural forms necessary for the provision or utilization of air rights sites for buildings to be used for residential, commercial, industrial, or other uses contemplated by the redevelopment plan.

33442 Disposition of land for public housing projects

An agency may sell, lease, grant, or donate real property owned or acquired by the agency in a survey area to a housing authority or to any public agency for public housing projects.

33443 Report of unsold property

Property acquired by an agency for rehabilitation and resale shall be offered for resale within one year after completion of rehabilitation, or an annual report shall be published by the agency in a newspaper of general circulation published in the community listing any rehabilitated property held by the agency in excess of such one-year period, stating the reasons such property remains unsold and indicating plans for its disposition.

33444 Annual report to Legislature

In undertaking rehabilitation of structures pursuant to this part, every redevelopment agency shall, on or before February 15th of each year, commencing with February 15, 1963, render a report to the Legislature setting forth in detail the activities of the agency involving rehabilitation, including, but not limited to, each of the following:

(a) Expenditure of public funds.

(b) Number and kinds of units rehabilitated.

(c) Disposition of rehabilitated units.

33444.5 Commercial rehabilitation loans

An agency may establish a program under which it loans funds to owners or tenants for the purpose of rehabilitating commercial buildings or structures within the project area.

33444.6 Financing of facilities/capital equipment: industrial or manufacturing projects

(a) Within a project area and as part of an agreement that provides for the development or rehabilitation of property that will be used for industrial or manufacturing purposes, an agency may assist with the financing of facilities or capital equipment, including, but not necessarily limited to, pollution control devices.

(b) Prior to entering into an agreement for a development that will be assisted pursuant to this section, the agency shall find, after a public hearing, that the assistance is necessary for the economic feasibility of the development and that the assistance cannot be obtained on economically feasible terms in the private market.

33445 Payment for publicly owned buildings, facilities, structures or other improvements

(a) Notwithstanding Section 33440, an agency may, with the consent of the legislative body, pay all or a part of the value of the land for and the cost of the installation and construction of any building, facility, structure, or other improvement that is publicly owned either within or without the project area, if the legislative body determines all of the following:

(1) That the buildings, facilities, structures, or other improvements are of benefit to the project area or the immediate neighborhood in which the project is located, regardless of whether the improvement is within another project area, or in the case of a project area in which substantially all of the land is publicly owned that the improvement is of benefit to an adjacent project area of the agency.

(2) That no other reasonable means of financing the buildings, facilities, structures, or other improvements, are available to the community.

(3) That the payment of funds for the acquisition of land or the cost of buildings, facilities, structures, or other improvements will assist in the elimination of one or more blighting conditions inside the project area or provide housing for low- or moderate-income persons, and is consistent with the implementation plan adopted pursuant to Section 33490.

(b) The determinations by the agency and the local legislative body pursuant to subdivision (a) shall be final and conclusive. For redevelopment plans, and amendments to those plans which add territory to a project, adopted after October 1, 1976, acquisition of property and installation or construction of each facility shall be provided for in the redevelopment plan. A redevelopment agency shall not pay for the normal maintenance or operations of buildings, facilities, structures, or other improvements that are publicly owned. Normal maintenance or operations do not include the construction, expansion, addition to, or reconstruction of, buildings, facilities, structures, or other improvements that are publicly owned otherwise undertaken pursuant to this section.

(c) When the value of the land or the cost of the installation and construction of the building, facility, structure, or other improvement, or both, has been, or will be, paid or provided for initially by the community or other public corporation, the agency may enter into a contract with the community or other public corporation under which it agrees to reimburse the community or other public corporation for all or part of the value of the land or all or part of the cost of the building, facility, structure, or other improvement, or both, by periodic payments over a period of years.

(d) The obligation of the agency under the contract shall constitute an indebtedness of the agency for the purpose of carrying out the redevelopment project for the project area, which indebtedness may be made payable out of taxes levied in the project area and allocated to the agency under subdivision (b) of Section 33670, or out of any other available funds.

(e) In a case where the land has been or will be acquired by, or the cost of the installation and construction of the building, facility, structure or other improvement has been paid by, a parking authority, joint powers entity, or other public corporation to provide a building, facility, structure, or other improvement that has been or will be leased to the community, the contract may be made with, and the reimbursement may be made payable to, the community.

(f) With respect to the financing, acquisition, or construction of a transportation, collection, and distribution system and related peripheral parking facilities, in a county with a population of 4,000,000 persons or more, the agency shall, in order to exercise the powers granted by this section, enter into an agreement with the rapid transit district that includes the county, or a portion thereof, in which agreement the rapid transit district shall be given all of the following responsibilities:

(1) To participate with the other parties to the agreement to design, determine the location and extent of the necessary rights-of-way for, and construct, the transportation, collection, and distribution systems and related peripheral parking structures and facilities.

(2) To operate and maintain the transportation, collection, and distribution systems and related peripheral parking structures and facilities in accordance with the rapid transit district's outstanding agreements and the agreement required by this paragraph.

(g) (1) Notwithstanding any other authority granted in this section, an agency shall not pay for, either directly or indirectly, with tax increment funds the construction, including land acquisition, related site clearance, and design costs, or rehabilitation of a building that is, or that will be used as, a city hall or county administration building.

(2) This subdivision shall not preclude an agency from making payments to construct, rehabilitate, or replace a city hall if an agency does any of the following:

(A) Allocates tax increment funds for this purpose during the 1988–89 fiscal year and each fiscal year thereafter in order to comply with federal and state seismic safety and accessibility standards.

(B) Uses tax increment funds for the purpose of rehabilitating or replacing a city hall that was seriously damaged during an earthquake that was declared by the President of the United States to be a natural disaster.

(C) Uses the proceeds of bonds, notes, certificates of participation, or other indebtedness that was issued prior to January 1, 1994, for the purpose of constructing or rehabilitating a city hall, as evidenced by documents approved at the time of the issuance of the indebtedness.

33445.3 California City Redevelopment Agency: limitations

Notwithstanding any other provision of law, the California City Redevelopment Agency shall not directly support the activities of, or pay for any part of the land or any building, facility, structure, or other improvements that specifically benefit, the California City Museum and Restoration Facility.

33445.5 School districts: overcrowding resulting from redevelopment plan

(a) If the governing board of a school district finds that conditions of overcrowding, as defined by subdivision (a) of Section 65973 of the Government Code, exist in one or more attendance areas within the district that serve pupils who reside in housing, located within or adjacent to a project area, and that the conditions of overcrowding result from actions taken by the redevelopment agency in implementing the redevelopment plan, the governing board may transmit a written copy of those findings, together with supporting information, materials, and documents, to the redevelopment agency. The redevelopment agency shall conduct a public hearing within 45 days after receiving the findings to receive public testimony identifying the effects of the redevelopment plan on the impacted attendance area or areas and suggesting revisions to the plan as adopted or amended by the legislative body that would alleviate or eliminate the overcrowding in the attendance area or areas caused by the implementation of the redevelopment plan. The redevelopment agency shall send written notice of the public hearing to, and at the hearing receive public testimony from, any affected taxing entity. After receiving that testimony at the hearing, the agency shall consider amendments of the plan necessary to alleviate or eliminate that overcrowding and may recommend those amendments for adoption by the legislative body.

(b) Section 33353 does not apply to an amendment of the plan proposed pursuant to subdivision (a) when both of the following occur:

(1) The amendment proposes only to add significant additional capital improvement projects to alleviate or eliminate the overcrowding in the attendance area or areas caused by the implementation of the plan.

(2) The amendment will delete capital improvement projects that are equivalent in financial impact on any affected taxing entity or otherwise modify the plan in a way that the agency finds there will be no additional financial impact or any affected taxing entity as a result of the amendment.

(c) Any funds received by a school district from a redevelopment agency to alleviate or eliminate the overcrowding in the attendance area or areas caused by implementation of a redevelopment plan as the result of a public hearing conducted pursuant to subdivision (a) shall be used only for capital expenditures.

(d) The governing body of a school district shall not make the findings permitted by subdivision (a) with respect to any project area more than once.

(e) This section applies only to redevelopment plans adopted prior to January 1, 1984.

33445.6 Fire protection districts: financial burden or detriment resulting from redevelopment plan

(a) If the governing board of a fire protection district finds that it is suffering a financial burden or detriment as a result of actions taken by the redevelopment agency in implementing the redevelopment plan, the district board may transmit a written copy of those findings, together with supporting information, materials, and documents, to the redevelopment agency. The redevelopment agency shall conduct a public hearing within 45 days after receiving the findings to receive public testimony identifying the effects of the redevelopment plan on the fire protection district and suggesting revisions to the redevelopment plan as adopted or amended by the legislative body that would alleviate or eliminate the financial burden or detriment in the area or areas caused by the implementation of the redevelopment plan. The redevelopment agency shall send written notice of the public hearing to, and at the hearing receive public testimony from, any affected taxing entity. After receiving that testimony at the hearing, the agency shall consider amendments of the plan necessary to alleviate or eliminate the financial burden or detriment in the area or areas caused by the implementation of the redevelopment plan. The agency may recommend those amendments for adoption by the legislative body.

(b) Section 33353 does not apply to an amendment of the plan proposed pursuant to subdivision (a) when both of the following occur:

(1) The amendment proposes only to add significant additional capital improvement projects to alleviate or eliminate the financial burden or detriment caused by the implementation of the plan.

(2) The amendment will delete capital improvement projects or otherwise modify the plan in a way that the agency finds will result in no additional financial impact on any affected taxing entity.

(c) Any funds received by a fire protection district from a redevelopment agency to alleviate or eliminate the financial burden or detriment caused by implementation of a redevelopment plan as a result of a public hearing conducted pursuant to subdivision (a) may be used for any lawful purpose of the district.

(d) The district board of a fire protection district shall not make the findings permitted by subdivision (a) with respect to any project area more than once.

(e) The agency may recover its actual costs of complying with the procedural requirements of this section from the fire protection district.

(f) This section applies only to redevelopment plans adopted prior to January 1, 1977.

33446 Construction and lease of buildings to school districts

The governing board of any school district may enter into an agreement with an agency under which the agency shall construct, or cause to be constructed, a building or buildings to be used by the district upon a designated site within a project area and, pursuant to the agreement, the district may lease the buildings and site. The agreement shall provide that the title to the building or buildings and site shall vest in the district at the expiration of the lease, and may provide the means or method by which the title to the building or buildings and the site shall vest in the district prior to the expiration of the lease, and shall contain other terms and conditions that the governing board of the district deems to be in the best interest of the district. The agreements and leases may be entered into by the governing board of any school district without regard to bidding, election, or any other requirement of Article 2 (commencing with Section 17400) of Chapter 4 of Part 10.5 of the Education Code.

33447 Payment for public improvements: City of Paramount

In addition to any other authority contained in this division and subject to the requirements of this section, taxes levied in a project area and allocated to the agency as provided in subdivision (b) of Section 33670 may be used as provided thereby anywhere within the territorial jurisdiction of the agency to finance the construction or acquisition of public improvements meeting the following criteria, as determined by resolution of the agency:

(a) The public improvements will enhance the environment of a residential neighborhood containing housing for persons and families of low or moderate income, as defined in Section 50093, including very low income households, as defined in Section 50105.

(b) The public improvements will be of benefit to the project area. That determination shall be final and conclusive as to the issue of benefit to the project area.

(c) Public improvements eligible for financing under this section shall be limited to the following:

(1) Street improvements.
(2) Water, sewer, and storm drainage facilities.
(3) Neighborhood parks and related recreational facilities.

This section shall be applicable to redevelopment projects within the City of Paramount for which the redevelopment plan authorizes tax-increment financing pursuant to Section 33670, whether the redevelopment plan is adopted prior or subsequent to January 1, 1978. Financing of public improvements pursuant to this section shall be authorized by the redevelopment plan or by resolution of the agency. Any ordinance or resolution implementing this section shall specify the public improvements to be financed thereunder.

As a condition to financing public improvements as provided in this section on or after January 1, 1983, the redevelopment agency of the City of Paramount shall establish a Low and Moderate Income Housing Fund, and, with respect to any project made subject to this section, shall deposit in that fund not less than 20 percent of that portion of revenues allocated and paid to the agency pursuant to subdivision (b) of Section 33670 on and after January 1, 1983, which is not required to pay the principal of, or interest on, bonds or other indebtedness of the agency issued or incurred prior to that date. Moneys deposited in the Low and Moderate Income Housing Fund pursuant to this section shall be used pursuant to Article 4 (commencing with Section 33330).

The Legislature finds and declares that effective redevelopment within the City of Paramount requires the existence of adequate public services and facilities for persons residing in the surrounding community, including persons employed by industry which is located in a redevelopment project, and that public improvements of the types specified in this section are particularly needed in the low- and moderate-income neighborhoods of the City of Paramount in order to encourage stability and prevent decline which could have serious negative impact on redevelopment, as well as necessitate additional redevelopment. Because of the unusually compelling need in the City of Paramount and because of the impracticability of financing all required improvements by other means, it is the intent of the Legislature in enacting this section to augment the powers of the redevelopment agency of the City of Paramount to permit the use of tax-increment revenues in the manner and for the purposes prescribed by this section.

33448 Counties over 4,000,000 persons or cities over 500,000 persons: transportation systems and peripheral parking facilities

In a county with a population of 4,000,000 persons or more, or in a city of 500,000 persons or more, an agency may, with the consent of the legislative body, acquire, construct, and finance by the issuance of bonds or otherwise a public improvement whether within or without a project area consisting of a transportation collection and distribution system and peripheral parking structures and facilities, including sites therefor, to serve the project area and surrounding areas, upon a determination by resolution of the agency and the legislative body that such public improvement is of benefit to the project area. Such determination by the agency and the legislative body shall be final and conclusive as to the issue of benefit to the project area.

The agency shall, in order to exercise the powers granted by this section, enter into an agreement with the rapid transit district which includes the county or city, or a portion thereof, in which agreement the rapid transit district shall be given all of the following responsibilities:

(a) To participate with the other parties to the agreement to design, determine the location and extent of the necessary rights-of-way for, and construct the transportation, collection, and distribution systems and related peripheral parking structures and facilities.

(b) To operate and maintain such transportation, collection, and distribution systems and related peripheral parking structures and facilities in accordance with the rapid transit district's outstanding agreements and the agreement required by this paragraph.

33449 Activities to provide affordable housing

Notwithstanding Section 33440, or any other provision of law, an agency may, inside or outside any project area, acquire land, donate land, improve sites, or construct or rehabilitate structures in order to provide housing for persons and families of low or moderate income, as defined in Section 41056, and very low income households, as defined in Section 41067, and may provide subsidies to, or for the benefit of, such persons and families or households to assist them in obtaining housing within the community.

Except as otherwise authorized by law, nothing in this section shall empower an agency to operate a rental housing development beyond such period as is reasonably necessary to sell or lease the housing development.

This section shall apply to all redevelopment project areas for which a redevelopment plan has been adopted, whether the redevelopment plan is adopted before or after January 1, 1976.

Article 12
Amendment of Redevelopment Plans

33450 Authority to amend redevelopment plan

If at any time after the adoption of a redevelopment plan for a project area by the legislative body, it becomes necessary or desirable to amend or modify such plan, the legislative body may by ordinance amend such plan upon the recommendation of the agency. The agency recommendation to amend or modify a redevelopment plan may include a change in the boundaries of the project area to add land to or exclude land from the project area. Except as otherwise provided in Section 33378, the ordinance shall be subject to referendum as prescribed by law for the ordinances of the legislative body.

33451 Public hearing by agency

Before recommending amendment of the plan the agency shall hold a public hearing on the proposed amendment.

33451.5 Public hearing by agency–plan amendment–report on blight

(a) This section shall apply only to proposed plan amendments that would do any of the following:

(1) Change the limitation on the number of dollars of taxes which may be divided and allocated to the redevelopment agency.

(2) Change the limit on the amount of bonded indebtedness that can be outstanding at one time.

(3) Change the time limit on the establishing of loans, advances, and indebtedness to be paid with the proceeds of property taxes received pursuant to Section 33670.

(4) Change the time limit on the effectiveness of the redevelopment plan.

(5) Change the boundaries of the project area.

(6) Merge existing project areas.

(b) No later than 45 days prior to the public hearing on a proposed plan amendment by an agency or the joint public hearing of the agency and the legislative body, the agency shall notify the Department of Finance and the Department of Housing and Community Development by first-class mail of the public hearing, the date of the public hearing, and the proposed amendment. This notice shall be accompanied by the report required to be prepared pursuant to subdivision (c).

(c) No later than 45 days prior to the public hearing on a proposed plan amendment by the agency or the joint public hearing by the agency and the legislative body, the agency shall prepare a report that contains all of the following:

(1) A map of the project area that identifies the portion, if any, of the project area that is no longer blighted, the portion of the project area that is blighted, and the portion of the project area that contains necessary and essential parcels for the elimination of the remaining blight.

(2) A description of the remaining blight.

(3) A description of the projects or programs proposed to eliminate any remaining blight.

(4) A description of how these projects or programs will improve the conditions of blight.

(5) The reasons why the projects or programs cannot be completed without the plan amendment.

(6) The proposed method of financing these programs or projects. This description shall include the amount of tax increment revenues that is projected to be generated as a result of the proposed plan amendment, including amounts projected to be deposited into the Low and Moderate Income Housing Fund and amounts to be paid to the affecting taxing entities. This description shall also include sources and amounts of moneys other than tax increment revenues that are available to finance these projects or programs. This description shall also include the reasons that the remaining blight cannot reasonably be expected to be reversed or alleviated by private enterprise or governmental action, or both, without the use of the tax increment revenues available to the agency because of the proposed amendment.

(7) An amendment to the agency's implementation plan that includes, but is not limited to, the agency's housing responsibilities pursuant to Section 33490. However, the agency shall not be required to hold a separate public hearing on the implementation plan pursuant to subdivision (d) of Section 33490 in addition to the public hearing on the amendment to the redevelopment plan.

(8) A new neighborhood impact report if required by subdivision (m) of Section 33352.

(d) Upon receiving the report, the Department of Finance shall prepare an estimate of how the proposed plan amendment will affect the General Fund. The Department of Finance shall determine whether the amendment will affect the need for school facilities.

(e) Within 21 days of the receipt of the report, the Department of Finance or the Department of Housing and Community Development may send any comments regarding the proposed plan amendment in writing to the agency and the legislative body. The agency and the legislative body shall consider these comments, if any, at the public hearing on the proposed plan amendment. If these comments are not available within the prescribed time limit, the agency and the legislative body may proceed without them.

(f) The Department of Finance or the Department of Housing and Community Development may also send their comments regarding the proposed plan amendment to the Attorney General for further action pursuant to Chapter 5 (commencing with Section 33501).

33452 Notice of public hearing by agency

(a) Notice of the hearing shall be published pursuant to Section 6063 of the Government Code prior to the date of hearing in a newspaper of general circulation, printed and published in the community, or, if there is none, in a newspaper selected by the agency. The notice of hearing shall include a legal description of the boundaries of the project area by reference to the description recorded with the county recorder pursuant to Section 33373 and of the boundaries of the land proposed to be added to the project area, if any, and a general statement of the purpose of the amendment.

(b) Copies of the notices published pursuant to this section shall be mailed by first-class mail, to the last known assessee of each parcel of land not owned by the agency within the boundaries referred to in subdivision (a), at his or her last known address as shown on the last equalized assessment roll of the county; or where a city assesses, levies, and collects its own taxes, as shown on the last equalized assessment roll of the city; or to the owner of each parcel of land within these boundaries as the ownership is shown on the records of the county recorder 30 days prior to the date the notice is published, and to persons, firms, or corporations which have acquired property within these boundaries from the agency, at his or her last known address as shown by the records of the agency.

(c) (1) Copies of the notice published pursuant to this section shall be mailed, by first-class mail, to all residents and businesses within the project area designated in the redevelopment plan as proposed to be amended at least 30 days prior to the hearing.

(2) The mailed notice requirement of this subdivision shall only apply when mailing addresses to all individuals and businesses, or to all occupants, are obtained by the agency at a reasonable cost. The notice may be addresses to "occupant." If the agency acted in good faith to comply with the notice requirements of this subdivision, the failure of the agency to provide the required notice to residents or businesses unknown to the agency or whose addresses cannot be obtained at a reasonable cost, shall not, in and of itself, invalidate an amendment to a redevelopment plan.

(d) Copies of the notices published pursuant to this section shall also be mailed to the governing body of each of the taxing agencies that levies taxes upon any property in the project area designated in the redevelopment plan as proposed to be amended. Notices sent pursuant to this subdivision shall be mailed by certified mail with return receipt requested.

33453 Submission of changes to planning commission

If after the public hearings the agency recommends substantial changes in the plan which affect the general plan adopted by the planning commission or the legislative body, such changes shall be submitted to the planning commission for its report and recommendation to the legislative body within 30 days after such submission. If the planning commission does not report upon the changes within 30 days after its submission by the agency, the planning commission shall be deemed to have waived its report and recommendations concerning such changes.

33454 Public hearing by legislative body

After receiving the recommendation of the agency concerning such changes in the plan, and not sooner than 30 days after the submission of changes to the planning commission, the legislative body shall hold a public hearing on the proposed amendment, notice of which hearing shall be published in a newspaper in the manner and at the times designated above for notice of hearing by the agency.

33455 Submission of further changes to planning commission; ordinance amending prior ordinance

After receiving the recommendation of the agency concerning such changes in the plan, the legislative body upon further recommendation by the agency, without additional agency public hearing, may make further changes, including changes in area or boundaries to exclude land from the project area, for consideration at the public hearing. If such changes are substantial changes in the plan which affect the master or community plan adopted by the planning commission or the legislative body, such changes shall be submitted to the planning commission for its report and recommendation to the legislative body within 30 days after such submission. If the planning commission does not report upon the changes within 30 days after its submission by the legislative body, the planning commission shall be deemed to have waived its report and recommendation concerning the changes. If after the public hearing the legislative body determines that the amendments in the plan, proposed by the agency, or the further recommended changes by the agency are necessary or desirable, the legislative body shall adopt an ordinance amending the ordinance adopting the plans thus amended. The legislative body shall consider any proposed changes at a public hearing reopened for that limited purpose.

33456 Recordation of amendments

(a) Not later than 60 days after the adoption of an amendment to a redevelopment plan pursuant to this article there shall be recorded with the county recorder of the county in which the project area is located a statement that the redevelopment plan has been amended. If the amendment adds territory to the redevelopment project area, the statement shall contain a description of the added territory, a prominent heading in boldface type noting that the property that is the subject of the statement is located within a redevelopment project, a general description of the provisions of the amended redevelopment plan, if any, that authorize the use of the power of eminent domain by the agency within the added territory, and a general description of any limitations on the use of the power of eminent domain within the added territory, including, without limitation, the time limit required by Section 33333.2. If the amendment changes any limitation on the use of eminent domain contained in the redevelopment plan, the statement shall contain a description of the land within the project area and a general description of the change.

(b) An agency shall not commence an action in eminent domain to acquire property located within territory added to a project area by an amendment to a redevelopment plan until the statement required by this section is recorded with the county recorder of the county in which the project area is located.

(c) Additional recordation of documents may be effected pursuant to Section 27295 of the Government Code.

33457 Transmittal of redevelopment plan amendment documents to taxing officials and entities

After the amendment of a redevelopment plan to add the provision permitted by Section 33670, or to increase or reduce the size of the project area, the clerk of the community shall transmit a copy of the ordinance amending the plan, a description of the annexed or detached land within the project area and a map or plat indicating the amendments to the redevelopment plan, to the following parties:

(1) The auditor and assessor of the county in which the project is located;

(2) The officer or officers performing the functions of the auditor or assessor for any taxing agencies which, in levying or collecting taxes, do not use the county assessment roll or do not collect taxes through the county;

(3) The governing body of each of the taxing agencies which levies taxes upon any property in the project area; and

(4) The State Board of Equalization.

Such documents shall be transmitted within 30 days following the adoption of the amended redevelopment plan. The legal effect of such transmittal shall be as set forth in Section 33674.

33457.1 Findings, reports and information required

To the extent warranted by a proposed amendment to a redevelopment plan, (1) the ordinance adopting an amendment to a redevelopment plan shall contain the findings required by Section 33367 and (2) the reports and information required by Section 33352 shall be prepared and made available to the public prior to the hearing on such amendment.

33458 Authority to hold joint public hearing

As an alternative to the separate public hearing required by Sections 33451 and 33454, the agency and the legislative body, with the consent of both, may hold a joint public hearing on the proposed amendment. The presiding officer of the legislative body shall preside over such joint public hearing. Prior to such joint public hearing, the agency shall submit the proposed changes to the planning commission as provided in Section 33453. Notice of the joint public hearing shall conform to all requirements of Section 33452. The joint public hearing shall thereafter proceed by the same requirements as are provided in Sections 33450 and 33454 to 33455, inclusive.

When a joint public hearing is held where the legislative body is also the agency, the legislative body may adopt the amended plan with no actions necessary by the agency, even as to the recommendations required of the agency by Sections 33454 and 33455.

Article 12.5
Hazardous Substance Release Cleanup

33459 Definitions

For purposes of this article, the following terms shall have the following meanings:

(a) "Department" means the Department of Toxic Substances Control.

(b) "Director" means the Director of Toxic Substances Control.

(c) "Hazardous substance" means any hazardous substance as defined in subdivision (h) of Section 25281, and any reference to hazardous substance in the definitions referenced in this section shall be deemed to refer to hazardous substance, as defined in this subdivision.

(d) "Local agency" means a single local agency that is one of the following:

(1) A local agency authorized pursuant to Section 25283 to implement Chapter 6.7 (commencing with Section 25280) of, and Chapter 6.75 (commencing with Section 25299.10) of, Division 20.

(2) A local officer who is authorized pursuant to Section 101087 to supervise a remedial action.

(e) "Qualified independent contractor" means an independent contractor who is any of the following:

(1) An engineering geologist who is certified pursuant to Section 7842 of the Business and Professions Code.

(2) A geologist who is registered pursuant to Section 7850 of the Business and Professions Code.

(3) A civil engineer who is registered pursuant to Section 6762 of the Business and Professions Code.

(f) "Release" means any release, as defined in Section 25320.

(g) "Remedy" or "remove" means any action to assess, evaluate, investigate, monitor, remove, correct, clean up, or abate a release of a hazardous substance or to develop plans for those actions. "Remedy" includes any action set forth in Section 25322 and "remove" includes any action set forth in Section 25323.

(h) "Responsible party" means any person described in subdivision (a) of Section 25323.5 of this code or subdivision (a) of Section 13304 of the Water Code.

33459.01 Title

This article shall be known, and may be cited as, the "Polanco Redevelopment Act."

33459.1 Remedy or removal of release

(a) (1) An agency may take any actions that the agency determines are necessary and that are consistent with other state and federal laws to remedy or remove a release of hazardous substances on, under, or from property within a project area, whether the agency owns that property or not, subject to the conditions specified in subdivision (b). Unless an administering agency has been designated under Section 25262, the agency shall request cleanup guidelines from the department or the California regional water quality control board before taking action to remedy or remove a release. The department or the California regional water quality control board shall respond to the agency's request to provide cleanup guidelines within a reasonable period of time. The agency shall thereafter submit for approval a cleanup or remedial action plan to the department or the California regional water quality control board before taking action to remedy or remove a release. The department or the California regional water quality control board shall respond to the agency's request for approval of a cleanup or remedial action plan within a reasonable period of time.

(2) The agency shall provide the department and local health and building departments, the California regional water quality control board, with notification of any cleanup activity pursuant to this section at least 30 days before the commencement of the activity. If an action taken by an agency or a responsible party to remedy or remove a release of a hazardous substance does not meet, or is not consistent with, a remedial action plan or cleanup plan approved by the department or the California regional water quality control board, the department or the California regional water quality control board that approved the cleanup or remedial action plan may require the agency to take, or cause the taking of, additional action to remedy or remove the release, as provided by applicable law. If an administering agency for the site has been designated under Section 25262, any requirement for additional action may be imposed only as provided in Sections 25263 and 25265. If methane or landfill gas is present, the agency shall obtain written approval from the California Integrated Waste Management Board prior to taking that action.

(b) Except as provided in subdivision (c), an agency may take the actions specified in subdivision (a) only under one of the following conditions:

(1) There is no responsible party for the release identified by the agency.

(2) A party determined by the agency to be a responsible party for the release has been notified by the agency or has received adequate notice from the department, a California regional water quality control board, the Environmental Protection Agency, or other governmental agency with relevant authority and has been given 60 days to respond and to propose a remedial action plan and schedule, and the responsible party has not agreed within an additional 60 days to implement a plan and schedule to remedy or remove the release that is acceptable to the agency and that has been found by the agency to be consistent, to the maximum extent possible, with the priorities, guidelines, criteria, and regulations contained in the National Contingency Plan and published pursuant to Section 9605 of Title 42 of the United States Code for similar releases, situations, or events.

(3) The party determined by the agency to be the responsible party for the hazardous substance release entered into an agreement with the agency to prepare a remedial action plan for approval by the department, the California regional water quality control board, or the appropriate local agency and to implement the remedial action plan in accordance with an agreed schedule, but failed to prepare the remedial action plan, failed to implement the remedial action plan in accordance with the agreed schedule, or otherwise failed to carry out the remedial action in an appropriate and timely manner. Any action taken by the agency pursuant to this paragraph shall be consistent with any agreement between the agency and the responsible party and with the requirements of the state or local agency that approved or will approve the remedial action plan and is overseeing or will oversee the preparation and implementation of the remedial action plan.

(c) Subdivision (b) does not apply to either of the following agencies:

(1) An agency taking actions to investigate or conduct feasibility studies concerning a release.

(2) An agency taking the actions specified in subdivision (a) if the agency determines that conditions require immediate action.

(d) An agency may designate a local agency in lieu of the department or the California regional water quality control board to review and approve a cleanup or remedial action plan and to oversee the remediation or removal of hazardous substances from a specific hazardous substance release site in accordance with the following conditions:

(1) The local agency may be so designated if it is designated as the administering agency under Section 25262. In that event, the local agency, as the administering agency, shall conduct the oversight of the remedial action in accordance with Chapter 6.65 (commencing with Section 25260) and all provisions of that chapter shall apply to the remedial action.

(2) The local agency may be so designated if cleanup guidelines were requested from a California regional water quality control board, and the site is an underground storage tank site subject to Chapter 6.7 (commencing with Section 25280) of Division 20, the local agency has been certified as a certified unified program agency pursuant to Section 25404.1, the State Water Resources Control Board has entered into an agreement with the local agency for oversight of those sites pursuant to Section 25297.1, the local agency determines that the site is within the guidelines and protocols established in, and pursuant to, that agreement, and the local agency consents to the designation.

(3) A local agency may not consent to the designation by an agency unless the local agency determines that it has adequate staff resources and the requisite technical expertise and capabilities available to adequately supervise the remedial action.

(4) (A) Where a local agency has been designated pursuant to paragraph (2), the department or a California regional water quality control board may require that a local agency withdraw from the designation, after providing the agency with adequate notice, if both of the following conditions are met:

(i) The department or a California regional water quality control board determines that an agency's designation of a local agency was not consistent with paragraph (2), or makes one of the findings specified in subdivision (d) of Section 101480.

(ii) The department or a California regional water quality control board determines that it has adequate staff resources and capabilities available to adequately supervise the remedial action, and assumes that responsibility.

(B) Nothing in this paragraph prevents a California regional water quality control board from taking any action pursuant to Division 7 (commencing with Section 13000) of the Water Code.

(5) Where a local agency has been designated pursuant to paragraph (2), the local agency may, after providing the agency with adequate notice, withdraw from its designation after making one of the findings specified in subdivision (d) of Section 101480.

(e) To facilitate redevelopment planning, the agency may require the owner or operator of any site within a project area to provide the agency with all existing environmental information pertaining to the site, including the results of any Phase I or subsequent environmental assessment, as defined in Section 25200.14, any assessment conducted pursuant to an order from, or agreement with, any federal, state or local agency, and any other environmental assessment information, except that which is determined to be privileged. The person requested to furnish the information shall be required only to furnish that information as may be within their possession or control, including actual knowledge of information within the possession or control of any other party. If environmental assessment information is not available, the agency may require the owner of the property to conduct an assessment in accordance with standard real estate practices for conducting phase I or phase II environmental assessments.

33459.3 Immunity from liability

(a) Notwithstanding any other provision of law, except as provided in Section 33459.7, an agency that undertakes and completes an action, or causes another person to undertake and complete an action, pursuant to Section 33459.1, as specified in subdivision (c), to remedy or remove a hazardous substance release on, under, or from property within a redevelopment project, in accordance with a cleanup or remedial action plan prepared by a qualified independent contractor and approved by the department or a California regional water quality control board or the local agency, as appropriate, pursuant to subdivision (b), is not liable, with respect to that release only, under Division 7 (commencing with Section 13000) of the Water Code or Chapter 6.5 (commencing with Section 25100), Chapter 6.7 (commencing with Section 25280), Chapter 6.75 (commencing with Section 25299.10), or Chapter 6.8 (commencing with Section 25300), of Division 20 of this code, or any other state or local law providing liability for remedial or removal actions for releases of hazardous substances. If the remedial action was also performed pursuant to Chapter 6.65 (commencing with Section 25260) of Division 20, and a certificate of completion is issued pursuant to subdivision (b) of Section 25264, the immunity from agency action provided by the certificate of completion, as specified in subdivision (c) of Section 25264, shall apply to the agency, in addition to the immunity conferred by this section. In the case of a remedial action performed pursuant to Chapter 6.65 (commencing with Section 25260) of Division 20, and for which the administering agency is a local agency, the limitations on the certificate of completion set forth in paragraphs (1) to (6), inclusive, of subdivision (c) of Section 25264 are limits on any immunity provided for by this section and subdivision (c) of Section 25264.

(b) Upon approval of any cleanup or remedial action plan, pursuant to applicable statutes and regulations, the director or the California regional water quality control board or the local agency, as appropriate, shall acknowledge, in writing, within 60 days of the date of approval, that upon proper completion of the remedial or removal action in accordance with the plan, the immunity provided by this section shall apply to the agency.

(c) Notwithstanding any provision of law or policy providing for certification by a person conducting a remedial or removal action that the action has been properly completed, a determination that a remedial or removal action has been properly completed pursuant to this section shall be made only upon the affirmative approval of the director or the California regional water quality control board or the local agency, as appropriate. The department, California regional water quality control board, or local agency, as appropriate, shall, within 60 days of the date it finds that a remedial action has been completed, notify the agency in writing that the immunity provided by this section is in effect.

(d) The approval of a cleanup or remedial action plan under this section by a local agency shall also be subject to the concurrent approval of the department or a California regional water quality control board when the agency receiving the approval was formed by the same entity of which the local agency is a part.

(e) Upon proper completion of a remedial or removal action, as specified in subdivision (c), the immunity from agency action provided by the certificate of completion provided pursuant to subdivision (c) of Section 25264 and the immunity provided by this section extends to all of the following, but only for the release or releases specifically identified in the approved cleanup or remedial action plan and not for any subsequent release or any release not specifically identified in the approved cleanup or remedial action plan:

(1) Any employee or agent of the agency, including an instrumentality of the agency authorized to exercise some, or all, of the powers of an agency within, or for the benefit of, a redevelopment project and any employee or agent of the instrumentality.

(2) Any person who enters into an agreement with an agency for the redevelopment of property, if the agreement requires the person to acquire property affected by a hazardous substance release or to remove or remedy a hazardous substance release with respect to that property.

(3) Any person who acquires the property after a person has entered into an agreement with an agency for redevelopment of the property as described in paragraph (2).

(4) Any person who provided financing to a person specified in paragraph (2) or (3).

(f) Notwithstanding any other provision of law, the immunity provided by this section does not extend to any of the following:

(1) Any person who was a responsible party for the release before entering into an agreement, acquiring property, or providing financing, as specified in subdivision (e).

(2) Any person specified in subdivision (a) or (e) for any subsequent release of a hazardous substance or any release of a hazardous substance not specifically identified in the approved cleanup or remedial action plan.

(3) Any contractor who prepares the cleanup or remedial action plan, or conducts the removal or remedial action.

(4) Any person who obtains an approval, as specified in subdivision (b), or a determination, as specified in subdivision (c), by fraud, negligent or intentional nondisclosure, or misrepresentation, and any person who knows before the approval or determination is obtained or before the person enters into an agreement, acquires the property or provides financing, as specified in subdivision (e), that the approval or determination was obtained by these means.

(g) The immunity provided by this section is in addition to any other immunity of an agency provided by law.

(h) This section does not impair any cause of action by an agency or any other party against the person, firm, or entity responsible for the hazardous substance release which is the subject of the removal or remedial action taken by the agency or other person immune from liability pursuant to this section.

(i) This section does not apply to, or limit, alter, or restrict, any action for personal injury, property damage, or wrongful death.

(j) This section does not limit liability of a person described in paragraph (3) or (4) of subdivision (e) for damages under the Comprehensive Environmental Response, Compensation, and Liability Act of 1980, as amended (42 U.S.C. Sec. 9601 et seq.).

(k) This section does not establish, limit, or affect the liability of an agency for any release of a hazardous substance that is not investigated or remediated pursuant to this section or Chapter 6.65 (commencing with Section 25260) of Division 20.

(l) The immunity provided for by this section is only conferred if both of the following apply:

(1) The action is in accordance with a cleanup or remedial action plan prepared by a qualified independent contractor and approved by the department or a California regional water quality control board or the local agency, as appropriate, pursuant to subdivision (b).

(2) The remedial or removal action is undertaken and properly completed, as specified in subdivision (c).

(m) The agency shall reimburse the department, the California regional water quality control board, and the local agency for costs incurred in reviewing or approving cleanup or remedial action plans pursuant to this section.

33459.4 Costs of remedy or removal of release

(a) Except as provided in Section 33459.7, if a redevelopment agency undertakes action to remedy or remove, or to require others to remedy or remove, including compelling a responsible party through a civil action, to remedy or remove a release of hazardous substance, any responsible party or parties shall be liable to the redevelopment agency for the costs incurred in the action. An agency may not recover the costs of goods and services that were not procured in accordance with applicable procurement procedures. The amount of the costs shall include the interest on the costs accrued from the date of expenditure and reasonable attorney's fees and shall be recoverable in a civil action. Interest shall be calculated based on the average annual rate of return on an agency's investment of surplus funds for the fiscal year in which costs were incurred.

(b) The only defenses available to a responsible party shall be the defenses specified in subdivision (b) of Section 25323.5.

(c) An agency may recover any costs incurred to develop and to implement a cleanup or remedial action plan approved pursuant to Sections 33459.1 and 33459.3, to the same extent the department is authorized to recover those costs. The scope and standard of liability for cost recovery pursuant to this section shall be the scope and standard of liability under the Comprehensive Environmental Response, Compensation, and Liability Act of 1980, as amended (42 U.S.C. Sec. 9601 et seq.) as that act would apply to the department; provided, however, that any reference to hazardous substance therein shall be deemed to refer to hazardous substance as defined in subdivision (c) of Section 33459.

(d) An action for recovery of costs of a remedy or removal undertaken by a redevelopment agency under this section shall be commenced within three years after completion of the remedy or removal.

(e) The action to recover costs provided by this section is in addition to, and is not to be construed as restricting, any other cause of action available to a redevelopment agency.

(f) Except as provided in subdivision (m) of Section 33459.3, notwithstanding any other provision of state law or policy, an agency that undertakes and completes a remedial action, or otherwise causes a remedial action to be undertaken and completed pursuant to Sections 33459.1 and 33459.3, shall not be liable based on its ownership of property after a release occurred, for any costs that any responsible party for that release incurs to investigate or remediate the release or to compensate others for the effects of that release.

33459.5 Enforcement of Water Code

Except as provided in Section 33459.3, nothing in this article shall limit the powers of the State Water Resources Control Board or a California regional water quality control board to enforce Division 7 (commencing with Section 13000) of the Water Code.

33459.8 Redevelopment plan amendments for remedial or removal actions

If an agency undertakes any action to remedy or remove a release of hazardous substances on, under, or from property within a project area, the agency shall amend its redevelopment plan and follow the same procedure, as specified, and the legislative body is subject to the same restrictions as provided for in Article 4 (commencing with Section 33330), for the adoption of a redevelopment plan, if the agency determines that as a result of the remedial or removal action, it will also be taking any of the following actions:

(a) Proposing to add new territory to the project area.

(b) Increasing either the limitation on the amount of funds to be allocated to the agency or the time limit on the establishing of loans, advances, and indebtedness established pursuant to subdivisions (1) and (2) of Section 33333.2.

(c) Lengthening the period during which the redevelopment plan is effective.

(d) Merging project areas.

(e) Adding significant additional capital improvement projects.

Article 14
Merger of Redevelopment Project Areas in the City of San Bernardino

33470 Amendment of redevelopment plans; continuation of each project under its own plan

For the purpose of allocating taxes pursuant to Section 33670 and subject to the provisions of this article, redevelopment project areas under the jurisdiction of the redevelopment agency of the City of San Bernardino, for which redevelopment plans have been adopted pursuant to Article 5 (commencing with Section 33360) of this chapter, may be merged, irrespective of contiguity, by the amendment of each affected redevelopment plan as provided in Article 12 (commencing with Section 33450) of this chapter. Upon merger, the provisions of subdivisions (a) and (c) of Section 33413 shall apply to the project areas merged pursuant to this article and the redevelopment agency shall use all reasonable efforts and all available subsidies to implement the provisions of subdivision (b) of Section 33413. Each constituent project area so merged, including, without limitation, those previously merged pursuant to this section, shall continue under its own redevelopment plan, but, except as otherwise provided in this article, taxes attributable to each project area merged pursuant to this section which are allocated to the redevelopment agency pursuant to Section 33670 shall be allocated, as provided in subdivision (b) of such section, to the entire merged project area for the purpose of paying the principal of and interest on loans, moneys advanced to, or indebtedness (whether funded, refunded, assumed, or otherwise) incurred by the redevelopment agency to finance or refinance, in whole or in part, such merged redevelopment project.

33471 Prior indebtedness of constituent project areas

If the redevelopment agency has, prior to merger of redevelopment project areas pursuant to Section 33470, incurred any indebtedness on account of a constituent project area so merged, taxes attributable to such area which are allocated to the agency pursuant to subdivision (b) of Section 33670 shall be first used to comply with the terms of any bond resolution or other agreement pledging such taxes from such constituent project area until a refunding has occurred which satisfies the terms of such resolution or agreement.

33471.5 Low and moderate income housing

After the refunding has occurred as provided in Section 33471, not less than 20 percent of all taxes which are allocated to the redevelopment agency pursuant to subdivision (b) of Section 33670 for redevelopment projects merged pursuant to this article shall be used by the agency for the purposes set forth in Section 33334.2, provided that such taxes shall first be used for the payment of principal, interest, and premium, if any, under the bond resolution or resolutions providing for the issuance of the refunding bonds and providing necessary reserves for such refunding bonds, but only to the extent that such refunding is necessary to refinance existing bonded obligations.

33472 Notice of public hearing by agency and legislative body

The redevelopment plan for a project area which is merged pursuant to Section 33470 shall be amended in the same manner as other redevelopment plans are amended. Notice of the public hearing shall be mailed to the last known assessee of each parcel of land not owned by the agency within the boundaries of the project area described in the redevelopment plan being amended. Notice of the public hearing need not be mailed to assessees of parcels of land within the boundaries of other project areas combined into a merged project area pursuant to Section 33470, except that notice of the public hearing shall be given to the project area committee for each project area which is part of the merged project area.

33473 Extension of duration of redevelopment plans

In the proceedings for the merger of a redevelopment project, pursuant to this article, the legislative body may provide for the extension of any termination date in the redevelopment plan for any particular project area to such date as will enable a refunding to be accomplished by the issuance of bonds for the merged project area which will extend debt service for the purpose of attempting to prevent default. The termination date may also be extended for the purpose of financing projects under Section 33334.2 or 33471.5 or for any other purposes permitted by law.

33475 Applicable only to City of San Bernardino; legislative findings and declarations

This article is, unless otherwise provided, applicable only to redevelopment projects of the redevelopment agency of the City of San Bernardino for which a final redevelopment plan was adopted by ordinance on or before January 1, 1978.

The Legislature finds and declares that conditions unique to the financing of redevelopment in the City of San Bernardino require the granting of authority to merge project areas in the manner provided in this article.

33476 Merger of project areas

Notwithstanding any other provision of this article, except Section 33471.5, for the purpose of allocating taxes pursuant to Section 33670 that are subject to this article, redevelopment project areas under the jurisdiction of the redevelopment agency of the City of San Bernardino designated Meadowbrook/Central City, Central City East, and Central City South, are hereby merged into one contiguous project area designated Central City. Each constituent project area so merged, shall continue under its own redevelopment plan for the longest term of the three plans, but, except as otherwise provided in this article, taxes attributable to each project area merged pursuant to this section that are allocated to the redevelopment agency pursuant to Section 33670 shall be allocated, as provided in subdivision (b) of that section, to the entire merged project area for the purpose of paying the principal of and interest on loans, moneys advanced to, or indebtedness, whether funded, refunded, assumed, or otherwise incurred by the redevelopment agency to finance or refinance, in whole or in part, the merged redevelopment project.

33476.3 Prior indebtedness of constituent project areas

If the redevelopment agency has, prior to merger of redevelopment project areas pursuant to Section 33476, incurred any indebtedness on account of a constituent project area so merged, taxes attributable to such area which are allocated to the agency pursuant to subdivision (b) of Section 33670 shall be first used to comply with the terms of any bond resolution or other agreement pledging such taxes from such constituent project area until a refunding has occurred which satisfies the terms of such resolution or agreement.

33476.5 Legislative findings and declarations

The Legislature finds and declares that the merger of the project areas specified in Section 33476 in the City of San Bernardino is necessary to prevent a default on the outstanding bonds of the Meadowbrook/Central City Project due to the drastic reduction in property taxes caused by the adoption of Article XIIIA to the Constitution. This project area is already substantially redeveloped, making it unlikely that further redevelopment can be used to increase the tax base. The Redevelopment Agency of the City of San Bernardino has already had to call on the state for support of its bonded debt. This is an undesirable burden on the state which can be avoided by merging the two contiguous project areas into the combined Central City Project so that the tax increment from the buildout in Central City East and Central City South Project areas, when added to the tax increment of the Meadowbrook/Central City Project Area, resulting from combining the project areas, can serve the debt of all three projects, or the debt as refunded, thus preventing an undesirable default, or, in lieu thereof, further draws on the funds of the state.

Article 14.5
Merger of Redevelopment Project Areas in the Cities of Richmond and Pittsburg

33478 Amendment of redevelopment plans; prior indebtedness of constituent project areas; fiscal review

(a) For the purpose of allocating taxes pursuant to Section 33670 and subject to the provisions of this article, redevelopment project areas under the jurisdiction of the redevelopment agency of the City of Richmond or the City of Pittsburg for which redevelopment plans have been adopted pursuant to Article 5 (commencing with Section 33360), may be merged, without regard to contiguity of such areas, by the amendment of each affected redevelopment plan as provided in Article 12 (commencing with Section 33450). Except as provided in subdivision (b), taxes attributable to each project area merged pursuant to this section which are allocated to the redevelopment agency pursuant to Section 33670 may be allocated, as provided in subdivision (b), to the entire merged project area for the purpose of paying the principal of, and interest on, indebtedness incurred by the redevelopment agency to finance or refinance, in whole or in part, such merged redevelopment project.

(b) If the redevelopment agency has, prior to merger of redevelopment project areas pursuant to subdivision (a), incurred any indebtedness on account of a constituent project area so merged, taxes attributable to that area which are allocated to the agency pursuant to Section 33670 shall be first used to comply with the terms of any bond resolution or other agreement pledging such taxes from the constituent project area.

(c) In connection with any amendment which proposes merger of redevelopment project areas pursuant to subdivision (a), the county or any affected taxing entity may call for the creation of a fiscal review committee as provided for in Article 4 (commencing with Section 33330).

(d) After merger of redevelopment projects pursuant to subdivision (a), the clerk of the legislative body shall transmit a copy of the ordinance amending the plans for projects to be merged to the governing body of each of the taxing agencies which levies taxes upon any property in the project.

33478.1 Low and moderate income housing

(a) Subject to the provisions of subdivisions (a) and (b) of Section 33478, not less than 20 percent of all taxes which are allocated to the redevelopment agency pursuant to Section 33670 for redevelopment projects merged pursuant to this article, irrespective of the date of adoption of the final redevelopment plans shall be deposited by the agency in the Low and Moderate Income Housing Fund established pursuant to Section 33334.3, or which shall be established for purposes of this section, except if the agency finds that not less than 4 percent of the housing units within its jurisdiction receive subsidies to make such units affordable to low- or moderate-income households. The agency shall use the moneys in such fund to assist in the construction or rehabilitation of housing units which will be available to, or occupied by, persons and families of low or moderate income, as defined in Section 50093, and very low income households, as defined in Section 50105, for a period of not less than 30 years. For the purposes of this subdivision, "construction and rehabilitation" shall include acquisition of land, improvements to land; the acquisition, rehabilitation, or construction of structures; or the provision of subsidies necessary to provide housing for persons and families of low or moderate income, as defined in Section 50093, and very low income households, as defined in Section 50105.

(b) The agency may use the funds set aside by subdivision (a) inside or outside the project area. However, the agency may only use these funds outside the project area upon a resolution of the agency and the legislative body that such use will be of benefit to the project. Such determination by the agency and the legislative body shall be final and conclusive as to the issue of benefit to the project area. The Legislature finds and declares that the provision of replacement housing pursuant to Section 33413 is of benefit to a project.

The Legislature finds and declares that expenditures or obligations incurred by the agency pursuant to this section shall constitute an indebtedness of the project.

(c) If moneys deposited in the Low and Moderate Income Housing Fund pursuant to this section have not been committed for the purposes specified in subdivisions (a) and (b) for a period of six years following deposit in that fund, the agency shall offer such moneys to the housing authority which operates within the jurisdiction of the agency, if activated pursuant to Section 34240, for the purpose of constructing or rehabilitating housing as provided in subdivisions (a) and (b).

(d) Notwithstanding subdivision (d) of Section 33413, any agency which merges its redevelopment project areas pursuant to this article shall be subject to the provisions of subdivisions (a) and (c) of Section 33413.

33478.2 Notice to Department of Housing and Community Development of intention to merge

Prior to merging project areas pursuant to Section 33478, the redevelopment agency shall notify the department of its intention to merge its project areas, which shall occur no later than 30 days prior to adoption of the ordinance which provides for merger.

33478.3 Applicable only to cities of Richmond and Pittsburg; legislative findings and declarations

This article shall be applicable to only those redevelopment projects of the City of Richmond for which a final redevelopment plan was adopted by ordinance on or before July 1, 1975, and amendments thereto adopted on or before June 1, 1980. This article shall be applicable to only those redevelopment projects of the City of Pittsburg for which a final redevelopment plan was adopted by ordinance on or before June 1, 1980, and amendments thereto adopted on or before June 1, 1980. The Legislature finds and declares that conditions unique to the financing of redevelopment in the City of Richmond and the City of Pittsburg require the granting of authority to merge project areas.

Article 15
Merger of Redevelopment Project Areas in the Cities of Chula Vista, San Jose, and Santa Fe Springs

33480 Amendment of redevelopment plans; continuation of each project under its own plan

For the purpose of allocating taxes pursuant to Section 33670 and subject to the provisions of this article, redevelopment project areas under the jurisdiction of the redevelopment agency of the Cities of Chula Vista, San Jose, and Santa Fe Springs, for which redevelopment plans have been adopted pursuant to Article 5 (commencing with Section 33360) of this chapter, may be merged, irrespective of contiguity, by the amendment of each affected redevelopment plan as provided in Article 12 (commencing with Section 33450) of this chapter. Each constituent project area so merged shall continue under its own redevelopment plan, but, except as otherwise provided in this article, taxes attributable to each project area merged pursuant to this section which are allocated to the redevelopment agency pursuant to Section 33670 may be allocated, as provided in subdivision (b) of such section, to the entire merged project area for the purpose of paying the principal of and interest on loans, moneys advanced to, or indebtedness (whether funded, refunded, assumed, or otherwise) incurred by the redevelopment agency to finance or refinance, in whole or in part, such merged redevelopment project.

33481 Prior indebtedness of constituent project areas

If the redevelopment agency has, prior to merger of redevelopment project areas pursuant to Section 33480, incurred any indebtedness on account of a constituent project area so merged, taxes attributable to that area which are allocated to the agency pursuant to Section 33670 shall be first used to comply with the terms of any bond resolution or other agreement pledging such taxes from the constituent project area.

33482 Notice of public hearing by agency and legislative body

The redevelopment plan for a project area which is merged pursuant to Section 33480 shall be amended in the same manner as other redevelopment plans are amended. Notice of the public hearing shall be mailed to the last known assessee of each parcel of land not owned by the agency within the boundaries of the project area described in the redevelopment plan being amended. Notice of the public hearing need not be mailed to assessees of parcels of land within the boundaries of other project areas combined into a merged project area pursuant to Section 33480, except that notice of the public hearing shall be given to the project area committee for each project area which is part of the merged project area.

33483 Low and moderate income housing

Not less than 20 percent of all taxes which are allocated to the redevelopment agency pursuant to Section 33670 for redevelopment projects merged pursuant to this article, irrespective of the date of adoption of the final redevelopment plans, shall be used for the purposes set forth in Section 33334.2.

33484 Applicable only to cities of Chula Vista, San Jose and Santa Fe Springs; legislative findings and declarations

This article shall be applicable only to redevelopment projects of the redevelopment agency of the Cities of Chula Vista, San Jose, and Santa Fe Springs for which a final redevelopment plan was adopted by ordinance on or before January 1, 1979.

The Legislature finds and declares that conditions unique to the financing of redevelopment in the Cities of Chula Vista, San Jose, and Santa Fe Springs require the granting of authority to merge project areas.

Article 16
Merger of Project Areas

33485 Legislative findings and declarations

The Legislature finds and declares that the provisions of this part, which require that taxes allocated pursuant to Section 16 of Article XVI of the California Constitution and Section 33670 be applied to the project area in which those taxes are generated, are designed to assure (1) that project areas are terminated when the redevelopment of those areas has been completed and (2) that the increased revenues which result from redevelopment accrue to the benefit of affected taxing jurisdictions at the completion of redevelopment activities in a project area. Mergers of project areas are desirable as a matter of public policy if they result in substantial benefit to the public and if they contribute to the revitalization of blighted areas through the increased economic vitality of those areas and through increased and improved housing opportunities in or near such areas. The Legislature further finds and declares that it is necessary to enact a statute that sets out uniform statewide standards for merger of project areas to assure that those mergers serve a vital public purpose.

33486 Amendment of redevelopment plans; prior indebtedness of constituent project areas

(a) For the purpose of allocating taxes pursuant to Section 33670 and subject to the provisions of this article, redevelopment project areas under the jurisdiction of a redevelopment agency for which redevelopment plans have been adopted pursuant to Article 5 (commencing with Section 33360), may be merged, without regard to contiguity of the areas, by the amendment of each affected redevelopment plan as provided in Article 12 (commencing with Section 33450). Before adopting the ordinance amending each affected redevelopment plan, the legislative body shall find, based on substantial evidence, that both of the following conditions exist:

(1) Significant blight remains within one of the project areas.

(2) This blight cannot be eliminated without merging the project areas and the receipt of property taxes.

(b) (1) Except as provided in paragraph (2), taxes attributable to each project area merged pursuant to this section that are allocated to the redevelopment agency pursuant to Section 33670 may be allocated to the entire merged project area for the purpose of paying the principal of, and interest on, indebtedness incurred by the redevelopment agency to finance or refinance, in whole or in part, the merged redevelopment project.

(2) If the redevelopment agency has, prior to merger of redevelopment project areas, incurred any indebtedness on account of a constituent project area so merged, taxes attributable to that area that are allocated to the agency pursuant to Section 33670 shall be first used to comply with the terms of any bond resolution or other agreement pledging the taxes from the constituent project area.

(c) After the merger of redevelopment projects pursuant to subdivision (a), the clerk of the legislative body shall transmit a copy of the ordinance amending the plans for projects to be merged to the governing body of each of the taxing agencies that receives property taxes from or levies property taxes upon any property in the project.

33487 Low and moderate income housing

(a) Subject to subdivisions (a) and (b) of Section 33486, not less than 20 percent of all taxes that are allocated to the redevelopment agency pursuant to Section 33670 for redevelopment projects merged pursuant to this article, irrespective of the date of adoption of the final redevelopment plans, shall be deposited by the agency in the Low and Moderate Income Housing Fund established pursuant to Section 33334.3, or that shall be established for purposes of this section. The agency shall use the moneys in this fund to assist in the construction or rehabilitation of housing units that will be available to, or occupied by, persons and families of low or moderate income, as defined in Section 50093, and very low income households, as defined in Section 50105, for the longest feasible time period but not less than 55 years for rental units and 45 years for owner-occupied units. For the purposes of this subdivision, "construction and rehabilitation" shall include acquisition of land, improvements to land; the acquisition, rehabilitation, or construction of structures; or the provision of subsidies necessary to provide housing for persons and families of low or moderate income, as defined in Section 50093, and very low income households, as defined in Section 50105.

(b) The agency may use the funds set aside by subdivision (a) inside or outside the project area. However, the agency may only use these funds outside the project area upon a resolution of the agency and the legislative body that the use will be of benefit to the project. This determination by the agency and the legislative body shall be final and conclusive as to the issue of benefit to the project area. The Legislature finds and declares that the provision of replacement housing pursuant to Section 33413 is of benefit to a project.

The Legislature finds and declares that expenditures or obligations incurred by the agency pursuant to this section shall constitute an indebtedness of the project.

(c) If moneys deposited in the Low and Moderate Income Housing Fund pursuant to this section have not been committed for the purposes specified in subdivisions (a) and (b) for a period of six years following deposit in that fund, the agency shall offer these moneys to the housing authority that operates within the jurisdiction of the agency, if activated pursuant to Section 34240, for the purpose of constructing or rehabilitating housing as provided in subdivisions (a) and (b). However, if no housing authority operates within the jurisdiction of the agency, the agency may retain these moneys for use pursuant to this section.

(d) If the agency deposits less than 20 percent of taxes allocated pursuant to Section 33670, due to the provisions of subdivisions (a) and (b) of Section 33486, in any fiscal year, a deficit shall be created in the Low- and Moderate Income Housing Fund in an amount equal to the difference between 20 percent of the taxes allocated pursuant to Section 33670 and the amount deposited in that year. The deficit, if any, created pursuant to this section constitutes an indebtedness of the project. The agency shall eliminate the deficit by expending taxes allocated in years subsequent to creation of the deficit, and until the time when that deficit has been eliminated, an agency shall not incur new obligations for purposes other than those set forth in Section 33487, except to comply with the terms of any resolution or other agreement pledging taxes allocated pursuant to Section 33670 that existed on the date of merger pursuant to this article.

(e) Notwithstanding subdivision (d) of Section 33413, any agency that merges its redevelopment project areas pursuant to this article shall be subject to subdivisions (a) and (c) of Section 33413.

33488 Notice to Department of Housing and Community Development of intention to merge

Prior to merging project areas pursuant to Section 33486, a redevelopment agency shall notify the department of its intention to merge its project areas, which shall occur no later than 30 days prior to adoption of the ordinance which provides for merger.

33489 Application of article

(a) Except as provided in subdivision (b), this article shall be exclusive authority for merger of redevelopment project areas on and after January 1, 1981. However, project areas merged prior to January 1, 1981, pursuant to other provisions of this chapter shall continue to be governed by such provisions.

(b) If Assembly Bill No. 3300 of the 1979–80 Regular Session is chaptered and becomes effective and adds Article 14.5 (commencing with Section 33478) to this chapter relating to the merger of project areas within the City of Richmond, any such project merger within the City of Richmond may be conducted either under this article or alternatively pursuant to the provisions of Article 14.5 (commencing with Section 33478).

Article 16.5
Adoption of Implementation Plans

33490 Adoption of implementation plans every 5 years

(a) (1) (A) On or before December 31, 1994, and each five years thereafter, each agency that has adopted a redevelopment plan prior to December 31, 1993, shall adopt, after a public hearing, an implementation plan that shall contain the specific goals and objectives of the agency for the project area, the specific programs, including potential projects, and estimated expenditures proposed to be made during the next five years, and an explanation of how the goals and objectives, programs, and expenditures will eliminate blight within the project area and implement the requirements of Section 33333.10, if applicable and Sections 33334.2, 33334.4, 33334.6, and 33413. After adoption of the first implementation plan, the parts of the implementation plan that address Section 33333.10, if applicable, and Sections 33334.2, 33334.4, 33334.6, and 33413 shall be adopted every five years either in conjunction with the housing element cycle or the implementation plan cycle. The agency may amend the implementation plan after conducting a public hearing on the proposed amendment. If an action attacking the adoption, approval, or validity of a redevelopment plan adopted prior to January 1, 1994, has been brought pursuant to Chapter 5 (commencing with Section 33500), the first implementation plan required pursuant to this section shall be adopted within six months after a final judgment or order has been entered. Subsequent implementation plans required pursuant to this section shall be adopted pursuant to the terms of this section, and as if the first implementation plan had been adopted on or before December 31, 1994.

(B) Adoption of an implementation plan shall not constitute an approval of any specific program, project, or expenditure and shall not change the need to obtain any required approval of a specific program, project, or expenditure from the agency or community. The adoption of an implementation plan shall not constitute a project within the meaning of Section 21000 of the Public Resources Code. However, the inclusion of a specific program, potential project, or expenditure in an implementation plan prepared pursuant to subdivision (c) of Section 33352 in conjunction with a redevelopment plan adoption shall not eliminate analysis of those programs, potential projects, and expenditures in the environmental impact report prepared pursuant to subdivision (k) of Section 33352 to the extent that it would be otherwise required. In addition, the inclusion of programs, potential projects, and expenditures in an implementation plan shall not eliminate review pursuant to the California Environmental Quality Act (Division 13 (commencing with Section 21000) of the Public Resources Code), at the time of the approval of the program, project, or expenditure, to the extent that it would be otherwise required.

(2) (A) A portion of the implementation plan shall address the agency housing responsibilities and shall contain a section addressing Section 33333.10, if applicable, and Sections 33334.2, 33334.4, and 33334.6, the Low and Moderate Income Housing Fund, and, if subdivision (b) of Section 33413 applies, a section addressing agency developed and project area housing. The section addressing the Low and Moderate Income Housing Fund shall contain:

(i) The amount available in the Low and Moderate Income Housing Fund and the estimated amounts which will be deposited in the Low and Moderate Income Housing Fund during each of the next five years.

(ii) A housing program with estimates of the number of new, rehabilitated, or price restricted units to be assisted during each of the five years and estimates of the expenditures of moneys from the Low and Moderate Income Housing Fund during each of the five years.

(iii) A description of how the housing program will implement the requirement for expenditures of moneys in the Low and Moderate Income Housing Fund over a 10-year period for various groups as required by Section 33334.4. For project areas to which subdivision (b) of Section 33413 applies, the 10-year period within which Section 33334.4 is required to be implemented shall be the same 10-year period within which subdivision (b) of Section 33413 is required to be implemented. Notwithstanding the first sentence of Section 33334.4 and the first sentence of this clause, in order to allow these two 10-year time periods to coincide for the first time period, the time to implement the requirements of Section 33334.4 shall be extended two years, and project areas in existence on December 31, 1993, shall implement the requirements of Section 33334.4 on or before December 31, 2014, and each 10 years thereafter rather than December 31, 2012. For project areas to which subdivision (b) of Section 33413 does not apply, the requirements of Section 33334.4 shall be implemented on or before December 31, 2014, and each 10 years thereafter.

(iv) This requirement to include a description of how the housing program will implement Section 33334.4 in the implementation plan shall apply to implementation plans adopted pursuant to subdivision (a) on or after December 31, 2002.

(B) For each project area to which subdivision (b) of Section 33413 applies, the section addressing the agency developed and project area housing shall contain:

(i) Estimates of the number of new, substantially rehabilitated or price restricted residential units to be developed or purchased within one or more project areas, both over the life of the plan and during the next 10 years.

(ii) Estimates of the number of units of very low, low-, and moderate-income households required to be developed within one or more project areas in order to meet the requirements of paragraph (2) of subdivision (b) of Section 33413, both over the life of the plan and during the next 10 years.

(iii) The number of units of very low, low-, and moderate-income households which have been developed within one or more project areas which meet the requirements of paragraph (2) of subdivision (b) of Section 33413.

(iv) Estimates of the number of agency developed residential units which will be developed during the next five years, if any, which will be governed by paragraph (1) of subdivision (b) of Section 33413.

(v) Estimates of the number of agency developed units for very low, low-, and moderate-income households which will be developed by the agency during the next five years to meet the requirements of paragraph (1) of subdivision (b) of Section 33413.

(C) The section addressing Section 33333.10, if applicable, and Section 33334.4 shall contain all of the following:

(i) The number of housing units needed for very low income persons, low-income persons, and moderate-income persons as each of those needs have been identified in the most recent determination pursuant to Section 65584 of the Government Code, and the proposed amount of expenditures from the Low and Moderate Income Housing Fund for each income group during each year of the implementation plan period.

(ii) The total population of the community and the population under 65 years of age as reported in the most recent census of the United States Census Bureau.

(iii) A housing program that provides a detailed schedule of actions the agency is undertaking or intends to undertake to ensure expenditure of the Low and Moderate Income Housing Fund in the proportions required by Section 33333.10, if applicable, and Section 33334.4.

(iv) For the previous implementation plan period, the amounts of Low and Moderate Income Housing Fund moneys utilized to assist units affordable to, and occupied by, extremely low income households, very low income households, and low-income households; the number, the location, and level of affordability of units newly constructed with other locally controlled government assistance and without agency assistance and that are required to be affordable to, and occupied by, persons of low, very low, or extremely low income for at least 55 years for rental housing or 45 years for homeownership housing, and the amount of Low and Moderate Income Housing Fund moneys utilized to assist housing units available to families with children, and the number, location, and level of affordability of those units.

(3) If the implementation plan contains a project that will result in the destruction or removal of dwelling units that will have to be replaced pursuant to subdivision (a) of Section 33413, the implementation plan shall identify proposed locations suitable for those replacement dwelling units.

(4) For a project area that is within six years of the time limit on the effectiveness of the redevelopment plan established pursuant to Section 33333.2, 33333.6, 33333.7, or 33333.10, the portion of the implementation plan addressing the housing responsibilities shall specifically address the ability of the agency to comply, prior to the time limit on the effectiveness of the redevelopment plan, with subdivision (a) of Section 33333.8, subdivision (a) of Section 33413 with respect to replacement dwelling units, subdivision (b) of Section 33413 with respect to project area housing, and the disposition of the remaining moneys in the Low and Moderate Income Housing Fund.

(5) The implementation plan shall identify the fiscal year that the agency expects each of the following time limits to expire:

(A) The time limit for the commencement for eminent domain proceedings to acquire property within the project area.

(B) The time limit for the establishment of loans, advances, and indebtedness to finance the redevelopment project.

(C) The time limit for the effectiveness of the redevelopment plan.

(D) The time limit to repay indebtedness with the proceeds of property taxes.

(b) For a project area for which a redevelopment plan is adopted on or after January 1, 1994, the implementation plan prepared pursuant to subdivision (c) of Section 33352 shall constitute the initial implementation plan and thereafter the agency after a public hearing shall adopt an implementation plan every five years commencing with the fifth year after the plan has been adopted. Agencies may adopt implementation plans that include more than one project area.

(c) Every agency, at least once within the five-year term of the plan, shall conduct a public hearing and hear testimony of all interested parties for the purpose of reviewing the redevelopment plan and the corresponding implementation plan for each redevelopment project within the jurisdiction and evaluating the progress of the redevelopment project. The hearing required by this subdivision shall take place no earlier than two years and no later than three years after the adoption of the implementation plan. For a project area that is within three years of the time limit on the effectiveness of the redevelopment plan established pursuant to Section 33333.2, 33333.6, 33333.7, or 33333.10, the review shall specifically address those items in paragraph (4) of subdivision (a). An agency may hold one hearing for two or more project areas if those project areas are included within the same implementation plan.

(d) Notice of public hearings conducted pursuant to this section shall be published pursuant to Section 6063 of the Government Code, mailed at least three weeks in advance to all persons and agencies that have requested notice, and posted in at least four permanent places within the project area for a period of three weeks. Publication, mailing, and posting shall be completed not less than 10 days prior to the date set for hearing.

Chapter 4.5. MILITARY BASE CONVERSION REDEVELOPMENT AGENCIES

Article 1
General Provisions

33492   Legislative intent

With enactment of this chapter, it is the intent of the Legislature to do both of the following:

(a) Provide a means of mitigating the economic and social degradation that is faced by communities the jurisdictions of which include military bases that have been ordered to be closed or realigned by the federal Base Closure Commission.

(b) Enable redevelopment agencies to place in a project area portions of a military base that were previously developed, but that cannot be utilized in their present condition because of, in whole or in part, substandard infrastructure and buildings that do not meet state building standards. It is not the intent of the Legislature to encourage redevelopment agencies to include large areas of undeveloped land within project areas.

33492.1   Legislative intent

The Legislature finds and declares that extraordinary measures must be taken to mitigate the effects of the federal government's efforts to reduce the number of military bases throughout the country.

33492.3   Territory of project area

For any project area formed pursuant to this chapter, the project area may include all, or any portion of, property within a military base that the federal Base Closure Commission has voted to close or realign when that action has been sustained by the President and Congress of the United States, regardless of the percentage of urbanized land, as defined in Section 33320.1, within the military base. The project area may include territory outside the military base; however, all territory outside the military base included therein shall be characterized as predominantly urbanized, as that term is defined in subdivision (b) of Section 33320.1. The procedures authorized by this chapter may be used for the redevelopment of any closed or realigned military base, but shall not constitute the exclusive method by which redevelopment may occur on these bases.

33492.4   Applicability of other provisions

Chapter 4 (commencing with Section 33300) shall be applicable to any project area formed pursuant to this chapter, except to the extent that Chapter 4 is inconsistent with this chapter.

33492.5   Adoption of project area by city, county, city and county or joint powers redevelopment agency

(a) In any community in which a military base is located, the Base Closure Commission has voted to close that military base, and the action of the Base Closure Commission has been sustained by the President and Congress of the United States, a project area may be adopted pursuant to the following requirements:

(1) If the project area is located entirely within the boundaries of a city, or city and county, then the redevelopment agency of the city, or city and county, may adopt the redevelopment project area pursuant to this part as modified by this chapter.

(2) If the project area is located entirely within the unincorporated area of a single county, then the county redevelopment agency may adopt the redevelopment project area pursuant to this part as modified by this chapter.

(3) If the project area includes property within the jurisdictions of two or more cities, or two or more counties, or a city and a county, or any combination of the foregoing, then all of the cities and counties the jurisdictions of which include property within the boundaries of the military base and any other territory to be included within the redevelopment project area may enter into a joint powers agreement, an agreement entered into pursuant to Section 33210, or other appropriate agreement for the purpose of creating a redevelopment agency and adopting a project area pursuant to this part as modified by this chapter.

(b) A redevelopment agency to which this chapter is applicable may adopt a project area either pursuant to this chapter or pursuant to other relevant provisions of this part.

33492.7   Blight finding

(a) Paragraph (11) of subdivision (d) of Section 33367 shall not apply to the territory within the military base for any redevelopment project area adopted pursuant to this chapter.

(b) For any project area adopted pursuant to this chapter, Section 33492.11 may be used in lieu of Section 33031.

33492.9   County auditor to notify Director of Finance when $100,000 tax increments received

Notwithstanding any other provision of law, in each county in which a redevelopment agency is formed, or a redevelopment plan is adopted, pursuant to this chapter, the county auditor shall certify to the Director of Finance the date of the final day of the first fiscal year in which one hundred thousand dollars ($100,000) or more of tax increment funds from the redevelopment project area adopted pursuant to this chapter are paid to the redevelopment agency pursuant to subdivision (d) of Section 33675.

33492.10 Blighted areas defined

(a) For purposes of this chapter, a blighted area within the boundaries of a military base is an area in which the combination of two or more conditions set forth in Section 33492.11 is so prevalent and so substantial that it causes a reduction of, or lack of, proper utilization of the area to an extent that constitutes a serious physical and economic burden on the community which cannot reasonably be expected to be reversed or alleviated by private enterprise or governmental action, or both, without redevelopment.

(b) A project area adopted pursuant to this chapter may include territory outside the boundaries of the military base, as those boundaries exist on January 1, 1996; however, all territory outside the boundaries of the military base included in the project area shall be characterized by blight, as that term is defined in Sections 33030 and 33031. An area outside the boundaries of a military base may be included in the project area only upon a finding by the agency that the area is blighted and that its inclusion in the project area is necessary for effective redevelopment of the base property. The agency shall include evidence supporting this finding in the report submitted to the legislative body pursuant to Section 33352. An area outside the boundaries of a military base shall be deemed not necessary for effective redevelopment if the area is included only for the purpose of obtaining the allocation of taxes from the area pursuant to Section 33670 without other substantial justification for its inclusion.

(c) This section, as amended by the act that adds this subdivision, shall only be applicable to a redevelopment plan adopted or amended on or after the effective date of the act that adds this subdivision. A redevelopment plan adopted pursuant to this chapter prior to the effective date of the act that adds this subdivision shall be subject to this section as it was added by Chapter 944 of the Statutes of 1993.

33492.11 Physical and economic blight

(a) For purposes of this chapter, this section describes conditions that cause blight:

(1) Buildings in which it is unsafe or unhealthy for persons to live or work. These conditions can be caused by serious building code violations, dilapidation and deterioration, defective design or physical construction, faulty or inadequate infrastructure, or other similar factors.

(2) Factors that prevent or substantially hinder the economically viable reuse or capacity of buildings or areas. This condition can be caused by conditions including, but not limited to, all of the following: a substandard design; buildings that are too large or too small, given present standards and market conditions; age, obsolescence, deterioration, dilapidation, or other physical conditions, that could prevent the highest and best uses of the property. This condition can also be caused by buildings that will have to be demolished, or buildings or areas that have a lack of adequate parking.

(3) Adjacent or nearby uses that are incompatible with each other and that prevent the economic development of those parcels or other portions of the project area.

(4) Buildings on land that, when subdivided, or when infrastructure is installed, will not comply with community subdivision, zoning, or planning regulations.

(5) Properties currently served by infrastructure that does not meet existing adopted utility or community infrastructure standards.

(6) Buildings that, when built, did not conform to the then effective building, plumbing, mechanical, or electrical codes adopted by the community where the project area is located.

(7) Land that contains materials or facilities, including, but not limited to, materials for aircraft landing pads and runways, that will have to be removed to allow development.

(b) Pursuant to Section 33321, a project area need not be restricted to buildings, improvements, or lands which are detrimental or inimical to the public health, safety, or welfare, but may consist of an area where these conditions predominate and injuriously affect the entire area. A project area may include lands, buildings, or improvements which are not detrimental to the public health, safety, or welfare, but the inclusion of which is found necessary for the effective redevelopment of the area of which they are a part. Each area included under this section shall be necessary for effective redevelopment, and shall not be included for the purpose of obtaining the allocation of tax-increment revenue from the area pursuant to Section 33670 without other substantial justification for its inclusion.

(c) This section, as amended by the act that adds this subdivision, shall only be applicable to a redevelopment plan adopted or amended on or after the effective date of the act that adds this subdivision. A redevelopment plan adopted pursuant to this chapter prior to the effective date of the act that adds this subdivision shall be subject to this section as it was added by Chapter 944 of the Statutes of 1993.

33492.13 Limitations on tax increments, incurring and repaying indebtedness, duration of plan and use of eminent domain

(a) A redevelopment plan, adopted pursuant to this chapter and containing the provisions set forth in Section 33670, shall contain all of the following limitations:

(1) A limitation on the number of dollars of taxes which may be divided and allocated to the redevelopment agency pursuant thereto. Taxes shall not be divided and shall not be allocated to the redevelopment agency beyond this limitation, except by amendment of the redevelopment plan pursuant to Section 33354.6, or as necessary to comply with subdivision (a) of Section 33333.8.

(2) (A) The time limit on the establishing of loans, advances, and indebtedness to be paid with the proceeds of property taxes received pursuant to Section 33670 to finance in whole or in part the redevelopment project, which may not exceed 20 years from the date the county auditor certifies pursuant to Section 33492.9, except by amendment of the redevelopment plan as authorized by subparagraph (B). The loans, advances, or indebtedness may be repaid over a period of time longer than the time limit as provided in this section. No loans, advances, or indebtedness to be repaid from the allocation of taxes shall be established or incurred by the agency beyond this time limitation, except as necessary to comply with subdivision (a) of Section 33333.8.

(B) The time limitation established by subparagraph (A) may be extended only by amendment of the redevelopment plan after the agency finds, based on substantial evidence, that (i) substantial blight remains within the project area; (ii) this blight cannot be eliminated without the establishment of additional debt; and (iii) the elimination of blight cannot reasonably be accomplished by private enterprise acting alone or by the legislative body's use of financing alternatives other than tax increment financing. However, this amended time limitation may not exceed 30 years from the date the county auditor certifies pursuant to Section 33492.9, except as necessary to comply with subdivision (a) of Section 33333.8.

(3) A time limit, not to exceed 30 years from the date the county auditor certifies pursuant to Section 33492.9, on the effectiveness of the redevelopment plan. After the time limit on the effectiveness of the redevelopment plan, the agency shall have no authority to act pursuant to the redevelopment plan except to pay previously incurred indebtedness, comply with subdivision (a) of Section 33333.8, and enforce existing covenants or contracts.

(4) A time limit, not to exceed 45 years from the date the county auditor certifies pursuant to Section 33492.9, to repay indebtedness with the proceeds of property taxes received pursuant to Section 33670. After the time limit established pursuant to this paragraph, an agency may not receive property taxes pursuant to Section 33670, except as necessary to comply with subdivision (a) of Section 33333.8.

(5) The limitations contained in a redevelopment plan adopted pursuant to this section shall not be applied to limit allocation of taxes to an agency to the extent required to comply with Section 33333.8. In the event of a conflict between these limitations and the obligations under Section 33333.8 the limitation established in the ordinance shall be suspended pursuant to Section 33333.8.

(b) (1) A redevelopment plan, adopted pursuant to this chapter, that does not contain the provisions set forth in Section 33670 shall contain the limitations in paragraph (2).

(2) A time limit, not to exceed 12 years from the date the county auditor certifies pursuant to Section 33492.9, for commencement of eminent domain proceedings to acquire property within the project area. This time limitation may be extended only by amendment of the redevelopment plan.

33492.15 Allocations to school and community college districts

Notwithstanding any other provision of law, all of the following shall occur:

(a) The agency shall make the payments required by Section 33607.5, except that each of the time periods governing the payments shall be calculated from the date the county auditor makes the certification to the Director of Finance pursuant to Section 33492.9, instead of from the first year that the agency receives tax-increment revenue.

(b) Prior to incurring any bonded indebtedness, any agency administering a project area pursuant to this chapter may subordinate to the bonded debt the amount required to be paid to an affected school district or community college district pursuant to this section upon a finding, based upon substantial evidence, that the agency will have sufficient funds available to pay both the bonded debt payments and the payments required by this section.

33492.16 Deferral of housing set-aside requirement

(a) Notwithstanding Section 33334.2 or any other provision of law, an agency established or governed pursuant to this chapter may annually defer the requirement to allocate 20 percent of tax increment revenue to the Low and Moderate Income Housing Fund for a period of up to five years after the date of adoption of the redevelopment plan, based upon an annual finding of the legislative body that the funds are necessary for the effective redevelopment of base property and long-term tax generation, and that the vacancy rate for housing affordable to lower income households within the jurisdiction of the members of the agency is greater than 4 percent. The vacancy rate for housing affordable to lower income households shall be established by using the vacancy rates most recently published in the annual California Department of Finance Population and Housing Estimates (Report E-5, or a successor report).

The authority and procedures for deferral of allocation of tax increment revenue which is governed by this section shall not apply to the tax increment revenues attributable to the property that is located outside the military base which is allocated to the Low- and Moderate-Income Housing Fund.

(b) The amount of the deferral, if any, shall be considered an indebtedness of the agency, and shall be paid into the Low and Moderate Income Housing Fund no later than the end of the 20th fiscal year after the date on which the agency adopts its project. If the indebtedness is not eliminated by the end of the 20th fiscal year, the county auditor or controller, no later than March 15 of the 21st year, shall withhold from the portion of tax increment to which the redevelopment agency is otherwise entitled an amount equal to the indebtedness and deposit those funds into a separate Low and Moderate Income Housing Fund for use by the agency to meet its affordable housing requirements pursuant to this part. Under no circumstances shall this section be interpreted or applied in a manner that has the effect of reducing the tax increment payable or received by affected taxing entities pursuant to Section 33492.15.

33492.18 Exemption from CEQA

(a) Notwithstanding subdivision (k) of Section 33352, the California Environmental Quality Act (Division 13 (commencing with Section 21000) of the Public Resources Code) shall not apply to the adoption of a redevelopment plan prepared pursuant to this article if the redevelopment agency determines at a public hearing, noticed in accordance with this section, that the need to adopt a redevelopment plan at the soonest possible time in order to use the authority in this article requires the redevelopment agency to delay application of the provisions of the California Environmental Quality Act to the redevelopment plan in accordance with this section.

(b) If the redevelopment agency finds, pursuant to subdivision (a), that the application of the California Environmental Quality Act to the redevelopment plan is required to be delayed, the redevelopment agency or the community shall certify an environmental impact report for the redevelopment plan within 18 months after the effective date of the ordinance adopting the redevelopment plan. If, as a result of the preparation of the environmental document prepared pursuant to this subdivision, it is necessary to amend the redevelopment plan to mitigate any impacts, the agency shall amend the redevelopment plan according to the procedures of this part. If the environmental document is determined to be inadequate by a court of competent jurisdiction, the redevelopment agency shall not undertake additional projects that implement the redevelopment plan until an adequate environmental document has been certified. However, this determination shall not affect the validity of the redevelopment plan.

(c) Until the redevelopment agency or the community certifies an environmental impact report for the redevelopment plan, all projects, as defined in the California Environmental Quality Act, that implement the redevelopment plan shall be subject to the California Environmental Quality Act, including, but not limited to, specific plans and rezonings. The environmental document for any implementing project shall include an analysis and mitigation of potential cumulative impacts, if any, that otherwise would not be known until an environmental document for the redevelopment plan is certified or approved and shall also include a reporting or monitoring program required pursuant to Section 21081 of the Public Resources Code.

(d) The notice for the public hearing required by subdivision (a) shall comply with, and may be combined with, the notices in Section 33349 or 33361. The notice shall state that the agency intends to consider and act upon a determination that the need to adopt a redevelopment plan at the soonest possible time in order to use the authority in this article requires the redevelopment agency to delay application of the provisions of the California Environmental Quality Act to the redevelopment plan in accordance with this section.

33492.20 Inapplicable requirements

(a) (1) The redevelopment plan for the base need not include either of the following:

(A) The information required pursuant to subdivision (d) of Section 33324, relative to the contents of the preliminary plan.

(B) The finding required pursuant to paragraph (4) of subdivision (d) of Section 33367, relative to the consistency of the redevelopment plan to the community's general plan.

(2) The agency shall not expend any tax increment funds allocated to it from the project area for expenses related to carrying out the project, unless and until the legislative bodies of all the communities included in the project area have adopted findings that the redevelopment plan is consistent with the general plan of the community, including the housing element, which substantially complies with the requirements of Article 10.6 (commencing with Section 65580) of Chapter 3 of Division 1 of Title 7 of the Government Code.

(b) Notwithstanding Section 33328, the report required by that section need only be as complete as the information then available permits.

(c) Notwithstanding Section 33344.5, the preliminary report required by that section need only be as complete as the information then available permits, and need not contain the information required by subdivision (c) of Section 33344.5.

(d) The report submitted by the agency to the legislative body pursuant to Section 33352, need not contain the items listed in subdivisions (h), (j), and (k) of Section 33352, as modified by subdivision (b) of this section.

(e) The ordinance adopted by the legislative body pursuant to Section 33367 need not contain the items listed in paragraphs (4) and (12) of subdivision (d) of Section 33367.

33492.21 Environmental impact report: San Diego Naval Training Center Redevelopment Plan

(a) Notwithstanding the time limit in subdivision (b) of Section 33492.18, the City Council of the City of San Diego shall certify an environmental impact report for the Naval Training Center Redevelopment Plan within 30 months after the effective date of the ordinance adopting that redevelopment plan.

(b) The following provisions shall apply to the approval of projects that implement a redevelopment plan authorized by this article:

(1) For 18 months after the effective date of the ordinance adopting the redevelopment plan, or until the certification of an environmental impact report for the redevelopment plan if the report is certified during that 18-month period, subdivision (c) of Section 33492.18 shall apply.

(2) If an environmental impact report for the redevelopment plan is not certified within 18 months after the effective date of the ordinance adopting the plan, then during the succeeding 12 months or until the certification of an environmental impact report if the report is certified during that 12-month period, no project, as defined in Section 21065 of the Public Resources Code, that implements the redevelopment plan shall be approved by the agency or the community unless any of the following occurs:

(A) The agency or the community has approved a negative declaration or certified an environmental impact report, or has certified a subsequent or supplemental environmental impact report, for the project before the expiration of the 18-month period provided in Section 33492.18.

(B) The agency or the community has certified a subsequent or supplemental environmental impact report for the project where the environmental impact report for the project was certified before the expiration of the 18-month period provided in Section 33492.18.

(C) The agency or the community complies with Chapter 4.5 (commencing with Section 21156) of Division 13 of the Public Resources Code for the subsequent projects described in a master environmental impact report as being within the scope of the report, and that master environmental impact report was certified before the expiration of the 18-month period provided in Section 33492.18.

(D) The project is categorically exempt pursuant to Article 19 (commencing with Section 15300) of Chapter 3 of Division 6 of Title 14 of the California Code of Regulations.

33492.22 Environmental impact report: Hunter's Point Shipyard Redevelopment Plan

(a) Notwithstanding the time limit in subdivision (b) of Section 33492.18, the Planning Commission and the Redevelopment Commission of the City and County of San Francisco shall certify an environmental impact report for the Hunter's Point Shipyard Redevelopment Plan within 30 months after the effective date of the ordinance adopting the redevelopment plan.

(b) The following provisions shall apply to the approval of projects that implement a redevelopment plan authorized by this article:

(1) For 18 months after the effective date of the ordinance adopting the redevelopment plan, or until the certification of an environmental impact report for the redevelopment plan if the report is certified during that 18-month period, subdivision (c) of Section 33492.18 shall apply.

(2) If an environmental impact report for the redevelopment plan is not certified within 18 months after the effective date of the ordinance adopting the plan, then during the succeeding 12 months or until the certification of an environmental impact report if the report is certified during that 12-month period, no project, as defined in Section 21065 of the Public Resources Code,

that implements the redevelopment plan shall be approved by the agency or the community unless any of the following occurs:

(A) The agency or the community has approved a negative declaration or certified an environmental impact report, or has certified a subsequent or supplemental environmental impact report, for the project before the expiration of the 18-month period provided in Section 33492.18.

(B) The agency or the community has certified a subsequent or supplemental environmental impact report for the project where the environmental impact report for the project was certified before the expiration of the 18-month period provided in Section 33492.18.

(C) The agency or the community complies with Chapter 4.5 (commencing with Section 21156) of Division 13 of the Public Resources Code for subsequent projects described in a master environmental impact report as being within the scope of the report, and that master environmental impact report was certified before the expiration of the 18-month period provided in Section 33492.18.

(D) The project is categorically exempt pursuant to Article 19 (commencing with Section 15300) of Chapter 3 of Division 6 of Title 14 of the California Code of Regulations.

33492.28 Fiscal year defined

As used in this chapter, "fiscal year" means a year commencing on July 1 and ending on the next June 30.

33492.29 Required finding in ordinance that no significant financial burden or detriment to taxing agencies

An ordinance adopting a redevelopment plan under this chapter shall include a finding that the effect of tax increment financing will not cause a significant financial burden or detriment on any taxing agency deriving revenues from a project area. This finding shall only be required when the project is financed in part or in whole from revenues derived from the allocation of taxes pursuant to Section 33670.

Article 1.5
Norton Air Force Base and George Air Force Base Redevelopment Project Areas

33492.40 Creation of joint powers agency by communities with land in proximity to military facilities or installations in County of San Bernardino

(a) Notwithstanding Section 33320.1, the requirement that privately owned land within a project area be "predominantly urbanized," as that term is defined in subdivision (b) of Section 33320.1, shall not apply to privately owned land within a project area, if the privately owned land is adjacent or in proximity to a military facility or installation that is proposed to be closed pursuant to Public Law 100-526 and the inclusion of the privately owned land is found by an entity formed pursuant to subdivision (b) to be necessary for the effective redevelopment of the military facility or installation and the adjacent area.

(b) The legislative bodies for communities having territory within, adjacent to, or in proximity to a military facility or installation described in subdivision (a) may create a separate joint powers agency pursuant to Chapter 5 (commencing with Section 6500) of Division 7 of Title 1 of the Government Code, which shall have and exclusively exercise powers of an agency in furtherance of the redevelopment of a project area approved by the joint powers agency. The joint powers agency so formed shall include as one of its members the county in which the project area is located. In addition to the powers of an agency, the joint powers agency so formed shall also act as the legislative body and planning commission for all approvals and actions required by this part of legislative bodies and planning commissions for the adoption and implementation of a redevelopment plan. However, all land use, planning, and development decisions with regard to the land within the project area shall continue to be under the control and jurisdiction of each of the respective local legislative bodies or planning commissions, as applicable.

(c) The territory included within the project and project area may be contiguous or noncontiguous, and any project area may be located in whole or in part within one or more of the communities impacted by the closure of the military facility or installation, and the land to be included within the project area within the community or communities in proximity to the military facility or installation shall be found necessary for the effective redevelopment of the military facility or installation and the adjacent area. A project area shall not include territory outside the jurisdiction of the communities that are parties to the joint powers agency without the consent of the legislative body having jurisdiction over the territory proposed to be included within the project area.

(d) A redevelopment plan for the project area shall contain all of the provisions required by this part. However, if the agency finds, based on substantial evidence on the record, that compliance with the requirements of Sections 33333.2 and 33334.1 would make it impracticable to achieve the policies of this section, the agency may eliminate or modify the requirements of Sections 33333.2 and 33334.1.

(e) The redevelopment plan shall provide for either of the following:

(1) A Low- and Moderate-Income Housing Fund, as required by Section 33334.2.

(2) A deferral for depositing all or part of the 20 percent of taxes allocated to the agency pursuant to Section 33670 in the Low- and Moderate-Income Housing Fund if the agency, after conducting a noticed public hearing, makes, and the executive committee of the Southern California Association of Governments reviews and approves, findings supported by substantial evidence that all of the following apply:

(A) The military facility or installation cannot be acquired or developed by private enterprise without the assistance of the agency.

(B) There are no feasible alternative means of financing the acquisition or development of the military facility or installation other than by utilizing the low- and moderate-income housing portion of the taxes that are allocated to the agency pursuant to subdivision (b) of Section 33670.

(C) Failure of the agency to finance the acquisition or development of the military facility or installation would lead to serious economic hardship and job loss.

(D) The redevelopment plan shall specify the period during which less than 20 percent of the taxes that are allocated to the agency pursuant to subdivision (b) of Section 33670, is to be deposited in the Low- and Moderate-Income Housing Fund. The redevelopment plan shall also contain a repayment plan which specifies a date at which time the agency will have made up the deficit created by the deferral, including repayment of the interest at the highest rate received by the agency on funds it deposits during the period of deferral. The repayment plan shall reduce the deficit in the shortest feasible time consistent with the needs of the agency, as specified in the agency's findings.

(f) The joint powers agency acting as the agency, the legislative body or the planning commission, shall follow all procedures under this part applicable to the adoption and amendment of redevelopment plans, except with respect to Sections 33347.5, 33353 to 33353.6, inclusive, Sections 33354.4 to 33354.6, inclusive, and Section 33385.

(g) The agency shall create a fiscal advisory group to consult with each affected taxing agency and to advise and report to the agency in the manner required of a fiscal review committee by Section 33353.5 on any potential fiscal impact upon affected taxing agencies within the project area. The fiscal advisory group shall consist of the financial officer or treasurer of each city and each county that created the joint powers authority.

(h) The agency shall prepare and distribute to each affected taxing agency a report that includes the information required by Section 33328. The agency shall also prepare an analysis of the report required of a fiscal review committee pursuant to subdivision (m) of Section 33352 and an analysis of the report required of the fiscal advisory group pursuant to subdivision (g).

(i) As used in this section, "in proximity to" means within three miles of the boundary of Norton Air Force Base and within eight miles of George Air Force Base.

(j) The Legislature finds and declares that the closure of two or more military facilities or installations within the County of San Bernardino will cause serious economic hardship in that county, including loss of jobs, increased unemployment, deterioration of properties and land utilization and undue disruption of the lives and activities of the people. Therefore, the Legislature finds and declares that to avoid serious economic hardship and accompanying blight, it is necessary to enact this act which shall apply only within the County of San Bernardino. In enacting this act, it is the policy of the Legislature to assist communities within the County of San Bernardino in their attempt to preserve the military facilities and installations for their continued use as airports and aviation-related purposes.

It is the intent of the Legislature and the commitment of the local authorities to ensure that the existing airfields at both Norton Air Force Base and George Air Force Base are protected, developed, and enhanced as civil aviation public use airports. Therefore, the joint powers authorities authorized by this section should make every reasonable effort to guarantee that these vital airport facilities are retained for general aviation use now and into the future.

(k) Any joint powers agreement entered into pursuant to this section shall provide that the financial needs of each of the parties shall be considered prior to adoption of a redevelopment plan, and may provide that the number of years shall be limited during which bonded indebtedness may be paid using taxes that are allocated to the agency pursuant to subdivision (b) of Section 33670.

(1) A joint powers agency operating within the area of Norton Air Force Base shall appoint a project area citizens committee for the purpose of consultation and advice regarding policy matters that relate to planning and programs affecting the residents, businesses, and educational institutions within the project area, implementation of the redevelopment plan, and the development and implementation of amendments to the redevelopment plan.

(2) The committee shall be comprised of residential owners, residential tenants, business owners, small business owners, business tenants, educational institution representatives, and community groups currently operating, living, or working within the project area. The membership of the Project Area Citizens Committee shall be appointed by the legislative body of the agency and shall be representative, both racially and ethnically, of the people who live and work within the project area.

(3) For the purposes described above, the committee shall meet at least once quarterly or more often to review policy matters and implementation issues as determined necessary by the legislative body.

(l) Amendments to any redevelopment plans adopted pursuant to this section shall not be required to comply with the provisions of Section 33452, provided that notice of the public hearing for any amendment adopted pursuant to Article 12 (commencing with Section 33450 of Chapter 4), is published pursuant to Section 6063 of the Government Code and mailed by regular mail to the governing body of each of the taxing agencies that levies taxes upon any property in the project area designated in the redevelopment plan as proposed to be amended.

33492.41 Norton Air Force Base Redevelopment Plan Amendment: exemption from CEQA

(a) Notwithstanding Section 21090 of the Public Resources Code, the Inland Valley Development Agency may determine at a noticed public hearing that the amendment of a redevelopment plan for the Norton Air Force Base Redevelopment Project Area pursuant to this chapter is not subject to the California Environmental Quality Act (Division 13 (commencing with Section 21000) of the Public Resources Code), except that projects implementing the redevelopment plan, including specific plans, rezonings, and ministerial projects that may have a significant effect on the environment, shall be subject to the California Environmental Quality Act. The environmental document for any implementing project shall include an analysis and mitigation of potential cumulative impacts that otherwise will not be known until an environmental impact report for the redevelopment plan is certified.

(b) The notice of the public hearing required pursuant to subdivision (a) shall include the date, time, and place of the hearing, a brief description of the proposed project and its location, the date when notice will be provided pursuant to Section 21092 of the Public Resources Code, and the address where copies of the notice of exemption are available for review.

(c) The notice required by this section shall be given to all organizations and individuals who have previously requested notice pursuant to the California Environmental Quality Act, and shall be given by publication, no fewer times than required by Section 6061 of the Government Code, by the public agency in a newspaper of general circulation in the area affected by the proposed project.

(d) If the Inland Valley Development Agency determines, pursuant to subdivision (a), that the amendment of a redevelopment plan is not subject to the California Environmental Quality Act, the redevelopment agency shall prepare and certify an environmental impact report for the redevelopment plan amendment within 12 months after the effective date of the ordinance amending the redevelopment plan.

(e) An environmental impact report prepared and certified for a specific plan or other comprehensive land use plan for the applicable portion of the Inland Valley Redevelopment Project Area shall satisfy the requirement of subdivision (d) if the plan covers the same area and project as the amendment to the redevelopment plan and is certified within 12 months after the effective date of the ordinance amending the redevelopment plan.

(f) The redevelopment agency shall revise the redevelopment plan if necessary to mitigate any impacts and comply with the California Environmental Quality Act and adopt mitigation measures as conditions of project approval.

(g) This section shall only apply to a redevelopment plan amendment approved on or before September 1, 1995.

33492.42 Norton Air Force Base Redevelopment Plan Amendment: sewer and water pipelines

(a) The redevelopment agency referenced in Section 33492.41 may locate, construct, and maintain facilities and infrastructure for sewer and water pipelines or other facilities for sewer transmission and water supply or distribution systems along and across any street or public highway and on any lands that are now or hereafter owned by the state, for the purpose of providing facilities or services related to development, to or in that portion of, the redevelopment project area referenced in subdivision (e) of Section 33492.41 that, as of January 1, 2000, meets all of the following requirements:

(1) Is unincorporated territory.

(2) Contains at least 100 acres.

(3) Is surrounded or substantially surrounded by incorporated territory.

(4) Contains at least 100 acres zoned for commercial or industrial uses or is designated on the applicable county general plan for commercial or industrial uses.

(b) Facilities or services related to development may be provided by the redevelopment agency referenced in Section 33492.41 to all or any portion of the area defined in paragraphs (1) to (4), inclusive, of subdivision (a). Notwithstanding any other provision of the Government Code, building ordinances, zoning ordinances, and any other local ordinances, rules, and regulations of a city or other political subdivision of the state shall not apply to the location, construction, or maintenance of facilities or services related to development pursuant to this section.

Article 4
Redevelopment Agency of Fort Ord

33492.70 Legislative intent; establishment and authority of Redevelopment Agency of Fort Ord

(a) (1) This article shall govern the establishment and operation of all redevelopment project areas created within the area previously known as Fort Ord.

(2) It is the intent of the Legislature that the redevelopment of the territory of Fort Ord be conducted jointly, in part by redevelopment project areas established by cities and the county with jurisdiction over parts of the territory of what was previously known as Fort Ord, and in part by the Fort Ord Reuse Authority. It is further the intent of the Legislature that this joint redevelopment include the sharing of tax increment revenues pursuant to this article. The joint division of tax increment will enable the local redevelopment agencies to finance redevelopment activities which primarily affect their own jurisdictions, and the authority will have a revenue source to assist in financing redevelopment of facilities of basewide significance.

(b) The board of the Fort Ord Reuse Authority, as established by Title 7.85 (commencing with Section 67650) of the Government Code, may, by ordinance, establish in the area of Fort Ord a public body, corporate and politic, known as the Redevelopment Agency of Fort Ord. This agency may transact business and exercise its powers as a redevelopment agency upon the effective date of the establishing ordinance. The provisions of the Community Redevelopment Law (Part 1 (commencing with Section 33000) of Division 24), as modified by Chapter 4.5 (commencing with Section 33492) thereof, shall apply to the Redevelopment Agency of Fort Ord, and this agency shall have all powers of a redevelopment agency as provided in this part.

(c) In addition to the powers of an agency, the Redevelopment Agency of Fort Ord shall also act as the legislative body and the planning commission for all approvals and actions required and authorized by this part for the adoption and implementation of a redevelopment plan. However, subject to the consistency and appeal provision of Title 7.85 (commencing with Section 67650) of the Government Code and other applicable provisions of state law, all planning, zoning, and permitting decisions with regard to the land within the project area shall continue to be under the control and jurisdiction of each of the respective local legislative bodies, as applicable.

(d) For purposes of this article, "board" means the governing board of the Fort Ord Reuse Authority, as defined in Title 7.85 (commencing with Section 67650) of the Government Code. "Legislative body," as used elsewhere in this part, shall, for the purposes of this article when relating to the Redevelopment Agency of Fort Ord, also refer to the governing board of the Fort Ord Reuse Authority.

(e) The board may create a project area to include all or a portion or portions of the area of Fort Ord, except that the board shall not create a project area which overlays any territory included within a project area established by the redevelopment agency of a city or the county.

(f) A city or county redevelopment agency may establish a project area which includes any or all of the territory within the jurisdiction of the city or county which is also within the territory of Fort Ord, but only pursuant to the provisions of this section.

33492.71 Payments to affected taxing entities

(a) This section shall apply to each redevelopment project area created pursuant to this article with a redevelopment plan that contains the provisions required by Section 33670. All amounts calculated pursuant to this section shall be calculated after the amount required to be deposited in the Low and Moderate Income Housing Fund pursuant to Sections 33334.2, 33334.3, 33334.6, and 33492.76, and the amounts required to be paid by school and community college districts pursuant to Section 33492.78 have been deducted from the local tax increment funds received by the agency in the applicable fiscal year.

(b) The payments made pursuant to this section shall be in addition to any amounts the affected taxing entities receive pursuant to subdivision (a) of Section 33670. The agency shall reduce its payments pursuant to this section to the authority or an affected taxing entity by any amount the agency has paid, directly or indirectly, pursuant to Section 33445 and with the agreement of the authority or the affected taxing entity, or pursuant to any other provision of law other than this section for, or in connection with a public facility owned or leased by the authority or that affected taxing entity and with the agreement of the authority or that affected taxing entity.

(c) Commencing in the first fiscal year in which a redevelopment agency receives tax-increment revenue from a project area created pursuant to this article, the agency shall pay the following amounts to the following entities, and the agency shall not be obligated to pay any additional sums to any taxing entities pursuant to Section 33607.5 and subdivision (b) of Section 33676:

(1) (A) Thirty-five percent of the tax-increment revenue received by the agency after the amount required to be deposited in the Low and Moderate Income Housing Fund pursuant to Sections 33334.2, 33334.3, and 33334.6, as modified by Section 33492.76, has been deducted each fiscal year shall be paid to the authority to finance in whole or in part, its responsibilities in providing for the reuse of Fort Ord.

(B) Thirty-five percent of the tax-increment revenue received by the agency after the amount required to be deposited in the Low and Moderate Income Housing Fund pursuant to Sections 33334.2, 33334.3, and 33334.6 of, as modified by Section 33492.76, has been deducted each fiscal year shall be paid to or retained by the redevelopment agency of the city or county in which the project area is located, to finance, in whole or in part, its responsibilities in providing for the reuse of Fort Ord.

(C) Of the amount referenced in subparagraph (B), each city may elect to receive from its agency, and the agency shall pay, an amount not to exceed 25 percent of the tax-increment revenue generated from a project area established pursuant to this article, to alleviate the financial burden and detriment incurred as a result of the adoption of the redevelopment plan in each year until the sixth fiscal year after the year in which the agency is first allocated one hundred thousand dollars ($100,000) or more in tax-increment revenues.

(D) Upon dissolution of the authority, the amount allocated pursuant to this section shall continue to be paid to the accounts of the authority insofar as needed to pay principal and interest or other amounts on debt that was incurred by the authority. Funds that would be allocated pursuant to this section that exceed the amounts necessary to pay debt service on authority debt shall be divided as follows: 54 percent shall be allocated to the city or county redevelopment agency that establishes the project area; 38 percent shall be allocated to the county; and 8 percent shall be allocated to other affected taxing entities.

(2) Twenty-five percent of the tax-increment revenue received by the agency after the amount required to be deposited in the Low and Moderate Income Housing Fund pursuant to Sections 33334.2, 33334.3, and 33334.6, as modified by Section 33492.76, has been deducted each fiscal year shall be paid to the county to alleviate the financial burden and detriment to the county incurred because of the establishment of the project area.

(3) Not to exceed 5 percent of the tax-increment revenue received by the agency after the amount required to be deposited in the Low and Moderate Income Housing Fund pursuant to Sections 33334.2, 33334.3, and 33334.6, as modified by Section 33492.76, has been deducted each fiscal year shall be paid to other affected taxing entities as defined in Section 33492.27, but excluding the entities specified in paragraphs (1) and (2), and excluding school and community college districts, in order to alleviate the financial burden and detriment incurred by those affected taxing entities because of the establishment of the project area. If the total payments made pursuant to this paragraph are less than 5 percent of the tax increment revenue received by the agency pursuant to this article, the remaining portion of the revenue available as a result of this paragraph shall be allocated as follows: 37 percent to the agency, 37 percent to the authority, and 26 percent to the county.

(d) Notwithstanding subdivision (c), through and including the second fiscal year after the certification date established pursuant to Section 33492.9, the amount of tax increment revenue the redevelopment agencies of the Cities of Marina and Seaside or the County of Monterey are required to pay to other entities as prescribed in paragraph (1) shall be modified as follows:

(1) For each of those fiscal years, the board shall determine an amount equal to 100 percent of the revenue payable to the city or county establishing the project area from all ad valorem property taxes, including allocations of property tax increment revenues pursuant to subdivision (c), sales taxes, utility users taxes, business license taxes, real property transfer taxes, franchise taxes, transient occupancy taxes, and payments received as a result of vehicle and trailer coach registration, and cigarette and gasoline taxes except for payments received as a result of vehicle registrations because of military personnel occupying Fort Ord, attributable to the property, population, and economic activity that is within the jurisdiction of each local entity that has established a redevelopment project area pursuant to this subdivision and is also within the area of Fort Ord.

(2) If the amount determined pursuant to paragraph (1) for a fiscal year is less than four hundred thousand dollars ($400,000), the redevelopment agency of the local entity that established the project area shall retain tax-increment revenue received because of the project area so that the sum of the retained tax-increment revenue, exclusive of required deposits to the Low and Moderate Income Housing Fund and the amount of revenue determined pursuant to paragraph (1), equals four hundred thousand dollars ($400,000), but in no event exceeding 100 percent of the tax-increment revenue received for the project area for that fiscal year. Any tax-increment revenue received by the redevelopment agency that established the project area which exceeds the amount necessary to bring the total of the amount calculated pursuant to paragraph (1), plus the tax increment retained by the agency pursuant to this subdivision to four hundred thousand dollars ($400,000) shall be distributed pursuant to subdivision (c).

(e) The board may increase or decrease the qualified minimum level of increment funding set in paragraph (2) of subdivision (d) above four hundred thousand dollars ($400,000), if the board determines, based on substantial evidence, that the costs of providing police and fire protection services to the area of Fort Ord within the local agency's redevelopment agency's project area exceed or are less than this amount. In the event that any city which does not now have jurisdiction over territory within the area of Fort Ord subsequently annexes territory within the area of Fort Ord, the board may provide for a qualified minimum level of increment funding at a level that it determines, based on substantial evidence as to the cost of providing police and fire protection services to the area of Fort Ord within the local agency's redevelopment agency's project area is appropriate for a period not to exceed three years, but is under no obligation to do so.

(f) Because this article provides for an allocation of tax-increment revenue arising from the redevelopment of the area of Fort Ord among the affected taxing entities for the purpose of alleviating any financial burden or detriment that is caused by the redevelopment plan, the consultations with the affected taxing entities shall not include the payment of supplemental moneys, but may only include the discussion of possible modifications in the redevelopment plan, including, but not limited to, the timing of projects, selection of projects, scope of projects, and the type of financing that is being considered for the projects.

(g) (1) All moneys received by the authority from a redevelopment agency shall be deposited in a separate fund from all other moneys of the authority.

(2) The authority shall annually report on the total amount of moneys deposited into the fund during the year; the specific project and programs which were financed with the moneys, including amounts expended per project and program; and the beginning and ending balance of the fund.

(3) The moneys in the fund shall be exclusively expended for the purpose of financing the development and redevelopment of basewide facilities as identified in the basewide public capital facilities plan adopted pursuant to Section 67675 of the Government Code.

(4) The authority shall have an independent financial audit annually prepared on the fund in accordance with generally accepted auditing standards and rules of governing auditing reports promulgated by the California Board of Accountancy.

(h) Notwithstanding any other provision of law, no tax increment moneys, including moneys paid from a redevelopment agency to Fort Ord Reuse Authority or any affected taxing entity, shall finance the development or redevelopment of buildings owned or operated by the California State University or the University of California.

33492.72 Subordination of payments to affected taxing entities

(a) Prior to incurring any loans, or other indebtedness, except loans or advances from the local agency or the authority, the agency which established the redevelopment project area, or the board, may subordinate to the loans or other indebtedness the amounts required to be paid to all other local agencies pursuant to this section, provided that the agency or the board has approved these subordinations pursuant to this subdivision.

(b) At the time the agency or the board requests any other entity receiving tax-increment revenues pursuant to this section to subordinate the amount to be paid to it, the agency or the board seeking permission for subordination, shall provide the affected taxing entity with substantial evidence that sufficient funds will be available to pay both the debt service and the payments required by this section, when due.

(c) Within 45 days after receipt of the agency's or the board's request, the entities receiving tax-increment revenues pursuant to this section shall approve or disapprove the request for subordination. An entity other than the redevelopment agency or the board may disapprove a request for subordination only if it finds, based upon substantial evidence, that after the agency or the board pays the debt payments, the agency will not have sufficient funds to pay the amounts required to be paid to other entities pursuant to this section. The agency or the board may also disapprove a request for subordination if it finds that subordination would interfere with its ability to issue debt as needed to carry out its responsibilities. If an entity, the agency, or the board does not act within 45 days after receipt of the agency's request, the request to subordinate shall be deemed approved and shall be final and conclusive.

33492.73 Consistency with Fort Ord Reuse Plan

Any redevelopment or implementation plan prepared in conjunction with establishment or operation of a project area, and any subsequent amendment, update, or other modification of that plan or those plans, shall take effect only upon certification by the board of the consistency of that plan or those plans with the Fort Ord Reuse Plan in the same manner as for the local agency's general plan pursuant to Chapter 4 (commencing with Section 67675) of Title 7.85 of the Government Code.

33492.74 Blighted area and blight defined

(a) For purposes of this article, a blighted area may be a military base in which the combination of two or more of the conditions set forth in subdivision (b) or (c) of this section are so prevalent and so substantial that it causes a reduction of, or a lack of, proper utilization of the area to an extent that constitutes a serious physical and economic burden on the community that cannot reasonably be expected to be reversed or alleviated by private enterprise or governmental action, or both, without redevelopment.

(b) This subdivision, for purposes of this article, describes physical conditions that cause blight.

(1) Buildings in which it is unsafe or unhealthy for persons to live or work. These conditions can be caused by serious building code violations, dilapidation and deterioration, defective design or physical construction, faulty or inadequate infrastructure, or other similar factors.

(2) Factors that prevent or substantially hinder the economically viable reuse or capacity of buildings or areas. This condition can be caused by a substandard design; buildings that are too large or too small given present standards and market conditions; and age, obsolescence, deterioration, dilapidation, or other physical conditions that could prevent the highest and best uses of the property. This condition can also be caused by buildings that will have to be demolished or buildings or areas that have a lack of parking.

(3) Adjacent or nearby uses that are incompatible with each other and that prevent the economic development of those parcels or other portions of the project area.

(4) Buildings on land that, when subdivided or when infrastructure is installed, will not comply with normal subdivision, zoning, or planning regulations.

(c) This subdivision, for purposes of this article, describes economic conditions that cause blight:

(1) Land that contains materials, including, but not necessarily limited to, materials for airport runways that will have to be removed to allow development.

(2) Properties that contain hazardous wastes that may benefit from the use of agency authority as specified in Article 12.5 (commencing with Section 33459) of Chapter 4 in order to be developed by either the private or public sector or in order to comply with applicable federal or state standards. Notwithstanding any other provision of law, all redevelopment agencies with authority under this act are specifically prohibited from accepting

responsibility for, or using agency authority on behalf of, hazardous waste sites that are the responsibility of the federal government.

(d) For purposes of this article, a blighted area also may be one that contains one or more of the conditions described in subdivision (c) and is, in addition, characterized by the existence of inadequate public improvements, public facilities, and utilities, where these conditions are so prevalent and so substantial that it causes a reduction of, or a lack of, proper utilization of the area to an extent that it constitutes a serious physical and economic burden on the community that cannot reasonably be expected to be reversed or alleviated by private enterprise or governmental action, or both, without redevelopment.

33492.75 Adoption of redevelopment plan: modified requirements

(a) For purposes of adoption of a project area, the preliminary report prepared pursuant to Section 33344.5 is not required to contain the material identified in paragraphs (2), (3), and (4) of subdivision (c) of Section 33344.5.

(b) For purposes of adoption of a project area, the report prepared pursuant to Section 33352 shall be modified to require that the blight conditions specified in Section 33492.74 exist.

(c) A redevelopment plan adopted for a project area shall contain the limitations set forth in Section 33492.13, and shall not be subject to the limitations set forth in Section 33333.2.

(d) For purposes of redevelopment project areas within the area of Fort Ord, calculation of the amount determined pursuant to subdivision (a) of Section 33670 shall be based on the assessment roll used in connection with property within the project area last equalized prior to the date on which the board of the Fort Ord Reuse Authority adopts a Fort Ord Reuse Plan pursuant to Section 67675 of the Government Code, which shall be deemed to be a redevelopment plan for the area of the base, or the effective date of the ordinance approving a redevelopment plan for a specific project area within the area of Fort Ord, whichever occurs first for any project area.

33492.76 Low and moderate income housing obligations

(a) (1) Notwithstanding Section 33334.2 or any other provision of law, a redevelopment agency established or governed pursuant to this article may:

(A) Annually waive the requirement to allocate 20 percent of the total annual tax increment revenue from any project area established pursuant to this article to the Low- and Moderate-Income Housing Fund for a period of up to five years after the date on which the county auditor makes the certification pursuant to Section 33492.9.

(B) Annually waive the requirement to allocate half of the 20 percent of the total annual tax increment revenue to the Low- and Moderate-Income Housing Fund for a period of five years after the fifth year after the date on which the county auditor makes the certification pursuant to Section 33492.9.

(2) The agency may not waive its allocation in any year unless it first adopts a finding, based on substantial evidence, that the vacancy rate for rental housing affordable to lower income households is greater than 6 percent.

(b) Notwithstanding Section 33413, the redevelopment agency shall not be required to replace removed or demolished military barracks, which are located, as of January 1, 1995, within the boundaries of Fort Ord.

33492.78 Payments to affected school and community college districts

(a) Section 33607.5 shall not apply to an agency created pursuant to this article. For purposes of Sections 42238, 84750, and 84751 of the Education Code, funds allocated pursuant to this section shall be treated as if they were allocated pursuant to Section 33607.5.

(1) This section shall apply to each redevelopment project area created pursuant to a redevelopment plan that contains the provisions required by Section 33670 and is created pursuant to this article. All the amounts calculated pursuant to this section shall be calculated after the amount required to be deposited in the Low and Moderate Income Housing Fund pursuant to Sections 33334.2, 33334.3, and 33334.6, as modified by Section 33492.76, has been deducted from the total amount of tax-increment funds received by the agency in the applicable fiscal year.

(2) The payments made pursuant to this section shall be in addition to any amounts the school district or districts and community college district or districts receive pursuant to subdivision (a) of Section 33670. The agency shall reduce its payments pursuant to this section to an affected school or community college district by any amount the agency has paid, directly or indirectly, pursuant to Section 33445, 33445.5, or 33446, or any provision of law other than this section for, or in connection with, a public facility owned or leased by that affected school or community college district.

(3) (A) Of the total amount paid each year pursuant to this section to school districts, 43.9 percent shall be considered to be property taxes for the purposes of paragraph (1) of subdivision (h) of Section 42238 of the Education Code, and 56.1 percent shall not be considered to be property taxes for the purposes of that section, and shall be available to be used for educational facilities.

(B) Of the total amount paid each year pursuant to this section to community college districts, 47.5 percent shall be considered to be property taxes for the purposes of Section 84750 of the Education Code, and 52.5 percent shall not be considered to be property taxes for the purposes of that section, and shall be available to be used for educational facilities.

(C) Of the total amount paid each year pursuant to this section to county offices of education, 19 percent shall be considered to be property taxes for the purposes of paragraph (1) of subdivision (h) of Section 42238 of the Education Code, and 81 percent shall not be considered to be property taxes for the purposes of that section, and shall be available to be used for educational facilities.

(D) Of the total amount paid each year pursuant to this section to special education, 19 percent shall be considered to be property taxes for the purposes of paragraph (1) of subdivision (h) of Section 42238 of the Education Code, and 81 percent shall not be considered to be property taxes for the purposes of that section, and shall be available to be used for educational facilities.

(4) Local education agencies that use funds received pursuant to this section for educational facilities shall spend these funds at schools that are any one of the following:

(A) Within the project area.

(B) Attended by students from the project area.

(C) Attended by students generated by projects that are assisted directly by the redevelopment agency.

(D) Determined by a local education agency to be of benefit to the project area.

(b) Commencing with the first fiscal year in which the agency receives tax increments, and continuing through the last fiscal year in which the agency receives tax increments, a redevelopment agency created pursuant to this article shall pay to each affected school and community college district an amount equal to the product of 25 percent times the percentage share of total property taxes collected that are allocated to each affected school or community college district, including any amount allocated to each district pursuant to Sections 97.03 and 97.035 of the Revenue and Taxation Code times the total of the tax increments received by the agency after the amount required to be deposited in the Low and Moderate Income Housing Fund has been deducted.

(c) Commencing with the 11th fiscal year in which the agency receives tax increments and continuing through the last fiscal year in which the agency receives tax increments, a redevelopment agency created pursuant to this article shall pay to each affected school and community college district, in addition to the amounts paid pursuant to subdivision (b), an amount equal to the product of 21 percent times the percentage share of total property taxes collected that are allocated to each affected school or community college district, including any amount allocated to each district pursuant to Sections 97.03 and 97.035 of the Revenue and Taxation Code times the total of the first adjusted tax increments received by the agency after the amount required to be deposited in the Low and Moderate Income Housing Fund has been deducted. The first adjusted tax increments received by the agency shall be calculated by applying the tax rate against the amount of assessed value by which the current year assessed value exceeds the first adjusted base year assessed value. The first adjusted base year assessed value is the assessed value of the project area in the 10th fiscal year in which the agency receives tax increment.

(d) Commencing with the 31st fiscal year in which the agency receives tax increments and continuing through the last fiscal year in which the agency receives tax increments, a redevelopment agency shall pay to the affected school and community college districts, in addition to the amounts paid pursuant to subdivisions (b) and (c), an amount equal to 14 percent times the percentage share of total property taxes collected that are allocated to each affected school or community college district, including any amount allocated to each district pursuant to Sections 97.03 and 97.035 of the Revenue and Taxation Code times the total of the second adjusted tax increments received by the agency after the amount required to be deposited in the Low and Moderate Income Housing Fund has been deducted. The second adjusted tax increments received by the agency shall be calculated by applying the tax rate against the amount of assessed value by which the current year assessed value exceeds the second adjusted base year assessed value. The second adjusted base year assessed value is the assessed value of the project area in the 30th fiscal year in which the agency receives tax increments.

(e) (1) The Legislature finds and declares both of the following:

(A) The payments made pursuant to this section are necessary in order to alleviate the financial burden and detriment that affected school and community college districts may incur as a result of the adoption of a redevelopment plan, and payments made pursuant to this section will benefit redevelopment project areas.

(B) The payments made pursuant to this section are the exclusive payments that are required to be made by a redevelopment agency to affected school and community college districts during the term of a redevelopment plan.

(2) Notwithstanding any other provision of law, a redevelopment agency shall not be required, either directly or indirectly, as a measure to mitigate a significant environmental effect or as part of any settlement agreement or judgment brought in any action to contest the validity of a redevelopment plan pursuant to Section 33501, to make any other payments to affected school and community college districts, or to pay for public facilities that will be owned or leased to an affected school or community college district.

(f) As used in this section, a "local education agency" includes a school district, a community college district, or a county office of education.

Article 5
March Joint Powers Redevelopment Agency

33492.80 Legislative intent

For purposes of this article, it is the intent of the Legislature to provide a means of mitigating the economic and social degradation facing communities impacted by the realignment of March Air Force Base.

33492.81 Establishment and authority of March Joint Powers Redevelopment Agency

(a) The March Joint Powers Authority, a public entity created pursuant to Article 1 (commencing with Section 6500) of Chapter 5 of Division 7 of Title 1 of the Government Code, and composed of the Cities of Moreno Valley, Perris, and Riverside and the County of Riverside, is hereby authorized to establish the March Joint Powers Redevelopment Agency, with all of the powers, authority, and duties granted to it under this part, as a public body, corporate and politic, for the exclusive purpose of establishing the March Air Force Base Redevelopment Project Area pursuant to this article.

(b) The March Joint Powers Redevelopment Agency shall act as the legislative body and planning commission for all approvals and actions required or authorized for the adoption and implementation of a redevelopment plan. However, all land use planning and development decisions with regard to the land within the project area shall continue to be under the control and jurisdiction of each of the respective local legislative bodies or planning commissions, as applicable.

33492.82 Blighted area defined

(a) For purposes of this article, a blighted area within the boundaries of March Air Force Base, as those boundaries exist on January 1, 1995, is either one of the following:

(1) An area in which the combination of two or more of the conditions set forth in subdivision (a) or (b) of Section 33492.83 is so prevalent and so substantial that it causes a reduction of, or a lack of, proper utilization of the area to an extent that constitutes a serious physical and economic burden on the community that cannot reasonably be expected to be reversed or alleviated by private enterprise or governmental action, or both, without redevelopment.

(2) An area that contains one or more of the conditions described in subdivision (b) of Section 33492.83, the effect of

which is so prevalent and so substantial that it causes a reduction of, or a lack of, proper utilization of the area to an extent that constitutes a serious physical and economic burden on the community that cannot reasonably be expected to be reversed or alleviated by private enterprise, or governmental action, or both, without redevelopment, and is, in addition, characterized by the existence of inadequate public improvements, public facilities, and utilities that cannot be remedied by private or governmental action without redevelopment.

(b) For the purposes of this article, a blighted area outside the boundaries of March Air Force Base, as those boundaries exist on January 1, 1995, shall be an area that meets the requirements of Section 33030.

33492.83 Blight defined

(a) This subdivision, for purposes of this article, describes physical conditions that cause blight.

(1) Buildings in which it is unsafe or unhealthy for persons to live or work. These conditions can be caused by serious building code violations, dilapidation and deterioration, defective design or physical construction, faulty or inadequate infrastructure, or other similar factors.

(2) Factors that prevent or substantially hinder the economically viable reuse or capacity of buildings or areas. This condition can be caused by a substandard design; buildings that are too large or too small given present standards and market conditions; and age, obsolescence, deterioration, dilapidation, or other physical conditions that could prevent the highest and best uses of the property. This condition can also be caused by buildings that will have to be demolished or buildings or areas that have a lack of parking.

(3) Adjacent or nearby uses that are incompatible with each other and that prevent the economic development of those parcels or other portions of the project area.

(4) Buildings on land that, when subdivided or when infrastructure is installed, will not comply with normal subdivision, zoning, or planning regulations.

(b) This subdivision, for purposes of this article, describes economic conditions that cause blight:

(1) Land that contains materials or facilities, including, but not necessarily limited to, materials for airport runways that will have to be removed to allow development.

(2) Properties that contain hazardous wastes that may benefit from the use of agency authority as specified in Article 12.5 (commencing with Section 33459) of Chapter 4 in order to be developed by either the private or public sector or in order to comply with applicable federal or state standards. Notwithstanding any other provision of law, the March Joint Powers Redevelopment Agency is specifically prohibited from accepting responsibility for, or using agency authority on behalf of, hazardous waste sites that are the responsibility of the federal government.

(c) Pursuant to Section 33321, a project area need not be restricted to buildings, improvements, or lands which are not detrimental or inimical to the public health, safety, or welfare, but may consist of an area in which these conditions predominate and injuriously affect the entire area. A project area may include lands, buildings, or improvements which are not detrimental to the public health, safety, or welfare, but whose inclusion is found necessary for the effective redevelopment of the area of which they are a part. Each area included under this section shall be necessary for effective redevelopment and shall not be included for the purpose of obtaining the allocation of tax-increment revenue from the area pursuant to Section 33670 without other substantial justification for its inclusion.

33492.84 Redevelopment agency and agency defined

For purposes of this article, the terms "redevelopment agency" and "agency" refer to the March Joint Powers Redevelopment Agency, which is hereby authorized to engage in the redevelopment activities included in and referenced by this article.

33492.85 Limitations on incurring and repaying indebtedness, duration of plan and use of eminent domain

(a) A redevelopment plan for March Air Force Base, adopted pursuant to this chapter and containing the provisions set forth in Section 33670, shall contain all of the following limitations:

(1) (A) A time limit on the establishing of loans, advances, and indebtedness to be paid with the proceeds of property taxes received pursuant to Section 33670 to finance in whole or in part the redevelopment project, which may not exceed 20 years from the date the county auditor certifies pursuant to Section 33492.9, except by amendment of the redevelopment plan as authorized by subparagraph (B). The loans, advances, or indebtedness may be repaid over a period of time longer than the time limit as provided in this section. No loans, advances, or indebtedness to be repaid from the allocation of taxes shall be established or incurred by the agency beyond this time limitation.

(B) The time limitation established by subparagraph (A) may be extended only by amendment of the redevelopment plan after the agency finds, based on substantial evidence, that (i) substantial blight remains within the project area; (ii) this blight cannot be eliminated without the establishment of additional debt; and (iii) the elimination of blight cannot reasonably be accomplished by private enterprise acting alone or by the legislative body's use of financing alternatives other than tax increment financing. However, this amended time limitation may not exceed 30 years from the date the county auditor certifies pursuant to Section 33492.9.

(2) A time limit, not to exceed 30 years from the date the county auditor certifies pursuant to Section 33492.9, on the effectiveness of the redevelopment plan. After the time limit on the effectiveness of the redevelopment plan, the agency shall have no authority to act pursuant to the redevelopment plan except to pay previously incurred indebtedness and enforce existing covenants or contracts.

(3) A time limit, not to exceed 45 years from the date the county auditor certifies pursuant to Section 33492.9, to repay indebtedness with the proceeds of property taxes received pursuant to Section 33670. After the time limit established pursuant to this paragraph, an agency may not receive property taxes pursuant to Section 33670.

(b) (1) A redevelopment plan, adopted pursuant to this chapter, that does not contain the provisions set forth in Section 33670 shall contain the limitations in paragraph (2).

(2) A time limit, not to exceed 12 years from the date the county auditor certifies pursuant to Section 33492.9, for commencement of eminent domain proceedings to acquire property within the project area. This time limitation may be extended only by amendment of the redevelopment plan.

33492.86 Payments to affected school and community college districts; territory of March Air Force Base Project Area

(a) This section shall apply to a redevelopment project area the territory of which includes March Air Force Base, that is adopted pursuant to a redevelopment plan that contains the provisions required by Section 33670, and that is adopted pursuant to this chapter. The redevelopment agency shall make the payments to affected school districts and community college districts required by subdivision (a) of Section 33607.5, except that each of the time periods governing the payments shall be calculated from the date the county auditor makes the certification to the Director of Finance pursuant to Section 33492.9 instead of from the first fiscal year in which the agency receives tax-increment revenue.

(b) (1) Pursuant to Section 33492.3, the March Air Force Base Project Area adopted pursuant to this article may include all, or any portion of, property within the military base that the federal Base Closure and Realignment Commission has voted to realign when that action has been sustained by the President and the Congress of the United States, regardless of the percentage of urbanized land, as defined in Section 33320.1, within the military base.

(2) (A) Pursuant to Section 33492.3, the March Air Force Base Project Area may include territory outside the military base. The project area shall be entirely contained within a one-mile perimeter of the boundaries of March Air Force Base, as those boundaries exist on January 1, 1995. At no time shall the aggregate acreage of the project area outside the boundaries of March Air Force Base, as those boundaries exist on January 1, 1995, exceed 2 percent of the total acreage contained within that one-mile perimeter, and these areas may only be included in the project area upon a finding of benefit to the March Air Force Base Project Area and with the concurrence of the legislative bodies of the County of Riverside, the City of Moreno Valley, the City of Perris, and the City of Riverside.

(B) The agency for the March Air Force Base Project Area may, with the concurrence of the relevant legislative body pursuant to subparagraph (B), pay for all or a part of the value of land and the cost of the installation and construction of any structure or facility or other improvement that is publicly owned outside the jurisdiction of the agency, if the legislative body of the agency determines all of the following:

(i) That the structure, facility, or other improvement is of benefit to the project area.

(ii) That no other reasonable means of financing the facilities, structures, or improvements are available to the community.

(iii) That the payment of funds for the acquisition of land or the cost of facilities, structures, or other improvements will assist in the elimination of one or more blight conditions, as identified pursuant to Section 33492.83, inside the project area, or provide housing for low- or moderate-income persons.

(C) Concurrence of the relevant legislative body shall be demonstrated by the adoption of an ordinance by the community where the structure, facility, or other improvement is to be located that authorizes the redevelopment of the area within its territorial limits by the redevelopment agency for the March Air Force Base Project Area.

(D) All projects authorized by this subdivision shall be within communities that are contiguous to the March Air Force Base Project Area.

(c) Notwithstanding subdivision (a) of Section 33492.15 or any other provision of law, the March Joint Powers Redevelopment Agency shall not be obligated to make any payments required by subdivision (a) of Section 33492.15 to the County of Riverside, the County Free Library Fund, and the County Fire Fund. Instead, the March Joint Powers Redevelopment Agency shall be required to make those payments required under the Cooperative Agreement entered into among the County of Riverside, the March Joint Powers Authority, and the March Joint Powers Redevelopment Agency dated August 20, 1996, as that agreement may be amended from time to time.

33492.87 Low and moderate income housing obligations

(a) (1) Notwithstanding Section 33334.2 or any other provision of law, the agency established or governed pursuant to this article may annually defer the requirement to allocate 20 percent of tax-increment revenue to the Low and Moderate Income Housing Fund for a period of up to 5 years after the date on which the county auditor makes the certification pursuant to Section 33492.9.

(2) The agency shall not defer its allocation in any year unless it first adopts a finding based on substantial evidence that the vacancy rate for rental housing affordable to lower income households within the jurisdiction of the members of the agency is greater than 4 percent.

(3) The amount of the deferral, if any, shall be considered an indebtedness of the agency and shall be paid into the Low and Moderate Income Housing Fund no later than the end of the 10th fiscal year after the date on which the county auditor makes the certification pursuant to Section 33492.9. If the indebtedness is not eliminated by the end of the 10th fiscal year, the county auditor or controller shall, no later than March 15 of the 11th year, withhold an amount equal to the indebtedness and deposit those funds into a separate Low and Moderate Income Housing Fund for use by the redevelopment agency to meet its affordable housing requirements pursuant to this part.

(b) The agency shall not be required to replace barracks or dormitory-style housing or Arnold Heights housing that is adaptively reused, demolished, or removed within the boundaries of March Air Force Base.

33492.88 Use of funds to provide credit enhancements

Notwithstanding any other provision of law, as part of an agreement that provides for the development, rehabilitation, or improvement of buildings, structures, or facilities within the project area, the redevelopment agency may use any available funds, including moneys received pursuant to Section 33670, to provide credit enhancements, including, but not limited to, the ability to buy down interest rates, that are necessary for the project. Prior to entering into an agreement for a development that would be assisted pursuant to this section, the agency shall find, after a public hearing, that the assistance is necessary for the economic feasibility of the development and that the assistance cannot be obtained on economically feasible terms in the private sector.

33492.89 Prerequisite adoption of housing element by City of Perris

Notwithstanding any other provision of law, the March Joint Powers Redevelopment Agency shall not expend any tax-increment funds allocated to it for expenses related to carrying out the project until and unless the City of Perris adopts a housing element, pursuant to Section 65585 of the Government Code, that substantially complies with the requirements of Article 10.6 (commencing with Section 65580) of Chapter 3 of Division 1 of Title 7 of the Government Code.

Article 6
Mare Island Redevelopment Project Area

33492.90 Legislative intent

With the enactment of this article, it is the intent of the Legislature to provide for precise and specific means to mitigate the very serious economic effects of the closure of the Mare Island Naval Shipyard on the City of Vallejo and surrounding communities by enabling the City of Vallejo to facilitate the planning and implementation of the reuse and redevelopment of the lands comprising Mare Island Naval Shipyard and surrounding areas, in accordance with the city's land use plans and facilities financing plans, through the redevelopment process and prior to the disposition of lands by the federal government to public entities and private parties.

33492.91 Adoption of redevelopment plan: modified requirements

(a) (1) The redevelopment plan for the Mare Island Redevelopment Project Area need not include either of the following:

(A) The information required pursuant to subdivision (d) of Section 33324 relative to the contents of the preliminary plan.

(B) The finding required pursuant to paragraph (4) of subdivision (d) of Section 33367 relative to the conformity of the redevelopment plan to the community's general plan.

(2) The redevelopment agency shall not expend any tax increment funds allocated to it from the project area for expenses related to carrying out the project unless and until the City of Vallejo finds that the redevelopment plan conforms to the general plan of the city, including the housing element thereof.

(b) Notwithstanding Section 33328, the report required by that section need only be as complete as the information then available will permit.

(c) Notwithstanding Section 33344.5, the preliminary report required by that section need only be as complete as the information then available will permit and need not contain the information required by subdivision (c) of Section 33344.5.

(d) The report submitted by the redevelopment agency to the legislative body pursuant to Section 33352, need not contain the items listed in subdivisions (b), (c), (d), (h), (j), (k), (l), and (m) of Section 33352, as modified by subdivision (b) of this section, and the ordinance adopted by the legislative body pursuant to Section 33367 need not contain the items listed in paragraphs (4) and (12) of subdivision (d) of Section 33367.

33492.92 Payments to affected taxing entities

(a) This section shall apply to a redevelopment project area that is adopted pursuant to this article and the territory of which includes the Mare Island Naval Shipyard.

(b) Notwithstanding any other provision of law, the redevelopment agency shall make payments to affected taxing entities required by subdivision (a) of Section 33607.5, except that each of the time periods governing the payments shall be calculated from the date the county auditor makes the certification to the Director of Finance pursuant to Section 33492.9 instead of from the first fiscal year in which the agency receives tax-increment revenue.

33492.93 Territory of Mare Island Redevelopment Project Area

(a) The territory of the Mare Island Redevelopment Project Area shall include all of Mare Island except for the following areas:

(1) All wetlands and dredge ponds, active or inactive.

(2) Subarea 12.

(3) The expanded golf course (Subarea 11).

(4) The recreation/open-space area (Subarea 13).

(5) The residential areas of Farragut and Coral Sea Villages (Subareas 6 and 8).

(b) As used in this section:

(1) "Subarea 6" means an area bounded on the east by Cedar Avenue and Oak Avenue; on the south by the Rifle Range (Area 7), and the Building 866 parking area; on the north by Third Street; and on the west by the wetlands.

(2) "Subarea 8" means an area bounded on the south by Club Drive; on the east by Suisun Avenue; and on the north and west by Mesa Road.

(3) "Subarea 11" means an area bounded on the west, east, and south by Regional Park; and on the north by Coral Sea Village, Young Drive, and Recreation Wall.

(4) "Subarea 12" means an area bounded on the south by Carquinez Strait; on the west by the wetlands and the dredge ponds; on the east by Mare Island Strait and Railroad Avenue; and on the north by the golf course, Young Drive, and Recreation Wall.

(5) "Subarea 13" means an area surrounded by other excluded areas (wetlands and dredge ponds).

33492.94 Exemption from CEQA

(a) Notwithstanding Section 21090 of the Public Resources Code, the redevelopment agency for the City of Vallejo or the legislative body of the City of Vallejo may determine at a noticed public hearing that the adoption of a redevelopment plan for the Mare Island Redevelopment Project Area pursuant to this article is not subject to the California Environmental Quality Act (Division 13 (commencing with Section 21000) of the Public Resources Code), except that projects implementing the redevelopment plan, including specific plans, rezonings, and ministerial projects that may have a significant effect on the environment, shall be subject to the California Environmental Quality Act. The environmental document for any implementing project shall include an analysis and mitigation of potential cumulative impacts that otherwise will not be known until an environmental impact report for the redevelopment plan is certified.

(b) The notice of the public hearing required pursuant to subdivision (a) shall include the date, time, and place of the hearing, a brief description of the proposed project and its location, the date when notice will be provided pursuant to Section 21092 of the Public Resources Code, and the address where copies of the notice of exemption are available for review.

(c) The notice required by this section shall be given to all organizations that, and individuals who, have previously requested notice pursuant to the California Environmental Quality Act, and shall be given by publication, no fewer times than required by Section 6061 of the Government Code, by the public agency in a newspaper of general circulation in the area affected by the proposed project.

(d) If the redevelopment agency for the City of Vallejo or the legislative body of the City of Vallejo determines, pursuant to subdivision (a), that the adoption of a redevelopment plan is not subject to the California Environmental Quality Act, the redevelopment agency shall prepare and certify an environmental impact report for the redevelopment plan within 18 months after the effective date of the ordinance adopting the redevelopment plan. An environmental impact report prepared and certified jointly with the preparation of the environmental impact statement by the federal lead agency pursuant to the National Environmental Policy Act of 1969 (42 U.S.C. Sec. 4321, et seq.) shall satisfy the requirement of this subdivision.

33492.95 Blighted area defined

For purposes of this article, a blighted area within the boundaries of the Mare Island Redevelopment Project Area is either of the following:

(a) An area in which the combination of two or more of the conditions set forth in subdivision (a) or (b) of Section 33492.11 are so prevalent and so substantial that it causes a reduction of, or a lack of, proper utilization of the area to an extent that constitutes a serious physical and economic burden on the community that cannot reasonably be expected to be reversed or alleviated by private enterprise or governmental action, or both, without redevelopment.

(b) An area that contains one or more of the conditions described in subdivision (b) of Section 33492.11, the effect of which are so prevalent and so substantial that it causes a reduction of, or a lack of, proper utilization of the area to an extent that constitutes a serious physical and economic burden on the community that cannot reasonably be expected to be reversed or alleviated by private enterprise or governmental action, or both, without redevelopment, and is in addition characterized by the existence of inadequate public improvements, public facilities, and utilities, that cannot be remedied by private or governmental action, without redevelopment.

Article 7
Tustin Marine Corps Air Station

33492.100 Legislative intent

With the enactment of this article, it is the intent of the Legislature to provide for precise and specific means to mitigate the very serious economic effects of the closure of the Tustin Marine Corps Air Station on the City of Tustin, surrounding cities and the County of Orange by facilitating the planning and implementation of the reuse and redevelopment of the lands comprising Tustin Marine Corps Air Station and surrounding areas in accordance with land use plans and a redevelopment plan that is in effect prior to the disposition of lands by the federal government.

33492.102 Project area for Tustin Marine Corps Air Station Redevelopment Project

Notwithstanding the requirements of Section 33320.1, a redevelopment plan for the Tustin Marine Corps Air Station Redevelopment Project may be adopted pursuant to the provisions of this article for a redevelopment project area which may include the following areas:

(a) An area comprising the Tustin Marine Corps Air Station that is generally bounded by Edinger Avenue, Redhill Avenue, Barranca Road, and Harvard Road.

(b) An area that includes land contiguous with the Tustin Marine Corps Air Station, if necessary for the effective redevelopment of the project area, provided that this area does not exceed 52 acres and meets the requirements of Section 33320.1 without taking into account any of the lands described in subdivision (a). Notwithstanding any other provision of this part, a redevelopment plan adopted pursuant to this part shall not authorize the redevelopment agency to acquire by condemnation any lands authorized to be included in a project area pursuant to this subdivision.

33492.104 Blighted area defined

For the purposes of this article, a blighted area within the boundaries of the Tustin Marine Corps Air Station Redevelopment Project is an area described in subdivision (a) of Section 33492.102 in which the combination of two or more of the following conditions are so prevalent and so substantial that it causes a reduction of, or a lack of, proper utilization of the area to an extent that constitutes a serious physical and economic burden on the community that cannot reasonably be expected to be reversed or alleviated by private enterprise or governmental action, or both, without redevelopment:

(a) Buildings in which it is unsafe or unhealthy for persons to live or work. These conditions can be caused by serious building code violations, dilapidation and deterioration, defective design or physical construction, faulty or inadequate infrastructure, or other similar factors.

(b) Factors that prevent or substantially hinder the economically viable reuse or capacity of buildings or areas. This condition may be caused by conditions including, but not necessarily limited to, all of the following: a substandard design; buildings that are too large or too small given present standards and market conditions; and age, obsolescence, deterioration, dilapidation, or other physical conditions that could prevent the highest and best uses of the property. This condition also may be caused by buildings that must be demolished or buildings or areas that have a lack of parking.

(c) Adjacent or nearby uses that are incompatible with each other and that prevent the economic development of those parcels or other portions of the project area.

(d) Buildings on land that, when subdivided or when infrastructure is installed, would not comply with community subdivision, zoning, or planning regulations.

(e) Properties currently served by infrastructure that does not meet existing adopted utility or community infrastructure standards or the existence of inadequate public improvements, public facilities, and utilities that cannot be remedied by private or governmental action, without redevelopment.

(f) Buildings that, when built, did not conform to the then-effective building, plumbing, mechanical, or electrical codes adopted by the jurisdiction in which the project area is located.

(g) Land that contains materials or facilities, including, but not necessarily limited to, materials for aircraft landing pads and runways that would have to be removed to allow development.

(h) Properties that contain hazardous wastes that may benefit from the use of agency authority as specified in Article 12.5 (commencing with Section 33459) of Chapter 4 in order to be developed by either the private or public sector or in order to comply with applicable federal or state standards.

33492.106 Deferral of housing set-aside requirement

(a) Notwithstanding Section 33334.2, or any other provision of law, the redevelopment agency for the Tustin Marine Corps Air Station Redevelopment Project, may, for up to 10 years, defer depositing into the Low- and Moderate-Income Housing Fund up to 50 percent of the amount required by Section 33334.2. The amount of the deferral shall be considered an indebtedness and shall be repaid to the Low- and Moderate-Income Housing Fund during the period from the beginning of the 11th year to the end of the 20th year after the establishment of the Tustin Marine Corps Air Station Redevelopment Project area. If the indebtedness is not eliminated by the end of the 20th year, the county auditor or controller shall withhold an amount equal to the indebtedness and deposit those funds into a separate Low- and Moderate-Income Housing Fund for use by the redevelopment agency.

(b) This section shall not apply to the requirement that tax increment revenues attributable to the property that is located outside the military base be allocated to the Low- and Moderate-Income Housing Fund.

33492.108 Payments to affected taxing entities

Notwithstanding any other provision of law, the redevelopment agency shall make payments to affected taxing entities required by subdivision (a) of Section 33607.5, except that each of the time periods governing the payments shall be calculated from the date the county auditor makes the certification to the Director of Finance pursuant to Section 33492.9 instead of from the first fiscal year in which the agency receives tax increment revenue.

33492.110 Limited exemption from CEQA

(a) Notwithstanding subdivision (k) of Section 33352, the California Environmental Quality Act (Division 13 (commencing with Section 21000) of the Public Resources Code) shall not apply to the adoption of a redevelopment plan prepared pursuant to this article if the redevelopment agency determines at a public hearing, noticed in accord with this section, that the need to adopt a redevelopment plan at the soonest possible time in order to use the authority in this article requires the redevelopment agency to delay application of the provisions of the California Environmental Quality Act to the redevelopment plan in accordance with this section.

(b) If the redevelopment agency finds, pursuant to subdivision (a), that the application of the California Environmental Quality Act to the redevelopment plan is required to be delayed, the redevelopment agency or the community shall certify an environmental impact report for the redevelopment plan within 18 months after the effective date of the ordinance adopting the redevelopment plan. If, as a result of the preparation of the environmental document prepared pursuant to this subdivision, it is necessary to amend the redevelopment plan to mitigate any impacts, the agency shall amend the redevelopment plan according to the procedures of this part. If the environmental document is determined to be inadequate, the redevelopment agency shall not continue with projects that implement the redevelopment plan until an adequate environmental document has been certified; however, this determination shall not affect the validity of the redevelopment plan.

(c) Until the redevelopment agency or the community certifies an environmental impact report for the redevelopment plan, all projects, as defined in the California Environmental Quality Act, that implement the redevelopment plan shall be subject to the California Environmental Quality Act, including, but not limited to, specific plans and rezonings. The environmental document for any implementing project shall include an analysis and mitigation of potential cumulative impacts, if any, that otherwise would not be known until an environmental document for the redevelopment plan is certified or approved and shall also include a reporting or monitoring program required pursuant to Section 21081 of the Public Resources Code.

(d) The notice for the public hearing required by subdivision (a) shall comply with, and may be combined with, the notices in Section 33349 or 33361. The notice shall state that the agency intends to consider and act upon a determination that the need to adopt a redevelopment plan at the soonest possible time in order to use the authority in this article requires the redevelopment agency to delay application of the provisions of the California Environmental Quality Act to the redevelopment plan in accordance with this section.

33492.112 Consistency with general plan

The ordinance adopting the redevelopment plan for the Tustin Marine Corps Air Station Project Area shall not be required to include the finding required pursuant to paragraph (4) of subdivision (d) of Section 33367. However, the redevelopment agency shall not expend any tax increment funds allocated to it from the project area for expenses related to carrying out the project unless and until the City of Tustin finds that the redevelopment plan conforms to the general plan of the city, including the housing element.

33492.114 Land use or other approvals; conditions

If the City of Tustin, the Tustin Community Redevelopment Agency, or any agency or political subdivision of either, intends to or does acquire title to any real property that lies within the boundaries of the former Marine Corps Air Station-Tustin, then notwithstanding any other provision of law, including Section 33607.5, neither the City of Tustin, nor the Tustin Community Redevelopment Agency, and none of their respective agencies and political subdivisions may grant or issue any land use or other approvals, in the form of any general plan amendments, specific plans, zoning ordinances, redevelopment plans, development agreements, subdivision maps, or other development permits or entitlements, to allow any persons or entities to develop any commercial, residential, or other land uses on all or any portion of any real property at the Marine Corps Air Station-Tustin that the City of Tustin, the Tustin Community Redevelopment Agency, or any agency or political subdivision of either, intends to or does acquire from any source, unless those approvals require, as conditions of approval and mitigation measures for allowing the development of those land uses, the conveyance, or the irrevocable offer to dedicate, without charge, to the Santa Ana Unified School District and the Rancho Santiago Community College District, for purposes of constructing and operating a K-14 facility, (a) fee title to a 100-acre parcel of contiguous land situated within that portion of the Marine Corps Air Station-Tustin that falls within the existing boundaries of the Santa Ana Unified School District and the Rancho Santiago Community College District and includes all or some of the real property referred to as Parcels 4, 5, 6, 7, 8, and 14 as shown on Figure 2-3 of the approved Reuse Plan for the

Marine Corps Air Station-Tustin, or (b) fee title to a portion of the Marine Corps Air Station-Tustin that consists of a portion of land that is approved in writing by the Santa Ana Unified School District and the Rancho Santiago Community College District and that does not include any property designated in the Marine Corps Air Station-Tustin Base Reuse Plan for any other public entity or nonprofit organization, including, without limitation, the County of Orange, the Orange County Sheriff-Coroner, and the Orange County Rescue Mission, but excluding the South Orange County Community College District. Those conditions of approval and mitigation measures shall require that the conveyance or offer to dedicate that 100-acre parcel to those districts shall be made within 12 months of the date on which the City of Tustin, the Tustin Community Redevelopment Agency, or any agency or political subdivision of either, first acquires that property from any source. The requirements of this section shall be deemed satisfied upon the conveyance of the property, described in (a) or (b), to the Santa Ana Unified School District and the Rancho Santiago Community College District. Prior to conveyance of this property, the Santa Ana Unified School District and the Rancho Santiago Community College District shall agree upon a legal description of the property. Notwithstanding any other provision of law, for purposes of Article 7 (commencing with Section 1240.610) of Chapter 3 of Title 7 of Part 3 of the Code of Civil Procedure, use of land for classroom facilities, including, but not limited to, educational and training programs, by the Santa Ana Unified School District or the Rancho Santiago Community College District shall be irrebuttably presumed to be a more necessary public use than any other use at the Marine Corps Air Station-Tustin. This section shall apply retroactively to all land use or other approvals relating to the Marine Corps Air Station-Tustin that are granted or issued by the City of Tustin, the Tustin Community Redevelopment Agency, or any agency or political subdivision of either, on or after January 1, 2001. Any such land use or other approvals granted or issued by any of these entities that do not comply with this section shall be invalid and of no force or effect.

33492.116 Historic preservation program

(a) For purposes of the application of Section 106 of the National Historic Preservation Act (16 U.S.C. Sec. 470 et seq.) as it applies only to an area comprising the survey area created for redevelopment of the Tustin Marine Corps Air Station pursuant to Section 33310, if the City of Tustin's historic preservation program is certified pursuant to Section 101(c)(1) of that act (16 U.S.C. Sec. 470a(c)(1)), the City of Tustin may elect to assume any of the duties that are given to the state historic preservation officer by Part 800 of Title 36 of the Code of Federal Regulations or that originate from agreements concluded under those regulations. The state historic preservation officer shall agree to this assumption of duties by the City of Tustin.

(b) In assuming the duties of the state historic preservation officer pursuant to this section, the city shall ensure that a marketing and solicitation process is conducted to determine the feasibility of permanent reuse of Buildings 29 and 29A. The city shall be responsible for determining in good faith if there are qualified respondents to the marketing and solicitation process and determining if the permanent use of these properties in their historic condition is feasible. If it is determined that permanent use of these historic properties is not feasible, the city shall require mitigation for the adverse effect on these historic properties prior to approving any undertaking.

Article 8
The Alameda Naval Air Station and the Fleet Industrial Supply Center

33492.125 Legislative intent

With the enactment of this article, it is the intent of the Legislature to provide for precise and specific means to mitigate the very serious economic effects of the closure of the Alameda Naval Air Station and the Fleet Industrial Supply Center on the City of Alameda, surrounding cities, and the County of Alameda by facilitating the planning and implementation of the reuse and redevelopment of the lands comprising the Naval Air Station and the Fleet Industrial Supply Center located in the City of Alameda and the surrounding areas in accordance with land use plans and a redevelopment plan that are in effect prior to the disposition of lands by the federal government.

33492.127 Project area boundaries

(a) A redevelopment plan covering all or part of the lands of the Alameda Naval Air Station and the Fleet Industrial Supply Center Redevelopment Project may be adopted pursuant to Article 1 (commencing with Section 33492), provided that the project area shall not include territory outside the boundaries of the Alameda Naval Air Station and the Fleet Industrial Supply Center.

(b) Notwithstanding the time limit in subdivision (b) of Section 33492.18, the agency or the community shall certify an environmental impact report for the redevelopment plan adopted pursuant to this section within 30 months after the effective date of the ordinance adopting the redevelopment plan.

(c) The following provisions shall apply to the approval of projects that implement a redevelopment plan authorized by this article:

(1) For 18 months after the effective date of the ordinance adopting the redevelopment plan, or until the certification of an environmental impact report for the redevelopment plan if the report is certified during that 18-month period, subdivision (c) of Section 33492.18 shall apply.

(2) If an environmental impact report for the redevelopment plan is not certified within 18 months after the effective date of the ordinance adopting the plan, then during the succeeding 12 months or until the certification of an environmental impact report if the report is certified during that 12-month period, no project, as defined in Section 21065 of the Public Resources Code, that implements the redevelopment plan shall be approved by the agency or the community unless any of the following occurs:

(A) The agency or the community has approved a negative declaration or certified an environmental impact report, or has certified a subsequent or supplemental environmental impact report, for the project before the expiration of the 18-month period provided in Section 33492.18.

(B) The agency or the community has certified a subsequent or supplemental environmental impact report for the project where the environmental impact report for the project was certified before the expiration of the 18-month period provided in Section 33492.18.

(C) The agency or the community complies with Chapter 4.5 (commencing with Section 21156) of Division 13 of the Public Resources Code for subsequent projects described in a master environmental impact report as being within the scope of the report, and that master environmental impact report was certified before the expiration of the 18-month period provided in Section 33492.18.

(D) The project is categorically exempt pursuant to Article 19 (commencing with Section 15300) of Chapter 3 of Division 6 of Title 14 of the California Code of Regulations.

33492.129 Payments to affected taxing entities

Notwithstanding Section 33492.9 or any other provision of law, the redevelopment agency shall make payments to affected taxing entities required by Section 33607.5.

33492.131 Substantially rehabilitated dwelling units

(a) Dwelling units, as defined, in the Alameda Naval Air Station and the Fleet Industrial Supply Center Project Area made available to a member of the Homeless Collaborative pursuant to the Base Closure Community Redevelopment and Homeless Assistance Act of 1994 (Part A of Title XXIX of Public Law 101-510; 10 U.S.C. Sec. 2687 note), and in particular Section (7) (C) through (O) thereof, and thereafter substantially rehabilitated, shall be deemed substantially rehabilitated units for purposes of determining the compliance of the Alameda Naval Air Station and the Fleet Industrial Supply Center redevelopment agency with the provisions of subdivision (b) of Section 33413.

(b) For the purposes of this section, "dwelling units" means permanent or transitional residential units, and does not mean student dormitory rooms or overnight emergency shelter beds.

(c) For the purposes of this section, "substantially rehabilitated" means rehabilitation, the value of which constitutes 25 percent of the after rehabilitation value of the dwelling, inclusive of land value.

Article 9
Hamilton Army Airfield

33492.140 Payments to specified taxing agencies

Notwithstanding paragraph (1) of subdivision (f) of Section 33607.5, the redevelopment agency of the City of Novato may pay to the County of Marin, the Novato Fire Protection District, and the Marin Community College District any amounts of money that in the agency's determination are appropriate to alleviate any financial burden or detriment caused to the County of Marin, the Novato Fire Protection District, or the Marin Community College District by the Hamilton Field Redevelopment Project.

Chapter 4.6. CALIFORNIA STATE UNIVERSITY, CHANNEL ISLANDS SITE AUTHORITY

33498 Legislative intent

(a) For purposes of this chapter, the terms "authority" and "site" have the meaning given in Section 67472 of the Government Code.

(b) With enactment of this chapter, it is the intent of the Legislature to do both of the following:

(1) Provide a means of mitigating the harmful effects and potentially blighted conditions caused by the closure of the former Camarillo State Hospital.

(2) Enhance the economic, cultural, and social development of the region by facilitating the development of a state university campus and other compatible uses on the site.

(c) The Legislature finds that the closure and conversion of major state facilities can require use of the powers provided under this part and under Section 16 of Article XVI of the California Constitution, and that the closure of the Camarillo State Hospital and the development of a California State University campus on the site as well as the development of compatible uses on the site requires development of a reuse plan by the California State University, Channel Islands Site Authority.

33498.1 Reuse plan

(a) The reuse plan adopted by the authority shall provide for use of the site and allocation of tax revenues to the authority for reuse and development on the site with priority to development of California State University facilities on the site as set forth in Title 7.75 (commencing with Section 67470) of the Government Code. Except as provided in that title and this chapter, the authority shall be exempt from all other requirements of this part.

(b) The reuse plan shall include an implementation plan adopted and periodically revised pursuant to Section 33490.

(c) The authority shall comply with Article 6 (commencing with Section 33030) of Chapter 1.

33498.2 Housing

(a) The Legislature finds and declares that the provision of housing is itself a fundamental purpose of this part and of the authority. There is a generally inadequate supply of decent, safe, and sanitary housing on the site available to the faculty and staff of the California State University, Channel Islands, and to persons and families of low or moderate income, as defined by Section 50093. The inadequate supply of this housing threatens the accomplishment of the primary purposes of this part and of the authority. Therefore, the Legislature finds and declares that the provision of housing pursuant to this section and the use of taxes allocated to the authority pursuant to subdivision (b) of Section 33670 is of statewide benefit and of particular benefit and assistance to the redevelopment of the former Camarillo State Hospital as the site of a California State University campus.

(b) Not less than 20 percent of all taxes that are allocated to the authority pursuant to Section 33670 shall be deposited into a separate Low and Moderate Income Housing Fund, which is hereby created in the State Treasury, to be administered and used by the authority for the purposes of increasing, improving, and preserving both of the following:

(1) Housing on the site for the faculty and staff of the California State University, Channel Islands.

(2) Low- and moderate-income housing on the site available at affordable housing cost, as defined by Section 50052.5, to persons and families of low or moderate income, as defined in Section 50093, and very low income households, as defined in Section 50105.

(c) Any interest earned by the Low and Moderate Income Housing Fund and any repayments or other income to the authority for loans, advances, or grants, of any kind from the fund, shall accrue to and be deposited in the fund and may be used only in the manner prescribed for the fund.

(d) In carrying out the purposes of this section, the authority may, solely within the boundaries of the site, exercise any or all of the following powers:

(1) Acquire real property or building sites pursuant to Section 33334.16.

(2) Improve real property or building sites for the housing listed in subdivision (b) with onsite or offsite improvements, but only if the authority finds either of the following:

(A) The improvements are made as part of a program that results in the new construction or rehabilitation of housing.

(B) The improvements are necessary to eliminate one or more specific conditions that jeopardize the health or safety of residents.

(3) Donate real property to private or public persons or entities.

(4) Finance insurance premiums pursuant to Section 33136.

(5) Construct residential buildings or related structures.

(6) Acquire buildings or structures for residential and related uses.

(7) Rehabilitate buildings or structures for residential and related uses.

(8) Provide subsidies to, or for the benefit of, very low income persons or households, as defined by Section 50105, lower income persons or households, as defined by Section 50079.5, or persons and families of low or moderate income, as defined by Section 50093, to the extent that those persons or households cannot obtain housing at affordable costs on the open market in the vicinity of the site. These subsidies or benefits may include rental subsidies to low-income students at California State University, Channel Islands, who live in housing, including dormitories, on the site. Housing units available on the open market are those units developed without direct government subsidies.

(9) Develop plans, pay principal and interest on bonds, loans, advances, or other indebtedness, or pay financing or carrying charges.

(10) Maintain the supply of mobilehomes on the site.

(11) Preserve the availability to lower income households of affordable housing units that are assisted or subsidized by public entities and which are threatened with imminent conversion to market rates.

(12) Pay for planning and general administration costs pursuant to subdivision (e).

(e) The Legislature intends that the authority use the Low and Moderate Income Housing Fund to the maximum extent possible to defray the costs of production, improvement, and preservation of housing solely within the site, and that the amount of money spent for planning and general administrative activities associated with the development, improvement, and preservation of that housing not be disproportionate to the amount actually spent for the costs of production, improvement, and preservation of that housing. The authority shall annually determine that the planning and administrative expenses are necessary for the production, improvement, or preservation of housing on the site. Legal, architectural, and engineering costs and other salaries, wages, and costs directly related to the planning and execution of a specific housing project and which are incurred by a nonprofit housing sponsor are not "planning and administrative costs" for the purposes of this subdivision, but are instead project costs. Planning and general administrative costs which may be paid with moneys from the Low and Moderate Income Housing Fund are those expenses that the authority incurs that are directly related to the powers listed in subdivision (d), and are limited to the following:

(1) Costs incurred for salaries, wages, and related costs of the authority's staff or for services provided through interagency agreements, and agreements with contractors, including usual related indirect costs.

(2) Costs incurred by a nonprofit corporation that are not directly attributable to a specific housing project.

(f) Housing that is produced, improved, or preserved with moneys from the Low and Moderate Income Housing Fund shall remain available for the longest period of time, as follows:

(1) The authority shall require that housing that is produced, improved, or preserved for the faculty and staff of the California State University, Channel Islands, be subject to covenants or restrictions filed in the office of the county recorder perpetually limiting the residency to those persons.

(2) The authority shall require that housing that is produced, improved, or preserved for persons and households of low or moderate income and persons and households of very low income be subject to covenants or restrictions filed in the office of the county recorder limiting the residency to those persons as follows:

(A) For owner-occupied housing units, for a period of 10 years. However, the authority may permit sales of owner-occupied units prior to the expiration of the 10-year period for a price in excess of that otherwise permitted under this subdivision pursuant to an adopted program that protects the authority's investment of moneys from the Low and Moderate Income Housing Fund, including, but not limited to, an equity sharing program that establishes a schedule of equity sharing that permits retention by the seller of a portion of those excess proceeds based on the length of occupancy. The remainder of the excess proceeds of the sale shall be allocated to the authority and deposited in the Low and Moderate Income Housing Fund.

(B) For rental units, for a period of 15 years.

(g) The authority shall spend or encumber all property tax revenues deposited into the Low and Moderate Income Housing Fund within five years from the end of the fiscal year in which the funds were deposited into the fund. If the authority fails to spend or encumber those revenues in a timely manner, and thereafter until the authority has expended or encumbered those revenues, the agency shall not receive any property tax revenue from any source except as necessary to pay the following obligations, if any:

(1) Bonds, notes, interim certificates, debentures, or other obligations issued by the authority whether funded, refunded, assumed, or otherwise, pursuant to Article 5 (commencing with Section 33640) of Chapter 6.

(2) Loans or moneys advanced to the authority, including, but not limited to, loans from federal, state, or local agencies, or a private entity.

(3) Contractual obligations which, if breached, could subject the authority to damages or other liabilities or remedies.

(4) Obligations incurred pursuant to Section 33445.

(5) Indebtedness incurred pursuant to Section 33334.2 or 33334.6.

(6) Obligations incurred pursuant to Section 33401.

Chapter 5. LEGAL ACTIONS

Article 1
Actions Involving Redevelopment Plans or Bonds

33500   **Limitation on actions**

(a) Notwithstanding any other provision of law, including Section 33501, an action may be brought to review the validity of the adoption or amendment of a redevelopment plan at any time within 90 days after the date of the adoption of the ordinance adopting or amending the plan.

(b) Notwithstanding any other provision of law, including Section 33501, an action may be brought to review the validity of any findings or determinations by the agency or the legislative body at any time within 90 days after the date on which the agency or the legislative body made those findings or determinations.

33501 Validation actions

(a) An action may be brought pursuant to Chapter 9 (commencing with Section 860) of Title 10 of Part 2 of the Code of Civil Procedure to determine the validity of bonds and the redevelopment plan to be financed or refinanced, in whole or in part, by the bonds, or to determine the validity of a redevelopment plan not financed by bonds, including without limiting the generality of the foregoing, the legality and validity of all proceedings theretofore taken for or in any way connected with the establishment of the agency, its authority to transact business and exercise its powers, the designation of the survey area, the selection of the project area, the formulation of the preliminary plan, the validity of the finding and determination that the project area is predominantly urbanized, and the validity of the adoption of the redevelopment plan, and also including the legality and validity of all proceedings theretofore taken and (as provided in the bond resolution) proposed to be taken for the authorization, issuance, sale and delivery of the bonds and for the payment of the principal thereof and interest thereon.

(b) Notwithstanding subdivision (a), an action to determine the validity of a redevelopment plan, or amendment to a redevelopment plan, may be brought within 90 days after the date of the adoption of the ordinance adopting or amending the plan.

(c) For the purposes of protecting the interests of the state, the Attorney General and the Department of Finance are interested persons pursuant to Section 863 of the Code of Civil Procedure in any action brought with respect to the validity of an ordinance adopting or amending a redevelopment plan pursuant to this section.

(d) For purposes of contesting the inclusion in a project area of lands that are enforceably restricted, as that term is defined in Sections 422 and 422.5 of the Revenue and Taxation Code, or lands that are in agricultural use, as defined in subdivision (b) of Section 51201 of the Government Code, the Department of Conservation, the county agricultural commissioner, the county farm bureau, the California Farm Bureau Federation, and agricultural entities and general farm organizations that provide a written request for notice, are interested persons pursuant to Section 863 of the Code of Civil Procedure, in any action brought with respect to the validity of an ordinance adopting a redevelopment plan pursuant to this section.

33501.1 Intervention by Attorney General

Notwithstanding Chapter 9 (commencing with Section 860) of Title 10 of the Code of Civil Procedure, the Attorney General may, pursuant to subdivision (b) of Section 387 of the Code of Civil Procedure, intervene as of right in an action specified in Section 33501 challenging the validity of any finding and determination that a project area is blighted. The Attorney General may seek permissive intervention pursuant to subdivision (a) of Section 387 of the Code of Civil Procedure in any other action brought pursuant to Section 33501.

33501.2 Required objections prior to close of public hearing before bringing action

(a) An action shall not be brought pursuant to Section 33501 unless the alleged grounds for noncompliance with this division were presented to the agency or the legislative body orally or in writing by any person before the close of the public hearing required by this division.

(b) A person shall not bring an action pursuant to Section 33501 unless a person objected to the decision of the agency or the legislative body before the close of the public hearing required by this division.

(c) This section does not preclude any organization formed after the approval of a project from bringing an action pursuant to Section 33501 if a member of that organization has complied with subdivision (b).

(d) This section does not apply to the Attorney General.

(e) This section does not apply to any alleged grounds for noncompliance with this division for which there was no public hearing or other opportunity for members of the public to raise those objections orally or in writing before the decision by the agency or the legislative body, or if the agency or the legislative body failed to give the notice required by law.

33501.3 Service on Attorney General

If an action specified in Section 33501 challenging the validity of any finding and determination that the project area is blighted is filed in any court, each party filing any pleading or brief with the court in that proceeding shall serve, within three days of the filing with the court, a copy of that pleading or brief on the Attorney General. Relief, temporary or permanent, shall not be granted to a party unless that party files proof with the court showing that it has complied with this section. A court may, by court order, allow a party to serve the Attorney General after the three-day period, but only upon showing of good cause for not complying with the three-day notice requirement, and that late service will not prejudice the Attorney General's ability to review, and possibly participate in, the action.

33501.5 Service on Director of Housing and Community Development

In any judicial action specified in Section 33501 in which the validity of actions of the agency under Section 33334.2, 33334.3, or 33334.6 are in issue, the party initiating the judicial action or otherwise challenging the validity of those actions of the agency shall serve a copy of the complaint or answer alleging that invalidity upon the Director of Housing and Community Development within 10 days after filing that complaint or answer with the court. The court may render no judgment in the matter or provide other permanent or provisional relief to any party until proof of service of the Director of Housing and Community Development pursuant to this section has been submitted to the court. Nothing in this section shall be deemed to expand the scope of Section 33501.

33501.7 Agency precluded from requiring indemnification of agency as a condition of adopting or amending a redevelopment plan

Notwithstanding any other provision of law, an agency or legislative body shall not permit or require a property owner or a real party in interest to indemnify the agency or the legislative body against actions brought pursuant to Section 33501 to challenge the adoption or amendment of a redevelopment plan, as a condition of adopting or amending a redevelopment plan.

33502 Judgment

The judgment shall determine the validity or invalidity, respectively, of the matters specified in Section 33501. The judgment shall be subject to being reopened under Section 473 or Section 473.5 of the Code of Civil Procedure or otherwise only within 90 days after the entry of the judgment and petitioner and any person who has appeared in the special proceeding shall have the right to move for a new trial under proper circumstances and upon appropriate grounds and to appeal from the judgment.

33503 Effect of judgment

The judgment, if no appeal is taken, or if taken and the judgment is affirmed shall be forever binding and conclusive, as to all matters therein adjudicated or which at that time could have been adjudicated, against the agency and against all other parties and if the judgment determines that the agency is lawfully established, that the redevelopment plan is valid and effective, that the agency is authorized to issue such bonds and that such bonds when issued will be valid, the judgment shall permanently enjoin the institution by any person of any action or proceeding raising any issue as to which the judgment is binding and conclusive.

33504 Other actions by obligees

Other actions by obligees are authorized by Sections 33660 and 33661.

Article 2
Actions for Money or Damages

33510 Actions against agency for money or damages

All claims for money or damages against the agency are governed by Part 3 (commencing with Section 900) and Part 4 (commencing with Section 940) of Division 3.6 of Title 1 of the Government Code except as provided therein, or by other statutes or regulations expressly applicable thereto.

Article 3
Actions Involving Public Agencies

33515 Actions against certain public agencies prohibited

(a) A redevelopment agency shall not, either directly or indirectly, use its funds to file or maintain an action or proceeding in either of the following circumstances:

(1) Against a public agency that does not have jurisdiction to conduct its governmental activities within the jurisdiction of the redevelopment agency.

(2) The subject matter of the action involves real property outside the jurisdictional boundaries of the redevelopment agency.

(b) The prohibition in subdivision (a) shall not preclude a redevelopment agency from using its funds to:

(1) Defend itself against any action.

(2) File or maintain an action against a public agency or private entity regarding the interpretation or enforcement of a written agreement between the redevelopment agency and that public agency or private entity.

(c) No funds of a redevelopment agency shall be loaned or granted to any person, corporation, or public agency to finance, in whole or in part, an action the financing of which by a redevelopment agency is prohibited by subdivision (a). In addition, a redevelopment agency shall not borrow funds from its community or any other source to file or maintain an action which is prohibited by subdivision (a).

(d) Nothing in this section shall prohibit a community from filing or maintaining an action on behalf of the community and its redevelopment agency as long as funds of the redevelopment agency are not used, either directly or indirectly, on behalf of the lawsuit.

(e) For purposes of this article:

(1) "Finance" includes, but is not necessarily limited to, the payment of filing fees, attorneys' fees, service fees, expert witness fees, consultants' fees, or any other expenses or costs incurred in connection with an action.

(2) "Public agency" includes a local agency as defined in Section 54951 of the Government Code and includes a joint powers agency or authority and a redevelopment agency.

Chapter 6. FINANCIAL PROVISIONS

Article 1
General

33600 Authority of agency

An agency may accept financial or other assistance from any public or private source, for the agency's activities, powers, and duties, and expend any funds so received for any of the purposes of this part.

33601 Financial assistance; loans

An agency may borrow money or accept financial or other assistance from the state or the federal government or any other public agency for any redevelopment project within its area of operation, and may comply with any conditions of such loan or grant.

An agency may borrow money (by the issuance of bonds or otherwise) or accept financial or other assistance from any private lending institution for any redevelopment project for any of the purposes of this part, and may execute trust deeds or mortgages on any real or personal property owned or acquired.

33602 Bonds

"Bonds" means any bonds, notes, interim certificates, debentures, or other obligations issued by an agency pursuant to Article 5 (commencing with Section 33640) of this chapter.

33603 Authorized investments

An agency may invest any money held in reserves or sinking funds, or any money not required for immediate disbursement, in property or securities in which savings banks may legally invest money subject to their control.

33604 Surplus funds

If an agency ceases to function, any surplus funds existing after payment of all its obligations and indebtedness shall vest in the community.

33605 Delegation of power for preliminary loan notes

In connection with the issuance and sale of preliminary loan notes, secured by a requisition agreement with the United States of America, the agency may delegate to one or more of its agents or employees the powers or duties it deems proper.

33606 Annual budget

An agency shall adopt an annual budget containing all of the following specific information, including all activities to be financed by the Low and Moderate Income Housing Fund established pursuant to Section 33334.3:

(a) The proposed expenditures of the agency.

(b) The proposed indebtedness to be incurred by the agency.

(c) The anticipated revenues of the agency.

(d) The work program for the coming year, including goals.

(e) An examination of the previous year's achievements and a comparison of the achievements with the goals of the previous year's work program.

The annual budget may be amended from time to time as determined by the agency. All expenditures and indebtedness of the agency shall be in conformity with the adopted or amended budget.

When the legislative body is not the redevelopment agency, the legislative body shall approve the annual budget and amendments of the annual budget of the agency.

33607 Reimbursement of county expenses

A county may require a community redevelopment agency to reimburse the county for any expenses incurred by the county in performing any of the services required to be performed by the county for the redevelopment agency pursuant to Sections 33670, 33675, and 33676 for a project area as to which no payments are made by the agency to the county in accordance with subdivision (b) of Section 33401 and no agreement has been entered into and either of the following situations exist:

(a) A final redevelopment plan for the project area is adopted on or after January 1, 1986.

(b) A final redevelopment plan for the project area was adopted prior to January 1, 1986, but its boundaries are changed on or after January 1, 1986, to add land to, or to exclude land from, the project area. However, in the case of a project area which changes its boundaries on or after January 1, 1986, to add land to the project area, the reimbursement shall relate only to expenses incurred by the county with respect to the added area.

33607.5 Payments to affected taxing entities

(a) (1) This section shall apply to each redevelopment project area that, pursuant to a redevelopment plan which contains the provisions required by Section 33670, is either: (A) adopted on or after January 1, 1994, including later amendments to these redevelopment plans; or (B) adopted prior to January 1, 1994, but amended, after January 1, 1994, to include new territory. For plans amended after January 1, 1994, only the tax increments from territory added by the amendment shall be subject to this section. All the amounts calculated pursuant to this section shall be calculated after the amount required to be deposited in the Low and Moderate Income Housing Fund pursuant to Sections 33334.2, 33334.3, and 33334.6 has been deducted from the total amount of tax increment funds received by the agency in the applicable fiscal year.

(2) The payments made pursuant to this section shall be in addition to any amounts the affected taxing entities receive pursuant to subdivision (a) of Section 33670. The payments made pursuant to this section to the affected taxing entities, including the community, shall be allocated among the affected taxing entities, including the community if the community elects to receive payments, in proportion to the percentage share of property taxes each affected taxing entity, including the community, receives during the fiscal year the funds are allocated, which percentage share shall be determined without regard to any amounts allocated to a city, a city and county, or a county pursuant to Sections 97.68 and 97.70 of the Revenue and Taxation Code, and without regard to any allocation reductions to a city, a city and county, a county, a special district, or a redevelopment agency pursuant to Sections 97.71, 97.72, and 97.73 of the Revenue and Taxation Code and Section 33681.12. The agency shall reduce its payments pursuant to this section to an affected taxing entity by any amount the agency has paid, directly or indirectly, pursuant to Section 33445, 33445.5, 33445.6, 33446, or any other provision of law other than this section for, or in connection with, a public facility owned or leased by that affected taxing agency, except: (A) any amounts the agency has paid directly or indirectly pursuant to an agreement with a taxing entity adopted prior to January 1, 1994; or (B) any amounts that are unrelated to the specific project area or amendment governed by this section. The reduction in a payment by an agency to a school district, community college district, or county office of education, or for special education, shall be subtracted only from the amount that otherwise would be available for use by those entities for educational facilities pursuant to paragraph (4). If the amount of the reduction exceeds the amount that otherwise would have been available for use for educational facilities in any one year, the agency shall reduce its payment in more than one year.

(3) If an agency reduces its payment to a school district, community college district, county office of education, or for special education, the agency shall do all of the following:

(A) Determine the amount of the total payment that would have been made without the reduction.

(B) Determine the amount of the total payment without the reduction which: (i) would have been considered property taxes; and (ii) would have been available to be used for educational facilities pursuant to paragraph (4).

(C) Reduce the amount available to be used for educational facilities.

(D) Send the payment to the school district, community college district, or county office of education, or for special education, with a statement that the payment is being reduced and including the calculation required by this subdivision showing the amount to be considered property taxes and the amount, if any, available for educational facilities.

(4) (A) Except as specified in subparagraph (E), of the total amount paid each year pursuant to this section to school districts, 43.3 percent shall be considered to be property taxes for the purposes of paragraph (1) of subdivision (h) of Section 42238 of the Education Code, and 56.7 percent shall not be considered to be property taxes for the purposes of that section and shall be available to be used for educational facilities.

(B) Except as specified in subparagraph (E), of the total amount paid each year pursuant to this section to community college districts, 47.5 percent shall be considered to be property taxes for the purposes of Section 84751 of the Education Code, and 52.5 percent shall not be considered to be property taxes for the purposes of that section and shall be available to be used for educational facilities.

(C) Except as specified in subparagraph (E), of the total amount paid each year pursuant to this section to county offices of education, 19 percent shall be considered to be property taxes for the purposes of Section 2558 of the Education Code, and 81 percent shall not be considered to be property taxes for the purposes of that section and shall be available to be used for educational facilities.

(D) Except as specified in subparagraph (E), of the total amount paid each year pursuant to this section for special education, 19 percent shall be considered to be property taxes for the purposes of Section 56712 of the Education Code, and 81 percent shall not be considered to be property taxes for the purposes of that section and shall be available to be used for education facilities.

(E) If, pursuant to paragraphs (2) and (3), an agency reduces its payments to an educational entity, the calculation made by the agency pursuant to paragraph (3) shall determine the amount considered to be property taxes and the amount available to be used for educational facilities in the year the reduction was made.

(5) Local education agencies that use funds received pursuant to this section for school facilities shall spend these funds at schools that are: (A) within the project area, (B) attended by students from the project area, (C) attended by students generated by projects that are assisted directly by the redevelopment agency, or (D) determined by the governing board of a local education agency to be of benefit to the project area.

(b) Commencing with the first fiscal year in which the agency receives tax increments and continuing through the last fiscal year in which the agency receives tax increments, a redevelopment agency shall pay to the affected taxing entities, including the community if the community elects to receive a payment, an amount equal to 25 percent of the tax increments received by the agency after the amount required to be deposited in the Low and Moderate Income Housing Fund has been deducted. In any fiscal year in which the agency receives tax increments, the community that has adopted the redevelopment project area may elect to receive the amount authorized by this paragraph.

(c) Commencing with the 11th fiscal year in which the agency receives tax increments and continuing through the last fiscal year in which the agency receives tax increments, a redevelopment agency shall pay to the affected taxing entities, other than the community which has adopted the project, in addition to the amounts paid pursuant to subdivision (b) and after deducting the amount allocated to the Low and Moderate Income Housing Fund, an amount equal to 21 percent of the portion of tax increments received by the agency, which shall be calculated by applying the tax rate against the amount of assessed value by which the current year assessed value exceeds the first adjusted base year assessed value. The first adjusted base year assessed value is the assessed value of the project area in the 10th fiscal year in which the agency receives tax increment revenues.

(d) Commencing with the 31st fiscal year in which the agency receives tax increments and continuing through the last fiscal year in which the agency receives tax increments, a redevelopment agency shall pay to the affected taxing entities, other than the community which has adopted the project, in addition to the amounts paid pursuant to subdivisions (b) and (c) and after deducting the amount allocated to the Low and Moderate Income Housing Fund, an amount equal to 14 percent of the portion of tax increments received by the agency, which shall be calculated by applying the tax rate against the amount of assessed value by which the current year assessed value exceeds the second adjusted base year assessed value. The second adjusted base year assessed value is the assessed value of the project area in the 30th fiscal year in which the agency receives tax increments.

(e) (1) Prior to incurring any loans, bonds, or other indebtedness, except loans or advances from the community, the agency may subordinate to the loans, bonds or other indebtedness the amount required to be paid to an affected taxing entity by this section, provided that the affected taxing entity has approved these subordinations pursuant to this subdivision.

(2) At the time the agency requests an affected taxing entity to subordinate the amount to be paid to it, the agency shall provide the affected taxing entity with substantial evidence that sufficient funds will be available to pay both the debt service and the payments required by this section, when due.

(3) Within 45 days after receipt of the agency's request, the affected taxing entity shall approve or disapprove the request for subordination. An affected taxing entity may disapprove a request for subordination only if it finds, based upon substantial evidence, that the agency will not be able to pay the debt payments and the amount required to be paid to the affected taxing entity. If the affected taxing entity does not act within 45 days after receipt of the agency's request, the request to subordinate shall be deemed approved and shall be final and conclusive.

(f) (1) The Legislature finds and declares both of the following:

(A) The payments made pursuant to this section are necessary in order to alleviate the financial burden and detriment that affected taxing entities may incur as a result of the adoption of a redevelopment plan, and payments made pursuant to this section will benefit redevelopment project areas.

(B) The payments made pursuant to this section are the exclusive payments that are required to be made by a redevelopment agency to affected taxing entities during the term of a redevelopment plan.

(2) Notwithstanding any other provision of law, a redevelopment agency shall not be required, either directly or indirectly, as a measure to mitigate a significant environmental effect or as part of any settlement agreement or judgment brought in any action to contest the validity of a redevelopment plan pursuant to Section 33501, to make any other payments to affected taxing entities, or to pay for public facilities that will be owned or leased to an affected taxing entity.

(g) As used in this section, a "local education agency" is a school district, a community college district, or a county office of education.

33607.7 Payments to certain affected taxing entities upon amendment of plan

(a) This section shall apply to a redevelopment plan amendment for any redevelopment plans adopted prior to January 1, 1994, that increases the limitation on the number of dollars to be allocated to the redevelopment agency or that increases or eliminates pursuant to paragraph (1) of subdivision (e) of Section 33333.6, the time limit on the establishing of loans, advances, and indebtedness established pursuant to paragraphs (1) and (2) of subdivision (a) of Section 33333.6, as those paragraphs read on December 31, 2001, or that lengthens the period during which the redevelopment plan is effective if the redevelopment plan being amended contains the provisions required by subdivision (b) of Section 33670. However, this section shall not apply to those redevelopment plans that add new territory.

(b) If a redevelopment agency adopts an amendment that is governed by the provisions of this section, it shall pay to each affected taxing entity either of the following:

(1) If an agreement exists that requires payments to the taxing entity, the amount required to be paid by an agreement between the agency and an affected taxing entity entered into prior to January 1, 1994.

(2) If an agreement does not exist, the amounts required pursuant to subdivisions (b), (c), (d), and (e) of Section 33607.5, until termination of the redevelopment plan, calculated against the amount of assessed value by which the current year assessed value exceeds an adjusted base year assessed value. The amounts shall be allocated between property taxes and educational facilities according to the appropriate formula in paragraph (3) of subdivision (a) of Section 33607.5. In determining the applicable amount under Section 33607.5, the first fiscal year shall be the first fiscal year following the fiscal year in which the adjusted base year value is determined.

(c) The adjusted base year assessed value shall be the assessed value of the project area in the year in which the limitation being amended would have taken effect without the amendment or, if more than one limitation is being amended, the first year in which one or more of the limitations would have taken effect without the amendment. The agency shall commence making these payments pursuant to the terms of the agreement, if applicable, or, if an agreement does not exist, in the first fiscal year following the fiscal year in which the adjusted base year value is determined.

33607.8 Payments to state water supply contractors

(a) Notwithstanding any other provision of law, a redevelopment agency may make payments from tax increment funds to an affected taxing entity that is a state water supply contractor in accordance with both of the following requirements:

(1) The payment shall not exceed the amount that, but for the activities of the redevelopment agency, otherwise would have been received by the affected taxing entity pursuant to a tax that was originally approved by the state's voters prior to July 1, 1978.

(2) The payments shall be made for the purpose of funding the payments of the state water supply contractor pursuant to its water supply contract with the Department of Water Resources for the costs of building, operating, maintaining, and replacing the State Water Resources Development System.

(b) Allocations made by a redevelopment agency for payments made pursuant to subdivision (a) shall not cause any reduction in payments to an affected taxing entity pursuant to paragraph (2) of subdivision (a) of Section 33607.5.

(c) For purposes of this section:

(1) "State Water Resources Development System" has the same meaning as used in Section 12931 of the Water Code.

(2) "State water supply contractor" has the same meaning as used in Section 11975 of the Water Code.

33608 Validation of reimbursement agreements: charter cities

(a) All acts and proceedings heretofore or hereafter taken under color of law by a charter city meeting the criteria of subdivision (g) and its redevelopment agency in a county with a population over 4,000,000 with respect to a reimbursement agreement executed pursuant to Section 33445 of the Health and Safety Code dated July 7, 1986, and as amended as of July 13, 1987, are hereby confirmed, validated, and declared legally effective to the extent the agreement could have been authorized by the Legislature initially, except as to limitations imposed by the California and United States Constitutions. The validation provided by this section shall be the only determination necessary to satisfy the requirement of subdivision (e) of Section 33675 of the Health and Safety Code and those provisions shall not apply to the agreement otherwise. The Legislature finds and declares that this section is consistent with existing law and does not conflict with either Article XIII B or Section 16 of Article XVI of the California Constitution.

(b) If the commencement of reimbursement of the principal amount of indebtedness of the agency under an agreement referred to in subdivision (a), or any predecessor agreement executed pursuant to Section 33445 of the Health and Safety Code, is delayed beyond 10 years after the date of execution of the agreement for any reason, the agency and the city may amend or enforce the reimbursement agreement, or any predecessor thereto, to provide for the payment of interest. The interest may accrue, as to reimbursement for any particular property or improvement, from the date of acquisition, construction, or installation thereof until the date of the reimbursement agreement and thereafter, until payment of the principal and interest by the agency. The interest shall be at the rate specified in the reimbursement agreement, not to exceed the rate of interest earned by the treasurer of the city on investments of the city's pooled funds. Subject to that limitation, interest on the indebtedness may be calculated pursuant to any generally accepted method of computation, including, without limitation, any method which allows the compounding of interest monthly or at other appropriate intervals.

(c) Reimbursements for any indebtedness under the reimbursement agreement referred to in subdivision (a) shall be (1) first allocated for the funding requirements of the fire and police retirement fund of the city and (2) then deposited into the Low and Moderate Income Housing Fund of the agency. However, this section shall not be construed to authorize any reimbursement of indebtedness which is not permissive under Section 16 of Article XVI of the California Constitution.

(d) The reimbursement agreement shall not be amended without the approval of the Legislature, by statute, and the obligation created by the reimbursement agreement shall terminate on December 31, 2014.

(e) In addition to any amounts provided to the city's fire and police retirement system under the reimbursement agreement, to the extent permitted by law, the city shall undertake, by ordinance, to contribute additional moneys from its general fund annually and transfer assets (including, without limitation, income producing assets such as parking garages) as necessary and actuarially appropriate to satisfy its fire and police retirement fund obligation. When this obligation has been actuarily funded, all assets contributed pursuant to this section shall revert to the city.

(f) The obligations created by the reimbursement agreement specified in subdivision (a) shall be deemed to be existing obligations for purposes of subdivision (d) of Section 33334.6 incurred by the agency to finance a redevelopment project existing on, and created prior to, January 1, 1986. The statement of existing obligations required by subdivision (f) of Section 33334.6 shall be deemed amended to include the obligations created by this reimbursement agreement. The agency shall make deposits into the Low and Moderate Income Housing Fund of the agency in accordance with the reimbursement agreement. These deposits shall be the only obligations that the agency shall have to deposit money in the Low and Moderate Income Housing Fund under subdivision (a) of Section 33334.2 or Section 33334.6, with respect to the project area subject to the reimbursement agreement, notwithstanding any other provision of law.

(g) This section applies to any charter city meeting all of the following criteria:

(1) The city's retirement system is part of the city's charter and was approved by the voters before July 1, 1978.

(2) The city did not levy a separate ad valorem property tax rate to support the retirement system in the 1983–84 fiscal year.

(3) The retirement system provides for a cost-of-living adjustment which is indexed to a consumer price index and does not limit the annual increases which may be paid to members after their retirement.

(4) The retirement system is not currently available to newly hired fire and police employees and will not be available in the future.

(5) Before January 1, 1985, the city unsuccessfully litigated a limit to the cost-of-living adjustment which may be paid to members of the retirement system after their retirement.

(6) The governing body of the city has, by resolution, elected to make this section applicable to it. This election shall be final and binding and may not be revoked for any reason.

(h) "Agency," as used in this section, includes a community development commission exercising the powers of a redevelopment agency pursuant to Section 34141.

Article 2
Community Redevelopment Agency Administrative Fund

33610 Appropriations by legislative body for administrative expenses and overhead

At any time after the agency created for any community becomes authorized to transact business and exercise its powers, the legislative body of the community may appropriate to the agency such amounts as the legislative body deems necessary for the administrative expenses and overhead of the agency. The money appropriated may be paid to the agency as a grant to defray the expenses and overhead, or as a loan to be repaid upon such terms and conditions as the legislative body may provide.

In addition to the common understanding and usual interpretation of the term, "administrative expense" includes, but is not limited to, expenses of redevelopment planning and dissemination of redevelopment information.

33611 Submission of agency budget to legislative body

Each agency transacting business and exercising powers under this part shall annually submit to the legislative body of the community a proposed budget of its administrative expenses.

33612 Adoption of agency budget by legislative body

The legislative body may adopt an annual budget for the administrative expenses of the agency in such amounts as it deems necessary and may provide such conditions and restrictions upon the expenditure or encumbrance of the money appropriated pursuant to the budget as it deems advisable.

33613 Community redevelopment agency administrative fund

The money appropriated for administrative expenses shall be kept in the treasury of the community in a special fund to be known as the community redevelopment agency administrative fund, and money shall be drawn from the fund to meet the administrative expenses of the agency in substantially the same manner as money is drawn by other agencies and departments of the community subject to budgetary control.

33614 Money appropriated to administrative fund

The money appropriated by the legislative body to the community redevelopment agency administrative fund is money granted by the community to defray the administrative expenses of the agency which is performing a public function of the community.

33615 Report of transactions by agency

Each such agency shall file with the legislative body a detailed report of all its transactions, including a statement of all revenues and expenditures, at monthly, quarterly, or annual intervals as the legislative body may prescribe.

Article 3
Redevelopment Revolving Fund

33620 Establishment of fund

At any time after it has adopted a resolution declaring that there is a need for an agency to function in the community, the legislative body may establish a redevelopment revolving fund to be kept in the treasury of the community.

33621 Appropriation of moneys for fund

For the purpose of raising money to be deposited in the redevelopment revolving fund, the legislative body may appropriate money or the community may issue and sell its general obligation bonds.

33622 Expenditures from fund

By resolution of the legislative body adopted by a majority vote, any money in the redevelopment revolving fund may be expended from time to time for:

(a) The acquisition of real property in any project area.

(b) The clearance, aiding in relocation of site occupants, and preparation of any project area for redevelopment.

33623 Payment of money from fund to agency

By resolution of the legislative body adopted by a two-thirds vote, any money in the redevelopment revolving fund may be paid to the agency, upon such terms and conditions as the legislative body may prescribe for any of the following purposes:

(a) Deposit in a trust fund to be expended for the acquisition of real property in any project area.

(b) The clearance of any project area for redevelopment.

(c) Any expenses necessary or incidental to the carrying out of a redevelopment plan which has been adopted by the legislative body.

33624 Redeposit of excess money into fund

All money received by the agency from the sale, lease, or encumbering of property acquired with money from the redevelopment revolving fund in excess of the money required to repay the loans and interest thereon authorized by this part shall be redeposited in the fund.

33625 Financing provisions subject to Sections 33433, 33434 and 33624

All other provisions of this part that relate to financing are subject to Sections 33433, 33434, and 33624.

33626 Abolition of revolving fund

The legislative body of any community may abolish the redevelopment revolving fund whenever it finds that the purposes for which it was established have been accomplished.

The legislative body of any community may, with the consent of the agency, withdraw money from the redevelopment revolving fund whenever and to the extent that it finds that the amount of money therein exceeds the amount necessary to finance existing or planned purposes for which its expenditure is authorized by the provisions of this article. All money withdrawn from the fund by reason of its being reduced in size, or its abolition, and all money which, after abolition, would have been required to be deposited or redeposited in the fund, shall be transferred to the general obligation bond redemption fund of the community or to the general fund of the community, as directed by the legislative body.

Article 4
Community Appropriations and General Obligation Bonds

33630 Community general obligation bonds

The community may issue and sell its general obligation bonds for any or all of the following purposes: raising money to be deposited in the redevelopment revolving fund, or providing funds with which to redeem before maturity, retire at maturity, or purchase agency bonds issued under Article 5 (commencing with Section 33640) of this chapter. General obligation bonds issued pursuant to this article may be authorized and issued in a principal amount sufficient to provide funds for the payment of any or all of the following:

(a) The estimated amount of money to be raised to be deposited in the redevelopment revolving fund.

(b) The principal amount of agency bonds proposed to be so redeemed, retired or purchased.

(c) The estimated amount of any premiums required to be paid in connection with the redemption or purchase of such agency bonds.

(d) The estimated amount of any due and unpaid interest or accrued interest on such agency bonds which must be paid at the time the same are redeemed, retired or purchased.

(e) The amount of interest on such general obligation bonds estimated to accrue during the period from the date thereof until the portion of taxes allocated to and paid into the special fund of the redevelopment agency under the provisions of Section 33670 pledged or to be pledged to the repayment of an advance to the agency for any purpose authorized by this article or by Article 3 (commencing with Section 33620) of this chapter equals the annual amount of the interest upon such bonds due and payable thereon in the next succeeding year, such period not to exceed 10 years from the date of such general obligation bonds or the first series thereof; provided, that such amount shall not include any interest estimated to accrue during any year for which interest on agency bonds proposed to be so redeemed, retired or purchased has been provided from the proceeds of sale of such agency bonds.

(f) The estimated amount of all expenses incidental to or connected with the redemption, retirement or purchase of such agency bonds and the authorization, issuance and sale of such general obligation bonds.

All agency bonds redeemed, retired or purchased with the proceeds of such general obligation bonds shall be canceled and shall not be reissued.

The legislative body may fix a date, not more than 10 years from the date of issuance of any such general obligation bonds, for the earliest maturity of each issue or series of such bonds.

33631 Loan of bond proceeds to agency

If the redevelopment plan contains the provision authorized by Section 33670, the agency and the legislative body of the community may, either before or after the authorization of general obligation bonds for the purposes permitted by Section 33630, enter into an agreement that the principal amount of any such general obligation bonds sold for such purposes, together with all interest which the community may pay thereon, shall constitute a loan by the community to the agency for the purpose of refinancing the redevelopment project, and that, subject to any prior pledge of or claim upon the moneys in the special fund provided for in said section 33670, the moneys accruing to such special fund are irrevocably pledged to the repayment of such loan until there has been repaid to the community from time to time from such special fund the principal amount of such general obligation bonds plus all interest which the community may pay thereon, less such part, if any, of the proceeds of such general obligation bonds which were not used for such purposes, and less any premiums and accrued interest received by the community upon the sale of such general obligation bonds.

33632 Bond redemption fund surplus

Any surplus existing in the general obligation bond redemption fund after payment of principal and interest shall be transferred to the general fund of the community.

33633 Authorization and issuance of bonds

Except as otherwise provided in this part, any general obligation bonds issued by any community pursuant to this article shall be authorized and issued in the manner and within the limitations prescribed by law or the charter of the community for the issuance and authorization of such bonds for public purposes generally. Irrespective of any limitation as to the amount of general obligation bonds which may be issued a community may issue such bonds for the purposes prescribed in this article, in excess of the limitation, in such amount as may be authorized by the voters of the community at any general or special election.

Article 5
Agency Bonds

33640   Authority to issue bonds

From time to time an agency may, subject to the approval of the legislative body, issue bonds for any of its corporate purposes. An agency may also, subject to the approval of the legislative body, issue refunding bonds for the purpose of paying or retiring bonds previously issued by it.

**33641   Types of bonds;
sources of repayment**

An agency may issue any types of bonds which it may determine, including bonds on which the principal and interest are payable:

(a) Exclusively from the income and revenues of the redevelopment projects financed with the proceeds of the bonds, or with the proceeds together with financial assistance from the state or federal government in aid of the projects.

(b) Exclusively from the income and revenues of certain designated redevelopment projects whether or not they were financed in whole or in part with the proceeds of the bonds.

(c) In whole or in part from taxes allocated to, and paid into a special fund of, the agency pursuant to the provisions of Article 6 (commencing with Section 33670).

(d) In whole or in part from taxes imposed pursuant to Section 7280.5 of the Revenue and Taxation Code which are pledged therefor.

(e) From its revenues generally.

(f) From any contributions or other financial assistance from the state or federal government.

(g) By any combination of these methods.

**33641.5   Pledge of collateral
by agency**

(a) As used in this section:

(1) "Collateral" means any revenues, moneys, accounts receivable, contracts rights, and other rights to payment of whatever kind or other property subject to the pledge provided for or created in a pledge document.

(2) "Pledge document" means the resolution, indenture, trust agreement, loan agreement, lease, installment sale agreement, reimbursement agreement, pledge agreement, or similar agreement in which the pledge is provided for or created.

(3) "Pledge" means a commitment of, by the grant of a lien on and a security interest in, the collateral referred to in a pledge document.

(b) A pledge of collateral by a redevelopment agency to secure, directly or indirectly, the payment of the principal or redemption price of, or interest on, any bonds, or any reimbursement agreement with any provider of credit to bonds, which is issued by or entered into by an agency shall be valid and binding in accordance with the terms of the pledge document from the time the pledge is made for the benefit of pledgees and successors thereto.

The collateral shall immediately be subject to the pledge, and the pledge shall constitute a lien and security interest which immediately shall attach to the collateral and be effective, binding, and enforceable against the pledgor, its successors, purchasers of the collateral, creditors, and all others asserting the rights therein, to the extent set forth, and in accordance with, the pledge document irrespective of whether those parties have notice of the pledge and without the need for any physical delivery, recordation, filing, or further act.

33642   Additional security

Any of such bonds may be additionally secured by a pledge of any revenues or by an encumbrance by mortgage, deed of trust, or otherwise of any redevelopment project or other property of the agency or by a pledge of the taxes referred to in subdivision (c) of Section 33641, or by any combination thereof.

**33643   Exemption from
personal liability**

Neither the members of an agency nor any persons executing the bonds are liable personally on the bonds by reason of their issuance.

**33644   Limitation
on indebtedness**

The bonds and other obligations of any agency are not a debt of the community, the State, or any of its political subdivisions and neither the community, the State, nor any of its political subdivisions is liable on them, nor in any event shall the bonds or obligations be payable out of any funds or properties other than those of the agency; and such bonds and other obligations shall so state on their face. The bonds do not constitute an indebtedness within the meaning of any constitutional or statutory debt limitation or restriction.

**33645   Authorization
by resolution**

The agency may authorize bonds by resolution. The resolution, trust indenture, or mortgage may provide for:

(a) The issuance of the bonds in one or more series.

(b) The date the bonds shall bear.

(c) The maturity dates of the bonds.

(d) The rate or maximum rate of interest on the indebtedness, which shall not exceed the maximum rate permitted by Section 53531 of the Government Code, and need not be recited if the rate does not exceed 4 1/2 percent. The interest may be fixed or variable and may be simple or compound. The interest shall be payable at the time or times determined by the agency.

(e) The denomination of the bonds.

(f) Their form, either coupon or registered.

(g) The conversion or registration privileges carried by the bonds.

(h) The rank or priority of the bonds.

(i) The manner of their execution.

(j) The medium of payment.

(k) The place of payment.

(l) The terms of redemption with or without premium to which the bonds are subject.

(m) The maximum amount of bonded indebtedness in compliance with, and not to exceed, the limit specified in the redevelopment plan as required in Section 33334.1.

The resolution, trust indenture, or mortgage shall provide that tax-increment funds allocated to an agency pursuant to Section 33670 shall not be payable to a trustee on account of any issued bonds when sufficient funds have been placed with the trustee to redeem all outstanding bonds of the issue.

33645.5 Exception to maximum interest rate limitation

Notwithstanding Section 33645 or any other provision of law, the rate of interest on any indebtedness or obligation of an agency which is payable to the federal government or any agency or instrumentality thereof or on any such indebtedness or obligation guaranteed by the federal government or any instrumentality thereof may be at a rate higher than the limitation established in Section 33645, or any other law, if such rate is the rate established by the federal government or any instrumentality thereof. Any such indebtedness or obligation shall be in such form and denomination, have such maturity, and be subject to such conditions as may be prescribed by the federal government or agency or instrumentality thereof.

33646 Sale of bonds

The bonds may be sold at no less than par less a discount of not to exceed 5 percent, at public sale held after notice published once at least five days prior to the sale in a newspaper of general circulation published in the community, or, if there is none, in a newspaper of general circulation published in the county. The bonds may be sold at not less than par to the federal government at private sale without any advertisement.

The amendment to this section made at the 1969 Regular Session of the Legislature shall be applicable to bonds of a redevelopment agency which have been authorized by the agency prior to the effective date of the amendment but which have not been issued prior to such date.

33647 Effectiveness of signature of ex-member or officer

If any agency member or officer whose signature appears on bonds or coupons ceases to be such member or officer before delivery of the bonds, his signature is as effective as if he had remained in office.

33648 Negotiability

Bonds issued pursuant to this part are fully negotiable.

33649 Validity of bonds

In any action or proceedings involving the validity or enforceability of any bonds or their security, any such bond reciting in substance that it has been issued by the agency to aid in financing a redevelopment project is conclusively deemed to have been issued for a redevelopment project and the project is conclusively deemed to have been planned, located, and constructed pursuant to this part.

33650 Additional powers of agency

In connection with the issuance of bonds, and in addition to its other powers, an agency has the powers prescribed in Sections 33651 to 33659, inclusive.

33651 Pledge of revenues; encumbrance of property

An agency may:

(a) Pledge all or any part of its gross or net rents, fees, or revenues to which its right then exists or may thereafter come into existence.

(b) Encumber by mortgage, deed of trust, or otherwise all or any part of its real or personal property, then owned or thereafter acquired.

33652 Covenants as to debts and obligations

An agency may covenant:

(a) Against pledging all or any part of its rents, fees, and revenues.

(b) Against encumbering all or any part of its real or personal property, to which its right or title then exists or may thereafter come into existence.

(c) Against permitting any lien on such revenues or property.

(d) With respect to limitations on its right to sell, lease, or otherwise dispose of all or part of any redevelopment project.

(e) As to what other, or additional debts or obligations it may incur.

33653 Covenants as to use of proceeds, replacement, repayment and redemption

An agency may:

(a) Covenant as to the bonds to be issued, as to the issuance of such bonds in escrow or otherwise, and as to the use and disposition of the bond proceeds.

(b) Provide for the replacement of lost, destroyed, or mutilated bonds.

(c) Covenant against extending the time for the payment of its bonds or interest.

(d) Redeem the bonds, covenant for their redemption, and provide the redemption terms and conditions.

33654 Covenants as to revenues

An agency may:

(a) Covenant as to the consideration or rents and fees to be charged in the sale or lease of a redevelopment project, the amount to be raised each year or other period of time by rents, fees, and other revenues, and as to their use and disposition.

(b) Create or authorize the creation of special funds for money held for redevelopment or other costs, debt service, reserves, or other purposes, and covenant as to the use and disposition of such money.

33655 Contracts with bondholders

An agency may prescribe the procedure, if any, by which the terms of any contract with bondholders may be amended or abrogated, the amount of bonds whose holders are required to consent thereto, and the manner in which such consent may be given.

33656 Covenants as to use and maintenance of property

An agency may covenant:

(a) As to the use of any or all of its real or personal property.

(b) As to the maintenance of its real and personal property, its replacement, the insurance to be carried on it, and the use and disposition of insurance money.

33657 Covenants as to defaults

An agency may:

(a) Covenant as to the rights, liabilities, powers and duties arising upon the breach by it of any covenant, condition, or obligation.

(b) Covenant and prescribe as to events of default and terms and conditions upon which any or all of its bonds or obligations become or may be declared due before maturity, and as to the terms and conditions upon which such declaration and its consequences may be waived.

33658 Vesting of rights in trustee

An agency may:

(a) Vest in a trustee or the holders of bonds or any proportion of them the right to enforce the payment of the bonds or any covenants securing or relating to the bonds.

(b) Vest in a trustee the right, in the event of a default by the agency, to take possession of all or part of any redevelopment project, to collect the rents and revenues arising from it and to dispose of such money pursuant to the agreement of the agency with the trustee.

(c) Provide for the powers and duties of a trustee and limit his liabilities.

(d) Provide the terms and conditions upon which the trustee or the holders of bonds or any proportion of them may enforce any covenant or rights securing or relating to the bonds.

33659 Additional covenants and powers of agency

An agency may:

(a) Exercise all or any part or combination of the powers granted in Sections 33651 to 33658 inclusive.

(b) Make covenants other than and in addition to the covenants expressly authorized in such sections of like or different character.

(c) Make such covenants and to do any and all such acts and things as may be necessary, convenient, or desirable to secure its bonds, or, except as otherwise provided in this part, as will tend to make the bonds more marketable notwithstanding that such covenants, acts, or things may not be enumerated in this part.

33660 Rights of obligees

In addition to all other rights which may be conferred on him, and subject only to any contractual restrictions binding upon him, an obligee may:

(a) By mandamus, suit, action, or proceeding, compel the agency and its members, officers, agents, or employees to perform each and every term, provision, and covenant contained in any contract of the agency with or for the benefit of the obligee, and require the carrying out of any or all such covenants and agreements of the agency and the fulfillment of all duties imposed upon it by this part.

(b) By suit, action, or proceeding in equity, enjoin any acts or things which may be unlawful, or the violation of any of the rights of the obligee.

33661 Grant of rights to obligees

By its resolution, trust indenture, mortgage, lease, or other contract, an agency may confer upon any obligee holding or representing a specified amount in bonds, the following rights upon the happening of an event or default prescribed in such resolution or instrument, to be exercised by suit, action, or proceeding in any court of competent jurisdiction:

(a) To cause possession of all or part of any redevelopment project to be surrendered to any such obligee.

(b) To obtain the appointment of a receiver of all or part of any redevelopment project of the agency and of the rents and profits from it. If a receiver is appointed, he may enter and take possession of the redevelopment project or any part of it, operate and maintain it, collect and receive all fees, rents, revenues, or other charges thereafter arising from it, and shall keep such money in separate accounts and apply it pursuant to the obligations of the agency as the court shall direct.

(c) To require the agency and its members and employees to account as if it and they were the trustees of an express trust.

33662 Tax-exempt status of bonds

The bonds are issued for an essential public and governmental purpose, and together with interest on them and income from them are exempt from all taxes.

33663 Status of bonds as legal investments

Notwithstanding any restrictions on investments contained in any laws, the state and all public officers, municipal corporations, political subdivisions, and public bodies, all banks, bankers, trust companies, savings banks and institutions, building and loan associations, savings and loan associations, investment companies, and other persons carrying on a banking business, all insurance companies, insurance associations, and other persons carrying on an insurance business, and all executors, administrators, guardians, conservators, trustees, and other fiduciaries may legally invest any sinking funds, money, or other funds belonging to them or within their control in any bonds or other obligations issued by an agency. Such bonds and other obligations are authorized security for all public deposits. It is one of the purposes of this part to authorize any persons, firms, corporations, associations, political subdivisions, bodies and officers, public and private, to use any funds owned or controlled by them, including, but not limited to, sinking, insurance, investment, retirement, compensation, pension, and trust funds, and funds held on deposit, for the purchase of any such bonds or other obligations. This part does not relieve any person, firm, or corporation from any duty of exercising reasonable care in selecting securities.

33664 Agency may purchase its own bonds

(a) An agency may purchase its bonds as follows:

(1) At a price not more than the sum of their principal amount and accrued interest plus (if the bonds purchased are callable at a premium) an amount not to exceed the premium that would be applicable if the bonds were purchased on the next following call date.

(2) At a higher price if a majority of the members of the agency determine, based upon substantial evidence, that under then prevailing conditions the purchase would be of financial advantage to the agency. Prior to purchasing bonds pursuant to this paragraph, the agency shall adopt a resolution designating paragraph (1), (2), or (3) of subdivision (b) as the financial advantage accruing to the agency from the bond purchase or specifying in

detail any alternative basis for the agency's finding of financial advantage. Unless the legislative body has designated itself as the redevelopment agency, the agency shall additionally obtain the approval of the legislative body for repurchase of agency bonds under this subdivision and, if applicable, under Section 33640.

A resolution of the legislative body approving repurchase of agency bonds under this subdivision shall be operative only for the period specified in the resolution of the legislative body, not to exceed five years. However, the authorization may be renewed by an appropriate resolution of the legislative body and the expiration of the legislative body's resolution shall in no way impair the obligation of bonds previously issued by the agency to refund bonds purchased under this subdivision.

(b) "Financial advantage," as used in subdivision (a), includes, but is not limited to, each of the following:

(1) A reduction in the aggregate debt service on the agency's outstanding bonds.

(2) The creation of opportunities to more efficiently leverage revenues of the agency.

(3) Cancellation of agency bonds subject to adverse provisions of, or tax consequences under, the laws of the United States.

(c) Any bond purchases made pursuant to this section shall be (1) identified in the agency's annual fiscal year report required by Section 33080.1 for the fiscal year in which the purchase was made and (2) reflected in the agency's statement of indebtedness filed pursuant to Section 33675.

(d) Within two weeks following a purchase of bonds pursuant to paragraph (2) of subdivision (a), the redevelopment agency shall transmit to the California Debt Advisory Commission a copy of the agency's resolution specifying the financial advantage to the agency in making the purchase, together with a covering letter that includes all of the following information respecting the bonds purchased:

(1) The date of the agency's resolution authorizing the bonds, the date of issuance of the bonds, and any other information necessary to identify the particular issuance or series of bonds.

(2) The terms of redemption to which the bonds were originally subject.

(3) The denominations and interest rates of the bonds purchased.

(4) The purchase price.

(e) All bonds purchased pursuant to this section shall be canceled.

33665 Applicability of revolving fund limitations

All of the provisions of this article are subject to the limitations of Article 3 (commencing with Section 33620) of this chapter.

Article 6
Taxation

33670 Division and allocation of property taxes

Any redevelopment plan may contain a provision that taxes, if any, levied upon taxable property in a redevelopment project each year by or for the benefit of the State of California, any city, county, city and county, district, or other public corporation (hereinafter sometimes called "taxing agencies") after the effective date of the ordinance approving the redevelopment plan, shall be divided as follows:

(a) That portion of the taxes which would be produced by the rate upon which the tax is levied each year by or for each of the taxing agencies upon the total sum of the assessed value of the taxable property in the redevelopment project as shown upon the assessment roll used in connection with the taxation of that property by the taxing agency, last equalized prior to the effective date of the ordinance, shall be allocated to and when collected shall be paid to the respective taxing agencies as taxes by or for the taxing agencies on all other property are paid (for the purpose of allocating taxes levied by or for any taxing agency or agencies which did not include the territory in a redevelopment project on the effective date of the ordinance but to which that territory has been annexed or otherwise included after that effective date, the assessment roll of the county last equalized on the effective date of the ordinance shall be used in determining the assessed valuation of the taxable property in the project on the effective date); and

(b) Except as provided in subdivision (e) or in Section 33492.15, that portion of the levied taxes each year in excess of that amount shall be allocated to and when collected shall be paid into a special fund of the redevelopment agency to pay the principal of and interest on loans, moneys advanced to, or indebtedness (whether funded, refunded, assumed, or otherwise) incurred by the redevelopment agency to finance or refinance, in whole or in part, the redevelopment project. Unless and until the total assessed valuation of the taxable property in a redevelopment project exceeds the total assessed value of the taxable property in that project as shown by the last equalized assessment roll referred to in subdivision (a), all of the taxes levied and collected upon the taxable property in the redevelopment project shall be paid to the respective taxing agencies. When the loans, advances, and indebtedness, if any, and interest thereon, have been paid, all moneys thereafter received from taxes upon the taxable property in the redevelopment project shall be paid to the respective taxing agencies as taxes on all other property are paid.

(c) In any redevelopment project in which taxes have been divided pursuant to this section prior to 1968, located within any county with total assessed valuation subject to general property taxes for the 1967–68 fiscal year between two billion dollars ($2,000,000,000) and two billion one hundred million dollars ($2,100,000,000), if the total assessed valuation of taxable property within the redevelopment project for the 1967–68 fiscal year was reduced, the total sum of the assessed value of taxable property used as the basis for apportionment of taxes under subdivision (a) shall be reduced by 10 percent for the 1968–69 fiscal year and fiscal years thereafter.

(d) For the purposes of this section, taxes shall not include taxes from the supplemental assessment roll levied pursuant to Chapter 3.5 (commencing with Section 75) of Part 0.5 of Division 1 of the Revenue and Taxation Code for the 1983–84 fiscal year.

(e) That portion of the taxes in excess of the amount identified in subdivision (a) which are attributable to a tax rate levied by a taxing agency for the purpose of producing revenues in an amount sufficient to make annual repayments of the principal of, and the interest on, any bonded indebtedness for the acquisition or improvement of real property shall be allocated to, and when collected shall be paid into, the fund of that taxing agency. This subdivision shall only apply to taxes levied to repay bonded indebtedness approved by the voters of the taxing agency on or after January 1, 1989.

33670.5 Fulfillment of intent of Constitution

Section 33670 fulfills the intent of Section 16 of Article XVI of the Constitution. To further carry out the intent of Section 16 of Article XVI of the Constitution, whenever that provision requires the allocation of money between agencies such allocation shall be consistent with the intent of the people when they approved Section 16 of Article XVI of the Constitution. Whenever money is allocated between agencies by means of a comparison of assessed values for different years, that comparison shall be based on the same assessment ratio. When there are different assessment ratios for the years compared, the assessed value shall be changed so that it is based on the same assessment ratio for the years so compared.

33670.8 Adjustments to assessment roll: cities of Santa Cruz and Watsonville

(a) With respect to the allocation of taxes pursuant to Section 33670 in redevelopment project areas within the incorporated City of Santa Cruz, which were already approved on October 17, 1989, the otherwise applicable provisions of this part shall be modified as specified in this subdivision.

For the purpose of determining the portion of taxes to be paid annually to the Redevelopment Agency of the City of Santa Cruz pursuant to Sections 33328, 33670, and 33675 for any redevelopment project which was approved on or before October 17, 1989, "assessment roll . . . last equalized" and "base-year assessment roll" mean the last equalized assessment roll determined pursuant to subdivision (a) of Section 33670 reduced by the same amount as the amount of reduction in the current assessment roll determined pursuant to Section 170 of the Revenue and Taxation Code.

(b) With respect to the allocation of taxes pursuant to Section 33670 in redevelopment project areas within the incorporated City of Watsonville, which were already approved on October 17, 1989, the otherwise applicable provisions of this part shall be modified as specified in this subdivision.

For the purpose of determining the portion of taxes to be paid annually to the Redevelopment Agency of the City of Watsonville pursuant to Sections 33328, 33670, and 33675 for any redevelopment project which was approved on or before October 17, 1989, "assessment roll . . . last equalized" and "base-year assessment roll" mean the last equalized assessment roll determined pursuant to subdivision (a) of Section 33670 reduced by the same amount as the amount of reduction in the current assessment roll determined pursuant to Section 170 of the Revenue and Taxation Code.

(c) In claiming an allocation of taxes pursuant to Section 33675, as adjusted pursuant to subdivision (b), the redevelopment agency of the City of Watsonville shall consider the economic impact of the allocation on other agencies which have sustained substantial disaster damage and shall negotiate and enter into an agreement with the County of Santa Cruz to avoid further economic hardship.

(d) Within 30 days after receipt of a notice from the Assessor of the County of Santa Cruz establishing the adjustment in the assessment roll pursuant to subdivision (b), the Redevelopment Agency of the City of Watsonville may elect not to be subject to this section by giving written notice of its decision to the County of Santa Cruz. Notwithstanding an election by the Redevelopment Agency of the City of Watsonville not to be subject to this section pursuant to this subdivision, it shall still reimburse the County of Santa Cruz for its cost of revising the property tax assessment rolls and allocations.

(e) Subdivisions (a) and (b) shall apply to allocation of taxes levied on the 1990 and subsequent equalized assessment rolls, upon the request of the redevelopment agencies of the Cities of Santa Cruz and Watsonville, and those agencies shall reimburse the County of Santa Cruz for its cost of revising the property tax assessment rolls and allocations.

(f) (1) The county auditor shall certify to the director of finance of each city which includes a redevelopment project subject to this section when the total sum of the assessed value of the taxable property in each redevelopment project subject to this section as shown upon each current year's equalized assessment roll becomes equal to the total sum of the assessed value of the taxable property in each redevelopment project as shown upon the assessment roll last equalized before October 17, 1989, adjusted by the change in the Consumer Price Index for the San Francisco/Oakland Metropolitan Area between 1989 and the date of the certification pursuant to this subdivision. On the July 1 following the date of certification and each July 1 thereafter, the county auditor shall increase the total sum of the assessed value of the taxable property in each redevelopment project as shown upon the assessment roll adjusted pursuant to subdivision (a) or (b) by 10 percent of the difference between the total sum of the assessed value of the taxable property in each redevelopment project determined pursuant to subdivision (a) of Section 33670 and the total sum of the assessed value of the taxable property in each redevelopment project as adjusted pursuant to subdivision (a) or (b), until the two total assessed values are equal, and shall report this adjusted value to the other county officials charged with the responsibility of allocating taxes pursuant to Sections 33670 and 33675, who shall use this assessed value in determining the portion of taxes to be paid annually to the redevelopment agency subject to this section.

(2) For purposes of this subdivision only, in the event that any redevelopment project area within the incorporated area of the City of Santa Cruz already approved on October 17, 1989, is amended to add territory to the project area, the assessed value of taxable property in the territory added shall be computed separately and the county assessor shall not take the assessed value into account in determining when the total sum of the assessed value of the taxable property in the redevelopment project becomes equal to the total sum of the assessed value of the taxable property as shown on the assessment roll last equalized prior to October 17, 1989, as adjusted pursuant to this subdivision.

(g) With respect to an area added to a redevelopment project by the City of Santa Cruz or the City of Watsonville pursuant to Sections 33458.5 and 33477, the terms "assessment roll" and "last equalized assessment roll" as used in Section 33670 shall mean and refer to the assessment roll as reduced in accordance with the provisions of subdivision (b) of Section 170 of the Revenue and Taxation Code.

33670.9 Orange County bailout

(a) For a period of 20 years commencing on July 1, 1996, the Orange County Development Agency shall transfer to the general fund of the County of Orange an amount equal to four million dollars ($4,000,000) a year in two equal installments on June 15 and February 15 of each year. The Orange County Development

Agency shall not incur any obligation with respect to loans, advances of money, or indebtedness, whether funded, refunded, assumed, or otherwise, that would impair its ability to make the foregoing transfers or that would cause the foregoing transfers to violate Section 16 of Article XVI of the California Constitution or subdivision (b) of Section 33670. Funds allocated to low- and moderate-income housing pursuant to Section 33334.2 shall not be used for purposes of this section.

(b) This section shall not take effect unless and until (1) a plan of adjustment is confirmed in Case No. SA-94-22272-JR in the United States Bankruptcy Court for the Central District of California or (2) a trustee is appointed pursuant to Chapter 10 (commencing with Section 30400) of Division 3 of Title 3 of the Government Code.

33670.95 Orange County repayment

(a) The board of supervisors of a county of the second class may, upon adoption of a resolution or resolutions approved by a majority of all of its members, provide for the repayment by the county's redevelopment agency of its debt to the county for general and specific benefits previously provided by the county to redevelopment project areas within the county. Such resolution or resolutions may provide for the transfer of (1) amounts equal to four million dollars ($4,000,000) a year in two equal installments on June 15 and February 15 of each year and (2) such additional amounts, at such times as are specified in the resolution or resolutions, as may be necessary to assure full repayment of the debt, provided that those additional amounts shall not exceed, in the aggregate, the sum of any amounts required to be repaid by the county to the redevelopment agency pursuant to, or as a consequence of, the final determination described in subdivision (c).

(b) A redevelopment agency of a county of the second class shall not incur any obligation with respect to loans, advances of money, or indebtedness, whether funded, refunded, assumed, or otherwise, that would impair its ability to make the transfers described in subdivision (a) or that would cause those transfers to violate Section 16 of Article XVI of the California Constitution or subdivision (b) of Section 33670. Funds allocated to low- and moderate-income housing pursuant to Section 33334.2 shall not be used for purposes of this section.

(c) This section shall become operative on the earlier of the date that a court of appellate jurisdiction renders a final determination invalidating Chapter 745 of the Statutes of 1995 or the date of a court action suspending or preventing the operation of any provision of Chapter 745. This section shall become inoperative on July 1, 2016, and, as of January 1, 2017, is repealed, unless a later enacted statute, that becomes operative on or before January 1, 2017, deletes or extends the dates on which it becomes inoperative and is repealed.

33671 Pledge of tax revenues for payment of indebtedness

In any redevelopment plan or in the proceedings for the advance of moneys, or making of loans, or the incurring of any indebtedness (whether funded, refunded, assumed, or otherwise) by the redevelopment agency to finance or refinance, in whole or in part, the redevelopment project, the portion of taxes mentioned in subdivision (b) of Section 33670 may be irrevocably pledged for the payment of the principal of and interest on such loans, advances, or indebtedness.

33671.5 Pledge of tax revenues; priority over other claims

Whenever any redevelopment agency is authorized to, and does, expressly pledge taxes allocated to, and paid into a special fund of, the agency pursuant to Section 33670, to secure, directly or indirectly, the obligations of the agency including, but not limited to, bonded indebtedness and agreements pursuant to subdivision (b) of Section 33401, then that pledge heretofore or hereafter made shall have priority over any other claim to those taxes not secured by a prior express pledge of those taxes.

33672 Taxes defined

As used in this article the word "taxes" shall include, but without limitation, all levies on an ad valorem basis upon land or real property. As used in this article, "taxes" shall not include any amounts of money deposited in a Sales and Use Tax Compensation Fund pursuant to Section 97.68 of the Revenue and Taxation Code or a Vehicle License Fee Property Tax Compensation Fund pursuant to Section 97.70 of the Revenue and Taxation Code.

33672.5 Statements regarding determination and allocation of tax revenues

(a) Upon the written request of a redevelopment agency for the purpose of assisting the agency, the county auditor or other officer responsible for allocation of tax revenues pursuant to Section 33670 shall prepare a statement each fiscal year, commencing with the 1992–93 fiscal year, for each redevelopment project area and each area added to a redevelopment project area by amendment, which provides for all the following:

(1) The total taxable assessed value of secured, unsecured, and state-assessed railroad and nonoperating, nonunitary property.

(2) The total taxable assessed value used by the county auditor to determine the division of taxes required by subdivision (a) of Section 33670.

(3) The total taxable assessed value used by the county auditor to determine the division of taxes required by subdivision (b) of Section 33670.

(4) The estimated amount of taxes calculated pursuant to subdivision (b) of Section 33670, as adjusted by subdivision (e) of Section 33670 and subdivision (a) of Section 33676. The statement shall specify the gross amount of tax-increment revenue allocated to the agency and any payments to other taxing entities that are deducted from the gross amount allocated.

(5) The estimated amount of taxes to be allocated pursuant to subdivisions (c) and (d) of Section 100 of the Revenue and Taxation Code.

(b) If requested to provide a statement pursuant to subdivision (a), the county auditor shall deliver each statement to the respective redevelopment agencies receiving property tax revenue on or before November 30 of each year.

(c) (1) Upon the request of a redevelopment agency pursuant to subdivision (a), and concurrently with the disbursement of those property tax revenues, the county auditor shall prepare a statement which provides the amount of disbursement made pursuant to all of the following:

(A) Section 33670.

(B) Section 100 of the Revenue and Taxation Code.

(C) Supplemental property tax revenues allocated pursuant to Sections 75 to 75.80 of the Revenue and Taxation Code, inclusive.

(2) The statement provided pursuant to this subdivision shall also include corrections, updates, or adjustments, if any, to the property tax revenue amounts and taxable assessed values reported pursuant to subdivision (a) of Section 33670.

(d) The county auditor shall also provide to a redevelopment agency, no later than 30 days after the receipt of a written request from that agency, information or clarification with respect to any statement issued pursuant to this section.

(e) If any redevelopment agency requests a statement or information pursuant to this section, the agency shall reimburse the county auditor for all actual and reasonable costs incurred.

33673 Taxation of property leased from agency

Whenever property in any redevelopment project has been redeveloped and thereafter is leased by the redevelopment agency to any person or persons or whenever the agency leases real property in any redevelopment project to any person or persons for redevelopment, the property shall be assessed and taxed in the same manner as privately owned property, and the lease or contract shall provide that the lessee shall pay taxes upon the assessed value of the entire property and not merely the assessed value of his or its leasehold interest.

33673.1 Notice to local assessor of lease of property

Every redevelopment agency shall provide notice to the local assessor within 30 days whenever the agency leases real property in a redevelopment project to any person or persons for redevelopment. The notice shall provide the date on which the lessee acquires the beneficial use of the leased property. The notice shall be accompanied by a memorandum of lease and a map of the leased property.

33674 Time for first allocation of tax increments from project area

The portion of taxes mentioned in subdivision (b) of Section 33670 shall not be allocable and payable for the first time until the tax year which begins after the December 1st next following the transmittal of the documents as required in Section 33375 or Section 33457.

33675 Procedure for allocation and payment of taxes to agency

(a) The portion of taxes required to be allocated pursuant to subdivision (b) of Section 33670 shall be allocated and paid to the agency by the county auditor or officer responsible for the payment of taxes into the funds of the respective taxing agencies pursuant to the procedure contained in this section.

(b) Not later than October 1 of each year, for each redevelopment project for which the redevelopment plan provides for the division of taxes pursuant to Section 33670, the agency shall file, with the county auditor or officer described in subdivision (a), a statement of indebtedness and a reconciliation statement certified by the chief financial officer of the agency.

(c) (1) For each redevelopment project for which a statement of indebtedness is required to be filed, the statement of indebtedness shall contain all of the following:

(A) For each loan, advance, or indebtedness incurred or entered into, all of the following information:

(i) The date the loan, advance, or indebtedness was incurred or entered into.

(ii) The principal amount, term, purpose, interest rate, and total interest of each loan, advance, or indebtedness.

(iii) The principal amount and interest due in the fiscal year in which the statement of indebtedness is filed for each loan, advance, or indebtedness.

(iv) The total amount of principal and interest remaining to be paid for each loan, advance, or indebtedness.

(B) The sum of the amounts determined under clause (iii) of subparagraph (A).

(C) The sum of the amounts determined under clause (iv) of subparagraph (A).

(D) The available revenues as of the end of the previous year, as determined pursuant to paragraph (10) of subdivision (d).

(2) The agency may estimate the amount of principal or interest, the interest rate, or term of any loan, advance, or indebtedness if the nature of the loan, advance, or indebtedness is such that the amount of principal or interest, the interest rate or term cannot be precisely determined. The agency may list on a statement of indebtedness any loan, advance, or indebtedness incurred or entered into on or before the date the statement is filed.

(d) For each redevelopment project for which a reconciliation statement is required to be filed, the reconciliation statement shall contain all of the following:

(1) A list of all loans, advances, and indebtedness listed on the previous year's statement of indebtedness.

(2) (A) A list of all loans, advances, and indebtedness, not listed on the previous year's statement of indebtedness, but incurred or entered into in the previous year and paid in whole or in part from revenue received by the agency pursuant to Section 33670. This listing may aggregate loans, advances, and indebtedness incurred or entered into in the previous year for a particular purpose (such as relocation expenses, administrative expenses, consultant expenses, or property management expenses) into a single item in the listing.

(B) For purposes of this section, any payment made pursuant to Section 33684 shall be considered as payment against existing passthrough payment indebtedness as listed on the agency's statement of indebtedness. If the most recent statement of indebtedness documents failed to include all or a part of the agency's obligation to the passthrough payments, those obligations shall be added to the next statement of indebtedness to be filed and shall include both current payments plus all future passthrough obligations.

(3) For each loan, advance, or indebtedness described in paragraph (1) or (2), all of the following information:

(A) The total amount of principal and interest remaining to be paid as of the later of the beginning of the previous year or the date the loan, advance, or indebtedness was incurred or entered into.

(B) Any increases or additions to the loan, advance, or indebtedness occurring during the previous year.

(C) The amount paid on the loan, advance, or indebtedness in the previous year from revenue received by the agency pursuant to Section 33670.

(D) The amount paid on the loan, advance, or indebtedness in the previous year from revenue other than revenue received by the agency pursuant to Section 33670.

(E) The total amount of principal and interest remaining to be paid as of the end of the previous fiscal year.

(4) The available revenues of the agency as of the beginning of the previous fiscal year.

(5) The amount of revenue received by the agency in the previous fiscal year pursuant to Section 33670.

(6) The amount of available revenue received by the agency in the previous fiscal year other than pursuant to Section 33670.

(7) The sum of the amounts specified in subparagraph (D) of paragraph (3), to the extent that the amounts are not included as available revenues pursuant to paragraph (6).

(8) The sum of the amounts specified in paragraphs (4), (5), (6), and (7).

(9) The sum of the amounts specified in subparagraphs (C) and (D) of paragraph (3).

(10) The amount determined by subtracting the amount determined under paragraph (9) from the amount determined under paragraph (8). The amount determined pursuant to this paragraph shall be the available revenues as of the end of the previous fiscal year.

(e) For the purposes of this section, available revenues shall include all cash or cash equivalents held by the agency that were received by the agency pursuant to Section 33670 and all cash or cash equivalents held by the agency that are irrevocably pledged or restricted to payment of a loan, advance, or indebtedness that the agency has listed on a statement of indebtedness. In no event shall available revenues include funds in the agency's Low and Moderate Income Housing Fund established pursuant to Section 33334.3. For the purposes of determining available revenues as of the end of the 1992–93 fiscal year, an agency shall conduct an examination or audit of its books and records for the 1990–91, 1991–92, and 1992–93 fiscal years to determine the available revenues as of the end of the 1992–93 fiscal year.

(f) For the purposes of this section, the amount an agency will deposit in its Low and Moderate Income Housing Fund established pursuant to Section 33334.3 shall constitute an indebtedness of the agency. For the purposes of this section, no loan, advance, or indebtedness that an agency intends to pay from its Low and Moderate Income Housing Fund established pursuant to Section 33334.3 shall be listed on a statement of indebtedness or reconciliation statement as a loan, advance, or indebtedness of the agency. For the purposes of this section, any statutorily authorized deficit in or borrowing from an agency's Low and Moderate Income Housing Fund established pursuant to Section 33334.3 shall constitute an indebtedness of the agency.

(g) The county auditor or officer shall, at the same time or times as the payment of taxes into the funds of the respective taxing entities of the county, allocate and pay the portion of taxes provided by subdivision (b) of Section 33670 to each agency. The amount allocated and paid shall not exceed the amount determined pursuant to subparagraph (C) of paragraph (1) of subdivision (c) minus the amount determined pursuant to subparagraph (D) of paragraph (1) of subdivision (c).

(h) (1) The statement of indebtedness constitutes prima facie evidence of the loans, advances, or indebtedness of the agency.

(2) (A) If the county auditor or other officer disputes the amount of loans, advances, or indebtedness as shown on the statement of indebtedness, the county auditor or other officer shall, within 30 days after receipt of the statement, give written notice to the agency thereof.

(B) The agency shall, within 30 days after receipt of notice pursuant to subparagraph (A), submit any further information it deems appropriate to substantiate the amount of any loans, advances, or indebtedness which has been disputed. If the county auditor or other officer still disputes the amount of loans, advances, or indebtedness, final written notice of that dispute shall be given to the agency, and the amount disputed may be withheld from allocation and payment to the agency as otherwise required by subdivision (g). In that event, the auditor or other officer shall bring an action in the superior court in declaratory relief to determine the matter not later than 90 days after the date of the final notice.

(3) In any court action brought pursuant to this section, the issue shall involve only the amount of loans, advances, or indebtedness, and not the validity of any contract or debt instrument or any expenditures pursuant thereto. Payments to a trustee under a bond resolution or indenture of any kind or payments to a public agency in connection with payments by that public agency pursuant to a lease or bond issue shall not be disputed in any action under this section. The matter shall be set for trial at the earliest possible date and shall take precedence over all other cases except older matters of the same character. Unless an action is brought within the time provided for herein, the auditor or other officer shall allocate and pay the amount shown on the statement of indebtedness as provided in subdivision (g).

(i) Nothing in this section shall be construed to permit a challenge to or attack on matters precluded from challenge or attack by reason of Sections 33500 and 33501. However, nothing in this section shall be construed to deny a remedy against the agency otherwise provided by law.

(j) The Controller shall prescribe a uniform form of statement of indebtedness and reconciliation statement. These forms shall be consistent with this section. In preparing these forms, the Controller shall obtain the input of county auditors, redevelopment agencies, and organizations of county auditors and redevelopment agencies.

(k) For the purposes of this section, a fiscal year shall be a year that begins on July 1 and ends the following June 30.

33676 Election of specified tax allocation by affected taxing entity

(a) Prior to the adoption by the legislative body of a redevelopment plan providing for tax increment financing pursuant to Section 33670, any affected taxing agency may elect to be allocated, and every school district and community college district shall be allocated, in addition to the portion of taxes allocated to the affected taxing agency pursuant to subdivision (a) of Section 33670, all or any portion of the tax revenues allocated to the agency pursuant to subdivision (b) of Section 33670 attributable to one or more of the following:

(1) Increases in the rate of tax imposed for the benefit of the taxing agency which levy occurs after the tax year in which the ordinance adopting the redevelopment plan becomes effective.

(2) If an agency pursuant to Section 33354.5 amends a redevelopment plan which does not utilize tax increment financing to add tax increment financing, and pursuant to subdivision (a) of Section 33670 uses the assessment roll last equalized prior to the effective date of the ordinance originally adopting the redevelopment plan, an affected taxing agency may elect to be allocated all or any portion of the tax revenues allocated to the agency pursuant to subdivision (b) of Section 33670 which the affected taxing agency would receive if the agency were to use the assessment roll last equalized prior to the effective date of the ordinance amending the redevelopment plan to add tax increment financing.

(b) (1) Any local education agency that is a basic aid district or office at the time the ordinance adopting a redevelopment plan is adopted and that receives no state funding, other than that provided pursuant to Section 6 of Article IX of the California Constitution, pursuant to Section 2558, 42238, or 84751, as appropriate, of the Education Code, shall receive annually its percentage share of the property taxes from the project area allocated among all of the affected taxing entities during the fiscal year the funds are allocated, increased by an amount equal to the lesser of the following:

(A) The percentage growth in assessed value that occurs throughout the district, excluding the portion of the district within the redevelopment project area.

(B) Eighty percent of the growth in assessed value that occurs within the portion of the district within the redevelopment project area.

(2) Subparagraphs (A) and (B) of paragraph (1) shall not apply to a redevelopment plan adopted by the legislative body of a community if both of the following occur:

(A) The median household income in the community in which the redevelopment project area is located is less than 80 percent of the median household income in the county in which the redevelopment project area is located.

(B) The preliminary plan for the redevelopment plan was adopted on or before September 1, 1993, and the redevelopment plan was adopted on or before August 1, 1994.

(3) Any local education agency that is a basic aid district or office at the time the ordinance amending a redevelopment plan is adopted pursuant to Section 33607.7 and that receives no state funding, other than that provided pursuant to Section 6 of Article IX of the California Constitution, pursuant to Section 2558, 42238, or 84751, as appropriate, of the Education Code, shall receive either of the following:

(A) If an agreement exists that requires payments to the basic aid district, the amount required to be paid by an agreement between the agency and the basic aid district entered into prior to January 1, 1994.

(B) If an agreement does not exist, the percentage share of the increase in property taxes from the project area allocated among all of the affected taxing entities during the fiscal year the funds in the project area are allocated, derived from 80 percent of the growth in assessed value that occurs within the portion of the district within the redevelopment project area from the year in which the amendment takes effect pursuant to subdivision (c) of Section 33607.7.

(4) The redevelopment agency shall subtract from any payments made pursuant to this section the amount that a basic aid district receives pursuant to Sections 33607.5 and 33607.7 for the purposes of either paragraph (1) of subdivision (h) of Section 42238 of the Education Code or either Section 2558 or 84751 of the Education Code.

(c) The governing body of any affected taxing agency, other than a school district and a community college district, electing to receive allocation of taxes pursuant to this section in addition to taxes allocated to it pursuant to subdivision (a) of Section 33670 shall adopt a resolution to that effect and transmit the same, prior to the adoption of the redevelopment plan, to (1) the legislative body, (2) the agency, and (3) the official or officials performing the functions of levying and collecting taxes for the affected taxing agency. Upon receipt by the official or officials of the resolution, allocation of taxes pursuant to this section to the affected taxing agency which has elected to receive the allocation pursuant to this section by the adoption of the resolution and allocation of taxes pursuant to this section to every school district and community college district shall be made at the time or times allocations are made pursuant to subdivision (a) of Section 33670.

(d) An affected taxing agency, at any time after the adoption of the resolution, may elect not to receive all or any portion of the additional allocation of taxes pursuant to this section by rescinding the resolution or by amending the same, as the case may be, and giving notice thereof to the legislative body, the agency, and the official or officials performing the functions of levying and collecting taxes for the affected taxing agency. After receipt of a notice by the official or officials that an affected taxing agency has elected not to receive all or a portion of the additional allocation of taxes by rescission or amendment of the resolution, any allocation of taxes to the affected taxing agency required to be made pursuant to this section shall not thereafter be made but shall be allocated to the agency and the affected taxing agency shall thereafter be allocated only the portion of taxes provided for in subdivision (a) of Section 33670. After receipt of a notice by the official or officials that an affected taxing agency has elected to receive additional tax revenues attributable to only a portion of the increases in the rate of tax, only that portion of the tax revenues shall thereafter be allocated to the affected taxing agency in addition to the portion of taxes allocated pursuant to subdivision (a) of Section 33670, and the remaining portion thereof shall be allocated to the agency.

(e) As used in this section, "affected taxing agency" means and includes every public agency for the benefit of which a tax is levied upon property in the project area, whether levied by the public agency or on its behalf by another public agency.

(f) This section shall apply only to redevelopment projects for which a final redevelopment plan is adopted pursuant to Article 5 (commencing with Section 33360) of Chapter 4 on or after January 1, 1977.

33677 Tax allocation computation for merged project areas

The amount of taxes allocated to the redevelopment agency pursuant to Section 33670 shall be separately computed for each constituent project area merged into a single project area pursuant to Section 33460, and for the original project area and each separate addition of land to the project area made by amendment of the redevelopment plan pursuant to Section 33450. The section is declaratory of existing law with respect to amendments to redevelopment plans.

33677.5 Offset of excess tax revenues

A county auditor shall only offset excess amounts of property tax revenues allocated to a redevelopment project against property tax revenues of that redevelopment project, and not against the property tax revenues of another redevelopment project governed by the same redevelopment agency.

33678 Redevelopment tax increment revenues not deemed proceeds of taxes under Article XIII B

(a) This section implements and fulfills the intent of this article and of Article XIII B and Section 16 of Article XVI of the California Constitution. The allocation and payment to an agency of the portion of taxes specified in subdivision (b) of Section

33670 for the purpose of paying principal of, or interest on, loans, advances, or indebtedness incurred for redevelopment activity, as defined in subdivision (b) of this section, shall not be deemed the receipt by an agency of proceeds of taxes levied by or on behalf of the agency within the meaning or for the purposes of Article XIII B of the California Constitution, nor shall such portion of taxes be deemed receipt of proceeds of taxes by, or an appropriation subject to limitation of, any other public body within the meaning or for purposes of Article XIII B of the California Constitution or any statutory provision enacted in implementation of Article XIII B. The allocation and payment to an agency of this portion of taxes shall not be deemed the appropriation by a redevelopment agency of proceeds of taxes levied by or on behalf of a redevelopment agency within the meaning or for purposes of Article XIII B of the California Constitution.

(b) As used in this section, "redevelopment activity" means either of the following:

(1) Redevelopment meeting all of the following criteria:

(A) Is redevelopment as prescribed in Sections 33020 and 33021.

(B) Primarily benefits the project area.

(C) None of the funds are used for the purpose of paying for employee or contractual services of any local governmental agency unless these services are directly related to the purpose of Sections 33020 and 33021 and the powers established in this part.

(2) Payments authorized by Section 33607.5.

(c) Should any law hereafter enacted, without a vote of the electorate, confer taxing power upon an agency, the exercise of that power by the agency in any fiscal year shall be deemed a transfer of financial responsibility from the community to the agency for that fiscal year within the meaning of subdivision (a) of Section 3 of Article XIII B of the California Constitution.

33679 Use of tax increments to pay for publicly-owned buildings; public hearing requirement

Before an agency commits to use the portion of taxes to be allocated and paid to an agency pursuant to subdivision (b) of Section 33670 for the purpose of paying all or part of the value of the land for, and the cost of the installation and construction of, any publicly owned building, other than parking facilities, the legislative body shall hold a public hearing.

Notice of the time and place of the public hearing shall be published in a newspaper of general circulation in the community for at least two successive weeks prior to the public hearing. There shall be available for public inspection and copying, at a cost not to exceed the cost of duplication, a summary which includes all of the following:

(a) Estimates of the amount of such taxes proposed to be used to pay for such land and construction of any publicly owned building, including interest payments.

(b) Sets forth the facts supporting the determinations required to be made by the legislative body pursuant to Section 33445.

(c) Sets forth the redevelopment purpose for which such taxes are being used to pay for the land and construction of such publicly owned building.

The summary shall be made available to the public for inspection and copying no later than the time of the first publication of the notice of the public hearing.

Article 7
School Finance

33680 Financial assistance to schools; legislative findings and declarations

(a) The Legislature finds and declares that the effectuation of the primary purposes of the Community Redevelopment Law, including job creation, attracting new private commercial investments, the physical and social improvement of residential neighborhoods, and the provision and maintenance of low- and moderate-income housing, is dependent upon the existence of an adequate and financially solvent school system which is capable of providing for the safety and education of students who live within both redevelopment project areas and housing assisted by redevelopment agencies. The attraction of new businesses to redevelopment project areas depends upon the existence of an adequately trained work force, which can only be accomplished if education at the primary and secondary schools is adequate and general education and job training at community colleges is available. The ability of communities to build residential development and attract residents in redevelopment project areas depends upon the existence of adequately maintained and operating schools serving the redevelopment project area. The development and maintenance of low- and moderate-income housing both within redevelopment project areas and throughout the community can only be successful if adequate schools exist to serve the residents of this housing.

(b) Redevelopment agencies have financially assisted schools which benefit and serve the project area by paying part or all of land and the construction of school facilities and other improvements pursuant to the authority in Section 33445. Redevelopment agencies have financially assisted schools to alleviate the financial burden or detriment caused by the establishment of redevelopment project areas pursuant to the authority in Sections 33401 and 33445.5. Funds also have been allocated to schools and community colleges pursuant to the authority in Section 33676.

(c) The Legislature further finds and declares that, because of the reduced funds available to the state to assist schools and community colleges which benefit and serve redevelopment project areas during the 1992–93, 1993–94, and 1994–95 fiscal years, it is necessary for redevelopment agencies to make additional payments to assist the programs and operations of these schools and colleges in order to ensure that the objectives stated in this section can be met. The Legislature further finds and declares that the payments to schools and community college districts pursuant to Section 33681 are of benefit to redevelopment project areas.

(d) The Legislature further finds and declares all of the following:

(1) Because of the reduced funds available to the state to assist schools that benefit and serve redevelopment project areas during the 2008-09 fiscal year, it is necessary for redevelopment agencies to make additional payments to assist the programs and operations of these schools to ensure that the objectives stated in this section can be met.

(2) The payments to schools pursuant to Section 33684 are of benefit to redevelopment project areas.

33681.6 Downtown project areas in charter cities

Notwithstanding any other provision of this article to the contrary, the amount determined pursuant to subparagraphs (A) and (B) of paragraph (2) of subdivision (a) of Section 33681.5 shall not include any tax increment apportioned to the downtown project area of a charter city meeting all of the criteria specified in Section 33608.

33681.7 Educational revenue augmentation fund; 2002–2003 fiscal years; additional allocations

(a) (1) During the 2002–03 fiscal year, a redevelopment agency shall, prior to May 10, remit an amount equal to the amount determined for that agency pursuant to subparagraph (I) of paragraph (2) to the county auditor for deposit in the county's Educational Revenue Augmentation Fund created pursuant to Article 3 (commencing with Section 97) of Chapter 6 of Part 0.5 of Division 1 of the Revenue and Taxation Code.

(2) For the 2002–03 fiscal year, on or before October 1, the Director of Finance shall do all of the following:

(A) Determine the net tax increment apportioned to each agency pursuant to Section 33670, excluding any amounts apportioned to affected taxing agencies pursuant to Section 33401 or 33676, in the 2000–01 fiscal year.

(B) Determine the net tax increment apportioned to all agencies pursuant to Section 33670, excluding any amounts apportioned to affected taxing agencies pursuant to Section 33401 or 33676, in the 2000–01 fiscal year.

(C) Determine a percentage factor by dividing thirty-seven million five hundred thousand dollars ($37,500,000) by the amount determined pursuant to subparagraph (B).

(D) Determine an amount for each agency by multiplying the amount determined pursuant to subparagraph (A) by the percentage factor determined pursuant to subparagraph (C).

(E) Determine the total amount of property tax revenue apportioned to each agency pursuant to Section 33670, including any amounts apportioned to affected taxing agencies pursuant to Section 33401 or 33676, in the 2000–01 fiscal year.

(F) Determine the total amount of property tax revenue apportioned to all agencies pursuant to Section 33670, including any amounts apportioned to affected taxing agencies pursuant to Section 33401 or 33676, in the 2000–01 fiscal year.

(G) Determine a percentage factor by dividing thirty-seven million five hundred thousand dollars ($37,500,000) by the amount determined pursuant to subparagraph (F).

(H) Determine an amount for each agency by multiplying the amount determined pursuant to subparagraph (E) by the percentage factor determined pursuant to subparagraph (G).

(I) Add the amount determined pursuant to subparagraph (D) to the amount determined pursuant to subparagraph (H).

(J) Notify each agency and each legislative body of the amount determined pursuant to subparagraph (I).

(K) Notify each county auditor of the amounts determined pursuant to subparagraph (I) for each agency in his or her county.

(b) (1) Notwithstanding Sections 33334.2, 33334.3, and 33334.6, and any other provision of law, in order to make the full allocation required by this section, an agency may borrow up to 50 percent of the amount required to be allocated to the Low and Moderate Income Housing Fund pursuant to Sections 33334.2, 33334.3, and 33334.6 during the 2002–03 fiscal year, unless executed contracts exist that would be impaired if the agency reduced the amount allocated to the Low and Moderate Income Housing Fund pursuant to the authority of this subdivision.

(2) As a condition of borrowing pursuant to this subdivision, an agency shall make a finding that there are insufficient other moneys to meet the requirements of subdivision (a). Funds borrowed pursuant to this subdivision shall be repaid in full within 10 years following the date on which moneys were borrowed.

(c) In order to make the allocation required by this section, an agency may use any funds that are legally available and not legally obligated for other uses, including, but not limited to, reserve funds, proceeds of land sales, proceeds of bonds or other indebtedness, lease revenues, interest, and other earned income. No moneys held in a low- and moderate-income fund as of July 1 of that fiscal year may be used for this purpose.

(d) The legislative body shall by March 1 report to the county auditor as to how the agency intends to fund the allocation required by this section.

(e) The allocation obligations imposed by this section, including amounts owed, if any, created under this section, are hereby declared to be an indebtedness of the redevelopment project to which they relate, payable from taxes allocated to the agency pursuant to Section 33670, and shall constitute an indebtedness of the agency with respect to the redevelopment project until paid in full.

(f) It is the intent of the Legislature, in enacting this section, that these allocations directly or indirectly assist in the financing or refinancing, in whole or in part, of the community's redevelopment projects pursuant to Section 16 of Article XVI of the California Constitution.

(g) In making the determinations required by subdivision (a), the Director of Finance shall use those amounts reported as the "Tax Increment Retained by Agency" for all agencies and for each agency in Table 7 of the 2000–01 fiscal year Controller's State of California Community Redevelopment Agencies Annual Report.

(h) If revised reports have been accepted by the Controller on or before January 1, 2003, the Director of Finance shall use appropriate data that has been certified by the Controller for the purpose of making the determinations required by subdivision (a).

33681.8 Deferral of additional allocations; educational revenue augmentation fund; 2002–2003 fiscal years

(a) (1) For the purposes of this section, "existing indebtedness" means one or more of the following obligations incurred by a redevelopment agency prior to the effective date of this section, the payment of which is to be made in whole or in part, directly or indirectly, out of taxes allocated to the agency pursuant to Section 33670, and that is required by law or provision of the existing indebtedness to be made during the fiscal year of the relevant allocation required by Section 33681.7:

(A) Bonds, notes, interim certificates, debentures, or other obligations issued by the agency, whether funded, refunded, assumed, or otherwise, pursuant to Article 5 (commencing with Section 33640).

(B) Loans or moneys advanced to the agency, including, but not limited to, loans from federal, state, or local agencies, or a private entity.

(C) A contractual obligation that, if breached, could subject the agency to damages or other liabilities or remedies.

(D) An obligation incurred pursuant to Section 33445.

(E) Indebtedness incurred pursuant to Section 33334.2.

(F) An amount, to be expended for the operation and administration of the agency, that may not exceed 90 percent of the amount spent for those purposes in the 2000–01 fiscal year.

(G) Obligations imposed by law with respect to activities that occurred prior to the effective date of the act that adds this section.

(2) Existing indebtedness incurred prior to the effective date of this section may be refinanced, refunded, or restructured after that date, and shall remain existing indebtedness for the purposes of this section, if the annual debt service during that fiscal year does not increase over the prior fiscal year and the refinancing does not reduce the ability of the agency to make the payment required by subdivision (a) of Section 33681.7.

(3) For the purposes of this section, indebtedness shall be deemed to be incurred prior to the effective date of this section if the agency has entered into a binding contract subject to normal marketing conditions, to deliver the indebtedness, or if the redevelopment agency has received bids for the sale of the indebtedness prior to that date and the indebtedness is issued for value and evidence thereof is delivered to the initial purchaser no later than 30 days after the date of the contract or sale.

(b) During the 2002–03 fiscal year, an agency that has adopted a resolution pursuant to subdivision (c) may, pursuant to subdivision (a) of Section 33681.7, allocate to the auditor less than the amount required by subdivision (a) of Section 33681.7, if the agency finds that either of the following has occurred:

(1) That the difference between the amount allocated to the agency and the amount required by subdivision (a) of Section 33681.7 is necessary to make payments on existing indebtedness that are due or required to be committed, set aside, or reserved by the agency during the applicable fiscal year and that are used by the agency for that purpose, and the agency has no other funds that can be used to pay this existing indebtedness, and no other feasible method to reduce or avoid this indebtedness.

(2) The agency has no other funds to make the allocation required by subdivision (a) of Section 33681.7.

(c) (1) Any agency that, pursuant to subdivision (b), allocates to the auditor less than the amount required by subdivision (a) of Section 33681.7 shall adopt, prior to December 31, 2002, after a noticed public hearing, a resolution that lists all of the following:

(A) Each existing indebtedness incurred prior to the effective date of this section.

(B) Each indebtedness on which a payment is required to be made during the 2002–03 fiscal year.

(C) The amount of each payment, the time when it is required to be paid, and the total of the payments required to be made during the 2002–03 fiscal year. For indebtedness that bears interest at a variable rate, or for short-term indebtedness that is maturing during the fiscal year and that is expected to be refinanced, the amount of payments during the fiscal year shall be estimated by the agency.

(2) The information contained in the resolution required by this subdivision shall be reviewed for accuracy by the chief fiscal officer of the agency.

(3) The legislative body shall additionally adopt the resolution required by this section.

(d) (1) Any agency that, pursuant to subdivision (b), determines that it will be unable in the 2002–03 fiscal year, to allocate the full amount required by subdivision (a) of Section 33681.7 shall, subject to paragraph (3), enter into an agreement with the legislative body by February 15, 2003, to fund the payment of the difference between the full amount required to be paid pursuant to subdivision (a) of Section 33681.7 and the amount available for allocation by the agency.

(2) The obligations imposed by paragraph (1) are hereby declared to be indebtedness incurred by the redevelopment agency to finance a portion of a redevelopment project within the meaning of Section 16 of Article XVI of the California Constitution. This indebtedness shall be payable from tax revenues allocated to the agency pursuant to Section 33670, and any other funds received by the agency. The obligations imposed by paragraph (1) shall remain an indebtedness of the agency to the legislative body until paid in full, or until the agency and the legislative body otherwise agree.

(3) The agreement described in paragraph (1) shall be subject to these terms and conditions specified in a written agreement between the legislative body and the agency.

(e) If the agency fails, under either Section 33681.7 or subdivision (d), to transmit the full amount of funds required by Section 33681.7, is precluded by court order from transmitting that amount, or is otherwise unable to meet its full obligation pursuant to Section 33681.7, the county auditor, by no later than May 15, 2003, shall transfer any amount necessary to meet the obligation determined for that agency in subparagraph (D) of paragraph (2) of subdivision (a) of Section 33681.7 from the legislative body's property tax allocation pursuant to Chapter 6 (commencing with Section 95) of Part 0.5 of Division 1 of the Revenue and Taxation Code.

33681.9 Allocations to the educational revenue augmentation fund 2003–04

(a) (1) During the 2003–04 fiscal year, a redevelopment agency shall, prior to May 10, remit an amount equal to the amount determined for that agency pursuant to subparagraph (I) of paragraph (2) to the county auditor for deposit in the county's Educational Revenue Augmentation Fund created pursuant to Article 3 (commencing with Section 97) of Chapter 6 of Part 0.5 of Division 1 of the Revenue and Taxation Code.

(2) For the 2003–04 fiscal year, on or before October 1, the Director of Finance shall do all of the following:

(A) Determine the net tax increment apportioned to each agency pursuant to Section 33670, excluding any amounts apportioned to affected taxing agencies pursuant to Section 33401, 33607.5, or 33676, in the 2001–02 fiscal year.

(B) Determine the net tax increment apportioned to all agencies pursuant to Section 33670, excluding any amounts apportioned to affected taxing agencies pursuant to Section 33401, 33607.5, or 33676, in the 2001–02 fiscal year.

(C) Determine a percentage factor by dividing sixty-seven million five hundred thousand dollars ($67,500,000) by the amount determined pursuant to subparagraph (B).

(D) Determine an amount for each agency by multiplying the amount determined pursuant to subparagraph (A) by the percentage factor determined pursuant to subparagraph (C).

(E) Determine the total amount of property tax revenue apportioned to each agency pursuant to Section 33670, including any amounts apportioned to affected taxing agencies pursuant to Section 33401, 33607.5, or 33676, in the 2001–02 fiscal year.

(F) Determine the total amount of property tax revenue apportioned to all agencies pursuant to Section 33670, including any amounts apportioned to affected taxing agencies pursuant to Section 33401, 33607.5, or 33676, in the 2001–02 fiscal year.

(G) Determine a percentage factor by dividing sixty-seven million five hundred thousand dollars ($67,500,000) by the amount determined pursuant to subparagraph (F).

(H) Determine an amount for each agency by multiplying the amount determined pursuant to subparagraph (E) by the percentage factor determined pursuant to subparagraph (G).

(I) Add the amount determined pursuant to subparagraph (D) to the amount determined pursuant to subparagraph (H).

(J) Notify each agency and each legislative body of the amount determined pursuant to subparagraph (I).

(K) Notify each county auditor of the amounts determined pursuant to subparagraph (I) for each agency in his or her county.

(b) (1) Notwithstanding Sections 33334.2, 33334.3, and 33334.6, and any other provision of law, in order to make the full allocation required by this section, an agency may borrow up to 50 percent of the amount required to be allocated to the Low and Moderate Income Housing Fund pursuant to Sections 33334.2, 33334.3, and 33334.6 during the 2003–04 fiscal year, unless executed contracts exist that would be impaired if the agency reduced the amount allocated to the Low and Moderate Income Housing Fund pursuant to the authority of this subdivision.

(2) As a condition of borrowing pursuant to this subdivision, an agency shall make a finding that there are insufficient other moneys to meet the requirements of subdivision (a). Funds borrowed pursuant to this subdivision shall be repaid in full within 10 years following the date on which moneys were borrowed.

(c) In order to make the allocation required by this section, an agency may use any funds that are legally available and not legally obligated for other uses, including, but not limited to, reserve funds, proceeds of land sales, proceeds of bonds or other indebtedness, lease revenues, interest, and other earned income. No moneys held in a low- and moderate-income fund as of July 1 of that fiscal year may be used for this purpose.

(d) The legislative body shall by March 1 report to the county auditor as to how the agency intends to fund the allocation required by this section, or that the legislative body intends to remit the amount in lieu of the agency pursuant to Section 33681.11.

(e) The allocation obligations imposed by this section, including amounts owed, if any, created under this section, are hereby declared to be an indebtedness of the redevelopment project to which they relate, payable from taxes allocated to the agency pursuant to Section 33670, and shall constitute an indebtedness of the agency with respect to the redevelopment project until paid in full.

(f) It is the intent of the Legislature, in enacting this section, that these allocations directly or indirectly assist in the financing or refinancing, in whole or in part, of the community's redevelopment projects pursuant to Section 16 of Article XVI of the California Constitution.

(g) In making the determinations required by subdivision (a), the Director of Finance shall use those amounts reported as the "Tax Increment Retained by Agency" for all agencies and for each agency in Table 7 of the 2001–02 fiscal year Controller's State of California Community Redevelopment Agencies Annual Report.

(h) If revised reports have been accepted by the Controller on or before January 1, 2004, the Director of Finance shall use appropriate data that has been certified by the Controller for the purpose of making the determinations required by subdivision (a).

33681.10 Educational revenue augmentation fund during 2003–04— existing indebtedness defined

(a) (1) For the purposes of this section, "existing indebtedness" means one or more of the following obligations incurred by a redevelopment agency prior to the effective date of this section, the payment of which is to be made in whole or in part, directly or indirectly, out of taxes allocated to the agency pursuant to Section 33670, and that is required by law or provision of the existing indebtedness to be made during the fiscal year of the relevant allocation required by Section 33681.9:

(A) Bonds, notes, interim certificates, debentures, or other obligations issued by the agency, whether funded, refunded, assumed, or otherwise, pursuant to Article 5 (commencing with Section 33640).

(B) Loans or moneys advanced to the agency, including, but not limited to, loans from federal, state, or local agencies, or a private entity.

(C) A contractual obligation that, if breached, could subject the agency to damages or other liabilities or remedies.

(D) An obligation incurred pursuant to Section 33445.

(E) Indebtedness incurred pursuant to Section 33334.2.

(F) An amount, to be expended for the operation and administration of the agency, that may not exceed 90 percent of the amount spent for those purposes in the 2001–02 fiscal year.

(G) Obligations imposed by law with respect to activities that occurred prior to the effective date of the act that adds this section.

(2) Existing indebtedness incurred prior to the effective date of this section may be refinanced, refunded, or restructured after that date, and shall remain existing indebtedness for the purposes of this section, if the annual debt service during that fiscal year does not increase over the prior fiscal year and the refinancing does not reduce the ability of the agency to make the payment required by subdivision (a) of Section 33681.9.

(3) For the purposes of this section, indebtedness shall be deemed to be incurred prior to the effective date of this section if the agency has entered into a binding contract subject to normal marketing conditions, to deliver the indebtedness, or if the redevelopment agency has received bids for the sale of the indebtedness prior to that date and the indebtedness is issued for value and evidence thereof is delivered to the initial purchaser no later than 30 days after the date of the contract or sale.

(b) During the 2003–04 fiscal year, an agency that has adopted a resolution pursuant to subdivision (c) may, pursuant to subdivision (a) of Section 33681.9, allocate to the auditor less than the amount required by subdivision (a) of Section 33681.9, if the agency finds that either of the following has occurred:

(1) That the difference between the amount allocated to the agency and the amount required by subdivision (a) of Section 33681.9 is necessary to make payments on existing indebtedness that are due or required to be committed, set aside, or reserved by the agency during the applicable fiscal year and that are used by the agency for that purpose, and the agency has no other funds that can be used to pay this existing indebtedness, and no other feasible method to reduce or avoid this indebtedness.

(2) The agency has no other funds to make the allocation required by subdivision (a) of Section 33681.9.

(c) (1) Any agency that, pursuant to subdivision (b), intends to allocate to the auditor less than the amount required by subdivision (a) of Section 33681.9 shall adopt, prior to December 31, 2003, after a noticed public hearing, a resolution that lists all of the following:

(A) Each existing indebtedness incurred prior to the effective date of this section.

(B) Each indebtedness on which a payment is required to be made during the 2003–04 fiscal year.

(C) The amount of each payment, the time when it is required to be paid, and the total of the payments required to be made during the 2003–04 fiscal year. For indebtedness that bears interest at a variable rate, or for short-term indebtedness that is maturing during the fiscal year and that is expected to be refinanced, the amount of payments during the fiscal year shall be estimated by the agency.

(2) The information contained in the resolution required by this subdivision shall be reviewed for accuracy by the chief fiscal officer of the agency.

(3) The legislative body shall additionally adopt the resolution required by this section.

(d) (1) Any agency that, pursuant to subdivision (b), determines that it will be unable in the 2003–04 fiscal year, to allocate the full amount required by subdivision (a) of Section 33681.9 shall, subject to paragraph (3), enter into an agreement with the legislative body by February 15, 2004, to fund the payment of the difference between the full amount required to be paid pursuant to subdivision (a) of Section 33681.9 and the amount available for allocation by the agency.

(2) The obligations imposed by paragraph (1) are hereby declared to be indebtedness incurred by the redevelopment agency to finance a portion of a redevelopment project within the meaning of Section 16 of Article XVI of the California Constitution. This indebtedness shall be payable from tax revenues allocated to the agency pursuant to Section 33670, and any other funds received by the agency. The obligations imposed by paragraph (1) shall remain an indebtedness of the agency to the legislative body until paid in full, or until the agency and the legislative body otherwise agree.

(3) The agreement described in paragraph (1) shall be subject to these terms and conditions specified in a written agreement between the legislative body and the agency.

(e) If the agency fails, under either Section 33681.9 or subdivision (d), to transmit the full amount of funds required by Section 33681.9, is precluded by court order from transmitting that amount, or is otherwise unable to meet its full obligation pursuant to Section 33681.9, the county auditor, by no later than May 15, 2004, shall transfer any amount necessary to meet the obligation determined for that agency in paragraph (1) of subdivision (c) of Section 33681.9 from the legislative body's property tax allocation pursuant to Chapter 6 (commencing with Section 95) of Part 0.5 of Division 1 of the Revenue and Taxation Code.

33681.11 Inability to make payments to educational revenue augmentation fund during 2003–04 — Legislative body to make payment

(a) In lieu of the remittance required by Section 33681.9, during the 2003–04 fiscal year, a legislative body may, prior to May 10, 2004, remit an amount equal to the amount determined for the agency pursuant to subparagraph (I) of paragraph (2) of subdivision (a) of Section 33681.9 to the county auditor for deposit in the county's Educational Revenue Augmentation Fund created pursuant to Article 3 (commencing with Section 97) of Chapter 6 of Part 0.5 of Division 1 of the Revenue and Taxation Code.

(b) The legislative body may make the remittance authorized by this section from any funds that are legally available for this purpose. No moneys held in an agency's Low and Moderate Income Housing Fund shall be used for this purpose.

(c) If the legislative body, pursuant to subdivision (d) of Section 33681.9, reported to the county auditor that it intended to remit the amount in lieu of the agency and the legislative body fails to transmit the full amount as authorized by this section by May 10, 2004, the county auditor, no later than May 15, 2004, shall transfer an amount necessary to meet the obligation from the legislative body's property tax allocation pursuant to Chapter 6 (commencing with Section 95) of Part 0.5 of Division 1 of the Revenue and Taxation Code. If the amount of the legislative body's property tax allocation is not sufficient to meet this obligation, the county auditor shall transfer an additional amount necessary to meet this obligation from the property tax increment revenue apportioned to the agency pursuant to Section 33670, provided that no moneys allocated to the agency's Low and Moderate Income Housing Fund shall be used for this purpose.

33681.12 Allocations to the educational revenue augmentation fund 2004–05 and 2005–06

(a) (1) During the 2004-05 fiscal year, a redevelopment agency shall, prior to May 10, remit an amount equal to the amount determined for that agency pursuant to subparagraph (I) of paragraph (2) to the county auditor for deposit in the county's Educational Revenue Augmentation Fund created pursuant to Article 3 (commencing with Section 97) of Chapter 6 of Part 0.5 of Division 1 of the Revenue and Taxation Code. During the 2005-06 fiscal year, a redevelopment agency shall, prior to May 10, remit an amount equal to the amount determined for that agency pursuant to subparagraph (I) of paragraph (2) to the county auditor for deposit in the county's Educational Revenue Augmentation Fund created pursuant to Article 3 (commencing with Section 97) of Chapter 6 of Part 0.5 of Division 1 of the Revenue and Taxation Code.

(2) For the 2004-05 and 2005-06 fiscal years, on or before November 15, the Director of Finance shall do all of the following:

(A) Determine the net tax increment apportioned to each agency pursuant to Section 33670, excluding any amounts apportioned to affected taxing agencies pursuant to Section 33401, 33607.5, or 33676.

(B) Determine the net tax increment apportioned to all agencies pursuant to Section 33670, excluding any amounts apportioned to affected taxing agencies pursuant to Section 33401, 33607.5, or 33676.

(C) Determine a percentage factor by dividing one hundred twenty-five million dollars ($125,000,000) by the amount determined pursuant to subparagraph (B).

(D) Determine an amount for each agency by multiplying the amount determined pursuant to subparagraph (A) by the percentage factor determined pursuant to subparagraph (C).

(E) Determine the total amount of property tax revenue apportioned to each agency pursuant to Section 33670, including any amounts apportioned to affected taxing agencies pursuant to Section 33401, 33607.5, or 33676.

(F) Determine the total amount of property tax revenue apportioned to all agencies pursuant to Section 33670, including any amounts apportioned to affected taxing agencies pursuant to Section 33401, 33607.5, or 33676.

(G) Determine a percentage factor by dividing one hundred twenty-five million dollars ($125,000,000) by the amount determined pursuant to subparagraph (F).

(H) Determine an amount for each agency by multiplying the amount determined pursuant to subparagraph (E) by the percentage factor determined pursuant to subparagraph (G).

(I) Add the amount determined pursuant to subparagraph (D) to the amount determined pursuant to subparagraph (H).

(J) Notify each agency and each legislative body of the amount determined pursuant to subparagraph (I).

(K) Notify each county auditor of the amounts determined pursuant to subparagraph (I) for each agency in his or her county.

(3) The obligation of any agency to make the payments required pursuant to this subdivision shall be subordinate to the lien of any pledge of collateral securing, directly or indirectly, the payment of the principal, or interest on any bonds of the agency including, without limitation, bonds secured by a pledge of taxes allocated to the agency pursuant to Section 33670.

(b) (1) Notwithstanding Sections 33334.2, 33334.3, and 33334.6, and any other provision of law, in order to make the full allocation required by this section, an agency may borrow up to 50 percent of the amount required to be allocated to the Low and Moderate Income Housing Fund pursuant to Sections 33334.2, 33334.3, and 33334.6 during the 2004-05 fiscal year and, if applicable, the 2005-06 fiscal year, unless executed contracts exist that would be impaired if the agency reduced the amount allocated to the Low and Moderate Income Housing Fund pursuant to the authority of this subdivision.

(2) As a condition of borrowing pursuant to this subdivision, an agency shall make a finding that there are insufficient other moneys to meet the requirements of subdivision (a). Funds borrowed pursuant to this subdivision shall be repaid in full within 10 years following the date on which moneys are remitted to the county auditor for deposit in the county's Educational Revenue Augmentation Fund pursuant to subdivision (a).

(c) In order to make the allocation required by this section, an agency may use any funds that are legally available and not legally obligated for other uses, including, but not limited to, reserve funds, proceeds of land sales, proceeds of bonds or other indebtedness, lease revenues, interest, and other earned income. No moneys held in a low- and moderate-income fund as of July 1 of the applicable fiscal year may be used for this purpose.

(d) The legislative body shall by March 1 report to the county auditor as to how the agency intends to fund the allocation required by this section, or that the legislative body intends to remit the amount in lieu of the agency pursuant to Section 33681.14.

(e) The allocation obligations imposed by this section, including amounts owed, if any, created under this section, are hereby declared to be an indebtedness of the redevelopment project to which they relate, payable from taxes allocated to the agency pursuant to Section 33670, and shall constitute an indebtedness of the agency with respect to the redevelopment project until paid in full.

(f) It is the intent of the Legislature, in enacting this section, that these allocations directly or indirectly assist in the financing or refinancing, in whole or in part, of the community's redevelopment project pursuant to Section 16 of Article XVI of the California Constitution.

(g) In making the determinations required by subdivision (a), the Director of Finance shall use those amounts reported as the "Tax Increment Retained by Agency" for all agencies and for each agency in the most recent published edition of the Controller's Community Redevelopment Agencies Annual Report made pursuant to Section 12463.3 of the Government Code.

(h) If revised reports have been accepted by the Controller on or before September 1, 2005, the Director of Finance shall use appropriate data that has been certified by the Controller for the purpose of making the determinations required by subdivision (a).

(i) (1) Notwithstanding any other provision of law, a county redevelopment agency may enter into a loan agreement with the legislative body to have the agency remit to the county's Educational Revenue Augmentation Fund for each of the 2004–05 and 2005–06 fiscal years an amount greater than that determined pursuant to subparagraph (I) of paragraph (2) of subdivision (a) if all of the following conditions are met:

(A) The agency does not exercise its authority under subdivision (b) to borrow from its Low and Moderate Income Housing Fund to finance its payments to the county's Educational Revenue Augmentation Fund.

(B) The agency does not have any outstanding loans from its Low and Moderate Income Housing Fund that were made under subdivision (b) of Section 33981.5, subdivision (b) of Section 33681.7, or subdivision (b) of Section 33681.9.

(C) The loan agreement requires the county to repay any excess remitted amounts, including interest, to the agency within three fiscal years subsequent to the fiscal year in which the loan is made.

(D) The agency making the loan does not participate in pooled borrowing under Section 33681.15.

(2) A loan agreement described in paragraph (1) shall be transmitted to the county auditor not later than December 1 of the fiscal year in which the loan is made. Any amount remitted by the agency to the county Educational Revenue Augmentation Fund for the 2004–05 or 2005–06 fiscal year in excess of the amount determined pursuant to paragraph (1) of subdivision (a) shall be credited to the amount that would otherwise be subtracted by the county auditor pursuant to subdivision (a) of Section 97.71 of the Revenue and Taxation Code for, as applicable, the 2004–05 and 2005–06 fiscal years.

(3) Notwithstanding subparagraph (C) of paragraph (1), a county redevelopment agency and a legislative body that have entered into a loan agreement under paragraph (1) may, by mutual consent, adopt either or both of the following modifications to that agreement:

(A) The repayment period may be extended, but the full repayment shall be completed no later than June 30, 2021.

(B) The repayment obligation may be offset by the amount of any expenditures by the county for capital improvements or deferred maintenance that substantially benefit any or all of the redevelopment project areas of the redevelopment agency if the agency approves the expenditure and the agency adopts a finding that the expenditure furthers the goals and objectives of the agency's redevelopment plan or plans.

33681.13 Inability to make payments to education revenue augmentation funds during 2004-05 and 2005-06; *existing indebtedness* defined

(a) (1) For the purpose of this section, "existing indebtedness" means one or more of the following obligations incurred by a redevelopment agency prior to the effective date of this section, the payment of which is to be made in whole or in part, directly or indirectly, out of taxes allocated to the agency pursuant to Section 33670, and that is required by law or provision of the existing indebtedness to be made during the fiscal year of the relevant allocation required by Section 33681.12.

(A) Bonds, notes, interim certificates, debentures, or other obligations issued by the agency whether funded, refunded, assumed, or otherwise pursuant to Article 5 (commencing with Section 33640).

(B) Loans or moneys advanced to the agency, including, but not limited to, loans from federal, state, or local agencies, or a private entity.

(C) A contractual obligation that, if breached, could subject the agency to damages or other liabilities or remedies.

(D) An obligation incurred pursuant to Section 33445.

(E) Indebtedness incurred pursuant to Section 33334.2.

(F) An amount, to be expended for the operation and administration of the agency, that may not exceed 90 percent of the amount spent for those purposes in the 2002-03 fiscal year.

(G) Obligations imposed by law with respect to activities that occurred prior to the effective date of the act that adds this section.

(2) Existing indebtedness incurred prior to the effective date of this section may be refinanced, refunded, or restructured after that date, and shall remain existing indebtedness for the purposes of this section, if the annual debt service during that fiscal year does not increase over the prior fiscal year and the refinancing does not reduce the ability of the agency to make the payment required by subdivision (a) of Section 33681.12.

(3) For the purposes of this section, indebtedness shall be deemed to be incurred prior to the effective date of this section if the agency has entered into a binding contract subject to normal marketing conditions, to deliver the indebtedness, or if the redevelopment agency has received bids for the sale of the indebtedness prior to that date and the indebtedness is issued for value and evidence thereof is delivered to the initial purchaser no later than 30 days after the date of the contract or sale.

(b) During the 2004-05 and 2005-06 fiscal years, an agency that has adopted a resolution pursuant to subdivision (c) may, pursuant to subdivision (a) of Section 33681.12, allocate to the auditor less than the amount required by subdivision (a) of Section 33681.12, if the agency finds that either of the following has occurred:

(1) That the difference between the amount allocated to the agency and the amount required by subdivision (a) of Section 33681.12 is necessary to make payments on existing indebtedness that are due or required to be committed, set aside, or reserved by the agency during the applicable fiscal year and that are used by the agency for that purpose, and the agency has no other funds that can be used to pay this existing indebtedness, and no other feasible method to reduce or avoid this indebtedness.

(2) The agency has no other funds to make the allocation required by subdivision (a) of Section 33681.12.

(c) (1) Any agency that, pursuant to subdivision (b), intends to allocate to the auditor less than the amount required by subdivision (a) of Section 33681.12 shall adopt, prior to December 31 of the applicable fiscal year, after a noticed public hearing, a resolution that lists all of the following:

(A) Each existing indebtedness incurred prior to the effective date of this section.

(B) Each indebtedness on which a payment is required to be made during the applicable fiscal year.

(C) The amount of each payment, the time when it is required to be paid, and the total of the payments required to be made during the applicable fiscal year. For indebtedness that bears interest at a variable rate, or for short-term indebtedness that is maturing during the fiscal year and that is expected to be refinanced, the amount of payments during the fiscal year shall be estimated by the agency.

(2) The information contained in the resolution required by this subdivision shall be reviewed for accuracy by the chief fiscal officer of the agency.

(3) The legislative body shall additionally adopt the resolution required by this section.

(d) (1) Any agency that, pursuant to subdivision (b), determines that it will be unable either in the 2004-05 or the 2005-06 fiscal year, to allocate the full amount required by subdivision (a) of Section 33681.12 shall, subject to paragraph (3), enter into an agreement with the legislative body by February 15 of the applicable fiscal year, to fund the payment of the difference between the full amount required to be paid pursuant to subdivision (a) of Section 33681.12 and the amount available for allocation by the agency.

(2) The obligations imposed by paragraph (1) are hereby declared to be indebtedness incurred by the redevelopment agency to finance a portion of a redevelopment project within the meaning of Section 16 of Article XVI of the California Constitution. This indebtedness shall be payable from tax revenues allocated to the agency pursuant to Section 33670, and any other funds received by the agency. The obligations imposed by paragraph (1) shall remain an indebtedness of the agency to the legislative body until paid in full, or until the agency and the legislative body otherwise agree.

(3) The agreement described in paragraph (1) shall be subject to these terms and conditions specified in a written agreement between the legislative body and the agency.

(e) If the agency fails, under either Section 33681.12 or subdivision (d), to transmit the full amount of funds required by Section 33681.12, is precluded by court order from transmitting that amount, or is otherwise unable to meet its full obligation pursuant to Section 33681.12, the county auditor, by no later than May 15 of the applicable fiscal year, shall transfer any amount necessary to meet the obligation determined for that agency in paragraph (1) of subdivision (c) of Section 33681.12 from the legislative body's allocations pursuant to Chapter 6 (commencing with Section 95) of Part 0.5 of Division 1 of the Revenue and Taxation Code.

33681.14 Inability to make payments to educational revenue augmentation fund during 2004–05 and 2005–06— Legislative body to make payment

(a) In lieu of the remittance required by Section 33681.12, during either the 2004–05 or 2005–06 fiscal year, a legislative body may, prior to May 10 of the applicable fiscal year, remit an amount equal to the amount determined for the agency pursuant to subparagraph (I) of paragraph (2) of subdivision (a) of Section 33681.12 to the county auditor for deposit in the county's Educational Revenue Augmentation Fund created pursuant to Article 3 (commencing with Section 97) of Chapter 6 of Part 0.5 of Division 1 of the Revenue and Taxation Code.

(b) The legislative body may make the remittance authorized by this section from any funds that are legally available for this purpose. No moneys held in an agency's Low and Moderate Income Housing Fund shall be used for this purpose.

(c) If the legislative body, pursuant to subdivision (d) of Section 33681.12, reported to the county auditor that it intended to remit the amount in lieu of the agency and the legislative body fails to transmit the full amount as authorized by this section by May 10 of the applicable fiscal year, the county auditor, no later than May 15 of the applicable fiscal year, shall transfer an amount necessary to meet the obligation from the legislative body's allocations pursuant to Chapter 6 (commencing with Section 95) of Part 0.5 of Division 1 of the Revenue and Taxation Code. If the amount of the legislative body's allocations are not sufficient to meet this obligation, the county auditor shall transfer an additional amount necessary to meet this obligation from the property tax increment revenue apportioned to the agency pursuant to Section 33670, provided that no moneys allocated to the agency's Low and Moderate Income Housing Fund shall be used for this purpose.

33681.15 Loans to agencies unable to make payments required by Section 33681.12; authorized issuer defined

(a) For the purposes of this section, an "authorized issuer" is limited to a joint powers entity created pursuant to Article 1 (commencing with Section 6500) of Chapter 5 of Division 7 of Title 1 of the Government Code that consists of no less than 100 local agencies issuing bonds pursuant to the Marks-Roos Local Bond Pooling Act of 1984 (commencing with Section 6584) of the Government Code.

(b) An authorized issuer may issue bonds, notes, or other evidence of indebtedness to provide net proceeds to make one or more loans to one or more redevelopment agencies to be used by the agency to timely make the payment required by Section 33681.12.

(c) With the prior approval of the legislative body by adoption of a resolution by a majority of that body that recites that a first lien on the property tax revenues allocated to the legislative body will be created in accordance with subdivision (h), an agency may enter into an agreement with an authorized issuer issuing bonds pursuant to subdivision (b) to repay a loan used to make the payment required by Section 33681.12, notwithstanding the expiration of the time limit on establishing loans, advances, advances and indebtedness, and the time limit on repayment of indebtedness. For the purpose of calculating the amount that has been divided and allocated to the redevelopment agency to determine whether the limitation adopted pursuant to Section 33333.2 or 33333.4 or pursuant to an agreement or court order has been reached, any funds used to repay a loan entered into pursuant to this section shall be deducted from the amount of property tax revenue deemed to have been received by the agency.

(d) A loan made pursuant to this section shall be repayable by the agency from any available funds of the agency not otherwise obligated for other uses and shall be repayable by the agency on a basis subordinate to all existing and future obligations of the agency.

(e) Upon making a loan to an agency pursuant to this section, the trustee for the bonds issued to provide the funds to make the loan shall timely pay, on behalf of the agency, to the county auditor of the county in which the agency is located the net proceeds (after payment of costs of issuance, credit enhancement costs, and reserves, if any) of the loan in payment in full or in part, as directed by the agency, of the amount required to be paid by the agency pursuant to Section 33681.12 and shall provide the county auditor with the repayment schedule for the loan, together with the name of the trustee.

(f) In the event the agency shall, at any time and from time to time, fail to repay timely the loan in accordance with the schedule provided to the county auditor, the trustee for the bonds shall promptly notify the county auditor of the amount of the payment on the loan that is past due.

(g) The county auditor shall reallocate from the legislative body and shall pay, on behalf of the agency, the past due amount from the first available proceeds of the property tax allocation that would otherwise be transferred to the legislative body pursuant to Chapter 6 (commencing with Section 95) of Part 0.5 of Division 1 of the Revenue and Taxation Code. This transfer shall be deemed a reallocation of the property tax revenue from the legislative body to the agency for the purpose of payment of the loan, and not as a payment by the legislative body on the loan.

(h) To secure repayment of a loan to an agency made pursuant to this section, the trustee for the bonds issued to provide the funds to make the loan shall have a lien on the property tax revenues allocated to the legislative body pursuant to Chapter 6 (commencing with Section 95) of Part 0.5 of Division 1 of the Revenue and Taxation Code. This lien shall arise by operation of this section automatically upon the making of the loan without the need for any action on the part of any person. This lien shall be valid, binding, perfected, and enforceable against the legislative body, its successors, creditors, purchasers, and all others asserting rights in those property tax revenues, irrespective of whether those persons have notice of the lien, irrespective of the fact that the property tax revenues subject to the lien may be commingled with other property, and without the need for physical delivery, recordation, public notice, or any other act. This lien shall be a first priority lien on these property tax revenues. This lien shall not apply to any portion of the property taxes allocated to the agency pursuant to Section 33670.

33682 Inability to make payments to educational revenue augmentation funds during 1992–93; existing indebtedness defined

(a) (1) For the purposes of this section, "existing indebtedness" means one or more of the following obligations incurred by a redevelopment agency prior to the effective date of the statute that adds this chapter, the payment of which is to be made in whole or in part, directly or indirectly, out of taxes allocated to the agency pursuant to Section 33670, and which is required by law or provision of the existing indebtedness to be made during the 1992–93 fiscal year:

(A) Bonds, notes, interim certificates, debentures, or other obligations issued by an agency (whether funded, refunded, assumed, or otherwise) pursuant to Article 5 (commencing with Section 33640).

(B) Loans or moneys advanced to the agency, including, but not limited to, loans from federal, state, or local agencies, or a private entity.

(C) A contractual obligation which, if breached, could subject the agency to damages or other liabilities or remedies.

(D) An obligation incurred pursuant to Section 33445.

(E) Indebtedness incurred pursuant to Section 33334.2.

(F) An amount, to be expended for the operation and administration of the agency, which may not exceed 90 percent of the amount spent for those purposes in the 1991–92 fiscal year.

(G) Obligations imposed by law with respect to activities which occurred prior to the effective date of the act that adds this chapter.

(2) Existing indebtedness incurred prior to the effective date of the statute that adds this article may be refinanced, refunded, or restructured after that date, and shall remain existing indebtedness for the purposes of this section, if the annual debt service during the 1992–93 fiscal year does not increase and the refinancing does not reduce the ability of the agency to make the payment required by subdivision (a) of Section 33681.

(3) For the purposes of this section, indebtedness shall be deemed to be incurred prior to the effective date of this chapter if the agency has entered into a binding contract subject to normal marketing conditions, to deliver the indebtedness, or if the redevelopment agency has received bids for the sale of the indebtedness prior to that date and the indebtedness is issued for value and evidence thereof is delivered to the initial purchaser no later than 30 days after the date of the contract or sale.

(b) During the 1992–93 fiscal year, an agency that has adopted a resolution pursuant to subdivision (c) may, pursuant to subdivision (a) of Section 33681, allocate to the auditor less than the amount required by subdivision (a) of Section 33681, if the agency finds that either of the following has occurred:

(1) That the difference between the amount allocated and the amount required by subdivision (a) of Section 33681 is necessary to make payments on existing indebtedness that are due or required to be committed, set aside, or reserved by the agency during the 1992–93 fiscal year and that are used by the agency for that purpose, and the agency has no other funds that can be used to pay this existing indebtedness, and no other feasible method to reduce or avoid this indebtedness.

(2) The agency has no other funds to make the allocation required by subdivision (a) of Section 33681.

(c) (1) Any agency that, pursuant to subdivision (b), allocates to the auditor less than the amount required by subdivision (a) of Section 33681 shall adopt, prior to December 31, 1992, for the 1992–93 fiscal year, after a noticed public hearing, a resolution which lists all of the following:

(A) Each existing indebtedness incurred prior to the effective date of the act that adds this article.

(B) Each indebtedness on which a payment is required to be made during the 1992–93 fiscal year.

(C) The amount of each payment, the time when it is required to be paid, and the total of the payments required to be made during the 1992–93 fiscal year. For indebtedness that bears interest at a variable rate, or for short-term indebtedness that is maturing during the fiscal year and expected to be refinanced, the amount of payments during the fiscal year shall be estimated by the agency.

(2) The information contained in the resolution required by this subdivision shall be certified by the chief fiscal officer of the agency.

(3) The legislative body shall additionally adopt the resolution required by this section.

(d) (1) Any agency that, pursuant to subdivision (b), determines that it will be unable to allocate the full amount required by subdivision (a) of Section 33681 shall, subject to paragraph (3), enter into an agreement with the legislative body by February 15, 1993, to fund the payment of the difference between the full amount required to be paid pursuant to subdivision (a) of Section 33681 and the amount available for allocation by the agency.

(2) The obligations imposed by paragraph (1) are hereby declared to be indebtedness incurred by the redevelopment agency to finance a portion of a redevelopment project within the meaning of Section 16 of Article XVI of the California Constitution. This indebtedness shall be payable from tax revenues allocated to the agency pursuant to Section 33670, and any other funds received by the agency. The obligations imposed by paragraph (1) shall remain an indebtedness of the agency to the legislative body until paid in full, or until the agency and the legislative body otherwise agree.

(3) The agreement described in paragraph (1) shall be subject to these terms and conditions specified in a written agreement between the legislative body and the agency.

(e) If the agency fails, under either Section 33681 or subdivision (d), to transmit the full amount of funds required by Section 33681, is precluded by court order from transmitting that amount, or is otherwise unable to meet its full obligation pursuant to Section 33681, the county auditor, by no later than May 15, 1993, shall transfer any amount necessary to meet the obligation determined for that agency in subparagraph (D) of paragraph (2) of subdivision (a) of Section 33681 from the legislative body's property tax allocation pursuant to Chapter 6 (commencing with Section 95) of Part 0.5 of Division 1 of the Revenue and Taxation Code.

(f) It is the intent of the Legislature in enacting this section that this section supersede and be operative in place of Section 33682 of the Health and Safety Code as added by Senate Bill 617 of the 1991–92 Regular Session.

33682.1 Inability to make payments to educational revenue augmentation funds: existing indebtedness further defined

For purposes of Section 33682, "existing indebtedness" also means an obligation incurred pursuant to a reimbursement agreement made for the purpose of funding an unfunded liability of a fire and police retirement system of a charter city meeting all of the criteria specified in Section 33608. This section shall not be applied retroactively.

33682.5 Inability to make payments to educational revenue augmentation funds during 1993–94 or 1994–95; existing indebtedness defined

(a) (1) For the purposes of this section, "existing indebtedness" means one or more of the following obligations incurred by a redevelopment agency prior to the effective date of the statute that adds this chapter, the payment of which is to be made in whole or in part, directly or indirectly, out of taxes allocated to the agency pursuant to Section 33670, and which is required by law or provision of the existing indebtedness to be made during the fiscal year of the relevant allocation required by Section 33681.5:

(A) Bonds, notes, interim certificates, debentures, or other obligations issued by an agency (whether funded, refunded, assumed, or otherwise) pursuant to Article 5 (commencing with Section 33640).

(B) Loans or moneys advanced to the agency, including, but not limited to, loans from federal, state, or local agencies, or a private entity.

(C) A contractual obligation that, if breached, could subject the agency to damages or other liabilities or remedies.

(D) An obligation incurred pursuant to Section 33445.

(E) Indebtedness incurred pursuant to Section 33334.2.

(F) An amount, to be expended for the operation and administration of the agency, that may not exceed 90 percent of the amount spent for those purposes in the 1991–92 fiscal year.

(G) Obligations imposed by law with respect to activities which occurred prior to the effective date of the act that adds this chapter.

(2) Existing indebtedness incurred prior to the effective date of the statute that adds this article may be refinanced, refunded, or restructured after that date, and shall remain existing indebtedness for the purposes of this section, if the annual debt service during that fiscal year does not increase over the prior fiscal year and the refinancing does not reduce the ability of the agency to make the payment required by subdivision (a) of Section 33681.5.

(3) For the purposes of this section, indebtedness shall be deemed to be incurred prior to the effective date of this chapter if the agency has entered into a binding contract subject to normal marketing conditions, to deliver the indebtedness, or if the redevelopment agency has received bids for the sale of the indebtedness prior to that date and the indebtedness is issued for value and evidence thereof is delivered to the initial purchaser no later than 30 days after the date of the contract or sale.

(b) During the 1993–94 or 1994–95 fiscal year, an agency that has adopted a resolution pursuant to subdivision (c) may, pursuant to subdivision (a) of Section 33681.5, allocate to the auditor less than the amount required by subdivision (a) of Section 33681.5, if the agency finds that either of the following has occurred:

(1) That the difference between the amount allocated and the amount required by subdivision (a) of Section 33681.5 is necessary to make payments on existing indebtedness that are due or required to be committed, set aside, or reserved by the agency during the applicable fiscal year and that are used by the agency for that purpose, and the agency has no other funds that can be used to pay this existing indebtedness, and no other feasible method to reduce or avoid this indebtedness.

(2) The agency has no other funds to make the allocation required by subdivision (a) of Section 33681.5.

(c) (1) Any agency that, pursuant to subdivision (b), allocates to the auditor less than the amount required by subdivision (a) of Section 33681.5 shall adopt, prior to December 31 of the relevant fiscal year, after a noticed public hearing, a resolution which lists all of the following:

(A) Each existing indebtedness incurred prior to the effective date of the act that adds this article.

(B) Each indebtedness on which a payment is required to be made during the relevant fiscal year.

(C) The amount of each payment, the time when it is required to be paid, and the total of the payments required to be made during the relevant fiscal year. For indebtedness that bears interest at a variable rate, or for short-term indebtedness that is maturing during the fiscal year and expected to be refinanced, the amount of payments during the fiscal year shall be estimated by the agency.

(2) The information contained in the resolution required by this subdivision shall be reviewed for accuracy by the chief fiscal officer of the agency.

(3) The legislative body shall additionally adopt the resolution required by this section.

(d) (1) Any agency that, pursuant to subdivision (b), determines that it will be unable in either the 1993–94 or 1994–95 fiscal year to allocate the full amount required by subdivision (a) of Section 33681.5 shall, subject to paragraph (3), enter into an agreement with the legislative body by February 15 of the relevant fiscal year to fund the payment of the difference between the full amount required to be paid pursuant to subdivision (a) of Section 33681.5 and the amount available for allocation by the agency.

(2) The obligations imposed by paragraph (1) are hereby declared to be indebtedness incurred by the redevelopment agency to finance a portion of a redevelopment project within the meaning of Section 16 of Article XVI of the California Constitution. This indebtedness shall be payable from tax revenues allocated to the agency pursuant to Section 33670, and any other funds received by the agency. The obligations imposed by paragraph (1) shall remain an indebtedness of the agency to the legislative body until paid in full, or until the agency and the legislative body otherwise agree.

(3) The agreement described in paragraph (1) shall be subject to these terms and conditions specified in a written agreement between the legislative body and the agency.

(e) If the agency fails, under either Section 33681.5 or subdivision (d), to transmit the full amount of funds required by Section 33681.5, is precluded by court order from transmitting that amount, or is otherwise unable to meet its full obligation pursuant to Section 33681.5, the county auditor, by no later than May 15 of the fiscal year, shall transfer any amount necessary to meet the obligation determined for that agency in subparagraph (D) of paragraph (2) of subdivision (a) of Section 33681.5 from the legislative body's property tax allocation pursuant to Chapter 6 (commencing with Section 95) of Part 0.5 of Division 1 of the Revenue and Taxation Code.

33683 Payments to educational revenue augmentation funds not counted toward tax increment caps

For the purpose of calculating the amount wthat has been divided and allocated to the redevelopment agency to determine whether the limitation adopted pursuant to Section 33333.2 or 33333.4 or pursuant to agreement or court order has been reached, any payments made pursuant to subdivision (a) of Sections 33681, 33681.5, 33681.7, 33681.9, and 33681.12 or subdivision (d) of Sections 33681.8, 33681.10, 33682, and 33682.5 with property tax revenues shall be deducted from the amount of property tax dollars deemed to have been received by the agency.

33684 Obligation to file passthrough payment report with county auditor

(a) (1) This section shall apply to each redevelopment project area that, pursuant to a redevelopment plan that contains the provisions required by Section 33670, meets any of the following:

(A) Was adopted on or after January 1, 1994, including later amendments to these redevelopment plans.

(B) Was adopted prior to January 1, 1994, but amended after January 1, 1994, to include new territory. For plans amended after January 1, 1994, only the tax increments from territory added by the amendment shall be subject to this section.

(2) This section shall apply to passthrough payments, as required by Sections 33607.5 and 33607.7, for the 2003-04 to 2008-09, inclusive, fiscal years. For purposes of this section, a passthrough payment shall be considered the responsibility of an agency in the fiscal year the agency receives the tax increment revenue for which the passthrough payment is required.

(3) For purposes of this section, "local educational agency" is a school district, a community college district, or a county office of education.

(b) On or before October 1, 2008, each agency shall submit a report to the county auditor and to each affected taxing entity that describes each project area, including its location, purpose, date established, date or dates amended, and statutory and contractual passthrough requirements. The report shall specify, by year, for each project area all of the following:

(1) Gross tax increment received between July 1, 2003, and June 30, 2008, that is subject to a passthrough payment pursuant to Sections 33607.5 and 33607.7, and accumulated gross tax increments through June 30, 2003.

(2) Total passthrough payments to each taxing entity that the agency deferred pursuant to a subordination agreement approved by the taxing agency under subdivision (e) of Section 33607.5 and the dates these deferred payments will be made.

(3) Total passthrough payments to each taxing entity that the agency was responsible to make between July 1, 2003, and June 30, 2008, pursuant to Sections 33607.5 and 33607.7, excluding payments identified in paragraph (2).

(4) Total passthrough payments that the agency disbursed to each taxing entity between July 1, 2003, and June 30, 2008, pursuant to Sections 33607.5 and 33607.7.

(5) Total sums reported in paragraph (4) for each local educational agency that are considered to be property taxes under the provisions of paragraph (4) of subdivision (a) of Sections 33607.5 and 33607.7.

(6) Total outstanding payment obligations to each taxing entity as of June 30, 2008. This amount shall be calculated by subtracting the amounts reported in paragraph (4) from paragraph (3) and reporting any positive sum.

(7) Total outstanding overpayments to each taxing entity as of June 30, 2008. This amount shall be calculated by subtracting the amounts reported in paragraph (3) from paragraph (4) and reporting any positive sum.

(8) The dates on which the agency made payments identified in paragraph (6) or intends to make the payments identified in paragraph (6).

(2) A revised estimate of the agency's total outstanding passthrough payment obligation to each taxing agency pursuant to paragraph (6) of subdivision (b) and paragraph (6) of subdivision (c) and the dates on which the agency intends to make these payments.

(c) On or before October 1, 2009, each agency shall submit a report to the county auditor and to each affected taxing entity that describes each project area, including its location, purpose, date established, date or dates amended, and statutory and contractual passthrough requirements. The report shall specify, by year, for each project area all of the following:

(1) Gross tax increment received between July 1, 2008, and June 30, 2009, that is subject to a passthrough payment pursuant to Sections 33607.5 and 33607.7.

(2) Total passthrough payments to each taxing entity that the agency deferred pursuant to a subordination agreement approved by the taxing entity under subdivision (e) of Section 33607.5 and the dates these deferred payments will be made.

(3) Total passthrough payments to each taxing entity that the agency was responsible to make between July 1, 2008, and June 30, 2009, pursuant to Sections 33607.5 and 33607.7, excluding payments identified in paragraph (2).

(4) Total passthrough payments that the agency disbursed to each taxing entity between July 1, 2008, and June 30, 2009, pursuant to Sections 33607.5 and 33607.7.

(5) Total sums reported in paragraph (4) for each local educational agency that are considered to be property taxes under the provisions of paragraph (4) of subdivision (a) of Sections 33607.5 and 33607.7.

(6) Total outstanding payment obligations to each taxing entity as of June 30, 2009. This amount shall be calculated by subtracting the amounts reported in paragraph (4) from paragraph (3) and reporting any positive sum.

(7) Total outstanding overpayments to each taxing entity as of June 30, 2009. This amount shall be calculated by subtracting the amounts reported in paragraph (3) from paragraph (4) and reporting any positive sum.

(8) The dates on which the agency made payments identified in paragraph (6) or intends to make the payments identified in paragraph (6).

(d) If an agency reports pursuant to paragraph (6) of subdivision (b) or paragraph (6) of subdivision (c) that it has an outstanding passthrough payment obligation to any taxing entity, the agency shall submit annual updates to the county auditor on October 1 of each year until such time as the county auditor notifies the agency in writing that the agency's outstanding payment obligations have been fully satisfied. The report shall contain both of the following:

(1) A list of payments to each taxing agency and to the Educational Revenue Augmentation Fund pursuant to subdivision (j) that the agency disbursed after the agency's last update filed pursuant to this subdivision or, if no update has been filed, after the agency's submission of the reports required pursuant to subdivisions (b) and (c). The list of payments shall include only those payments that address obligations identified pursuant to paragraph (6) of subdivision (b) and paragraph (6) of subdivision (c). The update shall specify the date on which each payment was disbursed.

(2) A revised estimate of the agency's total outstanding passthrough payment obligation to each taxing agency pursuant to paragraph (6) of subdivision (b) and paragraph (6) of subdivision (c) and the dates on which the agency intends to make these payments.

(e) The county auditor shall review each agency's reports submitted pursuant to subdivisions (b) and (c) and any other relevant information to determine whether the county auditor concurs with the information included in the reports.

(1) If the county auditor concurs with the information included in a report, the county auditor shall issue a finding of concurrence within 45 days.

(2) If the county auditor does not concur with the information included in a report or considers the report to be incomplete, the county auditor shall return the report to the agency within 45 days with information identifying the elements of the report with which the county auditor does not concur or considers to be incomplete. The county auditor shall provide the agency at least 15 days to respond to concerns raised by the county auditor regarding the information contained in the report. An agency may revise a report that has not received a finding of concurrence and resubmit it to the county auditor.

(3) If an agency and county auditor do not agree regarding the passthrough requirements of Sections 33607.5 and 33607.7, an agency may submit a report pursuant to subdivisions (b) and (c) and a statement of dispute identifying the issue needing resolution.

(4) An agency may amend a report for which the county auditor has issued a finding of concurrence and resubmit the report pursuant to paragraphs (1), (2), and (3) if any of the following apply:

(A) The county auditor and agency agree that an issue identified in the agency's statement of dispute has been resolved and the agency proposes to modify the sections of the report to conform with the resolution of the statement of dispute.

(B) The county auditor and agency agree that the amount of gross tax increment or the amount of a passthrough payment to a taxing entity included in the report is not accurate.

(5) The Controller may revoke a finding of concurrence and direct the agency to resubmit a report to the county auditor pursuant to paragraphs (1), (2), and (3) if the Controller finds significant errors in a report.

(f) On or before December 15, 2008, and annually thereafter through 2014, the county auditor shall submit a report to the Controller that includes all of the following:

(1) The name of each redevelopment project area in the county for which an agency must submit a report pursuant to subdivision (b) or (c) and information as to whether the county auditor has issued a finding of concurrence regarding the report.

(2) A list of the agencies for which the county auditor has issued a finding of concurrence for all project areas identified in paragraph (1).

(3) A list of agencies for which the county auditor has not issued a finding of concurrence for all project areas identified in paragraph (1).

(4) Using information applicable to agencies listed in paragraph (2), the county auditor shall report all of the following:

(A) The total sums reported by each redevelopment agency related to each taxing entity pursuant to paragraphs (1) to (7), inclusive, of subdivision (b) and, on or after December 15, 2009, pursuant to paragraphs (1) to (7), inclusive, of subdivision (c).

(B) The names of agencies that have outstanding passthrough payment obligations to a local educational agency that exceed the amount of outstanding passthrough payments to the local educational agency.

(C) Summary information regarding agencies' stated plans to pay the outstanding amounts identified in paragraph (6) of subdivision (b) and paragraph (6) of subdivision (c) and the actual amounts that have been deposited into the county Educational Revenue Augmentation Fund pursuant to subdivision (j).

(D) All unresolved statements of dispute filed by agencies pursuant to paragraph (3) of subdivision (e) and the county auditor's analyses supporting the county auditor's conclusions regarding the issues under dispute.

(g) (1) On or before February 1, 2009, and annually thereafter through 2015, the Controller shall submit a report to the Legislative Analyst's Office and the Department of Finance and provide a copy to the Board of Governors of the California Community Colleges. The report shall provide information as follows:

(A) Identify agencies for which the county auditor has issued a finding of concurrence for all reports required under subdivisions (b) and (c).

(B) Identify agencies for which the county auditor has not issued a finding of concurrence for all reports required pursuant to subdivision (b) and all reports required pursuant to subdivision (c) or for which a finding of concurrence has been withdrawn by the Controller.

(C) Summarize the information reported in paragraph (4) of subdivision (f). This summary shall identify, by local educational agency and by year, the total amount of passthrough payments that each local educational agency received, was entitled to receive, subordinated, or that has not yet been paid, and the portion of these amounts that are considered to be property taxes for purposes of Sections 2558, 42238, and 84751 of the Education Code. The report shall identify, by agency, the amounts that have been deposited to the county Educational Revenue Augmentation Fund pursuant to subdivision (j).

(D) Summarize the statements of dispute. The Controller shall specify the status of these disputes, including whether the Controller or other state entity has provided instructions as to how these disputes should be resolved.

(E) Identify agencies that have outstanding passthrough payment liabilities to a local educational agency that exceed the amount of outstanding passthrough overpayments to the local educational agency.

(2) On or before February 1, 2009, and annually thereafter through 2015, the Controller shall submit a report to the State Department of Education and the Board of Governors of the California Community Colleges. The report shall identify, by local educational agency and by year of receipt, the total amount of passthrough payments that the local educational agency received from redevelopment agencies listed in subparagraph (A) of paragraph (1).

(h) (1) On or before April 1, 2009, and annually thereafter until April 1, 2015, the State Department of Education shall do all of the following:

(A) Calculate for each school district for the 2003–04 to 2007–08, inclusive, fiscal years the difference between 43.3 percent of the amount reported pursuant to paragraph (2) of subdivision (g) and the amount subtracted from each school district's apportionment pursuant to paragraph (6) of subdivision (h) of Section 42238 of the Education Code.

(B) Calculate for each county superintendent of schools for the 2003–04 to 2007–08, inclusive, fiscal years the difference between 19 percent of the amount reported pursuant to paragraph (2) of subdivision (g) and the amount received pursuant to Sections 33607.5 and 33607.7 and subtracted from each county superintendent of schools apportionment pursuant to subdivision (c) of Section 2558 of the Education Code.

(C) Notify each school district and county superintendent of schools for which any amount calculated in subparagraph (A) or (B) is nonzero as to the reported change and its resulting impact on apportionments. After April 1, 2009, however, the department shall not notify a school district or county superintendent of schools if the amount calculated in subparagraph (A) or (B) is the same amount as the department calculated in the preceding year.

(2) On or before April 1, 2010, and annually thereafter until April 1, 2015, the State Department of Education shall do all of the following:

(A) Calculate for each school district for the 2008-09 fiscal year the difference between 43.3 percent of the amount reported pursuant to paragraph (2) of subdivision (g) and the amount subtracted from each school district's apportionment pursuant to paragraph (6) of subdivision (h) of Section 42238 of the Education Code.

(B) Calculate for each county superintendent of schools for the 2008-09 fiscal year the difference between 19 percent of the amount reported pursuant to paragraph (2) of subdivision (g) and the amount received pursuant to Sections 33607.5 and 33607.7 and subtracted from each county superintendent of schools apportionment pursuant to subdivision (c) of Section 2558 of the Education Code.

(C) Notify each school district and county superintendent of schools for which any amount calculated in subparagraph (A) or (B) is nonzero as to the reported change and its resulting impact on revenue limit apportionments. After April 1, 2010, however, the department shall not notify a school district or county superintendent of schools if the amount calculated in subparagraph (A) or (B) is the same amount as the department calculated in the preceding year.

(3) For the purposes of Article 3 (commencing with Section 41330) of Chapter 3 of Part 24 of Division 3 of the Education Code, the amounts reported to each school district and county superintendent of schools in the notification required pursuant to subparagraph (C) of paragraph (1) and subparagraph (C) of paragraph (2) shall be deemed to be apportionment significant audit exceptions and the date of receipt of that notification shall be deemed to be the date of receipt of the final audit report that includes those audit exceptions.

(4) On or before March 1, 2009, and annually thereafter until March 1, 2015, the Board of Governors of the California Community Colleges shall do all of the following:

(A) Calculate for each community college district for the 2003-04 to 2007-08, inclusive, fiscal years the difference between 47.5 percent of the amount reported pursuant to paragraph (2) of subdivision (g) and the amount subtracted from each district's total revenue owed pursuant to subdivision (d) of Section 84751 of the Education Code.

(B) Notify each community college district for which any amount calculated in subparagraph (A) is nonzero as to the reported change and its resulting impact on apportionments. After March 1, 2009, however, the board shall not notify a school district or county superintendent of schools if the amount calculated in subparagraph (A) is the same amount as the board calculated in the preceding year.

(5) On or before March 1, 2010, and annually thereafter until March 1, 2015, the Board of Governors of the California Community Colleges shall do all of the following:

(A) Calculate for each community college district for the 2003-04 to 2007-08, inclusive, fiscal years the difference between 47.5 percent of the amount reported pursuant to paragraph (2) of subdivision (g) and the amount subtracted from each district's total revenue owed pursuant to subdivision (d) of Section 84751 of the Education Code.

(B) Notify each community college district for which any amount calculated in subparagraph (A) is nonzero as to the reported change and its resulting impact on revenue apportionments. After March 1, 2010, however, the board shall not notify a community college district if the amount calculated in subparagraph (A) is the same amount as the board calculated in the preceding year.

(6) A community college district may submit documentation to the Board of Governors of the California Community Colleges showing that all or part of the amount reported to the district pursuant to subparagraph (B) of paragraph (4) and subparagraph (B) of paragraph (5) was previously reported to the California Community Colleges for the purpose of the revenue level calculations made pursuant to Section 84751 of the Education Code. Upon acceptance of the documentation, the board of governors shall adjust the amounts calculated in paragraphs (4) and (5) accordingly.

(7) The Board of Governors of the California Community Colleges shall make corrections in any amounts allocated in any fiscal year to each community college district for which any amount calculated in paragraphs (4) and (5) is nonzero so as to account for the changes reported pursuant to paragraph (4) of subdivision (b) and paragraph (4) of subdivision (c). The board may make the corrections over a period of time, not to exceed five years.

(i) (1) After February 1, 2009, for an agency listed on the most recent Controller's report pursuant to subparagraph (B) or (E) of paragraph (1) of subdivision (g), all of the following shall apply:

(A) The agency shall be prohibited from adding new project areas or expanding existing project areas. For purposes of this paragraph, "project area" has the same meaning as in Sections 33320.1 to 33320.3, inclusive, and Section 33492.3.

(B) The agency shall be prohibited from issuing new bonds, notes, interim certificates, debentures, or other obligations, whether funded, refunded, assumed, or otherwise, pursuant to Article 5 (commencing with Section 33640).

(C) The agency shall be prohibited from encumbering any funds or expending any moneys derived from any source, except that the agency may encumber funds and expend funds to pay, if any, all of the following:

(i) Bonds, notes, interim certificates, debentures, or other obligations issued by an agency before the imposition of the prohibition in subparagraph (B) whether funded, refunded, assumed, or otherwise, pursuant to Article 5 (commencing with Section 33460) of this chapter.

(ii) Loans or moneys advanced to the agency, including, but not limited to, loans from federal, state, local agencies, or a private entity.

(iii) Contractual obligations that, if breached, could subject the agency to damages or other liabilities or remedies.

(iv) Obligations incurred pursuant to Section 33445.

(v) Indebtedness incurred pursuant to Section 33334.2 or 33334.6.

(vi) Obligations incurred pursuant to Section 33401.

(vii) An amount, to be expended for the monthly operation and administration of the agency, that may not exceed 75 percent of the average monthly amount spent for those purposes in the fiscal year preceding the fiscal year in which the agency was first listed on the Controller's report pursuant to subparagraph (B) or (E) of paragraph (1) of subdivision (g).

(2) After February 1, 2009, an agency identified in subparagraph (B) or (E) of paragraph (1) of subdivision (g) shall incur interest charges on any passthrough payment that is made to a local educational agency more than 60 days after the close of the fiscal year in which the passthrough payment was required. Interest shall be charged at a rate equal to 150 percent of the current Pooled Money Investment Account earnings annual yield rate and shall be charged for the period beginning 60 days after the close of the fiscal year in which the passthrough payment was due through the date that the payment is made.

(3) The Controller, with the concurrence of the Director of Finance, may waive the provisions of paragraphs (1) and (2) for a period of up to 12 months if the Controller determines all of the following:

(A) The county auditor has identified the agency in its most recent report issued pursuant to paragraph (2) of subdivision (f) as an agency for which the auditor has issued a finding of concurrence for all reports required pursuant to subdivisions (b) and (c).

(B) The agency has filed a statement of dispute on an issue or issues that, in the opinion of the Controller, are likely to be resolved in a manner consistent with the agency's position.

(C) The agency has made passthrough payments to local educational agencies and the county Educational Revenue Augmentation Fund, or has had funds previously withheld by the auditor, in amounts that would satisfy the agency's passthrough payment requirements to local educational agencies if the issue or issues addressed in the statement of dispute were resolved in a manner consistent with the agency's position.

(D) The agency would sustain a fiscal hardship if it made passthrough payments to local educational agencies and the county Educational Revenue Augmentation Fund in the amounts estimated by the county auditor.

(j) Notwithstanding any other provision of law, if an agency report submitted pursuant to subdivision (b) or (c) indicates outstanding payment obligations to a local educational agency, the agency shall make these outstanding payments as follows:

(1) Of the outstanding payments owed to school districts, including any interest payments pursuant to paragraph (2) of subdivision (i), 43.3 percent shall be deposited in the county Educational Revenue Augmentation Fund and the remainder shall be allocated to the school district or districts.

(2) Of the outstanding payments owed to community college districts, including any interest payments pursuant to paragraph (2) of subdivision (i), 47.5 percent shall be deposited in the county Educational Revenue Augmentation Fund and the remainder shall be allocated to the community college district or districts.

(3) Of the outstanding payments owed to county offices of education, including any interest payments pursuant to paragraph (2) of subdivision (i), 19 percent shall be deposited in the county Educational Revenue Augmentation Fund and the remainder shall be allocated to the county office of education.

(k) (1) This section shall not be construed to increase any allocations of excess, additional, or remaining funds that would otherwise have been allocated to cities, counties, cities and counties, or special districts pursuant to clause (i) of subparagraph (B) of paragraph (4) of subdivision (d) of Section 97.2 of, clause (i) of subparagraph (B) of paragraph (4) of subdivision (d) of Section 97.3 of, or Article 4 (commencing with Section 98) of Chapter 6 of Part 0.5 of Division 1 of, the Revenue and Taxation Code had this section not been enacted.

(2) Notwithstanding any other provision of law, no funds deposited in the county Educational Revenue Augmentation Fund pursuant to subdivision (j) shall be distributed to a community college district.

(l) A county may require an agency to reimburse the county for any expenses incurred by the county in performing the services required by this section.

33685 Payments to the educational revenue augmentation fund during 2008-09

(a) (1) For the 2008-09 fiscal year a redevelopment agency shall remit, as determined by the Director of Finance, prior to May 10, an amount equal to the amount determined for that agency pursuant to subparagraph (K) of paragraph (2) to the county auditor for deposit in the county Educational Revenue Augmentation Fund, created pursuant to Article 3 (commencing with Section 97) of Chapter 6 of Part 0.5 of Division 1 of the Revenue and Taxation Code. Notwithstanding any other provision of law, in the 2008-09 fiscal year, no funds deposited in the county Educational Revenue Augmentation Fund pursuant to this section shall be distributed to a community college district.

(2) On or before November 15, 2008, the Director of Finance shall do all of the following:

(A) (i) Determine the value of five percent of the statewide total property tax revenue apportioned to agencies pursuant to Section 33670.

(ii) If the value determined pursuant to clause (i) exceeds three-hundred fifty million dollars ($350,000,000), the value determined in clause (i) shall be allocated to each agency as provided in paragraphs (B) to (J), inclusive.

(iii) If the value determined pursuant to clause (i) does not exceed three-hundred fifty million dollars ($350,000,000), three-hundred fifty million dollars ($350,000,000) shall be allocated to each agency as provided in subparagraphs (B) to (J), inclusive.

(B) Determine the net tax increment apportioned to each agency pursuant to Section 33670, excluding any amounts apportioned to affected taxing entities pursuant to Section 33401, 33607.5, or 33676.

(C) Determine the net tax increment apportioned to all agencies pursuant to Section 33670, excluding any amounts allocated to affected taxing entities pursuant to Section 33401, 33607.5, or 33676.

(D) Determine a percentage factor by dividing the amount determined pursuant to subparagraph (A) by two and then by the amount determined pursuant to subparagraph (C).

(E) Determine an amount for each agency by multiplying the amount determined pursuant to subparagraph (B) by the percentage factor determined pursuant to subparagraph (D).

(F) Determine the total amount of property tax revenue apportioned to each agency pursuant to Section 33670, including any amounts allocated to affected taxing entities pursuant to Section 33401, 33607.5, or 33676.

(G) Determine the total amount of property tax revenue apportioned to all agencies pursuant to Section 33670, including any amounts allocated to affected taxing entities pursuant to Section 33401, 33607.5, or 33676.

(H) Determine a percentage factor by dividing the amount determined pursuant to subparagraph (A) by two and then by the amount determined pursuant to subparagraph (G).

(I) Determine an amount for each agency by multiplying the amount determined pursuant to subparagraph (F) by the percentage factor determined pursuant to subparagraph (H).

(J) Add the amount determined pursuant to subparagraph (E) to the amount determined pursuant to subparagraph (I).

(K) Notify each agency, each legislative body, and each county auditor of each agency's amount. The county auditor shall deposit these amounts in the county Educational Revenue Augmentation Fund pursuant to paragraph (1).

(3) The obligation of any agency to make the payments required pursuant to this subdivision shall be subordinate to the lien of any pledge of collateral securing, directly or indirectly, the payment of the principal, or interest on any bonds of the agency including, without limitation, bonds secured by a pledge of taxes allocated to the agency pursuant to Section 33670. Agencies shall factor in the fiscal obligations created by this subdivision when issuing bonded indebtedness.

(b) (1) Notwithstanding any other provision of law, to make the full allocation required by this section, an agency may borrow up to 50 percent of the amount required to be allocated to the Low and Moderate Income Housing Fund, pursuant to Sections 33334.2, 33334.3, and 33334.6, unless, in a given fiscal year, executed contracts exist that would be impaired if the agency reduced the amount allocated to the Low and Moderate Income Housing Fund pursuant to the authority of this subdivision.

(2) As a condition of borrowing pursuant to this subdivision, an agency shall make a finding that there are insufficient other moneys to meet the requirements of subdivision (a). Funds borrowed pursuant to this subdivision shall be repaid in full within 10 years following the date on which moneys are remitted to the county auditor for deposit in the county Educational Revenue Augmentation Fund pursuant to subdivision (a).

(c) To make the allocation required by this section, an agency may use any funds that are legally available and not legally obligated for other uses, including, but not limited to, reserve funds, proceeds of land sales, proceeds of bonds or other indebtedness, lease revenues, interest, and other earned income. No moneys held in a low- and moderate-income fund as of July 1 of the applicable fiscal year may be used for this purpose.

(d) The legislative body shall by March 1 of each year report to the county auditor as to how the agency intends to fund the allocation required by this section, or that the legislative body intends to remit the amount in lieu of the agency pursuant to Section 33687.

(e) The allocation obligations imposed by this section, including amounts owed, if any, created under this section, are hereby declared to be an indebtedness of the redevelopment project to which they relate, payable from taxes allocated to the agency pursuant to Section 33670, and shall constitute an indebtedness of the agency with respect to the redevelopment project until paid in full.

(f) It is the intent of the Legislature, in enacting this section, that these allocations directly or indirectly assist in the financing or refinancing, in whole or in part, of the community's redevelopment project pursuant to Section 16 of Article XVI of the California Constitution.

(g) In making the annual determinations required by subdivision (a), the Director of Finance shall use those amounts reported in "Table 7, Assessed Valuation, Tax Increment Distribution and Statement of Indebtedness" for all agencies and for each agency in the most recent published edition of the Controller's Community Redevelopment Agencies Annual Report made pursuant to Section 12463.3 of the Government Code.

(h) If revised reports have been accepted by the Controller on or before September 1 of the applicable fiscal year, the Director of Finance shall use appropriate data that has been certified by the Controller for the purpose of making the determinations required by subdivision (a).

(i) Nothing in this section shall be construed as extending the time limits on the ability of agencies to do any of the following:

(1) Establish loans, advances, or indebtedness.

(2) Receive tax increment revenues.

(3) Exercise eminent domain powers.

33686 Inability to make payments to educational revenue augmentation fund during 2008-09–existing indebtedness defined

(a) (1) For purposes of this section, "existing indebtedness" means one or more of the following obligations incurred by a redevelopment agency prior to the effective date of this section, the payment of which is to be made in whole or in part, directly or indirectly, out of taxes allocated to the agency pursuant to Section 33670, and that is required by law or provision of the existing indebtedness to be made during the fiscal year of the relevant allocation required by Section 33685:

(A) Bonds, notes, interim certificates, debentures, or other obligations issued by the agency whether funded, refunded, assumed, or otherwise pursuant to Article 5 (commencing with Section 33640).

(B) Loans or moneys advanced to the agency, including, but not limited to, loans from federal, state, or local agencies, or a private entity.

(C) A contractual obligation that, if breached, could subject the agency to damages or other liabilities or remedies.

(D) An obligation incurred pursuant to Section 33445.

(E) Indebtedness incurred pursuant to Section 33334.2.

(F) An amount, to be expended for the operation and administration of the agency, that may not exceed 90 percent of the amount spent for those purposes in the 2005-06 fiscal year.

(G) Obligations imposed by law with respect to activities that occurred prior to the effective date of the act that adds this section.

(2) Existing indebtedness incurred prior to the effective date of this section may be refinanced, refunded, or restructured after that date, and shall remain existing indebtedness for the

purposes of this section if the annual debt service during that fiscal year does not increase over the prior fiscal year and the refinancing does not reduce the ability of the agency to make the payment required by subdivision (a) of Section 33685.

(3) For purposes of this section, indebtedness shall be deemed to be incurred prior to the effective date of this section if the agency has entered into a binding contract subject to normal marketing conditions or to deliver the indebtedness, or if the redevelopment agency has received bids for the sale of the indebtedness prior to that date and the indebtedness is issued for value and evidence thereof is delivered to the initial purchaser no later than 30 days after the date of the contract or sale.

(b) For the 2008-09 fiscal year, an agency that has adopted a resolution pursuant to subdivision (c) may allocate, pursuant to subdivision (a) of Section 33685, to the auditor less than the amount required by subdivision (a) of Section 33685 if the agency finds that any of the following has occurred:

(1) That the difference between the amount allocated to the agency and the amount required by subdivision (a) of Section 33685 is necessary to make payments on existing indebtedness that are due or required to be committed, set aside, or reserved by the agency during the 2008-09 fiscal year and that are used by the agency for that purpose, and the agency has no other funds that can be used to pay this existing indebtedness and no other feasible method to reduce or avoid this indebtedness.

(2) The agency has no other funds to make the allocation required by subdivision (a) of Section 33685.

(c) (1) Any agency that intends to allocate, pursuant to subdivision (b), to the auditor less than the amount required by subdivision (a) of Section 33685 shall adopt, prior to December 31, 2008, after a noticed public hearing, a resolution that lists all of the following:

(A) Each existing indebtedness incurred prior to the effective date of this section.

(B) Each indebtedness on which a payment is required to be made during the applicable fiscal year.

(C) The amount of each payment, the time when it is required to be paid, and the total of the payments required to be made during the applicable fiscal year. For indebtedness that bears interest at a variable rate, or for short-term indebtedness that is maturing during the fiscal year and that is expected to be refinanced, the amount of payments during the fiscal year shall be estimated by the agency.

(2) The information contained in the resolution required by this subdivision shall be reviewed for accuracy by the chief fiscal officer of the agency.

(3) The legislative body shall additionally adopt the resolution required by this section.

(d) (1) Any agency that determines, pursuant to subdivision (b), that it will be unable in the 2008-09 fiscal year to allocate the full amount required by subdivision (a) of Section 33685 may enter into, subject to paragraph (3), an agreement with the legislative body by February 15, 2009, to fund the payment of the difference between the full amount required to be paid pursuant to subdivision (a) of Section 33685 and the amount available for allocation by the agency.

(2) The obligations imposed by paragraph (1) are hereby declared to be indebtedness incurred by the agency to finance a portion of a redevelopment project within the meaning of Section 16 of Article XVI of the California Constitution. This indebtedness shall be payable from tax revenues apportioned to the agency pursuant to Section 33670, and any other funds received by the agency. The obligations imposed by paragraph (1) shall remain an indebtedness of the agency to the legislative body until paid in full, or until the agency and the legislative body otherwise agree.

(3) The agreement described in paragraph (1) shall be subject to those terms and conditions specified in a written agreement between the legislative body and the agency.

(e) If the agency fails to provide to the county auditor the full payment required under Section 33685, or fails to arrange for full payment to be provided on the agency's behalf pursuant to subdivision (d) or by Section 33687 or 33688, all of the following shall apply:

(1) The agency shall be prohibited from adding new project areas or expanding existing project areas. For purposes of this paragraph, "project area" has the same meaning as in Sections 33320.1 to 33320.3, inclusive, and Section 33492.3.

(2) The agency shall be prohibited from issuing new bonds, notes, interim certificates, debentures, or other obligations, whether funded, refunded, assumed, or otherwise, pursuant to Article 5 (commencing with Section 33640) of this chapter.

(3) The agency shall be prohibited from encumbering any funds or expending any moneys derived from any source, except that the agency may encumber funds and expend funds to pay, if any, all of the following:

(A) Bonds, notes, interim certificates, debentures, or other obligations issued by an agency before the imposition of the prohibition in paragraph (2), whether funded, refunded, assumed, or otherwise, pursuant to Article 5 (commencing with Section 33460) of this chapter.

(B) Loans or moneys advanced to the agency, including, but not limited to, loans from federal, state, local agencies, or a private entity.

(C) Contractual obligations that, if breached, could subject the agency to damages or other liabilities or remedies.

(D) Obligations incurred pursuant to Section 33445.

(E) Indebtedness incurred pursuant to Section 33334.2 or 33334.6.

(F) Obligations incurred pursuant to Section 33401.

(G) An amount, to be expended for the monthly operation and administration of the agency, that may not exceed 75 percent of the average monthly amount spent for those purposes in the fiscal year preceding the fiscal year in which the agency failed to make the payment required by subdivision (a) of Section 33685.

(f) The prohibitions identified in subdivision (e) shall be lifted once the county auditor certifies to the Director of Finance that the payment required by Section 33685 has been made by the agency, or that payment has been made on the agency's behalf pursuant to this section or to Section 33687 or 33688.

33687 In-lieu payments by legislative body to educational revenue augmentation fund during 2008-09

(a) In lieu of the remittance required by Section 33685, for the 2008-09 fiscal year, a legislative body may remit, prior to May 10, 2009, an amount equal to the amount determined for the agency pursuant to subparagraph (J) of paragraph (2) of subdivision (a) of Section 33685 to the county auditor for deposit in the county Educational Revenue Augmentation Fund, created pursuant to

Article 3 (commencing with Section 97) of Chapter 6 of Part 0.5 of Division 1 of the Revenue and Taxation Code. Notwithstanding any other provision of law, in the 2008-09 fiscal year, no funds deposited in the county Educational Revenue Augmentation Fund pursuant to this section shall be distributed to a community college district.

(b) The legislative body may make the remittance authorized by this section from any funds that are legally available for this purpose. No moneys held in an agency's Low and Moderate Income Housing Fund, pursuant to Sections 33334.2, 33334.3, and 33334.6, shall be used for this purpose.

(c) If the legislative body, pursuant to subdivision (d) of Section 33685, reported to the county auditor that it intended to remit the amount in lieu of the agency and the legislative body fails to transmit the full amount as authorized by this section by May 10, 2009, the county auditor, no later than May 15, 2009, shall transfer an amount necessary to meet the obligation from the legislative body's allocations pursuant to Chapter 6 (commencing with Section 95) of Part 0.5 of Division 1 of the Revenue and Taxation Code. If the amount of the legislative body's allocations are not sufficient to meet this obligation, the county auditor shall transfer an additional amount necessary to meet this obligation from the property tax increment revenue apportioned to the agency pursuant to Section 33670, provided that no moneys allocated to the agency's Low and Moderate Income Housing Fund shall be used for this purpose.

33688 Issuance of bonds to make payments to educational revenue augmentation funds during 2008-09

(a) For purposes of this section, an "authorized issuer" is limited to a joint powers entity created pursuant to Article 1 (commencing with Section 6500) of Chapter 5 of Division 7 of Title 1 of the Government Code that consists of no less than 100 local agencies issuing bonds pursuant to the Marks-Roos Local Bond Pooling Act of 1984 (Article 4 (commencing with Section 6584) of Chapter 5 of Division 7 of Title 1 of the Government Code).

(b) An authorized issuer may issue bonds, notes, or other evidence of indebtedness to provide net proceeds to make one or more loans to one or more agencies to be used by the agency to timely make the payment required by Section 33684.

(c) With the prior approval of the legislative body by adoption of a resolution by a majority of that body that recites that a first lien on the property tax revenues allocated to the legislative body will be created in accordance with subdivision (h), an agency may enter into an agreement with an authorized issuer issuing bonds pursuant to subdivision (b) to repay a loan used to make the payment required by Section 33685. For the purpose of calculating the amount that has been divided and allocated to the agency to determine whether the limitation adopted pursuant to Section 33333.2 or 33333.4 or pursuant to an agreement or court order that has been reached, any funds used to repay a loan entered into pursuant to this section shall be deducted from the amount of property tax revenue deemed to have been received by the agency.

(d) A loan made pursuant to this section shall be repayable by the agency from any available funds of the agency not otherwise obligated for other uses and shall be repayable by the agency on a basis subordinate to all existing and future obligations of the agency.

(e) Upon making a loan to an agency pursuant to this section, the trustee for the bonds issued to provide the funds to make the loan shall timely pay, on behalf of the agency, to the county auditor of the county in which the agency is located the net proceeds (after payment of costs of issuance, credit enhancement costs, and reserves, if any) of the loan in payment in full or in part, as directed by the agency, of the amount required to be paid by the agency pursuant to Section 33685 and shall provide the county auditor with the repayment schedule for the loan, together with the name of the trustee.

(f) In the event the agency shall fail to repay timely, at any time and from time to time, the loan in accordance with the schedule provided to the county auditor, the trustee for the bonds shall promptly notify the county auditor of the amount of the payment on the loan that is past due.

(g) The county auditor shall reallocate from the legislative body and shall pay, on behalf of the agency, the past due amount from the first available proceeds of the property tax allocation that would otherwise be transferred to the legislative body pursuant to Chapter 6 (commencing with Section 95) of Part 0.5 of Division 1 of the Revenue and Taxation Code. This transfer shall be deemed a reallocation of the property tax revenue from the legislative body to the agency for the purpose of payment of the loan, and not as a payment by the legislative body on the loan.

(h) To secure repayment of a loan to an agency made pursuant to this section, the trustee for the bonds issued to provide the funds to make the loan shall have a lien on the property tax revenues allocated to the legislative body pursuant to Chapter 6 (commencing with Section 95) of Part 0.5 of Division 1 of the Revenue and Taxation Code. This lien shall arise by operation of this section automatically upon the making of the loan without the need for any action on the part of any person. This lien shall be valid, binding, perfected, and enforceable against the legislative body, its successors, creditors, purchasers, and all others asserting rights in those property tax revenues, irrespective of whether those persons have notice of the lien, irrespective of the fact that the property tax revenues subject to the lien may be commingled with other property, and without the need for physical delivery, recordation, public notice, or any other act. This lien shall be a first priority lien on these property tax revenues. This lien shall not apply to any portion of the property taxes allocated to the agency pursuant to Section 33670.

33689 Payments to educational revenue augmentation funds for 2008-09 not counted toward tax increment caps

For the purpose of calculating the amount that has been divided and allocated to the agency to determine whether the limitation adopted pursuant to Section 33333.2 or 33333.4 or pursuant to agreement or court order that has been reached, any payments made pursuant to subdivision (a) of Section 33685 with property tax revenues shall be deducted from the amount of property tax dollars deemed to have been received by the agency.

Chapter 7.5. LOANS TO TAX-EXEMPT ORGANIZATIONS

33740 Legislative findings and declarations

The Legislature hereby finds and declares that it would be beneficial to empower redevelopment agencies to issue tax-exempt revenue bonds for the purpose of lending the proceeds to nonprofit organizations exempt from federal income taxation pursuant to Section 501(c)(3) of the Internal Revenue Code of 1986, as amended (26 U.S.C. Sec. 501(c)(3)), for the housing purposes specified in Section 33741.

33741 Issuance of bonds for multifamily rental housing development

An agency may issue bonds to provide funds to be loaned by the agency to nonprofit organizations exempt from federal income taxation under Section 501(c)(3) of the Internal Revenue Code of 1986, as amended (26 U.S.C. Sec. 501(c)(3)), for use by the organization to finance the acquisition, construction, rehabilitation, refinancing, or development of multifamily rental housing, including mobilehome parks that are or will be nonprofit or cooperatively owned, or both, in which residents rent spaces and either rent or own the mobilehomes occupying these spaces, to provide housing within the territorial jurisdiction of the agency in accordance with the organization's tax-exempt purposes under that federal law. The bonds shall be issued so as to satisfy the requirements of Section 145 of the Internal Revenue Code of 1986, as amended (26 U.S.C. Sec. 145).

33742 Affordability restrictions

(a) Occupancy and rent restrictions with respect to housing acquired pursuant to this chapter shall either meet the requirements of subparagraphs (A) and (B) of paragraph (1) or the requirements of paragraph (2), as follows:

(1) (A) Not less than 20 percent of the total number of units in a multifamily rental housing development financed, or for which financing has been extended or committed, pursuant to this chapter from the proceeds of the sale of bonds of each bond issuance of the agency shall be for occupancy on a priority basis by lower income households, as defined by Section 50079.5. If a multifamily rental housing development is located within a targeted area project, as defined by Section 103(b)(12)(A) of Title 26 of the United States Code, not less than 15 percent of the total number of units financed, or for which financing has been extended or committed pursuant to this chapter, shall be for occupancy on a priority basis by lower income households. Not less than one-half of the units required for occupancy on a priority basis by lower income households shall be for occupancy on a priority basis for very low income households, as defined by Section 50105.

(B) (i) With respect to multifamily rental developments that are not mobilehome parks, the rental payments on the units required for occupancy by very low income households paid by the persons occupying the units (excluding any supplemental rental assistance from the state, the federal government, or any other public agency to those persons or on behalf of those units) shall not exceed 30 percent of an amount equal to 50 percent of area median income. If the nonprofit organization elects to establish a base rent for all or part of the units for lower income households and very low income households, the base rents shall be adjusted for household size. In adjusting rents for household size for this purpose, it shall be assumed that one person will occupy a studio unit, two persons will occupy a one-bedroom unit, three persons will occupy a two-bedroom unit, four persons will occupy a three-bedroom unit, and five persons will occupy a four-bedroom unit.

(ii) With respect to mobilehome parks:

(I) Where a resident rents both the mobilehome and the space occupied by the mobilehome, for spaces and mobilehomes required for occupancy by very low income households, the total rental payments paid by the household on the mobilehome and the space occupied by the mobilehome (excluding any supplemental rental assistance from the state, the federal government, or any other public agency to that household or on behalf of that space and mobilehome) shall not exceed 30 percent of an amount equal to 50 percent of the area median income, adjusted for household size as appropriate for the unit that occupies the space.

(II) Where a resident is both the registered and legal owner of the mobilehome, is not making mortgage payments for the purchase of that mobilehome, and rents the space that the mobilehome occupies, for spaces and mobilehomes required for occupancy by very low income households, the total rental charge for occupancy of that space, excluding a reasonable allowance for other related housing costs determined at the time of acquisition of the mobilehome park by the nonprofit corporation, excluding any supplemental rental assistance from the state, the federal government, or any other public agency to that household on behalf of that space and mobilehome, shall not exceed 30 percent of 50 percent of the area median income, adjusted for household size as appropriate for the unit that occupies the space.

(III) Where a resident is the registered owner of the mobilehome, is making mortgage payments for the purchase of that mobilehome, and rents the space occupied by the mobilehome, for spaces and mobilehomes required for occupancy by very low income households, the rental charge for occupancy of a space by a mobilehome, exclusive of any charges for utilities and storage (excluding any supplemental rental assistance from the state, the federal government, or any other public agency to that household or on behalf of that space and mobilehome), shall not exceed 15 percent of 50 percent of the area median income, adjusted for household size as appropriate for the unit that occupies the space.

(IV) In adjusting rents for household size, either the occupancy standards established in clause (i) of subparagraph (B) of paragraph (1) of subdivision (a) or the alternative standards that assume that one person will occupy a recreational vehicle, two persons will occupy a single-wide mobilehome, and three persons will occupy a multisectional mobilehome may be utilized.

(2) The multifamily rental housing development is a "qualified low-income housing project," within the meaning of Section 42(g) of the federal Internal Revenue Code (26 U.S.C. Sec. 42), because it meets the criteria set forth in Section 42(g)(1)(B) and (2) of the federal Internal Revenue Code.

(b) If at the time of acquisition any of the units or mobilehome spaces are occupied by ineligible households, that fact alone shall neither constitute a cause for the tenant's eviction nor render the project ineligible. Upon vacation of any unit initially occupied by an ineligible household, that unit shall be rented to an eligible household until the required residency by eligible households is attained.

(c) As a condition of financing pursuant to this chapter, the nonprofit organization shall enter into a regulatory agreement with the agency, which shall require that units reserved for occupancy by lower income households shall remain available on a priority basis for occupancy for the term of the bonds issued to provide the financing or 30 years, whichever is greater. The regulatory agreement shall contain a provision making the covenants and conditions of the agreement binding upon successors in interest of the nonprofit organization. The regulatory agreement shall be recorded in the office of the county recorder of the county in which the multifamily rental housing development is located. The regulatory agreement shall be recorded in the grantor-grantee index to the name of the property owner as grantor and to the name of the agency as grantee.

33743 Authority to acquire commercial property; limitations

An agency may, in conjunction with the financing of multifamily rental housing pursuant to this chapter, finance the acquisition of commercial property for lease, subject to all of the following conditions:

(a) No more than 10 percent of the proceeds of any revenue bonds issued pursuant to this chapter may be used to acquire the commercial property for lease.

(b) The commercial property acquired will be located on the same parcel or on a parcel adjacent to a multifamily rental housing development.

(c) As a condition of the financing, any lease payments collected in excess of payments necessary for debt service, operating expenses and any required reserves related to the property, shall be used to reduce rents or units reserved for occupancy by lower income households and very low income households in a multifamily rental housing development.

33744 Violation of affordability restrictions; remedies

Whenever a complaint is received concerning a violation of the restrictions imposed pursuant to Section 33742, the agency shall investigate promptly and make a report to the complaining party on whether the violation existed and whether it persists, and if it persists, what action the agency will take to remedy the violation. When the agency determines that a violation exists, whether determined upon an investigation of a complaint or on its own motion, the agency shall take all appropriate action, including necessary legal action, to promptly eliminate the violation.

Notwithstanding other provisions of this section, any person aggrieved by a violation of the restrictions imposed pursuant to Section 33742 may seek a judicial remedy without regard to whether a complaint has been made to the agency or whether the agency is then taking any action to remedy the violation.

33745 Payment of administrative costs

For the purposes of this chapter, an agency shall have the power to issue its bonds to defray, in whole or in part, the costs of studies and surveys, insurance premiums, underwriting fees, and legal, accounting and marketing services incurred in connection with the issuance and sale of bonds pursuant to this chapter, including bond and mortgage reserve accounts, trustee, custodian, and rating agency fees, and any other costs which are reasonably related to the foregoing.

33746 Repayment of bonds; tax-exempt status

(a) Bonds issued pursuant to this chapter shall be repayable solely from payments of principal and interest on account of the loans funded thereby. The agency may pledge all or any portion of these payments to secure the bonds.

(b) Neither the members of the agency nor any person executing the bonds shall be personally liable on the bonds or be subject to any personal liability or accountability by reason of the issuance thereof.

(c) The exercise of the powers granted by this chapter shall be in all respects for the benefit of the people of this state and for their health and welfare. Any bonds issued under this chapter, their transfer, and income therefrom shall at all times be free from taxation of every kind by the state and by the municipalities and political subdivisions of the state, except estate taxes.

(d) This chapter provides an alternative method for issuing bonds and lending moneys for acquisition of multifamily rental housing by private nonprofit organizations.

Chapter 8. REDEVELOPMENT CONSTRUCTION LOANS

Article 1
General Provisions and Definitions

33750 Legislative findings and declarations

The Legislature finds and declares that it is necessary and essential that redevelopment agencies be authorized to make long-term, low-interest loans through qualified mortgage lenders to finance residential construction in order to encourage investment and upgrade redevelopment project areas and increase the supply of housing. Unless redevelopment agencies intervene to generate mortgage funds and to provide some form of assistance to finance residential construction, many redevelopment areas will stagnate and deteriorate because owners and investors are not able to obtain loans from private sources.

The Legislature further finds and declares that financing of rehabilitation, as provided in this chapter, serves an essential public purpose for the economic renewal of our cities.

33751 Further legislative findings and declarations

The Legislature further finds and determines that a program to provide residential construction financing would accomplish the following:

(a) Facilitate increasing the supply of urban housing and ease the housing shortage that exists in many parts of the state.

(b) Encourage Californians of all social and economic positions to reinhabit urban areas, thereby rendering these areas more socially balanced and economically self-sufficient.

(c) Reduce pressures for suburbanization and thereby mitigate many of the problems caused by urban migration, including inefficient use of scarce energy resources and urban sprawl.

(d) Stimulate urban building and construction activity and thereby increase urban employment and improve the urban tax base.

33751.5 Further legislative findings and declarations

The Legislature further finds and declares that the construction and rehabilitation of residences intended for occupancy primarily by persons and families of low or moderate income, as defined in Section 50093, is properly included within redevelopment plans whether or not such construction or rehabilitation is to occur within a redevelopment area, since redevelopment agencies have specific obligations for development of housing whether or not such development is feasible within specific redevelopment project areas.

33752 Legislative intent

It is the intent of the Legislature, in enacting this chapter, to strengthen the vitality and promote the completion of urban redevelopment for the general public benefit. The construction of federally assisted housing for low- and moderate-income households is not a primary purpose of this chapter. However, nothing in this chapter shall be deemed to prohibit financing of federally assisted housing for low- and moderate-income households when such housing is consistent with the redevelopment plan and the loan is directly or indirectly insured.

33753 Definitions

The definitions set forth in Article 1 (commencing with Section 33000) of Chapter 1 of this part shall govern the construction of this chapter. Additionally, as used in this chapter:

(a) "Construction loan" means a loan to finance residential construction under this chapter, whether such loan is insured or uninsured.

(b) "Financing" means the lending of moneys or any other thing of value for the purpose of facilitating residential construction pursuant to this chapter, including the making of construction loans and mortgage loans to purchasers of newly constructed and newly rehabilitated residences and the making of loans to qualified mortgage lenders, and the making of mortgage loans to purchasers of newly constructed or existing residences located in targeted areas as provided in Section 33760.

(c) "Local codes" means applicable local, state and federal standards for residential construction or rehabilitation, including any other standards adopted by the agency for a redevelopment project area or as part of its redevelopment program.

(d) "Mortgage loan" means a long-term loan which is secured by a mortgage and is made for permanent financing of residences, pursuant to this chapter.

(e) "Participating party" means any person, corporation, partnership, firm, or other entity or group of entities requiring financing for residential construction pursuant to the provisions of this chapter. No elective officer of the state other than officers provided for by Article VI of the California Constitution, and no employee or member of the redevelopment agency, shall be eligible to be a participating party under the provisions of this chapter. If any elected officer of any political subdivision of the state participates in deliberations or votes on a financing plan, redevelopment plan, or bond issue, that person shall not be eligible to be a participating party for bonds issued pursuant to those plans or issues.

(f) "Qualified mortgage lender" means a mortgage lender authorized by a redevelopment agency to do business with the agency and to aid in financing pursuant to this chapter on behalf of the agency, for which service the qualified mortgage lender will be reasonably compensated. Such a mortgage lender shall be a state or national bank, federal or state-chartered savings and loan association, or trust company or mortgage banker which is capable of providing service or otherwise aiding in the financing of mortgages on residential construction within the jurisdiction of the agency. Nothing in any other provision of state law shall prevent such a lender from serving as a qualified mortgage lender pursuant to this chapter.

(g) "Redevelopment project area" means a project area, as defined in Section 33320.1, for which a final redevelopment plan has been adopted pursuant to Section 33365.

(h) "Rehabilitation" means repairs and improvements to a substandard residence necessary to make it meet local codes; and also means the acquisition of substandard residences for purposes of repairs and improvements where the cost of such repairs and improvements equals or exceeds 25 percent of the cost of the acquisition. As used in this section, "substandard residence" has the same meaning as the term "substandard building," as defined in Section 17920.3, except that "substandard residence" shall include all property improved with any structure defined in subdivision (j) of this section as a "residence," with respect to which any of the conditions listed in Section 17920.3 exist.

(i) "Residential construction" means the construction of new residences or the rehabilitation and improvement of substandard residences to meet requirements of local codes and the redevelopment plan. "Residential construction" also means the improvement of residences as provided in subdivision (h).

(j) (1) "Residence" means real property improved with a residential structure and within a redevelopment project area real property improved with a commercial structure (or structures) or a mixed residential and commercial structure, which the redevelopment agency determines to be an integral part of a residential neighborhood. For purposes of determining the integrality of new construction for such purpose, a proposed commercial or mixed residential and commercial structure shall be located within or immediately adjacent to a neighborhood primarily residential in character.

(2) "Residence" also means residential hotels in which not less than one-half of the occupied dwelling units are occupied on a nontransient basis. A dwelling unit shall be deemed to be used on a nontransient basis if the term of the tenancy is one month or longer or if the tenant has resided in the unit for more than 30 days. In a residential hotel, individual dwelling units shall lack either cooking facilities or individual sanitary facilities, or both. However, for purposes of this paragraph, a residential hotel does not include dormitories, fraternity and sorority houses, hospitals, sanitariums, rest homes, or trailer parks and courts.

New construction of any commercial structure, or of the commercial portion of any mixed residential and commercial structure, financed under this chapter shall not exceed 80,000 square feet of gross building area per development. Any suit challenging such finding shall be filed within 60 days, or the findings of the agency shall be conclusive.

An agency may not provide long-term financing pursuant to this chapter for new construction of a commercial structure or the commercial portion of a mixed residential and commercial structure if conventional financing in an amount sufficient to complete the construction has been obtained for the construction of such structure or portion thereof.

Prior to the financing of any commercial structure within a redevelopment project area, the agency shall adopt a financing plan by resolution, which may include commercial and residential structures. The square footage of the commercial structures shall not exceed 30 percent of the aggregate square footage of all the commercial and residential structures within the project area and financed pursuant to the financing plan. The financing plan for the commercial and residential structures shall include structures that have been, or are being, financed pursuant to this chapter or under federal or state financial assistance programs or local assistance programs of any kind whatsoever. However, such a financing plan shall not be required for an agency that has financed residential structures with the proceeds of bonds issued prior to September 30, 1980, nor shall such amendments affect the validity of the tax-exempt status of bonds issued pursuant to this chapter prior to such date.

Additionally, any financing for a commercial structure or a mixed residential and commercial structure authorized or preliminarily approved by resolution adopted by a redevelopment agency or community development commission established pursuant to Section 33201 either (1) on or before June 3, 1980, in furtherance of which the agency or any person or entity has expended substantial funds or committed to reimburse another person or entity which has expended substantial funds; provided that if the long-term permanent financing is in excess of five million dollars ($5,000,000) on any one project from all financing sources, including conventional and tax-exempt financing, a redevelopment agency or community development commission shall not provide such long-term permanent financing unless such agency or commission adopted a resolution before January 1, 1981, officially approving and authorizing the sale of revenue bonds to provide such long-term permanent financing, and the bonds were sold and delivered before March 1, 1981; or (2) before October 31, 1980, in furtherance of which the agency has expended funds in connection with such financing or plans relating to such financing if the structure to be financed is located within a city designated pursuant to Section 119 of federal Public Law 95-128, as amended, or within a city designated as of September 30, 1980, under Title IX of federal Public Law 89-136, as amended, as a long-term economic deterioration area, or financing for a commercial structure or mixed residential and commercial structure as to which bonds have been delivered on or before July 31, 1980 (without regard to the date the bonds were authorized or received preliminary approval), shall not be subject to new requirements or conditions of this subdivision enacted by Chapter 1331 of the Statutes of 1980.

"Residence" includes condominium and cooperative dwelling units, and includes both real property improved with single-family residential structures and real property improved with multiple-family residential structures.

(k) "Revenue bonds" means any bonds, notes, interim certificates, debentures, or other obligations issued by an agency pursuant to this chapter and which are payable exclusively from revenues and from any other funds specified in this chapter upon which the revenue bonds may be made a charge and from which they are payable.

(l) "Revenues" means all amounts received as repayment of principal, interest, and all other charges received for, and all other income and receipts derived by, the redevelopment agency from the financing of residential construction, including moneys deposited in a sinking, redemption, or reserve fund or other fund to secure the revenue bonds or to provide for the payment of the principal of, or interest on, the revenue bonds.

(m) "Target areas" has the same meaning as in Section 103A of the Federal Internal Revenue Code of 1954, as amended.

Article 2
Powers and Procedures

33760 Residential mortgage or construction loans; affordability restrictions

(a) Within its territorial jurisdiction, an agency may determine the location and character of any residential construction to be financed under this chapter and may make mortgage or construction loans to participating parties through qualified mortgage lenders, or purchase mortgage or construction loans without premium made by qualified mortgage lenders to participating parties, or make loans to qualified mortgage lenders, for financing any of the following:

(1) Residential construction within a redevelopment project area.

(2) Residential construction of residences in which the dwelling units are committed, for the period during which the loan is outstanding, for occupancy by persons or families who are eligible for financial assistance specifically provided by a governmental agency for the benefit of occupants of the residence.

(3) To the extent required by Section 103A of Title 26 of the United States Code, as amended, to maintain the exemption from federal income taxes of interest on bonds or notes issued by the agency under this chapter, residences located within targeted areas, as defined by Section 103(b)(12)(A) of Title 26 of the United States Code. Any loans to qualified mortgage lenders shall be made under terms and conditions which, in addition to other provisions as determined by the agency, shall require the qualified mortgage lender to use all of the net proceeds thereof, directly or indirectly, for the making of mortgage loans or construction loans in an appropriate principal amount equal to the amount of the net proceeds. Those mortgage loans may, but need not, be insured.

(b) (1) Not less than 20 percent (15 percent in target areas) of the units in any residential project financed pursuant to this section on or after January 1, 1986, shall be occupied by, or made available to, individuals of low and moderate income, as defined by Section 103(b)(12)(C) of Title 26 of the United States Code. If the sponsor elects to establish a base rent for units reserved for lower income households, the base rents shall be adjusted for household size, as determined pursuant to Section 8 of the United States Housing Act of 1937 (42 U.S.C. Sec. 1437f), or its successor, for a family of one person in the case of a studio unit, two persons in the case of a one-bedroom unit, three persons in the case of a two-bedroom unit, four persons in the case of a three-bedroom unit, and five persons in the case of a four-bedroom unit.

(2) Not less than one-half of the units described in paragraph (1) shall be occupied by, or made available to, very low income households, as defined by Section 50105. The rental payments for those units paid by the persons occupying the units (excluding any supplemental rental assistance from the state, the federal government, or any other public agency to those persons or on behalf of those units) shall not exceed the amount derived by multiplying 30 percent times 50 percent of the median adjusted gross income for the area, adjusted for family size, as determined pursuant to Section 8 of the United States Housing Act of 1937 (42 U.S.C. Sec. 1437f), or its successor, for a family of one person in the case of a studio unit, two persons in the case of a one-bedroom unit, three persons in the case of a two-bedroom unit, four persons in the case of a three-bedroom unit, and five persons in the case of a four-bedroom unit.

(c) Units required to be reserved for occupancy as provided in subdivision (b) and financed with the proceeds of bonds issued on or after January 1, 1986, shall remain occupied by, or made available to, those persons until the bonds are retired.

(d) (1) When issuing tax-exempt bonds for purposes of this section, the regulatory agreement entered into by the agency shall require that following the expiration or termination of the qualified project period, except in the event of foreclosure and redemption of the bonds, deed in lieu of foreclosure, eminent domain, or action of a federal agency preventing enforcement, units required to be reserved for occupancy for low-or very low income households and financed or refinanced with proceeds of bonds issued pursuant to this section on or after January 1, 2006, or refinanced with the proceeds of bonds issued pursuant to Section 53583 of the Government Code or any charter city authority on or after January 1, 2007, shall remain available to any eligible household occupying a reserved unit at the date of expiration or termination, at a rent not greater than the amount set forth by the regulatory agreement prior to the date or expiration or termination, until the earliest of any of the following occur:

    (A) The household's income exceeds 140 percent of the maximum eligible income specified in the regulatory agreement for reserved units.

    (B) The household voluntarily moves or is evicted for "good cause." "Good cause" for the purposes of this section, means the nonpayment of rent or allegation of facts necessary to prove major, or repeated minor, violations of material provisions of the occupancy agreement which detrimentally affect the health and safety of other persons or the structure, the fiscal integrity of the development, or the purposes or special programs of the development.

    (C) Thirty years after the date of the commencement of the qualified project period.

    (D) The sponsor pays the relocation assistance and benefits to tenants as provided in subdivision (b) of Section 7264 of the Government Code.

(2) As used in this subdivision, "qualified project period" shall have the meaning specified in, and shall be determined in accordance with the provisions of, subsection (d) of Section 142 of the Internal Revenue Code of 1986, as amended, and United States Treasury regulations and rulings promulgated pursuant thereto.

(3) The amendment to this subdivision made during the 2005-06 Regular Session of the Legislature that is set forth in paragraph (1) is declaratory of existing law.

(e) This section shall become operative January 1, 1996.

33760.5   Residential mortgage or construction loans outside redevelopment project areas in jurisdictions of more than 600,000 persons

(a) Notwithstanding the requirements of Section 33760, agencies which operate within a jurisdiction, the population of which is in excess of 600,000 persons, as determined by the Department of Finance, may additionally provide financing for residential construction of multifamily rental units outside of a redevelopment project area as set forth in and subject to the limitations of this section.

(b) Within its territorial jurisdiction, an agency may determine the location and character of any residential construction to be financed under this chapter and may make mortgage or construction loans to participating parties through qualified mortgage lenders, or purchase mortgage or construction loans without premium made by qualified mortgage lenders to participating parties for financing residential construction of multifamily rental units.

(c) Not less than 20 percent (15 percent in target areas) of the units in each project financed pursuant to this section shall be occupied by, or made available to, individuals of low and moderate income, as defined in Section 103(b)(12)(C) of Title 26 of the United States Code. If the sponsor elects to establish a base rent for units reserved for lower income households, the base rents shall be adjusted for household size, as determined pursuant to Section 8 of the United States Housing Act of 1937 (42 U.S.C. Sec. 1437f), or its successor, for a family of one person in the case of a studio unit, two persons in the case of a one-bedroom unit, three persons in the case of a two-bedroom unit, four persons in the case of a three-bedroom unit, and five persons in the case of a four-bedroom unit.

(d) Not less than one-half of the low- and moderate-income units described in subdivision (c) shall be occupied by, or made available to, very low income households, as defined in Section 50105. The rental payments for those units paid by the persons occupying the units (excluding any supplemental rental assistance from the state, the federal government, or any other public agency to those persons or on behalf of those units) shall not exceed the amount derived by multiplying 30 percent times 50 percent of the median adjusted gross income for the area, adjusted for family size, as determined pursuant to Section 8 of the United States Housing Act of 1937, (42 U.S.C. Sec. 1437f), or its successor, for a family of one person in the case of a studio unit, two persons in the case of a one-bedroom unit, three persons in the case of a two-bedroom unit, four persons in the case of a three-bedroom unit, and five persons in the case of a four-bedroom unit.

(e) No agency may issue any bonds on or after January 1, 1986, until the information required to be filed pursuant to Section 8855.5 of the Government Code has been filed with the California Debt Advisory Commission and the Treasurer certifies to the Legislature that the agency has filed that information.

(f) Units required to be reserved for occupancy by subdivisions (c) and (d) and financed with the proceeds of bonds issued on or after January 1, 1986, shall remain occupied by, or made available to, those persons until the bonds are retired.

(g) This section shall become operative January 1, 1996.

33760.7   Notice requirements

The same notice requirements as specified in Section 65863.10 of the Government Code shall apply to multifamily rental housing that receives financial assistance pursuant to Section 33760 or 33760.5.

33761   Authority to issue revenue bonds

An agency may issue revenue bonds for the purpose of financing residential construction authorized by this chapter and for the purpose of funding or refunding previously issued revenue bonds. An agency may also issue revenue bonds for the purpose of refunding bonds previously issued by another political subdivision of the state for the purpose of financing residential construction authorized by this chapter for projects within the jurisdiction of the agency. For the purposes of this section, "political subdivision" means a city, a housing authority, or a nonprofit corporation acting on behalf of a city or a housing authority, all of which operate within the jurisdiction of the agency. Any savings that accrue to the agency from refunding bonds previously issued by another political subdivision shall be limited to the expenditures authorized in subdivision (e) of Section 33334.2.

33761.5   Requirements for refunding previously issued bonds

(a) (1) When refunding revenue bonds for multifamily housing which were previously issued pursuant to this chapter, the agency shall ensure that rental units required, by this chapter or by applicable federal law at the time the original bonds were issued, to be reserved for occupancy for low- and very low income households shall remain occupied by, or made available to, those persons at least until the later of the following:

(A) The date originally so required.

(B) As long as any bonds remain outstanding with respect to the development.

(2) For bonds previously issued to finance a development where all of the units, other than management units, are, at the time of the refunding, subsidized by a housing assistance payments contract for new construction and substantial rehabilitation pursuant to Section 8 of the United States Housing Act of 1937 (42 U.S.C. Sec. 1437f), subparagraph (B) of paragraph (1) shall mean a period of time until the termination of the contract.

(b) The agency may determine that the period set forth in paragraph (1) of subdivision (a) shall not apply to the refunding of previously issued revenue bonds for which there is a mandatory redemption or acceleration as a result of default under the terms of the existing loan agreement or other security documents.

33762 Limitations on fees, charges and interest rates for financing residential construction

An agency may establish limitations respecting fees, charges, and interest rates to be used by qualified mortgage lenders for financing residential construction pursuant to this chapter and may from time to time revise such fees, charges, and interest rates to reflect changes in interest rates on the agency's revenue bonds, losses due to defaults, changes in loan-servicing charges, or other expenses related to administration of the residential construction financing program. Any change in interest rate shall conform to the provisions of Section 1916.5 of the Civil Code, except that paragraph (3) of subdivision (a) of Section 1916.5 shall not apply and that the "prescribed standard" specified in Section 1916.5 shall be periodically determined by the redevelopment agency after hearing preceded by public notice to affected parties, and shall reflect changes in interest rates on the agency's bonds, and bona fide changes in loan servicing charges related to the administration of a program under the provisions of this chapter. An agency may purchase mortgage or construction loans made by a qualified mortgage lender without premium or may itself pay such fees and charges incurred in lending money for the purpose of residential construction and may collect and disburse, or may contract to pay any person, partnership, association, corporation, or public agency for, collection and disbursal of payments of principal, interest, taxes, insurance, and mortgage insurance. An agency may hold deeds of trust or mortgages, including mortgages insured under Title II of the National Housing Act, as security for financing residential construction and may pledge or assign the same as security for repayment of revenue bonds. Such deeds of trust or mortgages may be assigned to, and held on behalf of the agency by, any bank or trust company appointed to act as trustee or fiscal agent by the agency in any indenture or resolution providing for issuance of bonds pursuant to this chapter. An agency may establish the terms and conditions of financing, which shall be consistent with the provisions of any applicable federal or state law under which the financing is to be insured.

33763 Additional requirements for mortgage loans

(a) No loan shall be made for financing except through a qualified mortgage lender.

(b) All mortgage loans made for financing pursuant to this chapter from the proceeds of bonds issued on or before October 1, 1983, shall be insured or guaranteed, in whole or in part, by any instrumentality of the United States, or the State of California, or by any person licensed to insure mortgages in this state. Mortgage loans made for financing pursuant to this chapter from the proceeds of bonds issued after October 1, 1983, may be insured or guaranteed, in whole or in part by those entities or persons. However, nothing in this subdivision shall impair any contractual rights which may have vested in bondholders or other persons prior to October 1, 1983.

33763.5 Additional requirements for loans

All loans made by a redevelopment agency shall be made according to a regulation that contains standards, qualifications, and criteria for the making and approval of loans and that has been adopted by the redevelopment agency at a public meeting.

33764 Employment of consultants

An agency may employ engineering, architectural, accounting, collection, or other services, including services in connection with the servicing of loans made to participating parties, as may be necessary in the judgment of the agency for the successful financing of residential construction pursuant to this chapter. An agency may pay the reasonable costs of consulting engineers, architects, accountants, and other experts, if, in the judgment of the agency, such services are necessary to the successful financing of any residential construction and if the agency is not able to provide such services. An agency may employ and fix the compensation of financing consultants, bond counsel, and other advisers as may be necessary in its judgment to provide for the issuance and sale of any revenue bonds of the agency.

33765 Additional powers

In addition to all other powers specifically granted by this chapter, an agency may do all things necessary or convenient to carry out the purposes of this chapter.

33766 Repayment of revenue bonds

Revenues and the proceeds of mortgage insurance or guarantee claims, if any, shall be the sole source of funds pledged by an agency for repayment of its revenue bonds. Revenue bonds issued under this chapter do not constitute a debt or liability of the agency or the state for which the faith and credit of the agency or the state is pledged but shall be payable solely from revenues and the proceeds of mortgage insurance or guarantee claims, if any.

33767 Rules and regulations for residential construction; property acquisition and disposition

All residential construction shall be undertaken or completed subject to the rules and regulations of the agency. An agency may acquire by deed, purchase, lease, contract, gift, devise, or otherwise any real or personal property, structures, rights, rights-of-way, franchises, easements, and other interests in lands necessary or convenient for the financing of residential construction, upon such terms and conditions as it deems advisable, and may lease, sell, or dispose of the same in such manner as may be necessary or desirable to carry out the objectives and purposes of this chapter.

33768 Relocation assistance laws not applicable to acquisition for loan default

The provisions of Chapter 16 (commencing with Section 7260) of Division 7 of Title 1 of the Government Code shall not apply to owners or tenants of any property acquired by foreclosure, trust deed, sale or other proceeding resulting from default on a loan made by the agency.

33769 Prohibition against discrimination

(a) An agency shall require that any residence that is constructed with financing obtained under this chapter shall be open, upon sale or rental of any portion thereof, to all regardless of any basis listed in subdivision (a) or (d) of Section 12955 of the Government Code, as those bases are defined in Sections 12926, 12926.1, subdivision (m) and paragraph (1) of subdivision (p) of Section 12955, and Section 12955.2 of the Government Code. The agency shall also require that contractors and subcontractors engaged in residential construction financed under this chapter shall provide equal opportunity for employment, without discrimination as to any basis listed in subdivision (a) of Section 12940 of the Government Code, as those bases are defined in Sections 12926 and 12926.1 of the Government Code, and except as otherwise provided in Section 12940 of the Government Code. All contracts and subcontracts for residential construction financed under this chapter shall be let without discrimination as to any basis listed in subdivision (a) of Section 12940 of the Government Code, as those bases are defined in Sections 12926 and 12926.1 of the Government Code, and except as otherwise provided in Section 12940 of the Government Code. It shall be the policy of an agency financing residential construction under this chapter to encourage participation by minority contractors, and the agency shall adopt rules and regulations to implement this section.

(b) Notwithstanding subdivision (a), with respect to familial status, subdivision (a) shall not be construed to apply to housing for older persons, as defined in Section 12955.9 of the Government Code. With respect to familial status, nothing in subdivision (a) shall be construed to affect Sections 51.2, 51.3, 51.4, 51.10, 51.11, and 799.5 of the Civil Code, relating to housing for senior citizens. Subdivision (d) of Section 51 and Section 1360 of the Civil Code and subdivisions (n), (o), and (p) of Section 12955 of the Government Code shall apply to subdivision (a).

Article 3
Bonds and Notes

33775 Issuance of revenue bonds and bond anticipation notes

(a) An agency may, from time to time, issue its negotiable revenue bonds for the purpose of making or purchasing mortgage or construction loans, or making loans to qualified mortgage lenders, to finance residential construction. In anticipation of the sale of bonds, the agency may issue negotiable bond anticipation notes and may renew the notes from time to time. Bond anticipation notes may be paid from the proceeds of sale of the bonds of the agency in anticipation of which they were issued. Bond anticipation notes and agreements relating thereto and the resolution or resolutions authorizing the notes and agreements may contain any provisions, conditions, or limitations which a bond, agreement relating thereto, or bond resolution of the agency may contain except that any note or renewal thereof shall mature at a time not later than five years from the date of the issuance of the original note.

(b) Every issue of its revenue bonds shall be a special obligation of the redevelopment agency payable from all or any part of the revenues specified in this chapter. The revenue bonds shall be negotiable instruments for all purposes, subject only to the provisions of the bonds for registration.

33775.5 Costs of issuance

In determining the amount of bonds to be issued, the agency may include all costs of the issuance of such revenue bonds, bond reserve funds, and bond interest estimated to accrue for a period not exceeding 12 months from the date of issuance of the bonds.

33776 Resolution of the agency; types and terms of bonds

The revenue bonds may be issued as serial bonds or as term bonds, or the redevelopment agency, in its discretion, may issue revenue bonds of both types. The revenue bonds shall be authorized by resolution of the agency and shall bear such date or dates, mature at such time or times, not exceeding 50 years from their respective dates of issuance, bear interest at such fixed or variable rate or rates, be payable at such time or times, be in such denominations, be in such form either coupon or registered, carry such registration privileges, be executed in such manner, be payable in lawful money of the United States of America at such place or places, and be subject to such terms of redemption as the resolution or resolutions of the redevelopment agency may provide. The bonds may be sold at either a public or private sale and for such prices as the agency shall determine. Pending preparation of the definitive bonds, the agency may issue interim receipts, certificates, or temporary bonds, which shall be exchanged for such definitive bonds.

33777 Contract with bondholders

Any resolution or resolutions authorizing any revenue bonds or any issue of revenue bonds may contain provisions respecting any of the following terms and conditions, which shall be a part of the contract with the holders of the revenue bonds:

(a) The pledge of all or any part of the revenues, subject to such agreements with bondholders as may then exist.

(b) The interest and principal to be received and other charges to be charged and the amounts to be raised each year thereby, and the use and disposition of the revenues.

(c) The setting aside of reserves or sinking funds and the regulation and disposition thereof.

(d) Limitations on the purposes to which the proceeds of a sale of any issue of revenue bonds, then or thereafter issued, may be applied, and pledging such proceeds to secure the payment of the revenue bonds or any issue of revenue bonds.

(e) Limitations on the issuance of additional revenue bonds, the terms upon which additional revenue bonds may be issued and secured, and the refunding of outstanding revenue bonds.

(f) The procedure, if any, by which the terms of any contract with bondholders may be amended or abrogated, the amount of revenue bonds the holders of which must consent thereto, and the manner in which such consent may be given.

(g) Limitation on expenditures for operating, administration, or other expenses of the agency.

(h) Specification of the acts or omissions to act which shall constitute a default in the duties of the redevelopment agency to holders of its revenue bonds, and providing the rights and remedies of such holders in the event of default.

(i) The mortgaging of any residence and the site thereof for the purpose of securing the bondholders.

(j) The mortgaging of land, improvements, or other assets owned by a participating party for the purpose of securing the bondholders.

33777.5 Interim investment of revenues and proceeds of bonds

When not immediately required to provide financing under this chapter, revenues and the proceeds of revenue bonds may be invested in any securities or obligations authorized by the resolution providing for issuance of the bonds or authorized by its trust indenture. Such investments may include mortgage obligations on single-family dwellings purchased from a state or federally chartered bank or savings and loan association pursuant to a repurchase agreement under which the bank or savings and loan association will repurchase the mortgage obligation on or before a specified date and for a specified amount, provided that the mortgage or the repurchase agreement shall be insured by a mortgage insurance company licensed to insure mortgages in the State of California and qualified to provide insurance on mortgages purchased by the Federal Home Loan Mortgage Corporation or the Federal National Mortgage Association.

The authority provided in this section is additional and alternative to any other authorization for investments contained in this part, including Section 33782, or in other provisions of law.

33778 No personal liability

Neither the members of the agency nor any person executing the revenue bonds shall be liable personally on the revenue bonds or be subject to any personal liability or accountability by reason of the issuance thereof.

33779 Agency may purchase its own revenue bonds

The agency shall have the power out of any funds available therefor to purchase its revenue bonds. The agency may hold, pledge, cancel, or resell such revenue bonds, subject to and in accordance with agreements with the bondholders.

33780 Security for repayment of bonds

In the discretion of the agency, any revenue bonds issued under the provisions of this chapter may be secured by a trust agreement by and between the agency and a corporate trustee or trustees, which may be any trust company or bank having the powers of a trust company within or without this state. Such a trust agreement or the resolution providing for the issuance of revenue bonds may pledge or assign the revenues to be received or proceeds of any contract or contracts pledged, and may convey or mortgage any residence the construction of which is to be financed out of the proceeds of such revenue bonds. Such trust agreement or the resolution providing for the issuance of bonds may provide for the assignment to such corporate trustee or trustees of mortgage or construction loans or loans to qualified mortgage lenders, to be held by such trustee or trustees on behalf of the agency for the benefit of the bondholders. Such trust agreement or resolution providing for the issuance of revenue bonds may contain such provisions for protecting and enforcing the rights and remedies of the bondholders as may be reasonable and proper and not in violation of law, including such provisions as may be included in any resolution or resolutions of the agency authorizing the issuance of the revenue bonds. Any bank or trust company doing business under the laws of this state which may act as depositary of the proceeds of revenue bonds or of revenues or other moneys may furnish such indemnity bonds or pledge such securities as may be required by the agency. Any such trust agreement may set forth the rights and remedies of the bondholders and of the trustee or trustees, and may restrict the individual right of action by bondholders. In addition to the foregoing, any such trust agreement or resolution may contain such other provisions as the agency may deem reasonable and proper for the security of the bondholders. All expenses incurred in carrying out the provisions of such trust agreement or resolution may be treated as a part of the cost of residential construction.

33781 Rights of bondholders to enforce obligations

Any holder of revenue bonds issued under the provisions of this chapter or any of the coupons appertaining thereto, and the trustee or trustees appointed pursuant to any resolution authorizing the issuance of such revenue bonds, except to the extent the rights thereof may be restricted by the resolution authorizing the issuance of the revenue bonds, may, either at law or in equity, by suit, action, mandamus, or other proceedings, protect or enforce any and all rights specified in the laws of this state or in such resolution, and may enforce and compel the performance of all duties required by this chapter or by such resolution to be performed by the agency or by any officer, employee, or agent thereof, including the fixing, charging, and collecting of rates, fees, interest, and charges authorized and required by the provisions of such resolution to be fixed, established, and collected.

33782 Refunding or redemption of bonds

Any agency may provide for the issuance of the revenue bonds of the agency for the purpose of refunding any revenue bonds of the agency then outstanding, or for the purpose of refunding any revenue bonds of another political subdivision of the state then outstanding pursuant to Section 33761, including the payment of any redemption premiums thereof and any interest accrued or to accrue to the earliest or subsequent date of redemption, purchase, or maturity of the bonds, and, if both (a) deemed advisable by the agency, and (b) projects financed with the bonds fall within the jurisdiction of the agency, for the additional purpose of paying all or any part of the cost of additional residential construction.

The proceeds of revenue bonds issued pursuant to this section may, in the discretion of the agency, be applied to the purchase or retirement at maturity or redemption of outstanding revenue bonds, either at their earliest or any subsequent redemption date or upon the purchase or retirement at the maturity thereof and, pending that application, the portion of the proceeds allocated for that purpose may be placed in escrow, to be applied to the purchase or retirement at maturity or redemption on that date, as may be determined by the agency. Pending use for purchase, retirement at maturity, or redemption of outstanding revenue bonds, any proceeds held in such an escrow may be invested and reinvested as provided in the resolution authorizing the issuance of the refunding bonds. Any interest or other increment earned or realized on any such investment may also be applied to the payment of the outstanding revenue bonds to be refunded. After the terms of the escrow have been fully satisfied and carried out, any balance of the proceeds and any interest or increment earned or realized from the investment thereof may be returned to the agency to be used by it for any lawful purpose under this chapter. That portion of the proceeds of any revenue bonds issued pursuant to this section which is designated for the purpose of paying all or any part of the cost of additional residential construction may be invested and reinvested in obligations of, or guaranteed by, the United States of America or in certificates of deposit or time deposits secured by obligation of, or guaranteed by, the United States of America, maturing not later than the time or times when the proceeds will be needed for the purpose of paying all or any part of the cost.

All revenue bonds issued pursuant to this section shall be subject to this chapter in the same manner and to the same extent as other bonds issued pursuant to this chapter.

33783 Status of bonds as legal investments

Notwithstanding any other provision of law, revenue bonds issued pursuant to this chapter shall be legal investments for all trust funds, insurance companies, savings and loan associations, investment companies and banks, both savings and commercial, and shall be legal investments for executors, administrators, guardians, conservators, trustees, and all other fiduciaries. Such bonds shall be legal investments for state school funds and for any funds which may be invested in county, municipal, or school district bonds, and such bonds shall be deemed to be securities which may properly and legally be deposited with, and received by, any state or municipal officer or by any agency or political subdivision of the state for any purpose for which the deposit of bonds or obligations of the state is now, or may hereafter be authorized by law, including deposits to secure public funds.

33784 Tax-exempt status of bonds

The exercise of the powers granted by this chapter shall be in all respects for the benefit of the people of this state and for their health and welfare. Any revenue bonds issued under the provisions of this chapter, their transfer and the income therefrom, shall at all times be free from taxation of every kind by the state and by the municipalities and other political subdivisions of the state, except inheritance and gift taxes.

Article 4
Residential Construction

33790 Agreements for residential construction required

An agency may not finance mortgage or construction loans which have not been authorized by prior written agreement between the agency and the participating party. All agreements for such loans shall provide that the architectural and engineering design of the residential construction shall be subject to such standards as may be established by the agency and that the work of such residential construction shall be subject to such supervision as the agency deems necessary.

33791 Loan agreements for residential construction

An agency may enter into loan agreements with any participating party relating to residential construction of any kind or character. The terms and conditions of such loan agreements may be as mutually agreed upon, but such terms and conditions shall not be inconsistent with the provisions of this chapter or regulations adopted pursuant thereto. Any such loan agreement may provide the means or methods by which any mortgage taken by the agency shall be discharged, and it shall contain such other terms and conditions as the agency may require. An agency may fix, revise, charge and collect interest and principal and all other rates, fees, and charges with respect to financing of residential construction. Such rates, fees, charges and interest shall be fixed and adjusted so that the aggregate of such rates, fees, charges, and interest will provide funds sufficient with other revenues and moneys which it is anticipated will be available therefor, if any, to all of the following:

(a) Pay the principal of, and interest on, outstanding revenue bonds of the agency issued to finance such residential construction as the same shall become due and payable.

(b) Create and maintain reserves required or provided for in any resolution authorizing such revenue bonds. A sufficient amount of the revenues derived from residential construction may be set aside at such regular intervals as may be provided by the resolution in a sinking or other similar fund, which is hereby pledged to, and charged with, the payment of the principal of and interest on such revenue bonds as the same shall become due, and the redemption price or the purchase price of revenue bonds retired by call or purchase as therein provided. Such pledge shall be valid and binding from the time the pledge is made. The rates, fees, interest, and other charges, revenues, or moneys so pledged and thereafter received by the agency shall immediately be subject to the lien of such pledge without any physical delivery thereof or further act, and the lien of any such pledge shall be valid and binding as against all parties having claims of any kind in tort, contract, or otherwise against the agency, irrespective of whether such parties have notice thereof. Neither the resolution nor any loan agreement by which a pledge is created need be filed or recorded except in the records of the agency. The use and disposition of moneys to the credit of such sinking or other similar fund shall be subject to the provisions of the resolution authorizing the issuance of such revenue bonds. Except as may otherwise be provided in the resolution, such sinking or other similar fund may be a fund for all revenue bonds of the agency issued to finance the construction of the residence of a particular participating party without distinction or priority. The agency, however, in any such resolution may provide that such sinking or other similar fund shall be the fund for particular project or projects of residential construction and for the bonds issued to finance such project or projects and may, additionally, authorize and provide for the issuance of revenue bonds having a lien with respect to the security authorized by this section which is subordinate to the lien of other revenue bonds of the agency, and in such case, the agency may create separate sinking or other similar funds securing the revenue bonds having the subordinate lien.

(c) Pay operating and administrative costs of the agency incurred in the administration of the program authorized by this chapter.

33792 Revenues deemed trust funds

All moneys received pursuant to the provisions of this chapter, whether revenues or proceeds from the sale of revenue bonds or proceeds of mortgage insurance or guarantee claims, shall be deemed to be trust funds to be held and applied solely for the purposes of this chapter. Any bank or trust company in which such moneys are deposited shall act as trustee of such moneys and shall hold and apply the same for the purposes specified in this chapter, subject to the terms of the resolution authorizing the revenue bonds.

33795 Liberal construction of chapter

This chapter being necessary for the welfare of the state and its inhabitants, shall be liberally construed to effect its purposes.

33796 Immaterial omissions or defects in proceedings

If the jurisdiction of the agency to order a proposed act is not affected, an omission of any officer or the agency in proceedings under this chapter or any other defect in the proceedings shall not invalidate the proceedings or revenue bonds issued pursuant to this chapter.

33797 Full authority to issue bonds

This chapter is full authority for the issuance of bonds by an agency for the purpose of financing residential construction.

33798 Authority supplemental to other laws

This chapter shall be deemed to provide a complete, additional, and alternative method for doing the things authorized thereby, and shall be regarded as supplemental and additional to the powers conferred by other laws. The issuance of revenue bonds and refunding revenue bonds under the provisions of this chapter need not comply with the requirements of any other law applicable to the issuance of bonds.

33799 Validation actions

An action may be brought pursuant to Chapter 9 (commencing with Section 860) of Title 10 of Part 2 of the Code of Civil Procedure to determine the validity of any issuance or proposed issuance of revenue bonds under this chapter and the legality and validity of all proceedings previously taken or proposed in a resolution of an agency to be taken for the authorization, issuance, sale, and delivery of the revenue bonds and for the payment of the principal thereof and interest thereon.

Chapter 9. SPECIAL ASSESSMENTS

Article 1
Definitions

33800 Construction of chapter

The definitions contained in this article govern the construction of this chapter, unless the context requires otherwise.

33801 Indebtedness defined

"Indebtedness" means any obligations incurred by a redevelopment agency prior to July 1, 1978, the payment of which is to be made in whole or in part out of taxes allocated to the agency pursuant to Section 33670 and includes:

(a) Bonds, notes, interim certificates, debentures, or other obligations issued by an agency (whether funded, refunded, assumed or otherwise) pursuant to Article 5 (commencing with Section 33640) of Chapter 6 of this part.

(b) Loans or moneys advanced to the agency, including, but not limited to, loans from federal, state or local agencies.

(c) A contractual obligation which, if breached, could subject the agency to damages or other liabilities or remedies.

(d) An obligation incurred pursuant to Section 33445.

(e) Indebtedness incurred pursuant to Section 33334.2.

(f) Obligations imposed by law with respect to activities which occurred prior to July 1, 1978.

33802 Indebtedness further defined

"Indebtedness" also means a loan from the Local Agency Indebtedness Fund pursuant to Article 6.5 (commencing with Section 16496) of Chapter 3 of Part 2 of Division 4 of Title 2 of the Government Code for the purpose of making payments of principal or interest with respect to indebtedness specified in Section 33801.

33803 Payment defined

"Payment" means any payment of principal or interest payable with respect to indebtedness payable from taxes allocated pursuant to subdivision (b) of Section 33670, which is as defined in Section 33801 or 33802, including redemption payments and any administrative costs associated with the payment of such indebtedness.

33804 Persons and families of low or moderate income defined

"Persons and families of low or moderate income" has the same meaning as defined in Section 50093.

Article 2
Findings and Declarations

33810 Legislative findings and declarations

The Legislature finds and declares that the security of millions of dollars of indebtedness incurred prior to July 1, 1978, and dependent upon taxes allocated pursuant to Section 16 of Article XVI of the California Constitution and subdivision (b) of Section 33670 for its security is seriously threatened.

33811 Further legislative findings and declarations

The Legislature further finds and declares that unless supplemental sources of revenue for the payment of such indebtedness can be established, a substantial portion of such indebtedness will not be repaid, which will include the default of bonds and the breach of contractual obligations, and that if such defaults and breaches of contract occur, the credit and future borrowing capacity of both local agencies and the state may be impaired.

33812 Further legislative findings and declarations

The Legislature further finds and declares that such defaults and breach of contracts may result in lengthy and costly legal actions against public agencies for the impairment of contractual rights.

33813 Further legislative findings and declarations

The Legislature further finds and declares that there is a need to establish a flexible procedure to enable legislative bodies to obtain necessary supplemental revenues to pay the incurred indebtedness because the need for state funds for such purpose will be decreased and because the facts and circumstances surrounding each project and the indebtedness incurred are different and different solutions may be required.

33814 Further legislative findings and declarations

The Legislature further finds and declares that certain properties within the boundaries of redevelopment project areas established pursuant to the Community Redevelopment Law have increased in value and have received and will continue to receive special benefits from redevelopment activities undertaken by agencies, including, but not limited to, acquisition, assembly and disposition of lands, demolition and site clearance and the construction of public improvements financed by the proceeds of indebtedness incurred by redevelopment agencies.

33815 Further legislative findings and declarations

The Legislature further finds and declares that the establishment of special assessments on the properties so specially benefited from the activities described in Section 33814 is the most equitable method for providing supplemental revenues to be used to pay the indebtedness.

33816 Purpose to authorize special assessment areas within redevelopment project areas

It is the purpose of this chapter to authorize and provide for the establishment of special assessment areas within redevelopment project areas and for the levy of special assessments on properties within such special assessment areas to obtain supplemental revenues to be used for the payment of indebtedness incurred prior to July 1, 1978, and temporary borrowing from the state incurred to avoid default thereon.

33817 Special assessment area defined

A special assessment area may include any or all property within a project area as the project area existed on July 1, 1978, established pursuant to Chapter 4 (commencing with Section 33300) of this part, and may, but need not be, coterminous with such project area; however, only properties benefited by redevelopment activities described in Section 33814 shall be included within the special assessment area. The properties included in a special assessment area may be either contiguous or noncontiguous; however, only properties within a single project area may be included within a single special assessment area.

Article 3
Proceedings

33820 Authority to establish special assessment areas and levy special assessments

Special assessment areas wholly within redevelopment project areas may be established and special assessments levied within such special assessment areas pursuant to this chapter.

33821 Report to legislative body

When, in the opinion of the governing board of an agency, it is determined that there will be insufficient tax revenues allocated to the agency to pay its incurred indebtedness, the agency shall file with the legislative body a report.

33822 Contents of report to legislative body

The report shall contain all of the following:

(a) The total amount of outstanding indebtedness incurred by the agency with respect to the project area containing the special assessment area, a listing of the different kinds of indebtedness incurred together with the amount of debt incurred for each separate kind of indebtedness, and the annual payment required to be made for each such kind of indebtedness for each year during which the debt is outstanding.

(b) An estimate of the amount of taxes which will be received by the agency pursuant to subdivision (b) of Section 33670 which will be available to make payments on the different kinds of indebtedness when due.

(c) A description and estimated amounts of other revenues, funds and other moneys, other than tax revenues described in subdivision (b), which are or will be available to the agency for making the payments.

(d) An estimate of the total and annual amounts of the payments which the agency will be unable to make because of the insufficiency of funds available for that purpose.

(e) A schedule of payments and either (1) copies of contracts, agreements, or other documents creating the indebtedness, or (2) a list (including a summary of parties and purpose) of contracts, agreements, and other documents creating the indebtedness.

(f) A description of the redevelopment activities which have been or will be undertaken by the agency with the proceeds derived from the indebtedness.

(g) A diagram showing the following:

(1) The boundaries of a special area of the redevelopment project area which, in the opinion of the agency, has been specially benefited.

(2) The dimensions or description of the parcels of property within the special area as they existed at the time of making the report. Each such subdivision shall be given a separate number upon the diagram.

(3) The proposed assessment on each of the parcels of property within the special assessment area levied in proportion to benefits.

(h) A statement as to whether the proposed assessment district includes property containing residential dwelling units, an estimate of the number of such dwelling units occupied by persons and families of low or moderate income, and an estimate of the total amount of assessments to be levied on such dwelling units occupied by persons and families of low or moderate income.

(i) A request that the legislative body proceed with the formation of a special assessment area and levy a special assessment on properties in the special assessment area.

(j) For each fiscal year in which the special assessment is proposed to be levied, the amount of taxes which was projected to be available for allocation to the agency pursuant to subdivision (b) of Section 33670, based on the actual tax rates in effect for the 1977–78 fiscal year and on the projected assessed values under the applicable laws in effect for the 1977–78 fiscal year, with respect to its indebtedness incurred prior to July 1, 1978. The statement shall contain information upon which the assessed values were projected. If any bonds have been issued and the official statement or bond resolution for such bonds contained an estimate of projected tax revenues which were to be received by the agency pursuant to subdivision (b) of Section 33670, the information shall refer to the official statement or bond resolution.

33822.5 Documents to be available to public

Copies of contracts, agreements, and other documents specified in subdivision (e) of Section 33822 shall be made available to the public at the time the report is filed with the legislative body.

33822.7 Notice to Department of Housing and Community Development

The agency shall notify the Department of Housing and Community Development within five days following the filing of a report with the legislative body pursuant to Section 33821.

33823 Resolution of intention by legislative body

After the receipt of the report, the legislative body may adopt a resolution of intention to form a special assessment area and to levy special assessments on properties located therein to provide supplemental revenues for the purpose of making payments on the indebtedness when due.

33824 Contents of resolution of intention

The resolution of intention shall:

(a) Describe the exterior boundaries of the special assessment area.

(b) Include the estimated annual amounts needed to be levied on the properties within such area for the purpose of making such payments and the period during which such special assessments will be required, which in no case shall be longer than the time by which the debt is to be repaid.

(c) Include the proposed assessments.

The resolution shall incorporate by reference the report required by Section 33822.

33825 Notice of hearing by legislative body required

The resolution shall contain a notice of the time and place at which any person may appear before the legislative body and object to the formation of the special assessment area and the levy of special assessments therein. The hearing shall be held not less than 30 days after the passage of the resolution.

33826 Contents of notice of hearing

The notice shall contain all of the following:

(a) A statement of the time, place, and purpose of the hearing on the resolution of intention and report of the agency.

(b) A statement of the total estimated payments of principal and interest and other payments required.

(c) The amounts as shown on the report of the agency, to be assessed against each parcel of property annually.

(d) A statement that any owner of property within the proposed assessment area may file a written protest as provided in Section 33831.

(e) A statement that the city or county will pay the assessment levied on that portion of real property containing residential dwelling units occupied by persons and families of low or moderate income. The statement shall set forth a schedule of the applicable maximum annual incomes by family size which may be received by persons and families of low or moderate income and notice as to where applications and information regarding the payments may be obtained.

33827 Clerk to give notice of hearing by legislative body

The clerk of the legislative body shall give notice of the time and place in the resolution of intention as provided in Section 33825.

33828 Publication, mailing and posting of notice of hearing by legislative body

The notice shall be published pursuant to Section 6066 of the Government Code, the first publication of which shall be at least 20 days prior to the date set for hearing. Copies of the notice shall (1) be mailed by first class mail, postage prepaid, to the owners of property in the proposed special assessment area at the addresses of such owners as shown on the last equalized assessment roll used for tax purposes or as otherwise known to the clerk, (2) be mailed postage prepaid to the occupants of property in the proposed special assessment area, and (3) be posted conspicuously on all streets within the proposed special assessment area, not more than 300 feet apart on each street so posted, but not less than three in all. If property assessed pursuant to Section 19 of Article XIII of the Constitution is within such special assessment area, such notice shall be mailed to the owner of such property as shown on the roll last transmitted by the State Board of Equalization to the county auditor.

33829 Substantial compliance required

No proceeding shall be held invalid for the failure to mail notice to any property owner or occupant or to post the notice if there has been substantial compliance with the requirements of this article.

33830 Newspaper for publication

If no newspaper is published and circulated in the city, the notice shall be published in a newspaper published in any county in which the city is located.

33831 Written protests; time for filing

Any owner of property within the proposed special assessment area may protest the formation of the special assessment area, the extent thereof, or the proposed assessment by filing a written protest with the clerk of the legislative body at or before the time set for the hearing. Such protest shall contain a description of the property sufficient to identify the same and, if the signer is not shown on the last equalized assessment roll as the owner of such property, shall contain or be accompanied by written evidence that such signer is the owner of such property. The clerk shall endorse on each protest the date of its receipt and at the time appointed for the hearing shall present to the legislative body all protests filed. No other protests shall be considered by the legislative body.

33832 Hearing by legislative body

At the time and place set for hearing on the formation of the special assessment area and levy of special assessments, the legislative body shall consider the report of the agency and hear and pass upon all written protests. Such hearing may be continued from time to time by the legislative body.

33833 Majority protest

If protests are filed against the special assessment area, and the legislative body finds that such protests are signed by the owners of more than one-half of the area of the property included within the proposed special assessment area, all further proceedings under the resolution of intention are barred, and no new resolution of intention for the same shall be passed within six months after the decision of the legislative body on the hearing, unless the protests are overruled by an affirmative vote of four-fifths of the members of the legislative body.

33834 Determination of existence of majority protest

If it is necessary, in order to find whether a majority protest exists, to determine whether any or all of the signers of written protests are the "owners" of property to be assessed, the legislative body shall make such determination from the last equalized assessment roll or the roll specified in Section 33828, any written evidence submitted with a written protest and any other evidence received at the hearing. The legislative body shall be under no duty to obtain or consider any other evidence as to ownership of property and its determination of ownership shall be final and conclusive.

33835 Findings and determinations of legislative body

Prior to final action on the report, the legislative body shall find and determine, based on evidence submitted at the public hearing, (a) whether the properties proposed to be assessed are specially benefited by the redevelopment activities described in Section 33814, and are capable of bearing the burden of the proposed assessment, (b) whether the assessments have been apportioned in proportion to such benefits, (c) whether property within the assessment area contains residential dwelling units, and (d) for each fiscal year in which the special assessment is proposed to be levied, the amount of taxes which was projected to be available for allocation to the agency pursuant to subdivision (b) of Section 33670, based on the actual tax rates in effect for the 1977–78 fiscal year and on the projected assessed values under the applicable laws in effect for the 1977–78 fiscal year, with respect to its indebtedness incurred prior to July 1, 1978.

33835.3 Limitation on amount of special assessment

In no event shall a special assessment be levied pursuant to this chapter if the amount specified in the adopted report pursuant to subdivision (b) of Section 33822 is equal to or greater than the amount determined by legislative body pursuant to subdivision (d) of Section 33835. If the amount established pursuant to subdivision (b) of Section 33822 in the adopted report is less than the amount determined pursuant to subdivision (d) of Section 33835, then the maximum amount which can be levied by special assessment pursuant to this chapter is the dollar difference between the amounts described in those two subdivisions plus any indebtedness described in Section 33802.

33835.5 Findings and determinations of legislative body

Prior to taking final action on the report pursuant to either Section 33821 or 33837, the legislative body shall find and determine that the total amount of revenues received by levying a special assessment pursuant to this chapter, plus the taxes which the legislative body has determined will be received pursuant to subdivision (b) of Section 33822 of the adopted report, does not exceed the amount determined pursuant to subdivision (d) of Section 33835 plus any indebtedness described in Section 33802.

33836 Formation of special assessment area and levy of special assessments

If written protests by more than one-half of the area of the property in the special assessment area are either not received or are received and are overruled the legislative body may, by resolution, confirm, modify, or correct the report and order the formation of the special assessment area, and levy the assessments shown on the report as confirmed, modified or corrected. The resolution shall be final as to all persons and the assessments thereby levied upon the respective subdivisions of land in the special assessment area until changed pursuant to Section 33838. However, for the purposes of Section 33838, the assessment levied pursuant to this section shall be the assessment for the first fiscal year.

33837 Annual report of proposed special assessments

Prior to May 15th of each year, after the first fiscal year, during which the assessment district is to continue, the agency shall file with the legislative body a report which shall contain (1) an estimate of the total amount of funds including taxes received by the agency pursuant to subdivision (b) of Section 33670 which will be available to pay the indebtedness for the next fiscal year, (2) an estimate of the amount of payments specified in the report pursuant to Section 33822 which the agency will be unable to pay because of insufficient funds, and (3) a diagram and a proposed assessment to be levied upon each parcel of property in the area for the next fiscal year.

33838 Adoption of annual report of proposed special assessments by legislative body

After receiving a report pursuant to Section 33837, the legislative body shall review and adopt the report, either as presented or as modified, and shall take one of the following actions:

(a) Find that the existing levy will raise substantially the same amount as is needed to make the payments, in which case no change to the existing levy is needed.

(b) Find that the existing levy will raise more than is needed to make the payments, in which case the legislative body shall reduce the levy for that fiscal year to an amount sufficient to make the payments.

(c) Find that the existing levy will not raise sufficient funds to make the payments, in which case the legislative body may, after a notice and hearing pursuant to Sections 33825 to 33835, inclusive, levy an increased assessment for that fiscal year in an amount sufficient to make the payments.

33839 Tax increments to be used first to pay indebtedness

Notwithstanding any other provision of this chapter, all tax increments allocated to the agency pursuant to subdivision (b) of Section 33670 with respect to a redevelopment project for which a special assessment district has been created pursuant to this chapter, shall first be used to pay indebtedness, as defined in this chapter.

Article 4
Collection of Assessments

33840 Filing of diagram and assessment with county auditor

Immediately after the levy, but in all cases before July 15th, a certified copy of the diagram and assessment shall be filed with the county auditor. The county auditor shall enter the amounts of the respective assessments on the county tax roll opposite the respective parcels of property. Immediately upon such recording, each of such assessments shall be a lien upon the property against which it is made and shall only be discharged by payment of the assessment and, if applicable, penalties, costs, or other charges resulting from delinquency in the payment of the assessment.

33840.5 Payment by city or county of assessments on property occupied by persons and families of low or moderate income

A city or county which levies assessments pursuant to this chapter shall pay to the county tax collector all such assessments levied on real property containing one or more dwelling units occupied by persons and families of low or moderate income; provided, that where such real property contains uses other than residential dwelling units occupied by persons and families of low or moderate income only that portion of the assessment attributable to the portion of the property occupied by persons and families of low or moderate income shall be paid by the city or county. The city or county shall establish a reasonable method for determining such apportionments.

33840.7 Procedure for payment by city or county of assessments on property occupied by persons and families of low or moderate income

(a) Each city or county which makes a finding that the assessment area includes property containing residential dwelling units shall establish procedures to enable persons and families of low or moderate income who occupy dwelling units within the assessment area, or owners of such dwelling units as provided in subdivision (b), to apply to the city or county to have the assessment paid. Such procedures may include (1) reasonable time deadlines for application, which, if not met by the applicant, will extinguish the obligation of the city or county to pay the assessment for that year and (2) a requirement that the applicant, not more than once each year, provide information which will enable the city or county to determine the dwelling unit in which the applicant resides and whether the applicant is a person or family of low or moderate income.

(b) As to properties or portions of properties in which the occupancy of dwelling units is restricted by a written agreement or by operation of law to persons and families of low or moderate income, the owner of the property may apply to the city or county to have the assessment paid on all such dwelling units and as to those properties or portions of properties the use of which the city or county knows is restricted by a written agreement or by operation of law to persons and families of low or moderate income, the city or county shall pay the assessment without requiring any application to be submitted. The city or county may require the owners of such properties to provide a copy of the subject written agreement, if any, and to provide other information annually which will enable the city or county to determine the number of dwelling units actually occupied by persons or families of low or moderate income.

(c) Except as to dwelling units in which the occupancy is restricted by law to persons and families of low or moderate income, the information required of applicants may include copies of federal and state income tax returns of the subject low or moderate income residents.

(d) The procedures established by a city or county pursuant to this section shall provide for annual reviews as to whether real property within the assessment area containing residential dwelling units is occupied by persons and families of low or moderate income. The procedures shall additionally provide for notice to occupants and owners of property within the special assessment area of the maximum annual income by family size which may be received by persons and families of low or moderate income; the notices shall be mailed to such occupants and owners not less than 30 days prior to the final date for receiving applications for payment of the assessment pursuant to Section 33840.5.

33841 Priority of assessment liens

The lien of an assessment levied pursuant to this chapter shall be subordinate to all fixed special assessment liens previously imposed upon the same property but it shall have priority over all fixed special assessment liens which may thereafter be created against the property.

33842 Applicability of Revenue and Taxation Code

Assessments levied under this chapter shall be subject to all the provisions of Division 1 (commencing with Section 101) of the Revenue and Taxation Code applicable to the collection, penalties, costs, or other charges resulting from delinquency, redemption, and sale for nonpayment of taxes on the county tax roll.

33843 Continuation of special assessments

The special assessments provided for in the resolution adopted pursuant to Section 33836 shall be deemed to have been levied in each succeeding year until the assessment is revised pursuant to Section 33838 or rescinded and the county auditor is given notice thereof.

33844 Transfer of proceeds to agency

All the proceeds of the assessment shall be placed in a separate fund of the legislative body and shall be transferred to the agency only for the payment of indebtedness.

33845 Proceeds to be used for payment of indebtedness

Upon receipt of any proceeds from the legislative body pursuant to Section 33844, the agency shall either immediately use such proceeds for the payment of indebtedness or it shall place such proceeds in a separate fund and shall thereafter only be removed and expended for the purpose of making such payments.

Article 5
Legal Actions, Exceptions

33850 Limitation of actions

The validity of any assessment levied under this chapter shall not be contested in any action or proceeding unless commenced within 60 days after the levy thereof. The provisions of Chapter 9 (commencing with Section 860) of Title 10 of Part 2 of the

Code of Civil Procedure shall be applicable to any such action or proceeding.

33851 Sale or issuance of bonds not authorized

Nothing in this chapter shall be construed as authorizing the sale or issuance of bonds.

33852 Exemption from CEQA

All proceedings and decisions undertaken or made pursuant to this chapter shall be exempt from the requirements of Division 13 (commencing with Section 21000) of the Public Resources Code.

33853 Special Assessment Investigation, Limitation and Majority Protest Act of 1931 not applicable

The Special Assessment Investigation, Limitation and Majority Protest Act of 1931, Division 4 (commencing with Section 2800) of the Streets and Highways Code, shall not apply to proceedings under this part.

33854 Severability

If any provision of this chapter or the application thereof to any person or circumstances is held invalid, such invalidity shall not affect other provisions or applications of this chapter which can be given effect without the invalid provision or application, and to this end the provisions of this chapter are severable.

33855 Limitation on severability

If Section 33840.5 or any portion thereof is held invalid such invalidity shall not affect other provisions of this chapter which can be given effect without such invalid section; however, after such section or portion thereof has been held to be invalid: (1) no assessment district shall be established which includes real property containing one or more residential dwelling units occupied by persons and families of low or moderate income; (2) no levy shall be imposed on any real property containing one or more residential dwelling units occupied by persons and families of low or moderate income; and (3) any existing levy imposed upon real property containing one or more residential units occupied by persons and families of low or moderate income shall be deemed to be rescinded and the lien discharged. If any provision in this section is held to be invalid no levy shall be imposed on any property within a special assessment area which includes real property containing one or more residential dwelling units occupied by persons and families of low or moderate income after such section or portion thereof is found to be invalid.

PART 1.5. COMMUNITY REDEVELOPMENT DISASTER PROJECT LAW

34000 Legislative findings and declarations

(a) (1) The Legislature finds and declares all of the following:

(A) Floods, fires, hurricanes, earthquakes, storms, tidal waves, or other catastrophes are disasters that can harm the public health, safety, and welfare. Communities need effective methods for rebuilding after disasters.

(B) The extraordinary powers of redevelopment agencies have been and can be useful in the reconstruction of buildings and in stimulating local economic activity.

(C) The procedures and requirements of the Community Redevelopment Law (Part 1 (commencing with Section 33000)) restrict the ability of local officials to respond quickly after disasters.

(2) In enacting this part, it is, therefore, the intent of the Legislature to provide communities with alternative procedures and requirements for redevelopment after disasters.

(b) Any redevelopment agency or project area established pursuant to the Community Redevelopment Financial Assistance and Disaster Project Law (former Part 1.5 (commencing with Section 34000)), as that law existed prior to the effective date of the act that repeals that law, shall remain in existence and subject to that law as if the Legislature had not repealed that law.

(c) This part shall apply only to redevelopment activities undertaken pursuant to its provisions on and after the effective date of the act that adds this part.

(d) This part is known and may be cited as the Community Redevelopment Disaster Project Law.

34001 Compliance with Community Redevelopment Law; timing of redevelopment plan adoption

(a) Except as specifically provided in this part, a community shall comply with the Community Redevelopment Law.

(b) A community may establish a redevelopment agency, and adopt and implement a redevelopment plan pursuant to this part, within a disaster area if the community has commenced the adoption of the redevelopment plan within six months after the President of the United States has determined the disaster to be a major disaster pursuant to paragraph (1) of subdivision (a) of Section 34002 and the legislative body has adopted the redevelopment plan within 24 months after the President of the United States has determined the disaster to be a major disaster pursuant to paragraph (1) of subdivision (a) of Section 34002.

34002 Definitions

(a) As used in this part:

(1) "Disaster" means any flood, fire, hurricane, earthquake, storm, tidal wave, or other catastrophe occurring on or after January 1, 1996, for which the Governor of the state has certified the need for assistance and which the President of the United States has determined to be a major disaster pursuant to the Robert T. Stafford Disaster Relief and Emergency Assistance Act (Public Law 93-288), as it may be from time to time amended.

(2) "Project area" is an area that meets both of the following requirements:

(A) It is an area that is predominantly urbanized, as that term is defined in paragraph (3).

(B) It is limited to an area in which the disaster damage has caused conditions that are so prevalent and so substantial that they have caused a reduction, or a lack, of the normal pre-disaster usage of the area to an extent that causes a serious physical and economic burden that cannot reasonably be expected to be reversed or alleviated during the term of the redevelopment plan by private enterprise or governmental action, or both, without redevelopment.

(3) "Predominantly urbanized" means that not less than 80 percent of the land in the project area meets the requirements of paragraphs (1) and (3) of subdivision (b) of Section 33320.1.

(4) "Redevelopment agency" means any agency provided for and authorized to function pursuant to the Community Redevelopment Law or this part.

(b) Except as otherwise provided in this part, all words, terms, and phrases in this part shall have the same meanings as set forth in the Community Redevelopment Law.

34003 Ordinance declaring need for redevelopment agency

Any community in which a disaster has occurred, and which prior to January 1, 1996, had not authorized a redevelopment agency to transact business or exercise any powers, may, by ordinance, declare the need for an agency to function in the community. The ordinance of the legislative body declaring that there is a need for an agency to function in the community and the ordinance adopting the redevelopment plan shall be subject to referendum as prescribed by law for the ordinances of the legislative body.

34004 Adoption of redevelopment plan: modified requirements

Notwithstanding any provision of the Community Redevelopment Law, any redevelopment agency may plan, adopt, and implement a redevelopment plan, and the redevelopment agency and the legislative body of the community may approve a redevelopment plan for a project in a disaster area pursuant to the Community Redevelopment Law, without regard to any of the following:

(a) The requirements of Sections 33301 and 33302 that there be a planning commission and a general plan.

(b) The requirements of Sections 33320.1 and 33322 that the project area be a blighted area or that the project area be selected by a planning commission.

(c) The requirement of Section 33331 that the redevelopment plan shall conform to a general plan.

(d) The requirement of Section 33346 that the redevelopment plan be submitted to the planning commission.

(e) The requirements of Section 33367 that the ordinance of the legislative body adopting the redevelopment plan shall contain findings (1) that the project area is a blighted area and (2) that the redevelopment plan conforms to the general plan of the community.

(f) The "relocation findings and statement" required by Section 33367 or the requirement of subdivision (f) of Section 33352 that a relocation plan be adopted prior to the adoption of the redevelopment plan. Nothing in this subdivision shall be construed to eliminate the requirement that a redevelopment agency comply with the California Real Property Acquisition and Relocation Assistance Act (Chapter 16 (commencing with Section 7260) of Division 7 of Title 1 of the Government Code).

(g) The time limits required by Section 33333.2. However, any redevelopment plan adopted pursuant to this part shall contain the following time limits:

(1) A time limit on the establishing of loans, advances, and indebtedness to be paid with the proceeds of property taxes received pursuant to Section 33670, which may not exceed 10 years from the adoption of the redevelopment plan.

(2) A time limit, not to exceed 10 years from the adoption of the redevelopment plan, on the effectiveness of the redevelopment plan.

(3) A time limit, not to exceed 30 years from the adoption of the redevelopment plan, to repay indebtedness with the proceeds of property taxes received pursuant to Section 33670.

34005 Limited exemption from CEQA

(a) Notwithstanding subdivision (k) of Section 33352, the California Environmental Quality Act (Division 13 (commencing with Section 21000) of the Public Resources Code) shall not apply to the adoption of a redevelopment plan prepared pursuant to this part if the redevelopment agency determines at a public hearing, noticed in accord with this section, that the need to adopt a redevelopment plan at the soonest possible time in order to use the authority in the Community Redevelopment Disaster Project Law requires the redevelopment agency to delay application of the provisions of the California Environmental Quality Act to the redevelopment plan in accordance with this section.

(b) If the redevelopment agency finds, pursuant to subdivision (a), that the application of the California Environmental Quality Act to the redevelopment plan is required to be delayed, the redevelopment agency shall prepare and certify an environmental impact report or approve a negative declaration for the redevelopment plan within 12 months after the effective date of the ordinance adopting the redevelopment plan. If, as a result of the preparation of the environmental document prepared pursuant to this subdivision, it is necessary to amend the redevelopment plan to mitigate any impacts, the agency shall amend the redevelopment plan according to the procedures of this part. If the environmental document is determined to be inadequate, the redevelopment agency shall not continue with projects which implement the redevelopment plan until an adequate environmental document has been certified; however, this determination shall not affect the validity of the redevelopment plan.

(c) Until the redevelopment agency certifies an environmental impact report or negative declaration for the redevelopment plan, all projects, as defined in the California Environmental Quality Act, which implement the redevelopment plan shall be subject to the California Environmental Quality Act, including, but not limited to, specific plans and rezonings. The environmental document for any implementing project shall include an analysis and mitigation of potential cumulative impacts, if any, that otherwise will not be known until an environmental document for the redevelopment plan is certified or approved and shall also include a reporting or monitoring program required pursuant to Section 21081 of the Public Resources Code.

(d) The notice for the public hearing required by subdivision (a) shall comply with and may be combined with the notices in Section 33349 or 33361. The notice shall state that the agency intends to consider and act upon a determination that the need to adopt a redevelopment plan at the soonest possible time in order to use the authority in the Community Redevelopment Disaster Project Law requires the redevelopment agency to delay application of the provisions of the California Environmental Quality Act to the redevelopment plan in accordance with this section.

34006 Last equalized assessment roll and base-year assessment roll defined

For purposes of Sections 33328, 33670, and 33675, and for purposes of allocation of taxes pursuant to Section 33670 and the provisions of any disaster area redevelopment plan, "last equalized assessment roll" and "base-year assessment roll" mean the assessment roll as reduced in accordance with subdivision (b) of Section 170 of the Revenue and Taxation Code.

34007 Limitation on use of tax increments

A redevelopment agency that has adopted a redevelopment plan pursuant to this part shall limit the use of the proceeds of taxes received pursuant to Section 33670 for the sole purpose of acquiring, demolishing, removing, relocating, repairing, restoring, rehabilitating, or replacing buildings, low- and moderate-income housing, facilities, structures, or other improvements, in accordance with applicable laws, which are within the project area, and which have been damaged or destroyed by the disaster, which are unsafe to occupy, or which are required to be acquired, demolished, altered, or removed because of the disaster. Nothing in this section shall be deemed to expand or diminish the authority of a redevelopment agency pursuant to the Community Redevelopment Law.

34008 Inclusion within separate redevelopment plan

A community that has adopted a redevelopment plan pursuant to this part may, prior to the termination of the plan, include all or a portion of the project area within a separate redevelopment plan pursuant to the Community Redevelopment Law. However, any portion of the project area included within the separate redevelopment plan shall meet all the requirements of the Community Redevelopment Law.

PART 1.7. Community Development Commission

Chapter 1. DEFINITIONS

34100 Community defined

"Community" means a city, county, city and county, or Indian tribe, band, or group which is incorporated or which otherwise exercises some local governmental powers.

34101 Commission defined

"Commission" means a community development commission created by this part.

34102 Redevelopment agency defined

"Redevelopment agency" means a redevelopment agency created pursuant to the Community Redevelopment Law, Part 1 (commencing with Section 33000).

34103 Housing authority defined

"Housing authority" means a housing authority created pursuant to the Housing Authorities Law, Chapter 1 (commencing with Section 34200) of Part 2.

34104 Legislative body defined

"Legislative body" means the city council, board of supervisors, or other legislative body of the community.

Chapter 2. ESTABLISHMENT, CREATION, AND SUSPENSION OF COMMISSION

Article 1
Declaration of Creation and Establishment

34110 Existence of community development commission

There is hereby created and established in each community a public body, corporate and politic, known as the community development commission.

34111 Existence of redevelopment agency and housing authority

There is also in each community a public body, corporate and politic, known as the redevelopment agency of the community. There is also in each community a public body, corporate and politic, known as the housing authority of the community. Nothing in this part changes the existence of such entities as separate public bodies, corporate and politic.

34112 Purpose of community development commission

The commission is created and established in order that a community may have the option of operating and governing its redevelopment agency, or its redevelopment agency and its housing authority, under a single operating entity and board. The commission is also created and established for the purpose of exercising any other powers regarding community development which the legislative body of a community may desire to delegate to the commission subject to such conditions as may be imposed by the legislative body.

Article 2
Procedures Making Commission Operative

34115 Ordinance declaring need for community development commission

A commission may not transact any business or exercise any powers under this part unless, by ordinance, the legislative body declares that there is need for a commission to function in the community. The ordinance of the legislative body declaring that there is need for a commission to function in the community shall be subject to referendum as prescribed by law for a county or a city ordinance.

34115.5 Function of community development commission

The ordinance of the legislative body declaring a need for a commission to function in the community may declare a need that the commission function only with respect to a redevelopment agency or that the commission function with respect to a redevelopment agency and a housing authority. If the ordinance declares a need that the commission function only with respect to a redevelopment agency, then the commission shall not have the powers, duties, and responsibilities of a housing authority and the provisions requiring that two of the commissioners be tenants of the housing authority shall be inapplicable.

34116 Filing of ordinance

The commission shall cause a certified copy of the ordinance to be filed with the Department of Housing and Community Development.

34117 Validity of establishment and authority of community development commission

In any proceeding involving the validity or enforcement of, or relating to, any contract by a commission, the commission is conclusively deemed to have been established and authorized to transact business and exercise its powers upon proof of the filing with the Secretary of State and with the Department of Housing and Community Development of such an ordinance.

34118 Authority of community development commission established prior to January 1, 1978

Notwithstanding Section 34140 or any other provision of this part, a commission established prior to January 1, 1978, shall not be vested with the powers, duties, and responsibilities of the commissioners of the housing authority, nor shall the commission operate and govern the housing authority, unless:

(a) The ordinance adopted by the legislative body declaring a need for the commission to function in the community declares, or is subsequently amended to declare, that the commission shall be vested with the rights, powers, duties, and responsibilities of the commissioners of the housing authority; or

(b) Prior to the effective date of this section, the commission has assumed and exercised the rights, powers, duties, and responsibilities of the commissioners of the housing authority.

Article 3
Legislative Body as Commission

34120 Declaration of legislative body as community development commission; appointment of tenant commissioners

(a) The legislative body may, at the time of the adoption of an ordinance declaring that there is a need for a commission to function in the community or at any time thereafter, by adoption of an ordinance, declare itself to be the commission, in which case all of the rights, powers, duties, privileges, and immunities vested by this part in a commission, except as otherwise provided in this part, shall be vested in the legislative body of the community.

However, in any community in San Bernardino County that is a charter city, the adoption of any order or resolution by the legislative body acting as the commission shall be governed by the same procedures as are set forth in the provisions of the charter, and the mayor shall be chairperson of the commission, having the same power and authority in the conduct of the commission and the meetings of the legislative body acting as the commission that the mayor has in the conduct of the affairs of the city.

(b) If the legislative body has declared itself to be the commission, the legislative body shall appoint two additional commissioners who are tenants of the housing authority if the housing authority has tenants. One tenant commissioner shall be over 62 years of age if the housing authority has tenants of that age. If the housing authority does not have tenants, the legislative body shall, by ordinance, provide for the appointment to the commission of two tenants of the housing authority, one of whom shall be over 62 years of age if the housing authority has tenants of that age, within one year after the housing authority first has tenants. The term of any tenant appointed pursuant to this subdivision shall be two years from the date of appointment. If a tenant commissioner ceases to be a tenant of the housing authority, he or she shall be disqualified from serving as a commissioner and another tenant of the housing authority shall be appointed to the remainder of the unexpired term. A tenant commissioner shall have all the powers, duties, privileges, and immunities of any other commissioner.

(c) As an alternative to the appointment of tenants of the housing authority as commissioners pursuant to subdivision (b), if a community development committee is created as provided in Section 34120.5, the governing body may make tenant appointments pursuant to subdivision (b) to the committee, rather than to the commission.

34120.5 Creation and function of community development committee

(a) A legislative body which has declared itself to be the commission pursuant to Section 34120 may, by ordinance, create a community development committee of not more than seven members, or not more than nine members if tenant appointments are made pursuant to Section 34120. The terms of office, qualifications, and method of appointment and removal shall be as provided by ordinance.

(b) If a community development committee is created, its function shall be to review and make recommendations on all matters to come before the commission prior to commission action, except emergency matters, and matters which the committee, by resolution, excludes from committee review and recommendation. The legislative body may provide for procedures for review and recommendation, and for further functions of the committee, by ordinance or resolution, and may delegate any of its functions as the community development commission to the committee.

34121 Determination that legislative body not to function as community development commission

A legislative body which has declared itself to be the commission pursuant to Section 34120 may at any time by resolution determine that it shall no longer function as the commission, in which event, the mayor or chairman of the board of supervisors or similar official, with the approval of the legislative body, shall appoint resident electors of the community as members of the commission, including two tenant commissioners as provided in Section 34130.

Article 4
Suspension of Commission

34125 Ordinance declaring no further need for community development commission

The legislative body of the community may by ordinance declare that there is no further need for the commission. Upon adoption of the ordinance the offices of the commissioners are vacated and the capacity of the commission to transact business or exercise any powers is suspended until the legislative body subsequently adopts an ordinance declaring the need for the commission to function. If the commission has outstanding bonded indebtedness issued in the name of the commission, the legislative body of the community may adopt an ordinance declaring there is no further need for the commission only if the unanimous consent of the commissioners is first obtained.

34126 Filing of ordinance

The legislative body of the community shall file with the Secretary of State and with the Department of Housing and Community Development a certified copy of any ordinance suspending a commission.

Chapter 3. APPOINTMENT, COMPENSATION, AND REMOVAL OF COMMISSIONERS

34130 Appointment of commissioners

(a) When the legislative body adopts an ordinance declaring the need for a commission, the mayor or chairman of the board of supervisors or similar official, with the approval of the legislative body, shall appoint the number of resident electors of the community as commissioners as the legislative body prescribes by ordinance. The legislative body by ordinance may increase or decrease the number of commissioners. The legislative body, except as otherwise expressly provided in subdivision (b), shall establish and provide for the terms and removal of the commissioners. The legislative body shall provide procedures for appointment or election of the officers of the commission.

(b) Two of the commissioners shall be tenants of the housing authority if the housing authority has tenants. One such tenant commissioner shall be over the age of 62 years if the housing authority has tenants of such age. If the housing authority does not have tenants, the legislative body shall, by ordinance, provide for appointment to the commission of two tenants of the housing authority within one year after the housing authority first does have tenants. The term of any tenant commissioner appointed pursuant to this subdivision shall be two years from the date of appointment. If a tenant commissioner ceases to be a tenant of the housing authority, he shall be disqualified from serving as a commissioner and another tenant of the housing authority shall be appointed to serve the remainder of the unexpired term. A tenant commissioner shall have all the powers, duties, privileges, and immunities of any other commissioner.

(c) Upon the appointment and qualification of a majority of the commissioners, the commission shall be vested with all the powers, duties, and responsibilities of the members of the redevelopment agency and, if the legislative body so elects, the commissioners of the housing authority. Members of the redevelopment agency and commissioners of a housing authority which has been placed under the jurisdiction of the commission shall have no powers, duties, and responsibilities as long as the commission functions.

34130.5 Compensation to commissioners

(a) Commissioners shall receive their actual and necessary expenses, including traveling expenses incurred in the discharge of their duties. The legislative body may also provide for other compensation pursuant to either subdivision (b) or (c).

(b) If the ordinance of the legislative body declaring the need for a commission to function within the community declares that need only with respect to a redevelopment agency, the compensation provided by the legislative body shall not exceed seventy-five dollars ($75) for each commissioner for each meeting of the commission attended by that commissioner. No commissioner shall receive compensation for attending more than two meetings of the commission in any calendar month.

(c) If the ordinance of the legislative body declaring the need for a commission to function within the community declares that need with respect to a redevelopment agency and a housing authority, the compensation provided by the legislative body shall not exceed one hundred fifty dollars ($150) for each commissioner for each meeting of the commission attended by that commissioner. No commissioner shall receive compensation for attending more than two meetings of the commission in any calendar month.

34131 Limitation on membership

A commissioner, unless the legislative body is the commission, may not be an elective officer or an employee of the community, but may be a member, commissioner, or employee of any other agency or authority in the community.

Chapter 4. NATURE, JURISDICTION, AND GENERAL POWERS OF COMMISSION

34140 Governmental functions

The powers, duties, and responsibilities of the commission, the redevelopment agency, and the housing authority are vested in the commissioners in office. Each commission exercises governmental functions and has the powers prescribed in this part. Each commission is performing a public function of the community.

34141 General powers

The nature, power, authority, functions and jurisdiction of the commission include, but are not limited to, all of the nature, power, authority, functions, and jurisdiction of redevelopment agencies and housing authorities. The commission also has the nature, power, authority, functions, and jurisdiction relating to community development as may be delegated to the commission by the legislative body, subject to such conditions as may be imposed by the legislative body.

34143 Additional powers

A commission may:

(a) Sue and be sued.

(b) Have a seal.

(c) Make and execute contracts and other instruments necessary or convenient to the exercise of its powers.

(d) Make, amend, and repeal bylaws and regulations not inconsistent with, and to carry into effect the powers and purposes of this part and all other powers and purposes delegated to them by the legislative body.

34144 Employment of personnel

(a) A commission may select, appoint, and employ such permanent and temporary officers, agents, counsel, and employees as it requires, and determine their qualifications, duties, benefits, and compensation, subject only to the conditions and restrictions imposed by the legislative body on the expenditure or encumbrance of the budgetary funds appropriated to the commission. The commission shall adopt personnel rules and regulations applicable to all its employees. Such rules shall contain procedures affecting conflicts of interest, use of funds, personnel procedures on hiring and firing including removal of personnel for inefficiency, neglect of duties, or misconduct in office. Such rules and regulations shall be a public record.

(b) A commission may contract with the Department of Housing and Community Development or any other agency or entity for the furnishing by the department, agency, or entity of any necessary staff services associated with or required and which could be performed by the staff of a commission.

34145 Employment of staff, contractors and consultants

In addition to all other powers and authorities of the commission, the commission may hire, employ, or contract for staff, contractors, and consultants, or the commission may use community staff, contractors or consultants under contract or other arrangements with the community at the expense of the commission, the community, the redevelopment agency, or the housing authority.

34146 Community development commission not a department of community

Any grants or loans of money appropriated by the legislative body of the community to the commission is not to be construed as making the commission a department of the community or placing the officers, agents, counsel, and employees under civil service of the community.

34147 Financial assistance

The commission may accept financial assistance from public or private sources for the purposes of this part.

34148 Other assistance

The commission may accept any other assistance from the state or federal government or any public or private source for any of the commission's activities, powers, and duties.

34149 Other authorized powers

The commission shall have such other powers as may be authorized by the legislative body of the community.

34150 Administration by general manager, executive director or administrator

The legislative body of the community may delegate to or establish in a general manager, executive director, or administrator of the community or of the commission any or all of the power and authority of the commission for the administration of the activities of the commission, the redevelopment agency, or the housing authority. The commission may also delegate and establish any or all of the power and authority of the commission in a general manager, executive director, or administrator of the community or commission.

34151 Charter cities

A chartered city may enact its own procedural ordinance and exercise powers granted by this part.

34152 Delegation of powers or functions by community development commission to community

A commission is authorized to delegate to a community any of the powers or functions of the commission and such community is hereby authorized to carry out or perform such powers or functions for the commission.

Chpater 5. COMMUNITY REDEVELOPMENT LAW AND HOUSING AUTHORITIES LAW

34160 Inconsistent provisions of Community Redevelopment Law and Housing Authorities Law not applicable

Inconsistent provisions of the Community Redevelopment Law Part 1 (commencing with Section 33000) and the Housing Authorities Law Chapter 1 (commencing with Section 34200) of Part 2 are inoperative during the time that an ordinance has been adopted declaring a need for the commission to function, the commissioners have been appointed and qualified or the legislative body has declared itself to be the commission, and no suspension ordinance has been adopted.

Appendix B

Illustrative Time Schedule and Procedural Guide for the Adoption of a Redevelopment Plan

Effective January 1, 2009

Appendix B

Illustrative Time Schedule and Procedural Guide for the Adoption of a Redevelopment Plan*

Effective January 1, 2009

Scheduled Date and Action

Month 1, Day 1

1. CITY COUNCIL designates survey area. § 33310.**

   Action or document required
   Council Resolution No._____

After Month 1, Day 1

2. AGENCY staff and consultants review General Plan for compliance with state law.

After Month 1, Day 1 and prior to Item No. 5

3. AGENCY staff and consultants identify property ownership and business interests, if any, of Agency, Council, and Planning Commission members and other City officials in the proposed Project Area and determine whether any conflicts exist.

   Action or document required
   Letter to Council and Agency regarding disclosure and disclosure forms. Review by City Attorney or Special Counsel of economic interests and identification of conflicts. §§ 33130; 33130.5; Gov. Code § 87100 *et seq.*

   NOTES

   If conflicts are discovered, review Cal. Code Regs., tit. 2, § 18701 regarding disclosure procedures for public officials who have financial interests in a decision and if rule of necessity must be invoked.

After Month 1, Day 1

4. AGENCY staff and consultants commence preparation of Preliminary Plan.

   Action or document required
   Preliminary Plan

Month 1, Day 16

5. PLANNING COMMISSION selects Project Area boundaries, approves Preliminary Plan, and forwards Preliminary Plan to Agency. §§ 33322 and 33325.

   Action or document required
   Planning Commission Resolution. No._____

Month 1, Day 25

6. CITY COUNCIL determines whether a Project Area Committee (PAC) is required and, if a PAC is required, publishes notice of a public hearing on the PAC Election Procedures (minimum 10-day notice). § 33385(d).

   Action or document required
   Notice; PAC Election Procedures

   NOTES

   - *Election of a Project Area Committee must be held within 100 days after the Project Area is selected if either (1) a substantial number of low and/or moderate-income persons reside within the Project Area and the Redevelopment Plan contains eminent domain authority to acquire property on which any persons reside, or (2) the Redevelopment Plan contains public projects that will displace a substantial number of low- and/or moderate-income persons.*

   - *If the project does not contain a substantial number of low- and moderate-income persons, the AGENCY must either (1) call upon the residents and community organizations to form a project area committee, or (2) consult with and obtain the advice of residents and community organizations and provide those persons and organizations with the Redevelopment Plan prior to submitting it for adoption.*

---

* For the purposes of this illustration, the following assumptions have been made: (1) Month 1, Day 1 is a Monday and all months have 30 days; (2) the Council and the Redevelopment Agency hold their regular meetings on the first and third Mondays of each month; (3) the Planning Commission holds its regular meetings on the first and third Tuesdays of each month; and (4) the City is a general law city.

** All references are to the Health and Safety Code unless otherwise noted.

Month 1, Day 25

7. AGENCY accepts Preliminary Plan, directs preparation of Redevelopment Plan, and authorizes transmittal of information to taxing agencies and officials.

    Action or document required
    Agency Resolution No._____

Month 1, Day 26

8. AGENCY staff and consultants commence preparation of Section 33344.5 Preliminary Report; Redevelopment Plan; Section 33352 Report, which includes reasons for selection of the Project Area, description of Project Area conditions, a five-year implementation plan, financing methods, relocation plan, neighborhood impact report, report of the County Fiscal Officer, analysis of same by the Agency, etc.; and Section 33328.1(b) Report, which includes population and school needs projections. AGENCY requests projections of school needs for the duration of the Project from each school district, county office of education and community college district for Section 33328.1(b) Report. §33328.1(b)

    Action or document required
    Section 33344.5 Preliminary Report; Redevelopment Plan; Section 33352 Report; Section 33328.1(b) Report

Month 2, Day 6

9. If a PAC is required, CITY COUNCIL holds public hearing and adopts PAC Election Procedures (if community-wide PAC Election Procedures have not been previously adopted) and procedures for formation of the Project Area Committee. § 33385.

    Action or document required
    Council Resolution No._____
    PAC Election Procedures;
    Procedures for Formation of PAC

Month 2, Day 7

10. AGENCY staff transmits (a) legal description and map of boundaries of the Project Area, (b) statement that Redevelopment Plan is being prepared, and (c) indication of the last equalized assessment roll proposed to be used for tax allocations to the County Auditor, Assessor, and Tax Collector, to the State Board of Equalization, and to the governing bodies of all taxing agencies in the Project Area. H&SC §§ 33327 and 33328

    Action or document required
    Letter and Statement of Preparation of Redevelopment Plan; Filing Fee (to State Board of Equalization)

Optional actions or documents

- *Agency may include a listing, by tax rate area, of all parcels within the Project Area and the value used for each such parcel on the secured property tax roll.*
- *Agency may also request County Auditor to include in its report assessed valuation data for the past five years (instead of the standard preceding one year data only).*

NOTES

- *If the Project Area boundaries are changed, AGENCY must notify taxing officials and State Board of Equalization within 30 days by transmitting description and map of each boundary change made. § 33327*
- *Upon receipt of this information, COUNTY FISCAL OFFICER begins preparation of report identifying total assessed valuation of all taxable property within Project Area for the preceding year (or, if requested by the Agency, for the preceding five years), each taxing agency levying taxes in the Project Area, amount of tax revenue derived by each taxing agency from the Project Area, total ad valorem tax revenue for each taxing agency from all property within its boundaries, estimated first year taxes available to the Agency, etc. § 33328*
- *If subsequent to receiving the report of the County Fiscal Officer a different assessment roll will be used, additional specific procedures will be required under section 33328.5.*

Month 2, Day 7

11. AGENCY staff finalizes and delivers to the Department of Finance (DOF) the Section 33328.1(b) Report, including population and school needs projections for the duration of the Project Area. § 33328.1(b)

    Action or document required
    Section 33328.1(b) Report; Transmittal Letter

Month 2, Day 7

12. AGENCY staff mails, via certified mail, return receipt requested, Notice of Preparation of Draft EIR to:

    (a) Responsible agencies (CEQA Guidelines § 15082(a));
    (b) Federal agencies (CEQA Guidelines § 15082(a));
    (c) Trustee agencies (CEQA Guidelines § 15082(a));
    (d) Affected taxing entities (§ 33333.3);
    (e) Cities and counties that border the City (Pub. Resources Code § 21153); and
    (f) If the Project has statewide, regional, or areawide significance, transportation planning agencies or public agencies with potentially affected transportation facilities. Pub. Resources Code § 21092.4

If any of the responsible agencies or trustee agencies are state agencies, a copy of the Notice must be sent to the State Clearinghouse. CEQA Guidelines § 15082(d). AGENCY staff posts the Notice with the County Clerk for 30 days. Pub. Resources Code § 21092.3. The Notice must state whether any portion of the Project Area is on the hazardous waste lists compiled under Government Code § 65962.5. Pub. Resources Code § 21092.6

Action or document required
Notice of Preparation

After Month 2, Day 7

13. AGENCY staff and consultants commence preparation of a Draft Environmental Impact Report.

Action or document required
Draft EIR

After Month 2, Day 7

14. *Additional EIR Consultations*

    (a) AGENCY staff may consult with Project opponents for the purpose of securing all conflicting views prior to final preparation of a Draft EIR. *Woodland Hills Residents Assn., Inc. v. City Council* (1980) 26 Cal. 3d 938

    Optional actions or documents

    Notice in local newspaper of general circulation advising community that an EIR is being prepared for the proposed Project and inviting comments; letters to Project Area owners and businesses; letters to other persons and groups; and/or staff and consultants hold community meeting for the purpose of providing a public forum for discussion of the proposed Project in terms of community concerns, Project alternatives, and environmental issues related to the Project.

    (b) AGENCY shall call at least one scoping meeting for either (i) a proposed Project which may affect highways or other facilities under the jurisdiction of the State Department of Transportation, if requested by the State Department of Transportation, or (ii) a project of statewide, regional, or areawide significance. Pub. Resources Code § 21083.9

    NOTES

    - *The AGENCY shall call the scoping meeting as soon as possible, but not later than 30 days after receiving the request from the State Department of Transportation.*
    - *The AGENCY* **must** *provide notice of such scoping meeting to cities and counties which border the city, any responsible agencies, any public agency that has jurisdiction by law with respect to the Project, and any organization or individual which has filed a written request for the notice.*

    (c) Prior to completion of the Draft EIR, the AGENCY **must** consult with and obtain comments from any city or county that borders on the City within which the Project is located. Pub. Resources Code § 21153

    (d) If a Project has statewide, regional, or areawide significance, the AGENCY **must** consult with transportation planning agencies and public agencies that have transportation facilities within the proposed Project Area that could be affected by the Project. Pub. Resources Code § 21092.4

Month 2, Day 17

15. If a PAC is required, AGENCY publishes a public notice of PAC informational meeting (minimum 10-day notice). § 33385

Month 2, Day 17

16. If a PAC is required, AGENCY mails to all residents, business, and property owners in the Project Area, notice of public informational meeting and PAC election (minimum 30 days notice prior to PAC formation). § 33385

Month 2, Day 27

17. If a PAC is required, AGENCY holds PAC informational meeting. § 33385

    Action or document required
    Procedures for formation of PAC;
    PAC Election Procedures;
    copies of §§ 33385, 33347.5,
    and 33366; Preliminary Plan

Month 3, Day 11

18. All comments due in response to Notice of Preparation of Draft EIR (30 days from receipt of NOP). Pub. Resources Code § 21080.4; CEQA Guidelines § 15082(b)

Month 4, Day 9 (or Month 5, Day 9)

19. County Fiscal Report due within 60 days (or, if Agency requests information for preceding five years, 90 days) of the date of filing by the Agency with the State Board pursuant to Section 33327, and is submitted to the Agency and all affected taxing agencies. § 33328

    Action or document required
    County Fiscal Report

NOTES

- *If the proposed base year assessment roll has not been equalized at the time the filing by the Agency is received, the County Fiscal Report is not due until 60 (or 90) days after the equalization date (August 20).*
- *If the County Fiscal Report is not received within the prescribed time, the AGENCY may proceed with the adoption of the Redevelopment Plan.*

After receipt of report in Item 19

20. AGENCY staff consults with each taxing agency that receives taxes from property in the Project Area and prepares a summary of the consultation. §§ 33328 and 33352

NOTES

This must occur prior to publication of the notice of public hearing on adoption of the Redevelopment Plan. The summary of this consultation must be included as part of the Agency's Section 33352 Report to the City Council.

Month 4, Day 16

21. AGENCY approves Preliminary Report and refers it to each affected taxing agency. § 33344.5

  Action or document required
  Agency Resolution No._____
  Preliminary Report; Transmittal Letter

After Month 4, Day 17

No later than 45 days prior to the public hearing.

22. AGENCY transmits a copy of the Preliminary Report to the governing board of each affected taxing agency. § 33344.6

  Action or document required
  Preliminary Report; Transmittal Letter

After Month 4, Day 17

No later than 45 days prior to the public hearing.

23. AGENCY delivers a copy of the Preliminary Report to DOF and the Department of Housing and Community Development (HCD) by first-class mail. § 33360.5(a)

  Action or document required
  Preliminary Report; Transmittal Letter

By Month 4, Day 26

24. If applicable, election of Project Area Committee must be held. § 33385(d)(1)

  Action or document required
  Forms and materials required for election

NOTES

If PAC is required, election of a Project Area Committee must be held within 100 days after the Project Area is selected.

Promptly after election in Item 24

25. If applicable, AGENCY staff transmits to City Council information concerning the actions taken to form the PAC, including the election results.

  Action or document required
  Election results

Month 5, Day 8

Within 21 days of receipt of the Preliminary Report delivered per Item 23.

26. DEPARTMENT OF FINANCE or DEPARTMENT OF HOUSING AND COMMUNITY DEVELOPMENT may send comments regarding the proposed Redevelopment Plan adoption. § 33360.5(c)

NOTES

If DOF or HCD comments are not available within the 21-day limit, the Agency and City Council may proceed without them.

Month 5, Day 11

27. If applicable, last day to file a challenge to the PAC election or the electoral procedure. § 33385

NOTES

Challenges must be filed with the legislative body no more than 15 calendar days after the election.

Month 5, Day 21

28. AGENCY determines adequacy of Draft EIR and approves Draft EIR for circulation. CEQA Guidelines § 15084

  Action or document required
  Agency Resolution No._____

Month 5, Day 21

29. AGENCY refers proposed Redevelopment Plan to Planning Commission and to the Project Area Committee, if applicable, or provides it to residents and community organizations with whom it has consulted. §§ 33346 and 33385

  Action or document required
  Agency Resolution No._____
  Redevelopment Plan

NOTES

Contents for Redevelopment Plan modified pursuant to SB 53, effective January 1, 2007.

Month 5, Day 21

30. If applicable, CITY COUNCIL adopts finding that its adopted procedures were followed in the election of the PAC. H&SC § 33385(d)(2).

   Action or document required
   Council Resolution No._____

   NOTES

   This must occur following the 15-day challenge period.

Month 5, Day 22

31. AGENCY staff files Notice of Completion with the Office of Planning and Research (Pub. Resources Code § 21161) and circulates Draft EIR to concerned agencies and individuals and to each affected taxing agency for minimum 30-day review period. AGENCY staff publishes notice inviting public comments on Draft EIR, and posts notice with the County Clerk for 30 days. Pub. Resources Code §§ 21092, 21092.3 and 21153; CEQA Guidelines § 15087; § 33333.3. (If State Clearinghouse is used, the review period is 45 days and the cover form required by the State Clearinghouse is used instead of the Notice of Completion form.)

   Action or document required
   Notice of Completion (or State
   Clearinghouse Form); Public Notice

Following Item 30

32. If applicable, PROJECT AREA COMMITTEE holds first meeting to (1) discuss election of chair and vice chair, and (2) review redevelopment plan adoption process, major issues, required documents, redevelopment goals and objectives, and programs. § 33385

   Action or document required
   PAC Bylaws; Redevelopment Plan, Draft EIR

Month 6, Day 20

33. PLANNING COMMISSION reviews proposed Redevelopment Plan and Draft EIR and submits report and recommendations concerning Redevelopment Plan to Agency within 30 days of referral. § 33347

   Action or document required
   Planning Commission Resolution No._____

Month 6, Day 26
(Month 7, Day 11, if State
Clearinghouse is required)

34. Last day for receipt of public comments on Draft EIR. AGENCY staff evaluates comments received from agencies and persons reviewing Draft EIR and prepares Final EIR. Pub. Resources Code §§ 21092 and 21153; CEQA Guidelines §§ 15087, 15088, and 15089

   Action or document required
   Final EIR

Month 7, Day 24

35. AGENCY staff and consultants complete preparation of Final EIR and Section 33352 Report to the City Council, and either mail responses to public agencies who commented on the Draft EIR or send the Final EIR to those commentors at least 10 days prior to the joint public hearing. Pub. Resources Code § 21092.5

   Action or document required
   Final EIR; Section 33352 Report;
   Send either Written Responses
   or Final EIR to commentors.

   NOTES

   Contents of Section 33352 Report to City Council changed pursuant to SB 1206, effective January 1, 2007.

Month 8, Day 1

36. AGENCY adopts its Report to the City Council on the Redevelopment Plan, submits Report, proposed Redevelopment Plan, and Final EIR to City Council, and requests holding joint public hearing on Redevelopment Plan. §§ 33351, 33352, and 33355

   Action or document required
   Agency Resolution No._____

   NOTES

   Check local City/Agency procedures to determine whether they require public hearing on Draft or Final EIR.

Month 8, Day 1

37. AGENCY adopts Rules for Owner Participation and Extension of Reasonable Preferences to Businesses. §§ 33339.5 and 33345

   Action or document required
   Agency Resolution No._____
   OP Rules

Month 8, Day 1

38. CITY COUNCIL receives documents from Agency and calls joint public hearing on Redevelopment Plan. § 33355

   Action or document required
   Council Resolution No._____

Month 8, Day 1

39. CITY COUNCIL elects to receive all or a portion of the tax revenues allocated to the Agency attributable to tax rate increases imposed for the City. § 33676

   Action or document required
   Council Resolution No._____

Month 8, Day 1

40. CITY COUNCIL elects to receive payment of its share of property taxes pursuant to section 33607.5. § 33607.5

   Action or document required
   Council Resolution No._____

Month 8, Day 4

Not later than 45 days prior to the hearing:

41. AGENCY staff mails, by first-class mail, copies of notice of joint public hearing to Department of Finance and HCD. § 33360.5(a)

   Action or document required
   Notice of Joint Public Hearing; Affidavit of Mailing

Month 8, Day 4

42. AGENCY staff sends to newspaper notice of joint public hearing on Redevelopment Plan. The notice must contain a legible map of the boundaries of the Project Area and a general statement of the scope and objectives of the Redevelopment Plan. Newspaper publishes notice once a week for four successive weeks, not later than Month 8, Day 22; and Month 8, Day 29; Month 9, Day 6; and Month 9, Day 13. §§ 33349 and 33361

   Action or document required
   Notice of Joint Public Hearing

   NOTES

   A legal description of the boundaries of the area(s) in the proposed redevelopment plan shall be prepared and available for public inspection during the Agency's normal business hours. The notice of joint public hearing shall state that a copy of the legal description is available upon request, free of charge.

Month 8, Day 20

At least 30 days prior to hearing

43. AGENCY staff mails, by first class mail, copies of notice of joint public hearing to all residents and businesses in the Project Area at least thirty (30) days prior to hearing (if cost of obtaining mailing addresses is reasonable). § 33349(c)

   Action or document required
   Notice; Affidavit of Mailing

   NOTES
   Notice may be addressed to "occupant."

Month 8, Day 20

44. AGENCY staff mails copies of notices of joint public hearing and statement regarding property acquisition to property owners in Project Area by first class mail. Notice and statement are mailed to last known assessee of each parcel of land at his last known address as shown on the last equalized assessment roll of the county, or to the owner of each parcel of land as shown on the records of the County Recorder 30 days prior to the date the notice is published. §§ 33349 and 33350

   Action or document required
   Notice; Statement;
   Affidavit of Mailing

Month 8, Day 20

45. AGENCY staff mails, certified mail, return receipt requested, copies of the notice of joint public hearing to the governing body of each of the taxing agencies which receives taxes from property in the Project Area. § 33349

   Action or document required
   Notice; Affidavit of Mailing

By Month 9, Day 6

46. AGENCY obtains court reporter for public hearing transcript.

By Month 9, Day 6

47. AGENCY staff prepares Procedural Outline and attaches certified copies of exhibits for the joint public hearing, including Affidavit of Publication, Affidavit of Mailing Notice to Property Owners, Affidavit of Mailing Notice to Taxing Agencies, Affidavit of Mailing Notice to Residents and Businesses, Certification of Certain Official Actions, Report of the Agency, Final EIR, Redevelopment Plan, Owner Participation Rules, and Written Comments Received.

   Action or document required
   Procedural Outline with exhibits listed above

By Month 9, Day 6

48. AGENCY staff reminds all scheduled speakers of hearing and sends them copies of the Procedural Outline.

By Month 9, Day 6

49. AGENCY staff prepares agenda and form for speakers at hearing.

   Action or document required
   Agenda; Speaker Form

Prior to Month 9, Day 20

50. If applicable, PROJECT AREA COMMITTEE reviews proposed Redevelopment Plan and may submit report and recommendations to the Agency and City Council. § 33347.5

    Action or document required
    PAC report and recommendations, if any

Month 9, Day 20

51. CITY COUNCIL and AGENCY hold joint public hearing on Redevelopment Plan and hear all evidence and testimony for and against adoption of Redevelopment Plan.

    NOTES

    Alternate Dates are given for Actions 46–56; if written objections to the proposed redevelopment plan are received at or prior to the joint public hearing, the alternate dates apply.

**Month 9, Day 20 or
Month 10, Day 4**

52. AGENCY acts on adoption of Redevelopment Plan and certification of Final EIR.

    (a) AGENCY adopts resolution certifying completion of and making findings based upon consideration of the Final EIR. CEQA Guidelines §§ 15090, 15091, 15092, 15093

    Action or document required
    Agency Resolution No._____

    (b) AGENCY adopts resolution finding that the use of taxes allocated from the Project for the purpose of improving and increasing the community's supply of low- and moderate-income housing outside the Project Area will be of benefit to the Project (required if the Project Area does not include sites for low- and moderate-income housing). § 33334.2(g)

    Action or document required
    Agency Resolution No._____

    ***(c) AGENCY adopts resolution approving Redevelopment Plan.

    Action or document required
    Agency Resolution No._____

**Month 9, Day 20 or
Month 10, Day 4**

53. CITY COUNCIL acts on adoption of Redevelopment Plan and consideration of Final EIR.

    (a) CITY COUNCIL considers Report of Agency, Final EIR, report and recommendations of Planning Commission, report and recommendations of Project Area Committee, if any, comments from the DOF or HCD, if any, and all evidence and testimony for and against the proposed Redevelopment Plan and adopts written findings in response to each written objection to the Redevelopment Plan from affected taxing entities and property owners. § 33363

    Action or document required
    Council Resolution No._____
    Written Findings

    (b) CITY COUNCIL adopts resolution finding that the use of taxes allocated from the Project for the purpose of improving and increasing the community's supply of low- and moderate-income housing outside the Project Area will be of benefit to the Project (optional, but required if the Project Area does not include sites for low- and moderate-income housing). § 33334.2(g)

    Action or document required
    Council Resolution No._____

    (c) CITY COUNCIL adopts resolution making findings based upon consideration of the Final EIR. CEQA Guidelines § 15096(e), (f), (g), and (h)

    Action or document required
    Council Resolution No._____

    (d) After consideration of all objections and adoption of written findings in response to written objections from property owners and affected taxing entities, if any, CITY COUNCIL introduces Ordinance adopting proposed Redevelopment Plan for first reading. § 33364

    Action or document required
    Ordinance No._____

    NOTES

    Required findings for Ordinance changed pursuant to SB 1206, effective January 1, 2007.

**Month 10, Day 4
or Month 10, Day 18**

54. CITY COUNCIL has second reading and adopts Ordinance adopting Redevelopment Plan. §§ 33365 and 33366

    Action or document required
    Ordinance No._____

**Month 10, Day 5
(*no later than Month 10, Day 11*)
or Month 10, Day 19
(*no later than Month 10, Day 25*)**

55. AGENCY SECRETARY/CITY CLERK files Notice of Determination re Final EIR with County Clerk and, if necessary,

*** Not required, if Agency and Council are the same.

the Office of Planning and Research within five working days (Pub. Resources Code § 21152; CEQA Guidelines §§ 15094 and 15096(i)), with payment of Department of Fish and Game fees required, if any. Pub. Resources Code § 21089

Action or document required
Notice of Determination

NOTES

- *Make sure Notice of Determination is filed on behalf of both the Agency (as lead agency) and the City (as a responsible agency).*
- *Make sure the County Clerk **posts** this Notice (Pub. Resources Code § 21152), as the 30-day statute of limitations doesn't run unless and until it is posted in the County Clerk's office.*

**Month 10, Day 5
or Month 10, Day 19**

56. CITY CLERK sends Ordinance to newspaper for publication.

**Month 10, Day 5
or Month 10, Day 19**

57. CITY CLERK sends copy of Ordinance adopting Redevelopment Plan to the Agency. § 33372

Action or document required
Letter from Clerk transmitting Ordinance

**Month 10, Day 5
or Month 10, Day 19**

Not later than 60 days after adoption

58. CITY CLERK records, with County Recorder, Notice of Redevelopment Plan, including a legal description of land in Project Area, statement that redevelopment activities have been commenced, and, if applicable, a general description of Agency's eminent domain authority. § 33373

Action or document required
Letter from Clerk filing documents; Notice of adoption of Redevelopment Plan to be recorded.

NOTES

- Must be recorded within 60 days after adoption of the Redevelopment Plan.
- Agency shall not commence an action in eminent domain until the Statement is recorded.
- Requirements for recorded Statement changed and time limit for recording of Statement added pursuant to SB 1809, effective January 1, 2007.

**Month 10, Day 5
or Month 10, Day 19**

59. CITY CLERK notifies the Building Department of the adoption of the Redevelopment Plan and its effect upon their operations. § 33374

Action or document required
Cover Letter; Redevelopment Plan

**By Month 10, Day 19
or Month 11, Day 3**

60. Ordinance is published. Government Code § 36933

**By Month 11, Day 4
or Month 11, Day 18**

Not later than 30 days following adoption

61. CITY CLERK transmits a copy of Ordinance adopting the Redevelopment Plan, legal description of land within the Project Area and map or plat indicating boundaries of Project Area to County Auditor and County Assessor, to State Board of Equalization and to all taxing agencies in Project Area. § 33375

Action or document required
Letter from Clerk transmitting documents

NOTES

- Must be transmitted within 30 days after adoption of the Redevelopment Plan.
- Recommend transmittal by certified or overnight mail carrier to obtain receipt/evidence of delivery.
- Transmittal of documents must occur by December 1 to obtain allocation of tax increments in the following tax year. § 33674

**Month 13, Day 4
or Month 13, Day 18**

62. Ordinance adopting Redevelopment Plan becomes effective 90 days after adoption. §§ 33365 and 33378

NOTES

- Ordinance is subject to 90-day referendum period, pursuant to SB 1206, effective January 1, 2007.
- Effective date of Ordinance is based on referendum period; transmittals of documents and other time limits run from the adoption of the ordinance adopting the Redevelopment Plan [Item 54].

Appendix C

Definitions of a "Displaced Person" under Federal DOT Land HUD Guidelines

Effective January 1, 2004

Appendix C

Definitions of a "Displaced Person" under Federal Department of Transportation and Housing and Urban Development Guidelines

Federal DOT Guidelines

Section 24.2 of the Federal DOT Guidelines states:

"Displaced Person—(1) *General.* The term "displaced person" means, except as provided in paragraph (2) of this definition, any person who moves from the real property or moves his or her personal property from the real property: (This includes a person who occupies the real property prior to its acquisition, but who does not meet the length of occupancy requirements of the Uniform Act as described at §§ 24.401(a) and 24.402(a)):

(i) As a direct result of a written notice of intent to acquire, the initiation of negotiations for, or the acquisition of, such real property in whole or in part for a project.

(ii) As a direct result of rehabilitation or demolition for a project; or

(iii) As a direct result of a written notice of intent to acquire, or the acquisition, rehabilitation or demolition of, in whole or in part, other real property on which the person conducts a business or farm operation, for a project. However, eligibility for such person under this paragraph applies only for purposes of obtaining relocation assistance advisory services under § 24.205(c), and moving expenses under § 24.301, § 24.302 or § 24.303.

(2) *Persons not displaced.* The following is a nonexclusive listing of persons who do not qualify as displaced persons under this part:

(i) A person who moves before the initiation of negotiations (see also § 24.403(d)), unless the Agency determines that the person was displaced as a direct result of the program or project; or

(ii) A person who initially enters into occupancy of the property after the date of its acquisition for the project; or

(iii) A person who has occupied the property for the purpose of obtaining assistance under the Uniform Act;

(iv) A person who is not required to relocate permanently as a direct result of a project. Such determination shall be made by the Agency in accordance with any guidelines established by the Federal agency funding the project (see also appendix A of this part); or

(v) An owner-occupant who moves as a result of an acquisition as described at §§ 24.101(a) (1) and (2), or as a result of rehabilitation or demolition of the real property (however, the displacement of a tenant as a direct result of any acquisition, rehabilitation or demolition for a Federal or federally assisted project is subject to this part); or

(vi) A person whom the Agency determines is not displaced as a direct result of a partial acquisition; or

(vii) A person who, after receiving a notice of relocation eligibility (described at § 24.203(b)), is notified in writing that he or she will not be displaced for a project. Such notice shall not be issued unless the person has not moved and the Agency agrees to reimburse the person for any expenses incurred to satisfy any binding contractual relocation obligations entered into after the effective date of the notice of relocation eligibility; or

(viii) An owner-occupant who voluntarily conveys his or her property, as described at § 24.101(a)(1) and (2), after being informed in writing that if a mutually satisfactory agreement on terms of the conveyance cannot be reached, the Agency will not acquire the property. In such cases, however, any resulting displacement of a tenant is subject to the regulations in this part; or

(ix) A person who retains the right of use and occupancy of the real property for life following its acquisition by the Agency; or

(x) An owner who retains the right of use and occupancy of the real property for a fixed term after its acquisition by the Department of Interior under Public Law 93-477 or Public Law 93-303, except that such owner remains a displaced person for purposes of subpart D of this part; or

(xi) A person who is determined to be in unlawful occupancy prior to the initiation of negotiations (see paragraph (y) of this section), or a person who has been evicted for cause, under applicable law, as provided for in § 24.206.

(xii) A person who is not lawfully present in the United States and who has been determined to be ineligible for relocation benefits in accordance with § 24.208.

Federal HUD Guidelines

Section 570.606 (b)(2) of the Federal HUD Guidelines states:

(2) *Displaced Person.* (i) For purposes of paragraph (b) of this section, the term "displaced person" means any person (family, individual, business, non-profit organization, or farm) that moves from real property, or moves his or her personal property from real property, permanently and involuntarily, as a direct result of rehabilitation, demolition, or acquisition for an activity assisted under this part. A permanent, involuntary move from an assisted activity includes a permanent move from real property that is made:

(A) After notice by the grantee (or the state recipient, if applicable) to move permanently from the property, if the move occurs after the initial official submission to HUD (or the State, as applicable) for grant, loan, or loan guarantee funds under this part that are later provided or granted.

(B) After notice by the property owner to move permanently from the property, if the move occurs after the date of the submission of a request for financial assistance by the property owner (or person in control of the site) that is later approved for the requested activity.

(C) Before the date described in paragraph (b)(2)(i)(A) or (B) of this section, if either HUD or the grantee (or State, as applicable) determines that the displacement directly resulted from acquisition, rehabilitation or demolition for the requested activity.

(D) After the "initiation of negotiations" if the person is the tenant-occupant of a dwelling unit and any one of the following three situations occurs:

(1) The tenant has not been provided with a reasonable opportunity to lease and occupy a suitable decent, safe, and sanitary dwelling in the same building/complex upon the completion of the project, including a monthly rent that does not exceed the greater of the tenants' monthly rent and estimated average utility costs before the initiation of negotiations or 30 percent of the household's average monthly gross income; or

(2) The tenant is required to relocate temporarily for the activity but the tenant is not offered payment for all reasonable out-of-pocket expenses incurred in connection with the temporary relocation, including the cost of moving to and from the temporary location and any increased housing costs, or other conditions of the temporary relocation are not reasonable; and the tenant does not return to the building/complex; or

(3) The tenant is required to move to another unit in the building/complex, but is not offered reimbursement for all reasonable out-of-pocket expenses incurred in connection with the move.

(ii) Notwithstanding the provisions of paragraph (b)(2)(i) of this section, the term "*displaced person*" does not include:

(A) A person who is evicted for cause based upon serious or repeated violations of material terms of the lease or occupancy agreement. To exclude a person on this basis, the grantee (or State or state recipient, as applicable) must determine that the eviction was not undertaken for purpose of evading the obligation to provide relocation assistance under this section;

(B) A person who moves into the property after the date of the notice described in paragraph (b)(2)(i)(A) or (B) of this section, but who received a written notice of the expected displacement before occupancy.

(C) A person who is not displaced as described in 49 CFR 24.2(g)(2).

(D) A person who the grantee (or State, as applicable) determines is not displaced as a direct result from the acquisition, rehabilitation, or demolition for an assisted activity. To exclude a person on this basis, HUD must concur in that determination.

(iii) A grantee (or State or state recipient, as applicable) may, at any time, request HUD to determine whether a person is a displaced person under this section.

Appendix D

Key Provisions of the California Health and Safety Code Regarding Affordable Housing Cost

APPENDIX D

Key Provisions of the California Health and Safety Code Regarding Affordable Housing Cost

§ 50052.5 Affordable housing cost

(a) For any owner-occupied housing that receives assistance prior to January 1, 1991, and a condition of that assistance is compliance with this section, "affordable housing cost" with respect to lower income households may not exceed 25 percent of gross income.

(b) For any owner-occupied housing that receives assistance on or after January 1, 1991, and a condition of that assistance is compliance with this section, "affordable housing cost" may not exceed the following:

(1) For extremely low income households the product of 30 percent times 30 percent of the area median income adjusted for family size appropriate for the unit.

(2) For very low income households the product of 30 percent times 50 percent of the area median income adjusted for family size appropriate for the unit.

(3) For lower income households whose gross incomes exceed the maximum income for very low income households and do not exceed 70 percent of the area median income adjusted for family size, the product of 30 percent times 70 percent of the area median income adjusted for family size appropriate for the unit. In addition, for any lower income household that has a gross income that equals or exceeds 70 percent of the area median income adjusted for family size, it shall be optional for any state or local funding agency to require that affordable housing cost not exceed 30 percent of the gross income of the household.

(4) For moderate-income households, affordable housing cost shall not be less than 28 percent of the gross income of the household, nor exceed the product of 35 percent times 110 percent of area median income adjusted for family size appropriate for the unit. In addition, for any moderate-income household that has a gross income that exceeds 110 percent of the area median income adjusted for family size, it shall be optional for any state or local funding agency to require that affordable housing cost not exceed 35 percent of the gross income of the household.

(c) The department shall, by regulation, adopt criteria defining, and providing for determination of, gross income, adjustments for family size appropriate to the unit, and housing cost for purposes of determining affordable housing cost under this section. These regulations may provide alternative criteria, where necessary to be consistent with pertinent federal statutes and regulations governing federally assisted housing. The agency may, by regulation, adopt alternative criteria, and pursuant to subdivision (f) of Section 50462, alternative percentages of income may be adopted for agency-assisted housing development.

(d) with respect to moderate- and lower income households who are tenants of rental housing developments and members or shareholders of cooperative housing developments, or limited equity cooperatives "affordable housing cost" has the same meaning as affordable rent, as defined in Section 50053.

(e) Regulations of the department shall also include a method for determining the maximum construction cost, mortgage loan, or sales price that will make housing available to an income group at affordable housing cost.

(f) For purposes of this section, "area median income" shall mean area median income as published by the department pursuant to Section 50093.

(g) For purposes of this section, "moderate income household" shall have the same meaning as "persons and families of moderate income" as defined in Section 50093.

(h) For purposes of this section, and provided there are no pertinent federal statutes applicable to a project or program, "adjusted for family size appropriate to the unit" shall mean for a household of one person in the case of a studio unit, two persons in the case of a one-bedroom unit, three persons in the case of a two-bedroom unit, four persons in the case of a three-bedroom unit, and five persons in the case of a four-bedroom unit.

§ 50053 Affordable rent

(a) For any rental housing development that receives assistance prior to January 1, 1991, and a condition of that assistance is compliance with this section, "affordable rent" with respect to lower income households shall not exceed the percentage of the gross income of the occupant person or household established by regulation of the department that shall not be less than 15 percent of gross income nor exceed 25 percent of gross income.

(b) For any rental housing development that receives assistance on or after January 1, 1991, and a condition of that assistance is compliance with this section, "affordable rent," including a reasonable utility allowance, shall not exceed:

(1) For extremely low income households the product of 30 percent times 30 percent of the area median income adjusted for family size appropriate for the unit.

(2) For very low income households, the product of 30 percent times 50 percent of the area median income adjusted for family size appropriate for the unit.

(3) For lower income households whose gross incomes exceed the maximum income for very low income households, the product of 30 percent times 60 percent of the area median income adjusted for family size appropriate for the unit. In addition, for those lower income households with gross incomes that

exceed 60 percent of the area median income adjusted for family size, it shall be optional for any state or local funding agency to require that affordable rent be established at a level not to exceed 30 percent of gross income of the household.

(4) For moderate-income households, the product of 30 percent times 110 percent of the area median income adjusted for family size appropriate for the unit. In addition, for those moderate-income households whose gross incomes exceed 110 percent of the area median income adjusted for family size, it shall be optional for any state or local funding agency to require that affordable rent be established at a level not to exceed 30 percent of gross income of the household.

(c) The department's regulation shall permit alternative percentages of income for agency-assisted rental and cooperative housing developments pursuant to regulations adopted under subdivision (f) of Section 50462. The department shall, by regulation, adopt criteria defining and providing for determination of gross income, adjustments for family size appropriate to the unit, and rent for purposes of this section. These regulations may provide alternative criteria, where necessary, to be consistent with pertinent federal statutes and regulations governing federally assisted rental and cooperative housing. The agency may, by regulation, adopt alternative criteria, and pursuant to subdivision (f) of Section 50462, alternative percentages of income may be adopted for agency-assisted housing developments.

For purposes of this section, "area median income," "adjustments for family size appropriate to the unit," and "moderate-income household" shall have the same meaning as provided in Section 50052.5.

§ 50079.5   Lower income households

(a) "Lower income households" means persons and families whose income does not exceed the qualifying limits for lower income families as established and amended from time to time pursuant to Section 8 of the United States Housing Act of 1937. The limits shall be published by the department in the California Code of Regulations as soon as possible after adoption by the Secretary of Housing and Urban Development. In the event the federal standards are discontinued, the department shall, by regulation, establish income limits for lower income households for all geographic areas of the state at 80 percent of area median income, adjusted for family size and revised annually.

(b) "Lower income households" includes very low income households, as defined in Section 50105, and extremely low income households, as defined in Section 50106. The addition of this subdivision does not constitute a change in, but is declaratory of, existing law.

(c) As used in this section, "area median income" means the median family income of a geographic area of the state.

§ 50093   Persons and families of low, moderate, and median income; definitions; filing and publication of standards and criteria

"Persons and families of low or moderate income" means persons and families whose income does not exceed 120 percent of area median income, adjusted for family size by the department in accordance with adjustment factors adopted and amended from time to time by the United States Department of Housing and Urban Development pursuant to Section 8 of the United States Housing Act of 1937. However, the agency and the department jointly, or either acting with the concurrence of the Secretary of the Business and Transportation Agency, may permit the agency to use higher income limitations in designated geographic areas of the state, upon a determination that 120 percent of the median income in the particular geographic area is too low to qualify a substantial number of persons and families of low or moderate income who can afford rental or home purchase of housing financed pursuant to Part 3 (commencing with Section 50900) without subsidy.

"Persons and families of low or moderate income" includes very low income households, as defined in Section 50105, extremely low income households, as defined in Section 50106, and lower income households as defined in Section 50079.5, and includes persons and families of extremely low income, persons and families of very low income, persons and families of low income, persons and families of moderate income, and middle-income families. As used in this division:

(a) "Persons and families of low income" or "persons of low income" means persons or families who are eligible for financial assistance specifically provided by a governmental agency for the benefit of occupants of housing financed pursuant to this division.

(b) "Persons and families of moderate income" or "middle-income families" means persons and families of low or moderate income whose income exceeds the income limit for lower income households.

(c) "Persons and families of median income" means persons and families whose income does not exceed the area median income, as adjusted by the department for family size in accordance with adjustment factors adopted and amended from time to time by the United States Department of Housing and Urban Development pursuant to Section 8 of the United States Housing Act of 1937.

As used in this section, "area median income" means the median family income of a geographic area of the state, as annually estimated by the United States Department of Housing and Urban Development pursuant to Section 8 of the United States Housing Act of 1937. In the event these federal determinations of area median income are discontinued, the department shall establish and publish as regulations income limits for persons and families of median income for all geographic areas of the state at 100 percent of area median income, and for persons and families of low or moderate income for all geographic areas of the state at 120 percent of area median income. These income limits shall be adjusted for family size and shall be revised annually.

For purposes of this section, the department shall file, with the Office of Administrative Law, any changes in area median income and income limits determined by the United States Department of Housing and Urban Development, together with any consequent changes in other derivative income limits determined by the department pursuant to this section. These filings shall not be subject to Article 5 (commencing with Section 11346) or Article 6 (commencing with Section 11349) of Chapter 3.5 of Part 1 of Division 3 of Title 2 of the Government Code, but shall be effective upon filing with the Office of Administrative Law and shall be published as soon as possible in the California Regulatory Code Supplement and the California Code of Regulations.

The department shall establish and publish a general definition of income, including inclusions, exclusions, and allowances, for qualifying persons under the income limits of this section and Sections 50079.5, 50105, and 50106 to be used where no other federal or state definitions of income apply. This definition need not be established by regulation.

Nothing in this division shall prevent the agency or the department from adopting separate family size adjustment factors or programmatic definitions of income to qualify households, persons, and families for programs of the agency or department, as the case may be.

§ 50105 Very low income households

(a) "Very low income households" means persons and families whose incomes do not exceed the qualifying limits for very low income families as established and amended from time to time pursuant to Section 8 of the United States Housing Act of 1937. These qualifying limits shall be published by the department in the California Code of Regulations as soon as possible after adoption by the Secretary of Housing and Urban Development. In the event the federal standards are discontinued, the department shall, by regulation, establish income limits for very low income households for all geographic areas of the state at 50 percent of area median income, adjusted for family size and revised annually.

(b) "Very low income households" includes extremely low income households, as defined in Section 50106. The addition of this subdivision does not constitute a change in, but is declaratory of, existing law.

(c) As used in this section, "area median income" means the median family income of a geographic area of the state.

§ 50106 Extremely low income households

"Extremely low income households" means persons and families whose incomes do not exceed the qualifying limits for extremely low income families as established and amended from time to time by the Secretary of Housing and Urban Development and defined in Section 5.603(b) of Title 24 of the Code of Federal Regulations. These limits shall be published by the department in the California Code of Regulations as soon as possible after adoption by the Secretary of Housing and Urban Development. In the event the federal standards are discontinued, the department shall, by regulation, establish income limits for extremely low income households for all geographic areas of the state at 30 percent of area median income, adjusted for family size and revised annually. As used in this section, "area median income" means the median family income of a geographic area of the state.

Bibliography

Ralph Anderson and Associates. *Redevelopment and Tax Increment Financing*, Sacramento, 1976

Ralph Anderson and Associates. *Redevelopment and Tax Increment Financing, Housing Supplement*, Sacramento (1977)

California Debt Advisory Commission. *Use of Redevelopment and Tax Increment Financing*, 1984

Department of Housing and Community Development, *Redevelopment Housing Activities in California, Fiscal Year 1992–93*, Sacramento (1994)

Department of Housing and Community Development, *Redevelopment Housing Activities in California, Fiscal Year 1997–98*, Sacramento (1999)

Department of Housing and Community Development, *Redevelopment Housing Activities in California, Fiscal Year 2000–2001*, Sacramento (2002)

Bernard J. Freiden and Lynn B. Sagalyn. *Downtown, Inc.*, MIT Press (1989)

Quinn Johnstone. "The Federal Urban Renewal Program." *University of Chicago Law Review*, no. 25 (1958): 301

Eugene B. Jacobs and Jack G. Levine. "Redevelopment: Making Misused and Disused Land Available and Useable." *Hastings Law Journal*, no. 8 (1957): 241

Matteoni & Veit. "Condemnation Practice in California." *Continuing Education of the Bar*, November 2003

Michael H. Remy, *et al. Guide to the California Environmental Quality Act (CEQA)*. Tenth edition. Solano Press Books, 1999

Richard G. Rypinski. *Eminent Domain: A Step-by-Step Guide to the Acquisition of Real Property*. Solano Press Books, 2002

State Controller, Annual Report 1987–88 and Annual Report 2001–02. *Financial Transactions Concerning Community Redevelopment Agencies of California*

List of Acronyms

ADC	=	Association of Defense Communities
ASTM	=	American Society for Testing and Material
BCT	=	BRAC cleanup team
BRAC	=	Base Realignment and Closure Commission
Cal/EPA	=	California Environmental Protection Agency
CDBG	=	Community Development Block Grant
CEQA	=	California Environmental Quality Act
CERCLA	=	Comprehensive Environmental Response, Compensation and Liability Act
CHFA	=	California Housing Finance Agency
CLEAN	=	Cleanup Loans and Environmental Assistance to Neighborhoods
CLRRA	=	California Land Reuse and Revitalization Act
CRA	=	California Redevelopment Association
DDA	=	Disposition and development agreement
DIR	=	Department of Industrial Relations
DOT	=	Department of Transportation
DTSC	=	Department of Toxic Substances Control
EDC	=	Economic development conveyance
EETP	=	Eastern Early Transfer Parcel
EIR	=	Environmental impact report
EIS	=	Environmental impact statement
EOA	=	Environmental Oversight Agreement
ERAF	=	Education Revenue Augmentation Fund
ERAP	=	Expedited Remedial Action Program
ESCA	=	Environmental Services Cooperative Agreement
ETCA	=	Early Transfer Cooperative Agreement
EUL	=	Enhanced use leasing
FHA	=	Farmers Home Administration
FNMA	=	Federal National Mortgage Association
FORA	=	Fort Ord Reuse Authority
FOSET	=	Finding of suitability for early transfer
FOST	=	Finding of suitability to transfer
FPPC	=	California Fair Political Practices Commission
FSLIC	=	Federal Savings and Loan Insurance Corporation
GSA	=	General Services Administration
HCD	=	Department of Housing and Community Development
HSAA	=	Carpenter-Presley-Tanner Hazardous Substance Account Act
HUD	=	U.S. Department of Housing and Urban Development
LAMBRA	=	Local Military Base Recovery Area
LIFOC	=	Lease in furtherance of conveyance
LRA	=	Local reuse authority
MEC	=	Munitions and explosives of concern
MERLO	=	Municipal Environmental Response and Liability Ordinance
MTBE	=	Methyl tertiary butyl ether
NEPA	=	National Environmental Policy Act
NFA	=	No-further-action
NLDC	=	New London Development Corporation
OEHHA	=	Office of Environmental Health Hazard Assessment
OPA	=	Owner participation agreement
PAC	=	Project area committee
PBC	=	Public benefit conveyance
PCB	=	Polychlorinated biphenyl
PEA	=	Preliminary Endangerment Assessment
PRP	=	Potentially responsible person
RAB	=	Restoration advisory board
RACM	=	Regulated, asbestos-containing materials
RFP	=	Request for Proposal
RFQ	=	Request for Qualifications
RLUIPA	=	Religious Land Use and Institutionalized Persons Act
ROD	=	Record of decision
RWQCB	=	Regional Water Quality Control Board
TSCA	=	Toxic Substance Control Act
US-EPA	=	United States Environmental Protection Agency
UST	=	Underground storage tank
UXO	=	Unexploded ordnance
VCP	=	Voluntary Cleanup Program

Table of Authorities

CASES

	page(s)
99 Cents Only Stores, Inc. v. Lancaster Redevelopment Agency (C.D. Cal. 2001) 237 F. Supp. 2d 1123	125
Anaheim Redevelopment Agency v. Dusek (1987) 193 Cal. App. 3d 249	112, 113, 121
Andrews v. City of San Bernardino (1959) 175 Cal. App. 2d 459	21, 204, 208, 209
Arcadia Redevelopment Agency v. Ikemoto (1991) 233 Cal. App. 3d 24	235
Arcadia Redevelopment Agency v. Ikemoto (1993) 16 Cal. App. 4th 444	235–236
Arnel Development Co. v. City of Costa Mesa (1980) 28 Cal. 3d 511	208
Associated Home Builders Etc., Inc. v. City of Livermore (1976) 18 Cal. 3d 582	208
Babcock v. Community Redevelopment Agency (1957) 148 Cal. App. 2d 38	319
Barthelemy v. Orange County Flood Control District (1998) 65 Cal. App. 4th 558	127
Beach-Courchesne v. City of Diamond Bar (2000) 80 Cal. App. 4th 388	43
Berman v. Parker (1954) 348 U.S. 26	38, 39, 110, 111
Bernardi v. City Council (1997) 54 Cal. App. 4th 426	318
Bi-Rite Meat and Provisions Co. v. Redevelopment Agency of the City of Hawaiian Gardens (2007) 156 Cal. App. 4th 1419	166
Blue v. City of Los Angeles (2006) 137 Cal. App. 4th 1131	65, 113, 321
Boelts v. City of Lake Forest (2005) 127 Cal. App. 4th 116	321
Border Business Park, Inc. v. City of San Diego (2006) 142 Cal. App. 4th 1538	133, 134
Bozek and Gonzales v. Redevelopment Agency of the City of Chula Vista, No. 684525 (San Diego Co. Sup. Ct., 1995)	252
Brown v. Fair Political Practices Comm. (2000) 84 Cal. App. 4th 137 (1-A091305, Div. 2)	99
Burbank-Glendale-Pasadena Airport Authority v. Hensler (1991) 233 Cal. App. 3d 577	117
California Housing Finance Agency v. Elliott (1976) 17 Cal. 3d 575	295
California Housing Finance Agency v. Patitucci (1978) 22 Cal. 3d 171	295
Cambria Spring Co. v. City of Pico Rivera (1985) 171 Cal. App. 3d 1080	133
Chhour v. Community Redevelopment Agency (1996) 46 Cal. App. 4th 273	128
Citizens for Responsible Equitable Environmental Development v. City of San Diego Redevelopment Agency (2005) 134 Cal. App. 4th 598	69, 71
City of Burbank v. Burbank-Glendale-Pasadena Airport Authority (2003) 113 Cal. App. 4th 465	208
City of Carmel-by-the-Sea v. Board of Supervisors (1977) 71 Cal. App. 3d 84	71
City of Carson v. City of La Mirada (2004) 125 Cal. App. 4th 532	227, 251
City of Dinuba v. County of Tulare (2007) 137 Cal. App. 4th 1387	234
City of Fremont v. Fisher (2008) 160 Cal. App. 4th 666	131
City of Lake Elsinore v. Ranel Dev. Co. (1998) 70 Cal. Rptr. 2d 715, Supreme Court Minute Order 04-01-1998	121
City of Lake Elsinore v. Ranel Development Co. (1998) 60 Cal. App. 4th 974	121
City of Lincoln v. Barringer (2002) 102 Cal. App. 4th 1211	124
City of Lodi v. Randtron (2004) 118 Cal. App. 4th 337	151
City of Long Beach v. Dept. of Industrial Relations (2004) 34 Cal. 4th 942	197
City of Los Angeles v. Decker (1977) 18 Cal. 3d 860	126

	page(s)
City of Modesto Redevelopment Agency v. Superior Court (2004) 119 Cal. App. 4th 28	142
City of Ontario v. Superior Court (1970) 2 Cal. 3d 335	314, 315
City of San Diego v. Barratt-American, Inc. (2005) 128 Cal. App. 4th 917	131
City of San Jose v. Great Oaks Water Co. (1987) 192 Cal. App. 3d 1005	117
City of Santa Clarita v. NTS Technical Systems (2006) 137 Cal. App. 4th 264	123
City of Vista v. Fielder (1996) 13 Cal. 4th 612	128, 129
Cline v. Lewis (1917) 175 Cal. 315	76
Coachella Valley Mosquito and Vector Control Dist. v. City of Indio (2002) 101 Cal. App. 4th 12	318
Committee of Seven Thousand v. Superior Court (1988) 45 Cal. 3d 491	208
Community Redevelopment Agency of Oxnard v. County of Ventura (2007) 152 Cal. App. 4th 1470	234
Community Redevelopment Agency v. Force Electronics (1997) 55 Cal. App. 4th 622	132
Community Redevelopment Agency v. Superior Court (1967) 248 Cal. App. 2d 164	77, 315
Community Redevelopment Agency v. World Wide Enterprises, Inc. (2000) 77 Cal. App. 4th 1156	131
Contra Costa Theatre, Inc. v. Redevelopment Agency (1982) 131 Cal. App. 3d 860	172, 212
Contra Costa Water District v. Vaquero Farms, Inc. (1997) 58 Cal. App. 4th 883	128, 134
Cooper Industries, Inc. v. Aviall Services, Inc. (2004) 543 U.S. 157	145
Cottonwood Christian Ctr. v. Cypress Redevelopment Agency (C.D. Cal. 2002) 218 F. Supp. 2d 1203	125
County of Riverside v. City of Murrieta (1998) 65 Cal. App. 4th 616	42, 43, 44
County of Riverside v. Superior Court (1997) 54 Cal. App. 4th 443	315
County of Santa Cruz v. City of Watsonville (1985) 177 Cal. App. 3d 831	35, 55
County of Solano v. Vallejo Redevelopment Agency (1999) 75 Cal. App. 4th 1262	242
County of Ventura v. Channel Islands Marina, Inc. (2008) 159 Cal. App. 4th 615	134-135
Craig v. Poway (1994) 28 Cal. App. 4th 319	259, 270, 276
Davis v. City of Berkeley (1990) 51 Cal. 3d 227	297
Dina v. The People ex rel. Department of Transportation (2007) 151 Cal. App. 4th 1029	123
Dolan v. City of Tigard (1994) 512 U.S. 374	133

	page(s)
Downey Cares v. Downey Community Development Com. (1987) 196 Cal. App. 3d 983	91
Emeryville Redevelopment Agency v. Harcros Pigments, Inc. (2002) 101 Cal. App. 4th 1083	126, 128, 129
Emmington v. Solano County Redevelopment Agency (1987) 195 Cal. App. 3d 491	41, 42
Evans v. City of San Jose (2005) 128 Cal. App. 4th 1123	44, 78, 321
Fellom v. Redevelopment Agency (1958) 157 Cal. App. 2d 243, cert. denied (1958) 358 U.S. 56	41, 181
Fireman's Fund Ins. Co. v. City of Lodi (E.D. Cal. 2003) 296 F. Supp. 2d 1197	151
Fireman's Fund Insurance Company v. City of Lodi (9th Cir. 2002) 302 F. 3d 928	151
First English Evangelical Lutheran Church v. Los Angeles County (1987) 482 U.S. 304	133
Fontana Redevelopment Agency v. Torres (2007) 153 Cal. App. 4th 902	241, 318
Fosselman's, Inc. v. City of Alhambra (1986) 178 Cal. App. 3d 806	41
Franklin-McKinley School Dist. v. City of San Jose (1991) 234 Cal. App. 3d 1599	57
Fraser-Yamor Agency, Inc. v. County of Del Norte (1977) 68 Cal. App. 3d 201	102
Freedom Newspapers, Inc. v. Orange County Employees Retirement System (1993) 6 Cal. 4th 821	189
Friedland v. City of Long Beach (1998) 62 Cal. App. 4th 835	318
Friends of Mammoth v. Town of Mammoth Lakes Redevelopment Agency (2000) 82 Cal. App. 4th 511	39, 43, 45, 66-68
Gibbs v. City of Napa (1976) 59 Cal. App. 3d 148 [130 Cal. Rptr. 382]	210
Gilmore v. Pearson (1925) 71 Cal. App. 284	76
Gleason v. City of Santa Monica (1962) 207 Cal. App. 2d 458	312
Gonzales v. City of Santa Ana (1993) 12 Cal. App. 4th 1335	42
Graber v. City of Upland (2002) 99 Cal. App. 4th 424	43, 45, 234
Graydon v. Pasadena Redevelopment Agency (1980) 104 Cal. App. 3d 631	221, 228-229, 316-317
Green v. Community Redevelopment Agency (1979) 96 Cal. App. 3d 491	313, 316
Greystone Homes, Inc. v. Cake (2005) 135 Cal. App. 4th 1	197
Hawaii Housing Authority v. Midkiff (1984) 467 U.S. 229	111
Hensler v. City of Glendale (1994) 8 Cal. 4th 1	134
Hesperia Citizens for Responsible Development v. City of Hesperia (2007) 151 Cal. App. 4th 653	252

	page(s)
HFH, Ltd. v. Superior Court (1975) 15 Cal. 3d 508	134
Hogar v. Community Development Commission (2003) 110 Cal. App. 4th 1288	272
Housing Authority v. City of Los Angeles (1952) 38 Cal. 2d 853	203, 208, 209
Huntington Park Redevelopment Agency v. Duncan (1983) 142 Cal. App. 3d 17	182
Huntington Park Redevelopment Agency v. Martin (1985) 38 Cal. 3d 100	250
Inglewood Redevelopment Agency v. Aklilu (2007) 153 Cal. App. 4th 1095	129
Kaatz v. City of Seaside (2006) 143 Cal. App. 4th 13	317
Katz v. Campbell Union High School District (2006) 144 Cal. App. 4th 1024	314
Kehoe v. City of Berkeley (1977) 67 Cal. App. 3d 666	26, 209
Kelo v. City of New London (2005) 545 U.S. 469	12–13, 112
Kleiber v. City and County of San Francisco (1941) 18 Cal. 2d 718	208–209
Klopping v. City of Whittier (1972) 8 Cal. 3d 39	133
Kunec v. Brea Redevelopment Agency (1997) 55 Cal. App. 4th 511	99
Langer v. Redevelopment Agency (1999) 71 Cal. App. 4th 998	134
League for Protection of Oakland's Architectural and Historic Resources v. City of Oakland (1997) 52 Cal. App. 4th 896	215
Long Beach Community Redevelopment Agency v. Morgan (1993) 14 Cal. App. 4th 1047	120
Los Angeles County Metropolitan Transportation Authority v. Continental Development Corporation (1997) 16 Cal. 4th 694	127
M&A Gabaee v. Community Redevelopment Agency (9th Cir. 2005) 419 F. 3d 1036	125
MacDonald, Sommer & Frates v. County of Yolo (1986) 477 U.S. 340	134
Marek v. Napa Community Redevelopment Agency (1988) 46 Cal. 3d 1070	246–247, 317
Meaney v. Sacramento Housing and Redevelopment Agency (1993) 13 Cal. App. 4th 566	213, 220–221
Melamed v. City of Long Beach (1993) 15 Cal. App. 4th 70	108
Merced Irrigation Dist. v. Woolstenhulme (1971) 4 Cal. 3d 478	131
Metropolitan Water Dist. of So. Cal. v. Campus Crusade for Christ (2007) 41 Cal. 4th 954	126
Midway Orchards v. County of Butte (1990) 220 Cal. App. 3d 765	37, 76
Millbrae School Dist. v. Superior Court (1989) 209 Cal. App. 3d 1494	316
Morgan v. Community Redevelopment Agency (1991) 231 Cal. App. 3d 243, cert denied (1992) 503 U.S. 937	41
Mt. San Jacinto Community College District v. Superior Court (2007) 40 Cal. 4th 648	130
National City Business Assoc. v. City of National City (1983) 146 Cal. App. 3d 1060	41
Neilson v. City of California City (2007) 146 Cal. App. 4th 633	45
New Haven Unified School District v. Taco Bell Corp. (1994) 24 Cal. App. 4th 1473	128
Nolan v. Redevelopment Agency (1981) 117 Cal. App. 3d 494	25
Nollan v. California Coastal Commission (1987) 483 U.S. 825	133
North Hollywood Project Area Committee v. City of Los Angeles (1998) 61 Cal. App. 4th 719	52
Old Town Dev. Corp. v. Urban Renewal Agency (1967) 249 Cal. App. 2d 313	176
Pacific Rock Etc. Co. v. City of Upland (1967) 67 Cal. 2d 666	208
Pacific States Enterprise, Inc. v. City of Coachella (1993) 13 Cal. App. 4th 1414	25
Pacific Tel. and Tel. Co. v. Redevelopment Agency of the City of Glendale (1978) 87 Cal. App. 3d 296	169
Pardee Construction Co. v. City of Camarillo (1984) 37 Cal. 3d 465	208
Penn Central Transp. Co. v. New York City (1978) 438 U.S. 104	134
People ex rel. Chapman v. Rapsey (1940) 16 Cal. 2d 636	28
People ex rel. Dept. of Transportation v. Muller (1984) 36 Cal. 3d 263	127–128
People ex rel. Dept. of Transportation v. Tanczos (1996) 42 Cal. App. 4th 1215	130
Planning and Conservation League v. Dept. of Water Resources (1998) 17 Cal. 4th 264	322
Plunkett v. City of Lakewood (1975) 44 Cal. App. 3d 344	312
Redevelopment Agency of San Diego v. Attisha (2005) 128 Cal. App. 4th 357	128
Redevelopment Agency of San Diego v. Mesdaq (2007) 154 Cal. App. 4th 1111	129, 133
Redevelopment Agency of the City of Chula Vista v. Rados Bros. (2001) 95 Cal. App. 4th 309	112–113
Redevelopment Agency of the City of San Diego v. Salvation Army (2002) 103 Cal. App. 4th 755	141
Redevelopment Agency of the City of San Diego v. San Diego Gas & Electric Company (2003) 111 Cal. App. 4th 912	142
Redevelopment Agency v. City of Berkeley (1978) 80 Cal. App. 3d 158	39, 210–211
Redevelopment Agency v. Commission on State Mandates (1997) 55 Cal. App. 4th 976	271

Table of Authorities 505

	page(s)
Redevelopment Agency v. Contra Costa Theatre, Inc. (1982) 135 Cal. App. 3d 73	133
Redevelopment Agency v. County of Los Angeles (1999) 75 Cal. App. 4th 68	233
Redevelopment Agency v. County of San Bernardino (1978) 21 Cal. 3d 255	232, 233
Redevelopment Agency v. Del-Camp Investments, Inc. (1974) 38 Cal. App. 3d 836	113, 312
Redevelopment Agency v. Hayes (1954) 122 Cal. App. 2d 777, cert. denied (1954) 348 U.S. 897	39, 41
Redevelopment Agency v. Herrold (1978) 86 Cal. App. 3d 1024	113, 312
Redevelopment Agency v. Norm's Slauson (1985) 173 Cal. App. 3d 1121	124, 180, 184–185
Redevelopment Agency v. Shepard (1977) 75 Cal. App. 3d 453	295
Redevelopment Agency v. Superior Court (1991) 228 Cal. App. 3d 1487	78, 319
Regents of University of California v. Sheily (2004) 122 Cal. App. 4th 824	128
Regus v. City of Baldwin Park (1977) 70 Cal. App. 3d 968	39, 41, 42, 78, 319
Resource Defense Fund v. County of Santa Cruz (1982) 133 Cal. App. 3d 800	37
Richmond American Homes of Colorado, Inc. v. U.S. (2007) 75 Fed. Cl. 376	307
San Diego Metropolitan Transit Development Board v. Handlery Hotel, Inc. (1999) 73 Cal. App. 4th 517	133
San Franciscans Upholding the Downtown Plan v. City and County of San Francisco (2002) 102 Cal. App. 4th 656	44
Sanguineti v. City Council (1965) 231 Cal. App. 2d 813	182
Santa Ana Unified School District v. Orange County Development Agency (2001) 90 Cal. App. 4th 404	235
Santa Cruz County Redevelopment Agency v. Izant (1995) 37 Cal. App. 4th 141	124

	page(s)
Saratoga Fire Protection Dist. v. Hackett (2002) 97 Cal. App. 4th 895	123, 130
Save Our NTC, Inc. v. City of San Diego (2003) 105 Cal. App. 4th 285	302
Save Tara v. City of West Hollywood (2008) 45 Cal. 4th 116	180, 214
Shasta Lake v. County of Shasta (1999) 75 Cal. App. 4th 1	82
Sibbet v. Board of Directors (1965) 237 Cal. App. 2d 731	77–78, 315
Starr v. City and County of San Francisco (1977) 72 Cal. App. 3d 164	204
State Building and Construction Trades Council of California v. Duncan (2008) 162 Cal. App. 4th 289	194
State Route 4 Bypass Authority v. Superior Ct. (2007) 153 Cal. App. 4th 1546	131
Stockton Newspapers, Inc. v. Members of the Redevelopment Agency of the City of Stockton (1985) 171 Cal. App. 3d 95	29
Sweetwater Valley Civic Assn. v. City of National City (1976) 18 Cal. 3d 270	41–42
Temple City Redevelopment Agency v. Bayside Drive Ltd. Partnership (2007) 146 Cal. App. 4th 1555	132
Terminals Equipment Co. v. City and County of San Francisco (1990) 221 Cal. App. 3d 234	134
Thomson v. Call (1985) 38 Cal. 3d 633	102–103
Torrance Redevelopment Agency v. Solvent Coating Company (C.D. Cal. 1991) 781 F. Supp. 650	141
Torres v. City of Yorba Linda (1993) 13 Cal. App. 4th 1035	320
United Auto Workers v. Department of Transportation (1993) 20 Cal. App. 4th 1462	156
United States v. Atlantic Research Corp. (2007) 551 U.S. 128, 127 S. Ct. 2331	145
Witt v. Morrow (1977) 70 Cal. App. 3d 817	91
Yost v. Thomas (1984) 36 Cal. 3d 561	208

U.S. Constitution

	page(s)
Fifth Amendment	12, 13, 110, 112
Fourteenth Amendment	110

Federal Statutes

10 U.S.C. Sec. 2667	306
10 U.S.C. Sec. 2687	303
10 U.S.C. Sec. 2687(f)(1)	305
10 U.S.C. Sec. 2687(f)(2)	305
10 U.S.C. Sec. 2905(b)(4)	304
15 U.S.C. Sec. 2601 *et seq.*	151
40 U.S.C. Sec. 471 *et seq.*	302
40 U.S.C. Secs. 484(a)(1)–(2)	305
40 U.S.C. Sec. 484(e)(3)(H)	305
42 U.S.C. Sec. 2000 *et seq.*	125
42 U.S.C. Sec. 2531(a)	143
42 U.S.C. Sec. 4601 *et seq.*	155
42 U.S.C. Sec. 4623(a)	165
42 U.S.C. Sec. 4630	158
42 U.S.C. Sec. 4636	168
42 U.S.C. Sec. 5301	277
42 U.S.C. Sec. 9601	143
42 U.S.C. Sec. 9601 *et seq.*	144, 306
42 U.S.C. Sec. 9601(35)(A)	144
42 U.S.C. Sec. 9601(35)(A)(ii)	144
42 U.S.C. Sec. 9601(39)(A)	139
42 U.S.C. Sec. 9601(39)(B)	139
42 U.S.C. Sec. 9601(39)(C)	139
42 U.S.C. Sec. 9601(39)(D)	139
42 U.S.C. Sec. 9606	145
42 U.S.C. Sec. 9607	145
42 U.S.C. Sec. 9607(a)	145
42 U.S.C. Sec. 9607(b)(3)	144
42 U.S.C. Sec. 9613	145
42 U.S.C. Sec. 9620(a)(2)	306
42 U.S.C. Sec. 9620(h)(3)(A)	306
42 U.S.C. Sec. 9620(h)(3)(A)(ii)(I)	308
42 U.S.C. Sec. 9620(h)(3)(C)	308
42 U.S.C. Sec. 12721	278

Federal Regulations

24 C.F.R. Part 42	156
24 C.F.R. Sec. 42.325	159
24 C.F.R. Sec. 42.375	290
24 C.F.R. Sec. 570.606(6)(2)	163
24 C.F.R. Sec. 570.606(c)	290
32 C.F.R. Part 174	303
32 C.F.R. Part 175	303
41 C.F.R. Part 101-47.304-9(a)(4)	305
49 C.F.R. Sec. 24.1 *et seq.*	155
49 C.F.R. Sec. 24.2(a)(9)(ii)(H)	169
49 C.F.R. Sec. 24.2	163
49 C.F.R. Sec. 24.10	167
49 C.F.R. Sec. 24.101(a)(2)	169
49 C.F.R. Sec. 24.101(b)(1)	169
49 C.F.R. Sec. 24.101(b)(2)	169
49 C.F.R. Sec. 24.205(a)	159
49 C.F.R. Sec. 24.205(c)	159
49 C.F.R. Sec. 24.206	167
49 C.F.R. Sec. 24.302	165
49 C.F.R. Sec. 24.304	164
49 C.F.R. Sec. 42.325	159
H.R. 2869/Pub. Law 107-118	144, 146
Public Law 101-510, Title XXIX	303
Public Law 102-484	306, 307

California Constitution

	page(s)
Article I, Sec. 19	107, 110
Article XIII, Sec. 19	5, 231
Article XIII, Sec. 29	253
Article XIIIA	9, 235
Article XIIIB	223, 248, 249, 271
Article XVI, Sec. 16	5, 231, 232, 233, 234, 235, 236, 249
Article XXXIV	214, 290, 294, 295, 296, 297
Article XXXIV, Sec. 1	296

California Statutes

Civil Code

Sec. 1087	109

Code of Civil Procedures

Sec. 387	316
Sec. 860	221, 229, 314, 317
Sec. 860 *et seq.*	77, 313, 314, 316, 318
Secs. 860–870	311, 313, 315, 316
Sec. 861	314
Sec. 861.1	314, 316
Sec. 863	314–315, 316, 321
Sec. 864	221
Sec. 866	319
Sec. 869	221, 315, 316
Sec. 870	314
Sec. 870(b)	322
Sec. 1230.010 *et seq.*	110, 119
Sec. 1240.030	185
Sec. 1245.220	120
Sec. 1245.230	121
Sec. 1245.235	120
Sec. 1245.240	120
Sec. 1245.255	124
Sec. 1245.270	124
Sec. 1250.310	122
Sec. 1250.360	124
Sec. 1250.370	124
Sec. 1250.410	132
Sec. 1250.410(e)	132
Sec. 1255.060	131
Sec. 1255.260	124
Sec. 1255.410 *et seq.*	122
Sec. 1255.410(c)	123
Sec. 1255.410(d)	122
Sec. 1255.410(e)(1)	122
Sec. 1255.450(b)	123
Sec. 1255.450(e)	122
Sec. 1260.040	123–124
Sec. 1260.110	124
Sec. 1260.110. *et seq.*	123
Sec. 1260.210	130
Sec. 1260.220(b)	130
Sec. 1263.010 *et seq.*	120
Sec. 1263.025	115
Sec. 1263.110 *et seq.*	123
Sec. 1263.320(b)	126
Sec. 1263.410 *et seq.*	127
Sec. 1263.510(a)	127, 128

	page(s)
Sec. 1263.510(b)	127
Sec. 1268.010	131–132
Sec. 1268.310	132
Sec. 1268.710	132
Tit. 7, Part III	110, 119
Tit. 10, Pt. 2, Chap. 9	312

Evidence Code

Sec. 822(a)(1)	127

Government Code

Sec. 860.2	234
Sec. 1090	53, 102–103
Sec. 1090 *et seq.*	102
Sec. 1091	102
Sec. 1091.5	102
Sec. 1091.6	103, 114
Sec. 1097	102
Sec. 1126	103
Sec. 6066	211
Sec. 6584 *et seq.*	261
Sec. 7105	302
Sec. 7260	291
Sec. 7260 *et seq.*	115, 155, 163
Sec. 7260(c)	162
Sec. 7262(b)	165
Sec. 7262.5(a)	166
Sec. 7263	165
Secs. 7267.1–7267.7	121
Sec. 7267.1(a)	115
Sec. 7267.1(b)	115, 116
Sec. 7267.2	108, 115, 116
Sec. 7267.2(a)	108
Sec. 7267.2(c)	115
Sec. 7267.2(d)	109
Sec. 7267.2(e)	109
Sec. 7267.5	117
Sec. 7267.7	117
Sec. 7267.8	115, 157
Sec. 7269	168
Sec. 7272.3	166
Sec. 7277	168
Sec. 7277(a)	109
Sec. 7277(b)	109
Sec. 8855	257
Sec. 33385	51
Sec. 53051	25
Sec. 53084	251
Sec. 53090(a)	209
Sec. 53091	209
Secs. 53314.6–53314.7	148
Sec. 53511	220, 316, 317, 318
Sec. 53311 *et seq.*	261
Sec. 53891	30
Sec. 54950 *et seq.*	28, 52
Sec. 54952(b)	189
Sec. 54954.2	29
Sec. 54954.3	121
Sec. 54954.5	29
Sec. 54956.8	28, 29, 189
Sec. 54956.9	29
Sec. 54957	29
Sec. 55704.5	253
Sec. 55707	253
Sec. 6040 *et seq.*	25
Sec. 65090	51
Sec. 65302(a)	37

	page(s)		page(s)		page(s)
Sec. 65302(b)	37	Sec. 33030(c)	218	Sec. 33321.5	46
Sec. 65302(c)	37	Sec. 33031	39, 72, 218, 267	Sec. 33322	48
Sec. 65302(d)	37			Sec. 33324	48
Sec. 65302(e)	37	Sec. 33031(a)	40	Sec. 33327	49
Sec. 65302(f)	37	Sec. 33031(a)(4)	46, 53	Sec. 33328	49, 50, 53, 73, 237
Sec. 65302(g)	37	Sec. 33031(b)	40		
Sec. 65361	37, 38	Sec. 33031(b)(2)	108, 138	Sec. 33328.1	49
Sec. 65361(e)	38	Sec. 33032(c)	218	Sec. 33328.1(a)	50
Sec. 65400(b)	273	Sec. 33035	267	Sec. 33328.1(a)(2)	49
Sec. 65402	72	Sec. 33037	39, 208	Sec. 33328.1(a)(3)	49
Sec. 65560	37	Sec. 33070	275, 294	Sec. 33328.1(a)(4)	49
Sec. 65580	37	Sec. 33071	275, 294	Sec. 33328.1(b)	49
Sec. 65584	84, 277	Sec. 33080	31	Sec. 33328.4	50
Sec. 65585	62	Sec. 33080.1	30, 31, 63	Sec. 33328.5	49
Sec. 65865 et seq.	204	Sec. 33080.1(a)	31, 63	Sec. 33328.7	49, 50
Sec. 67650 et seq.	301, 303	Sec. 33080.1(c)	297	Sec. 33332	55
Sec. 67800 et seq.	301, 303	Sec. 33080.4	30	Sec. 33333	57
Sec. 81000 et seq.	26, 52–53, 87	Sec. 33080.4	297	Sec. 33333(a)	55
		Sec. 33080.4(a)(10)	297	Sec. 33333(b)	55
Sec. 82003	26	Sec. 33080.4(a)(11)	297	Sec. 33333(c)	55
Sec. 82019	88	Sec. 33080.5	30	Sec. 33333(d)	55
Sec. 82030	90	Sec. 33080.6	31	Sec. 33333.10	59, 62, 63, 85, 278, 285, 290, 291, 292
Sec. 82033	90	Sec. 33080.7	30, 297		
Sec. 82034	90	Sec. 33080.8	33		
Sec. 82048	26	Sec. 33080.8(b)	63	Sec. 33333.10(a)	293
Sec. 83114	100	Sec. 33100	26	Sec. 33333.10(c)	59
Sec. 83114(b)	100	Sec. 33101	21, 24, 81	Sec. 33333.10(e)	61, 292
Sec. 83116	100	Sec. 33102	21	Sec. 33333.10(f)	61
Sec. 87100	89	Sec. 33110	21, 23	Sec. 33333.10(f)(1)	292
Sec. 87103	89, 91	Sec. 33111	28	Sec. 33333.10(f)(2)	292
Sec. 87103.5	90	Sec. 33112	26	Sec. 33333.10(g)(1)	292, 293
Sec. 87105	98	Sec. 33113	24	Sec. 33333.10(g)(2)	293
Sec. 87200	88	Sec. 33114	23, 25	Sec. 33333.10(g)(2)	293
Sec. 87300 et seq.	25	Sec. 33114.5	23, 25	Sec. 33333.10(g)(3)	293
Sec. 87302	27, 88	Sec. 33120	25, 106	Sec. 33333.10(g)(4)	293
Sec. 87302(b)	27	Sec. 33125	24, 26, 178, 311	Sec. 33333.10(g)(5)	293–294
Sec. 89503	91			Sec. 33333.10(h)	59
Sec. 91000	100	Sec. 33126	24, 26, 29	Sec. 33333.10(h)(1)	62
Sec. 91000(c)	100–101	Sec. 33127	26	Sec. 33333.10(h)(2)	63
Sec. 91002	100	Sec. 33128	29	Sec. 33333.11	59, 62, 63, 292
Sec. 91003	101	Sec. 33130	25, 27, 28		
Sec. 91005	100	Sec. 33130(a)	28, 101	Sec. 33333.11(c)	63
Sec. 91005.5	100	Sec. 33130(b)	101	Sec. 33333.11(d)	64
Sec. 91011(b)	100–101	Sec. 33130(c)	102	Sec. 33333.11(e)	64
		Sec. 33130.5	102	Sec. 33333.11(f)	64
Health and Safety Code		Sec. 33131	26	Sec. 33333.11(g)	64
Chap. 326	322	Sec. 33132	26, 36	Sec. 33333.11(h)	64
Sec. 25180.7	149	Sec. 33133	26, 36	Sec. 33333.11(h)(4)	63
Sec. 25205 et seq.	150	Sec. 33134	26	Sec. 33333.2	57, 76, 106, 290
Sec. 25220	148	Sec. 33140	33		
Sec. 25242 et seq.	149	Sec. 33141	33	Sec. 33333.2(a)	113
Sec. 25242(a)	149	Sec. 33142	33	Sec. 33333.2(a)(1)	78
Sec. 25242.2	149	Sec. 33200	21, 22	Sec. 33333.2(a)(1)(A)	57, 58
Sec. 25242–25242.3	149	Sec. 33200(a)	22	Sec. 33333.2(a)(1)(B)	58
Sec. 25249.5	149	Sec. 33210	36, 81	Sec. 33333.2(a)(2)	59, 78
Sec. 25249.5 et seq.	149	Sec. 33211	81	Sec. 33333.2(a)(3)	61
Sec. 25249.6	149	Sec. 33213	36, 81	Sec. 33333.2(a)(4)	65, 113, 321
Sec. 25299.50	143	Sec. 33214	36, 81	Secs. 33333.2(a)(4)(A)–(B)	113
Sec. 25299.79	143	Secs. 33214–33216	82	Sec. 33333.2(b)	65
Sec. 25300 et seq.	145	Sec. 33215	81	Sec. 33333.2(c)	62
Sec. 25319	145	Sec. 33216	81, 82	Sec. 33333.2(d)	62
Sec. 25351.2	146	Sec. 33217	82	Sec. 33333.3	71
Sec. 25363(e)	145	Sec. 33220	203, 254	Sec. 33333.4	85, 106, 248, 283
Sec. 25395.22 et seq.	153	Sec. 33220(b)	218		
Sec. 25396.60	146	Sec. 33220(c)	218	Sec. 33333.4(a)(1)	78
Sec. 33000 et seq.	5, 21	Sec. 33301	36	Sec. 33333.4(a)(2)	78
Sec. 33013	182, 212	Sec. 33302	36–37	Sec. 33333.4(a)(3)	65, 321
Sec. 33020	182, 248	Sec. 33310	38	Sec. 33333.4(g)(12)	65
Sec. 33021	248	Sec. 33320.1	39, 44	Sec. 33333.4(g)(2)	321
Sec. 33021(b)	218	Sec. 33320.2	41, 294	Sec. 33333.6	57, 63, 290, 291
Sec. 33030 et seq.	39	Sec. 33321	39, 41		

	page(s)		page(s)		page(s)
Sec. 33333.6(a)	59	Sec. 33339	36, 56, 65, 114, 180, 181	Sec. 33381	36
Sec. 33333.6(a)(1)	240			Sec. 33385	47, 50, 52, 96, 107, 114
Sec. 33333.6(a)(2)	240	Sec. 33339.5	36, 56, 65, 114, 180		
Sec. 33333.6(b)	61			Sec. 33385(b)(1)	50
Sec. 33333.6(c)	65	Sec. 33340	114, 180	Sec. 33385(b)(2)	51
Sec. 33333.6(c)(1)	65	Sec. 33341	56	Sec. 33385(b)(4)(A)	51
Sec. 33333.6(e)(2)	57	Sec. 33342	56, 112	Sec. 33385(b)(5)	51
Sec. 33333.6(e)(2)(B)	58	Sec. 33342.5	56, 107, 112	Sec. 33385(b)(6)	51
Sec. 33333.6(e)(2)(C)	62	Sec. 33342.7	56, 107, 112	Sec. 33385(b)(7)	51
Sec. 33333.6(e)(2)(D)	62	Sec. 33343	57	Sec. 33385(c)	51, 96
Sec. 33333.6(f)	61	Sec. 33344	57	Sec. 33385(d)(1)	52
Sec. 33333.6(g)	61	Sec. 33344.5	53, 54, 68	Sec. 33385(d)(2)	52
Sec. 33333.8	33, 61, 290	Sec. 33344.6	54	Sec. 33385(f)	50
Sec. 33333.8(a)	58, 59, 61	Sec. 33345	56, 65, 180	Sec. 33385.3	79
Sec. 33333.8(a)(1)	291	Sec. 33346	73	Sec. 33386	52
Secs. 33333.8(b)–(c)	291	Sec. 33347	73, 75	Sec. 33388	52
Sec. 33333.8(d)	291	Sec. 33347.5	51, 73	Sec. 33391	26, 56, 105, 106, 112, 113
Sec. 33333.8(e)	291	Sec. 33348	73, 75		
Sec. 33333.8(f)	291	Sec. 33349	74	Sec. 33391 et seq.	106
Sec. 33334	55	Sec. 33350	74	Sec. 33393	102, 113
Sec. 33334.1	55, 241, 242	Sec. 33352	49, 158, 319	Sec. 33394	106, 114
Sec. 33334.12	63, 274, 275, 291	Sec. 33352(a)	72	Sec. 33395	106, 114
		Sec. 33352(b)	72	Sec. 33399	114
Sec. 33334.14	282	Sec. 33352(c)	72, 222	Sec. 33400	135
Sec. 33334.16	63, 279	Sec. 33352(d)	72	Sec. 33401	32, 58, 220, 236
Sec. 33334.17	279	Sec. 33352(e)	72		
Sec. 33334.2	54, 56, 237, 242, 247, 272, 275, 283, 284, 291	Sec. 33352(f)	72	Sec. 33402	135
		Sec. 33352(g)	72	Secs. 33410–33418	210
		Sec. 33352(h)	72	Sec. 33410 et seq.	156, 291
		Sec. 33352(i)	72	Sec. 33411	158
Sec. 33334.2(a)	270, 273, 280, 298	Sec. 33352(j)	66, 73	Sec. 33411.1	158
		Sec. 33352(k)	73	Sec. 33411.3	289
Sec. 33334.2(a)(1)	273	Sec. 33352(l)	60, 73	Sec. 33413	47, 83, 84, 286, 289, 291, 298
Sec. 33334.2(a)(2)	273	Sec. 33352(m)	73		
Sec. 33334.2(a)(3)(A)	273	Sec. 33352(n)	73		
Sec. 33334.2(b)	273	Sec. 33353.2	236–237	Sec. 33413(a)	289
Sec. 33334.2(c)	273	Sec. 33354.5	78	Sec. 33413(b)	62, 278, 285, 288, 294
Sec. 33334.2(e)	276	Sec. 33354.6	78		
Sec. 33334.2(e)(2)(A)	277	Sec. 33355	73	Sec. 33413(b)(1)	84, 288
Sec. 33334.2(e)(2)(B)	277	Sec. 33360	73	Sec. 33413(b)(2)	84
Sec. 33334.2(e)(9)	275	Sec. 33360.5(a)	55, 73	Sec. 33413(b)(2)(A)(ii)	287
Sec. 33334.2(g)	275, 286	Sec. 33360.5(b)	55	Sec. 33413(b)(2)(A)(iii)	285
Sec. 33334.2(j)	272	Sec. 33360.5(c)	55, 74	Sec. 33413(b)(2)(A)(v)	287
Sec. 33334.25	279	Sec. 33360.5(d)	55	Sec. 33413(b)(2)(B)	287
Secs. 33334.25(c)–(d)	280	Sec. 33363	75	Sec. 33413(b)(2)(C)	287, 288
Sec. 33334.3	63, 237, 272, 291	Sec. 33363.5	75	Sec. 33413(b)(2)(i)	285
		Sec. 33364	74	Sec. 33413(b)(4)	286
Sec. 33334.3(b)	253	Sec. 33365	77, 209	Sec. 33413(c)	285, 289
Sec. 33334.3(e)	282	Sec. 33366	51, 52, 73, 75	Sec. 33413(c)(2)	286, 288
Sec. 33334.3(f)(1)(A)	281			Sec. 33413(d)(1)	278, 285, 289
Sec. 33334.3(f)(1)(B)	281	Sec. 33367	22, 75, 80, 112, 158	Sec. 33413.5	214, 289, 290
Sec. 33334.3(f)(1)(C)	282			Sec. 33417.5	167
Sec. 33334.3(f)(3)(B)	282	Sec. 33367(c)	75	Sec. 33418	298
Sec. 33334.3(f)(7)	282	Sec. 33367(d)	75, 319	Sec. 33418(c)	298
Sec. 33334.3(i)	272	Sec. 33367(d)(14)	75	Sec. 33420.2	250
Sec. 33334.3(j)	279	Sec. 33367(d)(4)	37	Sec. 33421	218, 223
Sec. 33334.4	84, 277, 278, 291	Sec. 33368	112	Sec. 33421.1	213, 219, 249
		Sec. 33372	76	Sec. 33422.1	228
Sec. 33334.4(a)	277	Sec. 33373	76	Sec. 33422.3	228
Sec. 33334.4(b)	278	Sec. 33373(a)	76	Secs. 33423–33426	228
Sec. 33334.4(c)	278	Sec. 33373(b)(1)	76	Sec. 33426.5	107, 193, 227, 252
Sec. 33334.4(d)	278	Sec. 33373(b)(2)	76		
Sec. 33334.5	56	Sec. 33373(b)(3)	76	Sec. 33426.5(a)	226, 251
Sec. 33334.6	237, 283, 291, 294, 298	Sec. 33373(c)	77	Sec. 33426.5(b)	227, 252
		Sec. 33373(d)	77, 107	Sec. 33426.7	193, 227, 251
		Sec. 33375	77, 244	Sec. 33431	171, 211, 212
Sec. 33335	56	Sec. 33378	49, 75, 77, 209	Sec. 33433	22, 172, 174, 194, 196, 197, 211, 212
Sec. 33336(a)	56				
Sec. 33336(b)	56	Sec. 33378(a)	77		
Sec. 33337	56	Sec. 33378(b)(2)	77	Sec. 33433(c)	212
Sec. 33338	56	Sec. 33380	36	Sec. 33435	173

Table of Authorities 509

	page(s)		page(s)		page(s)
Sec. 33436	56, 173	Sec. 33492.16	291, 301	Sec. 33684(i)(2)	32
Sec. 33437	173, 198	Sec. 33492.20	301	Sec. 33684(i)(3)	33
Sec. 33437.5	198	Sec. 33492.3	301	Sec. 33685	14, 250
Sec. 33438	173	Sec. 33492.9	300	Sec. 33701	181, 182
Sec. 33440	224, 276	Sec. 33500	77, 112, 311, 312	Sec. 33740 *et seq.*	261
Sec. 33444.5	250			Sec. 33741	294
Sec. 33444.6	250	Sec. 33501	77, 220, 311, 312, 313, 314, 315	Sec. 33745	181
Sec. 33445	56, 68, 107, 213, 219, 220, 221, 223, 226, 237, 243, 248, 249			Sec. 33750 *et seq.*	261
				Sec. 33763.5	262
		Sec. 33501(a)	312	Sec. 34000 *et seq.*	54, 85
		Sec. 33501(b)	77	Sec. 34001(b)	85
		Sec. 33501(c)	78	Sec. 34002	85
Sec. 33445(b)	222	Sec. 33501.1	78	Sec. 34004	86
Sec. 33445(c)	219	Sec. 33501.2	78, 313, 321	Sec. 34004(g)	86
Sec. 33445(d)	220	Sec. 33501.3	313	Sec. 34005	86
Sec. 33445(e)	220	Sec. 33501.7	313	Sec. 34007	86
Sec. 33445(g)	226, 248	Sec. 33515	322	Sec. 34110	23
Sec. 33445.5	223	Sec. 33601	36, 256	Sec. 34115	21
Sec. 33445.6	223	Sec. 33606	30	Sec. 34115.5	23
Sec. 33446	223, 237, 271	Sec. 33607.5	79, 236, 237, 238, 239, 240, 272, 300, 320	Sec. 34120(a)	23
Sec. 33448	223			Sec. 34130(a)	23
Sec. 33449	135, 275, 294			Sec. 37000 *et seq.*	294
Sec. 33450	78, 209			Sec. 37001.5	295, 296
Sec. 33450 *et seq.*	62	Sec. 33607.5(a)(2)	237	Sec. 43800	150
Sec. 33451	80	Sec. 33607.5(a)(3)	79	Sec. 46001	150
Sec. 33451.5	78	Sec. 33607.5(a)(5)	239	Sec. 50052.5	280
Sec. 33451.5(a)(3)	58	Sec. 33607.5(b)	58	Sec. 50053	280
Secs. 33451.5(a)(3)-(4)	62	Sec. 33607.5(c)	58	Sec. 50079.5	292
Sec. 33451.5(b)	59	Sec. 33607.5(d)	58	Sec. 50093	292
Sec. 33451.5(c)	65	Sec. 33607.5(e)	58	Sec. 50101	150
Sec. 33451.5(c)(1)	60	Sec. 33607.5(e)(3)	239	Sec. 50105	292
Sec. 33451.5(c)(2)	60	Sec. 33607.5(f)(2)	239	Sec. 50106	292
Sec. 33451.5(c)(3)	60	Sec. 33607.7	57, 79, 240, 272	Sec. 53511	318
Sec. 33451.5(c)(4)	60				
Sec. 33451.5(c)(5)	60	Sec. 33607.7(c)	80	**Labor Code**	
Sec. 33451.5(c)(6)	60	Sec. 33607.8	236, 240	Sec. 1720	194, 197
Sec. 33451.5(c)(7)	60, 83	Sec. 33610	254		
Sec. 33451.5(c)(8)	60	Sec. 33620 *et seq.*	244	**Public Contract Code**	
Sec. 33451.5(d)	60	Sec. 33624	253	Secs. 20688.1–20688.4	227
Sec. 33451.5(e)	60	Sec. 33640	256	Sec. 20688.2	228
Sec. 33451.5(f)	60	Sec. 33641	251	Sec. 20688.3	228
Sec. 33452	80	Sec. 33641.5(b)	61	Sec. 20688.4	228
Sec. 33453	80	Sec. 33670	49, 53, 57, 77, 241		
Sec. 33454	80			**Public Resources Code**	
Sec. 33455	80	Sec. 33670 *et seq.*	232	Sec. 21000 *et seq.*	25, 66
Sec. 33457	80	Sec. 33670(a)	233, 234	Sec. 21002.1	66
Sec. 33457.1	80	Sec. 33670(b)	80, 234	Sec. 21068.5	215
Sec. 33458	80	Sec. 33671.5	49, 61	Sec. 21081	71
Sec. 33459	40, 143	Sec. 33672.5	247	Sec. 21081.5	71
Sec. 33459 *et seq.*	16, 141	Sec. 33672.7	248	Sec. 21081.6	71, 300
Sec. 33459(c)	143	Sec. 33673	234	Sec. 21083.6	300
Sec. 33459.1(e)	140	Sec. 33673.1	234	Sec. 21083.7	300
Sec. 33459.3	139	Sec. 33674	77	Sec. 21083.8.1	300, 304
Sec. 33459.3(m)	142	Sec. 33675	244	Sec. 21090	66, 67, 68, 69, 214
Sec. 33459.4	141	Sec. 33675(b)	245		
Secs. 33459–33459.8	138	Sec. 33675(c)(1)(D)	245	Sec. 21090(b)	68
Sec. 33485 *et seq.*	284	Sec. 33675(d)	245	Sec. 21093	69, 215
Sec. 33486	80	Sec. 33675(g)	245, 247	Sec. 21150	73
Sec. 33486(a)	80	Sec. 33675(h)	246	Sec. 21157	67
Sec. 33487	284, 291	Sec. 33676	235, 240, 271	Sec. 21166	66, 68, 69, 214
Sec. 33487(d)	284	Sec. 33676(b)	239		
Sec. 33488	80	Sec. 33676(b)(3)	79	**Revenue and Taxation Code**	
Sec. 33490	60, 63, 83, 84, 222, 286	Sec. 33677.5	233		
		Sec. 33678	223, 248	Sec. 96.6	233
Sec. 33490(a)(2)(A)(iii)	277, 278	Sec. 33679	213, 222, 243, 249	Sec. 97235	236
Sec. 33490(a)(2)(A)(iv)	278			Sec. 97.5	236
Sec. 33492 *et seq.*	54, 299	Sec. 33684	31, 32, 241	Sec. 422	46
Sec. 33492.10	301	Sec. 33684(e)	31	Sec. 422.5	46
Sec. 33492.11	299, 301	Sec. 33684(e)(5)	32	Sec. 110.1(f)	236
Sec. 33492.13	301	Sec. 33684(f)	32		
Sec. 33492.15	300	Sec. 33684(i)(1)	32		

	page(s)
Sec. 2052	49
Sec. 7200.1	251
Sec. 7202.6	251
Sec. 7280.5	253
Sec. 43001 *et seq.*	150

Streets and Highways Code

Sec. 10000 *et seq.*	261

Water Code

Sec. 13304(a)	142

Session Laws

1992 Cal. Stats., chap. 697	236
1993 Cal. Stats., chap. 942	6, 8, 10, 193, 218, 236
1993 Cal. Stats., Sec. 5	218
1997 Cal. Stats., chap. 597	165
1997 Cal. Stats., chap. 898	302, 303

California Regulations
(including CEQA Guidelines)

2 Cal. Code Regs., Sec. 18110 *et seq.*	87
2 Cal. Code Regs., Sec. 18233	90
2 Cal. Code Regs., Sec. 18329(b)(6)	100
2 Cal. Code Regs., Sec. 18329(c)	100
2 Cal. Code Regs., Sec. 18700	89
2 Cal. Code Regs., Sec. 18701	88
2 Cal. Code Regs., Sec. 18702.1	89
2 Cal. Code Regs., Sec. 18702.2	89
2 Cal. Code Regs., Sec. 18702.3	89
2 Cal. Code Regs., Sec. 18702.4(b)(1)	89
2 Cal. Code Regs., Sec. 18703.1	90
2 Cal. Code Regs., Sec. 18703.2	90
2 Cal. Code Regs., Sec. 18703.3	90
2 Cal. Code Regs., Sec. 18703.3(c)(2)(B)	97
2 Cal. Code Regs., Sec. 18703.4	91
2 Cal. Code Regs., Sec. 18703.5	90
2 Cal. Code Regs., Sec. 18704.1	91
2 Cal. Code Regs., Sec. 18704.2	91
2 Cal. Code Regs., Sec. 18704.2(a)	92
2 Cal. Code Regs., Sec. 18704.5	91
2 Cal. Code Regs., Sec. 18705 *et seq.*	91
2 Cal. Code Regs., Sec. 18705.1	93, 98
2 Cal. Code Regs., Sec. 18705.2(a)	92
2 Cal. Code Regs., Sec. 18705.2(b)	92
2 Cal. Code Regs., Sec. 18705.3(a)	93
2 Cal. Code Regs., Sec. 18705.3(b)(2)	94
2 Cal. Code Regs., Sec. 18705.3(b)(3)(A)	93
2 Cal. Code Regs., Sec. 18705.3(b)(3)(B)	93
2 Cal. Code Regs., Sec. 18705.5	94
2 Cal. Code Regs., Sec. 18707	94
2 Cal. Code Regs., Sec. 18707.1	94
2 Cal. Code Regs., Sec. 18707.1(b)(1)(A)	94
2 Cal. Code Regs., Sec. 18707.1(b)(1)(B)	94
2 Cal. Code Regs., Sec. 18707.1(b)(1)(C)	95
2 Cal. Code Regs., Sec. 18707.1(b)(1)(D)	95
2 Cal. Code Regs., Sec. 18707.1(b)(1)(E)	95
2 Cal. Code Regs., Sec. 18707.4	98
2 Cal. Code Regs., Sec. 18707.9	97
2 Cal. Code Regs., Sec. 18707.10	96
2 Cal. Code Regs., Sec. 18708	98, 99
2 Cal. Code Regs., Sec. 18708(b)	99
2 Cal. Code Regs., Sec. 18708(b)(4)	99
2 Cal. Code Regs., Sec. 18708(c)(3)	99
14 Cal. Code Regs., Sec. 15000 *et seq.*	66
14 Cal. Code Regs., Sec. 15064	66
14 Cal. Code Regs., Sec. 15065	66
14 Cal. Code Regs., Sec. 15091	71
14 Cal. Code Regs., Sec. 15094	77
14 Cal. Code Regs., Sec. 15124	66
14 Cal. Code Regs., Sec. 15125	66
14 Cal. Code Regs., Sec. 15126	66
14 Cal. Code Regs., Sec. 15130	66
14 Cal. Code Regs., Sec. 15162	70
14 Cal. Code Regs., Sec. 15163	70
14 Cal. Code Regs., Sec. 15168	215
14 Cal. Code Regs., Sec. 15260 *et seq.*	214
14 Cal. Code Regs., Sec. 15300 *et seq.*	214
25 Cal. Code Regs., Chap. 1, Art. 5, Sec. 32	40
25 Cal. Code Regs., Sec. 6000 *et seq.*	156
25 Cal. Code Regs., Sec. 6006	157
25 Cal. Code Regs., Sec. 6008(c)(3)	158
25 Cal. Code Regs., Sec. 6008(d)	160
25 Cal. Code Regs., Sec. 6008(l)	160
25 Cal. Code Regs., Sec. 6010(a)(1)	157
25 Cal. Code Regs., Sec. 6010(a)(2)	157
25 Cal. Code Regs., Sec. 6010(a)(3)	157
25 Cal. Code Regs., Sec. 6010(a)(4)	157
25 Cal. Code Regs., Sec. 6038	158
25 Cal. Code Regs., Sec. 6040 *et seq.*	159
25 Cal. Code Regs., Sec. 6042(c)	162
25 Cal. Code Regs., Sec. 6052	157
25 Cal. Code Regs., Sec. 6058	167
25 Cal. Code Regs., Sec. 6088	166, 167
25 Cal. Code Regs., Sec. 6090(i)	164
25 Cal. Code Regs., Sec. 6100(f)	164
25 Cal. Code Regs., Sec. 6150	167
25 Cal. Code Regs., Sec. 6182(d)	116
25 Cal. Code Regs., Sec. 6184	116
25 Cal. Code Regs., Sec. 6910 *et seq.*	280

CEQA Guidelines

Sec. 15063(d)	215
Sec. 15091	216
Sec. 15092	216
Sec. 15093	216
Sec. 15094	216
Sec. 15161	67
Sec. 15162	66, 215
Sec. 15163	66
Sec. 15168	215
Sec. 15180	68, 215
Sec. 15180(b)	66

California Attorney General Opinions

63 Ops. Cal. Atty. Gen. 509 (1980)	253
69 Ops. Cal. Atty. Gen. 147 (1986)	225
76 Ops. Cal. Atty. Gen. 137 (1993)	271
82 Ops. Cal. Atty. Gen. 126 (1999)	53, 96

California Fair Political Practices Commission Opinions/Advice Letters

Hudson opinion, 4 FPPC Ops. 13 (1978)	99

	page(s)
In re Thorner, 1 FPPC Ops. 198 (1975)	91
Legan opinion, 9 FPPC Ops. 1 (1985)	94
Rotman opinion, 10 FPPC Ops. 1 (1987)	53, 88, 95
Rousch Advice Letter, FPPC No. A-88-404, December 7, 1988	88
Scudder Advice Letter, FPPC No. A-88-181, June 20, 1988	88

Public Works Cases

	page(s)
Public Works Case No. 2007-012, Sand City Design Center/Sand City Redevelopment Agency	195
Public Works Case No. 2004-035, Santa Ana Transit Village/ City of Santa Ana	172, 194, 196
Public Works Case No. 2005-016, Oxnard Marketplace Shopping Center—Fry's Electronics/ City of Oxnard	197
Public Works Case No. 2004-024, New Mitsubishi Auto Dealership/ Victorville Redevelopment Agency	195

California Legislative Counsel Opinions

	page(s)
Ops. Cal. Legis. Counsel, No. 23767 (October 27, 1999)	234

Index

A

AB 389, 146
AB 637, 12
AB 1290. *See also* blight
    blight definition, 10–11, 14, 39, 41–42
    discussed, 8–11, 39, 41, 42, 58, 107,
        193, 217, 218, 226, 236, 244,
        247, 248, 251, 299, 324
    statutory payments, 58
AB 1389, 13–14, 241
AB 2610, 148
administration building, 217, 226, 248
    See also buildings;
    public improvements
administrative record, 43, 220
    See also evidence; findings
    requirements; report
agricultural lands
    county agricultural
        commissioner, 54, 71
    inclusion in redevelopment
        plan, 46, 54
    Williamson Act lands, 46
air rights, 224, 229
alternatives. *See also* environmental
    impact report
    financing, 72, 257
    to a project in an EIR, 66, 70, 71, 215
AMEX, 93
annexation, effect on jurisdiction, 81–83
architectural review, 198
asbestos, 152
    See also environmental
    law; hazardous materials
assessment district, 54, 192, 224
    See also assessment role;
    financing; Mello-Roos
    Community Facilities Act
    bonds, 260–261
assessment roll, 228
    See also taxes
    "last equalized" rule,
        48–50, 232, 233–234
audit, 33, 63, 318
    See also financing
requirements, 30, 31
auto malls, 9, 251
    assistance to prohibited,
        11, 193, 217, 226–227, 251

B

bankruptcy, 206–207
Base Closure and Realignment
    Act, 303, 304
Base Closure Community Assistance Act, 303
Base Realignment and Closure
    Commission (BRAC),
    302–303, 305, 307
    See also military base
Berkeley, 209
blight. *See also* AB 1290; redevelopment plan
    amendment of redevelopment plan to
        add eminent domain authority required
        a finding of, 321
    definition and revision, 10–11, 14,
        39, 59, 217, 218, 265, 267, 324
    AB 1290 definition,
        42, 75, 217, 218, 251
    agricultural lands, 41
    contamination as a
        condition of, 107, 138
    individual property need
        not be blighted, 39, 41
    legislative definition, 39–40, 41
    military base, 299–300, 301
    must be predominantly
        urbanized, 39, 44–46,
    must burden existing uses, 41
    must predominate and apply
        to area as a whole, 39
    nonblighted properties, 39
    nonblighted, noncontiguous
        properties, 41, 43
    physical and economic burden, 35, 42
    determination, 36, 41, 53
    "dilapidation," 40, 43, 300
    findings requirements,
        42, 312, 313, 319
    elimination, reporting requirements, 212
    findings requirements, 30, 212
    in general, 38–39
        economic blight, 40
        nonblighted properties, 39, 41, 193
        physical blight, 40
    must be predominantly urbanized, 39
    80-percent test, 7, 44
bond counsel, 29, 189, 256, 257, 258, 276
bonds. *See also* financing; loans;
    tax-increment financing
    assessment district bonds, 260–261

bonds *continued*
    lease revenue bonds, 243, 259–260
    Mello-Roos bonds, 260, 261, 148–149
    private activity bonds, 263–265
    private business use test/
        private security payment
        test, 263–264, 265
    private loan financing test, 263, 264
    public purpose or governmental
        bonds, 263–264, 265
        private activity bonds, 263–265
        "qualified bonds," 263
    residential mortgage
        revenue bonds, 261–262
    tax allocation bonds, 14, 241–242,
        243–244, 257, 258–259, 260,
        261, 265–266, 192, 203, 275
BRAC. *See* Base Realignment
    and Closure Commission
bribe, 124
Brown Act. *See* Ralph M. Brown Act
brownfields
    See also hazardous materials
    CERCLA provisions, 144, 146, 147
    definition, 138–139
    US-EPA Brownfields
        Grant Program, 140
budget crisis, 10, 12, 255
buildings. *See also* administration
    building; city hall building;
    commercial development;
    public improvements
    historic, 44, 256
    identifying in
        redevelopment plan, 46
    redevelopment agency
        authorization to construct,
        191, 198, 199–200, 219
business. *See also* employment;
    ground lease; relocation
    goodwill
        definition, 127
        determination, 128, 129, 130
        loss of business goodwill, 127–129
            compensation for, 117, 120, 131
    owner participation rules, 65–66
    preference to displaced
        businesses, 65
    relocation assistance to, 159
business districts, 16, 18, 267

513

C

Cal/EPA, Office of Environmental
    Health Hazard Assessment, 149
California Commission on State
    Mandates, 271
California Debt Advisory
    Commission, 7, 268
California Environmental
    Quality Act (CEQA)
    See also environmental impact;
      environmental impact report;
      National Environmental
      Policy Act
    review requirements,
      25, 66–71, 77, 83, 86, 117,
      179, 211, 214–216, 300, 304
    California Environmental
      Quality Act (CEQA), 215
California Fair Political Practices
    Commission (FPPC), 52–53,
    87, 88, 89, 91, 94, 95, 97, 98–100
    opinions and advice,
      88, 91, 94, 95, 99, 100
    violations, 100
California Farm Bureau
    Federation, 54, 71
California Housing Finance
    Agency (CHFA), 255, 295
    CHFA Resale Program, 255
    Home Purchase
      Assistance Program, 255
    Matching Down
      Payment Program, 255
California Land Reuse and
    Revitalization Act, 146
California Redevelopment
    Association (CRA), 8–14, 112,
    139, 193, 241, 249, 275, 325
California Relocation Assistance
    Act of 1970, 155–156
CalSites validation program, 147
Carpenter-Presley-Tanner Hazardous
    Substance Account Act
    (HSAA), 145–146, 151
CDBG. *See* Community
    Development Block Grant
CEQA. *See* California Environmental
    Quality Act
CEQA Guidelines, 66, 67, 68,
    214–215, 216, 300
CERCLA. *See* Comprehensive
    Environmental Response,
    Compensation and Liability Act
certificate of participation, 260
CFHA. *See* California Housing
    Finance Authority
CHFA Resale Program, 255
city hall building, 217, 226, 248
    See also buildings;
      public improvements
CLEAN. *See* Cleanup Loans and
    Environmental Assistance
    to Neighborhoods
Cleanup Loans and Environmental
    Assistance to Neighborhoods
    (CLEAN), 153–154
coastal zone, 208
commercial development
    See also buildings; retail project
    mixed-use project, 18
    relation to residential development, 8
    use or redevelopment to attract, 279

community. *See also* public
    formal relationship with
      redevelopment agency, 21–23
    neighborhood impact
      report, 60, 64, 73
    redevelopment agency as
      separate entity from, 21–23, 294
community college district
    See also school district
    tax-increment financing, 49, 238–239
Community Development
    Block Grant (CDBG),
    156, 159, 163, 254, 255, 256, 277
    discussed, 255
    section 108(a) loan
      guarantee program, 255
    special requirements, 290
community development commission
    See also project area committee
    establishment, 21, 23
community organizations,
    PAC membership, 50–52
Community Redevelopment Act, 1, 5
Community Redevelopment
    Disaster Project Law, 54, 85–86
Community Redevelopment Law,
    1. 5, 8, 16, 18, 21, 23, 24, 26,
    27–28, 33, 36, 38, 43, 48, 53,
    54, 57, 73, 77, 78, 80, 81, 85–86,
    88, 96, 101–102, 105–106, 107,
    112, 113, 115, 117, 137, 138,
    156, 158, 167, 171, 178, 180–181,
    207–209, 210–211, 218, 219, 223,
    224, 228, 231, 234, 241, 244, 262,
    267, 285, 290, 297, 298, 299, 319, 323
    conflict of interest provisions,
      23–24, 101–102
Community Redevelopment Law
    Reform Act of 1993, 8
compensation. *See also* relocation
    110, 115–117, 120–124, 125–132,
    134, 155, 160, 186, 201
    property owner, 125–132
    redevelopment agency members,
      23, 25
Comprehensive Environmental
    Response, Compensation
    and Liability Act (CERCLA),
    139, 146, 151, 306, 309, 310
    See also environmental law
    application, 144–145
      military base, 306–308
    "bona fide purchaser" provisions,
      144, 146
    "innocent landowner"
      provisions, 140–141
    "innocent purchaser"
      provisions, 144
condemnation,
    74, 75, 125, 129, 130, 144, 312
    See also eminent domain;
      property acquisition
    authority for, 39, 110, 112–114, 122
    inverse condemnation,
      114, 124, 128, 132–135, 185, 186
      discussed, 117
      regulatory taking, 133, 134
Condemnation Practice in California
    (Matteoni & Veit), 129
conflict of interest. *See also* personnel
    Community Redevelopment
      Law, 23–24, 101–102
    "designated employees," 26–27, 88

conflict of interest *continued*
    disqualification, 26–27, 88, 89, 91, 97–98
      direct or indirect involvement
        in decision, 91
      distinguishable from the
        public generally, 94–95
      examples, 97–98
      in general, 89
      making or participating
        in decision, 89
      materiality, 91–94
      project area committees, 95–96
      reasonable foreseeability, 91
      residential properties, 97–98
      small cities, 96–97
      types of economic interests, 89–91
    FPPC opinions, advice, 100
    in general, 87
    incompatibility of office, 28
    legally required participation,
      rule of necessity, 98–100
    materiality, 91–94
      business entities, directly
        involved, 91, 93
      business entities, indirectly
        involved, 91, 93
      gifts, 99
      personal finances, 90, 91, 94
      real property, directly involved, 91–92
      real property, indirectly involved, 92
      sources of income, 97
    must adopt codes for, 25, 26, 87
    Political Reform Act of 1974, 25, 26–27
    recusal, 98
    violations, 100
    violations, effect on decisions, 101
consultant. *See also* personnel;
    specific consultants
    to redevelopment agency, 29–30,
      36, 88, 89, 258,
      agency may employ, 29, 189
contract
    contractual financial
      obligations, 242–246
    redevelopment agency
      may enter into, 26, 219–220
      indebtedness, 241, 242, 244–246
      requirements, 204, 227–228
county agricultural commissioner, 54, 71
    See also agricultural lands
county auditor, 15, 31–32, 77, 233, 234,
    241, 244–246, 247–248, 301
county clerk, 21, 25, 77
county farm bureau, 54, 71
county fiscal officer, report, 48–50, 53, 73
county office of education, 49
    See also schools
county recorder, 76, 107
covenants, 198, 287
CRA. *See* California
    Redevelopment Association
crime, 41, 42, 191
    See also blight
Cypress, 125

D

DDA. *See* disposition and
    development agreement
deed of trust, as property disposition, 171
Defense Base Closure and
    Realignment Act of 1990, 303
Department of Conservation, 54, 71

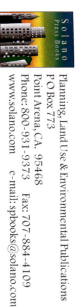

Solano Press Books

Planning, Land Use & Environmental Publications
P O Box 773
Point Arena, CA. 95468
Phone: 800-931-9373　Fax: 707-884-4109
www.solano.com　e-mail: spbooks@solano.com

Please make the following correction in your copy of

REDEVELOPMENT IN CALIFORNIA, 4th edition

ERRATA TO ITEM NO. 22 IN APPENDIX B —

Illustrative Time Schedule and Procedural Guide for the Adoption of a Redevelopment Plan – *Effective January 1, 2009*

Item No. 22 should read as follows:

After Month 4, Day 17
No later than **90** days prior to the public hearing.
22. AGENCY transmits a copy of the Preliminary Report to the governing board of each affected taxing agency. § 33344.6
Action or document required
Preliminary Report;
Transmittal letter

Department of Finance,
    10, 14, 32, 49, 55, 59, 60, 64,
    65, 73, 74, 78, 80, 193, 238, 313
Department of Housing and
        Community Development (HCD),
    14, 59, 60, 62–65, 74, 80, 156, 158,
    165, 254, 268, 269, 271, 273–275,
    280, 297, 298, 302, 318
    housing activities report, 268–269,
        271, 274
    loan and grant programs, 254
        Community Development
            Block Grant Program, 254
        Homeownership
            Assistance Program, 254
        Rental Housing
            Construction Program, 254
        Self-Help Housing Program, 254
    Model Relocation Plan, 158
    Relocation Assistance
        and Real Property
        Acquisition Guidelines, 156
    reports required by, 31, 55, 64, 73
Department of Industrial
    Relations (DIR), 172, 194–197
Department of Toxic Substances Control
        (DTSC), 139, 142, 146,
    149, 151, 307–308, 309
    See also environmental law
    CalSites database, 147
    CLEAN program, 153–154
        Preliminary Endangerment
            Assessment, 154
    Environmental
            Oversight Agreement, 139
    ERAP, 147
    institutional controls, 148
    Voluntary Cleanup Program, 147
        no-further-action letter, 147
Department of Transportation
    (DOT), 155, 255
Guidelines,
    156, 159, 163, 164, 167, 168, 169
design controls, 39
dilapidation, 40, 43, 300
    See also blight
    peeling paint, 43
dioxin, 152
DIR. *See* Department of Industrial Relations
disaster, 85–86, 226
    Community Redevelopment
        Disaster Project Law, 54, 85
discrimination, non-discrimination
        requirements, 56, 160,
    173, 174, 181, 198
disposition and development agreement
        (DDA), 88, 105, 120, 174, 178,
    179, 183, 185, 186, 187, 188,
    190, 196, 197, 202–206, 207,
    213, 214, 216, 246, 317
    See also property disposition
    discussed, 198–199
DTSC. *See* Department of Toxic
    Substances Control

E

earthquake, 226
economic interest. *See also* conflict
        of interest; financial disclosure
    disclosure, 26–27, 87–88
    materiality, 91–95, 97–99
    types of, 89–91

Education Revenue Augmentation
    Fund (ERAF), 11, 12, 14, 236
    challenges to, 325
    payments, 59, 61, 249–250
    extensions for, 62
EIR. *See* environmental impact report
EIS. *See* environmental impact statement
elderly. *See also* housing
    HUD programs, 256
eminent domain,
    1, 2, 13, 105, 144, 321, 323
    See also condemnation;
        property acquisition
    authorization in redevelopment
        plan, 74, 76–77
    compensation to owner, 125–130
        highest and best use, 125–126
        loss of business goodwill, 127–129
        severance damages, 127
        valuation techniques, 126–127
    conflict of interest, 103
    exercise of by redevelopment
        agency, 110–114, 144, 188, 191
    in general, 110
    justification for use of, 39
    owner participation, 180, 181
    PAC requirement, 47, 50, 79, 114
    political and policy concerns, 115
    precondemnation procedures, 115–119
        acquisition team, 117–119
        statutory requirements, 115–117
    procedures
        challenges to taking, 123–125, 186
        compensation to owner, 125–129
        compensation to owner,
            apportionment with tenant, 129–130
        complaint, 122
        deposit of probable compensation;
            order for possession, 122–123
        in general, 119
        judgment and appeal, 131–132
        resolution of necessity; notice;
            hearing, 120–122, 184
        time period for commencement,
            31, 57, 85, 186, 106–107, 113
        trial, 130–131
    property acquisition, 16, 25, 29, 106–107
    redevelopment bonds used for, 266
    redevelopment plan required
        elements, 56
    time limit on exercise of, 65
    waiver of right to, 199
Eminent Domain Law, 107, 110, 112,
    113, 115, 117, 119, 128, 184
    propositions challenging, 13–14, 107
Eminent Domain (Rypinski), 120, 129, 132
employment. *See also* business;
        prevailing wages
    highly trained workers, 71
environmental guidelines, redevelopment
    agency adoption, 24–25
environmental impact. *See also*
        environmental impact report
    alternatives, 66, 70, 71, 215
    cumulative impact, 67, 69
    mitigation measures, 66, 71, 73, 215
environmental impact report (EIR),
    36, 55, 71, 73, 300, 304
    See also California
        Environmental Quality Act
    challenges, 69
    discussed, 66–71
    draft EIR, 71

environmental impact report *continued*
    final EIR, 71
    focused EIR, 70
    initial study, 215
    joint EIR/EIS, 304
    master EIR, 67, 67n5, 214, 215
    notice of determination, 77, 216
    notice of preparation, 71
    program EIR, 67, 68, 69,
        70, 67n5, 69, 214–215
    project EIR, 67n5, 68, 214
    on redevelopment plan,
        67, 68, 69, 77, 86, 214, 216, 300
    statute of limitations, 77–78
    supplemental/subsequent EIR,
        66, 67, 70, 214, 215, 216
    tiering, 69
environmental impact statement
    (EIS), 300, 304
    joint EIR/EIS, 304
environmental law
    See also California
        Environmental Quality Act
    contaminated property,
        107–108, 137–138, 142, 145
    contaminated property cleanup
        government funds, 153–154
        insurance, 153
        redevelopment proponent, 138
    in general, 137–138
    governmental funding sources,
        153–154
    military base cleanup and reuse, 152
    state programs
        asbestos and lead, 152
        California Land Reuse and
            Revitalization Act, 146
        CalSites validation program, 147
        Carpenter-Presley-Tanner Hazardous
            Substance Account Act, 145–146
        Cleanup Loans and Environmental
            Assistance to Neighborhoods, 153–154
        cleanup-related taxes and fees, 150
        ERAP/SB 923, 147
        hazardous waste disposal
            on public land, 149
        institutional controls, 148
        local CERCLA-like ordinances, 151
        Mello-Roos Community
            Facilities Act, 148–149
        Polanco Act, 138–139
        Proposition 65, 149–150
        regulated, asbestos-containing
            materials, 152
        reporting requirements, 150–151
        Toxic Substances
            Control Act, 151–152
        Underground Storage Tank
            Cleanup Fund, 143, 153
        Voluntary Cleanup Program, 147
    Superfund, 140
        CERCLA, 140, 144–145
        federal, 137, 143, 144–145
        state, 140, 143, 145–146, 151
ERAF. *See* Education Revenue
    Augmentation Fund
ERAP. *See* expedited remedial
    action program
ESCA. *See* Environmental Cooperative
    Services Agreement
eviction, 159, 161, 167–168
    See also relocation; resident
    relocation agency policies, 159–160

evidence. *See also* administrative record;
findings requirements
in administrative record, 72–73
in agency report, 72–73
substantial evidence
requirements, blight, 41–44
"substantial evidence test," 71
exhaustion of administrative
remedies, 78, 319–321
See also judicial review;
validation litigation
expedited remedial action
program (ERAP), 147
See also environmental law

F

Farmers Home Administration
Program, 255, 256
Federal Aid Highway Act, 155
federal government
financing programs, 21–22, 283–284
CDBG, 156, 159, 163,
254, 256, 277, 290
other programs, 256
Section 108(a) loan
guarantee program, 255
Urban Mass Transit Program, 255
grants to local agencies, 4–5, 26
redevelopment programs historic, 2–5
residential portion, 3
Federal Highway Administration, 165
Federal Housing Administration (FHA), 2
Federal Property and Administrative
Services Act of 1949, 302
FHA. *See* Federal Housing Administration
financial disclosure
See also conflict of interest;
economic interest; personnel
Community Redevelopment
Law, 27–28, 101
in general, 25, 88, 90
Political Reform Act of 1974,
25, 26–27, 98–100
redevelopment agency
must adopt codes for, 26, 27
reporting requirements, 25, 26–27
financing. *See also* financing plan;
indebtedness; loans;
tax-increment financing; taxes
agency borrowing, 256–257
bonds
assessment district, 260–261
lease revenue, 192, 243, 259–260
Mello-Roos, 148–149, 260, 261
private activity bonds, 263–264
private business use test/
private security
payment test, 263, 265
private loan financing test, 263–264
public purpose or governmental
bonds, 263–264, 265
residential mortgage
revenue, 261–262
tax allocation bonds,
14, 192, 203, 229, 33, 241–244,
250, 257, 258–259, 260,
265–266, 275, 317
borrowing from developer
developer advances, 202–203
in general, 262
land sale proceeds, 253, 262–263
certificate of participation, 260

financing *continued*
governmental revenues
community funds, 254
federal, 255–256
revenue sharing, 253
state, 254–255
land sales proceeds and
lease revenues, 253, 262–263
in lieu guarantee of
tax increment, 263
miscellaneous expenditure
authority, 250
sales and use tax
financing, 250–253
statements of indebtedness
ERAF payments, 249–250
in general, 244–247
limitations upon use, 248–249
receipt by agency, 247–248
tax exemption, 257
financing plan. *See also*
tax-increment financing
considerations, 187
developer advances, 202–203
redevelopment plan as, 35
financing team. *See also* personnel
bond counsel,
29, 189, 256, 257, 258
financial advisor, 256, 257
fiscal agent/trustee, 256
fiscal consultant, 256
underwriter, 29, 189, 256, 257, 258
findings requirements
See also administrative
record; evidence
blight determination, 42, 44, 65, 312
designation of survey area, 38
environmental impact, 71
general plan adoption, 37
mergers, 75
prior determinations, 62
property acquisition, 117
property disposition,
172, 212, 213, 216
redevelopment plan adoption,
36, 42, 75, 312, 315, 319
fiscal agent/trustee, 256
flood control project, 225
foreclosure, 109, 168, 203, 205, 206, 207
Fort Ord, 152, 307, 310, 317
Fort Ord Reuse Authority Act, 301, 307
Fortune 500, 93
FPPC. *See* California Fair Political
Practices Commission
FPPC Form 700, 88
fraud, 312

G

gambling, 252
gas station. *See also* hazardous
materials; petroleum
underground tanks, 143, 153
general plan
must conform to state law, 36–38
housing element, 37
mandatory elements, 37
revision timelines, 37
redevelopment plan
must conform to, 36–38, 48
general plan amendment, timing,
redevelopment plan
adoption, 37–38

General Services Administration
(GSA), 302
goodwill. *See also* business
definition, 127
determination, 120, 127–129
loss of business goodwill,
117, 120, 127–129, 130, 131
gross abuse of discretion, 124, 185
ground lease, 198, 205
See also business; lease
discussed, 199–201
base rent, 200
holding rent, 200
participation rent, 200
percentage rent, 200
growth control, 206, 207
GSA. *See* General
Services Administration

H

Hamilton Air Force Base, 303
Hawaii Land Reform Act, 111
hazardous materials. *See also*
brownfields; environmental law
asbestos, 131, 152, 307
contaminated property,
107–108, 138–143,
146–150, 152–154
disposal on public land, 149
lead, 152
petroleum, 143, 145, 146, 150, 307
regulated, asbestos-containing
materials, 152
Superfund, 144–146
HCD. *See* Department of Housing
and Community Development
hearing. *See* public hearing
Hemet, 10
historic buildings, 44, 256
See also buildings;
historic landmarks
historic landmarks, 16
Home Investment Partnership
Program, 277
Home Owners and Private
Property Protection Act, 107
Home Purchase Assistance
Program (CHFA), 255
Homeownership Assistance
Program, 254
hotel, 16–18, 192, 226–228, 253
housing
additional authority, 294
affordable housing, 270, 280–281
affordability covenants, 287–288
Article XXXIV, 214, 290, 294–297
creation, 2, 12, 16, 47, 268, 274
elimination, 267–268
expenditures, 269
low-rent housing project, 294–296
maintaining affordability, 281–282
preservation, 166, 270
"qualified affordable housing
preservation project," 166
reporting and monitoring
requirements, 269
residents, 46
completion of housing
obligations, 290–291
"excess surplus," 274–275
"15 percent set-aside"
requirement, 285–286

housing *continued*
    in general, 267–270
    for homeless, 195–196
    housing fund monies, 275–280
        affordability, 280–282, 284
        limitations, 279
        merger of project areas, 284
        plans adopted before 1977, 283–284
        targeted expenditures, 278
        "targeting" requirements, 277–278
        use outside community, 279–280
    identifying in redevelopment plan, 56
    inclusionary housing requirements, 46–47
        aggregation between project areas, 287
        in general, 284–286
        implementation methods, 278, 286–288
        purchase of affordability covenants, 287
        sale of owner-occupied units, 288
        two-for-one alternative, 287
    Low- and Moderate-Income Housing Fund,
        8, 30, 58, 59, 60, 61, 63,
        84–85, 237–238, 242, 247,
        253, 258, 260, 268, 298, 301
        implementation plan discussion, 84
        reporting requirements, 297–298
    production housing requirements, 288
    rehabilitation, 47, 195, 276, 285
    relocation/replacement/
        20 percent tax increment, 46–47
    replacement housing requirements
        federal CDBG requirements, 290
        in general, 85, 288
        housing unit replacement, 289
        replacement housing plan, 289–290
    special provisions for time limit
        extension amendment deposits
        into housing fund, 292–293
        expenditures from housing fund, 292
        in general, 292
        plans adopted before 1976, 293–294
    "20 percent set-aside"
        requirement, 195, 270–272
        plans adopted before 1977, 272
        exceptions, 273–274
Housing Act of 1937, 2, 280
Housing Act of 1949, 3, 5, 8
housing element, 62, 63n4, 84, 273, 277
    See also general plan
    redevelopment plan must conform to, 37
Housing Element Law, 62*n*4
HSAA. *See* Carpenter-Presley-Tanner
    Hazardous Substance Account Act
HUD. *See* U.S. Department of Housing
    and Urban Development
Huntington Park, 184

I

implementation plan, for redevelopment
    plan, 60, 63, 64, 72, 83–85, 213,
    219, 222, 249, 277–278, 286
improvements. *See* public improvements
incompatibility of office
    See also conflict of interest
    discussed, 28
indebtedness. *See also* financing
    authority to use tax increment
        to repay, 231–232
    California Debt and Investment
        Advisory Commission, 257
    limitations on, 55
    pass-through agreements,
        11, 58, 235–237, 271–272

indebtedness *continued*
    Statement of Indebtedness
        ERAF payments, 249–250
        in general, 244–247
        limitations upon use, 248–249
        miscellaneous expenditure
            authority, 250
        receipt by agency, 247–248
    time limit on incurring,
        57–59, 85, 240
    time limit on repayment of, 61, 85
    special procedures applicable
        to SB 211 amendments, 62–65
    types of, 241–244
initial study, 215–216
    See also environmental impact report
initiative. *See* referendum/initiative process
insurance
    contaminated property cleanup
        using responsible parties'
        insurance policies, 153
    environmental insurance, 307, 310
    Labor Code section 1720, 194
    mortgage insurance, 255, 256
    redevelopment agency may carry, 26
    title insurance, 186
Internal Revenue Code, 264, 265
Isenberg, Phil, 8

J

judicial review. *See also* validation litigation
    exhaustion of administrative
        remedies, 78, 319–321
    redevelopment plan, 220

L

Lancaster, 125
landfill (dump), not an urban use, 45
lawsuit. *See also* validation litigation
    redevelopment agency
        may enter into, 26, 311
lead, 152
    See also environmental
        law; hazardous materials
lead agency, 69, 71
    See also California
        Environmental Quality Act
    redevelopment agency as, 24
lease. *See also* ground lease
    as property disposition, 171
legal counsel, 29, 30, 36, 119, 256
    See also personnel
legislative body. *See also* taxing agency
    as distinct from redevelopment agency, 23
    as redevelopment agency, 22
    relation to redevelopment
        agency, 26, 29, 30, 33
loans. *See also* bonds; financing
    below market rate loans, 256
    private loan financing test, 263, 264
    reporting requirements, 31
local reuse authority (LRA), 303, 307
    See also military base
Long Beach, Hyatt Regency
    convention center, 18
Los Angeles
    Bunker Hill Project, 232
    California Center Project, 18
    redevelopment, 1
    secession, 82
Los Angeles Redevelopment Agency, 18
Los Angeles Times, 10

Los Angeles Town Hall Report, 1
Low- and Moderate-Income Housing
    Fund, 8, 30, 58, 59, 60, 61,
    63, 84–85, 237–238, 242, 247,
    253, 258, 260, 268, 298, 301
LRA. *See* local reuse authority

M

map, for redevelopment plan,
    48, 50, 53, 60, 63, 72, 74, 118
Mare Island, 302, 309–310
Marks-Roos Local Bond
    Pooling Act of 1985, 261
Matching Down Payment
    Program (CHFA), 255
Matteoni & Veit, 117, 129
McKinney Homeless
    Assistance Act, 303, 304
meeting. *See also* public meeting;
    Ralph M. Brown Act
    closed session meeting, 28–29
    open meeting requirements, 28–29
    PAC meetings, 52
Mello-Roos Community Facilities Act
    contaminated land cleanup, 148–149
    Mello-Roos bonds, 148–249, 260, 261
Mello-Roos Community Facilities
    District, formation, 224–225, 261
MERLO. *See* Municipal Environmental
    Response and Liability Ordinance
military base. *See also* property
    acquisition; property disposition
    adoption of redevelopment
        plan, 299–302
    disposition procedures, 304–305
    early transfer pending
        remediation, 308–310
    EIS/EIR, 300, 304
    enhancing value, 305–306
    environmental cleanup
        before transfer, 306–308
    in general, 299
    hazardous waste contamination, 19
        cleanup and reuse, 152
    integration with BRAC process, 302–303
    Local Military Base Recovery Areas, 302
    local reuse authority
        establishment, 303
    reuse plan preparation
        and adoption, 303
Military Base Reuse Authority Act, 301
mining operation, not an urban use, 45
mitigation. *See also* environmental
    impact report
    environmental impact,
        66, 70, 71, 73, 215
mortgage
    as property disposition, 171
    residential mortgage revenue
        bond, 18, 184, 261–262
    tax-exempt mortgage revenue bonds, 260
mortgage assistance, 196
mortgage insurance, 255, 256
    See also insurance
MTBE, 143
Municipal Environmental Response
    and Liability Ordinance
    (MERLO), 151
Municipal Improvement
    Act of 1913, 260–261
museums, 18, 228
    See also public improvements

N

NASDAQ, 93
National Defense
    Authorization Act, 306
National Environmental Policy Act
    (NEPA), 300, 304
    See also California
    Environmental Quality Act
National Housing Act of 1934, 2
National Industrial Recovery
    Act of 1933, 2
National Priorities List, 308
negative declaration, 215
    See also environmental
    impact report
    mitigated negative declaration, 70, 216
neighborhood impact report,
    60, 64, 73
NEPA. *See* National
    Environmental Policy Act
new city, formation, effect on
    jurisdiction, 81–82
New Deal, 2
New Rule for All Appropriate
    Inquiries, 140, 146
New York, eminent domain
    redevelopment, 2
New York Stock Exchange, 93
newspaper, public notice publication,
    25, 51, 74, 211, 308, 314
nondiscrimination provisions,
    redevelopment plan, 56
"Norm's Slauson," 120, 184–187
    See also property disposition
notice of determination, 77, 216
    See also environmental
    impact report
Novato, 303

O

OEHHA. *See* Office of Environmental
    Health Hazard Assessment
office, equipment, supplies, 26, 52
Office of Environmental Health
    Hazard Assessment (OEHHA), 149
open space, 18, 55, 218, 224, 228, 233
    identifying in redevelopment
    plan, 46
open space element, 37
ordinance
    for redevelopment agency, 21
        adoption and filing, 21
        dissolution of agency, 33
    for redevelopment plan
        adoption, 37, 75–76, 81, 319
        amendment, 78–80
        notifications after plan
        adoption, 76–77
        subject to referendum, 77
owner participation. *See* property
    disposition; property owner

P

PAC. *See* project area committee
park, 213, 218, 254
    See also open space
parking facility, 18, 226–226,
    228, 233, 257, 259–260
    See also public improvements
pass-through agreements,
    11, 58, 235–237, 271–272
    See also tax-increment financing

PCBs. *See* polychlorinated biphenyls
personnel. *See also* conflict of interest;
    consultant; financial disclosure;
    financing team; public official
    closed session meetings about, 28–29
    "designated employees," disclosure
        requirements, 26–27, 88–89
    incompatibility of office, 28
    redevelopment agency
        may employ, 24, 25, 29
        acquisition team, 117–119
        redevelopment team, 36
petroleum. *See also* hazardous materials
    closed military base contamination, 307
    excluded from HSAA, 145
    remediation of contamination, 143
    UST Fund, 153
planning agency
    city must have, 36
    must select area boundary, 48
    redevelopment plan amendment
        review, 64–65, 73
    redevelopment plan review, 72, 73
playground, 213, 218
Polanco Redevelopment Act,
    16–17, 108, 133, 137–138,
    142, 143, 144–145, 146
    agency oversight, 142–143
    brownfields, definition, 138–139
    in general, 138–143
    investigation, 139–141
    remediation, 141–143
        environmental agency
        oversight, 142–143
        immunity from liability, 143
        notice requirements, 141
        petroleum, 143
        recovery of cleanup costs, 141–142
Political Reform Act of 1974,
    25, 52, 98, 100, 101, 102
    discussed, 26–27, 87–88
polychlorinated biphenyls (PCBs), 151–152
    See also hazardous materials
prevailing wages. *See also* employment
    triggers, 172, 194–197, 228, 229
project area committee (PAC)
    See also community; community
    development commission; personnel
    conflict of interest, 27, 53, 87, 92, 95–96
    discussed, 47, 50–53, 75, 114
        elections and voting, 51–52
        funds for operation, 52
        members are "public
        officials," 52–53, 88
        notification, 51
        review responsibilities,
        52, 64, 72, 73, 289
        who may serve,
        51–53, 65 79, 88, 95–96
    meetings, 52, 72, 76
    redevelopment plan
        amendment review, 61–62, 64, 78
property acquisition. *See also* eminent domain;
    property disposition
    acquisition team, 117–119
        acquisition agent, 118–119
        legal counsel, 118, 119
        relocation specialist, 118, 119
    appraisal of property, 115–116, 173
        appraiser, 118, 130–131
        impeachment of appraiser, 131
    authority and statutory
        requirements, 105–107

property acquisition *continued*
    closed session meeting allowance, 28, 29
    contaminated property, 107–108
    in general, 105, 156, 185, 187
    "redevelopment purpose," 107
    interim property management, 135
    inverse condemnation, 114, 132–135
    nonblighted properties, 41–44, 82
    owner notification, 74
    property "offered for sale"
        by owner, 109, 168–169
    reports about, 72, 73
    "uneconomic remnant," 117
    valuation techniques
        "cost approach," 126
        "income approach," 126
    voluntary sales, 108–109
        fair market value, 108–109
        "offered for sale," 109, 168–169
property disposition
    agency participation in cash flow, 201
    approval process, 211
    CEQA, 214–216 developer
    advances, 202–203
    developer selection
        combined RFQ/RFP, 175–177
        in general, 173–174
        highest bid/auction, 174
        master developer, 177–178
        negotiation with single developer
            without formal selection, 174–175
        request for proposal, 175
        request for qualifications, 175
    disposition and development
        agreement, 8, 105, 120, 174,
        178, 179, 183, 185, 186, 187, 188,
        190, 196, 198–199, 197, 202–206,
        207, 213, 214, 216, 246, 317
    documentation
        disposition and development
            agreements, 198–199
        in general, 198
        ground leases, 199–201
        owner participation agreement, 199
    exclusive negotiation
        agreements, 178–180
    fair reuse value determination, 173
    in general, 171–173
        "fair market price," 172, 194, 196
        fair market value, 173
        "fair reuse value," 172, 173, 196, 213
        highest and best use value, 131, 173
        "land write-down," 172, 191, 192
        prevailing wages,
        172, 194–197, 228, 229
    hearings, reports, findings,
        determinations, 211–214
    highest bid/auction, 174
    initiative, referenda, local
        legislative enactment, 207–211
    land sale proceeds, 253, 262–263
    lease returns, 253
    methods of assisting development
        when necessary, 191–193
        hotel uses, 192
        office uses, 192
        residential uses, 192
        retail uses, 192
    negotiations
        objectives, 187–188
        preparation, 188–190
        process structure, 190
    "Norm's Slauson" problem, 184–187

property disposition *continued*
   owner participation,
      general rules, 180–184
      prevailing wage considerations, 193–197
      renegotiation, 204–205
      subsequent discretionary
        approvals, 203–204
      unforeseen contingencies, 205–207
property management, 135
   interim property management, 135
property owner. *See also*
   relocation; resident
   compensation, 13, 125–132
      apportionment with tenant, 129–132
      severance damages, 127
   notification of redevelopment plan, 74
   owner participation agreement,
      163, 182, 198, 199, 241–242
   owner participation rules,
      55–57, 65–66, 96, 183
   owner may accompany appraiser, 116
   owner participation agreement, 199
   property disposition, 180–187
property taxes. *See also* taxes
   effect on of redevelopment plan, 77
   ERAF shift, 11, 325
Proposition 1C, 254
Proposition 4, 248
Proposition 13, 7–9, 192, 217
Proposition 65, 149–150
Proposition 90, 13, 112
Proposition 98, 13–14, 112, 250
Proposition 99, 13–14, 107, 112
Proposition 218, 253n1
public. *See also* community
   availability of documents for, 31, 74
   citizen input, 36
   with respect to PAC, 50, 95–96
public funds. *See also* financing
   authority for expenditure of, 39
public hearing, 14, 22
   condemnation, 117, 120–122
   general plan, 37–38
   implementation plan adoption, 83
   joint hearings, 24, 73
   property disposition,
      171, 172, 174, 179, 184, 211–214
   public improvements, 222
   redevelopment plan
      adoption, 73–76, 319–320
        administrative record creation, 76
   redevelopment plan amendment, 80
public housing, 2, 195
   See also housing
public improvements
   applications, typical, 224–225
   assistance to auto dealer, retail
      project prohibited, 226–227
   authorizations for specific projects
      air rights sites, 224
      buildings, 224
      in general, 223–224
   basic powers, 217
   city halls, county
      administration buildings, 226
   contracting requirements, 227–228
   convention facility, 18, 226, 228
   cultural facility, 18
   financing, 259–261
   implementation plan requirements, 222
   inadequacy no longer blight criteria, 218
   "integrally-related" improvements, 228–229
   prevailing wage considerations, 228

public improvements *continued*
   land and public buildings
      and facilities, 219–222
   maintenance and operations
      not authorized, 222
   off-site improvements, 218–219
   parking facilities, 225
   primary benefit to project area, 223
   prohibition on payments, 223
   public buildings, 225
   public hearing, 222
   redevelopment plan
      requirements, 56, 222
   Section 33445 findings, 219–222
public land, hazardous
   materials disposal, 149
public meeting. *See also* meeting
   Brown Act requirements, 28–29
   meeting agenda, 29
   joint meetings, 81
   PAC formation, 50
   redevelopment plan adoption, 28
public notice
   condemnation, 117, 121–121
   PAC formation, 50
   Polanco Act, 133
   proof of publication/
      certificates of mailing, 76
   redevelopment plan, 73–76
   redevelopment plan adoption, 28
   redevelopment plan amendment, 80
   required notices to persons
      being displaced, 161–162
public official. *See also* conflict
   of interest; personnel
   conflict of interest, 87, 88
   incompatibility of office, 28
   PAC member as, 52
public use, identifying in
   redevelopment plan, 55
public works project
   See also public improvements
   definition, 194

R

RACM. *See* regulated, asbestos-
   containing materials (RACM)
Ralph Andersen and Associates, 6n7, 268
Ralph M. Brown Act (Brown Act),
   28–29, 52, 118, 121, 189
   See also meeting
   discussed, 28–29
   PAC meetings subject to, 52
recession, 257
record of decision (ROD), 304
recreational facility, 18, 218
   See also public improvements
redevelopment
   definition, 182
   history
      application, 15–19
      federal, 2–5
      introduction, 1–2
      state, 5–15
   as state policy, 10, 21, 26, 39, 208
redevelopment agency
   agency activation, 24–25
      bylaws for officers, 24
      chairman/vice-chairman approval, 24
      environmental guidelines, 24–25
      personnel rules, 24
   agency dissolution, 33

redevelopment agency *continued*
   as agency of state, 10, 21, 26, 39, 208
   appointment of separate agency, 23
   audit requirements, 31
   budget, 29, 30
   as CEQA lead agency, 24, 71
   community development
      commission, establishment, 23
   compared to municipality, 111–112
   compensation, 23
   establishment, 21
      adoption of ordinance, 21
      referendum/initiative process, 24
   general powers/jurisdiction, 25–26
      may accept financial assistance, 25, 26
      may carry insurance, 26
      may employ staff and officers, 26
      may obtain office,
        equipment, supplies, 26
      may sue and be sued
        and make contracts, 26
   goals and objectives, 55, 72, 83
   housing agency and, 21, 23
   implementation plan, adoption, 83–85
   joint exercise or delegation of
      authority to redevelop, 81–83
   joint powers redevelopment agency, 19
   legislative body as, 22
   major violations, 33
   open meeting requirements, 28–29
   organization
      alternatives and advantages/
        disadvantages, 21–22
      filing of statement of, 25
   pass-through payments, 30–33
   relation with PAC, 52
   reporting requirements, 30–31
      preliminary report, 42, 53–55, 63, 64
   as separate legal entity, 24, 25
   staff and consultants, 29–30
redevelopment plan. *See also* blight
   AB 1290 time limits, 11
   adoption
      Community Redevelopment Disaster
        Project Law, 54, 85–86
      notifications after, 76–77
      objections, 74, 77–78
      ordinance for, 75–76, 81
      prerequisites, 36–38
      procedures, 36, 75
   amendment, 64
      discussed, 78–80
      effect on time limits, 54
      extensions, 59, 61
      ordinance for, 78–80
   approval
      public notice/public hearing, 73–76
      review by other bodies, 73
   area boundary, 25, 38
      housing, relocation, replacement, 46–47
      legal description, 74
      map, 48, 53
      other considerations, 47–48
      planning agency must select, 48
   authority for, 26
   challenges/legal actions, 77–78
   as charter, 35, 55
   EIR requirements, 66–71
   eminent domain, time limit
      on exercise of, 65
   failed plan, 207–208
   as financing plan, 35
   in general, 35–36, 222–223

redevelopment plan *continued*
   implementation plan, 83–85, 222
   joint exercise/delegation of
      authority to redevelop, 81–83
   judicial review, 76, 77–78
   mandatory elements, 55–57
      buildings, 55
      financing, 55
      housing, 55–56
      indebtedness, 55
      legal description of project, 55
      nondiscrimination provisions, 56
      open space description, 55
      optional provisions, 56
      owner participation provisions, 56
      property acquisition, 56
      public improvements, 56
      public purposes, 56
   merger, 80, 284
      discussed, 80
      effect on time limits, 65
   must conform to
      general plan, 36–37, 81
   owner participation rules,
      55–57, 65–66, 96, 183
   PAC must review, 52
   preparation
      county fiscal officer's report,
         48–50, 73
      initial feasibility study, 38
      preliminary report, 52–54
      project area committee, 50–53
   project area prerequisites
      agricultural lands, 46, 554
      blight, 38–44
      housing-relocation/replacement/
         20 percent tax
         increment, 41, 46–47
      other considerations, 47–48
      predominantly urbanized,
         44–46, 53, 301, 312
   redevelopment team, 36
   referenda, 77
   report to legislative body, 72–73
   SB 211 amendments
      extended consultations, 63–65
      in general, 62
      prior determination, 62–63
   SB 211 time limits, 14
   survey area designation, 38
   time limit on effectiveness, 59–60
   time limit on incurring
      indebtedness, 57–58
   time limit on repaying
      indebtedness, 61
redevelopment project, area
   boundary, 25, 38
referendum/initiative process
   redevelopment agency dissolution, 33
   redevelopment agency establishment, 24
   redevelopment plan
      adoption, 77, 207–211
Regional Water Quality Control
   Boards, 142–143, 146, 308
regulated, asbestos-containing
   materials (RACM), 152
   See also hazardous materials
Religious Land Use and Institutionalized
   Persons Act (RLUIPA), 125
relocation. *See also* business; compensation;
   property owner; resident
   agency relocation rules
      and regulations, 157

relocation *continued*
   authority to exceed
      minimum payments, 166
   comparable replacement
      dwelling units, 161–162
      definition, 161
      rental costs, 161
   eviction policies, 159, 167–168
   "Federal DOT Guidelines,"
      155, 156, 159, 163, 164, 167–169
   grievance procedures,
      157, 159, 161, 167
   history and law, 155–156
   last resort housing, 168
   payments not considered income, 168
   payments to businesses, 163–164
   payments to displaced persons, 162–163
      "displaced person"
         definition, 162–163
   payments to homeowner-
      occupants, 164–165
   payments to residential
      tenants, 165–166
   prior determination/
      assurances, 157–158
   property "offered for sale"
      by owner, 168–169
   record keeping, 168
   relocation assistance
      advisory program, 159–160
   relocation plans, 158–159
      key elements, 160–161
   required notices to persons
      being displaced, 161–162
   requirements prior to
      displacement, 156–159
   utilities, 169
Relocation Assistance and Real
   Property Acquisition
   Guidelines (HCD), 156
rental assistance, HUD section 8,
   18, 255, 256, 280
Rental Housing Construction
   Program (HCD), 254
report. *See also* administrative
   record; evidence
   assessed valuation
      of project area, 48
   county fiscal officer, 48–50, 53, 73
   neighborhood impact
      report, 60, 64, 73
   property disposition, 211–214
   redevelopment agency
      requirements, 30–31, 63–65
   redevelopment plan, 72–73
request for proposal (RFP)
   combined RFP/RFQ, 175–177
   discussed, 175
request for qualifications (RFQ)
   See also property disposition
   combined RFP/RFQ, 175–177
   in general, 175
resident. *See also* property
   owner; relocation
   compensation
      apportionment, 129–130
      displacement, 50–52, 109
      eviction, 167–168
      housing, relocation,
         replacement, 20 percent
         tax increment, 46–47, 73
      redevelopment impact
         on, 4, 47–48, 50–52

resolution of necessity
   condemnation, 113, 116,
      120–122, 124, 184–186
   adoption, 133
retail project. *See also*
   commercial development
   assistance to prohibited, 226, 227
RFP. *See* request for proposal
RFQ. *See* request for qualifications
RLUIPA. *See* Religious Land Use and
   Institutionalized Persons Act
roads, 218
ROD. *See* record of decision
Rypinski, Richard G., 120, 129, 132

S

Sacramento, Capitol Area
   Development Authority, 19
Sacramento Bee, 10
Safe Drinking Water and
   Toxic Enforcement Act
   of 1986. *See* Proposition 65
sale, as property disposition, 171, 198
sales tax. *See also* taxes
   AB 1290 changes,
      10–11, 192–193, 251–252
   auto malls and big-box retail, 9–10
   financing with, 250–253
   "two percent" inflation allocation, 9, 235
San Bernardino, 208
San Diego, Horton Plaza Project, 18
San Francisco, 181
   Yerba Buena Gardens Project, 18
San Joaquin County, MERLO, 151
San Jose, Fairmont hotel, 18
SB 53, 56, 65, 106
SB 211
   extended consultations, 63–65
   in general, 12, 57–58, 62, 324
   prior determination, 62–63
SB 527, 278
SB 649, 66–67
SB 1206, 14, 39, 41, 42, 44, 49, 55,
   58, 59, 62, 72, 73, 75–78,
   80, 83, 248, 311, 324
SB 1809, 76–77, 107
school district. *See also* community
   college district; schools
   Education Revenue
      Augmentation Fund, 11, 236
   tax-increment financing,
      10, 49, 232, 238
   "two percent" inflation
      allocation, 9, 235
schools
   county office of education, 238
      ERAF shift, 11
   facilities construction, 17, 223, 237
   funding sources, 10
   special education financing, 238
Secretary of State, 25, 33
Self-Help Housing Program (HCD), 254
shopping center, 16, 18, 172, 184,
   225–226, 228–229
   See also retail project
sidewalks, 191, 218, 224, 265
Small Business Liability
   Relief and Brownfields
   Revitalization Act, 144, 146
sovereignty, 110
special education. *See also* schools
   tax-increment financing, 238

State Board of Equalization, 48, 50, 77, 80
State Controller, 11, 14, 15, 30, 31, 32, 240, 244
Statement of Preparation, 48
statute of limitation. *See also* validation litigation
    EIR challenges, 77
    redevelopment plan challenges, 78, 100, 229, 311–312, 317
streets, 48, 169, 191, 203, 213, 218, 224, 265
    See also public improvements

T

taking. *See also* eminent domain; property acquisition
    challenges to, 123–125
    regulatory taking, 133–134
tax-increment financing, 234, 323
    See also financing; taxes; taxing agency
    authority for, 5
    background, 231–234
    community college districts, 238
    county offices of education, 238
    indebtedness, 241
        contingent/contractural obligations, 244
        direct bonded debt, 241–242
        miscellaneous expenditure authority, 250
        operational expenses, 243–244
        reimbursement debt, 243
        repayment debt, 242–243
    in lieu guarantee of tax increment, 263
    limits on, 7
        disaster project, 54, 85–86
        limitations upon receipt, 235–236
    notification of taxing agency, 76–77
    pass-through agreements, 11, 58, 235, 236, 237, 271, 272
    payments to taxing entities
        contingent/contractural obligations, 244
        direct bonded debt, 241–242
        in general, 236–241
        indebtedness, 241
        operational expenses, 243–244
        reimbursement debt, 243
        repayment debt, 242–243
    school districts, 238
    special education, 238
    statement of indebtedness
        ERAF payments, 249–250
        in general, 244–247
        limitations upon use, 248
        receipt by agency, 247–248
    "two percent" inflation allocation, 9, 235

Tax Reform Act of 1986, 257, 260, 261, 264, 275
taxes. *See also* sales tax; tax-increment financing; taxing agency
    assessment roll, 48–50, 228, 232, 233–234
    cleanup-related, 150
    "Gann limit," 223, 253
    "proceeds of taxes" limitations, 223
    property taxes, 6, 10–11, 32, 54, 61, 77, 79, 80, 192, 231–233, 235, 236–240, 247, 249, 280, 296, 320
    special taxes, 148, 224
    tax exemption, 2, 257–258, 259, 266, 295
    transient occupancy use tax, 253
taxing agency. *See also* legislative body
    agency meeting and comments, 63
    availability of documents for, 30–31
    environmental document review, 71
    redevelopment agency notification, 48–50, 63, 76–77
    equalized assessment role, 48–50
    reports, 53–54, 63–65
    Statement of Preparation, 48
telephone conversation
    See also meeting
    Brown Act requirements, 29
tenant. *See* resident
Toxic Substances Control Act (TSCA), PCBs, 151–152
Treasure Island Conversion Act of 1997, 302
Treasure Island Development Authority, 302
TSCA. *See* Toxic Substances Control Act
"two percent" inflation allocation, 9, 235

U

Underground Storage Tank Cleanup Fund (UST Fund), 143, 153
    See also petroleum
underwriter, 29, 189, 253, 257, 258
Uniform Relocation Act Amendments of 1987, 155
Uniform Relocation Assistance and Real Property Acquisition Policies Act of 1970, 155
Urban Mass Transit Program, 255
urban renewal, 3–4, 5, 180n1, 231, 268
U.S. Census Bureau, 278
U.S. Department of Housing and Urban Development (HCD) guidelines, 156, 159, 163, 165, 290
U.S. Environmental Protection Agency (USEPA), 144
USEPA. *See* U.S. Environmental Protection Agency

UST Fund. *See also* Underground Storage Tank Cleanup Fund
utilities, 243
    relocation, 169

V

validation litigation
    See also judicial review
    exhaustion of administrative remedies, 78, 319–321
    in general, 311
    in rem procedure, 313–314
    redevelopment plan, statute of limitation, 311–312
    restrictions on filing actions, 322
    standard of review, 318–319
    standing to sue, 319–321
    "interested person" definition, 321
    validating acts, 321–322
        appeal, 322
    validation procedures, 312–318
Vallejo, Mare Island, 302, 309, 310
VCP. *See* Voluntary Cleanup Program
Voluntary Cleanup Program (VCP), 147

W

Wal-Mart, 252
Williamson Act lands, 46
    See also agricultural lands

Y

Yorba Linda, 320

Other Guides and References

PLANNING . LAND USE . URBAN AFFAIRS . ENVIRONMENTAL ANALYSIS . REAL ESTATE DEVELOPMENT

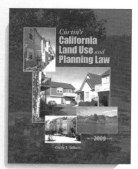

Cecily T. Talbert • Revised annually

Curtin's California Land Use and Planning Law

Well-known, heavily quoted, definitive summary of California's planning laws with expert commentary on the latest statutes and case law. Includes practice tips, graphics, a table of authorities, and an index. Cited by the California Courts, including the California Supreme Court, as an Authoritative Source.

William Fulton and Paul Shigley
2005 (third) edition

Guide to California Planning

All-new edition describes how planning really works in California, how cities, counties, developers, and citizen groups all interact with each other to shape California communities and the California landscape, for better and for worse. Recipient of the California Chapter APA Award for Planning Education.

California Environmental Law and Policy

The only book that covers the entire field of California environmental, land use, and natural resources law in a concise, user-friendly format. Comprehensively surveys the most important federal and state environmental statutes and regulatory programs. Highlights key permits, landmark court cases, and current policy issues. Provides practical tips and tools to guide your project through the regulatory process successfully.

Herson and Lucks • 2008

Ballot Box Navigator: A Practical and Tactical Guide to Land Use Initiatives and Referenda in California

The authoritative resource on securing a ballot title, qualifying an initiative or referendum for the ballot, and submitting a measure for an election. With short articles, practice tips, drawings, an index, glossary, and a table of authorities.

Michael Patrick Durkee et al. • 2003

California Public Contract Law

Public Contract Law is an easy-to-use, concise reference on State of California laws governing the public contracting processes used by federal, state, regional, and local agencies in California. The book reviews key requirements, suggests model provisions, and provides extensive references for relevant statutes and regulations. An important resource for bidders, agency administrators, and contractors involved in public contracting law in California.

Jeremy G. March • 2007

California School Facilities Planning

A single-source reference that offers a thorough discussion of laws and regulations that govern the planning, funding, siting, design, and construction of educational facilities. The book will guide the reader through every stage of the planning process—from initial conception through construction.

Maureen F. Gorsen et al. • 2005

CALL TOLL-FREE
(800) 931-9373

OR ORDER ONLINE AT
www.solano.com

Solano Press Books

www.solano.com . spbooks@solano.com . facsimile 707 884-4109

California Surface Mining Law: A Guide to Federal, State, and Local Requirements

The first and only book that comprehensively addresses the regulation of surface mining in California. Covers federal, state, regional, and local laws and regulations along with relevant cases, and provides extensive citations. Explains mining-specific concepts and offers practical advice for understanding and complying with the law.

Derek P. Cole • 2008

California Water II

Comprehensive guide to historical, legal, and policy issues affecting water use in California. This all-new edition discusses the historic Bay-Delta Accord, the crisis in the Delta, settlement of critical Colorado River issues, global warming, and the emergence of new supplies such as water transfers, conservation, recycling, and the conjunctive use of groundwater.

Littleworth and Garner • 2008 (second) edition

CEQA Deskbook

The practitioner's definitive guide to CEQA, explaining in clear language how to traverse the environmental review process, from beginning to end. Contains the full text of the Statutes and Guidelines. Recognized by the California Association of Environmental Professionals with an Award of Excellence. Cited as an Authoritative Source by the California Courts.

Bass, Bogdan, and Rivasplata • 2009 (third) edition

Eminent Domain: A Step-by-Step Guide to the Acquisition of Real Property

Explains the processes California public agencies must follow to acquire private property for public purposes through eminent domain—how to assemble required documents for the Resolution of Necessity, initial appraisal, acquiring contaminated property, goodwill valuation of machinery and equipment, and relocation assistance. Includes case law, legal references, tips, a table of authorities, sample letters and forms, a glossary, and an index.

Richard G. Rypinski • 2002 (second) edition

Guide to the California Environmental Quality Act

The professionals' guide to the California Environmental Quality Act presents an understandable, in-depth description of CEQA's requirements for adequate review and careful preparation of environmental impact reports and other environmental review documents. Includes extensive analyses of statutes, provisions of the CEQA Guidelines, and voluminous case law.

Remy, Thomas, Moose, and Manley • 2006 (eleventh) edition

Guide to the California Forest Practice Act and Related Laws: Regulation of Timber Harvesting on Private Lands in California

A comprehensive treatise on state and federal legislation that regulates timber harvesting on private lands in California. Includes short articles, charts, graphs, appendices, a table of authorities, and an index to help understand complex regulatory processes and how they interrelate.

Sharon E. Duggan and Tara Mueller • 2005

The NEPA Book

Practitioner's handbook that takes you through the critical steps, basic requirements, and most important decision points of the National Environmental Policy Act. With short articles, practice tips, tables, illustrations, charts, and sources of additional information.

Ronald E. Bass et al. • 2001 (second) edition

CALL TOLL-FREE
(800) 931-9373

OR ORDER ONLINE AT
www.solano.com

Solano Press Books

www.solano.com . spbooks@solano.com . facsimile 707 884-4109

Planning for Child Care in California

Presents basic child care information and guidelines for municipal, county, and school district planners, and for child care professionals and their advocates. The book includes examples of real child care projects, designs, and partnerships, along with numerous sources of funding and other implementation strategies.

Kristen M. Anderson • 2006

The Planning Commissioner and the California Dream: Plan It Again, Sam!

An easily readable reference and set of guidelines directed to the on-the-job needs of California's city and county planning commissioners. With interviews, case studies, tips on how to do the job well, photographs, illustrations, and a glossary of common terms.

Marjorie W. Macris, FAICP • 2004

Putting TDRs to Work in California

Using 27 case studies, the author explains how development rights can be formally and legally traded or transferred to protect open space and agricultural land, as well as natural resources, historic properties, and areas of historic value. Includes short articles, a model program, photos, and tables.

Rick Pruetz • 1993

Subdivision Map Act Manual

Comprehensive reference containing information needed to understand the legal provisions of the Subdivision Map Act, recent court-made law, and the review and approval processes. With the full text of the Map Act, practice tips, a table of authorities, and an index.

Daniel J. Curtin, Jr. and Robert E. Merritt • 2003 edition

Telecommunications

Detailed summary and analysis of federal and state laws governing the location and regulation of physical facilities including cable, telephone, and wireless systems (cellular, paging, and Internet), satellite dishes, and antennas. With practice tips, photos, a glossary, table of authorities, and an index.

Paul Valle-Riestra • 2002

Trail Planning for California Communities

Comprehensive guide for use at every stage of the trail development process. Provides guidance on planning, design, construction, funding, and maintenance of trails in California. Details relevant policies, legislation, and successful projects that lend support for planning and implementation of local trails.

Julie Bondurant and Laura Thompson et al. • 2009

Transportation Law in California

First complete collection of the most important laws and regulations affecting transportation planning in California. Includes ISTEA provisions, Title VI guidelines for mass transit, STIP Guidelines, provisions relating to air quality and equal employment opportunity, civil rights laws, a checklist for mandatory requirements for public outreach, and a glossary.

Jeremy G. March • 2000

Water and Land Use

First complete guide to address the link between California land use planning and the availability of water. Summarizes key statutes, policies and requirements, and current practices. With photos, illustrations, tables, flow charts, case studies, sample documents, practice tips, a glossary, references, and an index.

Karen E. Johnson and Jeff Loux • 2004

Wetlands, Streams, and Other Waters

A practical guide to federal and state wetland identification, regulation, and permitting processes. Provides detailed information, commentary, and practice tips for those who work with federal and state laws and are engaged in wetland conservation planning.

Paul D. Cylinder et al. • 2004 edition

CALL TOLL-FREE
(800) 931-9373

OR ORDER ONLINE AT
www.solano.com

Solano Press Books